# 54th Locarno In
## 2-12 August 2001

Adress: via Luini 3a
CH-6601 Locarno
Tel. +41 91 756 21 21
Fax +41 91 756 21 49
http://www.pardo.ch
e-mail: info@pardo.ch

# EDITED BY PETER COWIE

Managing Editor: Daniel Rosenthal

*faber and faber*
LONDON

**SILMAN-JAMES PRESS**
LOS ANGELES

# CONTENTS

**Editor**: Peter Cowie

**Managing Editor**: Daniel Rosenthal

**Consulting Editor**: Derek Elley

**Editorial Assistant**:  Damjana Finci

**Advertising Co-ordination**: Frederic Fenucci

**Cover Design**: Stefan Dreja

**Photo Consultants**: The Kobal Collection

9   Awards
13   Directors of the Year
13   Lasse Hallström
20   Neil Jordan
28   Goran Paskaljević
35   Steven Soderbergh
43   Edward Yang
50   DVD Round-Up
58   World Box-Office Survey

## WORLD SURVEY

69   Algeria
71   Argentina
75   Armenia
77   Australia
85   Austria
89   Belgium
93   Benin
95   Bosnia & Herzegovina
97   Brazil
99   Bulgaria
101   Canada
107   Chad
108   Chile
110   China
114   Croatia
117   Cuba
119   Czech Republic
123   Denmark
128   Egypt
131   Estonia
135   Finland
141   France

Editorial and Business Offices:
Variety
6 Bell Yard
London WC2A 2JR
Tel:  (020) 7520 5222
Fax: (020) 7520 5219

ISBN 0-571-20680-8 (United Kingdom)
ISBN 1-879505-58-4 (United States)
British Library Cataloging in Publication
Data
Variety International Film Guide 2001
1. Cowie, Peter
011.37

Published in the US by
Silman-James Press
Tel: (323) 661 9922
Fax: (323) 661 9933

Copyright © 2000 by
Variety Media Publications Ltd.

Photoset/Origination by Avonset, Bath
Printed and bound in Great Britain by
Cromwell Press Ltd.

# Dolby film sound—the complete service

Over the last 25 years, Dolby has built a network of international film sound specialists and service engineers who provide technical services to all areas of the film industry. Our complete service during the film production, distribution and exhibition stages gives filmmakers the confidence that their films will be presented all over the world exactly as they were intended to be.

**Film Production**
Dolby sound consultants work together with film production companies in over 200 Dolby film dubbing studios worldwide to help produce high-quality soundtracks for original films and foreign-language versions.

**Film Distribution**
We offer technical consulting to film laboratories on film sound printing, bulk print quality checking of both picture and sound, and technical assistance at screenings and festivals.

**Film Exhibition**
All over the world, Dolby Digital cinema installations continue to grow rapidly, ensuring the best motion picture experience to the widest possible audience. All Dolby cinemas are installed and maintained to our high specifications by Dolby-trained installation companies in over 50 countries.

**Film Advertising**
Dolby Digital is the one format that can be used for trailers and commercials in the cinemas. Audiences can now enjoy an *entire* presentation with the high-quality sound of Dolby Digital.

**Product Manufacture**
Dolby cinema processors have evolved from the early CP100 to the latest CP650, the new standard for high-quality cinema installations. This cinema processor replays all the Dolby film formats that have evolved over the years, including the latest development in film sound, Dolby Digital Surround EX.

**The Innovations Continue**
With our ongoing research and development programme, we continue to make films sound better than ever before. To review the latest sound innovations, please visit our website.

www.dolby.com

BREAKING SOUND BARRIERS
FOR 35 YEARS

Dolby Laboratories, Inc. • Wootton Bassett, Wiltshire SN4 8QJ, England • Tel (44) 1793-842100 • Fax (44) 1793-842101
100 Potrero Avenue, San Francisco, CA 94103-4813, USA • Tel (1) 415-558-0200 • Fax (1) 415-863-1373 • www.dolby.com
Dolby, the double-D symbol and Surround EX are trademarks of Dolby Laboratories ©2000 Dolby Laboratories, Inc. W00/121

# CONTENTS

147  Georgia
149  Germany
157  Greece
160  Hong Kong
164  Hungary
169  Iceland
172  India
178  Indonesia
181  Iran
189  Ireland
194  Israel
199  Italy
205  Japan
209  Kazakhstan
211  Latvia
213  Malaysia
215  Mexico
219  Morocco
220  Nepal
222  Netherlands
229  New Zealand
232  Norway
238  Pakistan
240  Peru
242  Philippines
243  Poland
247  Portugal
250  Puerto Rico
253  Romania
255  Russia
260  Serbia & Montenegro
264  Singapore
267  Slovakia
270  South Africa
274  South Korea
279  Spain
285  Sri Lanka
287  Sweden
292  Switzerland
297  Syria
299  Taiwan
302  Thailand
304  Tunisia
306  Turkey
308  United Kingdom
319  United States
331  Venezuela
336  Zimbabwe

339  Tribute: Karlovy Vary
     International Film
     Festival's First 35
     Years
349  Guide to Leading
     Festivals
395  Film Schools
398  Film Archives
403  Book Reviews
407  Film Bookshops,
     Posters & Records
410  Magazines
416  Index to Advertisers

## INTERNATIONAL LIAISON

*Africa*: Roy Armes (Algeria, Benin, Chad, Morocco, Tunisia, Zimbabwe)
*Armenia*: Sousanna Haroutiunian
*Australia*: David Stratton, Peter Thompson
*Austria*: Beat Glur
*Belgium*: Patrick Duynslaegher
*Bosnia & Hezegovina*: Rada Šesić
*Brazil*: Nelson Hoineff
*Bulgaria*: Pavlina Jeleva
*Canada*: Brendan Kelly
*Chile*: Luz María Vela
*Croatia*: Tomislav Kurelec
*Cuba*: Andrew Paxman
*Czech Republic*: Eva Zaoralová
*Denmark*: Ebbe Iversen
*Egypt*: Fawzi Soliman
*Estonia*: Jaan Ruus
*Far East*: Derek Elley (China, Hong Kong, Taiwan)
*Finland*: Antti Selkokari
*France*: Michel Ciment
*Georgia*: Goga Lomdize
*Germany*: Jack Kindred
*Greece*: Yannis Bacoyannopoulos
*Hungary*: Derek Elley

*Iceland*: Ásgrímur Sverrisson
*India*: Uma da Cunha
*Indonesia*: Marselli Sumarno
*Iran*: Jamal Omid
*Ireland*: Michael Dwyer
*Israel*: Dan Fainaru
*Italy*: Lorenzo Codelli
*Japan*: Frank Segers
*Kazakhstan*: Eugene Zykov
*Latvia*: Andris Rozenbergs
*Malaysia*: Baharudin A. Latif
*Mexico*: Tomás Pérez Turrent
*Nepal*: Uzzwal Bhandary
*Netherlands*: Pieter van Lierop
*New Zealand*: Peter Calder
*Norway*: Trond Olav Svendsen
*Pakistan*: Aijaz Gul
*Peru*: Isaac León Frías
*Philippines*: Agustin Sotto
*Poland*: Rick Richardson
*Portugal*: Martin Dale
*Puerto Rico*: José Artemio Torres
*Romania*: Cristina Corciovescu
*Russia*: Michael Brashinsky
*Serbia & Montenegro*: Goran Gocić
*Singapore*: Yvonne Ng
*Slovakia*: Hana Cielová
*South Africa*: Martin Botha
*South Korea*: Frank Segers
*Spain*: Peter Besas
*Sri Lanka*: Amarnath Jayatilaka
*Sweden*: Bengt Forslund
*Switzerland*: Michael Sennhauser
*Syria*: Rafik Atassi
*Thailand*: Anchalee Chaiworaporn
*Turkey*: Atilla Dorsay
*United Kingdom*: Philip Kemp
*United States*: Eddie Cockrell
*Venezuela*: Andreína Lairet Morreo

# US Academy Awards 1999

Best Film: *American Beauty*.
Best Direction: Sam Mendes for *American Beauty*.
Best Actor: Kevin Spacey for *American Beauty*.
Best Actress: Hilary Swank for *Boys Don't Cry*.
Best Supporting Actor: Michael Caine for *The Cider House Rules*.
Best Supporting Actress: Angelina Jolie for *Girl, Interrupted*.
Best Original Screenplay: Alan Ball for *American Beauty*.
Best Adapted Screenplay: John Irving for *The Cider House Rules*.
Best Cinematography: Conrad L. Hall for *American Beauty*.
Best Costume Design: Lindy Hemming for *Topsy-Turvy*.
Best Art Direction: Rick Heinrichs, Peter Young for *Sleepy Hollow*.
Best Editing: *The Matrix*.
Best Original Score: John Corgiliano for *The Red Violin*.
Best Original Song: 'You'll Be in My Heart', from *Tarzan* (music and lyrics, Phil Collins).
Best Sound: *The Matrix*.
Best Make-up: Christine Blundell and Trefor Proud for *Topsy-Turvy*.

*Kevin Spacey, left, and Sam Mendes, Oscar-winners for* AMERICAN BEAUTY
*photo: Lorey Sebastian/DreamWorks*

Best Visual Effects: *The Matrix*.
Best Sound Effects Editing: *The Matrix*.
Best Foreign-Language Film: *All About My Mother* (Spain).

# British Academy of Film and Television Awards 2000

Best Film: *American Beauty*.
Best British Film: *East Is East*.

*Jude Law, BAFTA's Best Supporting Actor for THE
TALENTED MR. RIPLEY*
*photo: Phil Bray/Paramount-Miramax*

Best Direction: Pedro Almodóvar for *All About My
Mother*.
Best Actor: Kevin Spacey for *American Beauty*.
Best Actress: Annette Bening for *American Beauty*.
Best Supporting Actor: Jude Law for *The Talented Mr
Ripley*.
Best Supporting Actress: Maggie Smith for *Tea with
Mussolini*.
Best Original Screenplay: Charlie Kaufman for *Being
John Malkovich*.
Best Adapted Screenplay: Neil Jordan for *The End of
the Affair*.
Best Foreign-Language Film: *All About My Mother*
(Spain).
Audience Award: *Notting Hill*.
Fellowship Award: Michael Caine, Stanley Kubrick.

# European Film Awards 1999

European Film: *All About My Mother* (Spain).
European Actor: Ralph Fiennes for *Sunshine*
(Hungary).
European Actress: Cecilia Roth for *All About My
Mother* (Spain).
European Screenwriter: István Szabó and Israel
Horovitz for *Sunshine* (Hungary).
European Cinematographer: Lajos Koltai for
*Sunshine* and *The Legend of 1900*.
European Achievement in World Cinema: Antonio
Banderas, Roman Polanski.
European Lifetime Achievement Award: Ennio
Morricone.
European Discovery – Fassbinder Award: Tim Roth
for *The War Zone* (UK).
European Documentary Award – Prix Arte: *Buena
Vista Social Club*, Dir: Wim Wenders.
European Critics' Award – Prix FIPRESCI: *Adieu
plancher des vaches* (France), Dir: Otar Iosseliani.
'Screen International' Award for a Non-European
film: *The Straight Story* (US), Dir: David Lynch.

European Short Film: *Benvenuto in San Salvario*, Dir:
Enrico Verra.
The People's Choice Awards (voted for by movie fans
across Europe) –
Best Director: Pedro Almodóvar for *All About My
Mother* (Spain).
Best Actor: Sean Connery for *Entrapment*.
Best Actress: Catherine Zeta-Jones for *Entrapment*.

# Australian Film Institute Awards 1999

Best Film: *Two Hands* (Producer: Marian Macgowan).
Best Direction: Gregor Jordan for *Two Hands*.
Best Original Screenplay: Gregor Jordan for *Two
Hands*.
Best Adapted Screenplay: Andrew McGahan for
*Praise*.
Best Actress: Sacha Horler for *Praise*.
Best Actor: Russell Dykstra for *Soft Fruit*.
Best Supporting Actress: Sacha Horler for *Soft Fruit*.
Best Supporting Actor: Bryan Brown for *Two Hands*.
Best Cinematography: Martin McGrath for *Passion*.
Best Editing: Lee Smith for *Two Hands*.
Best Original Music Score: David Bridie for *In a
Savage Land*.
Best Production Design: Murray Picknett for *Passion*.
Best Costume Design: Terry Ryan for *Passion*.
Best Foreign Film: *Life is Beautiful* (Italy).
Byron Kennedy Award for Excellence: Baz Luhrmann
and Catherine Martin.
Raymond Longford Award for Services to the
Industry: John Politzer.
Best Young Actor: Abbie Cornish for *Wildside*.

# Italian Donatello Awards 2000

Best Film: *Bread and Tulips* (*Pane e tulipani*).

*Charlie Kaufman won BAFTA's Best Original Screenplay
award for BEING JOHN MALKOVICH*
*photo: Melissa Moseley/Universal*

*THE WAR ZONE earned Tim Roth a European Film Award*
                    *photo: Jaap Buitendijk/Film Four*

*Winona Ryder, left, with Angelina Jolie, who won the Best Supporting Actress Oscar for GIRL, INTERRUPTED*
                    *photo: Suzanne Tenner/Columbia TriStar*

Best Director: Silvio Soldini for *Bread and Tulips*.
Best Debuting Director: Alessandro Piva for *La Capagira*.
Best Producer: Amedeo Pagani for *Garage Olimpo*.
Best Actor: Bruno Ganz for *Bread and Tulips*.
Best Actress: Licia Maglietta for *Bread and Tulips*.
Best Supporting Actor: Giuseppe Battiston for *Bread and Tulips*/Leo Gullotta for *A Respectable Man*.
Best Screenplay: Doriana Leondeff, Silvio Soldini for *Bread and Tulips*.
Best Cinematography: Luca Bigazzi for *Bread and Tulips*/Fabio Cianchetti for *Making Love* (*Canone Inverso*).
Best Music: Ennio Morricone for *Making Love*.
Best Art Direction: Francesco Bronzi for *Making Love*.
Best Costumes: Sergio Ballo for *The Wet Nurse*.
Best Editing: Carla Simoncelli for *Making Love*.
Best Sound: Maurizio Argentieri for *Bread and Tulips*.
Best Foreign Film: *All About My Mother* (Spain).

# French César Academy Awards 2000

Best Director: Tonie Marshall for *Venus Beauty*.
Best Film: *Venus Beauty*.
Best Actor: Daniel Auteuil for *The Girl on the Bridge*.
Best Actress: Karine Viard for *Raise the Heart*.
Best Supporting Actor: François Berleand for *My Little Business*.
Best Supporting Actress: Charlotte Gainsbourg for *Season's Beatings*.
Best Young Actor: Eric Caravaca for *What Is Life?*.
Best Young Actress: Audrey Tautou for *Venus Beauty*.
Best First Film: *Tracks*.
Best Foreign Film: *All About My Mother* (Spain).
Best Original Screenplay: Tonie Marshall for *Venus Beauty*.
Best Music: Bruno Coulais for *Caravan*.
Best Photography: Eric Guichard for *Caravan*.

Best Editing: Emmanuele Castro for *Tracks*.
Best Sets: Philippe Chiffre for *Rembrandt*.
Best Costumes: Catherine Leterrier for *The Messenger: The Story of Joan of Arc*.
Best Short Film: Delphine Gleize for *Sale Battars*.

# German Film Awards 2000

Best Film: *Nowhere to Go*.
Best Director: Pepe Danquart for *Home Game*.
Best Actor: Uwe Ochsenknecht for *Football Rules OK*.
Best Actress: Hannelore Elsner for *Nowhere to Go*.
Best Supporting Actor: Edgar Selge for *Three Chinamen with a Double Bass*.
Best Supporting Actress: Henriette Heinze for *Paths in the Night*.
Best Documentary: *Buena Vista Social Club*.
Best Children's Film: *Captain Blue Bear*.
Best Foreign Film: *All About My Mother* (Spain).
Prize of Honour: Gyula Trebitsch, producer.

# Belgian Joseph Plateau Awards 1999

Best Film: *Rosie*.
Best Director: Patrice Toye for *Rosie*.
Best Actor: Benoît Poelvoorde for *Les Convoyeurs attendent*.
Best Actress: Aranka Coppens for *Rosie*.
Special Joseph Plateau Award for Excellence in Film-making: Bonny Arnold, Peter Greenaway.
Special Joseph Plateau Award for Acting (international): Sandra Bullock.
Special Joseph Plateau Honorary Award: Irwin Winkler.
Special Joseph Plateau Lifetime Achievement Award: Stanley Donen, Ennio Morricone.

# At the top of Scandinavia

From now on you can reach the entire Scandinavian market, with more than 20 million people, through one new powerful film company.

In key cities of Denmark, Finland, Norway and Sweden 140 screens are waiting for you. And more well-equipped multi-movie theatres are under way.

So, whenever you are ready to launch a new film, welcome to the number one film company of Scandinavia.

# DIRECTORS
## of the year

## Lasse Hallström

### By Bengt Forslund

L asse Hallström is the first Swedish director to have forged a Hollywood career since Victor Sjöström in the 1920s. Sjöström made nine silent films between 1923 and 1929, with stars like Lillian Gish, Garbo and John Gilbert, and was regarded as one of 'the big four' from Europe, along with Chaplin, Lubitsch and von Stroheim. It was easier for film-makers from continental Europe at that time, since today Hollywood seems to prefer its international directors to come from English-speaking countries like Britain, Canada and Australia.

Ingmar Bergman almost made *The Merry Widow* with Barbra Streisand, but did not feel comfortable in Hollywood and changed his mind at the last minute. The next Swede to be invited to LA was Jan Troell, after his success with *The Emigrants*, and he made two Hollywood productions, another story about European settlers in America, *Zandy's Bride* (1974), and some years later *The Hurricane*. But Troell, being his own photographer and editor, was only allowed to work as a director, and that restriction led him to return home.

Although he also was his own cameraman and editor early in his career, Hallström is a different type of character. Long before he got an offer to shoot a film in America, thanks to the success of *My Life as a Dog* (1985), he had dreamed about a Hollywood career. His first 12 years in America were rather tough, and produced only three films, but he remained determined to build a real Hollywood career.

With the Oscar success of *The Cider House Rules* in 2000, he achieved his breakthrough and is now enjoying one of the most elusive positions for a director: being able to make definite plans for the film *after*

*Still from A LOVER AND HIS LASS, Hallström's debut feature*

*photo: Svensk Filmindustri*

the one you're currently working on. He enjoyed a comparable luxury in Sweden after he had, reluctantly, made his feature debut in 1975 with *A Lover and his Lass*. Reluctant? Yes, I was his producer, so I know. But let's take it from the beginning.

## Home movies

LASSE HALLSTRÖM was born in Stockholm in June 1946. His childhood was a happy one, in an artistic and rather wealthy family. His father was a dentist but also a devoted amateur film director, on 8mm and 16mm. His mother was a poet of some ability, and as her son had a musical ear he gained admission to the special musical high school in Stockholm, the Adolf Fredriks Musikskola.

A musical career was a possibility – and music has always played an important part in his movies – but the hobby of his father was more tempting. He made his first film aged just ten, *The Ghost Thief*, and in high school he went on making 8mm films for school shows, mostly comedies, with a good helping of slapstick, as his father had introduced him at a very early age to Chaplin's short films.

Television came to Sweden at the end of the 1950s, so Hallström belonged to the first generation of teenagers fascinated by this new medium, and it was natural for him to make his first more professional film with television in mind. It was about a popular pop group, The Mascots, whose members all attended Hallström's school. He made it on 16mm, and was his own photographer and editor. Swedish Television was not only happy to buy it, they asked for more, and as a freelance he made three variety entertainment series for young people, *Popside*, in 1967-68, followed by *Hug* (*Kram*) and *Laughter* (*Skratt*) in 1969.

That year Swedish Television launched its second channel and Hallström acquired his first permanent contract, as entertainment producer. Over the following years he made all kinds of programmes, mainly featuring music and comic sketches. He

*The fab four on tour in ABBA - THE MOVIE*
*photo: Kobal Collection*

had a close buddy from school, "Brasse" Brännström, and another one from university, Magnus Härenstam, whom he introduced, and the pair became a well known double-act, "Magnus & Brasse", in the 1970s.

## A reluctant debut

Hallström could have stayed with television (a job he enjoyed) if he had not made a one hour film in 1973, *Ska vi gå hem till mig eller dig eller var och en till sitt?* (literally, 'Shall we go back to my place, or is everyone going home?'). It was a charming contemporary comedy about young people with a passion for disco music, very much improvised with his friends. There was not much of a story, but great sympathy for everyday life: a film with a heart.

I had just taken on the responsibility for building up a production centre at the Swedish Film Institute, trying to find new talents, and I immediately contacted this promising young director. Why not make a real movie for the cinemas, I asked him. Usually young directors are only too eager to make their first movie. Hallström was not. He liked the short format, preferably sketches, and spending a year making just one film was not his style. *Ska vi gå hem...* had been an exception, and he had no faith in himself as a feature director.

It took me a year to convince him otherwise, but in 1974 we finally had a script – in the same spirit as *Ska vi gå hem...* – and could start shooting. Hallström was cameraman and co-writer; his pal, Brasse, the other writer, played the lead: a young, hypochondriac guy called Lasse, with no special ambitions, looking for girls and trying to find himself a place in life. The fictional Lasse was very much a composite portrait of the two men in their younger days.

The shooting took its time: 70 days. Hallström was nervous, improvised a lot, and shot a huge amount of footage – 100 hours' worth. As a result, post-production also took its time, with Hallström doing the editing himself, but when *A Lover and His Lass* finally opened in the summer of 1975, it was an immediate success with both critics and the public, attracting a million admissions within a few months. No more television for Hallström.

Svensk Filmindustri, the biggest Swedish production company, picked him up, but before signing a long-term contract with them he could not refuse another offer, a possibility to go back to his roots, by making a documentary about Swedish pop giants ABBA, during their 1976 tour of Australia. *ABBA – The Movie* gave Hallström a lot of money to spend – and to make. He enjoyed making it and the public enjoyed the film.

### Svensk's golden boy

Hallström went on to make six films for Svensk Filmindustri, all successful. *Father-to-be* (1979) and *Two Lovers and a Lass* (1983) were very much in the same style as his debut: partially improvised with his close

friends, Magnus and Brasse. Both films addressed the role of men in a society whose women were becoming ever stronger – a theme which one also could find in *The Rooster* (1981), an adaptation of a short story, *The Women Factory*, about an engineer who is the boss of a factory whose workers are all women.

While Hallström may not be regarded as an auteur in his more recent work, he certainly merited that description in these early films about his own generation. He calls them "recognition films", since he hopes that the male members of the audience will – with a smile – recognise themselves in the male protagonists' shame, clumsiness, stupidity. *Father-to-be* is a good example, a film about a man expecting his first child (Lasse's own situation in 1978-79) and contemplating the prison bars shutting out his happy bachelor life. His inspiration in those films came very much from John Cassavetes and Milos Forman, the two directors he admired most.

After his fabulous success in 1985 with *My Life as a Dog*, the moving and amusing tale of the emotional crises endured by 12-year-old Ingemar Johansson in a rural Swedish community in 1959, Lasse's insight into the adult world was pushed to one side. He had inspired such a memorable performance from young Anton Glanzelius as Ingemar that producers in Sweden and abroad were now more interested in his talent for directing kids.

*Still from FATHER-TO-BE, one of Hallström's "recognition films"*

*photo: Svensk Filmindustri*

*Anton Glanzelius, left, as the young hero of MY LIFE AS A DOG, with Tomas von Brömssen*

*photo: Svensk Filmindustri*

24 January - 4 February 2001

# 30th INTERNATIONAL FILM FESTIVAL ROTTERDAM

Lou Ye - Pablo Trapero - Karin Ottarsdóttir
Winners of the VPRO Tiger Award
International Film Festival Rotterdam 2000

www.filmfestivalrotterdam.com

*The eponymous heroes of CHILDREN OF BULLERBYN VILLAGE*

*photo: Svensk Filmindustri*

Sweden has a long tradition of making children's films, and by the mid-1980s there had been a film based on one of Astrid Lindgren's books released each Christmas for more than 20 years. Running out of unfilmed Lindgren titles, Svensk Filmindustri decided to start all over again, and Hallström was asked to shoot a remake of two early books: the stories about the kids in the little hamlet of Bullerbyn in the 1920s.

*Children of Bullerbyn Village* (1986) and *More About the Children of Bullerbyn* (1987) were well made and played, extremely beautiful, very nostalgic, and as successful as the earlier Lindgren films – but not very interesting. For Hallström as a director they were a step backwards, but during their production he received several offers from America, and told Swedish journalists: 'Hollywood, here I come!'

*My Life as a Dog* had received two Academy Award nominations in 1986, for Hallström as director and as Best Foreign Language Film, and was the most popular foreign film in America 1987. All the big companies lined up for Hallström. His agent, Spiros Skouras, wanted him to make a movie of *Peter Pan*, but Disney would not sell the rights and Steven Spielberg, who had initially encouraged Hallström in this project, decided to make his own modern version, *Hook*. The Swedish outsider had to think again.

## All American families

His Hollywood debut was the romantic

*Leonardo DiCaprio, left, Johnny Depp, centre, and Juliette Lewis in WHAT'S EATING GILBERT GRAPE?*

*photo: Kobal Collection*

comedy *Once Around* (1991), released in the same year as *Hook*. Neither was a success, but the critics agreed that *Once Around* – which unluckily opened on the weekend that the Gulf War erupted – was the better film. A heartbroken Holly Hunter, in a close Italian family, is courted by a very American salesman (Richard Dreyfuss), creating a collision between two cultures; something Hallström had started to learn about at first hand.

*What's Eating Gilbert Grape?*(1993) was, however, more his own choice, closer to the family relationship drama of *My Life as a Dog*, in telling the story of an obese mother and her adolescent kids in the countryside of Iowa. Having a Swedish producer and the Swedish cameraman Sven Nykvist by his side, Hallström felt more at home and he enjoyed working – and improvising (a method he is still very fond of) – with the young actors: Johnny Depp, Juliette Lewis and a teenage Leonardo DiCaprio, who was Oscar-nominated as Best Supporting Actor in his breakthrough role.

The next film – though not Hallström's first choice, as many prospective projects had fallen through in the interim – was a more conventional story about an unfaithful husband and his lass, *Something to Talk About* (1995). With Julia Roberts starring as the wronged wife, the film took $50m in America.

He then tried to find a project on which he could work with his wife, the actress Lena Olin, whom he had married in 1994. At least two ideas came close to realisation, but when offered *The Cider House Rules* by John Irving, he accepted the challenge. Other directors had been involved and departed; Irving knew precisely what he wanted and Hallström understood his wishes. He was fond of the very special characters in Irving's novel: the eccentric doctor fighting for the right to perform abortions, his timid pupil (a typical Hallström character, uncertain of himself, looking for meaning in life) and the strong girls around them; women are always stronger than men in a Hallström film.

And if the meaning of life is to find one's way, the boy in the film finally made it and so did Lasse Hallström. *The Cider House Rules* (1999) received no less than seven nominations for Academy Awards, among them Best Film and Best Director, making Hallström the first person to be nominated in that category for foreign-language and English-language films. In the end he had to be satisfied with two Oscars, for Irving's adapted screenplay, and Michael Caine as the abortionist. That success, and a US

*Kyra Sedgwick, left, Julia Roberts, centre, and Gena Rowlands in SOMETHING TO TALK ABOUT*
*photo: Demmie Todd/Warners*

gross of more than $50m, secured a solid future for Hallström in Hollywood.

As this article went to press he had finished shooting *Chocolat*, a comedy for Miramax about a single mother (Juliette Binoche) who opens a chocolate shop in a sleepy French village in the 1950s, disrupting the quiet lives of its residents. The cast also includes Lena Olin and Johnny Depp. Another film, starring Kevin Spacey, is in the pipeline. The future looks bright – or should we say brighter than ever. Hallström has always found himself on the sunny side of the street, though he is too shy, and too much of a hypochondriac to admit it.

BENGT FORSLUND was a well-known film producer for 30 years at Svensk Filmindustri, the Swedish Film Institute and Nordic Film & TV Fund. He is also a film historian and author of several books on cinema, including the definitive study of Victor Sjöström, and a volume on Sven Nykvist.

# Lasse Hallström Filmography

**1975**
**EN KILLE OCH EN TJEJ**
**(A Lover and His Lass)**

Script: LH, "Brasse" Brännströms. Direction: LH. Photography: LH, Lasse Karlsson. Editing: LH, Jan Pehrson. Music: Berndt Egerbladh. Production Design: Stig Limér. Players: "Brasse" Brännström (*Lasse*), Mariann Rudberg (*Lena*), Christer "Bonzo" Jonsson (*Bosse*). Produced by

Bengt Forslund, Olle Hellbom for Svenska Filminstitutet/Svensk Filmindustri (SF). 94 mins.

———

**1977**
**ABBA – THE MOVIE**

Documentary. Script: LH, Bob Caswell. Direction: LH. Photography: Jack Churchill, Paul Onorato. Editing: LH, Malou Hallström, Ulf Neidemar. Music: Benny Andersson, Stickan

Andersson, Björn Ulvaeus. Production Design: Åke Nordwall. Players: ABBA. Produced by Stig Andersson, Reg Grundy for Polar Music/Reg Grundy Prod. (Australia). 97 mins.

———

**1979**
**JAG ÄR MED BARN**
**(Father-to-be)**

Script: LH, Brasse Brännström, Olle Hellbom. Direction: LH.

Photography: Roland Lundin. Editing: LH. Music: Bengt Palmers. Production Design: Bengt Peters. Players: Magnus Härenstam (*Bosse, copywriter*), Anki Lidén (*Lena*), Micha Gabay (*Bosse's pal*). Produced by Olle Hellbom for SF. 107 mins.

## 1981
### TUPPEN (The Rooster)

Script: Olle Hellbom, LH, Catti Edfeldt, from a short story by Ivar Lo-Johansson. Direction: LH. Photography: Jörgen Persson. Editing: LH, Jan Persson. Music: Gunnar Svensson, Georg Riedel. Production Design: Lasse Westfelt, Tove Hellbom. Players: Magnus Härenstam (*Engineer Cederqvist*), Allan Edwall (*Hall porter*), Pernilla Wållgren (*Åsa*), Maria Johansson (*Hjördis*). Produced by Olle Hellbom for SF. 97 mins.

## 1983
### TVÅ KILLAR OCH EN TJEJ (Two Lovers and A Lass)

Script: LH, "Brasse" Brännström, Magnus Härenstam. Direction: LH. Photography: Roland Lundin. Editing: LH, Jan Persson. Music: Handel, Puccini, Verdi, Leoncavallo, Donizetti. Production Design: Lasse Westfelt. Players: "Brasse" Brännström (*Thomas*),

Magnus Härenstam (*Klasse*), Pia Green (*Anna*). Produced by Waldemar Bergendahl for SF. 111 mins.

## 1985
### MITT LIV SOM HUND (My Life as a Dog)

Script: LH, Reidar Jönsson, "Brasse" Brännström, Pelle Berglund, based on a novel by Reidar Jönsson. Direction: LH. Photography: Jörgen Persson. Editing: Christer Furubrand, Susanne Linnman. Music: Björn Isfält. Production Design: Lasse Westfelt. Players: Anton Glanzelius (*Ingemar Johansson*), Anki Lidén (*His mother*), Tomas von Brömssen (*His uncle*), Melinda Kinnaman (*Saga*). Produced by Waldemar Bergendahl for SF. 101 mins.

## 1986
### ALLA VI BARN I BULLERBYN (Children of Bullerbyn Village)

Script: Astrid Lindgren, based on her books. Direction: LH. Photography: Jens Fischer. Editing: Susanne Linnman. Music: Georg Riedel. Production Design: Lasse Westfelt. Players: Anna Sahlin (*Anna*), Henrik Larsson (*Bosse*), Linda Bergström (*Lisa*), Crispin Dickson Wendenius (*Lasse*). Produced by Waldemar

Bergendahl for SF. 90 mins.

## 1987
### MER OM OSS BARN I BULLERBYN (More About the Children of Bullerbyn)

Script: Astrid Lindgren, based on her books. Direction: LH. Photography: Jens Fischer. Editing: Susanne Linnman. Music: Georg Riedel. Production Design: Lasse Westfelt. Players: Anna Sahlin (*Anna*), Henrik Larsson (*Bosse*), Linda Bergström (*Lisa*). Crispin Dickson Wendenius (*Lasse*). Produced by Waldemar Bergendahl for SF. 89 mins.

## 1990
### ONCE AROUND

Script: Malia Scotch Marmo. Direction: LH. Photography: Theo van de Sande. Editing: Andrew Dunne. Music: James Horner. Production Design: David Gropman. Players: Holly Hunter (*Renata Bella*), Richard Dreyfuss (*Sam Sharpe*), Danny Aiello (*Joe Bella*), Laura San Giacomo (*Jan Bella*), Gena Rowlands (*Marilyn Bella*). Produced by Ami Robinson, Griffin Dunne for Universal Pictures. 115 mins.

## 1993
### WHAT'S EATING GILBERT GRAPE?

Script: Peter Hedges, based on his novel. Direction: LH. Photography: Sven Nykvist. Editing: Andrew Mondshein. Music: Alan Parker, Björn Isfält. Production Design: Bernt Capra. Players: Johnny Depp (*Gilbert Grape*), Juliette Lewis (*Becky*), Mary Steenburgen (*Betty Carver*), Leonardo DiCaprio (*Arnie Grape*), Darlene Cates (*Mommy*). Produced by Meir Teper, Bertil Ohlsson, David Matalon for J&M Entertainment. 118 mins.

*Richard Dreyfuss and Holly Hunter in ONCE AROUND*
*photo: Jim Bridges/Universal*

## 1995
### SOMETHING TO TALK ABOUT

Script: Callie Khouri. Direction: LH. Photography: Sven Nykvist.

Editing: Mia Goldman. Music: Hans Zimmer, Graham Preskett. Production Design: Mel Bourne. Players: Julia Roberts (*Grace*), Dennis Quaid (*Eddie*), Robert Duvall (*Wyly King*), Gena Rowlands (*Georgia*), Kyra Sedgwick (*Emma Rae*). Produced by Anthea Sylbert, Paula Weinstein for Spring Creek Production. 105 mins.

### 1999
### THE CIDER HOUSE RULES

Script: John Irving, based on his novel. Direction: LH. Photography: Oliver Stapleton. Editing: Lisa Zeno Churgin. Music: Rachel Portman. Production Design: David Gropman. Players: Tobey Maguire (*Homer*), Michael Caine (*Dr Larch*), Charlize Theron (*Candy Kendal*), Delroy Lindo (*Mr Rose*), Jane Alexander (*Sister Edna*). Produced by Richard Gladstein for Miramax. 126 mins.

*Hallström, centre, with Tobey Maguire, on location for THE CIDER HOUSE RULES*

photo: Stephan Vaughan/Miramax

### 2000
### CHOCOLAT

Script: Robert Nelson Jacobs, based on the novel by Joanne Harris. Direction: LH. Players: Juliette Binoche, Judi Dench, Johnny Depp, Alfred Molina, Carrie-Anne Moss, Lena Olin, Peter Stormare, Leslie Caron. Produced by David Brown, Kit Golden and Leslie Holleran for Miramax.

# Neil Jordan

### By Michael Dwyer

While it is not uncommon for novelists to turn occasionally to screenwriting, it is extremely unusual for a novelist to turn to film-making at the expense of his own writing career, and even more so for someone from a literary background to display the visual imagination and flair which has marked Neil Jordan's prolific career.

Having observed him at work on different sets throughout his career, it is evident that Jordan is equally at ease on a logistically difficult epic such as *Michael Collins* or an intimate, personal drama like *The Miracle*. It is also clear that he is consumed by writing. There are certain recurring motifs in his œuvre – the moral dilemmas of characters caught up in violence, the fantasy world of children, seaside locations and saxophone players – but his fertile, prolific imagination has turned out a remarkably diverse collection of scripts.

NEIL JORDAN was born by the sea, in County Sligo on the west coast of Ireland on February 25, 1950, the son of a teacher father and painter mother. The family moved to the east coast two years later, to a seaside suburb of Dublin. Jordan studied at University College Dublin, where he took a First in History, specialising in Early Christian History.

In the 1970s he was a founder of the Irish Writers Co-Op, which published his early short stories, and he acted, wrote and directed with the Children's T Company and with the Slot Players, a fringe theatre group which also included brothers Jim and Peter Sheridan, both also destined for film-making careers. Jordan idolised Charlie Parker, bought a saxophone and played with a Dublin band, which helps explain the prominence of this instrument in several of his movies.

His first work for the screen was the script for an Irish television film, *Memories and Miss Langan*. He adapted one of his finest short stories, 'Night in Tunisia', for an underestimated television film directed by Pat O'Connor, and scripted Joe Comerford's 1978 Irish feature, *Traveller*.

## Ulster's *Angel*, Carter's *Wolves*

Jordan worked with John Boorman on the final draft of the shooting script for *Excalibur* (1981), on which Jordan is credited as creative consultant, and made his directing debut with the documentary *The Making of Excalibur: Myth Into Movie*. "I had never even taken a photograph," Jordan admitted at the time. "I didn't know one end of a camera from the other." Jordan has always thanked Boorman for smoothing his transition from writing to film-making. "It also helped that [my] writing... was so heavily influenced by cinema that it was getting ridiculous for me to continue doing it as prose."

Boorman served as executive producer on Jordan's first feature, *Angel* (1982), an

*Stephen Rea as the hero of ANGEL, Jordan's feature debut*
*photo: Kobal Collection*

ironic exploration of the metaphysics of violence, with Stephen Rea as a dance band saxophonist traumatised by the murder of his manager and a mute girl fan by mobster paramilitaries in Northern Ireland. He is transformed into an angel of vengeance in this resonant and supremely stylish thriller, strikingly lit by Chris Menges.

Although too unconventional in form to make a mark commercially, *Angel* was widely embraced by critics at Cannes in 1982. Those excited included Stephen Woolley, who unsuccessfully tried to buy the UK rights for his then fledgling Palace Pictures. Woolley went on to produce all of Jordan's subsequent movies and the duo recently formed a production company whose first feature will be a film about actors, from the young, gifted Irish writer-director, Conor McPherson.

*The outlandish banquet from THE COMPANY OF WOLVES*
*photo: Palace/Kobal Collection*

Stephen Rea, whose complex central performance was the emotional heart of *Angel*, became a regular actor in Jordan's films, including *The Company of Wolves* (1984). This assured, inventive spin on the traditional werewolf movie grew from Jordan's collaboration with the English novelist Angela Carter. It expanded the genre to explore myths and fairytales, fear and desire and a 13-year-old girl's burgeoning sexuality, and was played out with a wry, knowing humour, on fantastical sets designed by Anton Furst. Woolley's Palace Pictures had the confidence to push the picture out of the arthouse market into mainstream cinemas in the UK and Ireland, where it became a surprise commercial success.

By contrast, Jordan's third feature, *Mona Lisa* (1986), confronted reality directly and again was rooted in fear and desire as it followed the relationship between a disillusioned ex-convict (Bob Hoskins) and the prostitute (Cathy Tyson) he is assigned to protect. Filmed on authentically sleazy locations in Brighton, it developed a touching and passionate love story at the core of a dark thriller. Jordan elicited memorable performances from Hoskins (named Best Actor at Cannes), Tyson and Michael Caine, oozing menace as a London mobster.

Jordan followed *Mona Lisa* with two US-financed comedies, neither of which impressed audiences or critics. Jordan intended *High Spirits* (1988) to blend humour and horror. Set in a rundown Irish stately home marketed as a haunted house and then invaded by real spirits, it was taken out of Jordan's hands during post-production; 20 minutes were removed, reducing the film to a whimsical farce.

Jordan's only film to date to be scripted by another writer, *We're No Angels* (1989), is a very loose reworking by David Mamet of the 1955 film of the same name, handsomely photographed but under-mined by mannered performances from Robert De Niro and Sean Penn as escaped convicts posing as priests in a Depression-stricken town renowned for its shrine to a weeping Madonna.

*Cathy Tyson and Bob Hoskins as prostitute and ex-con in* MONA LISA

*photo: Kobal Collection*

## A *Miracle* and a secret

*The Miracle* (1990) saw Jordan back on home ground – literally so, in that much of the film was shot in a house two doors away from his seafront home in Bray, Co. Wicklow. Summertime in Bray is the setting for this seductive story of two young dreamers, Jimmy and Rose (newcomers Niall Byrne and Lorraine Pilkington), 15-year-old friends indolently devising speculative scenarios for the various characters they observe on the promenade.

The pair become particularly intrigued by Renee (Beverly D'Angelo), an American actress in Dublin to perform in a tatty musical based on the Western *Destry Rides Again*. Jimmy's obsession with Renee turns into sexual attraction and he finds himself in too deep before discovering that she knows his father, Sam (Donal McCann), an alcoholic who plays saxophone with a local band. Finally, Jimmy realises that the object of his desire is his mother who, Sam had told him, had died a long time ago.

Charming, colourful and confidently unconventional, *The Miracle* requires and rewards the willing suspension of disbelief. When the narrative confronts the taboo theme of incest, Jordan's response is sure-footed and sensitive. Arguably Jordan's most underrated film, *The Miracle* was sparsely released internationally, despite some excellent reviews. Jordan's disillusionment at its fortunes deepened as he and Woolley struggled to raise the very

*Jaye Davidson, standing, and Miranda Richardson in*
*THE CRYING GAME*

photo: Kobal Collection

low budget for his next film, *The Crying Game* (1992).

He decided to abandon movies and return to writing novels if the project failed: "I just thought how making movies is all so much work, and if I'm not allowed to do anything interesting, and if people don't want to see the type of films I make, I don't want to make them anymore. I sat down and wrote a novel [*Sunrise With Sea Monster*]. Then *The Crying Game* came out and was very successful."

There are many unpredictable twists in this tantalising contemporary thriller, laced with dry, ironic humour and an unexpected vein of romance. Stephen Rea plays Fergus, an IRA volunteer asked by Jody (Forest Whitaker), the doomed black British soldier he is holding captive in Northern Ireland, to seek out his lover, Dil (Jaye Davidson, who resembles *Mona Lisa* star Cathy Tyson), in London. Fergus is

drawn into a complex multiple dilemma as Jordan turns up the tension, sexual and dramatic, exploring questions of loyalty, politics, love and desire. It's a heady, brilliantly sustained concoction.

The key to the film's commercial success was the clever campaign built by Miramax around the movie's central secret regarding Dil's gender. It built a momentum at the box-office, taking over $70m in the US and collecting six Oscar nominations, including Best Picture and Director, with Jordan deservedly receiving the statuette for Best Original Screenplay.

## Controversial horror, history

Suddenly, Jordan was a hot property and Warner Bros signed him to direct a lavish, big-budget genre piece, *Interview With the Vampire* (1994), based on the best-seller by Anne Rice, the first in a series featuring the vampire Lestat. An elegant and richly atmospheric Gothic horror movie, it features Brad Pitt as Louis, a vampire who tells a present-day journalist the story of how as a widowed New Orleans plantation manager in 1791 he fell in with the predatory Lestat (a comfortably cast-against-type Tom Cruise).

As Lestat initiates Louis into the life of a vampire, their relationship is charged with homoerotic tension, and the couple becomes a bizarre triangle with the addition of 12-year-old Claudia (Kirsten Dunst). Jordan taps into the Catholic guilt which suffuses Rice's novel, focusing on Louis' moral dilemma: he longs to be punished, though no punishment comes. The movie's closest reference point in Jordan's work is clearly *The Company of Wolves*, with both films drawn from stories by women writers who daringly connect sexuality and violence.

During production, Rice courted controversy by attacking the casting of Cruise, but when she saw the finished film, she changed her mind and took out full-page ads in the trade press to express her unqualified enthusiasm. Taking more than $200m worldwide, the film became

*Antonio Banderas, left, takes direction from Jordan for*
*INTERVIEW WITH THE VAMPIRE*
*photo: Geffen/Kobal Collection*

*Liam Neeson, centre, as MICHAEL COLLINS*
*photo: Tom Collins/Geffen*

Jordan's biggest commercial success, and encouraged Warner Bros to finance his long-cherished project, *Michael Collins* (1996). This biopic about the man who was a key political figure in Ireland from the 1916 uprising to his assassination in 1922, at the age of 31, is thrilling epic cinema, made with tremendous flair.

Jordan's film depicts Collins, robustly played by Liam Neeson, as a charming, seductive personality, a determined pragmatist who is not without self-doubt, capable of violence but able to realise when the fighting had to stop. A lucid, salutary history lesson, powerfully relevant to the ongoing schisms in Northern Ireland, Jordan's film was controversial, with many commentators attacking his allegedly anti-British interpretation of historical facts; although many of its early detractors ate their words after finally seeing the film.

*Michael Collins* is the most important film made in or about Ireland. Audiences unaccustomed to seeing their country's history brought so vividly to life made it Ireland's biggest-ever box-office success (although *Titanic* has since eclipsed the record). At Venice, it took the Golden Lion for Best Film and Neeson won Best Actor.

### Childhood trauma, past and present

Jordan's next film, *The Butcher Boy* (1997), was adapted from a 1992 novel by Patrick McCabe, which, with its stream-of-consciousness narration, had seemed unfilmable. Yet Jordan and McCabe's

screenplay produced a clear, surreal and distinctly unsettling film. Eamonn Owens, a gifted young newcomer, plays the title character, Francie Brady, an outwardly cheerful 13-year-old living in a small Irish town in the early 1960s, with his morose and feckless alcoholic father (Stephen Rea) and his manic depressive, suicidal mother (Aisling O'Sullivan).

Francie takes refuge from his dysfunctional family in an idyllic fantasy world of schoolboy games and comic-books. Left perplexed, insecure and alone in a threatening adult world after he loses both parents and then the company of his best friend, Francie releases his confused rage in an explosion of violence. This remarkable picture – which earned Jordan the Silver Bear for Best Director at Berlin – precisely catches the repression and hypocrisy of a small Irish town in the days when lace curtains were kept firmly drawn against anything that shattered the superficial contentment of daily life. The wild black humour which erupts uproariously at the most unlikely moments counterpoints the intensity of the drama – smiles abruptly wiped from the audience's faces.

With its heightened, stylised approach to an innocent child swept forward by fear and cruelty, *The Butcher Boy* again echoes *The Company of Wolves*, and both films are evoked in Jordan's *In Dreams* (1998), whose deeply disturbed protagonist, Vivian (Robert Downey Jr), has been irreparably damaged since childhood, when he was horrifically abused by his mother.

*Eamonn Owens as Francie Brady, THE BUTCHER BOY*
*photo: Geffen/Kobal Collection*

Claire Cooper (Annette Bening), a children's book illustrator, has vivid premonitions of a young girl being abducted in a forest, and these prove horribly true when her little daughter disappears during a woodland staging of *Snow White*. With accumulating intensity, *In Dreams* follows the distraught Claire and the disturbed Vivian along parallel lines, which begin to converge as the psycho-drama reaches its inevitable showdown.

It opened in the US at the beginning of 1999 to unfairly scathing reviews, which were in marked contrast to the many glowing notices accorded Jordan's Graham Greene adaptation, *The End of the Affair* (1999), when it opened towards the end of the same year. The narrative unfolds in an artfully devised, time-shifting structure, covering 1939-1946 and charting the passionate relationship between a self-absorbed, narcissistic novelist, Maurice Bendrix (Ralph Fiennes), and the emotionally repressed Sarah Miles (Julianne Moore), the wife of a dour, asexual civil servant, Henry (Stephen Rea).

The turning point of the story, a cataclysmic air raid vividly illustrated by Jordan from his protagonists' differing viewpoints, introduces a fourth character into the love triangle, God. As with the central revelation of Jordan's *The Crying Game*, this dramatic incident and its consequences demand a willing suspension of disbelief – which the film them amply rewards. Greene's novel, suffused by his preoccupation with sex, jealousy, God and death, had been filmed by Edward Dmytryk in an all-too-literal 1955 version, with the remarkable Deborah Kerr as Sarah and the blank, wooden Van Johnson as Bendrix. Jordan's altogether

*Julianne Moore and Ralph Fiennes in THE END OF THE AFFAIR*
*photo: Columbia TriStar*

superior treatment makes for haunting, quietly devastating cinema, powered by fine acting: Fiennes at his least mannered, Rea, as good as ever in his eighth Jordan film, and Moore, magnetic as the sensual, vulnerable Sarah.

Jordan and Moore reunited for the 14-minute *Not I*, the first film in the Samuel Beckett Film Project, which is adapting all 19 of Beckett's stage plays. Adhering firmly to the author's instructions, Jordan's film is an intense series of close-ups on the mouth of a woman (Moore) delivering a trauma-driven monologue with a hypnotic rhythm, heightened by seamless editing.

What Jordan does next remains to be seen. He has bought the film rights to another Patrick McCabe novel, *Breakfast On Pluto*, and is also contemplating a remake of Jean-Pierre Melville's 1955 film noir, *Bob le Flambeur*, in which Roger Duchesne played a retired bank robber and inveterate gambler planning a raid on the casino at Deauville. Jordan has also been writing *Lucrezia*, a screenplay about the Borgias, whose outrageous life stories would, he believes, make "a fascinating film... like *The Godfather* set in the Vatican."

Given his remarkably prolific output, his next feature is unlikely to be a long time coming. Over the past 18 years he has directed 12 features, writing or co-writing all but one of them, and written three novels. In 1991, commenting on having made six films in under 10 years, Jordan said: "I think you could make 20 films in the same time, if you could raise the money. After all, it takes only 10 to 14 weeks to shoot a film and about the same amount of time to cut it." Writing screenplays is a much quicker process than writing novels, he added. "A screenplay is about 100 pages long and there's a lot of space between the words."

MICHAEL DWYER has been Film Correspondent with *The Irish Times* in Dublin since 1988. He founded the Dublin Film Festival in 1985 and programmed it for its first six years, and has produced and presented three television series about movies.

# Neil Jordan Filmography

**1982**
**ANGEL**

US title: *Danny Boy*. Script and Direction: NJ. Photography: Chris Menges. Editing: Pat Duffner. Production Design: John Lucas. Players: Stephen Rea (*Danny*), Honor Heffernan (*Deirdre*), Veronica Quilligan (*Annie*), Peter Caffrey (*Ray*), Alan Devlin (*Bill*). Produced by Barry Blackmore. 92 mins.

**1984**
**THE COMPANY OF WOLVES**

Script: Angela Carter and NJ, based on short stories by Carter. Direction: NJ. Photography: Bryan Loftus. Editing: Rodney Holland. Music: George Fenton. Production Design: Anton Furst. Players: Angela Lansbury (*Granny*), David Warner (*Father*), Stephen Rea (*Young Groom*), Sarah Patterson (*Rosaleen*). Produced by Chris Brown and Stephen Woolley. 95 mins.

**1986**
**MONA LISA**

Script: NJ and David Leland. Direction: NJ. Photography: Roger Pratt. Editing: Lesley Walker. Music: Michael Kamen. Production Design: Jamie Leonard. Players: Bob Hoskins (*George*), Cathy Tyson (*Simone*), Michael Caine (*Mortwell*). Prod: Stephen Woolley and Patrick Cassavetti. 104 mins.

**1988**
**HIGH SPIRITS**

Script and Direction: NJ. Photography: Alex Thomson. Editing: Michael Bradsell. Music: George Fenton. Production Design: Anton Furst. Players: Peter O'Toole (*Peter Plunkett*), Daryl Hannah (*Mary Plunkett*), Steve Guttenberg (*Jack*), Liam Neeson (*Martin Brogan*), Beverly D'Angelo (*Sharon*), Jennifer Tilly (*Miranda*), Ray McAnally (*Plunkett Senior*). Produced by Stephen Woolley and David Saunders. 96 mins.

**1989**
**WE'RE NO ANGELS**

Script: David Mamet, based on Albert Husson's play, *La Cuisine des Anges*. Direction: NJ. Photography: Philippe Rousselot. Editing: Mick Audsley, Joke Van Wijk. Music: George Fenton. Production Design: Wolf Kroeger. Players: Robert De Niro (*Ned*), Sean Penn (*Jim*), Demi Moore

(*Molly*), Hoyt Axton (*Father Levesque*), Bruno Kirby (*Deputy*), Ray McAnally (*Warden*). Produced by Art Linson. 102 mins.

## 1990
## THE MIRACLE

Script and Direction: NJ. Photography: Philippe Rousselot. Editing Joke Van Wijk. Music: Anne Dudley. Production Design: David Wilson. Players: Beverly D'Angelo (*Renee Baker*), Donal McCann (*Sam Coleman*), Niall Byrne (*Jimmy Coleman*), Lorraine Pilkington (*Rose*). Produced by Stephen Woolley and Redmond Morris. 97 mins.

## 1992
## THE CRYING GAME

Script and Direction: NJ. Photography: Ian Wilson. Editing: Kant Pan. Music: Anne Dudley. Production Design: Jim Clay. Players: Stephen Rea (*Fergus*), Miranda Richardson (*Jude*), Jaye Davidson (*Dil*), Forest Whitaker (*Jody*), Adrian Dunbar (*Maguire*), Jim Broadbent (*Col*). Produced by Stephen Woolley. 112 mins.

## 1994
## INTERVIEW WITH THE VAMPIRE

Script: Anne Rice, based on her novel. Direction: NJ. Photography: Philippe Rousselot. Editing: Mick Audsley, Joke Van Wijk. Music: Elliot Goldenthal. Production Design: Dante Ferretti. Players: Tom Cruise (*Lestat de Lioncourt*), Brad Pitt (*Louis Pointe du Lac*), Antonio Banderas (*Armand*), Stephen Rea (*Santiago*), Kirtsen Dunst (*Claudia*), Christian Slater (*Daniel Malloy, the Interviewer*). Produced by Stephen Woolley and David Geffen. 122 mins.

## 1996
## MICHAEL COLLINS

Script and Direction: NJ. Photography: Chris Menges.

*Beverly D'Angelo and Niall Byrne in THE MIRACLE*
*photo: Richard Blanchard/Kobal Collection*

Editing: Patrick Duffner. Music: Elliot Goldenthal. Production Design: Tony Pratt. Players: Liam Neeson (*Michael Collins*), Julia Roberts (*Kitty Kiernan*), Aidan Quinn (*Harry Boland*), Alan Rickman (*Eamon De Valera*), Stephen Rea (*Ned Broy*), Ian Hart (*Joe O'Reilly*). Produced by Stephen Woolley. 132 mins.

## 1997
## THE BUTCHER BOY

Script: Patrick McCabe and NJ, from McCabe's novel. Direction: NJ. Photography: Adrian Biddle. Editing: Tony Lawson. Music: Elliot Goldenthal. Production Design: Anthony Pratt. Players: Eamonn Owens (*Francie Brady*), Stephen Rea (*Da Brady*), Aisling O'Sullivan (Ma Brady), Fiona Shaw (Mrs Nugent), Ian Hart (*Uncle Alo*), Alan Boyle (*Joe Purcell*), Brendan Gleeson (*Father Bubbles*), Milo O'Shea (*Father Sullivan*), Sinead O'Connor (*Our Lady*). Produced by Redmond Morris and Stephen Woolley. 110 mins.

## 1998
## IN DREAMS

Script: Bruce Robinson and NJ. Direction: NJ. Photography: Darius Khondji. Editing: Tony Lawson. Music: Elliot Goldenthal. Production Design: Nigel Phelps. Players: Annette Bening (*Claire Cooper*), Aidan Quinn (*Paul Cooper*), Robert Downey Jr (*Vivian Thompson*), Stephen Rea (*Dr Silverman*), Paul Guilfoyle (*Jack Kay*). Produced by Stephen Woolley. 99 mins.

## 1999
## THE END OF THE AFFAIR

Script: NJ, based on the novel by Graham Greene. Direction: NJ. Photography: Roger Pratt. Editing: Tony Lawson. Music: Michael Nyman. Production Design: Anthony Pratt. Players: Ralph Fiennes (*Maurice Bendrix*), Julianne Moore (*Sarah Miles*), Stephen Rea (*Henry Miles*), Ian Hart (*Mr Parkis*). Produced by Stephen Woolley and NJ. 102 mins.

# Goran Paskaljević

### By Deborah Young

As the dark curtain of the war in Kosovo rang down on the young nations that once comprised Yugoslavia, Serbian director Goran Paskaljević found himself the focus of international attention. Rabidly attacked by supporters of Yugoslav president Slobodan Milosević for his 1998 film *The Powder Keg* (released in the US and UK as *Cabaret Balkan*), Paskaljević won enthusiastic new admirers around the world for the movie's chilling depiction of a violent, inhuman society on the brink of exploding. It is curious that this passionate picture, the crowning achievement of a long and successful career, should come from a film-maker who has rarely dealt directly with politics and who prefers to leave social critique in the background, where he believes it is most effective.

A documentarist not afraid to use symbols in *Guardian Angel*, to tell a fable-like story in *A Time of Miracles*, or to adapt theatrical idiom to the screen in *The Powder Keg*, he has developed a body of work over the last 25 years that speaks directly to audiences, who have shown their appreciation by repeatedly selecting his films as their favourites at festivals. At times outpacing critical enthusiasm for his output (which has nonetheless always been considerable and consistent), Paskaljević's popularity results from a thoughtful, measured style, which blends laughter and drama with simple sincerity.

GORAN PASKALJEVIĆ was born in Belgrade on April 22, 1947. His mother, a history teacher, and father, a journalist and writer, divorced when he was two, and he was raised by his maternal grandparents in Nis, Serbia's second-largest city. His intimate early contact with his grandparents would inspire the many films in which he has dealt sympathetically with the aspirations and illusions of the elderly.

Returning to Belgrade at 16, he began to spend his time in the cinémathèque where his adoptive father, Filip Acimović, worked. His precocious interest in art and design, poetry and architecture, soon gave way to a passion for cinema. The film that made the most lasting impression on him was Vittorio De Sica's *Bicycle Thieves*, and the influence of Italian neo-realism – particularly the way in which De Sica, working from tiny budgets, used non-professional actors for maximum emotional effect – is apparent in Paskaljević's work; the simplicity of the characters and story are a channel for genuine emotion.

## FAMU and Film Noir

On Acimović's advice, Paskaljević enrolled in Prague's acclaimed film school, FAMU, alongside fellow students who were soon to become Yugoslavia's leading directors: Srdjan Karanović, Goran Marković, Rajko Grlić, Lordan Zafranović and, later, Emir Kusturica. Common to these directors, known as the 'School of Prague', are the professional look and strong narratives of their films, which have reached large audiences. All were strongly influenced by two movements: Yugoslavia's very political Film Noir and the Czech New Wave.

Film Noir, championed by directors like Zika Pavlović and Aleksandar Sasha Petrović, was largely a reaction against the tenets of socialist realism and it produced films with strong ideological positions. For Paskaljević, Film Noir lacked a sense of humour, which he found in abundance in the Czech New Wave – as well as on the

*Vojislav Brajović, Toni Mihajlovski and Mirjana Joković in THE POWDER KEG*

streets of Belgrade. He and other members of the School of Prague brought New Wave ideas back to Yugoslavia, specifically stories told from a humanistic viewpoint, taking a light-handed approach to social critique.

From 1967, when the Czech New Wave was at its height, to 1971, when it dissolved following the Warsaw Pact's invasion of Prague, he studied under Elmar Klos, the Oscar-winning co-director (with Jan Kadar) of *The Shop on Main Street*. It was at FAMU that he also came into contact with the work of two seminal East European film-makers whom he admired enormously, Sergei Paradjanov and Andrei Tarkovsky.

"Excess isn't part of my nature," Paskaljević has said. Being linked to a humanistic cinema, however, did not save him from censorship difficulties. The first short he made at FAMU, *Mr Hrtska*, was invited to the influential short film festival in Oberhausen in 1969, but the Czech authorities found it offensive to the socialist system and forbode its release. The hero was a simple working man who poses nude for an art class and jokingly strikes the classic pose of a socialist man of marble. Though it never came out, the film earned the young student the attention of leading New Wave directors like Věra Chytilová, Jiří Menzel, Milos Forman and Ivan Passer.

After a second FAMU short, *A Few Words About Love*, Paskaljević returned to Belgrade to scrape together money for his thesis film. *The Legend of Lapot*, a 30-minute movie which still rates among his best work, was produced by Filip David, the newly appointed head of fiction at Yugoslav television's second channel, and marked the beginning of their long creative association. It won a Silver Medal at the short film festival in Belgrade and was the first of the numerous examples of Paskaljević highlighting the plight of the elderly, in recounting the cruel Balkan practice of eliminating those too old to fend for themselves.

In the early 1970s, he continued making shorts and documentaries for television. *Children* (1973) introduced another important Paskaljević theme, the exploitation of young people, and won the Gold Medal at Belgrade. *The Burden* (1974) again dealt with the mistreatment of children and the elderly, revealing Paskaljević's emotional preoccupation with society's most vulnerable members, and his outrage at social injustice.

## The wait pays off

It took Paskaljević many years to settle on a script he felt was suitable for his feature debut. In 1976 he found it, in *The Beach Guard in Winter*, a comedy by Gordan Mihić, then known for his work with Film Noir master Pavlović. It recounts a bittersweet story of young love which cannot overcome family interference, and ends with the young hero more alone than ever, facing an unpromising future.

Though the Film Noir influence is apparent, the film is tinged with the cruel irony typical of Czech comedy of the period. Invited to compete at Berlin, it is reputed to have passed the local censors, despite ferocious reviews from 'communist' critics, thanks to the fact that Tito and his wife found it irresistibly funny. The picture became a huge hit in Yugoslavia, where it was proclaimed Film of the Year for 1976, and its success was instrumental in finding government support for the director's next projects.

Two years later, Paskaljević and Mihić were back with *The Dog Who Liked Trains*, a bittersweet satire that skilfully observed three characters following separate paths: a girl dreaming of Paris who escapes from prison, a boy raised in an orphanage who searches for his dog, and a cowboy stuntman who gives shows in small towns. This distinctive trio is drawn from Paskaljević's rich collection of down-and-out losers. Bata Zivojinović, the most famous Yugoslav actor of his time, as the

*Still from THE BEACH GUARD IN WINTER, Paskavljević's feature debut*

cowboy, and Irfan Mensur (the young boy from *Beach Guard*) as the orphan, bring violence and tenderness to a film which mixes humour and drama in typical Paskaljević fashion.

In 1979 he made *And the Days Go By* (originally shot for television in nine days on 16mm). This was a deeply moving comedy about two aged men sharing a room in a rest home. Shooting from his own script, Paskaljević utilised his early documentary experience, along with his uncanny ability to observe people and bring them to life on screen. Two non-professional actors, rest-home residents in real life, touchingly portray a good-humoured merchant marine captain and his crusty room-mate. Paskaljević's touch is light, never insistent, and always privileges simple emotions, a hallmark of his later work.

## One hit, one failure

Paskaljević's droll humour is present even in the chilling totalitarian allegory *Special Treatment*, which screened in competition at Cannes in 1980 and was nominated for a Golden Globe. Dr Ilić, who treats alcoholics in his clinic with a strict regime of exercise, diet, Wagner and enforced psychodrama, is gradually revealed to be a sadistic dictator with no desire to cure his patients. In a key scene, he takes them on a 'therapeutic' outing to a restaurant where all the waiters are tipsy. It is a film full of surprises and is marked by a great tenderness towards the poor souls forced to submit to the doctor's treatment. Extremely popular with Yugoslav audiences, it won first prize at the pan-Yugoslav Pula Film Festival.

This critical and commercial hit was followed by Paskaljević's least successful project, his 'American' film, *Twilight Time*, produced by MGM and United Artists. Set in a semi-deserted village in Istria, it describes the drama of people whose relatives have gone abroad, leaving them to look after the family property. Cut to the measure of star Karl Malden, the film lacked the emotional spontaneity that characterises Paskaljević's other work.

Returning to the safer ground of bittersweet comedy, *The Illusive Summer of '68* humorously chronicled the adventures of a young man who discovers girls, older women and finally love during that very special summer when momentous events were in the air, events it proves impossible for him to escape. Shot in 1984, the film casts an ironic backward glance at 1968, describing the generation gap between father and son and the rise of a new middle-class. Beautifully balancing humour and loss, Paskaljević had found his footing again in a film reminiscent of the Czech comedies of Menzel and Forman.

## Gypsies and Communists

The most poetically moving of all Paskaljević's films is perhaps *Guardian Angel* (1987), a dramatic, quasi-documentary story chronicling the plight of little Yugoslav gypsies sent to Italy to beg and steal by unscrupulous dealers in human traffic. This influential film (a precursor of Emir Kusturica's *Time of the Gypsies*) has often been compared to De Sica's post-war *Shoeshine*.

Its credibility and depth owe a great deal to the lead performance from a boy chosen from a real gypsy community and it makes

*Still from SPECIAL TREATMENT, which competed at Cannes in 1980*

a powerful statement against the horrific exploitation of children, without resorting to sensationalism. Paskaljević once again demonstrates that he is not a man of 'excess' but a film-maker of precision and restraint.

*Guardian Angel* burns with an underlying anger against the injustice it portrays, an anger that looks forward to the much edgier *Powder Keg*. Though undoubtedly building on the director's documentary experience and on seminal films like *And the Days Go By*, *Guardian Angel* has moments of highly lyrical symbolism (the slaughter of a lamb) that give the narrative a deeper resonance. In many ways it represents a high point in Paskaljević's career.

Arguably the director's most openly 'political' film is *The Time of Miracles* (1990), the first Yugoslav feature to deal openly with the subject of religious suppression under a Communist government (Boris Pekić, author of the book and script on which it is based, had spent seven years in prison for producing anti-Communist propaganda). The tale unfolds as the Second World War draws to a close, and the Communists take power in a small Orthodox village and begin their war on the people's religious beliefs. At the same time, strange events begin to occur which make the villagers think the Messiah has arrived. In depicting the conflict between Communist fanaticism and blind Christian fervour, Paskaljević depicts both as forms of illusion.

*Still from THE ILLUSIVE SUMMER OF '68*

*One of the young Yugoslav gypsies from GUARDIAN ANGEL*

The transition from the old order to the new also takes place filmically, through contrasting music and colours, often to comical effect. But behind the laughter lies a familiar human tragedy in which people's lives are dominated by lies. It was a great irony that the 1990 release of *The Time of Miracles*, which preaches love and tolerance, coincided with the outbreak of the war that would tear Yugoslavia to pieces for the next five years.

## A return to old age

The director's concern for the aged reappears in *Tango Argentino* (1992), a big-hearted picture that won the Grand Audience Prize at San Francisco. Miki Manojlović heads a familiar-looking Paskaljević family of argumentative losers, whose income derives from the mother's work looking after elderly folk. When 10-year-old Nikola takes charge of a group of oldsters, he revitalises them and they give him the love and affection he lacks at home. This likeable picture has the bittersweet, twilight feeling that marks the end of an epoch, like the one ending in Yugoslavia at that time.

Though artistically Paskaljević was treading water with *Tango Argentino*, it anticipated his next film. When Julio Popović, one of the elderly characters, finally admits that he's never been to Argentina, the land of his dreams and of a lifetime's reminiscence, he looks forward to *Someone Else's America* (1995). In the shadow of Manhattan, the characters sit around daydreaming in their broken-down shack, furnished with absurd souvenirs from the Old World. Although they come from completely different cultural backgrounds, the Serbian Bayo (Miki Manojlović) and the Hispanic Alonso (Tom Conti) instinctively understand each other's homesickness.

This gentle hymn to friendship across ethnic boundaries, a reverse image of the ferocious war in Yugoslavia, is full of pain, but also magical, humorous moments (like levitating car seats). Its feathery tone bears the hallmark of scriptwriter Gordan Mihić, in his fifth collaboration with Paskaljević. Shot largely in English, with finance from France, Germany, England and Greece, and a cast and crew representing 17 countries, it signalled the increasingly international road that Paskaljević's career was, of necessity, taking.

## The gunpowder plot

In February 1998, when the political crisis in Serbia, Montenegro and Kosovo seemed likely to precipitate another armed Balkan conflict, Paskaljević began shooting *The Powder Keg* in Belgrade. Based on a highly acclaimed stage play by Dejan Dukovski, this loosely interwoven series of stories leads to an inescapable conclusion about the violent, intolerant atmosphere reigning in the city, and its residents' inflammatory state of mind.

Set on the night when the Dayton pact was signed, the film has strong political and human dimensions. Paskaljević employs all his skill in portraying characters: a boxer mad with jealousy, a violent youth who hijacks a crowded bus, a man scheming to get back with his ex-lover, a girl and her boyfriend terrorised by deranged drug dealers, and a boy who, unable to find anything to believe in at home, roams the streets. The black humour reveals a previously unexplored level of desperation and pessimism in the director's work. The subject of the film is the evil existing within his fellow citizens, their hatred and violence untamed by the Dayton treaty.

For *How Harry Became a Tree*, which he was shooting in Ireland in summer 2000, Paskaljević wrote his own screenplay, adapted into English by Stephen Walsh. Starring Adrian Dunbar and Killian Murphy, this Italian/Irish co-production is Paskaljević's third film in English, a language he is likely to continue using, given the increasingly difficult political situation in Serbia. On the surface an extremely Irish tale about wilful stubbornness, its story of a small, hatred-infested village is ultimately a universal allegory.

Paskaljević plans to turn his attention in late 2001 to *The Legend of Tristan*, set in the twelfth century and scripted by Agnes Caffin. A long-cherished project, it seems certain to mark another turning point in Paskaljević's productive career.

**DEBORAH YOUNG** is an American writer, based in Rome since 1980. She reviews films for *Variety* and contributes to a number of other publications. She has selected films for the Venice and Taormina festivals.

*Still from TANGO ARGENTINO, winner of the Grand Audience Prize at San Francisco*

# Goran Paskaljević Filmography

Short films and television. 1969: *Pan Hrstka* (*Mr. Hrtska*), Czechoslovakia, FAMU; 1970: *Nekolik slov o lasce* (*A Few Words About Love*), Czechoslovakia, FAMU; 1971: *Legenda o Lapotu* (*The Legend of Lapot*), Yugoslavia, Famu graduation film; 1971-74: *Dosljaci* (*The Immigrants*), 30-part documentary series; 1973: *Deca* (*Children*), documentary; *Sluga* (*The Servant*), short fiction; 1974: *Teret* (*The Burden*), short documentary.

## 1976
## CUVAR PLAZE U ZIMSKOM PERIODU (The Beach Guard in Winter)

Script: Gordan Mihić. Direction: GP. Photography: Aleksandar Petković. Editing: Olga Skrigin. Music: Zoran Hristić. Production Design: Dragoljub Ivkov. Players: Irfan Mensur (*Dragan*), Gordana Kosanović (*Ljubica*), Danilo Stojković (*Father*), Mira Banjac (*Mother*), Dara Calenić (*Aunt*), Velimir Zivojinović (*Ljubica's father*). Produced by Centar Films (Belgrade). 89 mins.

## 1978
## PAS KOJI JE VOLEO VOZOVE (The Dog Who Liked Trains)

Script: Gordan Mihić. Direction: GP. Photography: Aleksandar Petković. Editing: Olga Skrigin. Music: Zoran Hristić. Production Design: Dragoljub Ivkov. Players: Svetlana Bojković (*Mika*), Irfan Mensur (*Young man*), Velimir Bata Zivojinović (*Cowboy*), Pavle Vuisić (*Uncle*), Danilo Stojković (*Father*), Dusan Janicijević (*Zuti*). Produced by Centar Films (Belgrade). 90 mins.

## 1979
## ZEMALJSKI DANI TEKU (And the Days Go By)

Script and Direction: GP. Photography: Milan Spasić.

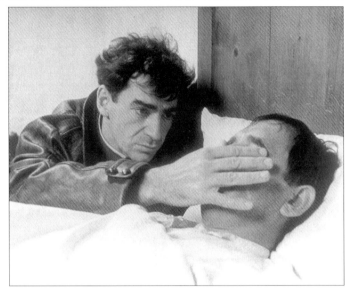

*Still from THE TIME OF MIRACLES*

Editing: Olga Skrigin. Music: Zoran Simjanović. Production Design: Dragoljub Ivkov. Players: Dimitrije Vujović (*The captain*), Obren Helcer (*Valet*), Sarlota Pesić (*Old lady*), Mila Keca (*Social worker*). Produced by Centar Films (Belgrade). 85 mins.

## 1980
## POSEBAN TRETMAN (Special Treatment)

Script: Dusan Kovacević, GP, Filip David. Direction: GP. Photography: Aleksandar Petković. Editing: Olga Skrigin. Music: Vojislav Kostić. Production Design: Dragoljub Ivkov. Players: Ljuba Tadić (*Dr Ilic*), Milena Dravić (*Social worker*), Petar Kralj (*Actor*), Radmila Zivković (*Prostitute*), Milan Srdoc (*Old man*), Bora Todorović (*Violinist*), Velimir Bata Zivojinović (*Restaurant manager*), Pavle Vuisić (*His father*). Produced by Centar Films (Belgrade)/Dan Tana Production (Los Angeles). 94 mins.

## 1982
## TWILIGHT TIME

Script: GP, Filip David. Direction: GP. Photography: Tomislav Pinter. Editing: Olga Skrigin. Music: Walter Scharf. Production Design: Niko Matul. Players: Karl Malden (*Marko*), Jodi Thelen (*Lena*), Demian Nash (*Ivan*), Mia Roth (*Ana*), Stojan Arandelović (*Matan*), Milan Srdoc (*Karlo*), Petar Bozović (*Rocky*), Dragan Maksimović (*Tony*). Produced by United Artists /MGM/Centar Films (Belgrade)/Dan Tana Production (Los Angeles). 102 mins

## 1984
## VARLJIVO LETO '68 (The Illusive Summer of '68)

Script: Gordan Mihić, GP. Direction: GP. Photography: Aleksandar Petković. Editing: Olga Skrigin. Music: Zoran Hristić. Production Design: Miljen Kljaković. Players: Slavko Stimac (*Petar*), Danilo Stojković (*Father*), Mija Aleksić (*Grandfather*), Mira Banjac (*Mother*), Sanja Vejnović

(*Ruzenka*). Produced by Centar Films (Belgrade). 88 mins.

## 1987
## ANDJEO CUVAR (Guardian Angel)

Script: GP. Direction: GP. Photography: Milan Spasić. Editing: Olga Skrigin, Olga Obradov. Music: Zoran Simjanović. Production Design: Milenko Jeremić. Players: Ljubisa Samardzić (*Dragan*), Neda Arnerić (*Mila*), Jakup Amzić (*Chayine*), Saban Bajramović (*Chayine's father*), Esmeralda Ametović (*Raba*), Mejaz-Majo Pasić (*Junko*), Trajko Demirović (*Moussa*). Produced by Singidunum Film Productions (Belgrade)/Jugoart (Zagreb). 88 mins.

## 1990
## VREME CUDE (The Time of Miracles)

Script: Borislav Pekić, GP. Direction: GP. Photography: Radoslav Vladić. Editing: Olga Skrigin, Olga Obradov. Music: Zoran Simjanović. Production Design: Miodrag Nikolić. Players: Predrag Miki Manojlović

(*Nicodemus*), Dragan Maksimović (*Lazarus*), Svetozar Cvetković (*Young man*), Mirjana Karanović (*Martha*), Danilo Bata Stojković (*John*), Mirjana Joković (*Maria*), Ljuba Tadic (*Pope Luke*), Slobodan Ninković (*Ozren*). Produced by Singidunum Film Productions (Belgrade)/Channel Four Television (UK)/Metropolitan Pictures. 98 mins.

## 1992
## TANGO ARGENTINO

Script: Gordan Mihić, GP. Direction: GP. Photography: Milan Spasić. Editing: Olga Skrigin. Music: Zoran Simjanović. Production Design: Miodrag Nikolić. Players: Nikola Zarkovic (*Nikola*), Mija Aleksic (*Popovic*), Predrag Miki Manojlović (*Father*), Pepi Laković (*Galitch*), Mica Tomić (*Mayor*), Rahela Ferrari (*Nana*), Ina Gogalova (*Mother*), Carna Manojlović (*Sister*). Produced by Singidunum Film Productions/Vans (Belgrade). 93 mins.

## 1995
## SOMEONE ELSE'S AMERICA

Script: Gordan Mihić. Direction:

GP. Photography: Yorgos Arvanitis. Editing: William Diver. Music: Andrew Dickson. Production Design: Wolf Seesselberg. Players: Tom Conti (*Alonso*), Miki Manojlović (*Bayo*), Maria Casares (*Alonso's mother*), Sergej Trifunović (*Luka*), Zorka Manojlović (*Bayo's mother*). Produced by Mact Production (France)/Intrinstica Films (UK)/Lichtblick (Germany). 95 mins.

## 1998
## BURE BARUTA (The Powder Keg; *US & UK title:* Cabaret Balkan)

Script: Dejan Dukovski, GP, with Filip David, Zoran Andrić. Direction: GP. Photography: Milan Spasić. Editing: Petar Putniković. Music: Zoran Simjanović. Production Design: Milenko Jeremić. Players: Miki Manojlović (*Mane*), Lazar Ristovski (*Boxer*), Mirjana Joković (*Ana*), Sergej Trifunović (*Youth on bus*), Dragan Nikolic (*Boxer's friend*), Milena Dravić (*Lady with hat on bus*). Produced by Mact Production/Ticket Productions (France)/Stefi (Greece)/Gradski Kina (Macedonia)/Mine Films (Turkey)/Vans (Serbia). 100 mins.

# Steven Soderbergh

## By Emanuel Levy

I t's hard to think of a more influential independent film-maker than Steven Soderbergh, whose first feature, *sex, lies, and videotape* (1989), remains one of the

most stunning debuts in American cinema history. It changed the public perception of indies and also put the Sundance Film Festival, where it premiered, on the map as the Mecca for the independent sector. It made Soderbergh, at 26, the youngest director ever to win the Palme d'Or. The movie also won Cannes' Best Actor for James Spader and was later nominated for the Best Original Screenplay Oscar. It established Soderbergh as the most promising director of his generation. Since then, with nine films to his credit, he has shown tremendous versatility, hopping from genre to genre while showing impressive technical command.

Soderbergh has also executive-produced *Suture*, *The Daytrippers* and *Pleasantville*, but he's still pigeonholed as the man who made *sex, lies...* – largely because it's one of his few movies to have earned money. "In

*Andie MacDowell as the unhappily married Ann in SEX, LIES, AND VIDEOTAPE*

*photo: Kobal Collection*

retrospect, that's the most memorable thing about it," Soderbergh has noted. "It's time for me to get a new middle name." And he did: his latest film, *Erin Brockovich*, became a massive hit, grossing more than $240m worldwide. A hot director again, Soderbergh is one of the few film-makers to navigate smoothly between big-budget Hollywood movies (*Out of Sight*) and small-scale indies (*The Limey*).

STEVEN SODERBERGH was born in Atlanta on January 14, 1963, and raised in Louisiana. He seemed destined to become a film-maker and began making movies at the age of 14, when his father, a college dean, enrolled him in a summer class at Louisiana State University. Upon graduation from a Baton Rouge high school, Soderbergh headed for Hollywood. It never occurred to him to go to film school. There was no need: he had spent his adolescence hanging around film students, borrowing equipment, arguing about movies. He had already cut his teeth making Super-8 shorts.

He experienced a frustrating spell in Hollywood with a routine job, holding cue cards for a TV talk show. After trying and failing to sell a script, he returned to Baton Rouge a year later feeling like a failure. Shortly afterwards, he got a job at a video arcade, wrote a number of scripts, and made some shorts. Soderbergh's break came in 1986, when the rock group Yes asked him to shoot some concert footage, which was later shaped into a Grammy-award winning video.

## Sex lives of the video generation

In 1987, Soderbergh, in his own words, put "an abrupt halt to all the bad personal stuff" that would become the basis for *sex, lies, and videotape*. He wrote the screenplay in motels, as he drove cross country heading West. With backing from RCA/Columbia Home Video, the $1.2m movie was completed a year later, packaging together emotions he had been carrying for years.

The most remarkable thing about *sex, lies...* was its freshness – it didn't recall any other film. Soderbergh spoke with a distinctive voice about issues that mattered. Intimate in scale, this finely-crafted, modern-day morality tale centres on Graham (James Spader), a handsome but sexually impotent man who derives gratification from recording women talking about their sex lives. A *Liaisons Dangereuses* for the video age, *sex, lies...* is an absorbing tale of desire and anxiety in which Graham's camera becomes the lead player.

The film is structured as a labyrinth in which the links among the partners are based on self-denial and deception. The unhappily married Ann (Andie MacDowell) is smart but confused. Behind a fragile, good-girl demeanour she hides a sexuality whose existence she can barely acknowledge. Her sexually confident sister, Cynthia (Laura San Giacomo), whom she describes as "extrovert and loud", is her opposite, and Cynthia's affair with Ann's husband, John (Peter Gallagher), stems as much from sibling rivalry as the thrill of deception and sexual heat.

Soderbergh directs the camera as if it were a natural storytelling device; he cuts fluidly from one pair to another, precisely revealing details both funny and chilling. Dialogue-driven, the movie contains long sequences shot in close-up and is far more accomplished than most feature debuts.

Every character is precisely constructed, but Graham is the most intriguing. With hesitant smile and tentative voice, he is both sweet and sinister. Ann, the film's most sympathetic character, recognises his vulnerability, perceiving him as a kindred repressed spirit. She responds to him sexually, but runs from friendship when she learns about his tapes. Like Antonioni's *Blow Up*, beneath the adulterous intrigue, *sex, lies...* poses questions about the potency of the video camera as an alternative to direct experience. Soderbergh's camera, like Graham's, is more concerned with talk than sex – dialogue carries the erotic charge.

But *sex, lies...* is by no means perfect. The characters' motivations are too simple: Cynthia needs to set herself apart from

*James Spader, left, with Soderbergh while filming SEX, LIES, AND VIDEOTAPE*

*photo: Kobal Collection*

Ann, and Ann rejects sex partly because of Cynthia. The resolution may be too neat given how messy the characters' lives are, and the formation of a new couple at the end may be too upbeat for this kind of tale. These aspects, added to his use of well-known actors rather than unknowns, positioned Soderbergh as a film-maker who wants to maintain his creative independence while staying close to the mainstream.

Even so, he deserves credit for not allowing audiences any distance, urging them to weigh the characters while evaluating their own morality. Each of the four principals turns out to be a liar, and it is our responsibility to assess their varying levels of dishonesty: is cheating on a sister worse than cheating on a spouse? Graham's recording of women's confessions is his means of seeking truth, but as the movie's title indicates, it's the dishonesty in *sex, lies and videotape* that gives it an edge.

## From Prague to St. Louis

After his breakthrough, Soderbergh made the visually striking but intellectually vapid *Kafka* (1991), which inadvertently gave credence to the theory of the sophomore directors' jinx. A thriller with a deliberately artificial style, *Kafka* felt much more like a first film than *sex, lies...* had done. Shot in black-and-white, with an impressive international cast, it was neither a biopic nor a mystery, its conventional plot too superficial to convey the spirit of Kafka as a modern, troubled Jewish intellectual.

In Lem Dobbs' script, Kafka (played by a miscast Jeremy Irons) is a quiet insurance company clerk who lives a routine life; at night, he writes stories for esoteric magazines. At his vast, impersonal office, Kafka is oppressed by a snooping overseer (Joel Grey) and criticised as a "lone wolf" by his boss (Alec Guinness). When a series of murders plagues the city, a police inspector (Armin Mueller-Stahl) begins an investigation. Through some puzzling events, Kafka finds himself carrying a bomb destined for an ominous castle which is the headquarters of a fascist government.

Instead of evoking the world of Kafka's writing, Soderbergh evokes old movies. The villain is named Murnau (after the German director) and the shadowy black-and-white imagery pays homage to German Expressionism. The tone vacillates between art film, absurdist comedy, horror movie and self-conscious thriller. Placing Kafka in a sinister Prague milieu that echoes the author's universe, proved to be a gimmick. The movie is a pastiche composed of borrowed parts, with the most obvious influence being *The Third Man* (in both location and Cliff Martinez's score), while Welles had himself filmed Kafka's *The Trial*.

Soderbergh's third outing, *King of the Hill* (1993), an adaptation of A.E. Hotchner's Depression memoir of his childhood in St. Louis, was a return to form, though few

*Ian Holm, left, with Jeremy Irons, right, as KAFKA*
*photo: Guild/Kobal*

people saw it. This coming-of-age story revolves around a bright 12-year-old, Aaron Kurlander (Jesse Bradford), who perseveres in the face of danger. Aaron is left alone in a spooky transient hotel that evokes Southern Gothic tradition. With plenty of time on his hands, the curious boy observes with fascination the strange people around him, soon finding himself entangled in their adventures. As a survival study of a kid who relies on his intuition, Aaron recalls the young protagonists of Twain and Dickens. The movie was intended as a tribute to the indomitable spirit of Jews who have fallen on hard times. A well-acted film, *King of the Hill* displayed Soderbergh's penchant for the realistic depiction of intimate dramas.

### Remake, documentary, comeback

His next film, *The Underneath* (1995), was an unsuccessful exercise in noir, a remake of the 1949 classic, *Criss Cross*. The weak dialogue and formulaic plot underlined again Soderbergh's need to work with a strong narrative. A realist by nature, with a sensitive feel for textures of domesticity, Soderbergh could not find a fresh perspective to elevate the pulpish material. Dismissed by most critics, *The Underneath* bombed at the box-office.

To break out of this stagnant phase, Soderbergh made the low-budget *Gray's Anatomy* (1996), a visually inventive version of the Spalding Gray stage monologue about an eye problem that sent Gray on a wild journey through alternative medicine before finally succumbing to surgery. The material is less funny than Gray's previous film-monologue, *Swimming to Cambodia*, but Soderbergh compensates with creepy, David Lynch-like visuals, and interviews with eccentric individuals who have suffered similar optical problems.

Soderbergh then put his own money into a personal, stylistic oddity, *Schizopolis* (1997), a satire which he wrote, directed and shot, as well as playing dual roles: as Fletcher Munson, a lethargic worker for a self-help corporation, and as his doppelganger, a dentist who is having an affair

*The Kurlander family in KING OF THE HILL*
*photo: Gramercy/Kobal Collection*

with Fletcher's wife. With its disdain for narrative coherence, this critique of modern life came straight out of the director's head, a sharp departure from the meticulous craftsmanship of *King of the Hill* and *The Underneath*, which were weighed down by intense concentration on form. Like *Gray's Anatomy*, *Schizopolis* took a long time to gain theatrical distribution, finally being picked up by a small company, Northern Arts.

*Schizopolis* turned out to be a wake-up call. Just when Hollywood was ready to write Soderbergh off, he rebounded with his best film to date, *Out of Sight* (1998), demonstrating again what a good actors' director he is – when working with the right material. In *Out of Sight*, Soderbergh had found a high-profile project that allowed him to exploit his creative energy. Cited as 1998's Best Film by the prestigious National Society of Film Critics, this is a terrific studio movie, made without studio compromise.

According to conventional Hollywood wisdom, you do not just hand over a $49m star vehicle like *Out of Sight* to someone with an arthouse reputation and commensurate box-office record. Indeed, Soderbergh had to convince Universal that he could handle the assignment, though once in the chair he was given free rein. The only pressure about making a big-budget movie came from within. "I wanted it to be good," he said, "because potentially more people would see it than any other film I'd made, and you don't want to blow that."

Soderbergh approached *Out of Sight* as a continuation of his creative rebirth, with playful energy, jump cuts, freeze frames, saturated colours and gritty textures. A sly, sexy version of Elmore Leonard's crime novel, *Out of Sight* contains a dozen off-beat characters and Scott Frank's witty, character-driven script contains snappy dialogue rarely heard in a mainstream picture. The complex structure, subtle humour and deliberate pacing all contribute to the overall artistic impact.

A romantic couple is front and centre. Standing on opposite sides of the law, the mismatched criminal Jack Foley (George Clooney) and Deputy Federal Marshal Karen Sisco (Jennifer Lopez) begin a courtship in the tight space of a car's trunk. *Out of Sight* contains priceless scenes, including a brilliantly-staged romantic interlude, and superb supporting performances by Ving Rhames, Billy Zahn, Don Cheadle, Dennis Farina, Catherine Keener and Albert Brooks.

*Out of Sight* grossed a so-so $37m in the US, and lacked the more facile commercial appeal of Leonard's *Get Shorty*, filmed by Barry Sonnenfeld in 1995, but it's a more satisfying work than Tarantino's *Jackie Brown* (based on Leonard's *Rum Punch*), which was low-key and lacked a strong romantic angle.

## Sixties icons and a 1990s superstar

*The Limey* (1999) continued Soderbergh's

*George Clooney and Jennifer Lopez in OUT OF SIGHT*
*photo: Merrick Morton/Universal*

*Peter Fonda, left, with Terence Stamp as THE LIMEY*
*photo: Bob Marshak/FilmFour*

artistic renewal, showing again what a consummate film-maker he is. The film suffered from a pretentious and under-developed script by Lem Dobbs, which promised more than it delivered. *The Limey*'s major asset was its casting of two icons of 1960s cinema, Britain's Terence Stamp and America's Peter Fonda, as enemies in what's basically a routine revenge thriller. Stamp plays Wilson, an ex-con who leaves London for the first time in his life, after spending nine years behind bars. Out of place in both time and space, Wilson sets out for LA to unravel the mystery surrounding his daughter's death.

Soderbergh took a standard crime melodrama and turned it into an accomplished movie. If *Out of Sight* employed stylistic devices associated with 1970s cinema, *The Limey* pays homage to – and is full of allusions to – 1960s international cinema, a feeling accentuated by the casting of Fonda and Stamp and the striking use of footage

showing the young Stamp in Ken Loach's *Poor Cow* (1967), as though it were a Wilson family home movie.

Soderbergh used Dobbs' script to fashion a contemplative, character-driven drama that underplays the familiar under-world milieu in favour of a meditation on crime, family and mortality. Ed Lachman's subtle lighting and inventive framing and Sarah Flack's astute cutting between past and present elevate *The Limey* way above its writing.

While the irresistibly charming *Erin Brockovich* (2000) is Soderbergh's most commercial work to date, it's also a compromised film, dominated by its star, Julia Roberts, Hollywood's highest-paid actress, who gives her most forceful dramatic performance yet. A feminist fairytale, the film is based on the true story of the former beauty queen-turned legal secretary who empowered herself by helping others gain justice in a notorious $333m lawsuit.

Assigned by her curmudgeonly boss (Albert Finney) to do some routine paper work, Erin (Roberts) stumbles upon a hidden epidemic: dozens of residents of Hinkley, California, have fallen victim to tumours and other afflictions. It turns out that Pacific Gas and Electric, the local industrial plant, has been contaminating the water supply with a deadly form of chromium. An old-fashioned crowd-pleaser, *Erin Brockovich* has twin messages about corporate malfeasance and the self-esteem gained by an uneducated, downtrodden woman.

With a working-class heroine who dares to fight the system, there are strong echoes here of *Norma Rae* and *Silkwood*, with a dash of the recent John Travolta corporate drama, *A Civil Action*. Like Erin, Roberts uses her allure for a good cause, putting her humour and feisty vulnerability at the service of a multi-shaded character. *Erin Brockovich* is entertaining, but seldom as gripping or surprising as *Out of Sight*.

*Erin Brockovich*'s mainstream success has enabled Soderbergh to work on two high-profile, back-to-back studio movies: the drug-smuggling thriller, *Traffic*, starring Michael Douglas and Catherine Zeta-Jones, and *Ocean's Eleven*, a remake of the 1960 crime comedy, which will reunite him with stars from whom he has already drawn fine performances: George Clooney and Julia Roberts.

EMANUEL LEVY is a senior film critic for *Variety*, a two-time president of the Los Angeles Film Critics Association, and the author of six film books, including *Cinema of Outsiders: The Rise of American Independent Film* (NYU Press, 1999).

# Steven Soderbergh Filmography

**1989**
**SEX, LIES AND VIDEOTAPE**

Script and Direction: SS. Photography: Walt Lloyd. Editing: SS. Music: Cliff Martinez. Production Design: Joanne Schmidt. Players: James Spader (*Graham*), Andie MacDowell (*Ann*), Peter Gallagher (*John*), Laura San Giacomo (*Cynthia*). Produced by John Hardy. 100 min.

**1991**
**KAFKA**

Script: Lem Dobbs. Direction: SS. Photography: Walt Lloyd. Editing: SS. Music: Cliff Martinez. Production Design: Gavin Bocket. Players: Jeremy Irons (*Kafka*), Theresa Russell (*Gabriela*), Joel Grey (*Burgel*), Ian Holm (*Doctor Murnau*), Armin Mueller-Stahl (*Grubach*). Produced by Harry Benn and Stuart Cornfeld. 98 min.

*Albert Finney with Julia Roberts as* ERIN BROCKOVICH

*photo: Columbia TriStar/Kobal Collection*

**1993**
**KING OF THE HILL**

Script and Direction: SS. Photography: Elliot Davis. Editing: SS. Music: Cliff Martinez. Production Design: Gary Frutkoff. Players: Jesse Bradford (*Aaron Kurlander*), Jeroen Krabbé (*Mr Kurlander*), Lisa Eichhorn (*Mrs Kurlander*), Karen Allen (*Miss Mathey*), Elizabeth McGovern (*Lydia*). Produced by Albert Berger. 109 min.

**1995**
**THE UNDERNEATH**

Script: Sam Lowry (pseudonym for SS). Direction: SS. Photography: Elliot Davis. Editing: Stan Salfas. Music: Cliff Martinez. Production Design: Howard Cummins. Players: Peter Gallagher (*Michael*), Allison Elliot (*Rachel*), William Fichtner (*Tommy*), Adam Trese (*David*), Paul Dooley (*Ed*). Produced by John Hardy. 99 min.

**1996**
**GRAY'S ANATOMY**

Script: Spalding Gray and Renee Shafransky. Direction: SS. Photography: Elliot Davis. Editing: Susan Littenberg. Production Design: Adele Plauche. Music: Cliff Martinez. Player: Spalding Gray. Produced by John Hardy. 80 min.

**1997**
**SCHIZOPOLIS**

Script and Direction: SS. Photography: SS. Editing: Sarah Flack. Players: Steven Soderbergh (*Fletcher Munson/Dr Jeffrey Korchek*), Betsy Brantley (*Mrs*

*Peter Gallagher as the hero of THE UNDERNEATH*

photo: Alan Pappe/Universal

*Munson*), David Jensen (*Elmo*), Mike Malone (*T. Azimuth Schwitters*). Produced by John Hardy. 99 min.

**1998**
**OUT OF SIGHT**

Script: Scott Frank, from the novel by Elmore Leonard. Direction: SS. Photography: Elliot Davis. Editing: Anne V. Coates. Music: David Holmes. Production Design: Gary Frutkoff. Players: George Clooney (*Jack Foley*), Jennifer Lopez (*Karen Sisco*), Ving Rhames (*Buddy Bragg*), Don Cheadle (*Maurice Miller*), Dennis Farina (*Marshall Sisco*), Albert Brooks (*Richard Ripley*). Produced by Danny DeVito, Michael Shamberg, Stacey Sher. 121 min.

**1999**
**THE LIMEY**

Script: Lem Dobbs. Direction: SS. Photography: Ed Lachman.

Editing: Sarah Flack. Music: Cliff Martinez. Production Design: Gary Frutkoff. Players: Terence Stamp (*Wilson*), Peter Fonda (*Valentine*), Lesley Ann Warren (*Elaine*), Luis Guzman (*Ed*), Barry Newman (*Avery*), Joe Dallessandro (*Uncle Harry*). Produced by John Hardy and Scott Kramer. 90 min.

**2000**
**ERIN BROCKOVICH**

Script: Susannah Grant. Direction: SS. Photography: Elliot Davis. Editing: Anne V. Coates. Music: Thomas Newman. Production Design: Philip Messina. Players: Julia Roberts (*Erin Brockovich*), Aaron Eckhart (*George*), Albert Finney (*Ed Masry*), Marg Helenberger (*Donna Jensen*), Peter Coyote (*Kurt Potter*). Produced by Danny DeVito, Michael Shamberg, Stacey Sher. 131 min.

# Edward Yang

### By Derek Elley

When Edward Yang became the first Taiwanese film-maker to win the Best Director award at Cannes, in May 2000, the jury's decision provided belated acknowledgement that for 18 years the island had been nurturing a world-class talent, a director who had never received his due acclaim beyond a relatively small circle of film buffs and East Asian aficionados. A writer-director of formidable intelligence and observation, and an Asian dealing with urban life rather than more 'exotic', pastoral stories, Yang is a resolutely modern director whose movies transcend their physical settings.

With an educational background in technology, and interests beyond movies, he brings a laser-like mind to the contra-dictions of contemporary life unmatched by any of his Chinese peers, portraying the small, often unwitting betrayals of friends and family, and the abiding power of memory and lost loves. Yang is simply the finest Taiwanese director of his generation.

EDWARD YANG was born in Shanghai, China, in September 1947, into a family from Meixian, Canton province (his name in Mandarin Chinese can be transliterated as Yang Te-ch'ang or Yang Dechang). In 1949 his parents moved to Taiwan, and he graduated there in Electrical Engineering

in 1969. Soon afterwards he moved to the US, gaining a Master's degree in Computer Sciences at Florida University in 1972 and two years later studying film briefly at the University of Southern California (USC). He subsequently worked as a computer designer at the University of Washington, Seattle, and only returned to Taiwan in 1981.

Yang's first film job was assisting on *The Winter of 1905* (directed by fellow USC student Yu Wei-cheng), for which he had written the original script. His first directing stint was *Floating Leaves* (*Fu ping*), an episode in Taiwan Television's video-shot series *11 Women* (1981), which was a major springboard for several of the New Taiwan Cinema generation.

At 146 minutes, Yang's episode was double the length of the others, and was broadcast in two parts on separate evenings. It was one of the series' best segments, and immediately demonstrated Yang's interest in contemporary city life, his avoidance of melodramatic clichés, and his seemingly natural talent for directing young actresses – here Ko Su-yun, excellent as a bored country girl who visits a friend in Taipei but slowly becomes disillusioned with big-city cynicism and mercenary values. When she finally returns home, she finds her boyfriend (Tso Ming-hsiang) has already married and gone to Germany to find work.

The fierce intelligence and freshness of vision which distinguishes all of Yang's work (even his less successful projects) was especially amazing for the time, when soupy melodrama was the order of the day on the island's television and the New Wave had yet to start.

### Teenage dreams

The film which officially gave birth to New Taiwan Cinema – largely invented by film-makers who had studied in the US, with the notable exception of Hou Hsiao-hsien – was *In Our Time*, a portmanteau movie produced by the government-funded Central Motion Picture Corporation

(CMPC). Shot and released in summer 1982, it teamed Yang with Jim Tao, Ko Yi-cheng and Chang Yi, each contributing an unrelated short episode in a film which built into a panorama of life from childhood to adulthood, from the 1960s to the present.

Set in 1967-68, Yang's episode, *Expectations*, was the second of the four and the most dream-like, centring on the romantic yearnings of a 13-year-old girl (Shih An-ni), her male friend (Wang Chi-kuang) and her elder sister (Chang Ying-chen). Both innocent and erotic, impressionistic and realistic, it's basically a sketch on which Yang was to build in subsequent films such as his first feature, *That Day, on the Beach*. Childhood and growing up were to become key themes for Taiwan's New Wave directors, but Yang, character-istically, was not to return to the subject for another decade, until *A Brighter Summer Day*.

At the time, Yang described *Expectations*, as "very simple. I tried to look at the subject very objectively. I chose to focus on this particular period of transition in the lives of teenagers because I think it's a very important stage for all of us: teenagers long to 'grow up', but they fear also the process."

## New Wave hits *Beach*

It is difficult nowadays to convey the sheer sense of excitement felt in Taiwan film circles when Yang's first feature, *That Day, on the Beach*, appeared in late 1983. Co-produced by CMPC and the Taipei branch of Hong Kong newcomer Cinema City, and running over two-and-a-half hours, nothing with this look or complexity had ever been produced on the island. The New Wave was already rolling, but this movie became its most contentious standard-bearer.

Commercially it did so-so business; critically it split the industry down the middle, deepening the division between the older, established generation (repre-sented by directors like Lee Hsing and Pai

*Teresa Hu in THAT DAY, ON THE BEACH*

Ching-jui) and the younger, foreign-trained film-makers. Praised by some for its trail-blazing qualities, it was damned by others for its supposed 'westernisation', and won only a few polite prizes at that year's Golden Horse Awards.

Yang had been developing the idea for about two years – a reminiscence of a past love, triggered by a death – but later expanded the original story, centred on one woman (Chia-li, played by Sylvia Chang, who had co-produced *11 Women*), to include that of a concert pianist (Ching-ching, played by model Teresa Hu). The two friends meet for the first time in 13 years and a complex series of flashbacks unfolds as the pair compare times past and present: Ching-ching has made a suc-cessful career in Europe, Chia-li has remained in Taiwan, married and been widowed by a presumed drowning accident (hence the title). But it emerges that their emotional lives have intertwined in hidden ways.

*That Day...* shot for 99 days (a huge schedule for an offshore Chinese film at the time), with the central section filmed first

*Still from MAHJONG, in which Taipei wannabes rub shoulders with the city's gangsters*

as Yang gradually forumlated the overall structure. The delicate photography (also new at the time) was chiefly due to Australian-born cameraman Christopher Doyle, the newcomer who shot most of the picture; a still photographer, he has since built a formidable reputation working for Chen Kaige and Wong Kar-wai.

The content reflects both the experiences of Yang himself, only recently returned from a decade in the US, and a whole stratum of Taiwan society coping with a rapidly westernised present, and memories of a simpler, more traditional and less cynical past. Like all of Yang's longer movies, *That Day...* fans out from a small event to build a complex web of memories and petty betrayals – a basically romantic view of life but told in a cool, often detached way punctuated by moments in which the story is magically transfigured into pure feeling.

Such moments – Chia-li's memories of seeing her father make love to a nurse (played to Beethoven's Pastoral Symphony)

or Ching-ching and her boyfriend dancing in an empty room – had no precursor in Chinese cinema of the time. Within the memorable gallery of performances, free of the usual stereotyping, Chang dominates, effortlessly moving from shy teenager to lonely wife in one of her finest screen performances.

## Darkness overcomes romance

*That Day, on the Beach* is still relatively little known, and greatly undervalued, in the West. It was Yang's next feature, *Taipei Story* (1984), that really established him internationally, probably because it better fitted western sensibilities. Gone is the underlying romanticism of his previous works: *Taipei Story's* microsopic examination of a young couple's scarred relationship is about wasted lives and the loneliness of failure.

The movie, wrote Yang, "is about how I felt about the city at the time – its past, its present, and its future." It was his most rapidly written and shot film to date, with only a week's post-production, in order to meet a pre-arranged release date. Partly due to the lack of proper publicity, it closed after only four days, and Yang subsequently re-edited it. Lung (played with sullen resignation by director Hou Hsiao-hsien, with whom Yang had formed Evergreen Films) is a businessman with financial problems and a lingering relationship with another woman (Lin Hsiu-ling); Chen (singer Tsai Chin, in her first screen role) is a minor executive recently made redundant.

There is only a minimal storyline; the characters reflect facets of modern-day Taipei life: the urge for escape (to the US), family commitments, the impermanent values of a status-orientated society, the loss of innocence. Yang's direction is cool, composed and unequivocal, with a bitter irony in the film's Chinese title, which literally translates as 'Green Plums and Toy Horses', a phrase referring to the charmed lives of childhood, of boys and girls growing up together.

For his third feature, *The Terroriser* (1986), Yang stayed with his favourite theme – contemporary urban relations – but returned to a more Chinese-box style, juggling several characters' lives. The film's complex structure, mingling fantasy with reality, teases the audience to a great degree, deliberately offering no firm conclusions. Referring to the film's title, Yang said: "There may be no Baader-Meinhof groups in this part of the world, but the bombs we planted deep within one another are ticking away."

The picture starts with an apparently senseless killing which gradually affects the lives of various characters: a bored novelist-housewife (Cora Miao), her weak husband (Li Li-chun), a young photographer (Ma Shao-chun) and a rebellious, often violent Eurasian girl (newcomer Wang An). There is a contained menace which underpins the film's self-conscious structure and portrait of urban alienation; the editing is tighter than in Yang's earlier films, the rhythm more urgent. But the basic theme is very simple: the volatility of urban emotions and the terrors inflicted by friends and enemies.

## In pursuit of perfection

As the initial impetus of the Taiwan New Wave burned out during the second half of the 1980s, and formerly close-knit relationships fragmented, Yang retreated into a kind of monastic perfection, preferring not to make films unless on his own terms. In 1986, the same year as *The Terroriser*, he also co-directed, with Hou Hsiao-hsien and critic Chen Kuo-fu, a music video, *Adult Games* (*Chengren youxi*), showcasing his new wife (Tsai Chin, from *Taipei Story*). Subsequently, he edited a comic-book collection and set up his own company, Yang & His Gang Filmmakers, for which he eventually made his next feature, *A Brighter Summer Day* (1991).

Set in the 1960s, and based on a true event in Taipei, the movie takes its English title from a line in the Elvis Presley song, 'Are You Lonesome Tonight', with the small change to the wording reflecting its mis-hearing by foreign ears. The Chinese title, *Incident of a Juvenile Murder on Kuling Street*, more accurately reflects the inspiration and content.

The three-hour picture is an astounding work that, again, takes a shocking incident – a street murder involving two teenagers – and uses it as the foundation for a complex portrait of family life, social tensions and youth culture, directed with Yang's customary finesse and surgical precision. The film shot on and off for over a year, because its principals were only available during school holidays. A relative success at the local box-office, it was later also made available in a four-hour version.

Increasingly, however, film-making was only one of several activities in which Yang was interested. In 1992 he renamed his company Atom Films & Theatre, and wrote and directed the one-act play *Likely Consequence* (*Ruguo*); he followed that in 1993 with the seven-acter *Growth Period* (*Chengzhang jijie*). When his next feature, *A*

*Yang, on bike, during the making of* A CONFUCIAN CONFUSION

*Confucian Confusion*, appeared in competition at Cannes in 1994, it showed several influences of his new interest: a more loquacious script, a looser feel to construction and, to the bafflement of most western audiences, a somewhat arcane theme elucidated more in theatrical than cinematic terms.

Its basic message, conveyed by a broad array of modern Taipei characters, is that Taiwan should rid itself of its confused Confucian heritage and go for honest, upfront relating. Opening with the chaotic rehearsals for an avant-garde playwright's first commercial production, the movie widens to embrace the yuppie owner of a PR company (Ni Shu-chun), her school-pal assistant (Chen Hsiang-chi) and her boyfriend (Wang Weiming), among many others. The female characters, as usual, are better drawn than the men, and clearly of more interest to Yang, though as a whole the movie buries its ideas far too deeply in the complex relationships plotting to engender much appeal.

The same fault afflicted *Mahjong* (1996), Yang's weakest movie to date, in which a group of young Taipei wannabes and foreign flotsam rub shoulders with one another and the city's underworld. Flawed by hit-and-miss performances (notably by the westerners, acting in stiff English) and

script, it touches on similar themes as *A Confucian Confusion*, but set lower on the social scale.

The story's trigger is the news that a businessman who owes $100m to Taipei's underworld has gone missing, and two hoods (Wu Nien-chen, Wang Po-sen) set out to track him down via his son, a young gang leader (Tang Tsung-sheng). They encounter a group of foreigners with whom a French girl (Virginie Ledoyen) has become involved after arriving in Taipei to continue her relationship with an Englishman (Nick Erickson). For two hours, Yang builds a tangled storyline in which the characters bounce off each other, fall in and out of love, and generally find their fates interwtined. As in *A Confucian Confusion*, there are playful elements throughout, but none of the masterly emotional or observational strokes that define Yang's best films.

## Return of the portrait artist

As after *The Terroriser*, Yang waited over four years before surfacing with his next feature, in between writing and directing a one-act play, *A 1997 Rhapsody* (*Jiu ge yu lao Qi*). But the wait was worth it, since *A One and a Two...* brought him triumph at Cannes and, at 52, re-established him as a world-class film-maker.

Though revisiting some of the themes of *That Day, on the Beach*, the movie is a more mature work by a writer-director now in calmer, less intense middle-age, with more assured variations in emotional tone and greater clarity. The central idea – a portrait of family, relatives and friends triggered by a sudden crisis – came from a real event 15 years earlier, when the father of one of Yang's friends was hit by a car and fell into a coma; the doctors gave up and told the family to take him home and talk to him, in an attempt to return him to consciousness.

*In A One and a Two...*, it is the collapse of a grandmother (Tang Ru-yun) which focuses the minds of a Taipei family, especially her teenage grand-daughter, Ting-ting (newcomer Kelly Lee). Among the large number of characters, however, it is her father, N.J. (scriptwriter Wu Nien-chen, who has appeared in several of Yang's films), who is the centre of the story, a businessman whose company is going through a sensitive merger with a Japanese firm, and whose first love from 30 years ago suddenly appears on the scene. N.J. is a man in the midst of a mid-life crisis, afflicted by a growing spiritual malaise which distances him from his business and his relatives, all of whom are experiencing some kind of emotional or financial confusion.

During the first half-hour Yang impressively juggles the characters, sowing seeds that will later grow. More gratifying is the way in which he paces the script over the almost three-hour running time, with N.J.'s visit to Japan, almost two

hours in, containing a major surprise that energises the final phase. Yang's wonderful assurance steers the viewer comfortably through the large number of characters, with moments of magical transfiguration (centred on Ting-ting's younger brother) that hark back to *That Day, on the Beach* in their combination of music and visuals.

For those familiar with the whole body of Yang's work across 20 years, the movie also completes a full circle: in the pivotal role of N.J.'s former lover is none other than Ko Su-yun, the young actress from Yang's debut film, *Floating Leaves*.

DEREK ELLEY has been associated with *IFG* for nearly 30 years, during which time he has written extensively on East Asian cinema. He is currently Senior Film Critic of *Variety*.

# Edward Yang Filmography

**1982**
**ZHIWANG (Expectations)**; one of four episodes within GUANGYINDE GUSHI (In Our Time)

Script and Direction: EY. Photography: Chen Chia-mo. Editing: Liao Ching-sung. Music: Beatles songs. Art Direction: Tsang Ping. Players: Shih An-ni (*Hsiao Fen*), Chang Ying-chen (*Elder sister*), Wang Chi-kuang (*Hsiao Hua*). Produced by Ming Ji for Central Motion Picture Corp. 28 mins. Total running time: 106 mins.

**1983**
**HAITANDE YITIAN (That Day, on the Beach)**

Script: EY, Wu Nien-chen. Direction: EY. Photography: Christopher Doyle, Chang Hui-kung. Editing: Liao Ching-sung. Art Direction: Tu Ta-hsiung, Li Pao-lin. Music: Violet Lam. Players: Sylvia Chang (*Lin Chia-li*), Teresa Hu (*Tan Wei-ching*), Tso Ming-hsiang (*Lin Chia-sen*), Hsu Ming (*Tsai*), Li Lieh (*Hsin-hsin*), Mao Hsueh-wei (*Cheng Te-wei*), Mei Fang (*Chia-li's mother*), Nan Chun (*Chia-li's father*), Yen

Feng-chiao (*Liu Hsiao-hui*), Hsiao Hu-tou (*Workman*), Yu Shou-jen (*Police officer*), Wu Shao-kang (*Ping-ping*), Sun Ming-chu (*Chia-li's servant*), Li Shu-chen (*Chia-li as a child*), Lo Wen-cheng (*Chia-sen as a child*), Huang Yu-hua (*Chia-sen's wife*), Li Meng-lin (*Teacher*), Jennifer O'Neal (*Bridget*). Produced by Ming Chi, Wang Ying-hsiang, Karl Maka for Central Motion Picture Corp. (Taiwan)/Cinema City & Films Co. (Hong Kong). 164 mins.

**1984**
**QINGMEI ZHUMA TAIPEI (Taipei Story)**

Script: EY, Chu Tien-wen, Hou Hsiao-hsien. Direction: EY. Photography: Yang Wei-han. Editing: Wang Chi-yang, Sung Fan-chen. Art Direction: Tsai Cheng-pin. Music: Beethoven cello solos, played by Yo-Yo Ma. Players: Tsai Chin (*Chen*), Hou Hsiao-hsien (*Lung*), Wu Nien-chen (*Chin*), Lin Hsiu-ling (*Ling*), Ko Yi-cheng (*Hsiao-ko*), Wu Ping-nan (*Chen's father*), Mei Fang (*Chen's mother*), Chen Shu-fang (*Mei*), Sun Peng (*The kid*), Lai Te-

nan (*Baseball coach*), Ko Su-yun (*Chuan*), Yang Li-yin (*Chin's wife*). Produced by Tan Yi-hua for Evergreen Films. 115 mins.

**1986**
**KONGBU FENZI (The Terroriser)**

Script: Hsiao Yeh, EY. Direction: EY. Photography: Chang Chan. Editing: Liao Ching-sung. Art Direction: Lai Ming-tang. Music: Weng Hsiao-liang. Players: Cora Miao (*Chou Yu-fen*), Li Li-chun (*Li Li-chung*), Chin Shih-chieh (*Yu-fen's lover*), Ku Pao-ming (*Detective*), Wang An ("*White Chick*"), Liu Ming (*Her mother*), Ma Shao-chun (*Photographer*), Huang Chia-ching (*His girlfriend*), Yu An-shun ("*Swen*"). Produced by Lin Teng-fei, Raymond Chow for Sunny Shareholding (Taiwan)/Golden Harvest (Hong Kong). 103 mins.

**1991**
**GULING JIE SHAONIAN REN SHIJIAN (A Brighter Summer Day)**

Script: EY, Yen Hung-ya, Yang Shun-ching, Lai Ming-tang.

Direction: EY. Photography: Chang Hui-kung, Li Lung-yu. Editing: Chen Po-wen. Art Direction: Yu Wei-yen, EY. Musical Supervision: Chang Hung-ta. Players: Chang Kuo-chu (*Father*), Elaine Jin (*Mother*), Chang Chen (*Hsiao Sze*), Chang Han (*Older brother*), Wang Chuan (*Older sister*), Lissa Yang (*Ming*). Produced by Yu Wei-yen for Yang & His Gang Filmmakers. 185 mins.

### 1994
### DULI SHIDAI (A Confucian Confusion)

Script and Direction: EY. Photography: Arthur Wong, Chang Chan, Li Lung-yu, Hung Wu-hsiu. Editing: Chen Po-wen. Art Direction: Tsai Chin, EY, Ernest Guan, Yao Jui-chung. Players: Chen Hsiang-chi (*Chi-chi*), Ni Shu-chun (*Molly*), Wang Wei-ming (*Ming*), Wang Chung-cheng (*Akeem*), Wang Ye-ming

(*Birdy*), Danny Deng (*Larry*), Yen Hung-ya (*Molly's brother-in-law*), Richie Li (*Feng*), Chen Li-mei (*Molly's sister*), Chen Yi-wen (*Li-jen*). Produced by Yu Wei-yen for Atom Films & Theatre. 133 mins.

### 1996
### MAJIANG (Mahjong)

Script and Direction: EY. Photography: Li Yi-hsu, Li Lung-yu. Editing: Chen Po-wen. Art Direction: Yu Wei-yen. Music: Forward Records. Players: Virginie Ledoyen (*Marthe*), Tang Tsung-sheng (*Red Fish*), Ko Yu-lun (*Lun-lun*), Chang Chen (*Hong Kong*), Wang Chi-tsan (*Little Buddha*), Nick Erickson (*Markus*), Chao Te (*Jay*), Ivy Chen (*Alison*), Andrew Tsao (*David*), Diana Dupuis (*Ginger*), Carrie Ng (*Angela*), Wu Nien-chen (*Older mobster*), Wang Po-sen (*Younger mobster*), Chang Kuo-chu (*Winston Chen*), Elaine Jin

(*Chen's wife*). Produced by Yu Wei-yen for Atom Films. 121 mins.

### 2000
### YIYI (A One and A Two...)

Script and Direction: EY. Photography: Yang Wei-han. Editing: Chen Po-wen. Art Direction: Peng Kai-li. Music: Peng Kai-li. Players: Wu Nien-chen (*N.J.*), Elaine Jin (*Min-min*), Issey Ogata (*Ota*), Kelly Lee (*Ting-ting*), Jonathan Chang (*Yang-yang*), Chen Hsi-sheng (*Di*), Ko Su-yun (*Sherry*), Michael Tao (*Da-da*), Hsiao Shu-shen (*Hsiao Yen*), Adrian Lin (*Li-li*), Yu-pang Chang (*Fatty*), Tang Ru-yun (*Min-min's mother*), Hsu Shu-yuan (*Li-li's mother*), Tseng Hsin-yi (*Yun-yun*). Produced by Shinya Kawai, Naoko Tsukeda for 1+2 Seisaku Iinkai (Japan)/Atom Films (Taiwan), for Pony Canyon/Omega Project (Japan). 173 mins.

*Kelly Lee, left, and Ruyun Tang in A ONE AND A TWO...*

*photo: Capitol Films*

# By Peter Cowie

It's playtime for film buffs as DVD explodes in the United States and begins to make an impact in Europe and further afield. Its global reach has been handicapped by the regional encoding that prevents US discs from being played abroad, and – in the Far East – by the cost-effective VCD format. Certainly no distributor in France or the UK will invest millions of dollars in restoring classic movies and adding commentaries and other bonus features unless there is a sufficiently large number of machines in local consumers' homes. The most remarkable figure of recent months has been the record first-week sales of 17,645 discs of *The Exorcist* in Britain, as part of a simultaneous video/DVD release.

The US public has always had both the curiosity and the cash to embrace consumer technology, and with some 15 million DVD players likely to be installed by the end of 2000, DVD is an established success. In the medium term it will displace VHS tape, and the advent of recordable DVD should provoke a further surge in purchases of machines and discs. Net-streaming may pose a threat to DVD in the long term, but for the foreseeable future the shiny platters will rule okay.

Most film buffs outside the US have had their machines "doctored", enabling them to play Region 1 DVDs and thus purchase discs from Amazon.com or during visits to America. Some companies, notably Criterion, do not regionally encode their discs, so that they can be played anywhere.

It's paradoxical that the only major problem besetting DVD is quality control. The technology can deliver superb sound and imagery, but the collector still needs to exercise caution when buying films. The major studios have kept their negatives in pretty good condition, going way back to the 1930s. Not so some of the independent companies, and certainly not so the European and Japanese film entities.

Labels such as Fox Lorber continue to put out discs often without even chapter stops, using murky materials that are no better than the average VHS cassette. Others still resist the wide-screen format (for example, PolyGram's release of *The Usual Suspects*), or do little to enhance a crackling soundtrack. One of the best elements of the new medium – the consumer's ability to switch subtitles on and off at will – is honoured by the majors but to a lesser degree by the independent labels, for whom it represents a considerable extra expense, and also because accurate spotting lists probably do not exist for many foreign films.

The most encouraging feature of the past year has been the sharp acceleration in classic releases (*Shane, Man with a Movie Camera, Cleo from 5 to 7* etc.). Even the Hollywood majors are foraging in their vaults instead of just pumping out second-rate Steven Seagal vehicles, as they were a year or two ago. The French are starting to motor, too, with Pathé nudging ahead with some high-quality editions.

### Restoration Heaven

Criterion has led the way in restoring classic films on DVD. To all but the youngest viewers, some of these releases

*LA REGLE DU JEU, available on DVD through French company Editions Montparnasse*
                                        *photo: Kobal Collection*

*GRAND ILLUSION has been restored from pristine elements by the Criterion Collection*
                                        *photo: Kobal Collection*

will come as a shock. Renoir's **Grand Illusion**, for example, looks absolutely marvellous in the Criterion edition. Working from the long-lost camera negative, engineers have also painstakingly eliminated scratches, flecks and tears from thousands of frames. In addition to an off-screen commentary by yours truly, the disc includes archival footage of Renoir and Erich von Stroheim, and numerous essays and cast biographies. If any single disc justifies the cost of converting to DVD, **Grand Illusion** is the one.

Equally stunning is the rehabilitation of Fellini's **Nights of Cabiria**, for which Criterion have located seven minutes of footage never included in US or UK release prints. Interviews with producer Dino De Laurentiis and Fellini assistant Dominique Delouche help recapture the atmosphere of filming in the mid-1950s. The film itself, like a great painting freshly cleaned, seems even more poignant than it did when watched on 16mm in the film societies of yore.

If the three-disc set devoted to Gilliam's *Brazil* was the highlight of Criterion's 1999 season, then the company's similar box, **The Orphic Trilogy**, dominates the 2000 catalogue. Containing Cocteau's three major films, *The Blood of a Poet*, *Orpheus* and *Testament of Orpheus*, the set also offers jewels such as Edgardo Cozarinsky's delightful study of Cocteau's career, and *Villa Santo Sospir*, a colour documentary by Cocteau himself about the principal

location for his testament. Criterion also release a rather less sparkling copy of **Beauty and the Beast**, enhanced by a commentary by the doyen of American film historians, Arthur Knight.

Running the Cocteau box a close second in Criterion's arsenal is a revelatory edition of Dreyer's **The Passion of Joan of Arc**. Found unexpectedly in a closet in a Norwegian asylum in 1981, the ur-version of this 1928 classic has been further digitally restored, and gleams with newly-minted confidence. Falconetti's committed performance as Joan can now be appreciated in even greater intimacy, and one of the disc's many supplementary goodies is an audio interview with the star's surviving daughter. Praise, too, for Richard Einhorn's *Voices of Light*, a chorale that seems to match the imagery to perfection.

The British Film Institute seeks to follow in Criterion's footsteps with its DVD editions, such as **Seven Samurai** (the full 190-minute version), with commentary on certain sequences by Philip Kemp, and **Man with a Movie Camera**, which offers not just a luminous transfer, but a choice of soundtracks (music, or a persuasive commentary by Russian scholar Yuri Tsivian). They offer excellent liner notes – something that's neglected by the Hollywood majors – and the packaging is imaginative, but the BFI needs to fine-tune its menu presentations, which are somewhat confusing on both discs.

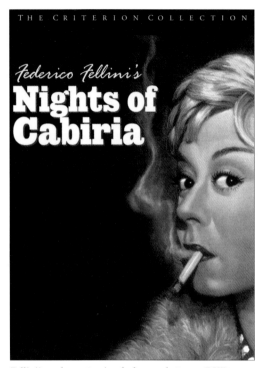

*Fellini's early masterpiece looks even better on DVD*

*The British Film Institute's admirable release of THE MAN WITH A MOVIE CAMERA*

## Westerns and Musicals

Studio restorations are more uneven in quality – and quantity. Columbia's **The Man from Laramie**, in its "Western Classics" series, looks better than on tape, but the colours remain insipid, and the sound muddy during action sequences. At least the disc offers optional French, Spanish and other subtitles. Fox's **South Pacific**, however, restores the original 1958 stereophonic track to all its glory (with the aid of THX digital mastering), and even the image, shot in Todd-AO, appears crisp and subtle in chromatic scale.

Warner's **An American in Paris** dates back even further, to 1951, when Minnelli's achingly romantic musical won the Academy Award for Best Picture. John Alton's luscious Technicolor cinematography can hardly have looked better even on first release; French subtitles are also available.

Warners have dedicated similar treatment to the DVD release of **My Fair Lady**, thanks to Robert Harris and James Katz

(who performed similar miracles on *Lawrence of Arabia* and *Vertigo*). The Dolby engineers deserve high marks for cleaning up the original mono score. **Casablanca**, on the other hand, has always been pretty well preserved in the Warner vaults, but the latest manifestation on DVD, though lacking in extras, gives one the original movie in as sparkling a state as one will ever see it.

Universal weighs in with a series of Hitchcock restorations. **Vertigo** had already seen the light of day on laser, and transfers to DVD with only marginal enhancement in quality, but **The Birds** recovers much of its original impact in the studio's DVD edition, which includes long, detailed interviews with surviving actors like Rod Taylor and Tippi Hedren.

Twentieth-Century Fox Home Entertainment's reissue of **Butch Cassidy and the Sundance Kid** has enjoyed the THX treatment, and offers an audio commentary by director George Roy Hill, cinematographer Conrad Hall and others, as well as a 45-minute documentary about the film's production. The colours are deliberately muted, to communicate the period mood, but the flesh-tones are accurate, and the monaural sound is free of hiss and crackle.

French companies have also begun foraging in the vaults. Editions Montparnasse offer a pristine transfer of Renoir's **La Règle du Jeu** (accompanied by optional subtitles in English, German or Spanish), with a short documentary about the making of the film, and DVD-ROM supplements too. It's the first time anyone has seen this particular masterpiece in such superb condition. Montparnasse have followed up their initiative with DVDs of Carné's **Drôle de drame** and Albert Lewin's **Pandora and the Flying Dutchman**.

With the French New Wave now 40 years old, Criterion has also started restoring some of its buried treasures. Agnès Varda's **Cleo from 5 to 7** appeared in 1962 and has been seen rarely in recent years. Now it surfaces as a Criterion DVD, in a transfer supervised by the director herself, from a 35mm fine-grain master-positive and a 35mm optical soundtrack print. Varda's skill as a documentary observer gives daily life in Paris a disturbing, almost nostalgic intimacy, like the photographs of Robert Doisneau, as Corinne Marchand's ailing singer drifts through the city while awaiting the results of some medical tests for cancer. The coda, involving a young soldier she meets in a park, becomes intensely moving. Relaxed and subtle at the same time, Varda's finest work never tumbles into sentimentality.

## Pushing the Envelope

DVD is perfectly suited to today's slam-bang, CG-effects-heavy cinema. Warner's **The Right Stuff**, directed by Philip Kaufman, pre-dated the explosion in special effects, but its soundtrack is a corker, and Sam Shepard's exploits as Chuck Yeager are rendered in sound infinitely richer and throatier than it was on the equivalent LD. The space-launch sequences are exhilarating, and Warners deserve a bouquet for the work that's clearly been devoted to this 1983 epic. Subtitles in most major languages are available on the wide-screen presentation.

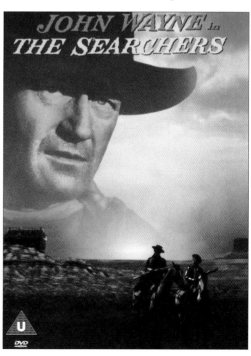

*Warners released EYES WIDE SHUT in Regions 1 and 2*

*Warner Home Video's latest version of THE SEARCHERS sets a new benchmark for Westerns on DVD*

Warner has also issued a spectacular disc for **The Matrix**, crammed with extra material such as documentaries, commentaries, a music-only audio track, and interfacing elements for DVD-ROM and the web. The movie's the thing, of course, although it's ironic than an older, more transient technology – laser disc – would have better enabled one to play sequences in slow-motion or frame by frame. Still, no carping: for *Matrix* mavens this is the ultimate trip, and this DVD has deservedly sold almost two million copies worldwide.

Columbia TriStar Home Video spent many months preparing its re-release of **Jaws** for DVD. For fans of Spielberg's breakthrough movie, the wait has been worthwhile. The disc bursts with extras: a 50-minute documentary with some perceptive remarks by Spielberg, Peter Benchley and the producers; deleted scenes; out-takes; three trailers; hundreds of production photos; and DVD-ROM features. The film itself, accompanied by optional subtitles in 21 languages, boasts a wide-ranging Dolby Digital soundtrack, although the image is furry in places and certainly no marked improvement over the Pioneer LD.

In terms of content, no film of the past decade has taken such outrageous risks as **Showgirls**, Paul Verhoeven's dazzling satire on American materialism, as exemplified in the microcosm of Las Vegas. MGM Home Video's luscious DVD edition enables one to reassess a film that was murdered by critics on its release in 1995. Verhoeven provided an invigorating commentary on the alternate track of *Starship Troopers*, so it's a pity that he did not do the same for *Showgirls*.

Ironically, Kubrick's final masterpiece, **Eyes Wide Shut**, was taken to task for not delivering the kind of in-your-face erotica of *Showgirls*. Viewing it in the intimacy of home cinema, one can admire the absolute assurance of this timeless, place-less meditation on death and morality. The Warner DVD includes brief interviews with Cruise, Kidman, and, for some reason, Spielberg, and adheres to Kubrick's

wish that it be presented in full-screen format for television.

The "director's cut" of **Apocalypse Now** should appear on DVD in 2001, but for now the film's legion of fans must be content with a Paramount release that does include one bonus item: the footage of Kurtz's temple being bombed, with Coppola talking over the silent images and explaining why they were never used in the film. The transfer, supervised by Vittorio Storaro and mastered at Zoetrope's own DVD lab in San Francisco, certainly marks a significant advance on all previous versions on cassette and laser disc.

## Auteurs Revived

Several of John Boorman's best films have been issued this year on DVD. Anchor Bay's **Hell in the Pacific** looks somewhat bland and a little fuzzy in the darker sequences, but it does include the alternate ending over which Boorman and his producer argued in the late 1960s. Warner Home Video has performed a better service to the director with their releases of the haunting **Deliverance** and the slumbrous **Excalibur**. *Deliverance* in particular has suffered, through generations of cassette and laser disc release, from gruesome hues and obvious day-for-night imagery. On DVD the film looks and sounds as compelling as it did in 1972. Both these Warner discs carry optional subtitles in ten languages.

Another Brit whose forays into film have been all too rare is Peter Brook. His 1963 version of **Lord of the Flies** has been given the Criterion treatment. Based on the relentless novel by William Golding about children marooned on a tropical island in the wake of a nuclear war, its stark black-and-white imagery makes *The Beach* pale by comparison, and under Brook's sensitive direction the youngsters mimic the fault-lines in the English class system. Brook's own commentary deserves a hearing, and his skills as a stage director are highlighted in Gerald Feil's documentary, included as a bonus on the disc.

*Hugh Edwards and James Aubrey in LORD OF THE FLIES, rescued from fading memory by Criterion*
*photo: Kobal Collection*

John Huston's work of the 1940s is emerging from the Warner vaults. **The Maltese Falcon** comes in a glorious transfer, with the fabled bird itself almost glowing with sheer blackness when it does appear, and Sydney Greenstreet effortlessly dominating a rather nervous Bogart. A TNT documentary built around trailers for Bogart movies fleshes out the disc. **Key Largo** is more sluggish as a film, but has not been seen in such pristine condition since it appeared in 1948. Optional subtitles are available in ten languages, and the Dolby Digital track eradicates much of the fuzz and crackle associated with the cassettes and 16mm prints of *Key Largo*.

Warners have also devoted a DVD to Howard Hawks' complex, prolix masterpiece of sorts, **The Big Sleep**, running the full 110 minutes (114 at 24 frames per second in theatres). The disc includes the original trailer, and optional subtitles in ten languages.

John Ford's **The Searchers**, already superb on laser disc, receives the DVD treatment from Warners on both sides of the Atlantic. The UK release is preferable, however, carrying subtitles in many more languages, and offering collectors a choice of viewing the film in either wide-screen or full-screen. Warner Home Video also includes on the disc various short documentaries about the making of the film against the backdrop of Ford's beloved Monument Valley.

Warner Home Video's release of Nicholas Ray's **Rebel Without a Cause** offers some engaging bonus material: off-screen footage of James Dean, Natalie Wood and Jim Backus, subtitles in ten languages, and a 2.55:1 wide-screen transfer. Digitally re-mastered from newly restored elements, this *Rebel* finally glows as it did on first release. Ray's direction may still appear theatrical and humourless, but Dean's presence and the contained anger of the piece make the film a true icon of the 1950s.

Bergman's work is well represented on DVD thanks to Criterion, and two additions to the canon have emerged this year. **The Magic Flute** was made in 1974 to celebrate the fiftieth anniversary of Swedish Radio, and so was never intended

*Mark Rylance and Alice Krige in INSTITUTE BENJAMENTA, by the Brothers Quay, which has been given a luscious transfer on DVD by Kino on Video. Kino's burgeoning collection also includes an array of Hollywood B movies, with a leaning towards noir (Budd Boetticher's BEHIND LOCKED DOORS, and Henry Fonda in THE LONG NIGHT, Litvak's remake of Carné's LE JOUR SE LEVE), and neglected classics such as Fritz Lang's HANGMEN ALSO DIE. Pride of place in the catalogue must go to THE TIN DRUM, which shared the Palme d'Or in Cannes with APOCALYPSE NOW, and has been released on DVD with a commentary by the director Volker Schlöndorff, and other extras.*

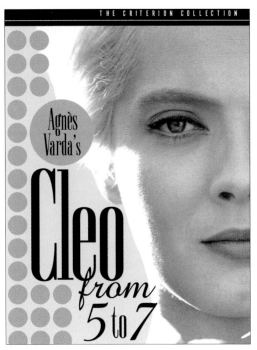

*Evocative box-cover for Criterion's restoration of CLEO FROM 5 TO 7*

for theatrical release. Criterion have gone back to the original stereo score and present it on the DVD in uncompressed PCM sound, so that the rendering of Mozart's music matches the exquisite photography of Sven Nykvist.

**Autumn Sonata** never looked very happy on laser disc, but Criterion's DVD, created from a 35mm colour reversal inter-negative, is a very different matter. The film's warm, glowing reds and browns create the right atmosphere for this psychological struggle between mother and daughter. There's an optional dubbed English-language track, and also a commentary by yours truly.

Pathé have released some of Claude Berri's most dramatic achievements as producer and/or director, among them *Germinal* and *La Reine Margot*. In **La Reine Margot**, directed with blood-curdling assurance by Patrice Chereau, Isabelle Adjani plays Marguerite de Valois, the heroine of Alexandre Dumas's novel about the 1572 Massacre of St. Bartholomew. The DVD features the full-length (143 min) version and a Dolby Stereo track.

**Germinal**, directed by Berri himself, captures the inexorable grimness of Zola's novel about miners in northern France. The historical background is well presented in some bonus materials on the DVD.

Finally, the ultimate auteur DVD boxed set: **Carnival of Souls**, better known in the US than in Europe, but a cult movie that has influenced many independent directors. Made by industrial documentary film-makers (Herk Harvey and friends) on a shoestring budget, this macabre ghost story unfolds in Kansas and Utah and works by turns as a pastiche of Dreyer, Cocteau and Bergman. The twin-disc release comprises the original theatrical version of *Carnival of Souls*, the extended director's cut, and an armful of extras, including documentaries, out-takes, interviews and commentaries. It's a wonderful example of the power of DVD to revive – and improve – what might otherwise have continued to be a bootlegged item beyond the reach of mainstream buffs.

*Note: for both DVD and LD collectors, Doug Pratt's* The DVD-Laser Disc Newsletter *remains an indispensable monthly read (PO Box 420, East Rockaway, NY 11518, USA).*

*THE RIGHT STUFF looks mint-fresh in the Warner Home Video transfer on DVD*

MC
MINISTÉRIO DA CULTURA

ICAM
INSTITUTO DO CINEMA
AUDIOVISUAL
E MULTIMEDIA

**ICAM – Instituto do Cinema, Audiovisual e Multimedia**
Rua São Pedro de Alcântara, 45, 1º
1269-138 Lisboa . Portugal
Tel.: + 351 . 213 230 800 . Fax: + 351 . 213 431 952
www.icam.pt . mail@icam.pt

PROMOTING AND SUPPORTING PORTUGUESE CINEMA, AUDIOVISUAL AND MULTIMEDIA

design **Vasco Colombo** e **Raquel Porto** | photo **Raquel Porto**

# World Box-Office Survey

## ARGENTINA

| | Admissions |
|---|---|
| 1.  Manuelita (Argentina) | 2,223,445 |
| 2.  Tarzan | 1,438,147 |
| 3.  The Sixth Sense | 1,328,240 |
| 4.  Star Wars: Episode I | 1,305,633 |
| 5.  Life is Beautiful (Italy) | 1,085,292 |
| 6.  The Mask of Zorro | 1,051,067 |
| 7.  The Mummy | 996,272 |
| 8.  That Damn Rib (Argentina) | 939,595 |
| 9.  Analyze This | 881,293 |
| 10. Dear Alma (Argentina) | 778,354 |

## AUSTRALIA

| | $ millions |
|---|---|
| 1.  Star Wars: Episode I | 25.6 |
| 2.  The Sixth Sense | 18.7 |
| 3.  Austin Powers: The Spy Who… | 14.8 |
| 4.  The Matrix | 14.7 |
| 5.  Notting Hill (UK) | 13.8 |
| 6.  The Mummy | 12 |
| 7.  Big Daddy | 9.7 |
| 8.  American Pie | 9.4 |
| 9.  The World Is Not Enough (UK/US) | 8.4 |
| 10. Toy Story 2 | 8.0 |

Source: AFMA.

## AUSTRIA

| | Admissions |
|---|---|
| 1.  Star Wars: Episode I | 686,000 |
| 2.  Notting Hill (UK) | 617,000 |
| 3.  Runaway Bride | 565,000 |
| 4.  Tarzan | 539,000 |
| 5.  The Matrix | 441,000 |
| 6.  Asterix & Obelix (France) | 435,000 |
| 7.  The Mummy | 407,000 |
| 8.  You've Got Mail | 388,000 |
| 9.  A Bug's Life | 386,000 |
| 10. Shakespeare in Love | 318,000 |

## BELGIUM

| | Admissions |
|---|---|
| 1  Star Wars: Episode I | 891,684 |
| 2.  The Matrix | 765,000 |
| 3.  The Mummy | 753,659 |
| 4.  Tarzan | 738,500 |
| 5.  Asterix & Obelix (France) | 703,093 |
| 6.  Entrapment | 533,036 |
| 7.  The World Is Not Enough (UK/US) | 510,000 |
| 8.  Shakespeare in Love | 505,009 |
| 9.  You've Got Mail | 430,000 |
| 10. A Bug's Life | 405,770 |

## BOSNIA & HERZEGOVINA

| |
|---|
| 1.  Tarzan |
| 2.  Life is Beautiful (Italy) |
| 3.  10 Things I Hate About You |
| 4.  All About My Mother (Spain) |
| 5.  Run Lola, Run (Germany) |
| 6.  A Bug's life |
| 7.  Enemy of the State |
| 8.  Instinct |
| 9.  The 13th Warrior |
| 10. The Buttoners (Czech Republic) |

For admissions in Sarajevo only.

## BRAZIL

| | Admissions |
|---|---|
| 1. The Sixth Sense | 4,830,542 |
| 2. Star Wars: Episode I | 3,457,844 |
| 3. Tarzan | 3,356,482 |
| 4. The Mummy | 2,457,566 |
| 5. A Bug's Life | 2,271,483 |
| 6. The Matrix | 2,055,797 |
| 7. Runaway Bride | 1,717,456 |
| 8. Notting Hill (UK) | 1,657,078 |
| 9. Life is Beautiful (Italy) | 1,593,756 |
| 10. Shakespeare in Love | 1,450,121 |

All titles are US productions unless otherwise indicated.
All figures are for January to December 1999 unless otherwise indicated.

*ANALYZE THIS, good business for the Mob in Bulgaria*
*photo: Phillip Caruso/Warners*

## CROATIA

| | Admissions |
|---|---|
| 1. Notting Hill (UK) | 159,664 |
| 2. Star Wars: Episode I | 121,709 |
| 3. Asterix & Obelix (France) | 117,319 |
| 4. There's Something About Mary | 91,404 |
| 5. The Mummy | 70,201 |
| 6. The Matrix | 70,152 |
| 7. Life is Beautiful (Italy) | 69,603 |
| 8. Marshal Tito's Spirit (Croatia) | 62,731 |
| 9. Entrapment | 52,539 |
| 10. Shakespeare in Love | 51,342 |

## BULGARIA

| | Admissions |
|---|---|
| 1. Star Wars: Episode I | 1 218,266 |
| 2. The Matrix | 187,920 |
| 3. The Mummy | 153,498 |
| 4. The 13th Warrior | 89,277 |
| 5. Entrapment | 64,526 |
| 6. Rush Hour | 63,946 |
| 7. Analyze This | 54,376 |
| 8. Blue Streak | 50,477 |
| 9. Meet Joe Black | 48,948 |
| 10. Ronin | 49,172 |

## CZECH REPUBLIC

| | Admissions |
|---|---|
| 1. Cosy Dens (Czech) | 914,442 |
| 2. The Mummy | 359,060 |
| 3. Helluva Good Luck (Czech) | 353,060 |
| 4. Star Wars: Episode I | 342,233 |
| 5. The Matrix | 256,877 |
| 6. Return of the Idiot (Czech) | 237,748 |
| 7. American Pie | 191,744 |
| 8. Shakespeare in Love | 178,238 |
| 9. Dr. Doolittle | 164,793 |
| 10. Saving Private Ryan | 150,459 |

## CHILE

| | Admissions |
|---|---|
| 1. Star Wars: Episode I | 873,553 |
| 2. The Sentimental Teaser (Chile) | 794,656 |
| 3. The Mummy | 625,307 |
| 4. Tarzan | 550,422 |
| 5. The Sixth Sense | 523,658 |
| 6. The Matrix | 433,146 |
| 7. Life is Beautiful (Italy) | 395,836 |
| 8. The Rugrats Movie | 382,916 |
| 9. A Bug's Life | 370,395 |
| 10. Saving Private Ryan | 258,664 |

## DENMARK

| | Admissions |
|---|---|
| 1. The One and Only (Denmark) | 840,442 |
| 2. Star Wars: Episode I | 542,174 |
| 3. Love at First Hiccup (Denmark) | 484,674 |
| 4. Tarzan | 476,471 |
| 5. Notting Hill (UK) | 354,126 |
| 6. Mifune (Denmark) | 350,861 |
| 7. Runaway Bride | 322,267 |
| 8. The Twopenny Dance (Denmark) | 318,030 |
| 9. The Matrix | 283,706 |
| 10. A Bug's Life | 280,029 |

*Above: Natalie Portman in STAR WARS: EPISODE I, a huge hit in Estonia, Finland and France. Opposite page: THE MATRIX, a virtual reality blockbuster in Germany and Greece*

## EGYPT $

| | |
|---|---|
| 1. Hammam in Amsterdam | 2,565,085 |
| 2. Aboud Ala El Hodood | 1,317,763 |
| 3. Marous, the Minister's Boy | 746,620 |
| 4. The Other | 695,211 |
| 5. No Intention | 339,805 |
| 6. Albanda | 269,934 |
| 7. The Empress | 245,440 |
| 8. Security Case | 212,578 |
| 9. The Leader | 189,737 |
| 10. Entrapment (US) | 187,142 |

$1 = 3.5 £E. All titles except Entrapment are Egyptian.

## FINLAND — Admissions

| | |
|---|---|
| 1. Star Wars: Episode I | 434,432 |
| 2. The Ambush (Finland) | 427,304 |
| 3. The Tough Ones (Finland) | 328,003 |
| 4. Tommy & the Wildcat (Finland) | 371,761 |
| 5. Notting Hill (UK) | 277,919 |
| 6. The World Is Not Enough (UK/US) | 262,077 |
| 7. The Swan & the Wanderer (Finland) | 232,912 |
| 8. The Matrix | 230,043 |
| 9. Shakespeare In Love | 202,487 |
| 10. Tarzan | 198,194 |

## ESTONIA — Admissions

| | |
|---|---|
| 1. The Matrix | 49,532 |
| 2. The Mummy | 35,902 |
| 3. Star Wars: Episode I | 39,105 |
| 4. Shakespeare in Love | 35,286 |
| 5. Big Daddy | 21,650 |
| 6. Wild Wild West | 21,004 |
| 7. Notting Hill (UK) | 20,257 |
| 8. Blue Streak | 19,540 |
| 9. Entrapment | 16,937 |
| 10. Analyze This | 16,753 |

## FRANCE — Admissions

| | |
|---|---|
| 1. Asterix & Obelix (France) | 8,944,457 |
| 2. Star Wars: Episode I | 7,157,124 |
| 3. Tarzan | 5,962,967 |
| 4. The Matrix | 4,676,807 |
| 5. Notting Hill (UK) | 4,501,631 |
| 6. A Bug's Life | 3,151,014 |
| 7. The Mummy | 3,140,417 |
| 8. Wild Wild West | 3,085,379 |
| 9. Joan of Arc (France) | 2,898,585 |
| 10. The World Is Not Enough (UK/US) | 2,894,192 |

## GEORGIA

1. Star Wars: Episode I
2. My Grandfather (Georgia)
3. The Mummy
4. Titanic
5. The Angels Fly Over (Georgia)
6. Armageddon
7. The World Is Not Enough (UK/US)
8. Here Comes the Down (Georgia)
9. The Graveyard of Dreams (Georgia)
10. The Lake (Georgia)

Chart is for Tiblisi only and is unconfirmed officially.

## GERMANY                                    $ millions

| | |
|---|---|
| 1. Star Wars: Episode I | 53.88 |
| 2. Notting Hill (UK) | 31.53 |
| 3. Runaway Bride | 29.62 |
| 4. The Mummy | 29.89 |
| 5. The Matrix | 27.63 |
| 6. Tarzan | 27.43 |
| 7. Enemy of the State | 20.64 |
| 8. Asterix & Obelix (France) | 19.75 |
| 9. A Bug's life | 17.94 |
| 10. You've Got Mail | 17.09 |

$1 = 1.84 DM.

## GREECE                                     Admissions

| | |
|---|---|
| 1. Safe Sex (Greece) | 900,000 |
| 2. The Sixth Sense | 360,000 |
| 3. American Beauty | 318,000 |
| 4. The Matrix | 230,000 |
| 5. The World Is Not Enough (UK/US) | 220,000 |
| 6. Tarzan | 212,000 |
| 7. Notting Hill (UK) | 201,000 |
| 8. The Green Mile | 182,000 |
| 9. End of Days | 180,000 |
| 10. Beware of Greeks... (Greece) | 179,000 |

Figures are for the Greater Athens area only, from August 1999 to May 2000; based on information from distribution offices and unconfirmed officially.

## HONG KONG                                  $ millions

| | |
|---|---|
| 1. The Ring (Japan) | 4.01 |
| 2. King of Comedy (Hong Kong) | 3.82 |
| 3. The Mummy | 3.56 |
| 4. Gorgeous (Hong Kong) | 3.52 |
| 5. A Man Called Hero (Hong Kong) | 3.01 |
| 6. Star Wars: Episode I | 2.87 |
| 7. The World Is Not Enough (UK/US) | 2.82* |
| 8. A Bug's Life | 2.47 |
| 9. The Sixth Sense | 2.45 |
| 10. The Legend of Speed (Hong Kong) | 2.43* |

$1 = HK$7.8. *Includes takings through mid-January 2000.

## INDIA

| | $ millions |
|---|---|
| 1. Kaho Na ... Pyar Hai | 33 |
| 2. Hum Saath-Saath Hai | 26 |
| 3. Taal | 17 |
| 4. Hum Dil De Chuke Sanam | 16 |
| 5. Sarfarosh | 14 |

Figures are for July 1999 to June 2000. Source: Film Information.

*NOTTING HILL, a romantic chart-topper in Italy*
*photo: Clive Coote/Universal*

## IRAN

| | $ |
|---|---|
| 1. Red | 446,780 |
| 2. Two Women | 390,646 |
| 3. Tutia | 265,232 |
| 4. The Girl in the Sneakers | 232,500 |
| 5. Siavash | 228,484 |
| 6. Sheyda | 173,604 |
| 7. The Color of God | 166,394 |
| 8. The Youth | 160,851 |
| 9. Love Beyond Borders | 148,127 |
| 10. Love + 2 | 147,532 |

All titles are Iranian. $1 = 8,000 rials.
Figures are for March 20, 1999 to March 19, 2000.

## ITALY

| | $ millions |
|---|---|
| 1. Notting Hill (UK) | 14.9 |
| 2. Shakespeare in Love | 13.7 |
| 3. The Sixth Sense | 13 |
| 4. That's Life (Italy) | 11.9 |
| 5. Tarzan | 11.6 |
| 6. The Mummy | 11.5 |
| 7. Star Wars: Episode I | 11.7 |
| 8. Eyes Wide Shut | 9.9 |
| 9. Runaway Bride | 8.4 |
| 10. Asterix & Obelix (France) | 8.2 |

## IRELAND

| | $ millions |
|---|---|
| 1. Star Wars: Episode I | 4.59 |
| 2. Notting Hill (UK) | 3.22 |
| 3. Austin Powers: The Spy Who... | 3.05 |
| 4. American Pie | 2.92 |
| 5. The Sixth Sense | 2.73 |
| 6. A Bug's Life | 2.26 |
| 7. Waking Ned | 2.23 |
| 8. The World Is Not Enough (UK/US) | 2.14 |
| 9. The Rugrats Movie | 2.09 |
| 10. The Blair Witch Project | 1.93 |

IR£1 = $1.3

## JAPAN

| | $ millions |
|---|---|
| 1. Armageddon | 78 |
| 2. Star Wars: Episode I | 72.9 |
| 3. The Matrix | 46.7 |
| 4. The Sixth Sense | 40.2 |
| 5. Pokémon 2 (Japan) | 33.6 |
| 6. Ring 2 (Japan) | 19.6 |
| 7. Poppoya – Railroad Man (Japan) | 19.2 |
| 8. Doraemon (Japan) | 18.7 |
| 9. The Mummy | 16.8 |
| 10. Eyes Wide Shut | 16.5 |

Figures are rentals (distribution income), not box-office gross. $1=107 yen.

## LATVIA

| | Admissions |
|---|---|
| 1. The Matrix | 66,500 |
| 2. The Mummy | 55,700 |
| 3. Star Wars: Episode I | 47,400 |
| 4. Shakespeare in Love | 42,000 |
| 5. The Parent Trap | 28,000 |
| 6. The Truman Show | 26,200 |
| 7. Big Daddy | 25,600 |
| 8. Cruel Intentions | 25,100 |
| 9. Babe 2: Pig in the City | 23,600 |
| 10. Elizabeth (UK) | 22,100 |

Source: Film Registry of the National Film Centre

*Disney's TARZAN swung to the number one position in Mexico*

*photo: Burroughs/Disney*

## MEXICO

| | Admissions |
|---|---|
| 1. Tarzan | 2,109,929 |
| 2. Sex, Shame and Tears (Mexico) | 1,905,198 |
| 3. Toy Story 2 | 1,822,674 |
| 4. Star Wars: Episode I | 1,741,653 |
| 5. The Sixth Sense | 1,716,530 |
| 6. The Mummy | 1,535,405 |
| 7. Stuart Little | 1,200,152 |
| 8. What Dreams May Come | 962,754 |
| 9. The Blair Witch Project | 952,577 |
| 10. The Matrix | 920,189 |

Figures are for Greater Mexico City only.
Source: Canacine.

## NEW ZEALAND

| | $ millions |
|---|---|
| 1. Star Wars: Episode I | 3.5 |
| 2. The Matrix | 2.5 |
| 3. Austin Powers: The Spy Who... | 2.2 |
| 4. The Sixth Sense | 1.95 |
| 5. What Becomes of the Broken Hearted (NZ) | 1.65 |
| 6. Shakespeare in Love | 1.5 |
| 7. Notting Hill (UK) | 1.5 |
| 8. A Bug's Life | 1.5 |
| 9. The Mummy | 1.2 |
| 10. Big Daddy | 1.15 |

## NETHERLANDS

| | Admissions |
|---|---|
| 1. Notting Hill (UK) | 1,060,000 |
| 2. Star Wars: Episode I | 966,000 |
| 3. The Matrix | 667,000 |
| 4. The World Is Not Enough (UK/US) | 613,000 |
| 5. Enemy of the State | 573,000 |
| 6. The Mummy | 563,000 |
| 7. Tarzan | 511,000 |
| 8. A Bug's Life | 488,000 |
| 9. Entrapment | 463,000 |
| 10. Runaway Bride | 406,000 |

## NORWAY

| | Admissions |
|---|---|
| 1. Notting Hill (UK) | 585,981 |
| 2. Fucking Åmål (Sweden) | 485,120 |
| 3. Star Wars: Episode I | 426,679 |
| 4. The Matrix | 388,000 |
| 5. The Prince of Egypt | 357,000 |
| 6. The World Is Not Enough (UK/US) | 356,523 |
| 7. Tarzan | 324,513 |
| 8. Olsen Gang – Final Mission (Norway) | 324,467 |
| 9. A Bug's Life | 261,192 |
| 10. Mulan | 260,540 |

*THE SIXTH SENSE, supernatural crowd-pleaser in Peru and Puerto Rico*

*photo: Spyglass*

## PAKISTAN

1. Bangles*
2. Bandit
3. End
4. Consent
5. Guns'n'Roses
6. Landlady
7. Law
8. Another Love Story
9. Revenge
10. Legacy

All titles are Pakistani. *Excludes 1998 gross.

## POLAND

| | Admissions |
|---|---:|
| 1. With Fire and Sword (Poland) | 7,135,915 |
| 2. Pan Tadeusz (Poland) | 5,504,111 |
| 3. Star Wars: Episode I | 1,369,664 |
| 4. Killer 2 (Poland) | 1,189,800 |
| 5. The Matrix | 718,551 |
| 6. The Mummy | 614,039 |
| 7. Asterix & Obelix (France) | 472,704 |
| 8. Tarzan | 451,336 |
| 9. A Bug's Life | 382,143 |
| 10. Prince of Egypt | 351,367 |

## PERU

1. Pantaleon and the Visitors (Peru)
2. Star Wars: Episode I
3. The Sixth Sense
4. Tarzan
5. The Mummy
6. The Matrix
7. Saving Private Ryan
8. Life is Beautiful (Italy)
9. Shakespeare in Love
10. Analyze This

## PUERTO RICO

| | $ millions |
|---|---:|
| 1. Star Wars: Episode I | 2.76 |
| 2. Toy Story 2 | 1.85 |
| 3. Stuart Little | 1.75 |
| 4. The Mummy | 1.59 |
| 5. Deep Blue Sea | 1.53 |
| 6. Tarzan | 1.52 |
| 7. The Sixth Sense | 1.42 |
| 8. End of Days | 1.29 |
| 9. Big Daddy | 1.25 |
| 10. Blue Streak | 1.22 |

*RUNAWAY BRIDE confirmed Julia Roberts' immense popularity in Serbia & Montenegro and Slovakia*
*photo: Paramount/Touchstone*

## ROMANIA

| | Admissions |
|---|---|
| 1. The Mummy | 249,448 |
| 2. Star Wars: Episode I | 221,008 |
| 3. Bean (UK) | 196,194 |
| 4. The Matrix | 147,548 |
| 5. Shakespeare in Love | 124,943 |
| 6. Knock Off | 124,842 |
| 7. Legionnaire | 96,211 |
| 8. Universal Soldier: The Return | 90,754 |
| 9. Meet Joe Black | 89,105 |
| 10. Wild Wild West | 76,140 |

## SERBIA & MONTENEGRO

| | Admissions |
|---|---|
| 1. Dagger (Serbia) | 521,727 |
| 2. Asterix & Obelix (France) | 402,560 |
| 3. The Barber of Siberia (Russia) | 274,806 |
| 4. Taxi (France) | 243,022 |
| 5. The White Suit (Serbia) | 218,577 |
| 6. Runaway Bride | 205,016 |
| 7. Notting Hill (UK) | 146,134 |
| 8. Wheels (Serbia) | 134,652 |
| 9. The 13th Warrior | 89,212 |
| 10. All About My Mother (Spain) | 76,360 |
| Source: Tuck. | |

## SINGAPORE

| | $ millions |
|---|---|
| 1. Star Wars: Episode I | 1.95 |
| 2. The Mummy | 1.87 |
| 3. Liang Po Po – The Movie (Singapore) | 1.75 |
| 4. The Sixth Sense | 1.58 |
| 5. The World Is Not Enough (UK/US) | 1.56 |
| 6. The Matrix | 1.54 |
| 7. Gorgeous (Hong Kong) | 1.15 |
| 8. The Ring (Japan) | 0.99 |
| 9. Deep Blue Sea | 0.98 |
| 10. A Man Called Hero (Hong Kong) | 0.97 |
| $1 = SG$1.73. | |

## SLOVAKIA

| | Admissions |
|---|---|
| 1. The Mummy | 144,003 |
| 2. A Bug's Life | 135,697 |
| 3. Fountain for Susannah III (Slovakia) | 105,810 |
| 4. The Matrix | 102,337 |
| 5. Star Wars: Episode I | 92,621 |
| 6. Asterix & Obelix (France) | 85,772 |
| 7. Runaway Bride | 80,328 |
| 8. Shakespeare in Love | 76,979 |
| 9. Life is Beautiful (Italy) | 74,231 |
| 10. You've Got Mail | 72,918 |

## SOUTH AFRICA

| | $ millions |
|---|---|
| 1. Notting Hill (UK) | 2.13 |
| 2. Star Wars: Episode I | 1.85 |
| 3. The Sixth Sense | 1.84 |
| 4. Runaway Bride | 1.76 |
| 5. Entrapment | 1.61 |
| 6. The Matrix | 1.34 |
| 7. Enemy of the State | 1.30 |
| 8. Bug's Life | 1.28 |
| 9. The World Is Not Enough (UK/US) | 1.24 |
| 10. Tarzan | 1.19 |

$1 = 6.66 rand.

## SPAIN

| | $ millions |
|---|---|
| 1. Star Wars: Episode I | 22.3 |
| 2. Life is Beautiful (Italy) | 16.1 |
| 3. Tarzan | 13.3 |
| 4. The Mummy | 12.9 |
| 5. Inspector Gadget | 12.3 |
| 6. Notting Hill (UK) | 12.1 |
| 7. Shakespeare in Love | 10.6 |
| 8. The Matrix | 10.3 |
| 9. Runaway Bride | 10.0 |
| 10. Entrapment | 9.6 |

$1 = 170 pesetas.

## SOUTH KOREA

| | $ millions |
|---|---|
| 1. Shiri (South Korea) | 25.0 |
| 2. The Mummy | 12.6 |
| 3. Attack on the Gas Station (South Korea) | 9.6 |
| 4. The Matrix | 9.1 |
| 5. The Sixth Sense | 8.4 |
| 6. Tarzan | 8.3 |
| 7. Star Wars: Episode I | 8.2 |
| 8. Tell Me Something (South Korea) | 7.4 |
| 9. Nowhere To Hide (South Korea) | 6.7 |
| 10. Love Letter (Japan) | 6.5 |

$1 = 1,200 won.

## SWEDEN

| | Admissions |
|---|---|
| 1. Tarzan | 1,150,000 |
| 2. Notting Hill (UK) | 900,000 |
| 3. The Health Farm (Sweden) | 850,000 |
| 4. Star Wars: Episode I | 810,000 |
| 5. The World Is Not Enough (UK/US) | 750,000 |
| 6. A Bug's Life | 635,000 |
| 7. Tsatsiki (Sweden) | 510,000 |
| 8. In Bed with Santa (Sweden) | 505,000 |
| 9. The Matrix | 465,000 |
| 10. Runaway Bride | 460,000 |

Includes admissions up to March 2000.

*SHIRI, the action-packed number one hit in South Korea*

## SWITZERLAND

| | Admissions |
|---|---|
| 1. Notting Hill (UK) | 670,464 |
| 2. The World Is Not Enough (UK/US) | 560,937 |
| 3. Star Wars: Episode I | 519,376 |
| 4. Tarzan | 460,495 |
| 5. Shakespeare in Love | 429,456 |
| 6. Runaway Bride | 428,252 |
| 7. You've Got Mail | 395,299 |
| 8. Asterix & Obelix (France) | 387,299 |
| 9. The Matrix | 379,613 |
| 10. The Mummy | 290,499 |

*YOU'VE GOT MAIL, a hit for Meg Ryan in Switzerland*
*photo: Brian Hamill/Warners*

## THAILAND

| | $ millions |
|---|---|
| 1. Nang Nak (Thailand) | 4.040 |
| 2. Star Wars: Episode I | 3.080 |
| 3. The Mummy | 2.972 |
| 4. The World Is Not Enough (UK/US) | 2.216 |
| 5. The Matrix | 2.040 |
| 6. The Sixth Sense | 1.702 |
| 7. Deep Blue Sea | 1.616 |
| 8. Enemy of the State | 1.491 |
| 9. Mighty Joe Young | 1.405 |
| 10. Tarzan | 1.298 |

$1 = 37 baht. Figures are based on information from distribution offices and are unconfirmed officially.

*THE GREEN MILE, a hit for Tom Hanks in Turkey*
*photo: Ralph Nelson/Kobal Collection*

## TURKEY

| | Admissions |
|---|---|
| 1. Byzance the Whore (Turkey) | 2,420,000 |
| 2. The Sixth Sense | 1,399,000 |
| 3. The Matrix | 1,330,000 |
| 4. Goodbye (Turkey) | 1,240,000 |
| 5. The Mummy | 1,106,000 |
| 6. Runaway Bride | 569,000 |
| 7. The Green Mile | 557,000 |
| 8. Life is Beautiful (Italy) | 543,000 |
| 9. American Beauty | 512,000 |
| 10. The Mask of Zorro | 502,000 |

## UNITED KINGDOM

| | $ millions |
|---|---|
| 1. Star Wars: Episode I | 83.7 |
| 2. Notting Hill (UK) | 50.6 |
| 3. A Bug's Life | 48.2 |
| 4. Austin Powers: The Spy Who... | 42.4 |
| 5. The World Is Not Enough (UK/US)* | 38.4 |
| 6. The Sixth Sense* | 33.9 |
| 7. Shakespeare in Love | 33.6 |
| 8. The Mummy | 28.7 |
| 9. The Matrix | 28.4 |
| 10. Tarzan | 27.8 |

*Still in release in 2000.

## UNITED STATES & CANADA   $ millions

| | |
|---|---|
| 1. Star Wars: Episode I | 430.4 |
| 2. The Sixth Sense | 276.3 |
| 3. Toy Story 2 | 208.8 |
| 4. Austin Powers: The Spy Who... | 205.4 |
| 5. The Matrix | 171.4 |
| 6. Tarzan | 170.9 |
| 7. Big Daddy | 163.4 |
| 8. The Mummy | 155.3 |
| 9. Runaway Bride | 152.0 |
| 10. The Blair Witch Project | 140.5 |

*THE MUMMY, effects-laden thrills in the US and Venezuela*

*photo: Keith Hamshere/Universal*

## VENEZUELA   $ millions

| | |
|---|---|
| 1. Tarzan | 2,040,060 |
| 2. The Mummy | 1,618,045 |
| 3. Star Wars: Episode I | 1,545,864 |
| 4. The Sixth Sense | 1,503,759 |
| 5. Life is Beautiful (Italy) | 1,353,383 |
| 6. The Matrix | 1,212,030 |
| 7. Glue Sniffer (Venezuela) | 819,549 |
| 8. The Final Day (Venezuela) | 723,308 |
| 9. Wild Wild West | 721,804 |
| 10. Toy Story 2 | 721,803 |

## WORLDWIDE   $ millions

| | |
|---|---|
| 1. Star Wars: Episode I | 920 |
| 2. The Matrix | 457 |
| 3. The Sixth Sense | 453 |
| 4. The Mummy | 413 |
| 5. Tarzan | 392 |
| 6. Notting Hill (UK) | 363 |
| 7. Austin Powers: The Spy Who... | 309 |
| 8. Runaway Bride | 308 |
| 9. Shakespeare in Love* | 283 |
| 10. The World Is Not Enough (UK/US) | 254 |

*Excludes 1998 gross.

*THE WORLD IS NOT ENOUGH, licensed to the number ten slot on the year's global box-office chart*

*photo: Danjaq/United Artists*

# WORLD SURVEY

# ALGERIA

Roy Armes

In the 1960s and early 1970s Algerian films seemed the model for a committed Third World cinema, relevant to local audiences. International acclaim arrived when Mohamed Lakhdar Hamina won the Palme d'Or at Cannes in 1975, with *Chronicle of the Years of Embers*. But the system – under which the state provided salaries and employment for film-makers but failed to invest sufficiently in infrastructure – proved unsustainable. The history of Algerian cinema in the 1980s and 1990s was one of constant bureaucratic reorganisation of film and television production.

Algerian film-making is still reeling from the most damaging of these developments, the sudden closure in 1997 and 1998 of all the principal government-funded production organisations: CAAIC (feature films), ENPA (television drama) and ANAF (news and current affairs). With no indication of what new structures would be put in place, four feature films – Sid Ali Fettar's *Meriem*, Ghaouti Bendeddouche's *The Neighbour*, Sid Ali Mazif's *Mimouna* and newcomer Abderrahim Laloui's *Scream* – were left uncompleted.

When this article went to press, there were still no formal structures in place and those plans that had been announced concentrated on television production, and seemed to exclude state aid for 35mm fiction features for cinema release. At the same time, a report indicated that annual cinema attendance had diminished from nine million in 1980 to just half a million

by 1992, while the number of film theatres had declined from 485 at the time of Independence to a bare dozen in 1999; most have been converted into video halls.

As a result, those few features which do get produced suffer enormous delays. Though Rachid Benbrahim did a symbolic first day's shooting for his second feature, *The Express from Oran*, in 1997, he was still awaiting full funding at the end of 1999. **Lotus Flower** (*Fleur de Lotus*), one of CAAIC's last productions, which occupied director Amar Laskri for most of the 1990s, was still having pre-release screenings at the end of 1999.

This ambitious Algerian-Vietnamese co-production (co-directed by Trân Dàc) chronicles some of the less predictable outcomes of colonial occupation and war, through the tale of a Vietnamese woman journalist, Houria, who arrives in Algiers

*Still from ALGERIA, LIFE ALL THE SAME*

to seek out her father. He had been sent to Vietnam as part of the French expeditionary forces in the 1940s, but had shifted his sympathies to the Vietnamese cause (in which Houria's mother was active) as a result of French massacres back home, before returning to Algeria to fight in the final liberation struggle.

## Dual perspectives

Even more delayed – partly because of financial difficulties experienced by the French co-producers – was Okacha Touita's 1990 film, **Cries of Men** (*Le Cri des hommes*), which received its first commercial screenings in 1999. The film is a sober reflection on the Algerian war of 1957, dealing with the lives of two policemen, one Algerian and one European, who find themselves on opposite sides of an increasingly savage combat.

Among Algerian feature directors living in exile, Rachid Benhadj has been shooting a low-budget but star-studded film, *Mirka*, set in the Balkans. Starring Gérard Depardieu, Vanessa Redgrave and the young Slovak actress Barbora Bobulova, it tells the story of a young mother who gives birth to a child who is the product of ethnic rape.

Merzak Allouache, having shot a television episode for the Arte Channel, is planning a new feature, *I've Dreamed New York*. There are also a number of younger film-makers of Algerian origin active in Europe, including Rachida Krim in France and Nasser Bakhti in Switzerland.

Particularly striking among this group is Djamila Sahraoui, who was born in Algeria in 1950 but has lived in France, where she studied film-making at IDHEC, since the early 1970s. To date she is best-known for *Half of Allah's Heaven*, her 1995 documentary study of Algerian women, from their active participation in the Algerian Independence struggle to their present oppression under the notorious Family Code of 1984, which makes divorced women responsible for their children but denies them any right to the family home.

Sahraoui's new documentary, **Algeria, Life All the Same** (*L'Algerie, La Vie Quand Meme*), which won the prize for best video documentary at the African Film Festival in Milan in 2000, is a penetrating and engaging look at Sadek and Abdenour, two unemployed young men in the Kabyle region, whose lives offer them nothing: no work, no living space, no girlfriends. Dreaming only of leaving Algeria (concluding that even Rwanda would be preferable!), they have only their friendship and humour to see them through the endless days.

ROY ARMES is the author of several books on film history and specialises in African cinema. He teaches film in London.

# Recent Films

**FLEUR DE LOTUS (Lotus Flower)**

Script and Dir: Amar Laskri and Trân Dàc. Phot: Rachid Merabtine, Phi Phenson and Ahmed Messad. Players: Nidhal El Melloughi, Nguyen Anchinh, Abdelhak Benmarouf, Le Khanh. Prod: CAAIC – ENPA (Algeria)/ Socofilms (Vietnam).

**LE CRI DES HOMMES (Cries of Men)**

Script: Okacha Touita and Mohamed Bouchibi. Dir: Okacha Touita. Phot: Allel Yahyaoui. Players: Miloud Khetib, Jean-Yves Gauthier, Nadia Samir, Roland Blanche. Prod: World Films Company/ENPA/Partenaires Associés/Wilaya   APC   de Mostaganem.

**L'ALGÉRIE, LA VIE QUAND MÊME (Algeria, Life All the Same)**

Documentary. Script and Dir: Djamila Sahraoui. Prod: Les Films d'Ici (Paris).

## Useful Address

**Cinémathèque Algérienne**
rue Larbi Ben M'Hidi
Algiers
Tel: (213 2) 638 301

# ARGENTINA
Alfredo Friedlander

For the second year in a row, the number of Argentine films has stabilised, with 35 released in 1999. The quantity produced in the same period is in fact far larger, since many Argentine movies never make it to the cinema, going straight to TV, or languishing on the shelf. In total, 260 new films were shown in the country in 1999, 50% of which came from the United States.

Last year's number one film was the excellent Argentine animated feature, **Manuelita**, following the adventures of the very popular, eponymous turtle. Its 2.2 million admissions pushed *The Sixth Sense* into second place. But while *Manuelita* was a huge commercial success, it also attracted controversy when it was selected as Argentina's entry for the Best Foreign Language Film Oscar and subsequently failed to be nominated.

Argentina now has two major festivals at which the most innovative local films have the opportunity to compete. In 1999, the 15th International Film Festival of Mar del Plata awarded prizes to Pablo Nisenson's **Angel, the Diva and I** (*Angel, la Diva y Yo*), but audience acclaim went to the much better **Just People** (*Solo Gente*), a medical drama from Roberto Maiocco, a physician whose film is partially based on his own experiences.

The second International Independent Film Festival of Argentina was held in Buenos Aires in April 2000. The competition fielded 16 films, three of which were from Argentina, including Daniel Burman's **Waiting for the Messiah** (*Esperando al Mesías*), which secured a prize for actor Enrique Pineyro. As with last year's winner, *Crane World*, the revelation of the event was another black-and-white movie with a social theme, **76 89 03**. The title refers to three years in the lives of three characters: 1976, during Argentina's military regime; 1989, in full democracy, and 2003.

The centenary of the birth of Jorge Luis Borges, the greatest Argentinean writer, was celebrated in 1999, and no fewer than four movies were planned to mark the anniversary. But none was ready for release before 2000. The first two to emerge in 2000 have been Tristan Bauer's **The Books and the Night** (*Los Libros y la Noche*) and Javier Torres' **A Borges Love** (*Un Amor de Borges*).

Some of Argentina's most compelling screen output recently has been set during the country's last military government (1976-1983). **Garage Olimpo**, which was shown in Un Certain Regard at Cannes in 1999, refers to the name given to a torture centre in Buenos Aires. Some graphic scenes make this drama hard to digest but at the same time a worthy experience. **Spoils of War** (*Botín de Guerra*) is a fine documentary which examines the experiences of children whose militant parents were killed by the military government, as the youngsters find themselves returned to their natural grandparents after living with adoptive families.

*Walter Santa Ana, left, and Leonardo Sbaraglia on location for THE BOOKS AND THE NIGHT*

*Eduardo Noriega, left, and Pablo Echarri in BURNT
MONEY*

Among recent releases, special mention should be made of Marcelo Piñeyro's fourth feature, **Burnt Money** (*Plata Quemada*). A factually-based thriller adapted from a best-selling book, it was shot in Argentina and Uruguay, with Hector Alterio and Leonardo Sbaraglia, who have appeared in all of Piñeyro's movies, cast opposite several of Argentina's most promising new actors.

ALFREDO FRIEDLANDER is a freelance film critic who writes regularly for the monthly *Cinetop* magazine. He also broadcasts on movie history and, above all, is a film buff.

# Recent and Forthcoming Films

## MANUELITA

Script and Dir: Manuel García Ferre. Music: María Elena Walsh, Néstor D'Alessandro, Roberto Lar. Prod: García Ferre Entertainment/ Telefe.

A beautiful animated feature that follows the adventures of a turtle called Manuelita, who travels to Paris to become an artist and then returns to Argentina in a hot-air balloon.

## ANGEL, LA DIVA Y YO (Angel, The Diva and I)

Script: Jose Pablo Feinman. Dir: Pablo Nisenson. Phot: Eduardo Pinto. Players: Pepe Soriano, Esther Goris, Boy Olmi, Florencia Peña, Ricardo Sandra, Margara Alonso, Salvador Sammaritano, Gogó Andreu.

When Julian is about to commit suicide a film can falls into his possession and changes his life. With the help of Diva, widow of Angel Ferreyros, a great film director, he will try to solve a mysterious puzzle: is Angel in fact still alive?

## SOLO GENTE (Only People)

Script and Direction: Roberto Maiocco. Phot: Carlos Torlaschi. Players: Pablo Echarri, Lito Cruz, Martin Adjemian, Walter Santa Ana, Ulises Dumont, Cristina Banegas, Tony Lestingi, Rodrigo Cameron.

A young man graduates from medical school, well-equipped with theoretical knowledge, and must come to terms with handling real patients.

## ESPERANDO AL MESIAS (Waiting for the Messiah)

Script: Daniel Burman, Emiliano Torres. Dir: Burman. Phot: Ramiro Civita. Players: Daniel Hendler, Enrique Pineyro, Hector Alterio, Melina Petriella, Stefania Sandrelli, Chiara Caselli, Gabriela Acher, Imanol Arias.

Two parallel and intersecting stories: a Jewish youth who gets involved with a bisexual girl; an unemployed man who meets a sympathetic woman. The film is a stark picture of end-of-the-century Buenos Aires.

## 76 89 03

Script and Dir: Christian Bernard, Flavio Nardini. Phot: Daniel Sotelo. Players: Sergio Baldrini, Gerardo Chendo, Diego Mackenzie, Claudio Rissi, Sol Alac. Prod: Flehner Films/La Produ 90/Film Suez.

The story of a dream shared by three guys: to make love to a famous model and TV actress. The story begins in 1976, when Argentina is under military rule, continues in 1989, under the democratically-elected government, and concludes in 2003, when their long-held dream finally comes true.

## LOS LIBROS Y LA NOCHE (The Books and the Night)

Script: Tristan Bauer, Carolina Scaglione. Dir: Bauer. Phot: Javier Julia. Players: Walter Santa Ana, Leonardo Sbaraglia, Lorenzo Quinteros, Hector Alterio, Ivonne Fournery, Lucas de Diego, Matías Fernandez Madris. Prod: Universidad Nacional de General San Martín/INCAA/Canal Plus (Spain).

This combination of fiction and fact portrays the life and work of one of the most remarkable Spanish-language writers, Jorge Luis Borges.

## UN AMOR DE BORGES (A Borges Love)

Script and Dir: Javier Torre. Phot: Mariano Cuneo. Players: Jean Pierre Noher, Ines Sastre, Inda Ledesma, Gigi Rua, Claudio Gallardou. Prod: Javier Torre Producciones.

Another examination of the very peculiar life of Jorge Luis Borges. His platonic love for the young Estela Canto is dominated by the strong presence of his mother.

## GARAGE OLIMPO

Script: Mario Bechis, Lara Fremder. Dir: Marco Bechis. Phot: Ramiro Civita. Music: Jacques Lederlin. Players: Antonella Costa,

Carlos Echevarría, Enrique Pineyro, Pablo Razuk, Dominique Sanda, Chiara Caselli, Miguel Oliveira, Paola Bechis.

Based on true events, this is the story of Maria, a 19-year-old militant, incarcerated at the "Garage Olimpo" torture centre, who discovers that one of her torturers was once her mother's tenant.

### BOTIN DE GUERRA (Spoils of War)

Script: Luisa Irene Ickowicz, David Blaustein. Dir: Blaustein. Phot: Marcelo Iaccarino. Prod: Zafra Difusion S.A. (Argentina)/ Tornasol Films S.A. (Spain).

This documentary focuses on the 'Plaza de Mayo Grandmothers', the organisation that for 20 years has highlighted the plight of babies who were raised by army and police families after their mothers had been detained and killed.

### PLATA QUEMADA (Burnt Money)

Script: Marcelo Figueras, Marcelo Piñeyro. Dir: Piñeyro. Phot: Alfredo Mayo. Players: Leonardo Sbaraglia, Eduardo Noriega, Pablo Echarri, Leticia Bredice, Ricardo Bartis, Dolores Fonzi, Carlos Roffe. Prod: Oscar Kramer/Cuatro Cabezas Film/ Tornasol Films (Spain)/Mandarin Films/Taxi Films.

Based on real life events from 1965, this thriller is Piñeyro's fourth movie. A conventional robbery of an armoured truck in Buenos Aires ends in a brutal massacre in Montevideo.

### EL MISMO AMOR, LA MISMA LLUVIA (The Same Love, the Same Rain)

Script: Fernando Castets, Juan Jose Campanella. Dir: Campanella. Phot: Daniel Schulman. Players: Ricardo Darin, Soledad Villamil, Ulises Dumont, Alfonso de Grazia, Alicia Zanca, Eduardo Blanco, Garciela Tenembaum.

Jorge, a journalist, and Laura, an aspiring actress, meet on a rainy day in 1980. The movie follows their encounters and disagreements across 20 years in a changing Argentina.

### EL MAR DE LUCAS (The Sea of Lucas)

Script: Mario Salinas. Dir: Victor Laplace. Phot: Fabian Giacometti. Players: Victor Laplace, Ana Maria Picchio, Pablo Rago, Betiana Blum, Virginia Innocenti, Norberto Diaz, Rodolfo Ranni, Ulises Dumont, Amelia Bence. Prod: Victor Laplace Producciones.

First feature from Victor Laplace, a popular Argentinean actor. It shows how the emerging love between Juan (Laplace) and Lucas, his previously unknown grandchild, will strengthen the bond between Juan and his son.

### LA EDAD DEL SOL (Age of the Sun)

Script: Luisa Irene Ickowicz. Dir: Ariel Piluso. Phot: Jorge Guillermo Behnisch. Players: Soledas Pastorutti, Celeste Garcia Satur, Ezequiel Abeijon, Karina Dali, Luciana Baskansky. Prod: Atomic Films/Naya Film S.A./ARTEAR.

Movie debut for Soledad Pastorutti, a popular Argentinean singer. In a mixture of fiction and reality, she portrays an artist forced to choose between her career (the build-up to a big show) and her friends (their graduation trip).

### OPERACION FANGIO (Operation Fangio)

Script: Claudia Furiati, Orlando Senna, Manuel Perez. Dir: Alberto Lecchi. Phot: Hugo Colace. Players: Dario Grandinetti, Ernesto Tapia, Laura Ramos, Gustavo Salmeron, Fernando Guillen, Arturo Maly. Prod: Aleph Producciones/ Productora Cinematografica ICAIC (Cuba)/El Paso Producciones (Spain).

This is the true story of the kidnapping of Juan Manuel Fangio, five-time world Formula One champion, in Havana, during the Cuban Revolution in 1958. The movie was shot in the actual locations where the abduction took place.

### NUECES PARA EL AMOR (Nuts for Love)

Script: Daniel Romanach, Daniel García Molt, Alberto Lecchi. Dir: Lecchi. Phot: Hugo Colace. Players: Ariadna Gil, Gaston Pauls, Malena Solda, Nicolas

Pauls, Gabriel Goity, Nancy Duplaa, Rodrigo de la Serna. Prod: Zarlek Producciones (Argentina)/ Tornasol Films S.A.(Spain).

Alberto Lecchi's fifth feature in only six years (quite a record in Argentina's present, tough movie-making climate) is not only a love story, but also a chronicle of events in Argentina over the past 25 years.

### CERCA DE LA FRONTERA (Near the Border)

Script: Rodolfo Duran, Eduardo Leiva Muller. Dir: Duran. Phot: Carlos Torlaschi. Players: Claudio Gallardou, Ulises Dumont, Leonor Manso, Victor Laplace, Alberto Benegas, Mirna Suarez, Paula Pourtale, Rene Olaguivel, Gonzalo Morales. Prod: Opera Prima srl/INCAA.

In 1978, under the military government, a threatened journalist tries to leave Argentina. He has to hide in a village near the border, where he establishes contact with the local priest, a brothel owner and a young militant who will dramatically change his life.

### SOLO POR HOY (Only for Today)

Script: Lautaro Nunez de Arce, Ariel Rotter. Dir: Rotter. Phot: Marcelo Lavitman. Players: Sergio Boris, Aili Chen, Damián Dreysik, Federico Esquerro, Mariano Martinez. Prod: Universidad del Cine.

A story of people struggling to survive; their motto is doing things "only for today".

## Producers

### Aleph Produciones S.A.
Constitucion 3156
Buenos Aires
Fax: (54 11) 4374 6448

### Argentina Sono Film
Lavalle 1860
1051 Buenos Aires
Fax: (54 11) 4374 9250

### Artear Group S.A.
Lima 1261
1138 Buenos Aires
Fax: (54 11) 4370 1309

*Sergio Boris, left, and Federico Esquerro in ONLY FOR TODAY*

**Atomic Films**
Castillo 1366
1414 Buenos Aires
Fax: (54 11) 4771 6003
www.flehnerfilms.com

**BD Cine**
Cabello 3650 1D
1425 Buenos Aires
Fax: (54 11) 4802 4218
e-mail: bdcine@movi.com.ar

**Film Suez S.A.**
Florida 681 2°
1375 Buenos Aires
Fax: (54 11) 4314 7800
e-mail: suez@interprov.com

**Imágen Satelital S.A.**
Avenida Melián 2752
1430 Buenos Aires
Fax: (54 11) 4546 8001

**Kompel Producciones S.A.**
Avenida Corrientes 1660
1042 Buenos Aires
Fax: (54 11) 4814 2657

**Oscar Kramer Producciones**
Figueroa Alcorta 3351 –
Piso 1° Of.104
1425 Buenos Aires
Fax: (54 11) 4807 3254
e-mail: okafilms@overnet.com.ar

**Patagonik Film Group S.A.**
Godoy Cruz 1540
1414 Buenos Aires
Fax: (54 11) 4778 0046
e-mail: patafilm@intermedia.com.ar

**POL-KA Producciones S.A.**
Jorge Newbery 3483
1427 Buenos Aires
Fax: (54 11) 4553 0588/0543
e-mail: cine@pol-ka.comar

**Telefe S.A.**
Pavón 2444
1248 Buenos Aires
Fax: (54 11) 4308 0054

**Tercer Milenio S.A.**
Fitz Roy 1940
1414 Buenos Aires
Fax: (54 11) 4771 2752
e-mail: aries@fibertel.com.ar

**U.C.G. Producciones S.A.**
Lavalle 1619 – 3° Piso E
1048 Buenos Aires
Fax: (54 11) 4373 8208
e-mail: cineojo@interlink.co.ar

# Distributors

**Alfa Films**
Av. Corrientes 2025 – 2° Piso A
1045 Buenos Aires
Fax: (54 11) 4951 9901
e-mail: alfafilms@ssdnet.com.ar

**Artistas Argentinos Asociados**
Lavalle 1977/79
1051 Buenos Aires
Fax: (54 11) 4811 5016/4371 3862
e-mail: artasoc@infovia.comar

**Columbia Tristar Film Gmbh**
Ayacucho 533

1026 Buenos Aires
Fax: (54 11) 4375 0133

**Cine3 S.A.**
Lavalle 1527 PB 2
1048 Buenos Aires
Fax: (54 11) 4374 4327
e-mail: cine3sa@cotelco.com.ar

**Distribution Company S.A.**
Ayacucho 595
1026 Buenos Aires
Fax: (54 11) 4372 9945/4371 3662
e-mail: dcazupnik@arnet.com.ar

**Eurocine S.A.**
Tucumán 1980 – P.B-
1050 Buenos Aires
Fax: (54 11) 4373 0547
e-mail: eurocine@navigo.com.ar

**IFA Argentina**
Riobamba 339 2° Piso A
1025 Buenos Aires
Fax: (54 11) 4373 7967
e-mail: ifa@cine3.com.ar

**Líder Films S.A.**
Lavalle 2086
1051 Buenos Aires
Fax: (54 11) 4953 7355
e-mail: liderstupia@infovia.com.ar

**Primer Plano Film Group S.A.**
Riobamba 477
1025 Buenos Aires
Fax: (54 11) 4374 0648/8435
e-mail: orlersa@comnet.com.ar

**UIP (United International Pictures) S.R.I.**
Ayacucho 520
1026 Buenos Aires
Fax: (54 11) 4373 5098
e-mail: zrossini@arnet.com.ar

**Warner Bros. – Fox**
Tucumán 1938
1050 Buenos Aires
Fax: (54 11) 4372 6094/97
e-mail: maicat@ssdnet.com.ar

# Useful Address

**INCAA (Instituto Nacional de Cine y Artes Audiovisuales)**
Lima 319
1073 Buenos Aires
Fax: (54 11) 4383 0029
e-mail: info@incaa.gov.ar

# ARMENIA

Susanna Harutiunian

With the tenth anniversary of Armenian state independence approaching in 2001, the difficult process of separating the film industry from the vestiges of state control and establishing a free market has been ongoing for a decade; so now is a good time to sum up. About 30 full-length features have been produced in Armenia in this period – not bad for a country which even during the Soviet years, when production had stable finance from the state, produced only three or four films a year.

The year 2000 can be considered as fruitful, with documentaries, animation films and video production, and no less than eight features released or scheduled for release, including Suren Babayan's *Crazy Angel* (*Khent Hreshtak*) and Albert Mkrtchian's *A Happy Bus* (*Avervats Kaghaki Meghedy*).

On the other hand, the production of some films has been delayed for many years and the necessary conditions for the development of independent film production still do not exist in Armenia. There is no legal framework, the state studios await redevelopment, the distribution network is inadequate, with just three cinemas operational in Yerevan, using old Soviet projection equipment.

Yet there are positive improvements to be noted within this knot of problems. In the spring of 2000, the Armenian National Assembly, after long and heated debates, finally voted in favour of Armenia joining the Bern Convention on Copyright Protection. This marked the start of a serious struggle against piracy within the local cinema and video markets. Opponents of this move claimed that because both local TV channels are

virtually bankrupt, the Armenian audience will be deprived of any possibility of watching new films – even if they are illegally screened.

That argument is indefensible. I still can't forget my astonishment when I saw Barry Levinson's *Wag the Dog* (1997) on television in Armenia just one month after its world premiere at the Berlin film festival. By the same token, illegally exported Armenian films are shown on some private TV channels abroad. Armenia now has a legitimate basis for developing relations with western distributors, and Haifilm studio has already launched two joint projects with France, both partially financed by the Centre National Cinématographique. One of them is Vigen Chaldranian's tale of a lunatic taking over an asylum, *Symphony of Silence* (see *IFG* 2000). The French company Boomerang Production was responsible for much of the post-production work, including sound mixing.

## Like a virgin

The second Armenian-French joint production is the new film from one of Armenia's best-known directors, Edgar Baghdassrian. Baghdassrian's previous work was the monumental documentary 'fresco', *Arratta – The Land of Holy Rituals*, which filmed in Iran, Turkey, Israel, Greece and Italy to mark the celebrations of the 1700th anniversary of the adoption of Christianity as the state religion in Armenia. Remarkably, *Arratta* was a completely independent production, with no money coming from the state, so great credit must go to the producer, Manouk Gevorkian.

Baghdassrian's new film, **Mariam**, is an astonishing story, a parable about a pure creature, Mariam (the Armenian name for

*Still from Albert Mkrtchian's A HAPPY BUS*

the Virgin Mary), a young woman of 35, who is a teacher and deaf and dumb interpreter at a boarding school for deaf children. She dwells on her virginity, and behaves so strangely that those around her, even her psychotherapist, cannot understand her. The psychotherapist thinks the only way to cure her mental disorders is to awaken her sensuality, but Mariam resists the idea.

Baghdassrian openly confronts the cult of sex that presently overwhelms so many art forms, including cinema. He chooses an unconventional path for his heroine, and the child she gives birth to at the end of the film does not appear to have been conceived from the sperm of an earthly donor; it's unclear whether the birth means the end or the beginning of the world.

Since the end of Soviet rule, professional links between members of the 'Armenian Diaspora' have become tighter and none of the expatriate Armenians to have made a name for themselves in cinema has been more successful than the outstanding Canadian-Armenian film-maker Atom Egoyan. His *Felicia's Journey* opened the First Festival of Armenian Films in Montreal in April-May 1999, which encompassed more than 30 films.

Special screenings of Armenian films followed in Ottawa (May-June) and Vancouver (July), and the organisers of the Montreal event hope it can become a regular meeting point for Armenian filmmakers now based in different parts of the world. It is to be hoped that such festivals may help Armenian cinema to overcome the numerous obstacles left behind by Soviet rule, and reduce its comparative isolation from the international filmmaking community.

SOUSANNA HAROUTIUNIAN graduated from Moscow's State Cinematographic Institute in 1987. She has contributed to numerous Armenian and Russian publications, has been film correspondent of the daily *Republica Armenia* since 1991 and is president of Armenia's Association of Film Critics and Cinema Journalists.

# Recent and Forthcoming films

**AVIRVATS KAGHAKI MEGHEDI (A Happy Bus)**

Script: Albert Mkrtchian, Mher Mkrtchian. Dir: Albert Mkrtchian. Phot: R.Vatinian. Players: M.Pogossian, G.Grigorian, A.Haroutiunian. Producer: Haifilm Studio.

**LRUTSIAN SIMPHONIA (Symphony of Silence)**

Script: Gurgen Khanjian, Vigen Chaldranian. Dir: Chaldranian. Phot: Artiom Melkonian. Players: M.Pogossian, K.Djanibekian, V.Msrian. Producer: Haifilm Studio.

**ARATTA – SRPAZAN TSESERY ERKIR (Aratta – The Land of Holy Rituals)**

Script and Dir: Edgar Baghdasarian. Phot: V.Ter-Hakopian, A.Mkrtchian. Producer: Manuk Gevorgian

**PERLEKINO**

Script and Dir: Tigran Xmalian. Phot: V.Ter-Hakopian. Players: V.Msrian, A.Khorenian, H.Haroutiunian, A. Haroutiunian. Producer: Yerevan Film Studio.

## Useful Addresses

**Armenian Union of Cinematographers**
18 Vardanats
Yerevan
Tel: (374 2) 570 528
Fax: (374 2) 570 136

**Armenian National Cinematheque**
25A,Tbilisskoye shosse
Yerevan
Tel: (374 2) 285 406

**Association of Film Critics and Cinema Journalists**
15 G.Lusavorich St
4th floor, #408
375 015 Yerevan
Tel: (374 2) 562 906
Fax: (374 2) 523 922
email: aafccj@arminco.com

**Association of Film Producers**
15, Amiryan St
Apt.85
375 010 Yerevan

**Film Department**
Ministry of Culture
5, Toumanian St
375 001 Yerevan
Tel: (374 2) 525 349
Fax: (374 2) 523 922

## Producers

**HAIFILM Studio**
50, Gevork Chaush
375088 Yerevan
Tel: (374 2) 343 000
Fax: (374 2) 523 922

**HAIK Documentary Studio**
50, Gevork Chaush
375088 Yerevan
Tel: (374 2) 354 590/357 032

**YEREVAN Studio**
47, Nork
375047 Yerevan
Tel: (374 2) 558 022
e-mail: tx-yes@media.internews.am

## Distributor

**Paradise**
18, Abovian
75001 Yerevan
Tel: (374 2) 521 271
Fax: (374 2) 521 302

# AUSTRALIA — David Stratton

The Australian film scene in 2000 looks very much as it has done for the last few years. Concerns about finding audiences for Australian films, both at home and overseas, continue to dominate industry debate. While our actors, directors and technicians continue to find work, and fame, overseas – Russell Crowe became a star in *The Insider* and *Gladiator*, and Heath Ledger took a big step up the ladder as Mel Gibson's son in *The Patriot* – Australia's production facilities are increasingly servicing Hollywood blockbusters.

On the day I completed this piece, newspaper reports announced that George Lucas had arrived in Sydney to start work on *Star Wars: Episode II* at the Fox Studios which previously hosted *Mission: Impossible 2* and *The Matrix*. Yet another big Hollywood production has been lured here by the expertise of local crews and a very favourable exchange rate; but while all this international activity goes on, authentic Australian films continually struggle to find an audience.

There has been intense speculation about the prospects of Baz Luhrmann's *Moulin Rouge*, starring Nicole Kidman and Ewan McGregor: a large-scale film with Hollywood backing, which had a lengthy rehearsal and shooting schedule. Other yet-to-be-released films that have been produced only with the help of international financing include *Bootmen*, a working-class musical, and Samantha Lang's *The Monkey's Mask*, her follow-up to *The Well*.

But commentators are beginning to ask if young Australian film-makers have lost that vital passion. Do they really *need* to make films, in the way their predecessors obviously did? Or do they just see it as a 'sexy' career? Even the best of the latest films tend to pale in comparison with the major productions of 20 years ago.

There is always an exception, however, and Jane Campion may be it. Not everyone liked **Holy Smoke**, which was an Australian production funded by Miramax, but the director's confrontational vision was well and truly to the fore in this superbly-acted piece. Kate Winslet's remarkable portrayal of a young Australian girl undergoing de-programming after joining a religious cult on a trip to India deserved greater recognition than it received. The scenes in which she turns the sexual tables on her de-programmer (Harvey Keitel) were quite remarkable.

### Tales from the melting pot

At a time when few local productions make their mark at the box-office, it was interesting that the two top-grossing Australian films of the year both dealt with ethnic minorities: crassly in the case of **The Wogboy**, tenderly in the case of *Looking for*

*Pia Miranda in LOOKING FOR ALIBRANDI*

*Alibrandi*. The former, directed by Aleksi Vellis, was inspired by a popular stage production, *Wogs Out of Work*, devised by lead actor Nick Giannopoulos. It is a perfunctorily made mixture of the amusing and the crass, in which Giannopoulos plays a happy-go-lucky unemployed man who falls foul of the vindictive Minister for Employment (Geraldine Turner, wickedly taking off a recognisable right-wing politician). A script re-write or three might have sharpened this rather lacklustre effort.

In complete contrast, Kate Woods' **Looking for Alibrandi**, a faithful adaptation of Melina Marchetta's popular autobiographical novel, centres on a lovely performance from first-time actress Pia Miranda. She plays Josephine, brought up by her single mother (Greta Scacchi) and beloved grandmother and other members of an extended Sicilian-Australian family. Josephine's journey through this very attractive film embraces tragedy (the suicide of a boy she fancies) and happiness (meeting her father, played by Anthony La Paglia, for the first time).

Continuing the ethnic theme, John Tatoulis' laid-back comedy, **Beware of Greeks Bearing Guns**, which as this report went to press had yet to open in Australia, has been a considerable success in Greece, partly because of the presence of popular entertainer Lakis Lazopoulos, who is excellent in the lead roles. He plays twin brothers, the gentle Manos and the macho George, involved in a long-standing family feud which starts off in wartime Crete and culminates in present-day Melbourne.

*Lakis Lazopoulos in BEWARE OF GREEKS BEARING GUNS*

Yet another film linking Australia with Mediterranean Europe is **The Missing**, in which Fabrizio Bentivoglio plays a Vatican priest who returns to Australia after many years away to search for his missing daughter. Manuela Alberti's chaotically incoherent film has elements borrowed from *The Last Wave* (a white man dreaming aboriginal dreams) and *Duel* (a sinister truck driver) but singularly fails to thrill or intrigue; yawning gaps in the narrative suggest a pile of film was left on the cutting room floor.

## Belgian lovers, French money

The protagonists of Paul Cox's serene **Innocence** came to Melbourne from Belgium many years ago. At the end of the Second World War, when they were in their twenties, Andreas (Charles Tingwell) and Claire (Julia Blake) were lovers. Now Andreas, a widower for 30 years, meets Claire again; she's in a contented but dull marriage and they resume their sexual

relationship, with somewhat surprising results. This is Cox working in the territory he knows best: a film about mature love, memory, loss, the ageing process – all elements found in his finest work (*Lonely Hearts*, *Man of Flowers*, *A Woman's Tale*). Since completing *Innocence*, he has been working on his long-cherished biopic, *Nijinsky*, to be released in 2001.

In June 2000, the re-vamped Sydney Film Festival opened with **Better Than Sex**, essentially a two-hander about a couple of strangers (David Wenham, Susie Porter) who meet for a one-night stand and fall in love during three days of concentrated sex. Terrific performances from the very likeable leads, and assured direction from first-timer Jonathan Teplitzky, who augments the basic material by inserting scenes in which a couple of Greek choruses, one male, one female, candidly comment on the action, ensure the success of this low-budget film, partly financed by French television.

French money, courtesy of Gaumont, entirely financed Pip Karmel's **Me, Myself, I**, a *Sliding Doors*-style comedy in which bachelor girl Rachel Griffiths (excellent) is given the opportunity to see how life might have turned out if she had married her first love several years before the film begins. The film's failure in France (where it opened several months before its Australian release) suggests similar funding deals may be harder to set up in future.

Several women directed their first features during the year, including Belinda

*Julia Blake and Charles Tingwell in INNOCENCE*

*David Wenham and Susie Porter in BETTER THAN SEX*

Chayko, whose **City Loop** was a low-budgeter set in Brisbane. It unfolds over one night and explores the lives of a handful of young people who work at a pizza parlour. Unfortunately, neither the characters nor their adventures (mostly sexual) are all that interesting, but Chayko's direction is good enough to promise better things when she finds stronger material.

Another low-budget film, **Mallboy**, by Vincent Giarrusso, proved to be a corrosive, rather sad study of a suburban

teenage boy, his family and friends, and their almost hopeless lives. One detects that Giarrusso admires Truffaut's *Les Quatre Cents Coups*, especially in the film's final image, but the young hero, played by Kane McNay, and his spaced-out mother (Nell Feeney), are really tragic figures. *City Loop* and *Mallboy* were funded by a low-budget feature scheme involving the Australian Film Commission, a free-to-air television network and a pay-TV channel.

### Have camera, will direct

Some film-makers, unable to find backers, just go out and shoot movies anyway, which in the age of digital video becomes easier all the time. Full marks to writer-producer-director Phillip Marzella, whose deliciously-titled **Low-Fat Elephants** is a promising situation comedy. Lesbian Greta (Tessa Wells), who shares an apartment with a heterosexual Chinese-Australian, Cassandra (Karen Pang), decides to put her flatmate off men for all time. She hires the shady Yuri, played by Marzella, to romance Cassandra, posing as a Frenchman, and then dump her. It is a

*Nell Feeney and Kane McNay in MALLBOY*
*photo: Beyond Films*

slight plot, but confidently handled, with particularly good performances from the women.

By contrast, **Muggers** is a slickly-filmed, 'Scope comedy starring Matt Day and Jason Barry as impoverished medical students who, in desperation, fund their studies by delving into the organ-stealing business. Though completely overlooked by critics and public alike, this clever film, well-directed by Dean Murphy, combines social criticism (government cutbacks in health and education) with a genuinely funny script, and there's a clutch of interesting character actors in support.

Less successful is Mark Lamprell's **My Mother Frank**, which also has a university setting, and which stars Sinead Cusack as a widowed mother who enrols as a student, to the embarrassment of her son, who is on the same campus. This was pretty thin material. Young people feature more interestingly in Clinton Smith's fast-paced, ebullient **Sample People**, in which the paths of 12 assorted characters cross on a hot Saturday night. Kylie Minogue appears to good effect as a young woman who works for a dangerous gang boss and plans to double-cross him.

Sadly, *Sample People* was another box-office catastrophe, though its failure was not as surprising as that of Kimble Rendall's **Cut**, a witty and accomplished slasher film in the *Scream* mould. Intelligently-plotted and benefiting, like *Scream 3*, from a film industry setting and a hefty marketing campaign, *Cut* could not attract the audiences who flock to its Hollywood equivalents.

The year's better documentaries included Trevor Graham's **Tosca: A Tale of Love and Torture**, a fly-on-the-wall look at Opera Australia rehearsals which at times threaten more violence than occurs in Puccini's opera. Also of great interest was Tom Zubrycki's **The Diplomat**, a study of East Timor's Jose Ramos Horta, which climaxed with the catastrophic events which occurred in that country in late 1999. On a lighter note was the seriously bizarre **Tackle Happy**, which follows two well-endowed young

*Nathalie Roy in SAMPLE PEOPLE*
photo: Rep Films

men who toured the country amusing mostly female audiences with what they call "puppetry of the penis".

Finally, it seems no year can pass without a front-page censorship scandal; the latest involved Catherine Breillat's pornographic *Romance*, which was initially banned by the Censorship Board, then passed on appeal. The conservative government's appointment of Des Clark as the new Chief Censor was something of a pleasant surprise, since he was formerly Chairman of the Board of the Melbourne International Film Festival. Meanwhile distributors complain privately about overly harsh classification decisions, and quietly clip their films – *Three Kings* is a recent example – to obtain milder ratings; without, of course, informing the public.

DAVID STRATTON was Director of the Sydney Film Festival (1966-1983) and is co-host of *The Movie Show*, a weekly programme on the SBS TV network. He also contributes reviews to *Variety* and *The Australian*, and lectures on film history at the University of Sydney.

*Jason Barry in MUGGERS*
photo: Rep Films

# Industry Survey

## by Peter Thompson

A quick snapshot: local production faltering, foreign companies moving in, commercial opportunities opening up but creative development in crisis. If 2000-2001 isn't a major turning point, for better or worse, it certainly feels like one. The production of feature films by Australians remains fairly static, as it has been for the last four years. During 1998-99, 41 films were made with a combined budget of $72m, but only a few had budgets over $3.5m and more than 16 were made for less than $600,000. The same trends continued in 1999-2000, with 36 features worth a total of $84m, a figure inflated by the inclusion of Baz Luhrmann's *Moulin Rouge*, which is regarded as Australian despite being totally financed by 20th Century Fox.

The increasing value of foreign production in Australia makes it hard to see the wood for the trees in gauging the health of the industry. Inward investment has been steadily climbing, boosting the total value of film and television drama in 1998-99 to over $405m. The success of *The Matrix*, *The Red Planet*, *Pitch Black* and *Mission: Impossible 2* has put a gloss on Australia's credibility as part of the global film business, with the next two *Star Wars* episodes, shooting at Fox Studios in Sydney, guaranteed to maintain that profile.

But 2000 was a defining year in many ways. It became clearer than ever that "the Australian film industry" as it's called, is in trouble, struggling for financial viability and creative direction. Symptomatic of the malaise was the formation at the end of 1999 of the Independent Producers Initiative. Twenty-four producers, including Jane Scott (*Shine*), Robert Connolly (*The Boys*), Hilary Linstead (*Bootmen*), Anthony Buckley (*The Potato Factory*) and Martha Coleman (*Praise*), submitted a strongly-worded statement to the Federal Government exposing their dire financial situation. The main state funding body, the Australian Film Finance Corporation (FFC), has driven increasingly tough deals

over the years, making it virtually impossible for producers to cover even their expenses, let alone participate in the profits if they happen to make a successful movie.

Some changes have now been implemented by both the FFC and the Australian Film Commission (AFC), which has traditionally supported script development. The FFC has loosened its grip on budgets, to acknowledge producers' real costs, and the AFC has begun funding producers directly, handing over a greater degree of creative responsibility. But there's also a cultural debate going on about the direction of Australian film-making.

## The economics, stupid!

Since the 1980s, Australia has been in the grip of economic rationalist ideology, with its devotion to the miraculous healing powers of the free market, low taxation, small government and deregulation. But these run counter to the realities of a domestic film industry heavily dependent on government investment and protective legislation. The success of the latter is borne out by the number of internationally accepted movies made since the 1970s and by the growth of an efficient film-making infrastructure, including creative personnel, technicians, laboratories and, more recently, computer-generated imagery. Nevertheless, the illusion persists in many quarters that the local industry can be self-supporting if only we can stop making bad movies. As the old joke goes, why not just make the commercially successful ones?

This sense of unreality is fostered by foreign companies arriving with bags full of money. As mentioned above, some high-profile Hollywood films have been made here and the hard currency that flows in is welcomed, not just by those who get jobs loading the cameras and driving the honey wagons. But Australia is also caught up in the rush towards globalisation. Australia can produce so-called "content" at bargain rates. So British, European, American and Japanese producers are seizing the opportunity. Pearson bought out Grundy many years ago. Granada took over Artist Services in 1999. Universal Pictures forged local links and Columbia TriStar launched a capital-raising venture to fund local production.

But Australia also offers a low-cost gateway into English-language production. Three German companies are now involved: MBP has signed a four-year financing agreement worth $31m with the film and television producer Beyond; EM.TV has taken a 50% share of Yoram Gross's animation studio; Ravensberger has bought 68% of rapidly expanding Energee Entertainment. French companies have invested in several local features, for instance Gaumont in *Me, Myself and I*, and Canal Plus in *The Monkey's Mask*. The obvious point needs to be made: much of this apparent boom depends on the low exchange rate of the Australian dollar: a fragile foundation on which to build.

There's a discernible shift to a 'commercial' frame of mind inside and outside the film community, especially in government, which increasingly expects the industry to pay its own way. That's fine, especially while foreign money is flowing in, but it hardly constitutes a cultural policy. Phrases such as "national identity" and "distinctly Australian" sound more and more hollow, especially on the lips of politicians. But hard questions need to be asked about what Australians want from their cinema: a mini-Hollywood or an indigenous industry striving above all to reflect and define something authentically Australian.

PETER THOMPSON is a writer, film-maker and critic who appears regularly on Australian national television.

# Producers

### Arenafilm
(Robert Connolly, John Maynard)
270 Devonshire Street
Surry Hills NSW 2010
Tel: (61 2) 9319 7011
Fax: (61 2) 9319 6906
e-mail: arenafilm@mpx.com.au

### Artist Services
(Andrew Knight, Steve Vizard)
33 Nott Street
Port Melbourne VIC 3207
Tel: (61 3) 9646 3388
Fax: (61 3) 9646 7644

### Barron Entertainment
(Paul Barron)
7/85 Forest St
Cottesloe WA 6011
Tel: (61 8) 9385 1551
Fax: (61 8) 9385 2299

### Bazmark Inq.
(Baz Luhrmann)
PO Box 430
Kings Cross NSW 1340
Tel: (61 2) 9361 6668
Fax: (61 2) 9361 6667
www.bazmark.com

### Beyond International
(Mikael Borglund)
53-55 Brisbane St
Surry Hills NSW 2010
Tel: (61 2) 9281 1266
Fax: (61 2) 9281 1261
www.beyond.com.au

### Bill Bennett Productions
(Bill Bennett)
PO Box 4117
Castlecrag NSW 2068
Tel: (61 2) 9417 7744
Fax: (61 2) 9417 7601
e-mail: billbenprods@aol.com

### Binnaburra Film Company
(Glenys Rowe)
PO Box 2124
Clovelly NSW 2031
Tel: (61 2) 9665 6135
Fax: (61 2) 9665 4378
e-mail: glenysmerle@one.act.au

### Cascade Films and Melbourne Film Studios
(David Parker, Nadia Tass)
117 Rouse St
Port Melbourne VIC 3207
Tel: (61 3) 9646 4022
Fax: (61 3) 9646 6336

e-mail: info@cascadefilms.com.au
www.cascadefilms.com.au

### David Hannay Productions
(David Hannay)
PO Box 175
Leura NSW 2780
Tel: (61 2) 4782 7111
Fax: (61 2) 4782 3711
e-mail: memdah@pnc.com.au

### Emcee Films
(Martha Coleman)
402 Bourke St
Surry Hills NSW 2011
Tel: (61 2) 9356 8040
Fax: (61 2) 9356 8050
e-mail: marthac@ozemail.com.au

### Energee Entertainment
(Gerry Travers)
1/706 Mowbray Rd
Lane Cove NSW 2066
Tel: (61 2) 9420 8864
Fax: (61 2) 9420 8861

### Fox Studios Australia
(Kim Williams)
Driver Avenue
Moore Park NSW 1363
Tel: (61 2) 9383 4000
Fax: (61 2) 9361 3106

**Great Scott Productions**
(Jane Scott)
27 Elizabeth St
Paddington NSW 2021
Tel: (61 2) 9331 3535
Fax: (61 2) 9360 5875
e-mail:greats@netspace.net.au

**House & Moorhouse Films**
(Lynda House, Jocelyn Moorhouse)
117 Rouse St
Port Melbourne VIC 3207
Tel: (61 3) 9646 4025
Fax: (61 3) 9646 6336

**Jan Chapman Productions**
(Jan Chapman)
PO Box 27
Potts Point NSW 1335
Tel: (61 2) 9331 2666
Fax: (61 2) 9331 2011

**Kennedy Miller**
(George Miller)
The Metro Theatre
30 Orwell Street
Kings Cross NSW 2011
Tel: (61 2) 9357 2322
Fax: (61 2) 9356 3162

**Matt Carroll Films**
(Matt Carroll)
12 Sloane Street
Newtown NSW 2042
Tel: (61 2) 9516 2400
Fax: (61 2) 9516 2099
e-mail: mcfilms@pop.real.com.au

**Palm Beach Pictures**
(David Elfick)
PO Box 409
Paddington NSW 2021
Tel: (61 2) 9365 1043
Fax: (61 2) 9365 1380
e-mail: palmbeach@infolearn.com.au

**RB Films**
(Rosemary Blight)
222 Johnston St
Annandale NSW 2038
Tel: (61 2) 9281 9550
Fax: (61 2) 9211 2281
rbfilms@ozemail.com.au

**REP Films**
(Richard Becker)
Level 2, 486 Pacific Highway
St Leonards NSW 1590
Tel: (61 2) 9438 3377
Fax: (61 2) 9439 1827

**Samson Productions**
(Sue Milliken)
Fox Studios
Driver Av
Moore Park NSW 1363
Tel: (61 2) 8353 2600
Fax: (61 2) 8353 2601
samson@samsonprod.com.au

**Serious Entertainment**
(Warwick Ross)
PO Box 600
North Sydney NSW 2059
Tel: (61 2) 9957 5375
Fax: (61 2) 9955 8600

**Smiley Films Pty Ltd**
(Richard Brennan)
Suite F14, 1-15 Barr St
Balmain NSW 2041
Tel: (61 2) 9818 7144
Fax: (61 2) 9818 7133
Mob: 61 407 439 776
e-mail: richbren@tech2u.com.au

**Southern Star Group**
(Errol Sullivan)
Level 9/8 West St
North Sydney NSW 2060
Tel: (61 2) 9202 8555
Fax: (61 2) 9925 0849
e-mail: general@sstar.com.au

**Stamen Films**
(Jonathan Shteinman)
PO Box 3226
Tamarama NSW 2026
Tel: (61 2) 9365 2284
Fax: (61 2) 9300 0264
e-mail: stamen@ozemail.com.au

**Tristram Miall Films**
(Tristram Miall)
270 Devonshire St
Surry Hills NSW 2010
Tel: (61 2) 9310 2422
Fax: (61 2) 9318 2542
e-mail: tmfilm@zeta.org.au

**Vertigo Productions**
(Rolf de Heer)
3 Butler Drive
Hendon SA 5014
Tel: (61 8) 8348 9382
Fax: (61 8) 8348 9347
e-mail: vertigo@adelaide.on.net

**Village Roadshow Pictures**
(Michael Lake)
Warner Roadshow Movie World

Studios
Pacific Highway
Oxenford QLD 4210
Tel: (61 7) 5588 6666
Fax: (61 7) 5573 3698
www.village.com.au

**Working Dog**
(Santo Cilauro, Tom Gleisner, Michael
Hirsh, Jane Kennedy, Rob Sitch)
PO Box 488
South Yarra VIC 3141
Tel: (61 3) 9826 4344
Fax: (61 3) 9826 4355
www.workingdog.com

# Distributors

Note: The Beyond Group, REP
Films and Southern Star are all
important distributors; see
Producers listings for contact
details.

**Buena Vista International
(Australia)**
Level 4
The Como Centre
650 Chapel St
South Yarra 3141
Tel: (61 3) 9826 5200
Fax: (61 3) 9826 6708

**Columbia TriStar Films**
GPO Box 3342
Sydney NSW 2001
Tel: (61 2) 9272 2900
Fax: (61 2) 9272 2991

**Dendy Films**
19 Martin Place
Sydney NSW 2000
Tel: (61 2) 9233 8558
Fax: (61 2) 9232 3841
e-mail: dendy@dendy.com.au

**Footprint Films Pty Ltd**
(same address as Arenafilm Pty Ltd)

**The Globe Film Company**
373 Liverpool St
Darlinghurst NSW 2010
Tel: (61 2) 9332 2722
Fax: (61 2) 9332 2888
e-mail: info@globefilm.com.au

**Newvision Film Distributors Pty
Ltd**
252 Bay St

Port Melbourne VIC 3207
Tel: (61 3) 9646 5555
Fax: (61 3) 9646 2411

**Palace Films**
233 Whitehorse Rd
Balwyn VIC 3103
Tel: (61 3) 9817 6421
Fax: (61 3) 9817 4921
e-mail: palace@netspace.net.au

**Roadshow Film Distributors**
GPO Box 1411M
Melbourne VIC 3000
Tel: (61 3) 9667 6666
Fax: (61 3) 9662 1449

**Ronin Films**
PO Box 1005
Civic Square ACT 2600
Tel: (61 6) 248 0851
Fax: (61 6) 249 1640
e-mail: roninfilms@netinfo.com.au

**Sharmill Films**
4/200 Toorak Road
South Yarra VIC 3141
Tel: (61 3) 9826 9077
Fax: (61 3) 9826 1935

**20th Century Fox
Film Distributors Pty Ltd**
505 George St
Sydney NSW 2000
Tel: (61 2) 9273 7300
Fax: (61 2) 9283 2191

**United International Pictures**
208 Clarence St
Sydney NSW 2000
Tel: (61 2) 9264 7444
Fax: (61 2) 9264 2499

## Useful Addresses

**Australian Film Commission**
150 William St
Wooloomooloo NSW 2011
GPO Box 3984
Sydney 2001
Tel: (61 2) 9321 6444
Fax: (61 2) 9357 3737
e-mail: info@afc.gov.au
www.afc.gov.au

**Australian Film Finance
Corporation**
130 Elizabeth St

Sydney NSW 2000
Postal address: GPO Box 3886
Sydney NSW 2001
Tel: (61 2) 9268 2555
Fax: (61 2) 9264 8551
www.ffc.gov.au

**Australian Film, Television
and Radio School**
PO Box 126
North Ryde NSW 2113
Tel: (61 2) 9805 6611
Fax: (61 2) 9887 1030
e-mail:
direct.sales@syd.aftrs.edu.au

**Film Australia**
101 Eton Rd
Lindfield NSW 2070
Tel: (61 2) 9413 8777
Fax: (61 2) 9416 9401

More information can be found via
the Web on www.nla.gov.au/oz/gov.
Also www.sna.net.au; for Screen
Network Australia which is a
gateway to more than 250 film and
television sites.

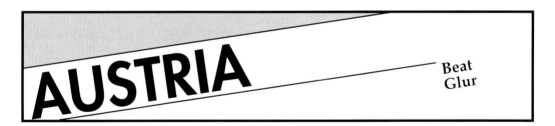

# AUSTRIA

Beat
Glur

In the aftermath of the election success of Jörg Haider's right-wing Freedom Party in 1999, Austrian film-makers found themselves in a very difficult position. On the one hand they protested vigorously against the new government, on the other they did not want international opposition to Haider to turn the country into a cultural 'no-go zone' and prevent foreign artists from coming to Austria, or Austrian films from being shown abroad. At the Berlin festival in February 2000, representatives of the Austrian film community held a press conference demanding the resignation of the new government, which they considered to be anti-democratic, xenophobic and anti-cultural.

Happily, things have cooled down since Haider's resignation as party leader, and the widely feared cuts in cultural budgets have not occurred. Yet there is still much to worry about. As Martin Schweighofer, managing director of the Austrian Film Commission, has said: "The Socialists did not show much interest in cinema, nor does the new right-wing government. They don't understand that the audiovisual industry is one of the big markets of the future, and that investment in that market would bring good returns for Austria." But there are positive signs too. The newly restored Vienna Film Fund has doubled its annual budget for film production to $8m (110m shilling) and the national broadcaster ORF has boosted its annual production fund to some $15m.

Other interesting developments saw three young directors, Barbara Albert, Jessica Hausner and Antonin Svoboda, together with the photographer Martin Gschlacht, found a new production company, Coop 99. Director and producer Reinhard Schwabenitzky's Starfilms Entertainment AG became the first Austrian film company to be registered on the Vienna stock market.

The year's new films included Harald Sicheritz's follow-up to 1998's *Hinterholz 8*, which with more than 600,000 admissions became Austria's biggest ever box-office hit (its star Roland Düringer was awarded the national prize for best actor in Spring 2000). The hero of Sicheritz's new comedy-drama, **Wanted**, is a doctor who, after carrying out an unsuccessful operation, decides to turn his back on real life and live in a psychiatric hospital. He makes his time bearable by imagining that he is in the Wild West. With 180,000 admissions, *Wanted* enjoyed solid commercial success.

Diego Donnhofer's debut, **The Virgin,** is an oddity for Austrian cinema: shot in English with American actors. There is not much of a story: three people (a brother and sister and a foreigner) are trying to survive in a place where drug abuse, prostitution and theft are part of the daily routine. The film totally divided the critics: some liked this descent to the very depths of human misery, others detested Donnhofer's pseudo-philosophical approach. Robert Dornhelm's **The Venice Project** is set during the art biennale in 1999. Featuring the likes of Lauren Bacall, Dennis Hopper, Anna Galiena and Hector Babenco, it is a cheerful reflection on the state and future of art at the end of the millennium.

## Fest success

With a total of 222 Austrian placements at international festivals, 1999 was perhaps the most important year ever for Austrian cinema abroad. The highlight was Barbara

Albert's 16mm feature debut, **North Side** (*Nordrand*), which won Nina Proll the prize for best young actress in Venice, and three further prizes at other festivals. It tells of five people from various ethnic backgrounds who meet on the north side of Vienna during the war in Yugoslavia, and share their dreams for a short time, all looking for happiness in a rather cruel world.

The most successful documentary was Nikolaus Geyrhalter's **Pripyat**, which was invited to 24 festivals worldwide and confirmed that Geyrhalter is one of the most interesting documentary directors in Austria. Pripyat is a town only five kilometres away from the Chernobyl nuclear power plant. Its population was 50,000 in 1986, the year of the disaster at Chernobyl, but has now diminished to 15,000, and Geyrhalter's film examines how the remaining inhabitants struggle for a decent life.

Michael Haneke's **Code Unknown** (*Code inconnu*), was shot in French, co-produced by the French company MK2 and chosen as one of the four French entries in official competition at Cannes 2000. Less disturbing than Haneke's last film, *Funny Games*, but still cold and far from accessible, the episodic plot features Juliette Binoche in the lead, as Anne, an actress, who becomes caught up in the xenophobia of present-day, multi-cultural Paris.

Last year was a relatively good one for Austria's distributors and exhibitors. Total admissions fell from 15.2 million in 1998 to 15.02 million in 1999 (still comfortably

*Ulrich Tukur in HUNTERS IN THE SNOW*

above the figures for 1996 and 1997). Vienna has become one of Europe's multiplex-capitals. In 1999, five new multi-screen theatres opened in the city; the largest, operated by Austrian firm Constantin, has 15 screens. Since 1994, Austria has gained more than 100 new screens and capacity in Vienna has risen by more than 50%, to a total of some 30,000 seats.

BEAT GLUR is a Swiss film and music critic, editor of the cultural department of the Swiss News Agency and a member of the Swiss Federal Film Commission and the Cultural Commission of Suissimage.

# Recent and Forthcoming Films

### ENE MENE MUH UND TOT BIST DU! (Eeeny, Meeny, Miny, Mo, You're the One That Has to Go!)

Script: Martin Betz. Dir: Houchang Allahyari. Phot: Hans Selikovsky. Players: Bibiana Zeller, Karl Merkatz, Waltraut Haas Prod: Terra Film.

### ERNTEDANK (Thanksgivin')

Script: Stephan Demmelbauer. Dir: Michael Pfeifenberger. Phot: Christian Giesser, Heinz Brandtner. Players: Alexander Pschill, Marianne Sägebrecht, Arthur Klemt. Prod: Demmelbauer Film.

### DIE FREMDE (The Stranger)

Script and Dir: Götz Spielmann. Phot: Fabian Eder. Players: Goya Toledo, Mertin Feifel, Nina Proll. Prod: Teamfilm.

### HEIMKEHR DER JÄGER (Hunters in the Snow)

Script: Michael Kreihsl, Barbara Zuber. Dir: Kreihsl. Phot: Oliver Bokelberg. Players: Ulrich Tukur, Julia Filimonov, Johannes Silberschneider. Prod: Wega Film

### HELLER ALS DER MOND (Brighter Than the Moon)

Script: Virgil Widrich, Enrico Jakob. Dir: Widrich. Phot: Martin Putz. Players: Christopher Buchholz, Piroska Székely, Lars Rudolph. Prod: Virgil Widrich Film

### NORDRAND (North Side)

Script and Dir: Barbara Albert. Phot: Christine A. Maier. Players: Nina Proll, Edita Malovcic, Tudor Chirilà. Prod: Lotus Film.

### PROFESSOR NIEDLICH

Script: Christian Fuchs. Dir: Lukas Stepanik. Phot: Jerzy Palacz. Players: Herbert Fux, Armin Paar, Nino Kratzer. Prod: SK-Film

### THE VIRGIN

Script and Dir: Diego Donnhofer. Phot: Peter Roehsler. Players: Kirsty Hinchcliffe, Joey Kern, Glen Cruz. Prod: Nanook Film.

### WANTED

Script: Alfred Dorfer. Dir: Harald Sicheritz. Phot: Helmut Pirnat. Players: Alfred Dorfer, Michael Niavarani, Eva Billisich. Prod: MR TV-Film.

### GELBE KIRSCHEDN (Yellow Cherries)

Script and Dir: Leopold Lummerstorfer. Phot: Robert Angst. Players: Martin Puntigam, Josef Hader. Prod: Aichholzer Film.

### DIE GOTTESANBETERIN (Praying Mantis)

Script: Susanne Freund, Gerda E. Grossmann. Dir: Paul Harather. Phot: Fabian Eder. Players: Christiane Hörbiger, Jan Niklas, Udo Kier. Prod: Allegro Film.

### HUNDSTAGE (Dog Days)

Script: Ulrich Seidl, Veronika Franz. Dir: Seidl. Phot: Wolfgang Thaler. Players: Alfred Mrva, Maria Hofstätter, Christine Jirku. Prod: Allegro Film.

### K.a.F.K.A. – FRAGMENT

Script and Dir: Christian Frosch. Phot: Johannes Hammel. Players: Lars Rudolph, Ursula Ofner. Prod: Johannes Hammel Film.

### KOMM, SÜSSER TOD (Come, Sweet Death)

Script: Wolfgang Murnberger, Wolfgang Haas. Dir: Murnberger. Phot: Peter von Haller. Players: Josef Hader, Barbara Rudnik, Simon Schwarz. Prod: Dor Film.

### LOVELY RITA

Script and Dir: Jessica Hausner. Phot: Martin Gschlacht. Players: Barbara Osika, Wolfgang Kostal. Prod: COOP 99/Prisma Film

### NACHTFALTER (Butterfly in the Night)

Script and Dir: Franz Novotny. Phot: Andreas Hutter. Players: Eva Lorenzo, Maria Schuster, Mickey Hardt. Prod: Novotny & Novotny Film.

### NICK KNATTERTON

Script: Philipp Weinges, Günter Knarr. Dir: Niki List, Marcus Rosenmüller. Phot: Hagen Bogdanski. Players: Jens Schäfer, Jeanette Hain, Wolfram Berger. Prod: Cult Film.

### TERNITZ TENNESSEE

Script: Manfred Rebhandl. Dir: Mirjam Unger Phot: Jürgen Jürges. Players: Sonja Romei, Nina Proll, Gerald Votava. Prod: Thalia Film.

### DER ÜBERFALL (The Hold-Up)

Script: Florian Flicker, Susanne Freund. Dir: Flicker. Phot: Helmut Pirnat. Players: Joachim Bissmeier, Roland Düringer, Josef Hader. Prod: Allegro-Film.

### DER UMWEG (The Detour)

Script and Dir: Frouke Foukkema. Phot: Wolfgang Simon. Players: Tamar van den Dop, Joachim Bissmeier. Prod: Lotus-Film.

# Producers

**Allegro Film Produktionsges.m.b.H.**
Helmut Grasser
Krummgasse 1a
A-1030 Vienna
Tel: (43 1) 712 5036
Fax: (43 1) 712 5036-20

**COOP 99 KEG**
Wasagasse 12/1/1
A-1090 Vienna
Tel: (43 1) 319 5825
Fax: (43 1) 319 5825-20
e-mail: coop99@chello.at

**Cult-Filmproduktionsges.m.b.H.**
Niki List
Spittelberggasse 3/7
A-1070 Vienna
Tel: (43 1) 526 0006
Fax: (43 1) 526 0006-16
e-mail: cultfilm@cultfilm.com
www.cultfilm.com

**Dor Film Produktionsges.m.b.H.**
Danny Krausz/Kurt Stocker
Bergsteiggasse 36
A-1170 Vienna
Tel: (43 1) 427 10-0
Fax: (43 1) 427 10-50
e-mail: dorfilm@magnet.at
www.members.magnet.at/dorfilm

**epo-film produktionsges.mbh.**
Dieter Pochlatko
Edelsinnstrasse 58
A-1120 Vienna
Tel: (43 1) 812 3718
Fax: (43 1) 813 8773
e-mail: office@epo-film.co.at
www.epo-film.co.at

**Lotus-Film Ges.m.b.H.**
Erich Lackner
Johnstrasse 83
A-1150 Vienna
Tel: (43 1) 786 3387
Fax: (43 1) 786 3387-11
e-mail: office@lotus-film.co.at
www.lotus-film.co.at/lotus

**Novotny & Novotny Filmproduktion GmbH**
Franz Novotny/Karin Novotny
Weimarerstrasse 22
A-1180 Vienna
Tel: (43 1) 478 7170
Fax: (43 1) 478 7170-20
e-mail: novotny@magnet.at

**Prisma Film Produktion GmbH**
Heinz Stussak/Michael Seeber
Neubaugasse 8/1
A-1070 Vienna
Tel: (43 1) 522 8325
Fax: (43 1) 522 8325-28
e-mail: film@prisma-wien.at

**Satel Fernseh- und Filmproduktionsges.m.b.H.**
Michael Wolkenstein
Wiedner Hauptstr. 68
A-1040 Vienna
Tel: (43 1) 588 72-0
Fax: (43 1) 588 72-106
e-mail: office@satel.at
produktion@satel.at
www.satel-film.com

**Star Film Ges.m.b.H.**
Reinhard Schwabenitzky
Paminagasse 46
A-1230 Vienna
Tel: (43 1) 662 4442
Fax: (43 1) 662 4443
e-mail: starfilm@compuserve.com
schwabenitzky@compuserve.com

**Terra Film Produktionsges.m.b.H.**
Norbert Blecha
Lienfeldergasse 39
A-1160 Vienna

Tel: (43 1) 484 1101-0
Fax: (43 1) 484 1101-27
e-mail: office@terrafilm.at
www.terrafilm.at

**Wega-Filmproduktionsges.m.b.H.**
Veit Heiduschka
Hägelingasse 13
A-1140 Vienna
Tel: (43 1) 982 5742
Fax: (43 1) 982 5833
e-mail: wegafilm@aon.at
Distributors

**Buena Vista International (Austria) Gmbh**
Ferdinand Morawetz
Hermanngasse 18
A-1071 Vienna
Tel: (43 1) 526 9467
Fax: (43 1) 526 9468-5
e-mail:
Ferdinand.Morawetz@disney.com
www.buenavista.at

**Concorde Media Beteiligungs GmbH**
Dr Herbert Kloiber
Neuer Markt 16
A-1010 Wien
Tel: (43 1) 513 2728
Fax: (43 1) 513 2728-11
e-mail: jth@concordemedia.co.at

**Constantin Film-Holding GmbH**
Christian Langhammer
Siebensterngasse 37
A-1070 Vienna
Tel: (43 1) 521 28-122
Fax: (43 1) 521 28-160
e-mail:
Constantin.Office@constantinfilm.at
www.cineplexx.at

**Filmladen**
Michael Stejskal
Mariahilfer Strasse 58
A-1070 Vienna
Tel: (43 1) 523 4362
Fax: (43 1) 526 4749
e-mail: m.stejskal@votivkino.at
www.filmladen.at

**Polyfilm Verleih**
Hans König, Christa Auderlitzky
Margaretenstrasse 78
A-1050 Vienna
Tel: (43 1) 581 3900-20
Fax: (43 1) 581 3900-39
e-mail: polyfilm@polyfilm.at
www.verleih.polyfilm.at

**Stadtkino**
Franz Schwartz
Spittelberggasse 3
A-1070 Vienna
Tel: (43 1) 522 4814
Fax: (43 1) 522 4815
e-mail: stadtkino@magnet.at

# Useful Addresses

**Association of the Audiovisual
and Film Industry**
Elmar A. Peterlunger
Wiedner Hauptstrasse 63
P.O. Box 327, A-1045 Vienna
Tel: (43 1) 501 05-3010
Fax: (43 1) 501 05-276
e-mail: film@fafo.at

**Austrian Film Commission**
Martin Schweighofer
Stiftgasse 6
A-1070 Vienna
Tel: (43 1) 526 3323
Fax: (43 1) 526 6801

e-mail: afilmco@magnet.at
www.afc.at

**Austrian Film Institute**
Gerhard Schedl
Spittelberggasse 3
A-1070 Vienna
Tel: (43 1) 526 9730-400
Fax: (43 1) 526 9730-440
e-mail: office@filminstitut.at

**Filmarchiv Austria**
Obere Augartenstrasse 1
A-1020 Vienna
Tel: (43 1) 216 1300
Fax: (43 1) 216 1300-100
e-mail: augarten@filmarchiv.at
www.filmarchiv.at

**Location Austria**
Austrian Business Agency
Opernring 3/2
A-1010 Vienna
Tel: (43 1) 588 5836
Fax: (43 1) 586 8659
e-mail: a.bohrer@aba.gv.at;

e.unterberger@aba.gv.at
www. location-austria.at

**ORF**
Austrian Broadcasting Corporation
Würzburggasse 30
A-1136 Vienna
Tel: (43 1) 878 78-0
www.orf.at/orf/home.htm

**Österreichisches Filmmuseum**
Augustinerstrasse 1
A-1010 Vienna
Tel: (43 1) 533 7054-0
Fax: (43 1) 533 7056-25
e-mail:
peter.konlechner@rs6000.univie.ac.at

**Vienna Film Fund**
Peter Zawrel
Stiftgasse 6/2/3
A-1070 Vienna
Tel: (43 1) 526 5088
Fax: (43 1) 526 5088-20
e-mail: wff@wff.at
www.wff.at/wff

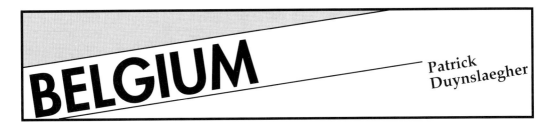

BELGIUM — Patrick Duynslaegher

The political scandals, murder cases and failings of the judicial system that rocked the nation a couple of years ago continued to inspire film-makers, bringing out the best in first-time director Willem Wallyn and the worst in veteran 'outcast' Rob Van Eyck, who gives amateurism a bad name.

Together with former NATO secretary-general Willy Claes, Willem Wallyn's father was one of the main players in the long-running Agusta affair. Wallyn junior's **Film 1** grew out of his ambivalent feelings towards the media-circus surrounding the corruption scandal that put his father on trial: the investigation into an alleged $1.25m (BF 50m) bribe in 1988 to secure the

contract for the purchase of Agusta S.p.A Helicopters.

In the film, the director's alter ego, Willy W. (Peter van den Begin), kidnaps a

*The kidnappers from FILM 1*

manipulative anchorman and gets even by delving into the private life of his victim, looking for the sordid details that can destroy a career. By employing the same methods as the shameless TV journalist, the hero loses not only his friends, but also his sanity and self-esteem. What makes the film work is not so much the morality of this fable about redemption and revenge, as Wallyn's genuine cinematic flair in mixing fact and fiction, the aesthetics of the reality show and the demands of the revenge thriller. By turns disturbing and provocative, *Film 1* is a remarkable debut.

One could call Rob Van Eyck the Flemish Ed Wood but that makes his work sound much more interesting than it is. In **Blue Belgium**, Van Eyck links the infamous Dutroux case (a previously convicted child rapist awaiting trial for the abduction and murder of young girls) to a global conspiracy, with a few powerful families pulling the strings in the corrupt Kingdom of Belgium. The result is a docu-drama that aims to shock and disturb, but the really frightening aspects are the pathetic writing and English-language 'acting'.

*Still from Chantal Akerman's THE CAPTIVE*

## Working-class struggles

Like *Blue Belgium*, Dominique Deruddere's **Everybody Famous** also centres on a kidnapping case – a favourite national pastime if the local film industry is to be believed. Josse De Pauw plays a proud father with great plans for the showbiz career of his beloved daughter, although the plain, overweight girl loses every singing contest she enters. Desperate after losing his factory job, the father turns to abduction and blackmail in an attempt to generate his darling's big break.

For a while, *Everybody Famous* tries to be a satire on media manipulation and an entertainment culture obsessed with fame, but its cliché-ridden script is not sharp enough to hit the target. The director clearly has no feeling for, or genuine interest in his working-class protagonists and has not made up his mind about the so-called talent of the aspiring singer. In one scene she's completely ridiculous, in the next the tone is patronising. All this results in crude characterisations and cheap sentiment. After *Suite 16* and *Hombres Complicades*, *Everybody Famous* is the third disastrous film in a row by the once promising director of *Crazy Love*.

A novel by Flemish writer Louis-Paul Boon has already produced one of the most successful Flemish films in recent memory, *Daens*. Alas, Luc Pien fared less well with his adaptation of an early Boon novel, **Street for Sale**. This is a group portrait of the working-class residents of a small dead-end street, and their struggles and solidarity when they face eviction. Among them is a celebrated writer (the stand-in for Boon) who observes the reactions of the colourful characters and dreams up a new street. Pien's heavy-handed approach prevents this social fable from taking flight.

Vincent Bal certainly found the right tone (intermittently joyful, poetic and melancholic) for his coming-of-age film, **Man of Steel**. During a holiday in a small coastal town, 13-year old Victor is looking for his first kiss, while also having to cope with the recent death of his father. This

*Still from Frédéric Fonteyne's UNE LIAISON PORNOGRAPHIQUE*

traumatic experience is mostly dealt with indirectly: through futuristic daydreams in which he sees himself as a comic-strip hero. Bal cleverly sets his story during the summer of 1993, when the sudden death of King Baudouin provoked an outpouring of emotion; the collective mourning is in sharp contrast with the bottled-up grief of the boy. Unfortunately the limited audience for a 'children's film' proved a major stumbling block when this promising first feature was released.

## Parisian lovers

In the critically acclaimed **A Pornographic Affair** (*Une Liaison pornographique*) there's nothing remotely pornographic on display. Whatever erotic activity makes the purely sexual relationship between a nameless man (Sergi Lopez) and woman (Nathalie Baye) so fulfilling, Frédéric Fonteyne leaves completely to the audience's imagination. Fonteyne anatomises their relationship in flashback, fake-documentary style (both are interrogated by an off-screen interviewer). Initially the two lovers, who meet through an ad placed by the woman in a magazine, are only interested in their shared sexual fantasy, but gradually they discover the emotional force of their encounters in an anonymous Paris hotel room. The director takes us through the various stages of this unusual love affair in a beautifully crafted and acted film.

Although set in contemporary Paris and immediately recognisable as a film by Chantal Akerman, **The Captive** (*La Captive*) is loosely based on *La Prisonnière*, the fifth volume of *Remembrance of Things Past*. In this story of two lovers sharing a Paris apartment, Akerman transforms the decor into a labyrinth of hidden rooms, closed doors and ominous corridors – the perfect setting for a tale of possession. Jealous rich kid Simon (Stanislas Merhar) puts his bisexual girlfriend Ariane (Sylvie Testud) under surveillance, has her accompanied wherever she goes and subjects her to endless questioning. Despite all his attempts to control her, she escapes him. His urge to enter her world grows obsessive and destructive.

This story of an impossible couple is told through intense, claustrophobic rituals, suddenly inter-cut with stunning moments of great visual beauty. Akerman's use of sound and gravely insistent music is also remarkable. The actors, especially Merhar, move through the film in Bressonian, somnambulistic mode. The scenes of a man trailing a woman in a nearly deserted Paris have a ghostly and dreamlike quality, not unlike the serials of Louis Feuillade.

---

PATRICK DUYNSLAEGHER is film critic for *Knack*, the leading Belgian weekly. His articles have appeared in *Variety*, *Sight and Sound* and other periodicals. He has written a book on André Delvaux, a guide for films on television and video, and a history, through 2,000 reviews, of a hundred years of cinema.

# Recent and Forthcoming Films

### VILLA DES ROSES

Script: Christophe Dirickx. Dir: Frank Van Passel. Phot: Jan Vancaillie. Players: Julie Delpy, Shaun Dingwall, Shirley Henderson, Harriet Walter, Timothy West. Prod: Dirk Impens & Rudy Verzyck (Favourite Films).

### POURQUOI SE MARIER LE JOUR DE LA FIN DU MONDE

Script and Dir: Harry Cleven. Phot: Zvonock C.L. Players: Elina Löwensohn, Pascal Greggory, Jean-Henri Compère. Prod: Patrick Quinet Artémis Productions (Belgium); Jani Thiltges-Samsa Film (Luxembourg).

### BLINKER

Script: Rudi Van Den Bossche. Dir: Filip Van Neyghem. Phot: Marijke Van Kets. Players: Joren Seldeslachts, Benny Claessens, Matthias Meersman, Chris Lomme. Prod: Antonio Lombardo-CINE 3.

### WILD BLUE

Script and Dir: Thierry Knauff. Phot: Antoine-Marie Meert. Players: Joan Leighton, Neela Bhagwat, Charläne Alenga, Dalida Amali. Prod: Les Productions du Sablier/ Artline Films/Man's Films, Navigator Films/RTBF/La Sept Arte.

### LUMUMBA

Script: Raoul Peck, Pascal Bonitzer. Dir: Peck. Phot: Bernard Lutic. Players: Eriq Ebouaney, Alex Descas, Théophile Moussa Sowie. Prod: JBA Production (France)/ Entre Chien et Loup (Belgium)/ Essential Filmproduktion (Germany)/ Velvet SA (Haiti)/ ARTE France Cinema/RTBF/ARTE/ ZDF.

### THE SEXUAL LIFE OF THE BELGIANS 4: ABOUT PLEASURE AND HYSTERIA

Script and Dir: Jan Bucquoy. Phot: Bucquoy, Nathalie Sartiaux, Michel Baudour, A.F.Bersou. Players: Evelyne Letawe, Marie Bucquoy, Gail Verhasselt, Anne Grandhenri. Prod: Francis De Smet/Transatlantic Films & De Smet Films.

### OLIVETTI 82

Script: Rudi Van Den Bossche, Ilse Somers. Dir: Van Den Bossche. Phot: Goert Giltaij. Players: Dirk Roofthooft, Hans De Munter, Gijs-Scholten Van Aschat, Ingrid De Vos, Hilde Heijnen. Prod: Antonio Lombardo/Prime Time/Antares Productions.

### SOFT SOAP

Script: Fernand Auwera, Robbe De Hert, Ruud den Drijver. Dir: Robbe De Hert. Phot: Piotr Kukla. Players: Koen De Bouw, Mike Verdrengh, Willeke van Ammelrooy, Sylvia Kristel, Jan Decleir. Prod: Ruud den Drijver, Michel Houdmont/ Cineventura/ Signature films.

### OSVETA

Script: Slobodan Despotovski, Jan Hintjes, Bob Goossens. Dir: Hintjens. Phot: Glynn Speeckaert, Louis-Philippe Capelle. Players: Refet Abazi, Ljupco Todorovski, Rik Van Uffelen, Christophe Vienne. Prod: Jan Hintjens – Nieuwe Media Produkties.

### THE JUST JUDGES

Script: Guido Van Meir. Dir: Vincent Rouffaer. Players: Maria Schneider, Dirk Roofthooft, Johan Leysen. Prod: Eric Kint – Itinera Films.

### AMOUR EN SUSPENS

Script: Micheline Hardy, Luc W.L.Janssen, Herman Van Eyken. Dir: Van Eyken. Phot: Rémon Fromont. Players: Marc Duret. Inge Paulussen, Andréa Ferreol, François Beukelaers. Prod: Jani Thiltges, Herman Van Eyken, Luis Galvao Teles.

### EN VACANCES (On Holiday)

Script: Yves Hanchar, Jacky Cukier. Dir: Hanchar. Phot: Virginie Saint-Martin. Players: Luc Picard, Catherine Hosmalin, Jérémy Lippman, Hilde Van Mieghem. Prod: Anne-Dominique Toussaint, Pascal Judelewicz.

**LE PRESSENTIMENT**

Script and Dir: Alex Stockman. Phot: Michel Baudour. Players: Stefan Perceval, Stefanie Bodien. Prod: Kaat Camerlynck.

**LE ROI DANSE (The King Dances)**

Script: Gérard Corbiau, Andrée Corbiau, Eve de Castro, Didier Decoin. Dir: Gérard Corbiau. Players: Boris Terral, Benoît Magimel, Tcheky Karyo, Colette Emmanuelle, Johan Leysen. Prod: Dominique Janne K2.

# Producers

**Alain Keytsman Production**
159, rue Berkendael
1050 Brussels
Tel: (32 2) 347 5710
Fax: (32 2) 347 2462

**Artémis Productions**
50, avenue Dailly
1030 Brussels
Tel: (32 2) 216 2324
Fax: (32 2) 216 2013

**K2**
81/3 Avenue Franklin Roosevelt
1050 Brussels

Tel: (32 2) 646 7270
Fax: (32 2) 646 9145

**Les Films de la Drève**
11, rue Simonis
4130 Esneux
Tel: (32 4) 380 5792
Fax: (32 4) 380 5790

**Corsan Productions**
J.De Hasquestraat 7
2000 Antwerp
Tel: (32 3) 234 2518
Fax: (32 3) 226 2158

**Favourite Films**
Vandenbusschestraat 3
1030 Brussels
Tel: (32 2) 242 4510
Fax: (32 2) 242 1408

**Kunst en Kino**
Avenue Louise 32/4
1050 Brussels
Tel: (32 2) 511 6341
Fax: (32 2) 512 6874

**Lamy Films**
Moensberg 57
1180 Brussels
Tel: (32 2) 375 3442
Fax: (32 2) 375 3271

**Man's Films**
Avenue Mostinck 65

1150 Brussels
Tel: (32 2) 771 7137
Fax: (32 2) 771 9612

**Multimedia**
Nieuwstraat 99
1730 Asse
Tel: (32 2) 453 0304
Fax: (32 2) 453 0920

**Flanders Image**
Handelskaai 18/2
1000 Brussels
Tel: (32 2) 219 3222
Fax: (32 2) 219 3402

**Communauté Française de Belgique**
Boulevard Léopold II, 44
1080 Brussels
Tel: (32 2) 413 2221
Fax: (32 2) 413 2068

**Ministry of the Flemish Community**
Koloniënstraat 29-31
1000 Brussels
Tel: (32 2) 510 3411
Fax: (32 2) 510 3651

**Wallonie Bruxelles Image**
Boulevard Adolphe Max 13
1000 Brussels
Tel: (32 2) 223 2304
Fax: (32 2) 218 3424

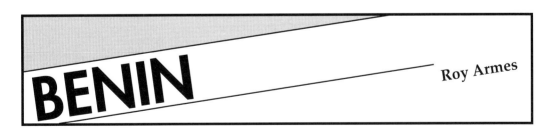

Roy Armes

Film-makers from Benin were active in the early years of cinema in Sub-Saharan Africa, when most directors were limited to using 16mm, and the principal source of funding was the French Ministry of Co-operation. In the late 1960s and early 1970s a range of short fiction films and documentaries were made, and even a few features, such as Pascal Abikanlou's *Sous le signe du vaudoun* (1974) and Richard de Medeiros's *Le nouveau venu* (1976). A decade later, François Sourou Okioh made a 35mm feature, *Ironou* (*Meditations*), but there was no sense of continuity as none of these three directors went on to make a second feature.

The emergence of Jean Odoutan (b.1965) with **Barbecue Pejo**, after a decade of silence broken only by a handful of short

*Still from Jean Odoutan's BARBECUE PEJO*

films and videos, is therefore to be warmly welcomed. Odoutan is typical of a new generation of African film-makers, having spent his formative years, from the age of 15, on the outskirts of Paris, and subsequently worked in France as actor, assistant and short film-maker. His production finance came from France's Centre National Cinématographique (which necessitated making the film in French) and the shooting marked the director's first visit to Benin for 20 years.

*Barbecue Pejo*, shown at the Milan 2000 African Film Festival, is a lively tragicomedy. The comedy comes from the frantic efforts of the hero, Baboucar, to make a living: investing in a taxi (which immediately breaks down), then using the vehicle's engine first to power a simple mill (another failure) and finally to barbecue corncobs. But the director does not romanticise the character's situation: while he struggles, his wife has to work as a prostitute to feed their family.

An interesting by-product of the project is *The Black Director* (*Le réalisateur noir*), a seven-minute documentary about what happens when 300 very diverse and emotional black actors turn up for a casting session for *Barbecue Pejo* and have to wait – because the director has been arrested by some very unsympathetic French policemen. By May 2000, Odoutan was already editing his second feature, *Djib*.

# Recent Film, Useful Addresses

**BARBECUE PEJO**

Script and Dir: Jean Odoutan. Phot: Valerio Truffa. Players: Odoutan, Laurentine Milébo, Didier Dorlipo, Adama Kouate, Koffi Gahou. Prod: 45 RDLC (Jean Odoutan; France)/ Tabou-Taba Film (Benin).

**Haute Authorité de l'Audiovisuel et de la Communication**
Tel: (229) 311 743
Fax: (229) 311 742

**Office de Radio Diffusion et Télévision de Bénin (ORTB)**
BP 366
Cotonou
Tel: (229) 300 628/349/301
Fax: (229) 300 448

# BOSNIA & HERZEGOVINA
Rada Šešić

Under socialist rule, film production and distribution in Bosnia and Herzegovina was completely organised by state-run institutions. Although one could have many objections about the way officials carried out their jobs, at least Bosnian cinema was still in motion. Every year about two features appeared, as well as ten to 15 shorts, animated films and documentaries. Films were sent to festivals and official international delegations of film-makers participated in exchange visits. Today, nothing of the sort is taking place.

The situation is not only due to post-war conditions. The indolence and apparent ignorance of the government is to blame, since they have yet to create an institution or department to finance regular production, manage international promotion or apply for international production finance. Film-makers who grew up in the socialist environment, and are inclined to see themselves as part of a society rather than individuals, lack the skills to take matters into their own hands. Production has come to a standstill.

For the moment, shorts and documentaries are all one can expect, with even these projects depending on the enthusiasm of individual film-makers eager to do something at any cost. They are mainly graduates from the Sarajevo Film Academy, all fed up with waiting for "better times" to come. They keep their budgets tiny, their shooting schedules short and work for nothing or a nominal fee. Their friends join the crews. Approximately five documentary and short fiction films were made this way in 1999-2000, most gaining a good response on the festival circuit.

The most successful is Srdjan Vuletić's short, *Hop, Skip & Jump*, co-produced by Slovenia's Arkadena Studio. It tells the story of a couple who parted during the Sarajevo Olympic Games in 1984. Nine years later they find themselves on opposing sides during the war: the woman is a sniper in the Serb army, the man, a Bosnian, is so desperate for food in besieged Sarajevo that he's desperately trying to trap a pigeon. Just 16 minutes long, this powerful film won a special award at the Berlin festival, where it was screened in the Panorama section, and major awards at the Slovenian national festival in Portoroz.

Aida Begić was a teenager when the war started in Bosnia. She studied film direction during the war and as her graduation project made a very interesting short, *Prvo Samrtno Iskustvo* (literally, *First Experience of the Agony of Death*). With a $10,000 budget (loans from friends and family, topped up a grant from the Soros Foundation), it follows a young man who is refused an ID card because, according to the statistics, he was killed in the war. He has to prove that he is alive. The ministry of culture refused to give any money to the project.

## True to life, and death

The documentary **Red Rubber Boots** (*Crvene Gumene Čizmice*) is a second film from Jasmila Žbanić, who was 15 when the war started. In it, a woman from Herzegovina searches for her children, who disappeared during the war. The camera follows the search team digging for mass graves and exploring underground caves for bodies, while the mother continuously reminds them to look for the little red rubber boots her child was wearing.

Films are very rarely produced in any part of Bosnia and Herzegovina other than

*A mother searches for her children in RED RUBBER BOOTS*

Sarajevo. In Bihać, a small town in northern Bosnia, local sponsors produced the documentary **The Pit** (*Bezdan*), directed by Adis Bakrać, which investigates a war tragedy in Bihać, where the Serbs threw their dead victims into a pit.

Vesna Ljubić, the respected Sarajevo director with a successful track record in features, made a documentary, **Adio Kerida**, supported by local sponsors and the Dutch Jan Vrijman fund. It focuses on the Jewish cemetery in Sarajevo; an old monument situated on top of a high hill, it was captured by the Serbs during the war and became one of the most notorious sniper positions.

The most blissful moments of Bosnian cinema, however, are not connected to production, but to special screenings. For six years, the Sarajevo International Film Festival has been held every August at an open air theatre with 2,400 seats and in the smaller but very modern 'Meeting Point' cinema. The event has grown every year and in 1999 attracted 55,000 people. There was a special focus on the work of actor Steve Buscemi, whose visit to the event was a highlight. Perhaps most importantly, the festival also links all the former Yugoslavian states. One could see new films from Serbia, Montenegro, Croatia, Slovenia and Macedonia, and listen to guests from all these states who still share a similar cultural background.

*Sarajevo*, the epic 'feature film-to-be' about the siege has already been mentioned in previous editions of *IFG*, and has now been in pre-production for three years. The producer and Veljko Bulajić, the director, have been involved in legal action, blaming each other for having spent about $500,000 without even starting to film. It is amazing and depressing to see how the government of Bosnia and Herzegovina has managed to throw away that kind of money, while film students have to work on antiquated editing tables.

RADA ŠEŠIĆ is a critic and film-maker. Since leaving Sarajevo in 1992 she has lived in the Netherlands and she writes for several magazines, specialising in Balkan and Indian cinema, about which she lectures at universities and festivals. Her third film, *In White Loneliness*, is in production.

# Producer:

**Saga Film Production**
Hakije Kulenovica 7
71000 Sarajevo
Fax: (387 71) 666 811
e-mail: saga@sagafilm.com

**Stop Film**
Buka 5
71000 Sarajevo
Tel/Fax: (387 71) 665 393
e-mail: jassen@bih.net.ba

**Ton-Light Film**
R. Abazovica 2
71000 Sarajevo

Tel/Fax: (387 71) 520 897
e-mail: dolina11@hotmail.com

**Kaleidoskop**
Kevrin potok 18-1
71000 Sarajevo
Tel: (387 71) 678 233
Fax: (387 71) 202 273

**HEFT Production Company**
71000 Sarajevo
Tel/Fax: (387 71) 133 568

**Sarajevo International
Production Company**
Marsala Tita 54-1
71000 Sarajevo

Tel: (387 71) 200 392
Fax: (387 71) 211 972

**Deblokada**
Kranjcevica 43
71000 Sarajevo
Tel/Fax: (387 71) 664 403
e-mail: deblok@bih.net.ba

# Useful Addresses

**National Film Archive of BiH**
Alipasina 19
71000 Sarajevo
Tel/Fax: (387 71) 668 678

**Sineast** [film magazine]
Strosmajerova 1
71000 Sarajevo
Tel: (387 71) 212 377
Fax: (387 71) 470 029
email: kinobih@bih.net.ba

**Sarajevo Film Festival**
Obala Kulina Bana
71000 Sarajevo
email: sff@sff.ba

**Association of Film Workers**
Strosmajerova 1
71000 Sarajevo

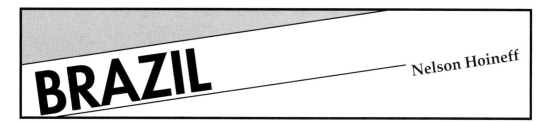

# BRAZIL — Nelson Hoineff

Nearly 30 Brazilian feature films were released in 1999, slightly more than the previous year. However, output is likely to drop, as local production faces huge financing problems because the tax-break laws (Rouanet and Audiovisual) are not working. Investors are not responding to most producers' projects, for various reasons, ranging from marketing questions to fears over the potential misuse of funding.

Article 3 of the audio-visual law, which allows foreign distributors to invest part of their profits in Brazilian production, needs to be improved, although the Hollywood majors have been funding local films: Fox partially financed *Xuxa Requebra*, following Warners' participation in 1999 in **Orfeu**, Cacá Diegues brilliant, modern-day inter-pretation of Vinicius de Moraes' play.

Among the most important 1999 releases, special attention should be devoted to **Here We Are, Waiting for You** (*Nos que Aqui Estamos Por Vós Esperamos*), a documentary directed by Marcelo Mazargao about some of the most important events of the twentieth century. This innovative, low-budget film won most of the national awards in 1999, and Best Picture at the Miami Festival of Brazilian Film, in 2000. Also impressive was **Midnight** (*O Primeiro Dia*), the new film by Walter Salles (co-directed by Daniela Thomas, who also worked with Salles on *Foreign Land*). This was a powerful portrayal of New Year's Eve 1999 in a disturbed Rio environment.

Carlos Reichembach's **Two Streams** (*Dois Córregos*) tells the story of a tormented man facing his past and his future. Well received by the critics it fared poorly in cinemas. With a budget of almost $4m, Sergio Rezende's **Maua – The Emperor and the King** (*Maua – O Imperador e o Rei*) was very expensive by Brazilian standards. It told the saga of the Baron of Maua, who 100 years ago was Brazil's most powerful entrepreneur and politician.

Released early in 2000, Luiz Alberto Pereira's **Hans Staden** is an impressive allegory about the sixteenth-century conflict between Portuguese conquerors and Brazilian native cannibals. Also in cinemas early in 2000 was **Villa-Lobos** (*Villa-Lobos – Uma Vida de Paixo*), directed by Zelito Vianna, a biopic about the most famous Brazilian classical composer. Villa-Lobos was played by Antonio Fagundes, who also stars in **Bossa Nova**, directed by Bruno Barreto, a musical comedy with a great score, co-starring Amy Irving.

*Bossa Nova* shows off Rio to very stylish effect, in complete contrast to one of the most intriguing recent Brazilian films, Sergio Bianchi's **Cronicamente Inviável** (literally, *Chronically Unfeasible*). In this tragi-comic story, Rio represents a country facing corruption and social injustice at all levels. In Bianchi's view, everybody is guilty in modern Brazilian society, regardless of their cultural, social or economic status. Despite its subtly ironic tone, the film was a surprise hit with public and critics in July 2000.

Despite the relatively low admission price (the average in 1999-2000 was $2.85, though a few first run theatres charge as much as $7.00), Brazil is one of the most important theatrical markets in the world. Nearly 70 million tickets were sold in 1999 (the same as in the previous year) generating $198m in grosses, with growth of 5-10% predicted for 2000. The multiplexes have consolidated their position as Brazil's leading exhibitors. Since July 1997, when the first local multiplex opened, nearly $200m has been invested by the leading chains, with Cinemark spending half that total.

NELSON HOINEFF is a journalist and film critic, president of the Association of Film Critics of Rio de Janeiro and a regular contributor to *Variety*.

# Recent and Forthcoming Films

### AMELIA

Script: Ana Carolina and José Antonio Pinheiro. Direction: Carolina. Phot: Rodolfo Sanchez. Players: Miriam Muniz, Camila Amado, Alice Borges, Marilia Pera, Beatrice Agemin. Prod: Cristal Produções.

### LAVOURA ARCAICA

Script: Luiz Fernando Carvalho, based on the book by Raduam Nassar. Dir: Carvalho. Phot: Walter Carvalho. Players: Selton Mello, Raul Cortez, Juliana Carneiro Cunha. Prod: Videofilmes.

### XANGO DE BAKER STREET

Script: Patricia Mello, Miguel Faria Jr, Marco

Bernstein, based on the book by Jo Soares. Dir: Faria Jr. Phot: Lauro Escolrel. Players: Joaquim de Almeida, Maria de Medeiros, Marco Nannini, Claudio Marzo, Claudia Abreu, Marcelo Anthony. Prod: Bruno Stroppiana/Skylight.

### CARANDIRU

Script: Hector Babenco, Fernando Bonassi, Victor Naves, based on the book by Brauzio Varella. Dir: Babenco. Phot: Lauro Escorel. Players: [to be confirmed]. Prod: HB Filmes.

### CRONICAMENTE INVIAVEL

Script: Gustavo Steinberg and Sergio Bianchi. Dir: Bianchi. Phot: Marcelo Coutinho and Antonio Penido. Players: Umberto Magnani, Cecil Thiré, Dira Paes, Betty Goffman. Prod: Agravo Produções.

### QUASE NADA

Script and Dir: Sergio Rezende. Phot: Guy Goncalves. Players: Augusto Pompeu, Genesio de Barros, Denise Wainberg, Caio Junqueira. Prod: Morena Filmes.

### MINHA VIDA EM SUAS MAOS

Script and Dir: Jose Antonio Garcia. Phot: Jose Tadeu Ribeiro.

Players: Maria Zilda, Caco Siockler, Cristina Ache, Ymara Reis. Prod: Roberaf Producoes.

### BRAVA GENTE BRASILEIRA

Script and Dir: Lucia Murat. Phot: Antonio Luiz. Players: Floriano Peixoto, Leonardo Villar, Buza Ferraz. Prod: Lucia Murat.

### ESTORVO

Script: Ruy Guerra, based on the book by Chico Buarque. Direction: Ruy Guerra. Phot:: Marcelo Durst. Players: Jorge Perrugoria, Bianca Byigton. Prod: Skylight.

### A 3a MORTE DE JOAQUIM BOLIVAR

Script and Dir: Flavio Candido. Phot: Cleumo Sigmond. Players: Jonas Bloch, Antonio Pitanga, Maria Lucia Dahl. Prod: Cinema Novo.

## Producers and Distributors

**Rio Vermelho Filmes**
(Cacá Diegues)
Rua Ataulfo de Paiva 527
22420-030 Rio de Janeiro
Tel: (55 21) 259 2289

**Cinédia**
(Alice Gonzaga)

Estrada do Soca s/n
Jacarepagua
Rio de Janeiro
Tel (55 21) 445 6868

**Comunicacao Alternativa**
(Marcos Rezende)
Rua Barío do Flamengo 32
22220-080 Rio de Janeiro
Tel: (55 21) 558 2825

**Filme B**
(Paulo Sergio Almeida)
Rua Alcindo Guanabara, 24
20038-900 Rio de Janeiro
Tel: (55 21) 240 8439

**Grupo Novo de Cinema e TV**
(Antonio Urano/Tarcisio Vidigal)
Av. Marechal Niemeyer 24
22251-060 Rio de Janeiro
Tel: (55 21) 266 3637

**HB Filmes**
(Hector Babenco)
Rua Emmanoel Kant, 39
Jardim Paulista
São Paulo
Tel (55 11) 883 7755

**Morena Filmes**
(Marisa Leão)
Rua Visconde de Pirajá 596/204
Ipanema
Rio de Janeiro
Tel: (55 21) 511 0754

**RioFilme**
(José Carlos Avellar)
Prana Floriano 19
20031-050 Rio de Janeiro
Tel: (55 21) 220 7090

# BULGARIA — Pavlina Jeleva

Sadly, 1999 was one of the most troubled years in the decade-long attempt to reconstruct Bulgaria's film industry. Hit by the irregularities of public financing, some producers were obliged to interrupt shooting, and the unstable economic situation, amongst other factors, prompted the Culture Minister to dismiss Dimitar Dereliev, director of the National Film Centre since 1991.

The radical anti-corruption series *Danube Bridge* (*Dunav Most*), written by Gueorgui Mishev, directed by Ivan Andonov and fully-financed by Bulgarian National Television was broadcast by its main Channel. The films, about the lives of several young couples in a fictional Bulgarian town, who dream of leaving the country via the Danube Bridge, provoked negative reactions from some important media commentators. Both authors defended their work with courage and accused their backers of offering them an insufficient budget to produce a 6x56-minute series to the necessary standards.

In order to prevent further over-emotional public discussions, the government's television committee temporally banned the children's series *The Big Schemes* (*Golemite Igri*), an ironic ten-part story about a 13-year-old boy and his newly-wealthy grandparents. The ban was lifted following vociferous protests from eminent scriptwriter Gueorgui Danailov and director Ivanka Grabcheva.

The 13-part series *Clinic on the Third Floor* (*Klinika Na Tretia Etaj*), by young director Nikolay Akimov, was an ironical Bulgarian version of a typical American or British hospital soap opera, full of beautiful doctors and nurses. It was so popular that a second, nine-part series was commissioned.

## Emergency appeal

Strongly supported by the Union of Bulgarian Film-makers, the Association of Bulgarian Producers and a large number of media outlets, an impressive group of famous directors created a "red cross committee" for the urgent preservation of Bulgarian film production. They almost succeeded in convincing the government to include cinema on its list of urgent economic priorities. A dose of hope arrived when the European Union Media II Audio-visual programme agreed to begin the process which should lead to Bulgaria gaining full membership.

Three Bulgarian feature films were distributed in the theatres in 1999: **Dan Kolov**, directed by young Mihail Getzov, was a biopic about a once-famous Bulgarian wrestler; **Magicians** (*Magiossnizi*) was an impressive, special effects-laden children's tale from young Ivan Gueorgiev; **Glass Bulls** (*Stakleni Topcheta*) was another intelligent examination by 40-year-old Ivan Cherkelov of the intellectual and emotional

*Still from BULGARIA, THAT IS ME*

A very positive point was a revival in documentary production. **Like in Cinema** (*Kato Na Kino*), by eminent director Iulii Stoianov, and **Accusation** (*Obvinenieto*), by Anna Petkova, both focused on former victims of the communist camps; **Useless** (*Izlishnite*), by Adela Peeva, told the powerful stories of members of the Muslim minority who are not allowed to leave Bulgaria. Nikolay Volev made *The Eternal Lover* (*Vechniat Liubovnic*), a pleasant short about a man and his strange film collections. The biggest foreign production entirely shot in Bulgaria was the French costume adventure *Vircingetorix*, directed by Jacques Dorfmann and starring Christopher Lambert.

problems of his generation (it was included in the Berlin Forum 2000). Svetoslav Ovcharov's second feature, **Bulgaria, that is Me**, told the story of the director's own family, and impressed the critics.

PAVLINA JELEVA has been a professional film critic and journalist since 1978 and is a regular contributor to Bulgarian newspapers and magazines. A former national representative on the boards of Eurimages Board and FIPRESCI, she is now artistic and foreign relations director for her own film company.

# Recent and Forthcoming Films

**PISMO DO AMERIKA (Letter to America)**

Script and Dir: Iglika Trifonova. Players: Vladimir Penev, Maria Sapoundjieva. Prod: Klas Film.

In a beautiful mountain village, the population is suddenly involved in a strange correspondence with a distant country.

**PANSION ZA KUCHETA (Dog House)**

Script: Uiri Datchev. Dir: Stefan Komandarev Prod: "Marten" OOD.

A famous opera singer and her closest friend run a dog kennel with some very strange clients.

**OPASHKATA NA DIAVOLA (Devil's Tale)**

Script and Dir: Dimitar Petkov. Prod: "Paralax" OOD.

A talented Bulgarian musician, Pavel, is torn between God and the Devil.

**GOSPOJA DINOSAVAR (Mrs Dinosaur)**

Script: Rada Moskova. Dir: Anri Kulev. Prod: Kulev Film productions.

Poetic, part-animated fairytale about the adventures of young Nusha.

# Producers

**Bulgarian Film Producers Association**
67 Dondukov Blvd
Sofia 1504
Tel: (359 2) 447 326
Fax: (359 2) 463 676

**Borough Film Ltd**
13 Krakra St
Sofia 1000

Tel: (359 2) 445 880
Fax: (359 2) 445 880
e-mail: borough@mbox.cit.bg

**Gala Film Ltd**
3 Uzundjovska St
Sofia 1000
Tel: (359 2) 981 4209
Fax: (359 2) 804 434

**Geopoly Ltd**
16 Kapitan Andreev St

Sofia 1421
Tel/Fax: (359 2) 963 0661
e-mail: geopoly@mail.techno-link.com

**Klas Film**
156 Kniaz Boris I St
Sofia 1000
Tel: (359 2) 523 580
Fax: (359 2) 527 451

**Paralax Ltd**
67 Dondukov Blvd
Sofia 1504
Tel: (359 2) 447 326
Fax: (359 2) 463 676
e-mail: dimo@omega.bg

## Distributors

**Alexandra Film**
17 Naycho Tzanov St
Sofia 1000
Tel: (359 2) 980 6070
Fax: (359 2) 981 0715

**Duga Entertainment**
141 Kniaz Boris I St
Sofia 1304
Tel: (359 2) 981 9584
Fax: (359 2) 980 8842

**Sofia Film**
26 Maria Luiza Blvd
Sofia 1000
Tel: (359 2) 835 584
Fax: (359 2) 833 707

**Sunny Films**
17-a Tzar Osvoboditel Blvd
Sofia 1000
Tel: (359 2) 943 4849
Fax: (359 2) 943 3703

## Useful Addresses

**Ministry of Culture**
17 Stamboliiski St
Sofia 1000
Tel: (359 2) 86111
Fax: (359 2) 877 339

**National Film Centre**
2-a Dondukov Blvd
Sofia 1000
Tel: (359 2) 803 134
Fax: (359 2) 873 626

**Union of Bulgarian Film Makers**
67 Dondukov Blvd
Sofia 1504
Tel/Fax: (359 2) 946 1068

**Bulgarian National Television**
29 San Srefano St
Sofia 1000
Tel: (359 2) 985 591
Fax: (359 2) 871 871

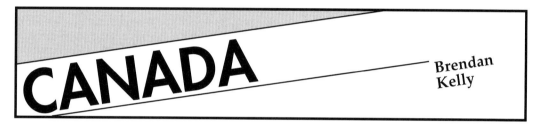

# CANADA

Brendan Kelly

These are boom times for the film biz in Canada. Too bad the boom has almost nothing to do with homegrown Canadian films. Box-office sales are soaring, thanks largely to the multiplex building spree powered by the rapid-fire expansion schemes of Famous Players, Cineplex Odeon, and newcomer AMC. Ticket sales in Canada hit the $449m (C$659m) mark in 1999, but the outstanding business was almost entirely due to a major upswing in sales for Hollywood blockbusters. The 1999 box-office Top Ten in the country was, as usual, a Maple Leaf-free zone. *Star Wars: Episode I* not surprisingly took the top spot with $32.3m, followed by *The Sixth Sense* and *Austin Powers: The Spy Who Shagged Me*.

In an all-too-familiar tale, Canadian-made features failed to make much of an impression with Canadian film-goers. The top English-Canadian performer in 1999 was seasoned Toronto auteur David Cronenberg's twisted sci-fi comedy *eXistenZ*, with a gross of just $885,000. No

other Canadian flick came close to that tally in 1999. Director Anne Wheeler's lesbian-themed drama *Better Than Chocolate* grossed $194,000 and, astonishingly – given its massive marketing campaign and generally favourable reviews – Atom Egoyan's *Felicia's Journey* managed to take just $122,000. In 1999, English-Canadian films grabbed a mere 0.5% of ticket sales across the country.

One of the few bright spots in this bleak picture was Montreal writer-director François Girard's ambitious, multi-lingual musical epic *The Red Violin*, which was released in Canada in late 1998. During a lengthy run in 1998 and early 1999, the Rhombus Media-produced pic garnered $2m in Canada and went on to become a surprise sleeper arthouse hit in the US in the summer of 1999, reaping $10m for Lions Gate Films.

The other good news comes from Quebec, where homegrown French-language films broke box-office records for the second consecutive year, garnering sales of $6.5m in 1999. That represented 7% of the province's total theatrical gross, whereas for most of the past 20 years, the market share of Quebec films was generally between 2% and 4%. The top box-office draw in Quebec in 1999 was maverick director Pierre Falardeau's low-brow comedy **Elvis Gratton II – Miracle in Memphis** (*Elvis Gratton II – Miracle à Memphis*), followed by hockey comedy sequel **Les Boys II**.

*Elvis Gratton II* is Falardeau's follow-up to his 1985 cult hit, and almost makes *There's Something About Mary* look like *Citizen Kane* in comparison. It is frequently quite funny, but, as is often the case, Falardeau simply can't stop himself from resorting to political haranguing and his film eventually becomes downright misanthropic. Julien Poulin showcases real comic skill in his portrayal of the eponymous Montreal Elvis impersonator.

**Laura Cadieux... The Sequel** (*Laura Cadieux... La Suite*) lacked the emotional resonance and memorable characters of the first *Laura Cadieux* pic, and eventually degenerated into rather tired slapstick. Writer-director Denise Filiatrault once again focused the cameras on a group of chubby middle-aged women from working-class East End Montreal; this time around they hit the water for a luxury cruise.

## Show us the money

Film production is booming in Canada, but it's mostly thanks to Hollywood film-makers taking advantage of the cheap Canadian dollar and making the trek to shoot north of the US border. In 1999, film-makers spent $680m in the west-coast province of British Columbia, up 32% from the previous year. Ontario also hit a record high, with film shoots worth $638m. Homegrown film-making is not expanding at the same rate, however, and according to figures from the Canadian Film and Television Production Association, the cumulative budget for Canadian features declined by 14% in 1998-1999 to $182m.

Canadian pics suffer from a chronic lack of funding. In Spring 2000, Federal Heritage Minister Sheila Copps was poised to announce a new $34m feature film fund, but at press time the announcement had been put on what looks like semi-permanent hold. Most in the industry figure this is due to the film funding and film and TV tax-credit scandal sparked by allegations of tax-credit abuse at Montreal-based TV company Cinar Corp. It is clearly not politically viable to inaugurate a new public film-funding policy while the industry is under a cloud of controversy.

Over the past year, film funding agency Telefilm Canada supported the production of 46 features, contributing $15.4m to their overall budgets of $89.2 m. That statistic aptly sums up the state of play in Canadian cinema – the entire overall budget of the year's production tally in Canada is about equal to the budget of a single major Hollywood film. The average budget for Canadian films this year was $1.3m.

## Arcand leads the auteurs

Denys Arcand finally returned with a major picture last year. Unfortunately, **Stardom** lacked the witty verve and personal insight of Arcand's best pictures, *The Decline of the American Empire* and *Jesus of Montreal*. The English-language film chronicles the rise and fall of a young girl who becomes an internationally-celebrated model, with a cast that includes newcomer Jessica Pare, Dan Aykroyd, Charles Berling, Thomas Gibson and Frank Langella.

Arcand's satirical points about super-ficial celebrity and entertainment culture are usually all-too-obvious and there's a sense of déjà-vu to the proceedings. Arcand shoots almost the entire film as if viewers are seeing action via the cameras of various TV shows, a highly-problematic device. First-off, it results in a picture that doesn't look great and it also makes it hard to showcase any in-depth psychology.

One of the more encouraging trends over the past couple of years has been the re-birth of auteur-style film-making in

*Jessica Paré and Dan Aykroyd in Denys Arcand's STARDOM*

Quebec. Positive news began with Swiss-Canadian helmer Lea Pool's festival hit *Set Me Free* (*Emporte-Moi*), the writer-director's most accomplished work yet. Pool shot her first English-language film last year, **Lost and Delirious**, based on the novel *Wives of Bath*, by Susan Swan. *Lost and Delirious* stars Piper Perabo (from *Coyote Ugly*), Jessica Pare and Mischa Barton (*The Sixth Sense*), and is shaping up as one of the most highly-anticipated 2001 releases from Canada.

There are also signs that a new wave of young and interesting French-Canadian directors is building, after years in which a relatively-unhealthy film scene was dominated by the same greying film-makers. Credit here has to be given to veteran Montreal producer Roger Frappier, who has dedicated his company, Max Films, to promoting up-and-coming talent.

Max produced **Matroni and Me** (*Matroni et Moi*), the feature directorial debut from Jean-Philippe Duval. It is a refreshing, off-beat comedy. This smart, funny tale of an intellectual egghead who runs into trouble with the neighborhood mafia kingpin features snappy writing (from Duval and Alexis Martin, who also stars), strong performances from Martin, Guylaine Tremblay and Pierre Lebeau. Split-screen work, freeze frames and odd close-ups give the film a 1960s New Wave feel.

## Dead men's blues

Perhaps the strongest French Quebec film of the past year was **Post Mortem**. A debut feature from video-maker Louis Belanger, it deservedly won major prizes at the Montreal World Film Festival, the Canadian Genie Awards and the Quebec Jutra Awards. Mixing formal innovation and intense emotional story-telling, *Post Mortem* tells the tale of a morose morgue attendant obsessed by the blues and a single mother who rips men off to provide for her five-year-old daughter. It is the most unlikely of love stories. The lead actors, Gabriel Arcand as the morgue mope and Sylvie Moreau as the criminal mom, are both top-notch.

Quebec-born film-maker Allan Moyle (*Pump Up the Volume*) returned from Hollywood obscurity with **New Waterford**

**Girl**, a charming-but-gritty coming-of-age story set in rough, rural Nova Scotia. Tricia Fish's finely-nuanced script follows two teenage girls frustrated by their dead-end lives in the tiny burg of New Waterford, Cape Breton. Moyle wisely keeps proceedings low-fi, never straying far from the tough humour of the piece and his no-frills approach packs a hefty emotional punch. Newcomer Liane Balaban gives a dynamite lead performance as the moody teen, Mooney Pottie.

## Back to the truth

Another hopeful glimmer on the Canadian horizon is the mini-renaissance of documentary film-making. Canada has a rich legacy in this area, largely thanks to the National Film Board of Canada's efforts, and the board helped produce two critically-acclaimed documentary features last year. Montreal director Peter Wintonick's **Cinéma Vérité: Defining the Moment** was a provocative and always-entertaining history of the cinema revolution of the 1950s and 1960s that introduced hand-held cameras and fly-by-the-seat-of-your-pants documentary film-making.

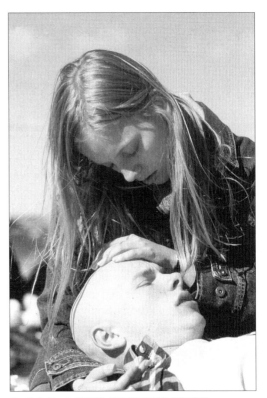

*Sarah Polley in THE LAW OF ENCLOSURES*

In 1999, **Just Watch Me: Trudeau and the '70s Generation** won the Toronto International Film Festival's award as Best First Canadian feature for director Catherine Annau, and her film met with remarkable success in Canada. It is an engaging portrait of the impact on ordinary Canadians of the policies – particularly his push for a fully-bilingual Canada – of influential former Prime Minister Pierre Trudeau. Jennifer Baichwal delivered an extraordinary portrait of legendary author Paul Bowles in **Let It Come Down: The Life of Paul Bowles**, and veteran film-maker Ron Mann did an entertaining job of charting the history of the US government's war on the wicked weed in **Grass**. Both films had limited runs in US cinemas.

**Pandora's Beauty** (*La Beauté de Pandore*), the final part of Charles Binamé's urban-angst trilogy – after *Eldorado* and *Le Coeur au Poing* – is the weakest. The visuals are strong, but the story of a man whose life is destroyed following an encounter with a shady seductress is clichéd and unbelievable. Rodrigue Jean's New Brunswick-set **Full Blast** is an attempt to capture the desperate bleakness of no-future youth but there simply aren't enough dramatic sparks to maintain interest.

Mort Ransen followed-up a hit, *Margaret's Museum*, with the ill-conceived **Touched**, the story (poorly-scripted by Ransen and Joan Hopper) of a May-to-December romance, featuring some terrible performances, notably a completely over-the-top turn from Lynn Redgrave as an old rebel. Jerry Ciccoritti's **The Life Before This** is a mostly-uninteresting look at the events leading up to a violent coffee-shop shoot-up. The philosophical points in the screenplay are mundane and the actors look lost in this misguided effort.

BRENDAN KELLY reports on the Canadian film scene and reviews films for *Variety*. He also writes about entertainment for *The Gazette*, Montreal, and is a columnist on CBC Radio.

# Recent and Forthcoming Films

### THE FAVOURITE GAME

Script: Bernar Hebert, Peter Putka. Dir: Hebert. Phot: TBA. Players: TBA. Prod: Cine Qua Non Films.

### GINGER SNAPS

Script: Karen Walton. Dir: John Fawcett. Phot: Thom Best. Players: Emily Perkins, Katherine Isabelle, Kris Lemche, Mimi Rogers. Prod: Oddbod Productions.

### THE LAW OF ENCLOSURES

Script: Dale Peck, John Greyson. Dir: Greyson. Phot: Kim Derko. Players: Sarah Polley, Brendan Fletcher, Sean McCann, Shirley Douglas, Diane Ladd. Prod: Buffalo Gal Pictures/Pluck.

### LOST AND DELIRIOUS

Script: Judith Thompson. Dir: Lea Pool. Phot: Pierre Gill. Players: Piper Perabo, Jessica Pare, Mischa Barton. Prod: Cite-Amerique, Dummett Films.

### MAELSTROM

Script and Dir: Denis Villeneuve. Phot: Andre Turpin. Players: Marie-Josee Croze, Jean-Nicholas Verreault, Stephanie Morgenstern. Prod: Max Films.

### MARINE LIFE

Script: Robert Forsyth, Lori Lansens. Dir: Anne Wheeler. Phot: David Pelletier. Players: Cybill Shepherd, Peter Outerbridge, Alexandra Purvis. Prod: Crescent Entertainment.

### POSSIBLE WORLDS

Script: John Mighton. Dir: Robert Lepage. Phot: Jonathan Freeman. Players: Tilda Swinton, Tom McCamus, Sean McCann. Prod: In Extremis Images/East Side Film Company.

### STARDOM

Script: Denys Arcand, Jacob Potashnik. Dir: Arcand. Phot: Guy Dufaux. Players: Jessica Pare, Dan Aykroyd, Frank Langella, Thomas Gibson, Robert Lepage, Charles Berling. Prod: Alliance Atlantis/Serendipity Point Films/Cinemaginaire/Cine b.

### SUSPICIOUS RIVER

Script and Dir: Lynne Stopkewich. Phot: Greg Middleton. Players: Molly Parker, Callum Keith Rennie. Prod: Suspicious Films.

### TWO THOUSAND AND NONE

Script and Dir: Arto Paragamian. Phot: Noraryr Kasper. Players: John Turturro, Oleg Kissellov, Katherine Borowitz. Prod: Galafilm.

### LA VIE APRES L'AMOUR (Life After Love)

Script: Ken Scott. Dir: Gabriel Pelletier. Phot: Eric Cayla. Players: Michel Cote, Sylvie Leonard, Patrick Huard. Prod: Max Films.

# Producers

**Accent Entertainment Corporation**
666B Queen St. W-Tor., Ont. M6J 1E5
Tel: (416) 867 8700
Fax: (416) 867 1764

**ACPAV**
1050 boul. René-Lévesque est, bur. 200
Montréal, QC H2L 2L6
Tel: (514) 849 2281
Fax: (514) 849 9487

**Alliance Atlantis Communications Corporation Head Office**
121 Bloor St. E., Ste. 1400
Toronto, ON M4W 3M5
Tel: (416) 967 1174
Fax: (416) 960 0971

**ASKA Film Productions Inc.**
1600 ave. de Lorimier, Ste. 211
Montréal, QC H2K 3W5
Tel: (514) 521 7103
Fax: (514) 521 6174

**Cinemaginaire International**
5144 boul. Saint-Laurent
Montréal, QC H2T 1R8
Tel: (514) 272 5505
Fax: (514) 272 9841

**Cine Qua Non Films**
5266 boul. St-Laurent
Montréal, QC H2T 1S1
Tel: (514) 271 4000
Fax: (514) 271 4005

**Filmline International Inc.**
410 St-Nicolas St., Ste. 10
Montréal, QC H2Y 2P5
Tel: (514) 288 5888
Fax: (514) 288 8083

**Galafilm**
5643 Clark, 3rd Floor
Montréal, H2T 2V5
Tel: (514) 273 4252
Fax: (514) 273 8689

**Nelvana Limited**
32 Atlantic Ave.
Toronto, ON M6K 1X8
Tel: (416) 588 5571
Fax: (416) 588 5588

**North American Pictures Ltd.**
808 Nelson St., Ste. 2105
Vancouver, BC V6Z 2H2
Tel: (604) 681 2165
Fax: (604) 681 5538

**Les Productions La Fête Inc.**
387 rue St. Paul o.
Montréal, QC H2Y 2A7
Tel: (514) 848 0417
Fax: (514) 848 0064

**Rhombus Media Inc.**
489 King St. W., Ste. 102
Toronto, ON M5V 1L3
Tel: (416) 971 7856
Fax: (416) 971 9647

**Shaftesbury Films**
264B Adelaide St. E.
Toronto, ON M5A 1N1
Tel: (416) 363 1411
Fax: (416) 363 1428

**Triptych Media Inc.**
788 King St. W. 2nd Floor
Tor. Omt. M5V 1N6
Tel: (416) 703 8866
Fax: (416) 703 8867

# Distributors

**Alliance Atlantis
Communications Corporation**
Head Office:
121 Bloor St. E., Ste. 1400
Toronto, ON M4W 3M5
Tel: (416) 967 1174
Fax: (416) 960 0971

**ASKA Film Distribution Inc.**
1600 av, de Lorimier, Ste. 211
Montréal, QC H2K 3W5
Tel: (514) 521 0623
Fax: (514) 521 6174

**Buena Vista Pictures
Distribution Canada**
Distributors of Walt Disney Pictures,
Touchstone Pictures and Hollywood
Pictures
Sales:
1235 Bay St., Ste. 901
Toronto, ON M5R 3K4
Tel: (416) 964 9275
Fax: (416) 964 8537

**Columbia Tristar Films of
Canada**
A Division of Columbia Pictures
Industries Inc.
1303 Yonge St., Ste. 100
Toronto, ON M4T 1W6
Tel: (416) 922 5740

**Compagnie France Film Inc.**
505 rue Sherbrooke est., Ste. 2401
Montréal, QC H2L 4N3
Tel: (514) 844 0680

**DreamWorks Distribution
Canada Co.**
2 Bloor St. W., Ste. 2510
Toronto, ON M4W 3E2
Tel: (416) 513 0312
Fax: (416) 513 0316

**Filmoption International**
3401 St-antoine
Westmount, QC H3Z 1X1
Tel: (514) 931 6180
Fax: (514) 939 2034

**Film Tonic Inc.**
5130 boul. St-Laurent, 4e étage
Montréal, QC H2T 1R8
Tel: (514) 272 4425
Fax: (514) 274 0214

**Film Transit International Inc.**
402 est rue Notre-Dame, Ste. 100
Montréal, QC H2Y 1C8
Tel: (514) 844 3358
Fax: (514) 844 7298

**Lions Gate Films Inc.**
2 Bloor St. W., Ste. 1901
Toronto, ON M4W 3E2
Tel: (416) 944 0104
Fax: (416) 944 2212

**MGM/UA Distribution Co.**
720 King St. W., Ste. 611
Toronto, ON M5V 2T3
Tel: (416) 703 9579

**Mongrel Media Inc.**
109 Mzlville
Toronto, ON M6G 1Y3
Tel: (416) 516 9775
Fax: (416) 516 0651

**TVA International Inc.**
A Coscient Group Company
465 McGill St.
Montréal, QC H2Y 4A6
Tel: (514) 284 2525

**North American Releasing Inc.**
808 Nelson st., Ste. 2105
Vancouver, BC V6Z 2H2
Tel: (604) 681 2165
Fax: (604) 681 5538

**Paramount Pictures Canada**
Viscom Enterprises Canada Limited
146 Bloor St. W.
Toronto, ON M5S 1M4
Tel: (416) 969 9901
Fax: (416) 922 0287

**Red Sky Entertainment**
Ste. 635 – The Landing
375 Water St.
Vancouver, BC V6B 5C6
Tel: (604) 899 0609
Fax: (604) 899 0619

**Societe De Distribution Cinema
Libre Inc.**
460 Ste-Catherine o, bur. 500
Montréal, QC H3B 1A7
Tel: (514) 861 9030
Fax: (514) 861 3634

**Twentieth Century Fox Film
Corporation**
33 Bloor St. E., Ste. 1106
Toronto, ON M4W 3H1
Sales: (416) 921 0001
Advertising: (416) 926 7317
Publicity: (416) 515 3365
Fax: (416) 921 9062

**Universal Films Canada**
2450 Victoria Park Ave.
Willowdale, ON M2J 4A2
Tel: (416) 491 3000
Fax: (416) 502 0323

**Warner Bros. Entertainment Inc.**
4576 Yonge St., 2nd Fl.
North York, ON M2N 6P1
Tel: (416) 250 8384
Fax: (416) 250 1898 (Advertising)
Fax: (416) 250 8930 (Sales)

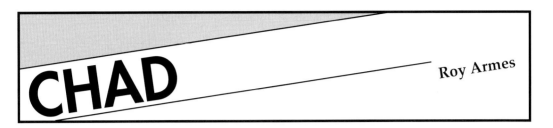

# CHAD — Roy Armes

Like many of the states formed from the massive French colonies of French West and Equatorial Africa, Chad had at least a minimal involvement in the 16mm film production fostered from the mid-1960s by the French Ministry of Co-operation, thanks to the documentary work of Edouard Sailly, who had studied at a French newsreel company.

In a very different context, Zara Mahamat Yacoub, who was born in Chad but studied audio-visual communication in France before working in South African television, made a short video documentary in 1994. *Le dilemme au féminin*, made as a collaboration between Canadian and Chad television, caused great controversy through its unflinching investigation of female circumcision.

In a very different vein is the work of Mahamat Saleh Haroun, who has just completed Chad's first fictional feature film. Born in 1961 in Chad, Haroun has the background typical of many of the younger African film-makers: he studied film at the Conservatoire Libre du Cinéma in Paris and then journalism in Bordeaux, where he has lived since 1982. He has worked in radio and journalism and made a number of documentaries through his Paris-based production company, Les Films de la Lanterne, the best-known of which is his study of the Malian actor and story-teller, Sotigui Kouyate.

His debut feature, **Bye Bye Africa**, which won the prize for best first film at

*Still from Mahamat Saleh Haroun's BYE BYE AFRICA*

the Milan African Film Festival in 2000, mixes documentary and fictional recon-struction, to recount his return to his native Chad after an absence of ten years. The very personal, at times almost home-movie style is a direct result of Haroun's innovative combination of digital shooting and editing, transferred to 35mm film to create the release print.

This was a system adopted by four out of ten of the films in competition in Milan, including Zimbabwean Michael Raeburn's *Home Sweet Home*. Haroun's work raises many fundamental issues about film and video, especially the confusions that can arise between filmed images and the reality they depict. More poignantly, showing documentary images of the cinemas in the capital N'djamena, all now at least partially destroyed by the civil war, it asks the question: how can one make films for a country where the cinema no longer exists?

## Recent Film

**BYE BYE AFRICA**

Script and Dir: Mahamat Saleh Haroun. Phot: Stéphane Legoux. Players: Haroun, Garba Issa, Aicha Yelena, Mahamat Saleh Abakar. Prod: Les Productions de la Lanterne (Paris).

## Useful Address

**Télé-Chad**
N'djamena
Chad
Tel: (235) 523 554
Fax: (235) 522 923

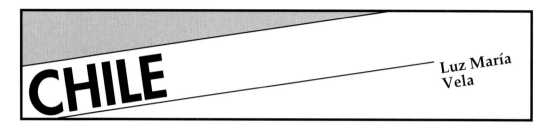

CHILE — Luz María Vela

Without question, 1999 was a landmark year in the history of Chilean cinema. **The Sentimental Teaser** (*El Chacotero Sentimental*), directed by Cristian Galaz, became the most successful domestic feature in history. With more than 950,000 spectators it reached the number two position on Chile's all-time box-office chart, pushing *The Lion King* into third, and almost sinking *Titanic*.

Based on a popular talk-radio show of the same name, *The Sentimental Teaser* presents three separate stories of love and sex in contemporary Chile. Simple in structure and colloquial in tone, mixing comedy and drama, it covers infidelity, incest and the struggle to find privacy for sex in an over-crowded house in the ghetto. It won Best Film at the International Latino Film Festival, New York.

The vast admissions figures revealed only part of the story of the film's phenomenal popularity; subsequent studies showed that 80% of *Sentimental Teaser*'s audience had not been to the movies for at least six years, and had never previously been into a multiplex. Even more astonishing than this one film's success was the explosion of native productions, with ten movies scheduled to debut in 2000, another ten announced for 2001, and 27 more in development. How is this possible in a country that normally produces between two and four movies a year, and where even the biggest native hits have never surpassed 100,000 spectators?

One of the keys is what Chilean film-makers call 'the consolidation of state support'. After getting burned in the early 1990s, the government had backed away from film-related investment. However, since 1998 diverse government agencies – CORFO, FONDART and now PROCHILE – have joined forces, step-by-step, to promote domestic feature production. Now, *Sentimental Teaser* should bring the state almost $3m in ticket-sales tax alone – quite a return on its $1m investment in the *entire* Chilean film industry in 1999.

## A lasting revival?

The second key factor in the recent improvements has been the multiplex boom which has seen total admissions increased from 6.5 million in 1996 to 13 million last year. Expansion has also brought diversification; Hollywood productions still dominate, but Latin and European offerings have a dedicated following, capturing an impressive 14% of ticket sales in 1999 (up from 9% in 1998). Even documentaries are finding a niche. Following the modest local success of Wim Wenders' *Buena Vista Social Club*, two controversial documentaries were scheduled to reach the nation's screens in the second half of 2000:*The Battle of Chile* (*La Batalla de Chile*), Patricio Guzman's legendary 1972-73 record of the demise of Salvador Allende's socialist government (never domestically released) and his 1997 sequel, *The Obstinate Memory* (*La Memoria Obstinada*).

Veteran director Silvio Caoizzi suggested these developments might herald "the definitive renaissance of Chilean cinema". Caoizzi's latest film, **Coronation** (*Coronacion*), drew more than 80,000 spectators in its initial six weeks on release. Andres Wood's **The Revenge** (*El Desquite*) filled 47,000 seats last year with its romantic tale of the affair between a wealthy landowner and a young servant in rural Chile in the early twentieth century. The film has been playing well at festivals (Toronto, San Sebastián, Huelva, Trieste, La

*Still from the enormously successful THE SENTIMENTAL TEASER*

*Still from Andres Wood's THE REVENGE*

Habana, Damascus), winning various awards. Wood's follow-up, *Loco Fever* (*La Fiebre del Loco*), is set to be released in 2001.

There was great anticipation prior to the Chilean release of Miguel Littín's **Tierra del Fuego**, an epic adventure yarn about the gold-digging Romanian engineer who exterminated Chilean Indians in the 1850s. Despite its poor reception at Cannes and by critics, it had done good business at cinemas in Spain and Portugal.

Whether the Chilean cinema is experiencing a lasting renaissance or just a temporary revival may be determined by two national productions announced for next year: *Black Angel* (*Angel Negro*), a thriller aimed at young audiences, and *Mampato y Ogú*, the first fully-animated

Chilean feature, based on two comic-strip characters who have been national icons for 30 years.

According to *Sentimental Teaser* director Galaz and others, a lasting Chilean cinema will only be possible with further support from the state, specifically a Cinema Law which would provide a legal framework for international co-productions, and create a new institution for co-ordinating government support. Happily, the government has unveiled plans to introduce such legislation by the start of 2001.

---

LUZ MARÍA VELA is a freelance journalist and video-maker who divides her time between Los Angeles and Santiago de Chile.

---

# Useful Addresses

**Arauco Film**
(production facility)
Silvina Hurtado 1789
Santiago
Tel: (56 2) 209 2091
Fax: (56 2) 204 5096

**Asociación de Productores de Cine de Chile**
Federico Froebel 1755
Providencia
Santiago
Tel: (56 2) 209 9031
Fax: (56 2) 204 8988

**Conate and Chile Films**
(studio, lab, distributor and exhibitor)

La Capitania 1200
Santiago
Tel: (56 2) 220 3086
Fax: (56 2) 211 9826

**Filmocentro**
(production facility)
Jorge Washington 302
Santiago
Tel: (56 2) 341 3100
Fax: (56 2) 209 1671

**Oficina de Difusión de la Cinematografia Chilena**
Villavicencio 352
Santiago
Tel: (56 2) 632 6565 or 632 6607
Fax: (56 2) 632 6389

**Roos Films**
(production facility)
Ricardo Matte Pérez 0216
Santiago
Tel: (56 2) 341 1188

**Augusto Ubilla**
(distributor)
General del Canto 10, 3°
Santiago
Tel: (56 2) 223 7685
Fax: (56 2) 235 2399

**Unicine**
(producers and directors union)
Huérfanos 587, Of.918
Santiago
Tel/Fax: (56 2) 273 1462

# CHINA

Derek Elley

The past year has been a good one for Asian cinema in general and mainland Chinese film-making in particular, ceremoniously anointed by the 2000 Cannes festival, which devoted unparalleled space in its competition to movies from the region. On the industry side, however, mainland China is still plagued by the same problems: thin audiences for local product, an exhibition sector still in need of heavy investment, and US studios relentlessly lobbying for a bigger slice of the market.

Following their major blunder in 1999, letting slip new films by Zhang Yimou (see *IFG* 2000), the Cannes' selectors went overboard on oriental fare in 2000. Actor Jiang Wen's second film as director, **Devils on the Doorstep** (*Guizi laile*), won the Special Jury Prize and caused the biggest hoo-ha since Zhang Yimou's *To Live* competed in 1994. Jiang had submitted the film without first securing official permission from Beijing's Film Bureau (mandatory for all movies sent abroad), and the Chinese tried to get it pulled before the festival by sending a delegation to Cannes head Gilles Jacob.

However, with prints already outside China, and even the negative stored in Australia, the festival went ahead. When Jiang won his prize, the event went unreported in Mainland newspapers. Subsequently, news filtered out that Jiang was to be forbidden from having any involvement with the film and TV industries (either as an actor or director) for seven years; one of his executive producers was to be carpeted for two.

As of late July, Jiang was still claiming he had not officially been told of any ban, and that the movie had obtained the necessary permissions throughout its writing and shooting (it was in production for two years, with plenty of press coverage). However, the Film Bureau has never taken kindly to being pressured into letting films attend festivals, so Jiang has only himself to blame. As in the past, a compromise will doubtless be worked out (after *To Live*, Zhang was forbidden from working on foreign co-productions for two years, and eventually wrote a self-criticism).

Like Pavlov's dog, the western press leapt to Jiang's defence, even though *Devils on the Doorstep* met a very mixed reception at Cannes. A black-and-white comedy-drama about ignorant but wily villagers dealing with two Japanese prisoners dumped on their doorstep by a member of the Resistance during the Second World War, it is extravagantly long at 162 minutes, shot in exhaustingly jittery style, and shows every sign of a film produced, directed, co-written and performed by an actor, with no one around to cry "Enough!". However, as his first film, *In the Heat of the Sun* (1994), had already demonstrated, Jiang is undoubtedly a considerable talent behind the camera; shorn of an hour, *Devils* could become the ironic fable it aspires to be.

## Zhang back on track

Though none were at Cannes, five pictures headlined on the 1999-2000 festival circuit. Zhang Yimou's **Not One Less** (*Yige dou bu neng shao*) and **The Road Home** (*Wode fuqin muqin*), which respectively competed at Venice 1999 and Berlin 2000, showed Zhang making a triumphant return to form after fears that his career, like Chen Kaige's, might have reached a plateau in middle age. Both films have a simplicity and emotional purity which are new to his work, despite again being set in the countryside.

*Not One Less*, about a teenage teacher going in search of a kid who's gone missing from her class, slightly recalls *The Story of Qiuju*, but carries greater emotional power. *The Road Home*, in which a son recalls his parents' love affair during the late 1950s, is an exercise in almost purely metaphysical film-making which deliberately ignores the human story's political background – one of the nastiest periods in China's recent history. Predictably, this device was criticised by some westerners, who missed the point completely. It also introduced a star in the making in young actress Zhang Ziyi, subsequently seen in Ang Lee's *Crouching Tiger, Hidden Dragon* (see Taiwan section).

Two other film-makers from different generations also made an impact. In **Seventeen Years** (*Guonian huijia*), a moving, beautifully observed chamber piece about the friendship between a prison guard and her female charge, Zhang Yuan surprised everyone with his almost classical restraint. With this, the first of his works to be officially released in China (in January 2000), former bad-boy Zhang officially rehabilitated himself after making provocative indies, and also showed a new maturity. His feature-length documentary **Crazy English** (*Fengkuang yingyu*) was entertaining but over-stretched: a portrait of born self-promoter Li Yang, who holds mass English-language teach-ins, the film blunted its commentary on modern China by being at least half-and-hour too long.

From the younger generation, Zhang Yang established his name internationally with **Shower** (*Xizao*), his second feature (after *Spicy Love Soup*) and the biggest hit so far for Beijing-based American producer Peter Loehr's Imar Films. Like *Seventeen Years*, *Shower* is emotionally powerful and low-key without being strenuously arty, sketching relations between two brothers and their aged father, who runs a traditional Beijing bathhouse due for demolition.

Finally, Lou Ye's third feature, **Suzhou River** (*Suzhou he*), established the director as a name to watch. His dreamlike, rather mournful and highly atmospheric

*Still from Lou Yi's SUZHOU RIVER*

mystery-cum-love story, set in Shanghai, caused heads to turn on the festival circuit following its premiere at Rotterdam early in 2000.

## Festival highlights, local hits

Among the best films making a smaller but very solid impression at festivals were Huo Jianqi's **Postmen in the Mountains** (*Na shan na ren na gou*), a delicate study of cross-generational bonding as a father hands over his 112-kilometre rural postal round to his son; Xu Geng's **Thatched Memories** (*Cao fangzi*), a beautifully shot coming-of-age story based around a rural school in the early 1960s; Sun Zhou's **Breaking the Silence** (*Piaoliang mama*), a Gong Li vehicle in which the putative star, playing a simple single mum with a deaf child, was overshadowed by the supporting cast; and young Beijinger Wang Quan'an's first feature, **Lunar Eclipse** (*Yueshi*), a cleverly constructed, noir-ish drama with a sly sense of humour. Wu Tianming's **An Unusual Love** (*Feichang aiqing*), which finally surfaced overseas in 1999, was a rather melodramatic tale of a young doctor who patiently nurses her brain-injured husband. After his 1995 *The King of Masks*, this was more local, commercial fare.

The hit-and-miss prospects of Mainland movies being screened abroad still result in many worthwhile items never – or only belatedly – receiving the attention they deserve. Three films dating from 1998-99 need mentioning here: Zhou Xiaowen's **The Common People** (*Guanyu ai de gushi*) is unlike any other Mainland movie to date, a boldly inventive comedy in *Idiots* style, set among cerebral palsy sufferers; Zhang Qian and Ma Weijun's **The Crossing** (*Tianzi matou*), a well-observed study of a Guangzhou family coping with unemployment; and Wang Xiaolie's **Seeing Chalila from Afar** (*Yaowang Chalila*), from Emei Studio, about a wife's journey to visit her husband in Tibet that turns into a kind of off-beat spiritual odyssey.

The local hit of the past year was the relationships comedy **Sorry Baby** (*Mei wan mei liao*), the third in a series directed by Feng Xiaogang and starring comedian Ge You (who always plays likeable rogues). Paired this time with Taiwanese actress Wu Chien-lien, Ge plays a tour-bus driver who inadvertently "kidnaps" his crooked boss' girlfriend and teams up with her to extract a debt from him. Less manicured and more laid-back than the previous *Party A Party B* (1997) and *Be There Or Be Square* (1998), *Sorry Baby* features wonderful ensemble playing, especially by Fu Biao as the corrupt entrepreneur. Released at Christmas 1999, the film took $1m (RMB 8.4 million) in Beijing alone, double the gross of its Hollywood competitor, *Enemy of the State*. Internet ticket sales accounted for a big chunk of its success.

*Sorry Baby* is typical of a growing number of Mainland movies which rarely make the festival circuit or gain distribution outside East Asia, but which show that, contrary to received opinion, China is capable of producing quality mainstream fare. Shanghai Film Studios' big-budget **Crash Landing** (*Jinji pojiang*), an undisguised rip-off of *Airport* directed by Zhang Jianya, is a slick thriller, with fine special effects, that's just as entertaining as anything from Hollywood or Hong Kong. The same studio's **Ice Speed** (*Bing yu huo*), by Hu Xueyang, about the dogged ambition of a young woman speed skater, is certainly on a par with, if not better than, a similar US movie like *The Cutting Edge*.

## Celebration and negotiation

As 1999 marked the fiftieth anniversary of the founding of the People's Republic, the latter half of the year was clogged up with celebratory works, some, like Wu Ziniu's **National Anthem** (*Guoge*), directed by names who were just marking time. In this category of old-fashioned film-making one must also file **Lover's Grief over the Yellow River** (*Huang he jue lian*), a ridiculous war movie that was the second in a "nationalistic trilogy" directed by journeyman Feng Xiaoning, following 1997's *Red River Valley*.

In May 2000 Hollywood made progress in trying to beat down China's protective door by exploiting the latter's desire to establish permanent normal trade relations with the US and also to join the World Trade Organisation. The annual quota of 10 foreign films (most, in practice American), imported on a 50-50 revenue sharing basis, is initially to be increased to 20. On the exhibition side, foreign firms will be allowed up to 49% ownership (unofficially, maybe more) of joint ventures.

As with everything in China, however, anything in the movie business can be changed at a moment's notice. Hollywood is playing a long waiting game, with reps from most of the majors already ensconced in Hong Kong or Beijing and paying lip service to the Chinese by financially seeding the occasional local production. Total US entertainment revenues from China are currently estimated at $20m a year, tiny considering the market's size.

Hollywood's relations with China always make the headlines, but the Mainland has for several years been going through a gradual, internal revolution with far less fanfare. Distribution companies in cities like Beijing, Shanghai, Guangzhou, Chengdu and Wuhan have been moving into exhibition, and strong local entities have formed, such as Shanghai Yongle Film Group, China Film Group and Shanghai Film Group. A considerable amount of Hong Kong money – both in exhibition and production – has also quietly been filtered into the Mainland.

Certain western commentators love to maintain the clichéd image of the Mainland being a hidebound, communist-party controlled megastate deprived of western "opportunities". However, in practice, its big cities are now modern, hip centres, with their own yuppies and wealthy entrepreneurs. Film is only one of many entertainment options, and traditional theatrical exhibition (still the lodestone in the US mindset, but decreasingly so in other countries) is only a small part of a much bigger, more complex leisure economy.

# The 19th Golden Rooster Awards

The following awards were made in Shenyang on October 20, 1999, alongside the 22nd Hundred Flowers Awards (voted by readers of the large-circulation monthly, *Popular Cinema*). Main prizes:

**Best Film:** *Postmen in the Mountains.*
**Best Director:** Zhang Yimou (*Not One Less*).
**Best Script:** Cao Wenxuan (*Thatched Memories*).
**Best Actor:** Teng Rujun (*Postmen in the Mountains*).
**Best Actress:** Ning Jing (*Lover's Grief over the Yellow River*).
**Best Supporting Actor:** Du Yuan (*Thatched Memories*).
**Best Supporting Actress:** Yuan Quan (*Spring Rhapsody*).
**Best Photography:** Zhao Fei (*The Emperor and the Assassin*).
**Best Art Direction:** Tu Juhua, Lin Qi (*The Emperor and the Assassin*).
**Best Editing:** Du Yuan, Liu Xiaoqin (*Love of the Internet Generation*).
**Best Music:** Li Ge (*Lover's Grief over the Yellow River*).

**Best Sound:** Tao Jing (*The Emperor and the Assassin*).
**Best First Work by a Director:** Jin Chen (*Love of the Internet Generation*).
**Best Documentary:** *Communist Party Chairman Liu Shaoqi.*
**Best Children's Film:** *Thatched Memories.*
**Best Special Effects:** *Lover's Grief over the Yellow River.*
**Special Jury Prizes:** *National Anthem; Spring Rhapsody; Lover's Grief over the Yellow River.*
**Honorary Award:** actor Xie Tian (*The Go-Between*).

# The 22nd Hundred Flowers Awards

**Best Films:** *House Husband, Wife Director; The Go-Between; Not One Less.*
**Best Actor:** Zhao Benshan *(House Husband, Wife Director).*
**Best Actress:** Liu Xin *(The Go-Between).*
**Best Supporting Actor:** Niu Ben *(Daughter-in-Law, You Manage Affairs).*
**Best Supporting Actress:** Li Xiaohong *(Love on the Silver Screen).*

# Forthcoming Films

**ALL THE WAY**
Dir: Shi Runjiu. Players: Jiang Wu, Karen Mok. Prod: Imar.

**LU ZHEN CHUANSHUO**
Dir: Gu Rong. Players: Guo Lun, Li Jiayao, Wei Qiming. Prod: Shanghai Yongle.

**NA SHI HUA KAI**
Dir: Gao Xiaosong. Players: Zhou Xun, Xia Yu, Bo Shu.

**NENG REN YU SI**
Dir: Wang Haowei.

**ZHONG SHI YIWANG**
Dir: A Nian. Players: Yan Danchen, Li Mengnan.

**SHUOCHU NIDE MIMI**
Dir: Huang Jianxin. Player: Jiang Shan.

**FEICHANG JIARI (A LINGERING FACE)**
Dir: Lu Xuechang. Players: Ma Xiaoqing, Li Min, Ge Yaming.

**BOLI SHI TOUMINGDE**
Dir: Xia Gang. Players: Huang Kai, Ma Yingli, Xu Xiaodan, Ma Lun.

# Useful Addresses

**August First Film Studio**
A1, Beili
Liuliqiao
Guanganmenwai
Beijing 100073
Tel: (86 10) 6681 2329
Fax: (86 10) 6326 7324

**Beijing Film Institute**
4 Xitucheng Rd
Haidian District
Beijing 100088
Tel: (86 10) 6201 8899
Fax: (86 10) 6201 3895

**Beijing Film Studio**
77 Beisanhuan Central Rd
Haidian District

Beijing 100088
Tel: (86 10) 6201 2067
Fax: (86 10) 6201 2312

**China Film Archive**
3 Wenhuiyuan Rd
Haidian District
Beijing 100088
Tel: (86 10) 6225 4422
Fax: (86 10) 6225 0362

**China Film Corp.**
(import, export)
25 Xinjiekouwai St
Beijing 100088
Tel: (86 10) 6225 4488
Fax: (86 10) 6225 0652

**China Film Coproduction Corp.**
5 Xinyuan South Rd

Chaoyang Distruct
Beijing 100027
Tel: (86 10) 6466 3330
Fax: (86 10) 6466 3983

**Imar Film Co.**
34, Guangximen Beili
Chaoyang District
Beijing 100028
Tel: (86 10) 6420 4646/4555
Fax: (86 10) 6422 1622

**Changchun Film Studio**
20 Hongqi St
Changchun 130021
Tel: (86 431) 595 3511
Fax: (86 431) 595 2747

**Guangxi Film Studio**
26 Youai North Rd
Nanning 530001

Tel: (86 771) 313 4261
Fax: (86 771) 313 3739

**Pearl River Film Production Co.**
352 Xingang Central Rd
Guangzhou 510311
Tel: (86 20) 8420 2238
Fax: (86 20) 8420 9584

**Shanghai Film Studio**
595 Caoxi North Rd
Shanghai 200030
Tel: (86 21) 6438 7100
Fax: (86 21) 6439 1650

**Xi'an Film Studio**
70 Xiying Rd
Xi'an 710054
Tel: (86 29) 552 2526
Fax: (86 29) 552 2611

# CROATIA — Tomislav Kurelec

The events of 1999 made it one of the most interesting years for the Croatian film industry in the decade since independence. Several events on the film scene anticipated the social changes and political conflicts which were to change Croatia following the death of president Franjo Tudjman in December, and the parliamentary elections in January 2000, which saw the defeat of Tudjman's previously all-powerful Croatian Democratic Union.

Public dissatisfaction with the government arose in August 1999 when the first international film festival was held in the Istrian town of Motovun. The event allowed Croatian audiences to see for the first time Bosnian director Adem Kenović's *Perfect Circle* and Serbian director Goran Paskaljević's *The Powder Keg*. There was a welcoming, small-town atmosphere, as predominantly young film enthusiasts rubbed shoulders with film-makers and critics from all over the world.

But this openness of spirit did not suit the authoritarian regime, which, either deliberately or out of sheer negligence, changed the dates of the national film festival, held annually in Pula, so that it clashed with the Motovun event, just 70km away. The Croatian film community, after a long period in the shadows, suddenly found itself at the centre of a media storm, although the controversy said more about politics than the films themselves.

Many journalists treated the new Croatian features as government stooges, a label certainly applicable to the only flop at Pula: veteran director Željko Senečić's **Dubrovnik Twilight**, an unconvincing melodrama which unfolds during the siege of Dubrovnik. Alos set against the backdrop of Croatia's struggle for independence, but far more successful, was **Madonna**, a revenge drama that was the debut feature from Neven Hitrec. Fine performances and the director's talent compensated for the inadequacies of the screenplay by Hrvoje Hitrec, the director's father, and *Madonna* won Pula's Grand Prix.

The Croatian film Critics Award at Pula went to the youngest director in competition, Ognjen Sviličić, and his exceptionally witty comedy **I Wish I Were a Shark**, which superbly conjures a Mediterranean atmosphere. However, one feels the story has been awkwardly lengthened from a shorter version intended for television.

## Power corrupts

The two other features presented at Pula criticised aspects of Croatian society, stressing the connection between political and criminal power. For its first two thirds, Dejan Šorak's **Garcia** is a superb thriller – the best-directed film seen in Croatia in the past year. Then, when the plot turns into a *Hamlet*-like family tragedy in the last couple of reels, it loses all conviction and viewers lose interest.

The awards for Best Director and Best Screenplay (shared with Goran Tribuson) went to Zrinko Ogresta for **Red Dust**. This is an intriguing, provocative story set in the dismal, crime-ridden Zagreb suburbs, and focusing on ordinary people living on the edge of poverty. It was invited to 15 international festivals, winning the Grand Prix in Rome and Haifa.

Vinko Brešan's **Marshal Tito's Spirit**, nominated for Best Film at Berlin's International Forum in 2000, is a sometimes grotesque comedy about the appearance of the ghost of the former Yugoslav president on a small Dalmatian island. In late 1999 and early 2000 it drew audiences of more than 100,000 to Croatian cinemas, outgrossing the latest Hollywood releases and reaching second place on the list of all-time domestic hits – behind Brešan's *How the War Started on My Island*. Its casual wit offended the authorities, who temporarily banned it from being advertised on Croatian Television, one of the film's co-producers.

*Still from Vinko Brešan's MARSHAL TITO'S SPIRIT*

By contrast, Jakov Sedlar's **Walking in Fours**, which was released just before the election, was advertised at every opportunity. Produced with official funding, and some finance from shady, untraceable sources, it was one of the most expensive and worst Croatian films ever made. Sedlar's film dealt with a very painful topic – the suffering of soldiers and civilians at the end of the Second World War as they retreated westwards to escape the violent revenge of the Communists – but served only as propaganda, its goal being to thwart the left-wing opposition party's victory in the elections, by branding them as the direct descendants of those responsible for the 1940s tragedy depicted on screen.

So determined was the government to use *Walking in Fours* for its own ends that after the film had played to virtually empty cinemas for ten days it was broadcast on Croatian Television. Happily, it could not prevent democratic change, which will undoubtedly offer Croatian cinema more freedom. However, we are now left to wonder whether the prevailing economic circumstances will allow film-makers to take advantage of that freedom.

TOMISLAV KURELEC has been a film critic since 1965, mostly on radio and television. He has directed five short films and many television items.

# Recent and Forthcoming Films

**BOGORODICA (Madonna)**

Script: Hrvoje Hitrec. Dir: Neven Hitrec. Phot: Stanko Herceg. Players: Ljubomir Kerekeš, Lucija Šerbedžija, Ivo Gregurević. Prod: Maxima Film/HRT – Croatian Television.

**CRVENA PRAŠINA (Red Dust)**

Script: Goran Tribuson, Zrinko Ogresta. Dir: Ogresta. Phot: Davorin Gecl. Players: Josip Kučan, Marko Matanović, Ivo Gregurević. Prod: Interfilm Zagreb.

**DA MI JE BITI MORSKI PAS (I Wish I Were a Shark)**

Script and Dir: Ognjen Sviličić. Phot: Vedran Šamanović. Players: Josip Zovko, Vedran Mlikota, Elvis Bošnjak, Bruna Bebić-Tudor, Edita Majić. Prod: HRT –

Croatian Television.

**DUBROVAČKI SUTON (Dubrovnik Twilight)**

Script: Željko Senečić, Tomislav Sabljak. Dir: Senečić. Phot: Sobodan Trninić. Players: Michaela Kezele, Slavko Juraga, Boris Cavazza. Prod: Patria Film.

**GARCIA**

Script and Dir: Dejan Šorak. Phot: Vjekoslav Vrdoljak. Players: Dubravko Šimek, Ksenija Pajić, Vanja Drach, Zoja Odak, Josip Genda, Linda Begonja. Prod: Ban Film Zagreb.

**MARŠAL (Marshal Tito's Spirit)**

Script: Ivo Brešan and Vinko Brešan. Dir: Vinko Brešan. Phot: Živko Zalar. Players: Dražen Kühn, Linda Begonja, Ilija Ivezić,

Boris Buzančić, Inge Appelt, Ivo Gregurević, Predrag Vušević. Prod: Interfilm Zagreb, HRT – Croatian Television.

**ČETVERORED (Walking in Fours)**

Script: Ivan Aralica. Dir: Jakov Sedlar. Phot: Igor Sunara. Players: Ivan Marević, Goran Navojec, Ena Begović, Ivica Vidović. Prod: Duga, HRT – Croatian Television.

**SRCE NIJE U MODI (Heart is Out of Fashion)**

Script: Goran Tribuson. Dir: Branko Schmidt. Phot: Vjekoslav Vrdoljak. Players: Graham Rock, Nataša Lušetić, Ivo Gregurević Franjo Dijak. Prod: Interfilm Zagreb, HRT – Croatian Television.

# Producers

**HRT – Croatian Television**
10000 Zagreb
Tel: (3851) 634 2634
Fax (3851) 634 3692

**Interfilm**
10000 Zagreb

Nova Ves 45
Tel: (3851) 466 7022

**Jadran Film**
10000 Zagreb
Oporovečka 12
Tel: (3851) 298 7222

**Maxima Film**
10000 Zagreb

Belostenčeva 6
Tel: (3851) 9953 5624

**Patria Film**
10000 Zagreb
Deželićeva
Tel: (3851) 370 7500

**Zagreb Film**
10000 Zagreb

Vlaška 70
Tel: (3851) 455 0489

## Distributors

**Adria Art Film**
10000 Zagreb
Ivanićgradska 64
Tel: (3851) 382 1172

**Blitz**
10000 Zagreb
Sv. Mateja 121
Tel: (3851) 665 9500

**Continental Film**
10000 Zagreb
Šoštarićeva 10
Tel: (3851) 481 8340

**Discovery**
10000 Zagreb
Veslačka 27
Tel: (3851) 619 2203

**Europa Film and Video**
10000 Zagreb
Šoštarićeva 10
Tel: (3851) 299 2694

**Kinematografi**
10000 Zagreb
Tuškanac 1
Tel: (3851) 483 4900

**Oscar Vision**
10000 Zagreb
Marulićev trg 17

**UCD**
10000 Zagreb
Ribnička 61
Tel: (3851) 363 0339

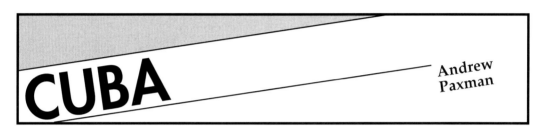

# CUBA
Andrew Paxman

Cuban cinema experienced a mini-revolution – or at least a change of dynasty – in March 2000, with the replacement of long-serving film institute chief Alfredo Guevara by industry newcomer Omar González. The transition comes just as production activity is gaining genuine momentum for the first time in a decade. It raises the question of whether the free-spirited formula for recent Cuban film, dependent upon Spanish co-producers and melding social observation with commercial sensibility, will survive or be replaced by something rather more grey.

Other Latin film industries, such as those in Brazil and Mexico, have since the mid-1990s been moving away somewhat from state-dependence, yet Cuban cinema remains controlled by national film institute the ICAIC, so the significance of Guevara's departure should not be under-estimated; all the more so, given his lengthy friendship with Fidel Castro. Said to be one of the few Cubans able to argue with the president, Guevara skilfully fostered projects that mocked the ineffi-ciencies of communist bureaucracy and cheerfully acknowledged black-market capitalism, despite occasional condemnation by Castro, who in a much-remarked 1998 speech railed against the satirical comedy *Guantanamera*.

Named head of the ICAIC at its foundation in 1959, Guevara oversaw the golden era of post-revolution film-making, serving until 1982, when he became Cuba's ambassador to UNESCO. He returned to the post in 1991, when Cuba was entering a period of major enconomic crisis and output was barely one picture per year, and oversaw a gradual rebirth through international co-production, chiefly with Spain, but also with Mexico, Argentina, France and Germany.

Guevara's exit was officially announced as retirement, and he retains the post of president of Havana's year-end film festival. This version of events was credible, as he is well into his seventies and has been frail for several years. But some allege that Castro has tired of films that sniped at the system, and that new ICAIC chief González, formerly head of the Cuban Book Institute, is likely to foster party-line films. Still, one good sign is that Camilo Vives, the dealmaker largely responsible for enticing Spanish producers to made-in-Cuba projects, remains the ICAIC production chief.

*Still from Juan Carlos Tabío's THE WAITING LIST*
*photo: Tornasol Films*

## Dumbing down?

Building on the critical and commercial success of Fernando Pérez's poetic study of denial and reconciliation in present-day Cuba, *Life is to Whistle* (*La Vida es Silbar*; 1998; reviewed in *IFG* 2000), which chalked up many international TV sales, Cuban cinema had a conspicuous presence at festivals in 2000. Gerardo Chijona's *A Paradise Under the Stars* (*Un Paraiso bajo las Estrellas*) was well-received at Sundance; Pastor Vega's *The Prophecies of Amanda* (*Las Profecías de Amanda*) played at the 40th Cartagena Film Festival in Colombia; Juan Carlos Tabío's **The Waiting List** (*La Lista de Espera*), a light-hearted comedy that uses a broken-down bus as a metaphor for modern-day Cuba, gained a slot in Un Certain Regard at Cannes.

As well as their guaranteed theatrical run in Spain, most of these titles have strong export potential, but some critics wonder whether the influence of Spanish co-producers has not made Cuban film a little too fluffy, even lowbrow. It is difficult to make such a judgment, since many of the anti-state jibes that these films contain, including plays-on-words and allusions to speeches by Castro, are too subtle for most foreign viewers. **A Paradise Under the Stars**, a crowd-pleasing romance set in the Tropicana night-club, typifies this debate, striking some as too improbable and wilfully quirky, and others as effectively interweaving a delightful comedy with worthwhile themes, such as the growing disposability of family in Cuban society.

Projects set to emerge in late 2000 and early 2001 include a film from veteran Humberto Solás, *Miel para Ochun*, about a Cuban-American who returns to the island in search of his mother, and *Hacerse el Sueco*, from Daniel Díaz Torres, a comedy about a Swede living in Havana. The latter marks another investment from Spain's Igeldo, which co-produced *The Prophecies of Amanda* and has also recently teamed up with ICAIC on a feture documentary, Ana Diez's **La Mafia en La Habana**, about US mafia operations in the Cuban capital in the 1950s.

Even more supportive is Wanda Films, headed by José María Morales, which having co-produced *Life is to Whistle* and *A Paradise Under the Stars*, is now preparing two more projects: *Loving Gilda* for Fernando Pérez, which is slated to film in Italy, and a comedy from Gerardo Chijona, *Corazón de Papel*.

Meanwhile, Cuban music continues its celluloid hot streak. In the wake of the immensely successful *Buena Vista Social Club* from Germany's Wim Wenders, and *Lagrimas Negras* by Holland's Sonia Helman Dolz (plus the less well-received *Cuba Feliz* from Frenchman Karim Dridi) two more music documentaries are emerging, again driven by foreign participation. One is *Latino Jazz*, from Spain's Fernando Trueba, which secured a distribution deal with Miramax even before the cameras rolled. The other, which will be released first, celebrates the island's long-established, Grammy-winning salsa combo, Los Van Van. Entitled *Van Van: The Party Begins* (*Van Van: Empezó la Fiesta*), the documentary is jointly directed by Liliana Mazure (Argentina) and Aarón Vega (Cuba).

ANDREW PAXMAN led *Variety* coverage of Latin America from 1994-99. He is co-author of *El Tigre: Emilio Azcárraga y su imperio Televisa*, a best-selling biography of Mexican media mogul Emilio Azcárraga Milmo.

# Recent and Forthcoming Films

**HACERSE EL SUECO**

Script: Eduardo del Llano, Daniel Díaz Torres. Dir: Díaz Torres. Phot: Raúl Pérez Ureta. Players: Peter Lohmeyer, Enrique Molina, Ketty de la Iglesia. Prod: ICAIC/Igeldo (Spain)/Impala (Spain)/Kinowelt (Germany).

**LA LISTA DE ESPERA (The Waiting List)**

Script: Juan Carlos Tabío, Senel Paz. Dir: Tabío. Phot: Hans Burmann. Players: Vladimir Cruz, Thaimi Alvarino, Jorge Perugorría. Prod: ICAIC/Tornasol Films (Spain)/DMVB (France)/Tabasco Films (Mexico).

**LAS NOCHES DE CONSTANTINOPLA** (*literally*, **Constantinople Nights**)

Script: Manuel A. Gutiérrez, Orlando Rojas. Dir: Rojas. Phot: Angel Alderete. Players: Rosita Fornés, Verónica Lynn, Liberto Rabal, Paco Rabal. Prod: ICAIC/El Paso Producciones (Spain).

**LAS PROFECIAS DE AMANDA (The Prophecies of Amanda)**

*Grammy-winning salsa combo and now documentary stars, Los Van Van*

Script: Aaron Vega, Pastor Vega. Dir: Pastor Vega. Phot: Rafael Solás. Players: Daisy Granados, Marisela Berti, Adolfo Llaurado. Prod: ICAIC/Igeldo (Spain)/Alter (Venezuela).

**UN PARAISO BAJO LAS ESTRELLAS (A Paradise Under the Stars)**

Script: Gerardo Chijona, Luis Agüero, Senel Paz. Dir: Chijona. Phot: Raúl Pérez Ureta. Players: Thaís Valdés, Vladimir Cruz, Enrique Molina. Prod: ICAIC/Wanda Films (Spain).

**VAN VAN, EMPEZO LA FIESTA (Van Van: The Party Begins)**

Script: Martín Salinas. Dir: Liliana Mazure, Aarón Vega. Phot: Marcelo Iaccarino. Players: Los Van Van. Prod: ICAIC/Arca Difusión (Argentina).

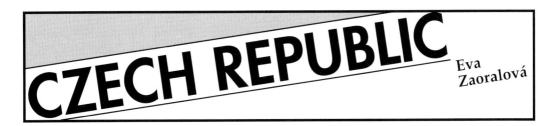

**CZECH REPUBLIC** Eva Zaoralová

Eighteen new Czech films competed for the top award in the national FINÁLE Plzeň competition 2000 – an indication of the comparatively healthy state of the local industry. The box-office chart for 1999 brought further good news. While in 1998, just one Czech title had made the list (*The Time of Debts*, in ninth place) in 1999 Jan Hřebejk's comedy about the Prague Spring, **Cosy Dens** (*Pelíšky*; reviewed in IFG 2000), reached the number one spot and went on to break box-office records early in 2000, by reaching more than one million admissions.

Zdenek Trosky's fairytale, **Helluva Good Luck** (*Z pekla štěstí*), reached third place on the table and Saši Gedeona's universally comprehensible modern adaptation of a tragicomic Dostoyevsky novel,

*Still from David Ondříček's LONERS*

**Return of the Idiot** (*Návrat idiota*), was the sixth most successful film of the year. All three, particularly Gedeona's film, which carried off most of the Czech Lion awards (the country's equivalent to the Oscars) at the beginning of 2000, also attracted attention at foreign festivals in Europe and the US. Such successes mean that the Oscar-winning Jan Svěrák (*Kolya*) is no longer the only name in the industry becoming familiar outside the Czech Republic

The new feature from Hrebejk (b.1967), **Divided We Fall** (*Musíme si pomáhat*), from a script by *Cosy Dens* writer Petr Jarchovský, is a bittersweet wartime comedy which tells of a married couple who, while feigning collaboration with the Nazis, are able to conceal the fact that they have been hiding a young Jewish man in their flat throughout the conflict. The film transcends its period setting in a fine exploration of real and false heroism, and the relativity of the seemingly unambiguous roles people assign themselves in extreme situations. It was awarded the main prize at FINÁLE Plzeň 2000.

Also conceived as a tragicomedy is a film by another representative of the younger generation, David Ondříček (b.1969), the son of a famous Czech cinematographer. His second film, **Loners** (*Samotári*), was

based on a screenplay by Petr Zelenka, director of 1997's very popular *The Buttoners*. In *Loners*, Zelenka's absurd humour pervades the present-day story of several young people trying to make major decisions in their lives but finding themselves unable to break free from well-worn paths, while the style recalls the lyricism of Ondříček's directing debut, *Whisper* (*Septej*, 1996).

## First-timers and veterans

The story of the debut film by recent FAMU graduate Alice Nellis (b.1971), with its somewhat mysterious and elusive title, **Ene Bene** (based on the words of a children's counting rhyme), comes considerably closer to Czech reality. The intimate, tragi-comic story innovatively links public and private issues and its author succeeds in combining humour with sensitivity to reflect the extremes of interpersonal relationships. The strength of this low-budget film, made with the support of Czech Television, lies in the performances of the three leading actors.

Two further debuts, **Eliska Loves it Wild** (*Eliška má ráda divočinu*) and **Very Ordinary Person** (*Kanárek*), made lesser impressions on critics and viewers, although the film-makers cannot be faulted for their originality and taste for experimentation. *Eliska Loves it Wild*, from the highly successful actor, screenwriter and director of music videos, Otakár Schmidt (b.1960), was a post-modern piece which assaults the senses with new visual and sound "attractions". *Very Ordinary Person* is the work of Viktor Tauš, a former FAMU student, and was based on his experiences of drug dependency. A documentary account of a therapeutic environment is combined with almost convulsively staged scenes in a style akin to Tarantino.

Vojtěch Jasný (b.1925), the man responsible for the once-celebrated features *That Cat, Desire* and *All Good Countrymen* (for which he received a share of the Best Director award at Cannes in 1969), returned after many years abroad, to film a kind of sequel to those 1960s films, **Which Side Eden?** (*Návrat ztraceného ráje*). This story of an émigré who returns after many years to the Moravian countryside where he grew up is, however, marred by excessive nostalgia and the creator's tendency to moralise.

Jasný's former colleague, the highly active Karel Kachyňa (b.1924), made **Hanele**, an adaptation of a classic Czech novel by Ivan Olbracht, set in a Jewish community in the Sub-Carpathian Ukraine during the 1930s. This work, in which strong tradition confronts the need for greater freedom, was less successful among Czech audiences and critics than it was at the Berlinale 2000, where it was screened in the Panorama section.

### Shooting the past

Another film seeking inspiration from the past is **Spring of Life** (*Pramen zivota*), directed by Milana Cieslara (b.1960); it was awarded the Jury Prize at the national competition. Based on a screenplay by the renowned writer Vladimíra Körnera (who consistently examines the history of the relationship between Czechs and Germans in the Czech border region), it describes the monstrous Nazi project known as "Der Lebensborn" which was to secure for the Third Reich perfect, racially pure descendants. Vladimír Drha (b.1944), in **The Conception of My Younger Brother** (*Početí mého mladšího bratra*), returns to an apartment block in the suburbs in the late 1940s, and paints the portraits of its diverse inhabitants during the course of a single night.

Among the most interesting forthcoming releases is the new work from Drahomíry Vihanové (b.1930), whose promising career was cut short at the start of the Communist regime and who, after a number of excellent documentaries, now presents what is only her third feature film, *The Pilgrimage of Students Peter and Jacob* (*Zpráva o putování studentu Petra a Jakuba*). It focuses on the current issue of the differing attitudes displayed by the Romany minority who encounter the racist views of "whites".

Successful director of photography F.A.Brabec is completing his second, somewhat risky feature. Having several years ago filmed an adaptation of Alfred Jarry's *King Ubu*, he has now turned his attention to a rhyming ballad by mid-nineteenth century Czech poet Karel Jaromír, *Erben*. After an extensive search for a producer Jan Svěrák is finally to make *The Blue World* (*Tmavomodrý svět*). In an ironic twist, this film about Czechoslovak airmen fighting the Germans from bases in England during the Second World War, will be made with German finance.

Petr Václav, whose *Marian* won the Silver Leopard at Locarno a while ago, is making *Parallel Worlds* (*Paralelní Světy*). Film editor Andrea Sedlácková is to make her feature film directing debut; for *Victims and Murderers* (*Oběti a vrahy*), she has cast major Czech stars Ivana Chylková and Karel Roden.

EVA ZAORALOVÁ is a Czech film critic and editor of the magazine *Film a doba*. The author of many essays and books on Italian, French and Czech cinema, she taught film history for ten years at FAMU in Prague, and is artistic director of the Karlovy Vary International Film Festival.

# Recent and Forthcoming Films

### ELIŠKA MÁ RÁDA DIVOČINU (Eliška Likes It Wild)

Script and Dir: Otakáro Schmidt. Phot: Martin Štrba. Players: Bolek Polívka, Zuzana Stivínová, Martin Dejdar, Veronika Žilková. Prod: M. D. M. Production/S Pro Alfa Film/Czech Television.

### ENE BENE (Ene Bene)

Script and Dir: Alice Nellis. Phot: Ramunas Breičius. Players: Iva Janžurová, Theodora Remundová, Leoš Suchařípa. Prod: Pozitiv s.r.o./ Czech Television.

### HANELE (Hanele)

Script: Jana Dudková, based on two novels by Ivan Olbracht. Dir: Karel Kachyňa. Phot: Petr Hojda. Players: Lada Jelínková, Miroslav Noga, Jiří Ornest, Táňa Fischerová. Prod: Czech Television.

*Still from* THE PILGRIMAGE OF STUDENTS PETER AND JACOB

## KANÁREK (Very Ordinary Person)

Script: Boris Hybner. Dir: Viktor Tauš. Phot: David Čálek. Players: Viktor Tauš, Milan Hlavsa, Vanda Hybnerová, František Černý. Prod: GagStones/Milk and Honey/Čzech Television.

## MUŚIME SI POMÁHAT (Divided We Fall)

Script: Petr Jarchovský. Dir: Jan Hřebejk. Phot: Jan Malíř. Players: Bolek Polívka, Anna Šišková, Jaroslav Dušek, Csongor Kassal. Prod: Total HelpArt/Czech Television.

## NÁVRAT ZTRACENÉHO RÁJE (Which Side Eden?)

Script and Dir: Vojtěch Jasný. Phot: Juraj Šajmovič. Players: Vladimír Pucholt, Ingrid Timková, Adam Davison, Jana Brejchová. Prod: Lumar Production l.t.d.

## PRAMEN ŽIVOTA (Spring of Life)

Script: Vladimír Körner. Dir: Milan Cieslar. Phot: Marek Jícha. Players: Monika Hilmerová, Michal Sieczkowski, Johanna Tesařová, Vilma Cibulková. Prod: Czech Television.

## SAMOTÁŘI (Loners)

Script: Petr Zelenka. Dir: David Ondříček. Phot: Richard Řericha. Players: Labina Mitevská, Jitka Schneiderová, Saša Rašilov, Jiří Macháček, Ivan Trojan, Miki Křen, Dana Sedláková. Prod: Lucky Man Films/Czech Television.

## TMAVOMODRÝ SVĚT (The Blue World)

Script: Zdeněk Svěrák. Dir: Jan Svěrák. Phot: Vladimír Smutný. Players: Ondřej Vetchý, Akryštof Hádek, Tara Fitzgerald. Prod: Tmavomodrý svět s.r.o./Helkon Media Filmproduktion g.m.b.h.

## ZPRÁVA O PUTOVÁNÍ STUDENTŮ PETRA A JAKUBA (The Pilgrimage of Students Petr and Jakub)

Script: Vladimír Vondra, Drahomíra Vihanová. Dir: Vihanová. Phot:: Juraj Šajmovič. Players: Andrej Jastraba, Gustav Řezníček, Zuzana Stivínová, Jolana Badžová. Prod: CINEART/Czech Television/Slovak Television.

## Producers

### Ateliéry Bonton Zlín
Filmová 174
761 79 Zlín

Tel: (420 6) 752 7200
Fax: (420 6) 752 7527

### Barrandov Biografia
(Also distributor)
Kříženeckého nám. 322
152 00 Praha 5
Tel: (420 2) 6707 1111
Fax: (420 2) 6707 2273

### BUC Film
Kříženeckého nám. 322
152 00 Praha 5
Tel: (420 2) 581 9441
Fax: (420 2) 6707 2125

### CINEART Productions
Vzdušná 817
140 00 praha 4
Tel: (420 2) 6171 1108
Fax: (420 2) 6171 1048

### Czech TV Productions
Kavčí hory
140 70 Praha 4
Tel: (420 2) 6121 2945
Fax: (420 2) 5121 1354

### NOVA TV
Vladislavova 20
110 00 Praha 1
Tel: (420 2) 2110 0113

### Febio Ltd.
Růžová 13
110 00 Praha 1
Tel: (420 2) 2421 3933
Fax: (420 2) 2421 4254

### NEGATIV
Švédská 21
150 00 Praha 5
Tel: (420 2) 5732 6042

### Space Films Ltd.
(also distributor)
Karlovo nám 19
120 00 Praha 2
Tel: (420 2) 2491 3043
Fax: (420 2) 2491 3045

### VaC – Vachler Art Company
Na Žertvách 40
180 00 Praha 8
Tel: (420 2) 683 2600

### Whisconti Prod.
Odborů 4
120 00 Praha 2
Tel/Fax: (420 2) 296 930

## Distributors

**Bonton Films**
Národní tř. 28
1120 00 Praha 1
Tel: (420 2) 2110 5248
Fax: (420 2) 2422 5263

**CINEMART a.s.**
Národní 28
110 00 Praha 1
Tel: (420 2) 2110 5235
Fax: (420 2) 2110 5220

**FALCON**
Stroupežnického 6
150 00 Praha 5
Tel: (420 2) 538 085
Fax: (420 2) 533 194

**Filmexport Prague**
Na Moráni 5
128 00 Praha 2
Tel: (420 2) 2491 5239
Fax: (420 2) 293 312

**Gemini Film**
V jámě 1
110 00 Praha 1
Tel: (420 2) 2416 2471
Fax: (420 2) 2422 6562

**Intersonic Taunus Prod. Ltd**
Palackého 15
110 00 Praha 1
Tel/Fax: (420 2) 2422 9007

## Useful Addresses

**Ministry of Culture**
Milady Horákové 139
160 00 Praha 6
Tel: (420 2) 5708 5111
Fax: (420 2) 2431 8155

**FITES (Association of
Czech Film Artists)**
Pod Nuselskými schody 3
120 00 Praha 2
Tel: (420 2) 691 0310
Fax: (420 2) 691 1375

**Union of Czech Distributors**
U Rajské zahrady 14
130 00 Praha 3
Tel: (420 2) 9000 2651

**Association of Producers in
the Audiovisual Industry
c/o SPACE Film**
Karlovo nám. 19
120 00 Praha 2
Tel: (420 2) 2491 3043

# DENMARK — Ebbe Iversen

For Danish cinema, the highlight of 1999-2000 occurred in May, when Lars von Trier was awarded the Palme D'Or in Cannes for his **Dancer in the Dark**, which also secured the Best Actress award for Icelandic singer Björk. This was the third such success for a Danish director, with von Trier following Bille August, who received the award in 1987 for *Pelle the Conqueror* and in 1992 for *Best Intentions*.

It was the fourth time that von Trier had been honoured in Cannes, previously having been awarded the Technical Prize in 1984 for *The Element of Crime*, the Jury Special Prize in 1991 for *Zentropa* and the Grand Prix in 1996 for *Breaking the Waves*; *The Idiots*, in competition in 1998, failed to win anything.

*Dancer in the Dark* got a very mixed reception in Cannes, being lauded by the French critics in particular, whereas the British and Americans generally had strong objections. Crafted as a musical – but shot on video, frequently with a hand-held camera, as in the Dogme films – it is set in the United States in the early 1960s and tells the very emotional, ultimately tragic story of a Czech immigrant, Selma (Björk), who, while gradually going blind, toils in a factory to raise money for a costly operation to prevent her young son from losing his sight.

With a budget of approximately $13m and an international cast including France's Catherine Deneuve, America's David Morse and Sweden's Peter Stormare, *Dancer in the Dark* is thematically close to *Breaking the Waves*: here is another story of a simple woman elevated to martyrdom

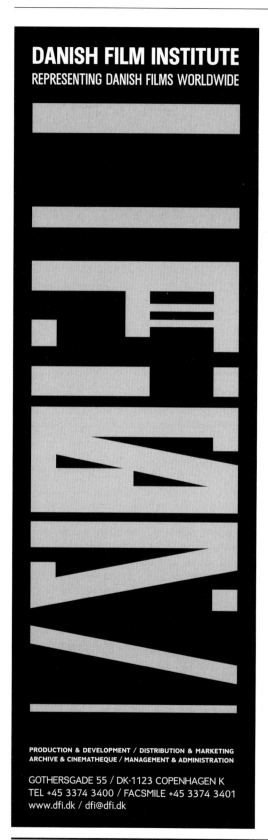

and almost sainthood by sacrificing herself. After the much-publicised conflicts between von Trier and Björk during shooting, the Cannes success was a new triumph for von Trier and producer Peter Aalbæk Jensen's Zentropa Entertainments. Zentropa is by far the most active production company in Denmark, operating through an intricate network of about 60 sub-companies in order to prevent the entire, financially rather fragile structure from collapsing, should one of the sub-companies be declared bankrupt.

Danish films also given their world premieres in Cannes in 2000 included Per Fly's **The Bench** (*Bænken*), a gritty drama about a middle-aged alcoholic on the slide, and Stefan Fjeldmark and Michael Hegner's ambitious **Help! I'm a Fish** (*Hjælp! Jeg er en fisk*), an animated family feature made on a technical level which compares favourably with Disney productions, and which should secure a solid international success.

### Dogme does Shakespeare

The fourth official Danish Dogme film, Kristian Levring's **The King Is Alive**, also premiered at Cannes. Shot in Namibia, it tells the harrowing story of a dozen European and American travellers stranded in a desert, where they attempt to perform *King Lear* while awaiting an unlikely rescue. The strong cast of this visually very powerful film includes Jennifer Jason Leigh, Janet McTeer and Bruce Davison.

Outside Denmark, five films bearing the official Dogme certificate had been produced by mid 2000, including Harmony Korine's rather weird American contribution, *Julien: Donkey-Boy*, which was presented at the 1999 Venice Film Festival. Four new Danish Dogme films are in production or pre-production, directed by Lone Scherfig, Henrik Ruben Genz, Ole Christian Madsen and Åke Sandgren. Sandgren's latest film, **Beyond** (*Dykkerne*), had its world premiere in Cannes, but its occult story for young audiences about teenagers exploring a sunken Nazi submarine full of ghosts, hardly caused a stir.

*Björk, centre, in Lars von Trier's DANCER IN THE DARK*

## Disappointments and rancour

The first half of 2000, however, saw a number of disappointments, although Kaspar Rostrup's **A Place Nearby** (*Her i nærheden*) was well-received as a tense psychological drama about the strained relationship between a protective mother and her autistic son, who is suspected of murder. First time director Trine Piil Christensen misfired with the incoherent crime drama **Rent a Family** (*Max*); Aage Rais made the ambitious, but dramatically uneven **Foreign Fields** (*På fremmed mark*), about wealthy tourists using the civil war in Bosnia as a playground for murderous manhunting, and in **The Lady of Hamre** (*Fruen på Hamre*) Katrine Wiedemann tried to bring tough violent realism to a simple novel by popular Danish writer Morten Korch. The result was an artistic and commercial disaster.

The Danish Film Institute (DFI), whose public funds are used to help finance almost every Danish feature, has a normal annual budget of around $35m, but for 2000 parliament granted an extra $14m, and $21m for both 2001 and 2002. The goal is to increase annual feature production from around 15 to 25 titles, but a new conflict has arisen in 2000, as a growing number of talented younger directors want to shoot their films in English and outside Denmark.

Thomas Vinterberg and Ole Bornedal

(*Night Watch*) have both been partially refused financial support from DFI as the institute does not consider their planned international co-productions to be basically Danish films; Bornedal had already secured support from the Swedish and Norwegian film institutes for his *Dina's Book*, based on a Norwegian novel.

The DFI's stance is in accordance with the film law, but it has prompted a debate in parliament, as most politicians are eager to support domestic film production. Suggestions have been put forward that financial support should not be channelled entirely through the Ministry of Culture, but also through the Ministry of Trade. The establishment of regional film funds has been proposed, as has a law to refund 50% of losses suffered by private investors in unsuccessful film productions.

Internationally, Danish films are doing

*Still from Åke Sandgren's BEYOND*
*photo: Henrik Ploug*

well, especially the Dogme instalments. *The Idiots* has been sold to 57 countries, Søren Kragh-Jacobsen's *Mifune* to 46 and Thomas Vinterberg's *The Celebration* to 40. At the domestic cinemas 1999 was an exceptionally good year for Danish films, which achieved a market share of 27% – almost twice that of 1998 and the best result since 1978.

Optimism prevails in the cinema business, and at least two new multiplexes, built by Germany's CinemaxX, were scheduled to open in Denmark in the autumn of 2000, one in Odense with seven screens, the other in Copenhagen, offering ten screens and 3,200 seats, making it the largest multiplex in Scandinavia.

Another conflict arose between film companies and the two national broadcasters, Danmarks Radio and TV 2, who, according to a new law, must invest approximately $5m annually in film production, but frequently choose to spend the money on films and series produced directly for television rather than feature films. Film companies have been demanding larger investments in features, but when this article went to press the conflict remained unresolved.

### News of the Oscar-winners

Among films currently in production, *Blinkende lygter* (no English title as yet) is eagerly awaited, as it is the first feature directed by the talented Anders Thomas Jensen, co-writer of *Mifune* and the 1999 Academy Award winner for Best Live Action Short, *Election Night*. Veteran director Gabriel Axel, Oscar-winner for *Babette's Feast*, has boldly shot his romantic love story *Laila the Pure* (*Laila den Rene*) in Morocco, without any dialogue, and Jan Jung, whose first film was the American-Russian co-production *Three Days in August*, has based his *Hannah Wolfe* on English novelist Sarah Dunant's detective novel *Under My Skin*.

Tomas Gislason, who has directed a number of interesting documentaries, shot his road movie *Like a Rock* in the US; horror

*Still from* THE LADY OF HAMRE

*photo: Per Folker*

expert Martin Schmidt has directed the supernatural thriller *Cat* (*Kat*); talented provocateur Søren Fauli's *Count Axel* (*Grev Axel*) is scripted by Anders Thomas Jensen and will be a satirical period drama; veteran actor Erik Wedersøe bows as director with *Anna*, based on a novel by prominent author Klaus Rifbjerg and featuring Swedish star Pernilla August as the eponymous ambassador's wife who goes on the run through Europe with an escaped convict.

Bille August's next film, *A Song for Martin* (*En sang for Martin*), will be a Danish-Swedish co-production, an intimate psychological drama about a husband hit by Alzheimer's Disease, and finally Søren Kragh-Jacobsen is planning *Skagerrak*, featuring Iben Hjejle, who shot to fame in *Mifune* and was last seen in Stephen Frears' *High Fidelity*.

EBBE IVERSEN has been film critic of *Berlingske Tidende* since 1973. He is a former co-editor of the magazine *Kosmorama*.

## Producers

**ASA Film Production A/S**
Avedøre Tværvej 10
Bygn 76
DK-2650 Hvidovre
Tel: (45) 3686 8747
Fax (45) 3649 8747
e-mail: asa@film.dk

**Bech Film ApS**
Langebrogade 6, J.4
DK-1411 København K.
Tel: (45) 3295 7111
Fax: (45) 3295 7112
e-mail: bechfilm@bechfilm.dk

**Buxton Ravn Production ApS**
Avedøre Tværvej 10
DK-2650 Hvidovre
Tel: (45) 3634 1212
Fax: (45) 3634 1717
e-mail: buxton@post2.tele.dk

**Crone Film Produktion A/S**
Blomstervænget 52
DK-2800 Lyngby
Tel: (45) 4587 2700
Fax: (45) 4587 2705

**Danish Film Studio**
Blomstervænget 52
DK-2800 Lyngby
Tel: (45) 4587 2700
Fax: (45) 4587 2705
e-mail: ddf@filmstudie.dk

**Grasten Filmproduktion ApS**
Lykkevej 6
DK-2920 Charlottenlund
Tel: (45) 3963 4424
Fax: (45) 3963 4192

**Holst Film A/S, Per**
Mosedalvej 14
DK-2500 Valby
Tel: (45) 3618 8666
Fax: (45) 3618 8655
e-mail: phf@hf.dk

**M&M Productions**
Blomstervænget 52
DK-2800 Lyngby
Tel: (45) 7020 3080
Fax: (45) 7020 3081
e-mail: mail@mmproductions.dk

**Magic Hour Films ApS**
Blomstervænget 52
DK-2800 Lyngby
Tel: (45) 4587 2700
Fax: (45) 4587 2705
e-mail: post@magic-hour-films.dk

**Metronome Productions A/S**
Jenagade 22
DK-2300 København S.
Tel: (45) 3264 6565
Fax: (45) 3264 6666

*Sidse Babette Knudsen in RENT A FAMILY*

**Nimbus Film Productions ApS**
Box 518, Avedøre Tværvej 10
DK-2650 Hvidovre
Tel: (45) 3634 0910
Fax: (45) 3634 0911
e-mail: nimbus@nimbusfilm.dk

**Nordisk Film A/S**
Mosedalvej 14
DK-2500 Valby
Tel: (45) 3618 8200
Fax: (45) 3616 8502
e-mail: production@nordiskfilm.dk

**Thura Film A/S**
Indiakaj 12
DK-2100 København Ø.
Tel: (45) 3544 1111
Fax: (45) 3543 4015
e-mail: thura@thura.com

**Zentropa Productions ApS**
Avedøre Tværvej 10
DK-2650 Hvidovre
Tel: (45) 3678 0055
Fax: (45) 3678 0077
e-mail: zentropa@zentropa-film.com

# Distributors

**All Right Film A/S**
Indiakaj 12
DK-2100 København Ø.
Tel: (45) 7026 7626
Fax: (45) 7026 7627

**Angel Film A/S**
Stockholmsgade 43
DK-2100 København Ø.
Tel: (45) 3525 3600
Fax: (45) 3525 3610
e-mail: info@angelfilms.dk

**Buena Vista International (Denmark) A/S**
Østergade 26 AB, 3.
DK-1100 København K.
Tel: (45) 3312 0800
Fax: (45) 3312 4332
e-mail:
erik_hamre@studio.disney.com

**Camera Film**
Mikkel Bryggers Gade 8
DK-1460 København K.
Tel: (45) 3313 6112
Fax: (45) 3315 0882
e-mail: camerafilm@grandteatret.dk

**Constantin Film**
Halmtorvet 29
DK-1700 København V.
Tel: (45) 3326 6868
Fax: (45) 3326 6859

**Gloria Film**
Rådhuspladsen 59
DK-1550 København V.
Tel: (45) 3312 8232
Fax: (45) 3312 0632

**Nordisk Film Biografdistribution A/S**
Halmtorvet 29
DK-1700 København V.
Tel: (45) 3326 6860
Fax: (45) 3326 6869

**Sandrew Metronome**

**Filmdistribution A/S**
Søndermarksvej 16
DK-2500 Valby
Tel. (45) 3515 9500
Fax: (45) 3615 9525
e-mail: filmdistribution@dk.
sandrewmetro

**SF Film**
Indiakaj 12
DK-2100 København Ø.
Tel: (45) 7026 7626
Fax: (45) 7026 7627
e-mail: sf-film@sf-film.dk

**United International Pictures**
Hauchsvej 13
DK-1825 Frederiksberg C.
Tel: (45) 3331 2330
Fax: (45) 3323 3420

**Zentropa PR**
Avedøre Tværvej 10
DK-2650 Hvidovre
Tel: (45) 3686 8777
Fax. (45) 3686 8789
e-mail: pr@zentropa-film.com

## Useful Addresses

**Danish Film Institute**
Gothersgade 55
DK-1123 København K.
Tel: (45) 3374 3400
Fax. (45) 3374 3401

**Danish Film Institute Workshop**
Gothersgade 55
DK-1123 København K.
Tel: (45) 3374 3480
Fax: (45) 3374 3490
e-mail: workshop@df.dk

**The Danish Film School**
Theodor Christensens Plads 1
DK-1437 København K.
Tel: (45) 3268 6400
Fax. (45) 3268 6410
e-mail: info@filmskolen.dk

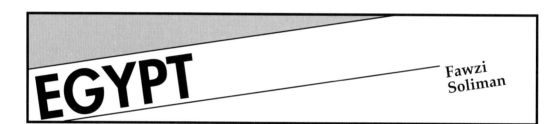

# EGYPT

Fawzi
Soliman

For the first time in Egyptian history, the top nine films in the box-office chart for 1999 were Egyptian, despite wide distribution of the latest Hollywood releases. A new trend saw producers and distributors reap quick profits from the stardom of comedians. After his massive hit, *An Upper Egyptian at AUC* (see *IFG* 2000), Mohamed Heneidy followed up with another success, **Hammam in Amsterdam** (*Hammam Fi Amsterdam*). Directed once again by Said Hamed, the movie is about young Egyptian immigrants in the Netherlands, overcoming various challenges. It became the year's most successful film.

Alaa Wali Eldin, another comic actor, had his first lead role, as a fat army recruit in **Aboud at the Borders** (*Aboud Ala El-houdod*), directed by Sherif Arafa, the number two film on the chart. Aboud's exhausting training and his exploits as a border guard, protecting Egypt from enemies and drug smugglers, arouse plenty of light-hearted laughs.

The third comedian with a hit this past year was Ashraf Abdel Baqui, in the musical comedy **The Cutest Guy in Roxy** (*Ashyak Wad Fi Roxy*). Adel Imam, the celebrated comedian, returned to the screen and had a more modest success with a satire on the American dream, **Hello America**. Directed by Nader Galal, it shows immigrants confronting the fragility of this dream in an increasingly violent and immoral society.

Radwan El Kashef's marvellous portrait of daily life in a village in southern Egypt, *Date Wine* (*Araak El-Balah*; see *IFG* 2000), has now received 22 awards at international and local festivals. **Land of Fear** (*Ard El-Khouf*), written and directed by Daoud Abdel-Sayed, won the Silver Pyramid Award at the 1999 Cairo International Film Festival. The movie brilliantly merges reality and metaphysics and offers a wonderful portrayal of Islamic Cairo (great credit is due to set designer Onsy Abu Seif), as well as mystic music from Rageh Dawoud, to whom the film is dedicated.

*Still from Ossama Fawzi's FALLEN ANGELS'*
*PARADISE*

*Still from Atef Hatata's THE CLOSED DOORS*

Ossama Fawzi's second film, **Fallen Angels' Paradise** (*Gannet Al Shayatin*), was freely adapted by Mostafa Zikry from Brazilian writer Jorge Amado's novel *The Man Who Died Twice*, and ironically tackles the issue of death, treating it as a philosophical notion within a story whose characters are all driven by their instincts. The film won major awards at the Alexandria and Damascus film festivals.

## New arrivals

In 1999-2000 several directors made promising debuts. Karim Gamal El-Din, who studied film-making in the US, directed **Hasan and Aziza** (*Hasan Wa Aziza-Amn Dawla*), a political comedy blending satirical reality with farcical fantasia. It mocks the state security service and the police and in its second half turns into an action movie. Sameh El Bagoury's musical drama **After Shocks** (*Koursy Fi El Kolob*) impressively recreates Egypt's October 1992 earthquake, and reveals how that disaster devastated souls as well as buildings. El Bagoury is a gifted director who successfully sustains a comic thread, despite the movie's grim theme.

After making several excellent shorts, Atef Hatata won Best Film at the first Bahrain film festival with **The Closed Doors** (*El Abwab El Moghlaka*), set against the backdrop of the Gulf War and tackling the issue of teenagers who fall prey to fundamentalists. Its hero is a teenager seeking salvation and struggling to come to terms with schisms in the Egyptian and Arab character.

With a lot of brilliant documentaries to his credit, Mohamed Shaaban made his first fiction feature, **Honour** (*El Sharaf*), which brilliantly dramatises the impact of the Six-Day War in 1967, as residents of the ruined Suez Canal towns were forced to migrate. The heroine is forced to give up all hope of love and she marries an elderly butcher.

Ahmad Atef, a film critic who has directed several shorts, made his feature debut with **Omar Alfeen** (*Omar 2000*). Khaled Youssef, who has co-written several of Youssef Chahine's movies, has also directed his first film, **The Storm** (*El Asefa*). Both Atef and Youssef try to trace the effect of domestic and international events on Egyptian youth. Yousry Nasallah won three awards at Locarno with his third film, **The Town** (*El Madina*). Shot on video and digitally enlarged to 35mm, its hero is a young man who abandons his family to pursue an acting career in Paris, where he encounters many frustrating obstacles.

Contemporary social issues always arouse directors' interests and **Forbidden Talk** (*Kalam Fi El Mamnou*) is a case in point. Directed by Omar Abdel Aziz, it discusses social corruption and stresses the unity of Muslims and Copts. The always daring Inas El Degheidy also tackles social corruption in her film about physical, moral and political prostitution, **Kalam El Leil** (literally, *Night Revelations*), which contains some steamy scenes and was originally entitled *Nudity* – until the censors insisted on a change.

Mohamed Abou Seif stressed the positive relations between teachers and pupils in **First Grade** (Oula Thanawy). One of the year's flops was **Star of the Orient** (*Kawkab El Shark*), directed by Mohamed Fadel, about the life of Arabic singing diva Oum Koulthom.

FAWZI SOLIMAN is a film journalist and critic who has contributed to magazines and newspapers in Egypt and the Arab world. He has served on the FIPRESCI jury at many film festivals.

*Still from Mohammed Abou Seif's FIRST GRADE*

# Recent and Forthcoming Films

**GANNET AL-SHAYATIN (Fallen Angels' Paradise)**

Script: Mostafa Zekri, inspired by George Amado's novel. Dir: Ossama Fawzi. Phot: Tarek El-Telmessany. Players: Lebleba, Mahomoud Hemeda, Caroline Khalil, Amr Waked, Salah Fahmi. Prod: Al-Batrik Art Production.

**OULA THANAWI (First Grade)**

Script: Ashraf Mohamed. Dir: Mohamed Abu Seif. Phot: Kamal Abdel Aziz. Players: Nour El-Sherif, Nervet Amin, Maher Essam. Prod: Shoa.

**EL SHARAF (Honour)**

Script: Mustafa Moharam. Dir: Mohamed Shaaban. Phot: Maher Radi. Players: Farouk El-Feshaui, Gihan Fadel, Magda Zaki. Prod: Shoa.

**AL-ABWAB AL MOGHLAKA (The Closed Doors)**

Script and Dir: Atem Hatata. Phot: Samir Bahzan. Players: Sawsan Badr, Ahmed Azmi, Mahmoud Heeida. Prod: Misr. International (Cairo)/Mediae Prod. (Paris).

**KORSI FI EL CLOB-TAWABEI (After Shocks)**

Script: Hani Fawzi. Dir: Sameh El-Bagouri. Phot: Samir Bahzan. Players: Lucy, Salah Abdallah, Medhat Saleh. Prod: El-Sultan Film.

**HASSAN & AZIZA AMN DAWLA (Hassan and Aziza)**

Script: Mostafa Mohamarm. Dir: Karim Gamal El-Din. Phot: Tarek El Telmessany. Players: Ashraf Abdel Baqui, Yousra, Magdi Kame. Prod: Elixir Aritistic Prod.

**EL-MEDINA (The Town)**

Script: Yousry Nasrallah, Nasser Abdel-Rahman and Claire Denis. Dir: Nasrallah. Phot: Samir Bahzan. Players: Bassam Samra, Abia Kamel, Ahmed Fouad Selim. Prod: Humbert Balsan (Paris)/ Misr International (Cairo).

**HAMMAM FI AMESTERDAM (Hammam in Amsterdam)**

Script: Mohamed El Adl. Dir: Saeed Hamed. Phot: Players: Mohamed Heneidi, Ahmed El-Sakka, Mona Liza. Prod: El-ADL Group.

**KALAM FI EL-MAMNOUE (Forbidden Talk)**

Script: Nagui George. Dir: Omar

Abdel Aziz. Phot: Samir Farag. Players: Nour El-Sherif, Maged El-Masri, Amina Rizk. Prod: Hani Fawzi.

**ANBAR WA ALWAN (Ambar and the Colours)**

Script: Summaya Eresha. Dir: Adel El-Aasar. Phot: Samir Farag. Players: Hussein Fahmy Maali Zayed, Mahmoud El-Headdiny.

# Producers/ Distributors

**Misr International**
35 Champolion St
Cairo
Tel: (20 2) 578 8124
Fax: (20 2) 578 8033

**SHOA's Cultural Media Arab Co.**
29 Yathreb St
Dokki
Cairo
Tel: (20 2) 336 9510
Fax: (20 2) 336 9511

**Egyptian Renaissance Co.**
11 Dr. Mohamed Mandour St
Rabaa El-Adawiya
Nasr City
Cairo
Tel: (20 2) 404 8869
Fax: (20 2) 404 8871

**Studio 13**
Soliman El-Halaby St
Cairo
Tel: (20 2) 574 8807
Fax: (20 2) 588 1406

**El-Sultan Film**
102 Al-Ahram Ave
Giza
Tel: (20 2) 304 7711
Fax: (20 2) 304 7744

**El-ADL Group**
3b – Soliman El-Halabi St
Cairo
Tel: (20 2) 574 8000
Fax: (20 2) 574 8100

**Al-Batrik Art Production and Cinema Services**
12 El-Ishaqi
Manshiyet Al-Bakri
Heliopolis
Cairo
Tel/Fax: (20 2) 452 9377

**Elixir Artistic Production & Distribution Co.**
13 El-Fardoos St

Agouza 12411
Cairo
Tel: (20 2) 349 9110 & 336 8697/8
Fax: (20 2) 335 3691

**Egyptian Radio & TV Union**
Kornish El-Nil
Maspero St
Cairo
Tel: (20 2) 576 0014 & 576 0058
Fax: (20 2) 579 9916

## Useful Addresses

**National Film Centre**
City of Arts
Al-Ahram Ave
Giza
Tel: (20 2) 585 4801
Fax: (20 2) 585 4701

**Cultural Development Fund**
Opera Gezira
Cairo
Tel: (20 2) 340 4234/7001
Fax: (20 2) 341 4634

**Chamber of Film Industry**
33 Oraby St
Cairo
Tel: (20 2) 574 1577
Fax: (20 2) 575 1583

**Alexandria International Film Festival**
Tel: (20 2) 574 1112
Fax: 578 376 727

**Cairo International Film Festival**
17 Kasr El-Nil St
Cairo
Tel: (20 2) 392 3562
Fax: (20 2) 393 8979

**Higher Film Institute**
Gamal El-Din El-Afaghani St
City of Arts
Pyramids Ave
Giza
Tel/Fax: (20 2) 586 8203

**National Archive**
c/o National Film Centre
Tel: (20 2) 585 4807
Fax: (20 2) 585 4701

# ESTONIA
Jaan Ruus

These days, the chances of any Estonian feature breaking into the box-office Top Ten are almost nil. The last film to have major public appeal was *My Old Love Letters* (*Minu vanad armastuskirjad*), the box-office number one in the year 1992; at present domestic films reach an average attendance of just 5,000.

The upper bound of domestic production in the near future, according to a Ministry of Culture estimate, is 20 hours of film per year, but achieving this would require at least a doubling of today's subsidies. In 1999, state support for film-related activities remained at the 1998 level, $1.6m (24m kroon), of which the Estonian Film Foundation gave around two thirds. The state is virtually the sole sponsor of film production, since producers can find very little financial support elsewhere.

In the summer of 1999 the new minister of culture installed a new board for the Estonian Film Foundation, including several experienced producers. A course was set for producing three feature films per year – the same amount as during the Soviet era. Since the Estonian market is limited, international co-productions remain the only alternative, and the ministry has allocated about $170,000 to forging better international links. Appeals for support have been made to local business circles but film production is not commercially viable, not least because the dozens of local film studios are on difficult terms with the banks. The financial difficulties of the one public service and three private television channels make co-production with the small screen difficult.

## Collected stories

In 1999, five newcomers made their first features. Recent film graduates Jaak Kilmi, Rainer Sarnet and Peter Herzog created a dashing game in their anthology **Happy Landing** (*Kass kukub käppadele*). Its three segments are all grotesque and all feature young male protagonists. Kilmi places an innocent young adventurer with a suicide-bound religious sect. Sarnet creates a world of doppelgangers to explore people's secret desires. Herzog tells a story of a fatally hypnotic tape recording.

The second anthology, **Three Stories About...** (*Sellised kolm lugu*), features three contrasting tales: an anecdote about cannibalism in the desert, from newcomer Ervin Õunapuu; an encounter between a police officer and a group of Kurdish refugees on a tiny island, by Peeter Simm; a love story set in the Riga underworld, by Latvian newcomer Askolds Saulitis. The film again highlighted the importance of Estonian-Latvian co-production. *Good Hands*, scheduled for release in spring 2001, will, it is hoped, be another valuable co-production, the budget shared equally by Estonia and Latvia.

Based on a successful stage play, the full-length feature **The Highway Crossing** (*Ristumine peateega*), directed by young cameraman Arko Okk, is a modern fable

*Andrus Varrik in THE HIGHWAY CROSSING*

*Still from the Nabokov-inspired AN AFFAIR OF HONOUR*

about the power of money. A magical goldfish has brought the strange hero $4 billion, with which he intends to purchase love. This theatrical, suggestive story, which features three characters and is in some ways reminiscent of Roman Polanski's *Cul-de-Sac*, has successfully represented Estonia at several festivals (Stockholm, Montevideo, Hong Kong).

In the third feature of the year, Valentin Kuik's perceptively psychological **An Affair Of Honour** (*Lurjus*), based on a story by Vladimir Nabokov, a modern husband fights a duel to defend his wife's honour. Standing up for this 'old-fashioned' concept enables the young man to find himself, and regain his wife's love.

In addition, there were new shorts from several promising directors. Estonian documentary has completely converted from film to video and is enjoying a productive period. Its geographical sweep reaches from Paris and Los Angeles to Tonga, from Siberia to Tibet, however, the films' perceptions rarely go beyond the levels of daily journalism. Animators, on the other hand, have retained a high reputation on festivals and, in view of the increasing need to seek outside production finance, have set about making humorous cartoon series for European TV channels.

## Too much for too few

The average ticket price rose to $3.15 in 1999 and caught up with the price of theatre tickets, making Estonia the most expensive cinema market of the former Eastern bloc countries. Two thirds of the cinemagoers live in the capital Tallinn and here they have to pay at least $4.1 for an evening show. After the *Titanic* phenomenon in 1998 the yearly admission figure for 1999 was down, at 874,560 (0.6 tickets per capita) – the lowest on record. It's hardly surprising with such high prices and so few screens: with a population of 400,000, Tallinn has just three cinemas.

In May 1999, Finnkino Ltd, a subsidiary of the Finnish company Rautakirja Ltd, acquired 90 % of the local distribution company MPDE, which accounts for three quarters of the total gross. In May 2000, Finnkino laid a cornerstone in Tallinn for an $10m, 11-screen multiplex scheduled for completion by May 2001. Meanwhile, video rental is a developing business. While licensed distributors continually add classic titles to the newest releases, the police are conducting regular raids on market stalls run by bootleggers who illegally import videos from Finland.

JAAN RUUS is film critic for the biggest Estonian weekly, the Tallinn-based *Eesti Ekspress*, and President of Estonian FIPRESCI. He is a member of the Estonian Film Foundation's Commisssion of Experts.

# Recent and Forthcoming Films

**KARU SÜDA (The Heart of the Bear)**

Script: Nikolai Baturin, Arvo Iho, Arvo Valton, Rustam Ibragimbekov. Dir: Iho. Phot: Rein Kotov. Players: Rain Simmul, Lembit Ulfsak, Merle Palmiste, Arvo Kukumägi, Dinara Drukarova, Iliana Pavlova. Prod: Cumulus Project, Faama Film (Estonia)/Lenfilm (Russia)/Fama 92 (Czech Republic).

Romantic drama about the loves and adventures of a hunter searching for spiritual harmony in Siberia.

**HEAD KÄED (Good Hands)**

Script: Toomas Raudam, Peeter Simm. Dir: Simm. Prod: Allfilm (Estonia)/F.O.R.M.A. (Latvia).

Tragi-comic story of a professional thief forced to become a 'housewife'.

**AGENT SINIKAEL (Agent Blueneck)**

Script: Marko Raat, Ervin Ounapuu. Dir: Raat. Prod: Suhkur Film.

Drama following the exploits of a controversial agent for an economic espionage bureau.

**DOOMINO (Domino)**

Script: William Aldridge, Jüri Sillart, Graham Dallas, Tiina Lokk, Maria Avdjushko. Dir: Sillart. Prod: Allfilm (Estonia).

A thriller with some esoteric elements.

**FORCE MAJEURE**

Script: Priit Pärn. Dir: Rao Heidmets. Prod: Rao Heidmetsa Filmistuudio.

Black comedy based on cross-cultural conflicts.

**LEND (The Flight)**

Script: Indrek Ude, Toomas Muru, Toomas Sula. Prod: Nikodemus Film (Estonia)/The Coproduction Office (Germany).

A romantic comedy.

**RAHVUSPARK (National Park)**

Script: Priit Pärn. Dir: Hardi Volmer. Prod: Faama Film.

Science fiction vision of Estonia's near future.

**P'RANDAALUNE (Underground)**

Script: Rainer Sarnet, Taavi Eelmaa. Dir: Sarnet. Prod: Suhkur Film.

Dostoyevsky's novel, *Notes from the Underground*, adapted to present-day Estonia.

**JA SINU KÄTES ON PORGUTULI (And There is Hellfire in Your Hands)**

Script and Dir: Valentin Kuik. Phot: Rein Kotov. Prod: F-Seitse.

Drama about a man searching for the possibility of living by his own rules.

**SOO (Swamp)**

Script: Arvo Valton. Dir: Renita and Hannes Lintrop.

A French artist in Estonia meets a mysterious girl and a group of smugglers.

# Producers

**A Film**
Kaare 15
Tallinn 11618
Tel: (37 2) 670 6485
Fax: (37 2) 670 6433
E-mail: afilm@online.ee

**Acuba Film**
Soo 37-2
Tallinn 10414
Tel/Fax: (37 2) 660 4724
e-mail. acuba@acuba.ee

**Allfilm**
Saue 11
Tallinn 10612
Tel: (37 2) 672 9070
Fax: (37 2) 672 9071
e-mail: allfilm@allfilm.ee

**Cumulus Project**
Köleri 32-2
Tallinn 10150
Tel: (37 2) 601 5401
Fax: (37 2) 640 9181
e-mail: iho@ tpu.ee

**Eesti Joonisfilm**
Laulupeo 2
Tallinn 10121
Tel/Fax: (37 2) 601 0275
e-mail: joonis@delfi.ee

**EXITfilm**
Kaupmehe 6
Tallinn 10114
Tel: (37 2) 631 7995
Fax: (37 2) 660 4121
e-mail: exitfilm@ online.ee

**Faama Film**
Gonsiori 27
Tallinn 10147
Tel: (37 2) 646 2027
Fax: (37 2) 646 2028
e-mail: faama@ etv.ee
www.etv.ee/faama

**FilmiMAX [also distributor]**
Nafta 1
Tallinn 10152
Tel: (37 2) 662 3597
Fax: (37 2) 662 3598
e-mail: filmimax@ uninet.ee

**Freyja Film**
Regati 8
Tallinn 11911
Tel: (37 2) 648 8222
Fax: (37 2) 648 8223
e-mail: freyjafilm@hot.ee

**F-Seitse**
Narva mnt 63
Tallinn 10152
Tel: (37 2) 601 5983
Fax: (37 2) 601 5982
e-mail: fseitse@online.ee

**Gaviafilm**
Kivila 42-61
Tallinn 13814
Tel: (37 2) 523 2554
Fax: (37 2) 641 1629

**Kairiin**
Söpruse pst 175-53
Tallinn 13413
Tel/Fax: (37 2) 752 0182
e-mail: jyri.sillart@mail.ee

**Lege Artis Film**
Uus 3
Tallinn 10111
Tel: (37 2) 648 8013
Fax: (37 2) 648 8014
e-mail: lehtmets@ uninet.ee

**Myth Film**
Nafta 1
Tallinn 10152
Tel/Fax: (37 2) 662 3703
e-mail: karis@ online.ee

**Nikodemus Film**
Kaupmehe 6
Tallinn 10114
Tel: (37 2) 642 6682
Fax: (37 2) 642 6682
e-mail: niko@online.ee

**Nukufilm**
Kaupmehe 6
Tallinn 10114
Tel: (37 2) 660 4040
Fax: (37 2) 660 4040
e-mail: nukufilm@ online.ee

**ONfilm**
Lasnamäe 24-12
Tallinn 11413
Tel: (37 2) 621 5296
e-mail: kuik@online.ee

**Polarfilm**
Suur-Sojamäe 10
Tallinn 11415
Tel: (37 2) 638 1052
Fax: (37 2) 638 1052
e-mail: polarfilm@ anet.ee

**Profilm**
PO Box 3181
Tallinn 10505
Tel: (37 2) 505 6691
Fax: (37 2) 646 6249
e-mail: paasu@hot.ee

**Q-film**
Mäe talu
Neeme küla
Harju mk. 74203
Tel: (37 2) 608 3742
Fax: (37 2) 601 5982

**Raamat-film**
Tähe 5-3
Tallinn 11619
Tel: (37 2) 670 0778
Fax: (37 2) 670 0778

**Rao Heidmets Filmstudio**
Müürivahe 31-16
Tallinn 10140
Tel: (37 2) 646 4299
Fax: (37 2) 646 4299
e-mail: raoheidmets@ hotmail.com

**Weiko Saawa Film**
Nikolai 15-4
Pärnu 80011
Tel: (37 2) 443 0772
Fax: (37 2) 443 0774
e-mail: docfest@chaplin.ee

# Distributors

**BDG**
Vana-Posti 8
Tallinn 10146
Tel: (37 2) 627 4770
Fax: (37 2) 631 3023
e-mail: bdg@bdg.ee

**MPDE**
Pärnu mnt 45
Tallinn 10119
Tel: (37 2) 631 4546
Fax: (37 2) 631 3671
e-mail: info@ kosmos.ee

# Useful Address

**Estonian Film Foundation**
Harju 9
Tallinn 10146
Tel: (37 2) 641 1120
Fax: (37 2) 644 2356
e-mail: film@ efsa.ee

# FINLAND

Antti
Selkokari

Finnish films enjoyed a long-awaited triumph in 1999. With a 25% market share, domestic features dominated the box-office to such an extent that even *The Phantom Menace* was in trouble. Finnish cinemas had not seen a rush like this since the heydays of the 1950s. Seven million admissions in 1999 was a record-breaking figure (up from 6.4 million in 1998), and 1.8 million of these were for local films.

The biggest hit was Olli Saarela's Second World War drama **The Ambush** (*Rukajärven tie*), with 426,000 admissions. The film appealed strongly to two distinct audiences: the veterans who for the first time were able to see images of their own combat hell depicted on screen, and younger cinemagoers, who were fascinated to see, as it were, their fathers and grandfathers fighting a war they had only heard stories about.

The romance of a young lieutenant (Peter Franzé) and his fiancée (Irina Björklund) helped to get the film through with the popcorn-consuming crowd. Impressively shot by Kjell Lagerroos, *The Ambush* also generated widespread discussion of the mental and physical scars left by the war.

A different take on the war was seen in Taru Mäkelä's **Little Sister** (*Pikkusisar*) which concentrated on women contributing to the war effort on the home front. Widowed by the Germans, Katri (Vera Kiiskinen) becomes a volunteer nurse to overcome her grief at losing a husband she never really got to know. At the hospital, Katri meets Arvo (Kai Lehtinen), a lumberjack who claims to have seen Katri in his dreams. This develops into a love triangle between Katri, Arvo and Eero (Tarmo Ruubel), Katri's childhood friend, who is sending her shy love letters from the front, and Katri cannot choose between

*Still from SEVEN SONGS FROM THE TUNDRA, which won the Nordic Amanda at Haugesund as Best Nordic Film of the Year*

the two.

This character-driven film, solidly performed and strong on repressed emotions, elegantly avoids the twin traps of cheap sentimentality and melodramatic nostalgia. Lehtinen's performance as the lumberjack was a breakthrough for this talented actor, whose rugged good looks should guarantee him a successful career; expect him to secure some 'lovable crook' roles.

Another war film with women taking the lead was Lauri Törhönen's **Abandoned Houses** (*Hylätyt talot autiot pihat*), about women in the town of Vyborg, looking after their families as Russian troops draw near. It bombed critically, but proved a hit with local audiences, attracting 180,000 spectators. Over-designed and poorly-directed, it tried hard to depict the panic in a town surrounded by enemy troops, and left you feeling as though you had merely skim-read the novel on which it was based.

## Tales of country and city

A strong tradition in Finnish film and literature has been rural drama, and one of the most popular settings for both has been

*Still from Lauri Törhönen's ABANDONED HOUSES*

Pohjanmaa (Ostrobothnia), a province known for its stubborn, violence-prone men. Their mentality was superbly captured in Aleksi Mäkelä's 1998 film *Tough Ones* (*Häjyt*; reviewed in *IFG* 2000). Longing for Ostrobothnia also fuels the fiction of Antti Tuuri, who helped adapt his novel into the screenplay for Ilkka Vanne's **Return to Plainlands** (*Lakeuden kutsu*). This is the story of a tax evader, Erkki (Kari Väänänen), who returns from Florida having become a millionaire as a used car salesman.

He is set to buy a metal workshop which would guarantee him the social status he needs to win back the heart of his estranged wife, Kaisu (Mari Rantasila). The film revels in home-grown fetishism (the names of particular places and neighbourhoods are repeated like mantras), and should ring a bell in the heart of anyone familiar with slow Finnish utterances. Lukewarm colour tones make the film a pleasure to watch.

Amidst the rural and war dramas, the debut of Esa Illi, **Monkey Business** (*Apinajuttu*), felt like a gust of hot, urban air. The story - a circle of friends gather for the wedding of one of their number - may not sound terribly original, but Illi handles it with precision, and devotion to his characters: thirtysomethings on the brink of making serious commitments.

Illi has studied directing under the tutelage of Actors Studio disciple Judith Weston, and it shows, because he perfectly captures tiny moments when nothing is really said. Just 55 minutes long, *Monkey Business* was Illi's breakthrough at the Tampere short film festival, and won the coveted Risto Jarva prize, the most prestigious film award in Finland

ANTTI SELKOKARI is a freelance film critic, based in Helsinki, and the president of the Finnish section of FIPRESCI.

# Recent and Forthcoming Films

### RUKAJÄRVEN TIE (Ambush)

Script: Antti Tuuri. Dir: Olli Saarela. Phot: Kjell Lagerroos. Players: Peter Franzén, Irina Björklund, Kari Heiskanen, Taisto Reimaluoto. Prod: Matila & Röhr MR Productions.

### APINAJUTTU (Monkey Business)

Script and Dir: Esa Illi. Phot: Pentti Keskimäki. Players: Ville Virtanen, Miia Lindström, Max Bremer, Niklas Häggblom. Prod: Kinotar Oy.

### PELON MAANTIEDE (Geography of Fear)

Script and Dir: Auli Mantila. Phot: Heikki Färm. Players: Tanjalotta Räikkä, Leea Klemola, Pertti Sveholm. Prod: Blind Spot Pictures Oy.

### HIGHWAY SOCIETY

Script: Paul Charles Bailly, Mika Kaurismäki. Dir: Kaurismäki. Phot: Timo Salminen. Players: Gitta Uhlig. Prod: Marianna Films/Mariette Rissenbeek Filmproduktion.

### PIKKUSISAR (Little Sister)

Script: Raija Talvio. Dir: Taru Mäkelä. Phot: Jouko Seppälä. Players: Vera Kiiskinen, Kai Lehtinen, Tarmo Ruubel, Seela Sella, Pirkko Hämäläinen, Anna-Lena Sipilä. Prod: Kinotar Oy.

### LEVOTTOMAT (The Restless)

Script: Aleksi Bardy. Dir: Aku Louhimies. Phot: Mac Ahlberg. Players: Mikko Nousiainen, Petteri Summanen, Valtteri Roiha, Laura Malmivaara, Irina Björklund, Matleena Kuusniemi. Prod: Solar Films Oy.

### LAKEUDEN KUTSU (Return to Plainlands)

Script: Antti Tuuri, Ilkka Vanne, based on Tuuri's novel. Dir:

Vanne. Phot: Olli Varja. Players: Kari Väänänen, Mari Rantasila, Martti Suosalo. Prod: Matila & Röhr Productions Oy.

### SEITSEMÄN LAULUA TUNDRALTA (Seven Songs from the Tundra)

Script: Anastasia Lapsui. Dir: Lapsui, Markku Lehmuskallio. Phot: Johannes Lehmuskallio. Players: Vitalina Hudi, Hatjako Yzangi, Nadeshda Horotetto. Prod: Jörn Donner Productions Oy.

### RAKKAUDELLA, MAIRE (Kiss Me in the Rain)

Script: Antti Karumo. Dir: Veikko Aaltonen. Phot: Pekka Uotila. Players: Eeva Litmanen, Esko Salminen, Matti Onnismaa, Minna Haapkylä. Prod: Kinotar.

### HÄJYT (Tough Ones)

Script: Aleksi Bardy. Dir: Aleksi Mäkelä. Players: Samuli Edelman, Teemu Lehtilä, Juha Veijonen, Kalevi Haapoja. Prod: Solar Films.

### ROLLING STONE ALEKSIS KIVEN ELÄMÄ (Rolling Stone)

Script and Dir: Jari Halonen. Players: Marko Tiusanen, Karoliina Kudjoi, Margit Lindeman, Helge Herala, Gustav Wiklund, Jari Salmi, Hannu Huuska. Prod: Halonen, Heikki Ahonius/Blacksmith Callahan's Filmworld.

### BADDING

Script: Heikki Metsämäki, Markku Pölönen. Dir: Pölönen. Phot: Kari Sohlberg. Players: Janne Reinikainen, Peter Franzén, Karoliina Blackburn. Prod: Fennada-Filmi Oy.

### CYCLOMANIA (Cyclomania)

Script and Dir: Simo Halinen. Phot: Pentti Keskimäki. Players:

Lauri Nurkse, Elena Leeve, Tommi Mujunen. Prod: Blind Spot Pictures Oy.

### LÄHIÖSATU (A Suburban Saga)

Script: Esko Salervo, Sakari Kirjavainen. Dir: Kirjavainen. Phot: Petri Rossi. Players: Antti Litja, Taisto Reimaluoto, Anna-Maija Valonen, Elena Leeve., Alain Azerot. Prod: Kinotar Oy.

### UMUR

Script: Kai Lehtinen, Petter Sairanen. Dir: Lehtinen. Players: Minna Turunen, Heikki Turunen. Prod: Fantasiafilmi Oy.

# Producers

**Artista Filmi Oy**
Friitalantie 11
FIN 28400 Ulvila
Tel: (358 2) 538 3665
Fax: (358 2) 538 3663
e-mail: artista@pekko.com

**Blind Spot Pictures Oy**
Merimiehenkatu 27
FIN 00150 Helsinki
Tel: (358 9) 622 2144
Fax: (358 9) 622 2307
e-mail: tero@blindspot.fi

**Dada-Filmi Oy/Fennada-filmi Oy**
Kolmas linja 5
FIN 00530 Helsinki
Tel: (358 9) 774 4780
Fax: (358 9) 730 734
e-mail: kari.sara@dada.pp. fi

**Ere Kokkonen Oy**
Viertolantie 7 B
FIN 01800 Klaukkala
Tel: (358 400) 416 730
Fax: (358 9) 2709 0535

**Fantasiafilmi Oy**
Tallberginkatu 1 A 141
FIN 00180 Helsinki
Tel: (358 9) 540 7850
Fax: (358 9) 5407 8530
e-mail: fantasiadilm@netlife. fi

**Filmikonttori/Wildcat Productions Oy**
Katajanokan laituri 11 B, K 13
FIN 00160 Helsinki
Tel: (358 9) 658 799
Fax: (358 9) 658 414
e-mail: filmikonttori@co.inet.fi

**GNUfilms Oy**
Aleksis Kiven katu 26 C
FIN 00500 Helsinki
Tel: (358 9) 726 1525
Fax: (358 9) 726 1536
e-mail: gnu@gnufilms.fi

**Illume Ltd. Oy**
Palkkatilankatu 7
FIN 00240 Helsinki
Tel: (358 9) 148 1489
Fax: (358 9) 148 148
e-mail: Illume@illume.fi

**Juniper Films Oy**
Työpajakatu 6 A
FIN 00580 Helsinki
Tel: (358 9) 774 0660
Fax: (358 9) 7740 6640
e-mail: outi.limnell@juniperfilms.fi

**Jörn Donner Productions Oy**
Pohjoisranta 12
FIN 00170 Helsinki
Tel: (358 9) 135 6060
Fax: (358 9) 135 7568

**Kinofinlandia Oy**
Maneesikatu 1-3 J
FIN 00170 Helsinki
Tel: (358 9) 278 1783
Fax: (358 9) 278 1763

**Kinoproduction Oy**
Katajanokankatu 6
FIN 00160 Helsinki
Tel: (358 9) 663 217
Fax: (358 9) 662 048
e-mail:
kinoproduction@kinoproduction.fi

**Kinotar Oy/For Real Productions Oy**
Meritullinkatu 33 E
FIN 00170 Helsinki
Tel: (358 9) 135 1864
Fax: (358 9) 135 7864
e-mail: kinotar@kinotar.com

**Kristallisilmä Oy/Crystal Eye Ltd**
Tallberginkatu 1/44

*Still from Aku Louhimies' THE RESTLESS*

FIN 00180 Helsinki
Tel: (358 9) 694 2308
Fax: (358 9) 694 7224
e-mail: pohjola@crystaleye.fi

**Lasihelmi Filmi Oy**
Päijänteentie 39-41
FIN 00510 Helsinki
Tel: (358 9) 774 830
Fax: (358 9) 7742 8350
e-mail: byro@lasihelmi.fi

**Lumifilm Oy**
Vuorimiehenkatu 10 E
FIN 00100 Helsinki
Tel: (358 9) 622 5882
Fax: (358 9) 622 5886
e-mail: hemila@lumifilm.fi

**Mandart Entertainment**
Kalevankatu 28 A 3
FIN 00100 Helsinki
Tel: (358 9) 694 3142
Fax: (358 9) 694 3136
e-mail: mandart@kolumbus.fi

**Mandrake Productions Oy**
Tehtaankatu 29 A, 8 krs
FIN 00150 Helsinki
Tel: (358 9) 6689 360
Fax: (358 9) 6689 3616
e-mail: jan@mandrake.fi

**Marianna Films Oy**
Pursimiehenkatu 25
FIN 00150 Helsinki
Tel: (358 9) 622 1811
Fax: (358 9) 622 3855
e-mail: mika@marfilm.fi

**Millennium Film Oy**
Maneesikatu 1-3 J
FIN 00170 Helsinki
Tel: (358 9) 686 0466
Fax: (358 9) 6860 4660
e-mail:
millennium@millenniumfilm.fi

**MRP Matila &Röhr Productions Oy**
Tallbrginkatu 1 A 141
FIN 00180 Helsinki
Tel: (358 9) 685 2227
Fax: (358 9) 685 2229
e-mail: mrp@surfnet.fi

**Perfecto Films Oy**
Vallilantie 21
00510 Helsinki
Tel: (358 9) 7269 5850
Fax: (358 9) 7269 5851
e-mail:
johannes.lassila@perfectofilms.com

**Seppä Callahanin Filmimaailma Oy/Blacksmith Callahan's Filmworld**
Telakkakatu 2
FIN 00150 Helsinki
Tel: (358 9) 278 4078
Fax: (358 9)278 4035

**Silva Mysterium Oy**
Laippatie 1
FIN 00880 Helsinki
Tel: (358 9) 7594 720
Fax: (358 9) 7594 7240
e-mail:
mika.ritalahti@silvamysterium.fi

**Smile Entertainment**
Indiakaj 12
DK 2100 Copenhagen
Denmark
Tel: (45 35) 441 105
Fax: (45 35) 434 008
e-mail: ttl@smile.dk

**Solar Films Oy**
Kiviaidankatu 1, 4.krs
FIN 00210 Helsinki
Tel: (358 9) 682 3622
Fax: (358 9) 682 3410
e-mail: jukka.helle@solarfilms.com

**Sputnik Oy**
Pursimiehenkatu 25
FIN 00150 Helsinki
Tel: (358 9) 622 1811
Fax: (358 9) 622 3855
e-mail: sputnik@saunalahti.fi

**Villealfa Filmproductions Oy**
Pursimiehenkatu 25
FIN 00150 Helsinki
Tel: (358 9) 622 1811
Fax: (358 9) 622 3855
e-mail: sputnik@saunalahti.fi

**Talent House**
Tallberginkatu 1A/141
FIN 00180 Helsinki
Tel: (358 9) 685 2227
Fax: (358 9) 685 2229

**Åke Lindman Film-Production Oy**
Elimäenkatu 14-16 C
FIN 00510 Helsinki
Tel: (358 9) 736 300
Fax: (358 9) 737 700

e-mail: hemila@medeia.com

# Distributors and Exhibitors

**Buena Vista Int. Finland Oy**
Kaisaniemenkatu 1 C 110
FIn 00100 Helsinki
Tel: (358 9) 25303200

**Cinema Mondo**
Unioninkatu10 A 27
FIN 00130 Helsinki
Tel: (358 9) 629 528
Fax: (358 9) 631 450
e-mail: mikas@clinet.fi

**Columbia Tristar Egmont Film Distributors Oy**
Runeberginkatu 60 B
FIN 00260 Helsinki
Tel: (358 9) 476 4460
Fax: (358 9) 4764 4650

**Finnkino Oy**
Koivuvaarankuja 2
FIN 01640 Vantaa
Tel: (358 9) 131 191
Fax: (358 9) 825 7206

**FS Film Oy**
Urho Kekkosenkatu 4-6 E
FIN 00100 Helsinki
Tel: (358 9) 695 580
Fax: (358 9) 694 0466
e-mail: lasse.hyyti@fsfilm.fi

**Kamras Film Group Oy**
Mikonkatu 19

FIN 00100 Helsinki
Tel: (358 9) 6220 0260
Fax: (358 9) 684 7263

**Oy Kinoscreen Ltd**
Katajanokankatu 6
FIN 00160 Helsinki
Tel: (358 9) 663 717
Fax: (358 9) 662 048

**Sandrew Metronome Finland Oy Ab**
Kaisaniemenkatu 1 B A 69
FIN 00100 Helsinki
Tel: (358 9) 616 651
Fax: (358 9) 6166 5655

**Sandrew Metronome Distribution Oy Ab**
Kaisaniemenkatu 1 B A 69
FIN 00100 Helsinki
Tel: (358 9) 8624 5806
Fax: (358 9) 8624 5810

**Senso Films Oy**
Pursimiehenkatu 25
FIN 00150 Helsinki
Tel: (358 9) 622 1811
Fax: (358 9) 622 3855

**United International Pictures Oy**
Kaisaniemenkatu 1 C 98
FIN 00100 Helsinki
Tel: (358 9) 684 1007
Fax: (358 9) 6841 0010

**Walhalla Ry**
PL 1134
FIN 00101 Helsinki
Tel: (358 9) 4541 9500
Fax: (358 9) 4541 9501

# Useful Addresses

**Finnish Film Foundation**
Kanavakatu 12
FIN 00160 Helsinki
Tel: (358 9) 622 0300
Fax: (358 9) 622 3060

**Finnish Cinema Association**
Finnish Film Chamber
Kaisaniemenkatu 3 B
FIN 00100 Helsinki
Tel: (358 9) 636 305
Fax: (358 9) 176 689

*Still from Auli Mantila's GEOGRAPHY OF FEAR*

# FRANCE

Michel Ciment

The American philosophy of commercial success as the ultimate criterion of value seems to be increasingly accepted in France, a country more often associated with elitism in art. The Cannes festival chose Luc Besson as its jury president for 2000 – a concession to youth culture and an *hommage* to a director who would judge the artistic achievement of some of his colleagues far superior to his own.

It was an unprecedented decision, when one thinks of the auras surrounding former jury presidents: Coppola, Polanski, Eastwood, Bertolucci, Scorsese, Wenders, Forman et al. Besson was also man of the year for the success of his own *Joan of Arc* and for his production of *Taxi II*, which has become one of the three top-grossing pictures in French history. The arrogance of the successful self-made man has never been more in evidence than when Besson rolled up for the Cannes screening of *In the Mood for Love* in a car daubed with publicity for *Taxi II* and mounted the stairs, eclipsing the presence of the film's director, Wong Kar-wai.

Besson's condescending comments about the American selection (*O Brother, Where Art Thou?* and *The Yards*) were all the more striking considering that *Taxi II* was one of the most vulgar, vapid films of recent years. Not surprisingly, however, the list of awards was culture-oriented, with several prizes going to Asian cinema, as if to prove that Besson could also be a keen film buff (though the jury of course had nine other members). The absence of awards for any French films – although four good ones were competing – was regretted by many observers.

## Good news on all fronts

The year proved once again the good health of French cinema in production, distribution and exhibition. An 8.8% fall in the number of tickets sold (155.5 million) can be attributed solely to the phenomenal success of *Titanic*, which had made 1998 an exceptional year. France was still ahead of Germany (149 million admissions), the UK (139.1 million), Spain (131.3 million) and Italy (118.5 million). Furthermore, French films' market share increased from 27.6% to 32.3% (50 million spectators), and ten French films each sold more than one million tickets. American films accounted for 53.5% of the gross, compared to 85.4% in Germany, 80.5% in the UK, 64.2% in Spain and 63.8% in Italy.

Yet these figures obscure a lack of curiosity amongst most cinemagoers. Overwhelmingly, French audiences view only local and Hollywood films. The 1999 statistics indicate a considerable appetite for non-French 'European' films only because of the popularity of *Notting Hill*, *Eyes Wide Shut* and *The World Is Not Enough*, which are counted as British but, culturally, can easily be confused with American films. This trio attracted 13.5 million admissions, whereas only 500,000 went to see German films and 400,000 to Italian films. The dominance of a limited number of titles is increasing; half of 1999's admissions were claimed by just 30 films; 84% by the top 100 amongst the 525 new releases (including 209 French and 175 American).

The mushrooming of multiplexes in the major towns and cities, stable ticket prices (because of intense competition between exhibitors) and the huge media coverage of cinema help explain why each spectator goes to the cinema, on average, at least five times a year – one of the highest figures in Europe. While French films fare well on their own turf, they struggle abroad.

Excluding Besson's *The Fifth Element* (French-produced and directed, but rightly perceived as an American action movie), French films' export revenues were down by $7.5m (52 million francs) in 1999; 46% of the foreign market is European, but Japan is the best single customer.

## Films galore

Production is also flourishing. Some 181 features were produced with French money in 1999, 150 of these with total (or majority) French backing, as against 148 in 1998. This is the highest level since the 1980s. There were 66 films produced with a foreign partner (mostly Spain, Belgium, Italy and Switzerland), a noticeable fall of 15% on 1998. Likewise, total production investment fell by 8.1%: $705m in 1998, $650m in 1999. The average feature film budget dropped from $2.9m to $2.5.

One third of the production was made up of first films (62), a sure enough sign of vitality, but only 16 second pictures were financed, a symptom of indifference towards newcomers who did not fulfil expectations. The role of the "advance against receipts" subsidy scheme for first features has dwindled; only one third were supported this way, compared to half in the early 1990s. One reason for this is the essential role now played by terrestrial and cable television in feature production, particularly of debuts (70% were pre-financed by Canal Plus). Television provided 40.2% of total feature investment (as against 38.5% in 1998 and 35.9% in 1997), with 140 features co-produced by Canal Plus.

The Franco-German channel, Arte, is playing an increasingly vital part in quality French films. Though originally TV films, more Arte-funded titles are being screened at international festivals, such as Dominique Cabrera's *Nadia et les hippopotames* at Cannes and Claire Denis' *Beau Travail* in Venice. The producers' associations have expressed concern at this trend, and have tried unsuccessfully to prevent such TV films from being screened in theatres. Television has also been crucial to the development of documentaries,

whose airtime increased by 28.5% in 1999, and of animated film (239 hours in 1999).

## Docus and doctors

Most of the grand old masters took a leave of absence in 1999: Godard, Resnais, Chabrol, Rohmer, Sautet, Cavalier. However, Chris Marker distinguished himself with his splendid documentary on Andrei Tarkovsky, **Une journée d'Andrei Arsenevich**, and another great documentary-maker, Agnès Varda, returned to top form with **Les Glaneurs et la glaneuse**, both a self-portrait at 70, and a look at the gleaners and scavengers in the fields and on the roads of France. This was Varda at her best: sharp, poetic, witty, always unpredictable.

Michel Deville's **La Maladie de Sachs** won several prizes (including the prize of the French Critics' Association) and deserved greater commercial success. In adapting a very successful book by Martin Winckler (a doctor-turned novelist), about the emotional depression and professional dedication of a physician (magnificently played by Albert Dupontel) in a small provincial town, Deville showed his best qualities: dazzling editing and a formally inventive approach to sound, dialogue and images. Grave and humorous, *La Maladie de Sachs* confirmed Deville as one of the best directors of his generation.

Claude Miller was also utterly convincing with **La Chambre des magiciennes** (which won the FIPRESCI

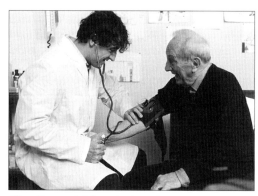

*Albert Dupontel, left, as the doctor hero of LA MALADIE DE SACHS*

*Anne Brochet in LA CHAMBRE DES MAGICIENNES*

*Daniel Auteuil and Juliette Binoche in LA VEUVE DE SAINT-PIERRE*

prize at Berlin), in which three women share a hospital room. The director deals playfully with one of his favourite subjects: the unease of a character who loses touch with reality. An anthropology student (Anne Brochet) finds herself in a clinic, suffering from anorexia and other dysfunctions. Her tense relationship with her two fellow patients is ominous and hilarious. By shooting on digital video, Miller seems to have recovered a bold creative freedom.

All the talent of Andrzej Zulawski – and also his capacity to waste it – were evident in **La Fidelité**, a modern variation on *La Princesse de Clèves*, about duty and fidelity (the novel was also recently adapted by Manoel de Oliveira as *The Letter*). The first part has an astonishing energy and formal invention, showing Sophie Marceau at her best as a photographer who meets and falls in love with a publisher (Pascal Greggory), but halfway along the narration goes berserk in a multiplicity of irrelevant incidents.

Claude Lelouch and Bertrand Blier both played in their traditional fields. Lelouch's **Une pour toutes** was a lightweight comedy about an airline desk receptionist who organises pseudo 'chance' meetings between young gold diggers and sugar daddies. As usual, when not in pretentious mood, Lelouch lights on some good gags and allows his actors some playful improvisation. Blier made his comedians the centre of his new film, **Les Acteurs**. Jean-Pierre Marielle, André Dussollier, Jean-Paul Belmondo and Alain Delon each

plays his own role, but this accumulation of stereotypes becomes an embarrassing self-parody, and what starts out as a tribute to actors ends as a sour and empty portrayal.

## The costume boom

One of the characteristics of the past year has been a widespread interest in costume drama. There have of course been some remarkable recent achievements in this genre, such as Patrice Leconte's *Ridicule*, but not in such concentrated numbers. Leconte confirmed his eclecticism by directing **La Veuve de Saint-Pierre**, a romantic drama set in the mid-nineteenth century on a small French island near the Canadian coast. A man condemned to death (Emir Kusturica, in a dazzling debut screen performance) is being cared for by the wife (Juliette Binoche) of the local garrison captain (Daniel Auteuil). The film is all restrained emotion and windswept landscape and its anachronistic yet beautiful style deserved a better reception.

Young directors Olivier Assayas, Arnaud Desplechin and Patricia Mazuy all found themselves selected for Cannes with costume pictures. Assayas' **Les Destinées sentimentales** is a faithful, three-hour adaptation of a sprawling pre-war novel by Jacques Chardonne, charting 30 years of a marriage against the background of France's porcelain and cognac industries and flawlessly acted by Charles Berling, Emmanuelle Béart and Isabelle Huppert. Desplechin's **Esther Kahn** was a boldly-drawn portrayal of the rise of a young actress in late nineteenth-century England. The lush photography and perfect reconstruction of the period mask the violence of the young woman's professional and romantic ordeals.

Equally bold and inventive was Mazuy's third feature, **Saint-Cyr**, an evocation of the school for young girls run by Louis XIV's mistress, Madame de Maintenon (Isabelle Huppert). She yearns to create a Utopian society in this pre-feminist institute, but ends by destroying the very youngsters she has helped emancipate. Mazuy's brash yet spare depiction of the past is strikingly realistic, avoiding all the pitfalls of academic reconstruction.

By contrast, Besson's **Joan of Arc** lacked a consistent artistic approach. It borrows shamelessly from recent cinema trends, with a particular weakness for New Age philosophy. The story is so strong that the film has more content than all Besson's other movies, but it fails to express the complexity of the historical background, preferring to liken Joan to a pop singer surrounded by her fans. If Besson avoids any kind of political perspective he has good reason: his decision to tell in English the story of a woman who died to keep France's political identity is sufficiently ironic.

## Jacquot's trio

Benoît Jacquot in **Sade** took us to 1794, to focus on a few days in the life of the 'divine Marquis', impressively played by Daniel Auteuil. Abandoning the gothic, satanic figure cherished by the surrealists, Jacquot instead shows a tired man who embodies the idea of freedom – the perfect foil to Robespierre's totalitarian spirit. This psychological interpretation and the rather conventional approach to the costume film were rather tame for such a daunting figure.

Strangely, a smaller film directed by Jacquot, **La Fausse Suivante**, from a little-known eighteenth-century play by Marivaux, had more charm, complexity and vivacity, with a quartet of superlative

*Legionnaires in Claire Denis' BEAU TRAVAIL*

comedians: Isabelle Huppert, Sandrine Kiberlain, Pierre Arditi and Mathieu Amalric. Here, in spite of the wigs, costumes and sets, we see only the complexity of human hearts and minds. More prolific than ever, Jacquot directed a third film this past year, **Pas de Scandale**, a contemporary study of social morals and manners, in which Fabrice Luchini plays an executive who finds it hard to readjust to life with his family after a spell in prison.

As usual, women directors offered strikingly original films. Laetitia Masson explored mental states in **Love Me**, about the journey to America of an amnesiac woman (Sandrine Kiberlain). Claire Denis, with **Beau Travail**, loosely inspired by Melville's *Billy Budd*, choreographed a fascinating and puzzling ballet of Foreign Legion soldiers, with homoerotic overtones. Laurence Ferreira Barbosa combined three stories of solitude in **La Vie Moderne**. Noemie Lvovsky's group portrait of teenage girls, **La Vie ne me fait pas peur**, was exhilaratingly dynamic.

Promising newcomers included Anne Villacèque with her **Petite Chèrie**, a bleak story of a lonely young girl and the pressures of family life, Christine Carrière with **Qui plume la lune?**, a humorous tale of a father raising his two daughters, and Helen Angel, who won the Golden Leopard at Locarno with **Peau d'homme, cœur de bête**, a violent rendering of peasant life and family feuds, shot like a Western. Emmanuel Bereot's **La Puce** was about a young girl who leads an older man in a ballet of seduction.

The year's most striking success was **Le goût des autres**, written, directed by and starring Agnès Jaoui (who co-wrote Resnais' two most recent films). A totally assured first feature, this is an incredibly funny and moving reflection on cultural prejudices, with a psychological sense worthy of Claude Sautet.

## Debuts, experts and sophomores

The new, talented male directors are less numerous, led by Laurent Cantet, who with **Ressources Humaines** produced a socially committed film about the son of a worker who becomes a minor executive, comes back to work at his father's factory and finds himself on the side of the management in a time of conflict.

On the lighter side, actor Sam Karman's debut, **Kennedy et moi**, offered the exceptional Jean-Pierre Bacri (also the star of *Le goût des autres* and a co-writer for Resnais) as a hypochondriac. But probably the most striking revelation was Orso Miret's **De l'histoire ancienne**, an investigation into the role of memory in relation to the years when France was occupied by the Germans, combined with a complex analysis of family relationships, told in an austere, dense style reminiscent of Bresson.

More seasoned directors had an uneven year. Régis Wargnier's direction was stilted in the curiously outmoded and un-convincing **Est-Ouest**, the story of a French woman (Sandrine Bonnaire, excellent) married to a Russian trapped in Moscow during the Cold War. **Tout va bien on s'en va**, by Claude Mourièra, is a fine ensemble portrayal of three sisters in the provinces who welcome their father 20 years after he disappeared from their lives. Comedian Michel Blanc shot his third successful film, **Mauvaise Passe**, in England, in English, on the provocative theme of a gigolo (Daniel Auteuil) offering his services to women in London after deserting his family in Paris.

Most rewarding of all was the confirmation of new talents with their second features. After *La vie rêvée des anges*, Erik Zonca shot **Le petit voleur** in urgent, Scorsese style, tracing the odyssey of a young baker who is fired, enters the underworld and becomes a boxer. Olivier Ducastel and Jacque Martineau followed their Aids musical *Jeanne et le garçon formidable* with **Drole de Felix**, a road movie about a gay man travelling south through France to meet his father. François Ozon, a promising but not always convincing exponent of provocative cinema, found the right material for his third film, **Goûttes d'eau sur pierre brûlante**, adapting an early play by Fassbinder about sadomasochistic homo- and heterosexual relationships, observed with a streak of dark humour.

The most successful second feature was **Harry, un ami qui vous veut du bien**, by Dominik Moll, the follow-up to his noted debut, *Intimité* (1995). This was a Hitchcock/Chabrol-type thriller about a man who, while on holiday with his wife and children, meets a former schoolmate, Harry (Sergi Lopez), for the first time in 20 years. Harry offers to make the man happy, but the price is a series of murders. At once funny and frightening, the film is greatly enhanced by the superb Lopez and three other fine performances.

MICHEL CIMENT is one of France's most eminent critics and commentators on cinema. An editor of *Positif*, and a lecturer on film at universities in France and abroad, he has also made documentaries on various directors.

*Still from Agnès Jaoui's LE GOUT DES AUTRES*

# Producers

**Alexandre Films**
14 Rue de Marignan
75008 Paris
Tel: (33 1) 4495 8989
Fax: (33 1) 4289 2689

**Alter Films**
4 Rue Treilhard
75008 Paris
Tel: (33 1) 4256 1297
Fax: (33 1) 4256 4574

**Caméra One**
19 Rue Tremoille
75008 Paris
Tel: (33 1) 5689 9200
Fax: (33 1) 5689 9216

**Cinéa**
87 Rue Taitbout
75009 Paris
Tel: (33 1) 4491 9414
Fax: (33 1) 4016 1911

**Film Par Film**
10 Avenue George V
75008 Paris
Tel: (33 1) 4073 8420
Fax: (33 1) 4723 9568

**Films Alain Sarde**
17 Rue Dumont d'Urville
75116 Paris
Tel: (33 1) 4443 4370
Fax: (33 1) 4720 6150

**Films Christian Fechner**
39 Rue des Tilleuls
92100 Boulogne
Tel: (33 1) 4699 0202
Fax: (33 1) 4699 0343

**Flach Films**
12 Rue Lincoln
75008 Paris
Tel: (33 1) 5669 3838
Fax: (33 1) 5669 3843

**Gaumont**
30 Avenue Charles de Gaulle
92200 Neuilly
Tel: (33 1) 4643 2000
Fax: (33 1) 4643 2168

**Hachette Première**
25 Rue François Premier
75008 Paris

Tel: (33 1) 4723 2500
Fax: (33 1) 4723 2510

**IMA Productions**
13 Avenue de Clichy
75008 Paris
Tel: (33 1) 4387 4041
Fax: (33 1) 4387 4050

**MACT Productions**
27 Rue de Fleurus
75006 Paris
Tel: (33 1) 4549 1010
Fax: (33 1) 4559 3060

**MK2 Productions**
55 Rue Traversière
75012 Paris
Tel: (33 1) 4467 3000
Fax: (33 1) 4341 3230

**Renn Productions**
10 Rue Lincoln
75008 Paris
Tel: (33 1) 4076 9100
Fax: (33 1) 4225 1289

**Le Studio Canal+**
17 Rue Dumont d'Urville
75116 Paris
Tel: (33 1) 4443 9800
Fax: (33 1) 4720 1358

**Téléma**
44 Rue Chaptal
92300 Levallois Perret
Tel: (33 1) 4149 6000
Fax: (33 1) 4149 6049

**UGC Images**
24 Avenue Charles de Gaulle
92200 Neuilly
Tel: (33 1) 4640 4400
Fax: (33 1) 4624 3728

# Distributors

**A.M.L.F.**
10 Rue Lincoln
75008 Paris
Tel: (33 1) 4076 9100
Fax: (33 1) 4225 1289

**Bac Films**
10 Avenue de Messine
75008 Paris
Tel: (33 1) 5353 5252
Fax: (33 1) 5353 5253

**Gaumont/BVI**

5 Rue du Colisée
75008 Paris
Tel: (33 1) 4643 2453
Fax: (33 1) 4643 2047

**Mars Films**
95 Blvd. Haussmann
75008 Paris
Tel: (33 1) 4494 9500
Fax: (33 1) 4494 9501

**Metropolitan Filmexport**
116 bis Avenue des Champs Elysées
75008 Paris
Tel: (33 1) 4563 4560
Fax: (33 1) 4563 7731

**MKL**
55 Rue Traversière
75012 Paris
Tel: (33 1) 4307 1510
Fax: (33 1) 4344 2018

**Pyramide Film**
5 Rue Richepanse
75008 Paris
Tel: (33 1) 4296 0101
Fax: (33 1) 4020 0221

**UFD**
2 Avenue Montaigne
75008 Paris
Tel: (33 1) 5367 1717
Fax: (33 1) 5367 1700

**UGC**
24 Avenue Charles de Gaulle
92200 Neuilly
Tel: (33 1) 4640 4400
Fax: (33 1) 4624 3728

**United International Pictures**
1 Rue Meyerbeer
75009 Paris
Tel: (33 1) 4007 3838
Fax: (33 1) 4007 3839

# Useful Addresses

**Centre National de la Cinématographie (CNC)**
12 Rue de Lubeck
75116 Paris
Tel: (33 1) 4434 3440
Fax: (33 1) 4755 0491

**Unifrance Film International**
4 Villa Bosquet
75007 Paris

# GEORGIA

Goga
Lomdize

Georgian cinema has gone through very difficult times for the past decade. The country's dire economic situation has meant that annual state subsidy for the entire film industry has fallen to just $450,000 – far too little to provide work for the country's 70 highly-trained directors, not to mention actors, cameramen and other technicians. Under Soviet rule Georgia produced around 14 features per year, but in 1998 there were just two new films and three in 1999.

Apart from the 75 year-old Georgia-Film, there are few independent producers. Adam & Eva, Sameba and Debiuti are the most important and produced three new features between them in the past two years. Inevitably, these circumstances have generated an increase in international co-production; in 1998-99 five Georgian-made features had backing from France, Germany, Russia, the UK or Denmark. There are still six cinemas in Tbilisi, including the recently refurbished Rustaveli theatre, but they all face increasing competition from terrestrial and satellite TV.

Yet despite these difficulties, Georgian film-makers continue to produce high-quality movies, with several on show at Cannes in 2000. In the Directors Fortnight, Nana Djordjadze, a former Cannes jury member (1992) and Oscar-nominee for *Chef in Love* (1996), premiered her romantic, lyrical **Summer, or 27 Missing Kisses** (*Zapkhuli*). The story of a teenage girl who arrives on holiday in a boring town and transforms the lives of its residents, it was

*Still from Nana Djordjadze's SUMMER, OR 27 MISSING KISSES*

*Still from Dito Tsintsadze's LOST KILLERS*
*photo: Rommel Film*

picked up for distribution in 35 countries.

Un Certain Regard presented Dito Tsintsadze's **Lost Killers** (*Dakargulu mkvlelebi*), which follows five fugitives trying to survive in Germany. Tsintsadze's breakthrough came in 1993 when his *On the Edge* won the Silver Leopard at Locarno. Otar Ioseliani headed the Cannes' Caméra D'Or jury, and the festival also presented his debut short, *April* (1962).

Giorgi Shengelaya's **Georgian Grapes** (*Sikvaruli venakhshi*) is a first for Georgian cinema: an erotic film which with humour and simplicity shows rural characters having their first sexual experiences. Shengelaya made an impetuous, rebellious debut with *Alaverdoba* (1962) and became

internationally known with *Pirosmani* (1969), about a self-taught artist. The emotional powerful of his work placed him in the front rank of the former USSR's film-makers.

Kakha Kikabidze made an interesting debut with **The Lake** (Georgian title not yet confirmed), the story of a village boy who has to get used to city life after his father is killed and his mother takes them away from the countryside. **Here Comes the Dawn** (*Ak tendeba*), by Zaza Urushadze, was Georgia's official entry for the Academy Awards. An unusual and touching story of a politician who abandons his successful career and runs away with his handicapped son, it won the jury's special prize at the 1998 Anapa festival in Russia.

At Anapa's most recent event, another Georgian, Goderdzi Chokheli, won Best Screenplay for **The Gospel According to St. Luke** (*Lukas sakhareba*), about an orphaned schoolboy who suffers at the hands of a despotic teacher. Chokheli became internationally known for his short, *Human Sadness*, which won the Grand Prize at Oberhausen in 1982.

GOGA LOMIDZE has lived in the Netherlands since 1994, teaching Russian and working as a freelance Russian-Dutch translator.

## Recent Films

**AK TENDEBA (Here Comes the Dawn)**

Script: Amiran Chichinadze, Zaza Urushadze. Dir: Urushadze. Players: Zura Begalishvili, Guram Pirtskhalava. Prod: Georgia-Film.

**ADIEU, PLANCHER LES VACHES!**

Script and Dir: Otar Ioseliani. Phot: William Lubtchansky. Players: Nico Tarielashvili, Lily Lavina, Philippe Bas, Ioseliani. Prod: Martine Marignac.

**DAKARGULI MKVLELEBI (Lost Killers)**

Script and Dir: Dito Tsintsadze.

Phot: Benedict Neuenfels. Players: Nicole Seeling, Lasha Bakradze, Misel Maticevic, Athanasios Cosmadakis. Prod: Home Run Pictures/Rommel Productions/ARTE/ZDF.

**MISTERIEBI (Mysteries)**

Script: Rustam Ibragimbekov, Micheil Kalatozishvili. Dir: Kalatozishvili. Players: Tolsty, Nodar Kalandaze, Nato Murvanidze.

**OTSNEBEBIS SASAPLAO (Graveyard of Dreams)**

Script: Giorgi Khaindrava,

Irakli Solomonashvili. Dir: Khaindrava. Phot: Khaindrava, Mikhail Magalashvili. Players: Giorgi Nakaschidse, Batscho Batschukaschwili, Tamas Berejiani. Prod: TMS-Invest/Coca-Cola/Potis Porti.

**SAMOTXIS CHITEBI (Birds of Paradise)**

Script and Dir: Goderdzi Chokheli. Phot: Jimy Kristesashvili. Players: Kakhi Kavsadze, Givi Berikashvili. Prod: Georgia-Film/Sameba.

**SIKVARULI   VENAKHSHI**

**(Georgian Grapes)**

Script: Georgi Shengelaya, Levan Kitia, Kote Djandieri. Dir: Shengelaya. Phot: Geno Tschiradze. Players: Ia Parulava, Zaza Papuashvili, Celina Wieczorek. Prod: Regina Ziegler Film.

---

**THE LAKE**

Script and Dir: Kakha Kikabidze. Phot: Igor Amasiysky. Players: Dimitry Shvelidze, Irakly Mshvildaze, Alina Nozadze. Prod: Georgia-Film

---

**ZAPKHULI (Summer, or 27 Missing Kisses)**

Script: Irakli Kvirikadze. Dir: Nana Djordjadze. Phot: Phedon Papamichael. Players: Nino Kukhianidze, Evgeni Sidichin, Shaco Iashvili, Pierre Richard. Prod: Egoli Films/ Canal Plus/ Moco Films/British Screen/Adam & Eva/Babelsberg/Wave Pictures.

## Producers

**Kartuli-Pilmi/Georgia-Film**
Akhmetelis Kucha 10a
380059 Tbilisi
Tel: (995) 3252 0627/0115
Fax: (995) 3252 0910

**Adam & Eva**
David Agmasheneblis Gamziri 164
380002 Tbilisi
Tel: (995) 3295 0305
Fax: (995) 3235 1109

**Kartulu Telepilmi**
Kostavas Kucha 68
380071 Tbilisi
Tel: (995) 3236 8796/8239
Fax: (995) 3233 2649

**Aisi**
Kostavas Kucha 36
380079 Tbilisi
Tel: (995) 3293 1037

**New Studio**
Gorgaslis Kucha 16
380014 Tbilisi
Tel/Fax: (995) 3298 7085

## Useful Addresses

**The Film House**
Dzmebi Kakabadzeebis Kucha 2
380008 Tbilisi
Tel:(995) 3298 8328/3293 4612
Fax: (995) 3293 5097

**Georgian State Institute of Theatre and Film**
Rustavelis Gamziri 19
380004 Tbilisi
Tel: (995) 3299 0438
Fax: (995) 3200 1153

# GERMANY
Jack Kindred

Germany's film landscape is improving rapidly. Distribution and production groups, flush with investment from their listings on Frankfurt's booming New Market, are merging, acquiring companies, buying rights and entering into high-budget co-production deals with independents and the Hollywood majors. It all adds up to an exciting new era for the German movie industry.

But some things never seem to change, namely the American majors' perennial domination of the exhibition market, and the film-going public's lust for Hollywood entertainment. No home-grown movies made 1999's top ten grossing list, which was headed by *Star Wars: Episode I*, followed by *Notting Hill* and *Runaway Bride*.

Nevertheless, domestic features held their own, attracting nearly 20 million visitors and capturing 14% of the market, up from 9.5% in 1998. Boosting German cinema's reputation were *Annaluise and Anton* (1.7 million admissions), *Aimee & Jaguar* (1.2 million) and Wim Wenders' surprising **Buena Vista Social Club**, which came close to the one million mark - a huge figure for a documentary. Wenders had high hopes of winning an Oscar for his film about a group of long-forgotten Cuban musicians, but the award went to *One Day in September*, about the massacre of Israeli

*Katje Flint as Dietrich in MARLENE*

athletes at the 1972 Munich Olympics.

Berlin Film Festival director Moritz de Hadeln chose Wenders' **The Million Dollar Hotel** as the event's opener, one of the rare occasions that a German film has been selected for this honour. The movie, shot in a seedy district in Los Angeles, had an impressive cast, headed by Jeremy Davies, Milla Jovovich and Mel Gibson, who were members of a gang of outcasts and misfits. Nevertheless, it failed to win a festival award and subsequently did poorly at the box-office.

Wenders was not the only German director to suffer major disappointments. Director-producer-cameraman Joseph Vilsmaier, who enjoyed success at home and abroad with 1997's *Comedian Harmonists*, appeared to have bitten off more than he could chew in attempting to re-create the myth and legend of Marlene Dietrich, in **Marlene**, an opulent, $8.5m production. The biopic flopped, pulling only 435,000 visitors after two months on release.

Vilsmaier's leading lady, Katje Flint, tried her best, but failed to make the fascination of Dietrich plausible to film fans; perhaps a hopeless task for any actress. The movie stretches from Dietrich's international breakthrough in *The Blue Angel*, through the 1930s, until the story ends during the Second World War. It stops short of her seven Hollywood films.

No German movie made the competition list at Cannes in 2000, but Jan Schütte's **The Farewell** (*Abschied*), a fictional account of seven hours in the life of German dramatist Bertolt Brecht, was included in Un Certain Regard. Scripted by Schütte in collaboration with Klaus Pohl, it starred Josef Bierbichler as Brecht, with Monica Bleibtreu as his wife, Helene Weigel.

## Tales from the East

With the acceptance of his **No Place to Go** (*Die Unberührbare*) in the Directors Fortnight, writer-director Oskar Roehler saved face, after the drama was turned down by the 2000 Berlinale. The movie is based on the tragic life of East German novelist Gisela Elsner, played by Hannelore Elsner (no relation), who committed suicide three years after the fall of the Berlin Wall.

Another film set in East Germany before the Wall came tumbling down, **The Eastie Boys** (*Sonnenallee*), was based on a best-selling novel by East German Thomas Brussig, and took a nostalgic look at growing up in the communist nation in the 1970s. Named after Sonnenallee, a street running from East to West Berlin that was cut in half by the Wall, this non-political movie, starring Alexander Scheer and Alexander Beyer, revolved around the very funny antics of a group of teenagers. It remained on the top ten box-office list for five weeks, pulling in 1.8 million patrons.

Still on an East German theme, the equally funny **Heroes Like Us** (*Helden wie wir*), directed by Sebastian Peterson, depicts dull, everyday life in the grim Stalinist country prior to the collapse of the Wall. The movie ends when the hero,

*The eponymous heroes of ERKAN & STEFAN*

played by Daniel Borgwardt, stumbles half-naked into a security zone, and the border guards are so astounded by the sight of his vast genitals that they inadvertently let down the barriers dividing East and West.

Also set in East Berlin under the communists, **Break Even** (*plus-minus-null*) has a simple storyline about a trio of losers living in a building site container at the Potsdamer Platz. In a five-week shooting schedule, during which dialogues were improvised, director Eoin Moore used hand-held cameras and jump cuts in a bid to give the movie a dynamic pace.

### Comic capers

Paying heed to youth, director Michael Herbig turned out a rollicking comedy featuring German-born ethnic Turks, **Erkan & Stefan**, with elements of MTV's cartoon characters, Beavis and Butthead. The dialogue is based on the odd slanguage used by young Turks and adopted by German teenagers, and the fast-moving plot revolves around a missing audio-cassette allegedly containing revelations about the mysterious death of a politician.

In possession of the tape, but unaware of its significance, Erkan and Stefan become the quarry in an hilarious chase, led by undercover CIA and German BDN intelligence officers who are determined to prevent the information becoming public. A booming soundtrack, with helicopters, shootings and explosions, forms an appropriate background to the spoof.

Both *Erkan & Stefan* and another Constantin release, Marc Rothemund's schoolboy comedy **Ants in the Pants** (*Harte Jungs*) spent weeks on the top ten list. *Ants in the Pants* was Germany's answer to *American Pie*, about nascent sex and the need for love. Klaus Krämer's feature debut was the comedy **Three Chinamen with a Double Bass** (*Drei Chinese mit dem Kontrabass*), with a plot involving the frantic efforts of two men, played by Boris Aljinovic and Jürgen Tarrach, to get rid of a corpse.

Fans of popular comedian Otto Waalkes have had to wait eight years for the $8.5m **Otto - The Disaster Movie** (*Otto - Der Katastrofenfilm*), the fifth in his hugely successful series. This time around, Otto is the reluctant captain of an ocean liner, who succeeds in knocking down the Statue of Liberty. Despite negative reviews, the slapstick comedian can do no wrong in the eyes of his youthful followers, and he attracted one million admissions.

Doris Dörrie's latest feature, **Enlightenment Guaranteed** (*Erleuchtung garantiert*), starred Uwe Ochsenknecht and Gustav Peter Wöhler as two brothers in mid-life crisis who seek Buddha at a Zen monastery in Japan. Despite its comic elements, involving the problems of being down and out in Tokyo, the movie failed to click with the public.

### What Lola did next

In Friedemann Fromm's thriller **Paradise Mall** (*Schlaraffenland*), bankable young star Franka Potente, acclaimed internationally for her role in *Run Lola Run*, teamed up with Heiner Lauterbach in a suspense story about a gang of youngsters who stage an illegal party at a huge shopping mall after it has closed for the night. The teenage prank turns into a deadly struggle when a blizzard cuts off the mall and disables the security system, trapping the young kids with four security guards, there to protect the central safe.

Potente also starred in the gruesome

**Anatomie**, the first cinema release from the newly established Deutsche Columbia Pictures Filmproduktion. Directed by Stefan Ruzowitzky, the plot focuses on a young medical student, Paula (Potente), who discovers on her dissection table the cadaver of a young man whom she saw alive only the previous day. Her professor and fellow students urge her not to delve further, otherwise her life could be in danger. The movie came close to hitting two million admissions, double the usual benchmark for a successful film in Germany.

As one of the production companies raising capital on the New Market, Helkon has completed post-production chores on the $40m, *Naked Gun*-style spoof, *2001 - A Space Travesty*, starring Leslie Nielsen. Adventure buffs can look forward to the high-budget **As Far as My Feet Will Carry Me** (*So Weit die Füsse Tragen*), the story of a German soldier's dramatic escape from a POW camp in Siberia just after the Second World War, and the hardships he endured during a three-year trek to freedom. Directed by Hardy Martins and featuring successful stage actor Bernhard Bettermann in his first film role, the film obliged cast and crew to endure the hardships of a Siberian winter.

Finally, the 51st Berlinale in February, 2001, will be director Moritz de Hadeln's last, after more than two decades at the helm of one of the two biggest cinema events in Europe.

JACK KINDRED, self-styled "expat country boy from South Dakota", keeps tab on film, television, video and new media developments in Germany from his Munich hideout.

# Recent and Forthcoming Films

### ABSCHIED (The Farewell)

Script: Klaus Pohl. Dir: Jan Schütte. Phot: Edward Klosinski. Players: Josef Bierbichler, Monica Bleibtreu. Prod: Novoskop Film.

### ANATOMIE (Anatomy)

Script and Dir: Stefan Ruzowitzky. Phot: Peter von Haller. Players: Franka Potente, Benno Fürmann, Anna Loos, Sebastian Blomberg. Prod: Deutsche Columbia Pictures Film Produktion.

### BODY FAITH

Script and Dir: Douglas Buck. Phot: Peter Przybyiski. Players: Gary Betsworth. Prod: Syrreal Entertainment.

### DER TOTE TAUCHER IM WALD (The Dead Diver in the Wood)

Script: Peter Dollinger. Dir: Marcus O. Rosenmüller. Phot: Ekkehart Pollack. Prod: Helkon Media Filmproduktion.

### DREI CHINESE MIT DEM KONTRABASS (Three Chinamen with a Double Bass)

Script and Dir: Klaus Krämer. Phot: Ralph Netzer. Players: Boris Aljinovic, Jürgen Tarrach, Claudia Michelsen, Ilja Richter. Prod: ndF.

### EINE HAND VOLL GRAS (A Handful of Grass)

Script: Uwe Timm. Dir: Roland Suso Richter. Phot: Martin Langer. Players: Oliver Korittke, Arman Kuru, Michael Gwisdek, Dieter Pfaff. Prod: Kinowelt Filmproduktion/ Bavaria Film.

### ERKAN & STEFAN

Script: Philip Weinges, Günther Knarr. Dir: Michael Herbig. Phot: Stephan Schuh. Players: Erkan Maria Moosleitner, Stefan Lust, Alexandra Neldel, Manfred Zapatka. Prod: Hofmann & Voges/ Constantin Film.

### ERLEUCHTUNG GARANTIERT (Enlightenment Guaranteed)

Script and Dir: Doris Dörrie. Phot: Hans Karl Hu. Players: Uwe Ochsenknecht, Gustav-Peter Wöhler, Petra Zieser, Ulrike Kriener. Prod: Megaherz TV Fernsehproduktion.

### FLASHBACK

Script: Natalie Scharf, Jimmy Sangster. Dir: Michael Karen. Players: Valerie Niehaus, Xaver Hutter, Alexandra Neidel, Simone Hanselmann, Elke Sommer, Detlev Buck. Prod: Tele-München/ Clasart Film Produktion.

### GOTT UND DIE WELT (God and the World)

Script and Dir: Thorsten Wettcke. Phot: Martin Ruhe. Players: Oscar Ortega Sanchez, Anna Loos, Oliver Korittke, Heike Makatsch, Martin Semmelrogge. Prod: Buena Vista Productions/ VCC Filmproduktions.

### GIERIG (Greedy)

Script and Dir: Oskar Roehler. Phot: Hagen Bogdanski. Players: Richy Müller, Jasmin Tabatabai, Gregor Törzs, Nele Mueller-Stöfen. Prod: Filmpool.

**HARTE JUNGS (Ants in the Pants)**

Script: Granz Henman. Dir: Marc Rothemund. Phot: Hans-Günther Bücking. Players: Tobias Schenke, Axel Stein, Luise Helm, Mina Tander, Sissi Perlinger. Prod: Constantin Film.

**HELDEN WIE WIR (Heroes Like Us)**

Script: Thomas Brussig, Sebastian Peterson, Markus Dittrich. Phot: Peter Przybylski. Players: Daniel Borgwardt, Adrian Heidenreich, Xenia Snagowski, Luca Lenz. Prod: Senator Film.

**I LOVE YOU, BABY**

Script: Ron Peer. Dir: Nick Lyon. Phot: Ekkehart Pollack. Players: Mark Keller, Jasmin Gerat, Maximilian Schell, Burkhard Driest. Prod: Two Guys and a Girl/ Warner Bros. Film Produktion.

**LAWYERS IN LOVE**

Script: Pascal Bancon. Dir: Simon Brook. Phot: Gernot Roll. Players: Kelly McGillis. Prod: Cinerenta Gesellschaft für Internationale Filmproduktion/ Axion Film/IMX Communication/ Babelsberg Film und Fernsehproduktions.

**LOST KILLERS**

Script and Dir: Dito Tsintsadze. Phot: Benedict Neuenfels. Players: Nicole Seelig, Misel Maticevic, Lasha Bakradze, Elie James Bleees. Prod: Home Run Pictures.

**MARLENE**

Script: Christian Pfannenschmidt. Dir and Phot: Joseph Vilsmaier. Players: Katja Flint, Herbert Knaup, Heino Ferch, Hans-Werner Meyer, Christiane Paul, Suzanne von Borsody, Armin Rohde. Prod: TPR/Perathon Film.

**THE MILLION DOLLAR HOTEL**

Script: Nicolaus Klein. Dir: Wim Wenders. Phot: Phedon Papamichael. Players: Jeremy Davies, Milla Jovovich, Mel Gibson, Peter Stormare, Jimmy Smits, Gloria Stuart, Bud Cort. Prod: Road Movies Filmproduktion.

**OTTO - DER KATASTROFENFILM (Otto - The Disaster Movie)**

Script: Bernd Eilert, Michel Bergmann, Otto Waalkes. Dir: NAME t.b.c. Phot: Hagen Bogdanski. Players: Otto Waalkes, Eve Hassmann, Reiner Schöne. Michael Schweighöfer. Prod: Rialto

**PARADISO**

Script and Dir: Rudolf Thome. Phot: Reinhold Vorschneider. Players: Hanns Zischler, Cora Frost, Adriana Altaras, Sabine Bach. Prod: Moanafilm.

**PLUS-MINUS NULL (Break Even)**

Script and Dir: Eoin Moore. Phot: Bernd Löhr, Eoin Moore. Players: Andreas Schmidt, Tamara Simunovic, Kathleen Gallego Zapata, Matthias Schmidt. Prod: dffb/ZDF/3sat.

**SCHLARAFFENLAND (Paradise Mall)**

Script: Christoph Fromm. Dir: Friedemann Fromm. Phot: Jo Heim. Players: Heiner Lauterbach, Franka Potente, Jürgen Tarrach, Roman Knizka. Prod: Hager Moss Film/Seven Pictures /Babelsberg Film.

**SCHNEE IN DER NEUJAHRSNACHT (Snow on New Year's Eve)**

Script: Stefan Kolditz. Dir: Thorsten Schmidt. Phot: Klaus Eichhammer. Players: Jürgen Tarrach, Tamara Simunovic, Hannes Jaenicke, Dieter Landuris, Barbara Rudnik. Prod: Ufa Filmproduktions.

**SO WEIT DIE FÜSSE TRAGEN (As Far As My Feet Will Carry Me)**

Script: Bernd Schwamm, Bastian Clevé. Dir: Hardy Martins. Phot: Sergei Yurisdizki. Players: Bernhard Bettermann, Michael Mendl, Analtoli Kotinyov, Irina Pantaeva. Prod: Cascadeur Filmproduktion.

**THE 13TH FLOOR**

Script: Josef Rusnak, Ravel Centeno-Rodriguez. Dir: Rusnak. Phot: Wedigo von Schultzendorff. Players: Craig Bierko, Gretchen Mol, Vincent D'Onofrio, Armin Mueller-Stahl, Dennis Haysbert. Prod: Centropolis Entertainment.

**DIE STILLE NACH DEM SCHUSS (Rita's Legends)**

Script: Wolfgang Kohlhaase. Dir: Volker Schlöndorff. Phot: Andreas Höfer. Players: Bibiana Beglau, Nadja Uhl, Martin Wuttke. Prod: Babelsberg Film/ MDR

**SONNENALLEE (The Eastie Boys)**

Script and Dir: Leander Haussmann. Phot: Peter J. Krause. Players: Alexander Scheer, Alexander Beyer, Katharina Thalbach, Henry Hübchen. Detlev Buck. Prod: Boje Buck Prod/Ö-Film.

**TROUBLE SHOOTER**

Script: Niki Müllerschön. Dir: Carl Schenkel. Phot: Egon Werdin. Players: Thomas Kretschmann, Désiré Nosbusch, Thure Riefenstein, Dirk Martens. Martin Semmelrogge, Klaus Löwitsch. Prod: ZDF/MPS Medienproduktion.

**DIE UNBERÜHRBARE (No Place to Go)**

Script and Dir: Oskar Roehler. Phot: Hagen Bagdanski. Players: Hannelore Elsner, Vadim Glowna, Tonio Arango, Michael Gwisdek, Nini Petri. Prod: Distant Dreams/ Geyer Werke.

# Producers

**Allianz Filmproduktion GmbH**
Leibnitzstr. 60
10625 Berlin
Tel: (49 30) 323 9011
Fax: (49 30) 323 1693

**Anthea Film GmbH**
Widenmayerstr. 4
80538 Munich
Tel: (49 89) 226 194
Fax: (49 89) 221 251

**Bavaria Film GmbH**
Bavariafilmplatz 7
80336 Geiselgasteig
Munich
Tel: (49 89) 6499 2389
Fax: (49 89) 649 2507

**BioSkop-Film GmbH**
Türkenstr. 91/111
80799 Munich
Tel: (49 89) 394 987
Fax: (49 89) 396 820

**Capitol Film + TV International
GmbH & Co. Vertriebs KG**
Harvestehuder Weg 43
20149 Hamburg 13
Tel: (49 40) 411 79-0
Fax: (49 40) 411 70-199

**Constantin Film AG**
Kaiserstr. 39
47441 Munich
Tel: (49 89) 3860 9221/2
Fax: (49 89) 3860 9242

**Franz Seitz Produktions GmbH**
Beichstr. 8
80802 Munich
Tel: (49 89) 391 1123
Fax: (49 89) 340 1291

**Willy Bogner Film GmbH**
Sankt Veitstr. 4
81673 Munich
Tel: (49 89) 436 06-0
Fax: (49 89) 436 06 429

**CCC Filmkunst GmbH**
Verlangerie Daumstr. 16
13599 Berlin
Tel: (49 30) 334 200-1
Fax: (49 30) 334 0418

**CineVox Film GmbH**
Bavaria Filmplatz 7

80336 Geiselgasteig
Tel: (49 89) 641 80-0
Fax: (49 89) 649 3288

**Manfred Durniok Produktion**
Hausotterstr. 36
13409 Berlin
Tel: (49 30) 491 8045
Fax: (49 30) 491 4065

**Hermes Film GmbH**
Kaiserplatz 7
47441 Munich
Tel: (49 89) 394 368
Fax: (49 89) 344 363

**Oko-Film GmbH**
Mauerkircherstr. 3
81679 Munich
Tel: (49 89) 987 666
Fax: (49 89) 987 602

**Olga Film GmbH**
Tengstr. 16
80798 Munich
Tel: (49 89) 271 2635
Fax: (49 89) 272 5768

**Regina Ziegler Filmproduktion**
Budapesterstr. 35
10789 Berlin
Tel: (49 30) 261 8071
Fax: (49 30) 262 8213

**Rialto Film GmbH**
Bismarckstr. 108
13469 Berlin
Tel: (49 30) 310 0000
Fax: (49 30) 3100 0559

**Roxy-Film GmbH**
Schützenstr. 1
80335 Munich 2
Tel: (49 89) 555 341
Fax: (49 89) 594 510

**Studio Hamburg**
Tonndorfer Hauptstr. 90
22045 Hamburg
Tel: (49 40) 66 880
Fax: (49 40) 665 601/6688 4370

**Tele-München GmbH**
Kaufingerstr. 25
80331 Munich
Tel: (49 89) 290 930
Fax: (49 89) 290 93129

**Vision Film GmbH**
Kurfürstenplatz 4

80796 Munich
Tel: (49 89) 390 029
Fax: (49 89) 395 569

**Von Vietinghoff Filmproduktion**
Potsdamerstr. 199
10783 Berlin
Tel: (49 30) 216 8931
Fax: (49 30) 215 8219

# Distributors

**Advanced Film Verleih**
Keltenring 11
82041 Oberhaching
Tel: (49 89) 613 805-5
Fax: (49 89) 613 805-61
www.@advanced-film.de

**Advanced Film Verleih**
Raiffeinsenallee 16
82041 Oberhaching
Tel: (49 89) 273 7610
Fax: (49 89) 273 76173

**Ascot Filmverleih GmbH**
St. Annastr. 16
80538 Munich
Tel: (49 89) 296 995
Fax: (49 89) 331 839

**Buena Vista International**
Kronstadter Strasse 9
81677 Munich
Tel: (49 89) 99 34 0-0
Fax: (49 89) 929 40 01

**Columbia TriStar
Filmgesellschaft GmbH**
Ickstattstr. 1
80469 Munich
Tel: (49 89) 236 90
Fax: (49 89) 264 380

**Columbia TriStar
Filmgesellschaft GmbH**
Kemperplatz 1
10785 Berlin
Tel: (49 30) 2575 5800
Fax: (49 30) 2575 5809
www.columbiatristar.de

**Concorde Filmverleih GmbH**
Rosenheimerstr. 143 B
81671 Munich
Tel: (49 89) 4506 100
Fax: (49 89) 4506 1014

**Constantin Film AG**

Kaiserstrasse 39
80801 Munich
Tel: (49 89) 386 090
Fax: (49 89) 386 09-242

**Delphi Filmverleih GmbH & Co. KG**
Kurfürstendamm 225
10719 Berlin
Tel (49 30) 885 974-0
Fax: (49 30) 885 974-15

**Filmverlag der Autoren**
Neue Schönhauserstrasse 20
10178 Berlin
Tel: (49 30) 300 697-0
Fax: (49 30) 300 697-11

**Helkon Filmverleih**
Rauchstrasse 9-11
81697 Munich
Tel: (49 89) 9980 5800
Fax: (49 89) 9980 5810
www.helkon.de

**Helkon Media Filmvertrieb GmbH**
Widenmayerstr. 36
80538 Munich
Tel: (49 89) 2916 0490
Fax: (49 89) 291 3720

**Jugend Film Verleih GmbH**
Reichsstrasse 15
14052 Berlin
Tel: (49 30) 300 6970
Fax: (49 30) 3006 9711

**Kinowelt Filmverleih GmbH**
Schwere-Reiterstrasse 35
Building 14
80797 Munich
Tel: (49 89) 307 960
Fax: (49 89) 3079 6701

**Progress Film Verleih**
Burgstrasse 27
10178 Berlin
Tel: (49 30) 2400 3400
Fax. (49 89) 2400 3459

**ScotiaFilm GmbH**
Possartstr. 14
81679 Munich
Tel: (49 89) 413 0900
Fax: (49 89) 470 6320

**SenatorFilm GmbH**
Kurfürstendamm 65
10707 Berlin
Tel: (49 30) 8809 1700
Fax: (49 30) 8809 1790

**20th Century Fox of Germany GmbH**
Postfach 70 11 22
60561 Frankfurt am Main
Tel: (49 69) 609 020
Fax: (49 69) 627 716

**TiMe Filmverleih GmbH**
Brüsselerstr. 89–93
50672 Cologne
Tel: (49 221) 952 9680
Fax: (49 221) 19529 6866

**TiMe Film Verleih**
Potsdam
Tel: (49 331) 721 5540
Fax: (49 331) 721 5570

**Tobis Studio Canal**
Pacellialle 47
14195 Berlin
Tel: (49 30) 839 007-0
Fax. (49 30) 8390 0765

**Transit Film GmbH**
Dachauerstrasse 35
80335 Munich
Tel: (49 89) 555 261
Fax: (49 89) 596 122

**Transit Film GmbH**
Dachauerstrasse 36
80335 Munich
Tel: (49 89) 599 885-0
Fax: (49 89) 599 885-20

**United International Pictures GmbH**
Hahnstr. 31-35
60528 Frankfurt am Main
Tel: (49 69) 669 8190
Fax: (49 69) 666 6509

**Warner Bros Film GmbH**
Hans-Henny-Jahn-Weg 35
22085 Hamburg
Tel: (49 40) 226 500
Fax: (49 40) 2265 0259

**Warner Bros. Film GmbH**
Jarrestrasse 4
22303 Hamburg
Tel: (49 40) 226 500
Fax: (49 40) 2265 0259

# Useful Addresses

**Verband der Filmverleiher e.V (49 VDI)**
(49 Assn. of Distributors)
Kreuzberger Ring 56
65205 Wiesbaden
Tel: (49 611) 778 920
Fax: (49 611) 778 9212

**Export Union**
Türkenstr. 93
80799 Munich
Tel: (49 89) 390 095
Fax: (49 89) 395 223

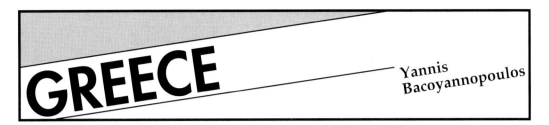

# GREECE

Yannis
Bacoyannopoulos

**M**ultiplex construction in Greece continues to outstrip consumer demand. Since January 2000, Village Park, the biggest complex in Greece, with 20 screens, has been doing excellent business in a rundown area near the centre of Athens. Traditional, isolated movie theatres have already suffered a devastating drop in admissions and several have closed. The relative difficulty in finding large enough chunks of real estate for new multiplexes in the centre of the major cities has made it possible for centrally located movie theatres to hang on to their audiences, but the prospects are grim.

The invasion of multi-screen theatres has secured the dominance of American cinema, with Hollywood films, and some other English-language productions now completely dominating the top 20 box-office spots. The notable exceptions to this rule were the Greek films which ranked first and tenth in the chart for 1999. In the number one spot, **Safe Sex**, directed and co-written by Thanassis Papathanassiou, broke the all-time box-office record for a Greek film, with 900,000 admissions in the Greater Athens area alone. A comedy that pokes fun at sexual behaviour in present-day Athens, it follows eight parallel stories, brief erotic adventures that take place in apartments and offices. In tenth place on the chart was **Beware of Greeks Bearing Guns**, a romantic comedy about a school-teacher heading a vendetta spanning three generations.

The public's preference for Greek films concerns mostly popular comedies like *Safe Sex*, which are to a certain degree extensions of hit television series. These films constitute an autonomous genre, comparable to the comedies of the old Greek cinema, but a number of more

demanding films did achieve respectable results, despite their limited distribution. These included Costas Kapakas' drama about a middle-aged man's reminiscence of childhood and adolescence, *Peppermint* (which swept most of the State Awards), and purely 'art' movies such as Michael Cacoyannis' *The Cherry Orchard* and Dimos Adveliodis' *The Four Seasons of the Law*. In total, the 15 Greek films released in 1999-2000 drew 2.3 million admissions nation-wide, the highest figure for 15 years.

Encouraged by this optimistic message, the Greek Film Centre (GFC), in collaboration with exhibitors, has proceeded with the creation of a small network of movie theatres that will support the distribution of Greek and European films, as well as arthouse retrospectives.

The expansion of financial resources available to Greek film-makers, thanks largely to the GFC, is combined with positive new developments in production. Independent producers are becoming more

*Still from Dionysis Gregoratos' TOO EARLY TO FORGET*

daring, well-established distributors are also investing in production, often as a film's principal investor, and independent television networks (following in the footsteps of state television) have begun to participate, either by co-producing the occasional film or by carrying out their legal obligation to invest 1.5% of their revenues in motion picture production.

Greek cinema is entering a promising phase.

YANNIS BACOYANNOPOULOS has written on film for Greek newspapers and magazines since 1960, and for the past 20 years has been film critic for the Athens daily *Kathimerini* and Greek State Television ET-1.

# Recent and Forthcoming Films

### BACKDOOR

Script: Yorgos Tsemberopoulos, Deni Iliadi. Dir: Tsemberopoulos. Prod: Ideefixe Ltd./Greek Film Centre (Greece)/BA Production (France)/FILMEX (Romania).

Coming-of-age story, set in Athens in 1966, a period of transformation and destruction when Greeks giddily sought role models in both East and West. A major building contractor dies suddenly of a heart attack when the new government forces him to stop building his life's work, a 12-storey high-rise in downtown Athens. His 13-year-old son, Dimitris, decides to bypass his childhood and grow up very fast.

### TOO EARLY TO FORGET

Dir: Dionyssis Gregoratos. Prod: Gregoratos/Hyperion S.A./Greek Film Centre/ERT.

Drama set in the near future, in a harbour threatened by ecological catastrophe. A missing sailor draws the group of people searching for him into his own bitter fate.

### THE MONKEY QUEEN

Script: Christopher Christophis, based on his book, *The Comedy of Mythomani*. Dir: Christophis. Prod: Greek Film Centre/Takis Zervoulakos.

A black-and-white situation comedy set in 1999 on a ship sailing from Montenegro to Piraeus. It is carrying fortune hunters and oddballs.

### GOLDEN FIELDS OF WHEAT

Script: Giorgos Zafiris and Christos Koulinos. Dir: Zafiris. Prod: Notos/GFC/ERT.

A young man who returns to his

homeland and finds it completely changed makes a wager with himself that he can rebuild the lost landscape of his memory.

### THE FOUR SEASONS OF THE LAW

Script and Dir: Dimos Avdeliodis. Prod: GFC/Avdeliodis/ET-1.

The island of Chios, 1960. Following the sudden death of the local rural guard, the council of the village of Tholopotami pressures the district agronomist to appoint a new man. Several rural guards refuse to go to the village, which has a bad reputation. Eventually four men volunteer for the post but each in turn fails in his mission and is dismissed.

### THE LIGHT THAT FADES

Script: Despina Tomazani. Dir: Vassilis Douros. Prod: Attika S.A.

Christos Myrisiotis, 12-year-old son of divorced parents, lives with his mother Eleni on a remote Aegean island. He has remarkable talent as a violinist, but is

going blind as a result of a rare disease. He has become an eccentric loner who creates a dream world in a cave, finds friendship with his classmate, Angeliki, and with the island's old lighthouse-keeper, Soursoumis. Everything changes when a new schoolteacher, Maria, arrives on the island.

### RISOTTO

Script: Olga Malea, Manina Zoumboulaki. Dir: Malea. Prod: Papandreou S.A.

Domestic comedy about Eugenia, a photographer, and Vicky, a stylist, who are both married with children. They have to cope with constant stress, fighting with their unhelpful husbands, and end up taking their frustrations out on their kids. When they move into the same house with both sets of kids, life becomes easier – until their husbands form an alliance to win them back, causing huge domestic and sexual mix-ups.

### HOME SWEET HOME

*Still from Dimos Avdeliodis' THE FOUR SEASONS OF THE LAW*

Dir: Phillippos Tsitos. Prod: Ideefixe Ltd./Twenty-Twenty vision (Germany).

A series of tragi-comic stories about a group of aimless people who run into each other in the course of a disastrous eve-of-wedding party in honour of an American guy and a German girl.

## THE OFFERING

Dir: Andreas Pantzis.

The adventures of a deeply religious man on Cyprus, who in his desperate desire to have a son makes an offering to Saint Andreas. When the son is born, the man starts a long journey on foot to the Saint's monastery on the other side of the island.

## THE BELLY OF THE BEE

Dir: Vassilis Eleftheriou.

Drama set in a riverside children's holiday camp.

## THE VERY POOR, INC.

Script: George Kotanidis. Dir: Antonis Kokkinos. Prod: Mythos/ Alpha TV/Odeon S.A./Protasis S.A./GFC/Filmnet.

Odysseus (Yannis Bezos), a brilliant scientist but also a confirmed workaholic, hopes to get his life back when he comes up with a unique system for utilising recycled garbage. A surrealistic, entertaining comedy unfolds against a

background of big-city paranoia.

## IN GOOD COMPANY

Script: Nikos Zapatinos. Dir: N. Zapatinos. Prod: Mythos/Alpha TV/Odeon S.A./Protasis S.A./ Filmnet.

A madman and an imprisoned robber, both given five days of freedom, meet as a result of a car crash in the middle of nowhere. They are observed by a doctor and his assistant who are studying the madman's behaviour, and by two cops trying to discover where the money from the robbery is hidden. The situation becomes even more complicated when they meet the madman's gorgeous aunt. A whimsical comedy, full of crazy situations.

# HONG KONG — Derek Elley

In late 1999 a sense of confidence started to return to the Hong Kong industry after three years of jitters, and by early 2000 the territory was consumed with dot.com fever as fresh money was pumped into the production sector and talent realigned itself. After the most prolonged shock to its system for several decades, it looked like it was back to business as usual by summer 2000, though with a strong sense of caution still apparent.

The doomsayers – both local and foreign – were proved wrong in writing off Hong Kong cinema, as it once again demonstrated its flexibility. After drawn-out internal "restructuring", Golden Harvest has remained committed to production; one-man industry Johnnie To jumped into bed with China Star to set up the Hundred Years of Cinema company, uniting himself with the likes of Tsui Hark and Ringo Lam. Media Asia is forging ahead with a double-edged slate of big-budget action pictures and high-profile movies attached to name directors; the Star East/Bob & Partners grouping, led by Wong Jing, remains devoted to the popular market.

Video distributor Mei Ah announced its own slate; sales company Golden Network moved into film and TV production with dot.com Cosmedia; and following his Hollywood film *The Love Letter*, Peter Chan "returned" to Hong Kong by attaching his name to a new company, Applause Pictures (backed by Star East).

This commitment to production is mostly to fuel the future demand for titles as the downloadable internet market dawns: much of the new money pumped into the market has come from internet companies investing in established production units. More and more – except in the US – theatrical revenues are becoming poor indicators of how a market is performing. The problem for statisticians is that reliable figures for other revenues are very hard to pin down – and impossible in East Asia, especially Hong Kong.

## The bottom line

For what they are worth, the theatrical figures for Hong Kong in 1999 showed

*Still from Johnnie To's THE MISSION*

little change in the trend of the past two years: an ever-increasing number of titles released (including, since summer 1999, some 53 shown in Beta or Digital Video), and fewer and fewer scoring at the box-office. No real lessons have been learned from the mid-1990s crisis, but at least Hong Kong has not lost its vitality and quick wits – both of which secure its place as the main engine room of Chinese-language production.

Excluding Beta/DV releases, 93 Hong Kong films were released in 1999, up from 84 in 1998, and the total gross was again down, to some $43m (HK$335m) against $53m the previous year. Much of this was made by a few titles: the Stephen Chiau comedy *King of Comedy* (1999's box-office champ with takings of around $3.8m), Jackie Chan's romantic action-comedy *Gorgeous*, and the Andrew Lau-directed *A Man Called Hero*. Solid mid-range successes (grossing around $1.3m-$2.6m) were dominated by popular Bob & Partners productions (*The Conmen in Las Vegas*, *Price Charming*, *The Tricky Master*, *The Legend of Speed*), plus three from Media Asia (*Gen-X Cops*, *Purple Storm*, *Tempting Heart*), and one each from Golden Harvest (*Fly Me to Polaris*) and China Star (*Running out of Time*).

Over Chinese New Year 2000 (February), three big productions joined battle, with Golden Harvest's *Tokyo Raiders* scoring $3.6m, Bob & Partners' swordplay adventure *The Duel* in second place with $2.7m, and Media Asia's Singapore-set actioner *2000 AD* earning $1.7m.

Mainland Chinese and Taiwanese movies still perform feebly in Hong Kong, despite being lauded at film festivals overseas. Chen Kaige's massive costume drama *The Emperor and the Assassin* made a paltry $24,000, and Hou Hsiao-hsien's *Flowers of Shanghai* around $125,000. The most successful Mandarin film was Zhang Yimou's *Not One Less*, with $320,000.

With all the talk in recent years of Hollywood taking over the market, it was, in fact, a Japanese film, "psycho-horror" *The Ring*, that was the year's top grosser, at $4m. This immediately sparked a flood of Japanese films into Hong Kong (plus local copycats); and at the end of the year the moderate success of South Korean actioner *Shiri* – the first Korean title released there in ages – underlined the new reality: that Hong Kong is now part of a broader East Asian market. Cross-financing with Japan had been growing throughout the 1990s; now Hong Kong producers gaze with interest at the newly-resurgent industry in Korea (previously only regarded as a location).

## Heroes and lovers

Artistically, the past year has been an interesting one. After a couple of lame ducks, director-producer Johnnie To had a critical success with **The Mission**, a wonderfully stylish, almost minimalist study of heroic codes, directed with restraint and featuring fine performances from his regular gallery of actors. Actress-director Sylvia Chang had her biggest success in some time with the very personal, cleverly constructed melodrama **Tempting Heart**, a love-triangle with Takeshi Kaneshiro, Gigi Leung and Karen Mok.

Ringo Lam branched out with the genre-mixing **Victim** (ghost story-meets action drama), with Lau Ching-wan and Tony Leung Kar-fai. The film's box-office failure, however, subsequently led Lam to accept a Hollywood-funded Jean-Claude Van Damme vehicle, *Replicant*, shot in Vancouver. One of the most original movies of the past year was scriptwriter

Riley Ip's **Metade Fumaca**, a beautiful meditation on memory and friendship, co-produced by Media Asia and UFO, but strongly suffused by the warm and richly-textured UFO style.

With Vincent Kuk directing, Jackie Chan made a bold career swerve with **Gorgeous**, pairing himself with Taiwanese-born actress Shu Qi in a charming, and finally moving, romantic comedy in which action was only one of several important ingredients (Chan effectively alternates between Hong Kong and Hollywood films nowadays, remaining loyal to his home market). Between summer 1999 and spring 2000, the prolific Andrew Lau had a bonanza year: the boldly-structured **A Man Called Hero**, set in turn-of-the-century New York; the above-average racing drama, **The Legend of Speed** (also with actor Ekin Cheng); the offbeat swordplay drama, **The Duel**; and the charming (if throwaway) San Francisco-set romancer, **Sausalito**, pairing Leon Lai and Maggie Cheung, the latter giving her most natural performance in years.

Among festival names, it was a mixed year. Stanley Kwan fell flat on his face with

*Still from Riley Ip's METADE FUMACA*

the pretentious, embarrassingly acted farrago **The Island Tales**, an allegory set on a quarantined island. After almost two years, Wong Kar-wai finally produced **In the Mood for Love**, which made the Cannes competition screening by a matter of hours and earned Tony Leung Chiu-wai the Best Actor palm. Immaculately shot (in Bangkok, by Christopher Doyle and Mark Lee) but dramatically shallow, the 1960s Hong Kong-set melodrama aims for a refined, stylised approach which is impressive, but there is very little else to this repetitious movie.

# The 19th Hong Kong Film Awards

The following awards were announced on April 16, 2000:

**Best Film:** *Ordinary Heroes*.
**Best Director:** Johnny To (*The Mission*).
**Best Actor:** Andy Lau (*Running Out of Time*).
**Best Actress:** Helena Law (*Bullets over Summer*).
**Best Supporting Actor:** Ti Lung (*The Kid*).
**Best Suppprting Actress:** Carrie Ng (*The Kid*).

**Best Newcomer:** Cecilia Cheung (*Fly Me to Polaris*).
**Best Script:** Sylvia Chang, Catherine Kwan (*Tempting Heart*).
**Best Photography:** Arthur Wong (*Purple Storm*).
**Best Action Design:** Tung Wai (*Purple Storm*).
**Best Art Direction:** Man Nim-chung (*Tempting Heart*).
**Best Costume Design:** Dora Ng (*Purple Storm*).
**Best Editing:** Kwong Chi-leong (*Purple Storm*).
**Best Sound Effects:** Tsang King-cheung (*Purple Storm*).
**Best Original Song:** "The Stars Speak My Heart's Desire" (from *Fly Me to Polaris*).
**Best Original Music:** Peter Kam.

# Recent and Forthcoming Films

### 2046

Dir: Wong Kar-wai. Players: Tony Leung Chiu-wai, Hirosuke Kimura, Chang Chen. Prod: Jet Tone.

### GEN-Y COPS

Dir: Benny Chan. Players: Nicholas Tse, Cecilia Cheung. Prod: Media Asia.

### LEGEND OF ZU

Dir: Tsui Hark. Players: Ekin Cheng, Louis Koo, Zhang Ziyi, Kristy Yang. Prod: China Star.

## THE TOUCH
Dir: Lee Chi-ngai. Players: Michelle Yeoh. Prod: Media Asia.

## PRINCESS D
Dir: Sylvia Chang. Prod: Media Asia.

## VISIBLE SECRET
Dir: Ann Hui. Prod: Media Asia.

## SPACKED OUT
Dir: Lawrence Ah Mon.

## THE ACCIDENTAL SPY
Dir: Benny Chan. Players: Jackie Chan, Vivian Hsu, Wu Hsing-kuo, Kim Mae. Prod: Golden Harvest.

## OKINAWA – RENDEZ-VOUS
Dir: Gordon Chan. Players: Leslie Cheung, Faye Wong, Tony Leung Kar-fai.

## LAVENDER
Dir: Riley Ip. Players: Takeshi Kaneshiro, Kelly Chan. Prod: UFO/Golden Harvest.

## SUMMER HOLIDAY
Dir: Jingle Ma. Players: Richie Ren, Sammi Cheng. Prod: Golden Harvest.

## BEIJING LOVE STORY
Dir: Mabel Cheung. Prod: Media Asia.

# Producers

**Bob & Partners Co.**
22/F, 83 Austin Rd.
Tsimshatsui
Tel: (852) 2314 7198
Fax: (852) 2314 7120

**Chang-Hong Channel Film & Video Co. (HK)**
5/F, Blk A, Full View Bldg.
3-7 Liberty Ave.
Kowloon
Tel: (852) 2762 2689
Fax: (852) 2762 2692

**China Star Entertainment Group**
Unit 503C, Miramar Tower
1-23 Kimberley Rd.
Tsimshatsui
Tel: (852) 2313 1888
Fax: (852) 2191 9888

**Eastern Production**
Kimberley Mansion, GA
15 Austin Ave.
Tsimshatsui
Tel: (852) 2367 3328
Fax: (852) 2367 5797

**Golden Harvest/Golden Communications**
8 King Tung St.
Hammer Hill Rd.
Kowloon
Tel: (852) 2352 8222
Fax: (852) 2351 1683

**Impact Films Production**
6/F, Blk 2, Tien Chu Centre
1E Mok Cheong St.

Tokwawan, Kowloon
Tel: (852) 2715 6545
Fax: (852) 2713 3390

**Ko Chi Sum Films Co.**
Room 617, Hewlett Centre
52-54 Hoi Yuen Rd.
Kwun Tong
Tel: (852) 2793 1123
Fax: (852) 2793 1134

**Long Shong Pictures (H.K.)**
G/F, Blk D, 272 Prince Edward Rd.
West Kowloon
Tel: (852) 2338 2211
Fax: (852) 2336 9911

**Mandarin Films (Singapore)**
1801-2 Westlands Centre
20 Westland Rd

Quarry Bay
Tel: (852) 2579 1718
Fax: (852) 2579 1707

**Media Asia Films**
Rm 412-416, 4/F, World Commercial Centre
11 Canton Rd
Tsimshatsui
Tel: (852) 2314 4288
Fax: (852) 2314 4247

**Mei Ah Films Production Co.**
Unit 15-28, 17/F, Metro Centre,
Phase 1
32 Lam Hing St
Kowloon Bay
Tel: (852) 2754 2855
Fax: (852) 2799 3643

*Still from the award-winning PURPLE STORM*

**Milkyway Entertainment Group**
22/F, Remington Centre
23 Hung To Rd
Kwun Tong
Kowloon
Tel: (852) 2718 8128
Fax: (852) 2718 8122

**Mobile Film Production**
Flat C, 2/F, Dorfu Court
5-6 Hau Fook St
Tsimshatsui
Tel: (852) 2301 3008
Fax: (852) 2732 5315

**Pineast Pictures**
Flat B, 8/F, Beauty Mansion
69-71 Kimberley Rd
Kowloon
Tel: (852) 2722 0896
Fax: (852) 2311 4167

**Salon Films (H.K.)**
6 Devon Rd
Kowloon Tong
Tel: (852) 2338 0505
Fax: (852) 2338 2539

**Seasonal Film Corp.**
12/F, Flat H, Kim Tak Bldg
328 Nathan Rd
Kowloon
Tel: (852) 2385 6125
Fax: (852) 2770 0583

**Southern Film Co.**
Rm 1902, Dominion Centre
43-59 Queen's Rd East

Hong Kong
Tel: (852) 2528 4787
Fax: (852) 2865 1449

**Tomson (H.K.) Films Co.**
Suite 1406-09, 14/F,
China Resources Bldg
26 Harbour Rd
Hong Kong
Tel: (852) 2848 1668
Fax: (852) 2877 0590

**United Filmmakers Organisation**
Unit B, 11/F, Prosperous Centre
1 Knutsford Terrace
Tsimshatsui
Tel: (852) 2336 3298
Fax: (852) 2339 0972

**Win's Entertainment**
2A Kimberley Mansion
15 Austin Ave
Tsimshatsui
Tel: (852) 2739 2877
Fax: (852) 2369 0981

**Wong Jing's Workshop**
PO Box 99093
Tsimshatsui
Tel: (852) 2314 7198
Fax: (852) 2314 7120

## Useful Addresses

**Hong Kong Film Archive**
Rm 176, 7/F, Camplex
123A Fa Yuen St
Mongkok
Tel: (852) 2739 2139
Fax: (852) 2311 5229

**Hong Kong Film Directors Guild**
2/F, 35 Ho Man Tin St
Kowloon
Tel: (852) 2760 0331
Fax: (852) 2713 2373

**Hong Kong Film Academy**
PO Box 71311
Kowloon
Tel: (852) 2786 9349
Fax: (852) 2742 7017

**Hong Kong Film Institute**
6/F, 295 Lai Chi Kok Rd
Kowloon
Tel: (852) 2728 2690
Fax: (852) 2728 5743

**Hong Kong Theatres Assn.**
21/F, Hongkong-Chinese Bank
42 Yee Woo St
Causeway Bay
Tel: (852) 2576 3833
Fax: (852) 2576 1833

**Performing Artists Guild of H.K.**
145 Waterloo Rd
Kowloon
Tel: (852) 2794 0388
Fax: (852) 2338 7742

# HUNGARY — Derek Elley

It has been the best and worst of years for some time in Hungarian cinema, with (on the artistic side) a visionary new film from maverick Béla Tarr standing high among a field of largely mediocre movies and (on the business side) multiplexes continuing to increase overall cinema attendance. As in 1998, a handful of local movies did very well at the box-office – confirming that the torch of commercial film-making is not totally extinguished – while the vast majority of other titles were seen by a handful of people and will only surface abroad at festivals (if they are lucky).

No director except István Szabó has yet cracked the code of making a quality movie which will also appeal to overseas markets. Szabó's three-hour long **Sunshine**, tracing the history of a Jewish family across several generations, split critics down the middle. With Ralph Fiennes in three roles, one's reaction to the movie – always made with the utmost care, as usual with Szabó – depended much upon one's reaction to the actor. There is, however, a dramatic lassitude about the film that is more troubling.

*Ralph Fiennes in István Szabó's SUNSHINE*

The box-office champion of 1999 was Róbert Koltai's comedy *Professor Albeit*, which was released at the end of 1998 and by the end of the following year had garnered a hefty 240,000 admissions. In second place was Tamás Sas' youth movie *Pirates* (aka *You or Me*) with 183,500 admissions, and in fourth Péter Tímár's football fantasy *6:3* with 113,500. Some way down were the thriller *Europa Express*, with 57,000, and Miklós Jancsó's *The Lord's Lantern in Budapest*, with a respectable 33,000 (all of these titles were discussed in *IFG* 2000). Other titles garnered a few thousand admissions each.

In third place for the calendar year was Barna Kabay and Katalin Petényi's **Hippolyt**, an updated remake of a 1931 comedy classic directed by István Szekely (later known in Hollywood as Steve Sekely). Released in early December, it had already achieved 132,000 admissions by the end of the month, and by spring 2000 topped out at around 300,000, a major hit by local standards. The film has little potential outside Central Europe but was a well-made and well-acted comedy about a snobbish, nouveau-riche family which hires a butler and soon finds its life taken over by him. The film-makers set up their own distribution company, CinemaStar, to release it and used marketing tactics like teaser trailers and a music CD.

Overall, 17 Hungarian features were released during 1999 (including two video works), for a total of 593,000 admissions (against 404,000 the previous year) and box-office gross of some $1.2m (240m forints), a considerable rise on the 1998 total of $715,000. The success of *Professor Albeit* and *Hippolyt* accounted for much of this increase. By the end of 1999, Hungary boasted 13 multiplexes, including a 14-screener in Westend City Centre (one of whose theatres is digitally-equipped) and a 12-screen complex in Campona Shopping Centre.

## A disappointing Week

The new fare at the 31st Hungarian Film Week in early February 2000 was the weakest for some years. Márta Mészáros went to the well one time too many with **Little Vilma: The Last Diary** (*Kisvilma: az utolsó napló*), which closed her *Diary* series (1982-90) with a whimper rather than a bang. This archly written and stiffly staged prequel to the trilogy, set amongst leftist intellectuals drawn to the Soviet experiment in the early 1930s, was notable only for some poetic photography of the Kirgiz landscape by Mészáros' son, Nyika Jancsó.

Nyika's father, veteran Miklós Jancsó, continued his new collaboration with writer-cameraman Ferenc Grunwalsky and his old one with writer Gyula Hernádi, in **Damn You! Mosquito** (*Anyad! A szúnyogok*), a companion piece to *Lord's Lantern* but considerably more shapeless and obscure to non-Hungarians. A meditation on Hungary's past and present, featuring the same two gravedigger characters, it does not represent a particularly rich new direction for the 79-year-old director, and clearly demonstrates his indifference to what people think of his work.

The variable Krisztina Deák, whose work has shown a tendency towards melodrama, filmed Hungary's top-selling novel of 1999, Pál Závada's **Jadviga's Pillow** (*Jadviga párnája*), centred on a fractured marriage in the Slovak community during the late 1910s and early 1920s. Rather too long for foreign tastes, at 134 minutes, it is essentially an intimate, small-scale drama, with a good central performance by Ildikó Tóth as the strong but unsatisfied wife married to an impetuous, immature young man (Viktok Bodó). Cutting would help to bring out the film's better qualities, which include a wedding night shown in painstaking detail.

The best film on show was a deceptively simple movie by András Surányi entitled **Film...**, which gave wonderful opportunities to two veteran players, Iván Darvas and Hédi Temessy, as an old couple who have spent a lifetime together and effectively closed themselves off from the world. Full of marvellous touches, and oblique references, it is a connoisseur's movie, faulted only by some pretentious bookends which could easily be removed.

### Views from bar and shop

Little else at the Film Week stood out from the pack, though some films had individual strengths. Andor Lukáts' characters-in-a-bar comedy **Portuguese** (*Portugál*), from the stage success by András Monori and Zoltán Egressy, boasts faultless ensemble playing (by many of the stage cast) and fully rounded performances, but its humour is too local. Even more familiar in tone and content was another rural comedy, György Molnár's **We Live Only Once** (*Egyszer élünk*), centred on a quirky family whose drunken father reappears after being presumed dead.

The highly-touted **Glamour**, by Frigyes Gödrös, which represented Hungary in Berlin's Panorama, turned out to be a wearying, corner-shop view of 80 years of Hungarian history through the eyes of a Jewish family. Five years in the making, it simply recalled earlier, far better neighbourhood movies by directors like Szabó (*25, Fireman's Street*; *Budapest Tales*).

After *Espresso* and *Pirates*, Tamás Sas came up with the disappointing **Bad Guys** (*Rosszfiúk*), a dramatically fuzzy drama set in an anarchic institution for delinquent boys. More interesting, though resolutely small-scale, was Mihály Buzás' lightly comic **The Little Voyage** (*A kis utazás*), following a group of high-school teenagers who win a trip to an East German holiday camp in the 1970s.

Two films had a non-Hungarian look and feel. Péter Meszáros' **The Foolish Pomegranate Tree** (*A bolond gránátamafa*) was a plotless mood piece shot in sepia and set among a group of eccentrics in old Tbilisi that was more Georgian in tone and humour. And, though a promising debut, András Fésős' **Seaside, Dusk** (*Balra a nap nyugszik*), an existential-flavoured movie about the weird relationship between a Budapest drifter and a solitary woman, was more German-looking, with strong shades of Wim Wenders.

### Overpowering *Harmonies*

Towering above all the year's other Hungarian films was Béla Tarr's **Werckmeister Harmonies** (*Werckmeister harmoniák*), his first feature since the stunning, seven-and-a-half-hour *Satan's Tango* (1994). One of the highlights of the Quinzaine at Cannes 2000, it belatedly helped to restore Hungary's reputation on the festival circuit.

Four years in the making, and a mere 145 minutes long, *Werckmeister* is a hypnotic meditation on Tarr's favourite themes of popular demagogy and mental manipulation, set in a wintry town visited by a strange, almost magical circus as jobless roam the streets and the country stands poised on the brink of revolution. The movie is almost like a boiled-down version of *Satan's Tango* but no less powerful, with a final half-hour that is overpoweringly moving and spiritually transcendent. Tarr's style of film-making will never solve the lingering problems of the Hungarian film industry, and is of an admittedly highly specialised nature; but he is that rare thing nowadays – a film-maker with a genuine vision rather than just a set of second-hand, pseudo-artistic attitudes.

The past year also saw the publication of an essential reference work for anyone interested in Hungarian cinema: *Hungarian Film Directors* (ISBN 963 03 8530 9; published jointly by the Hungarian Film Institute and Filmunio Hungary). This is an immensely valuable, English-language lexicon, collecting together material previously published in other books, but also updating it and adding new research. Each biofilmography is as complete as possible, and this 384-page hardback contains a large number of mugshots and stills. Where possible, entries also contain contact info, with telephone, fax and even e-mail details.

For the most comprehensive source of current information, listings and statistics,

*The poster image from WERCKMEISTER HARMONIES*

and anything else on the contemporary Magyar film industry, turn to the *Hungarian Film Guide 2000*. This handy, 224-page illustrated paperback is published by Montazs 2000, Harsfa utca 40, Budapest 1074; e-mail: montazs@mail.elender.hu; www.montazs2000.hu).

# 31st Hungarian Film Week Awards

**Best Film (shared):** *Glamour* and *Johnny Famous*.
**Best Director:** Miklós Jancsó (*Damn You! Mosquito*).
**Best Actress:** Hédi Temessy (*Film...*).
**Best Actor:** Iván Darvas (*Film...* and *The Morel Boy*)
**Best Script::** Sándor Tar (*We Live Only Once*).
**Best Photography:** András Nagy (*Seaside, Dusk*).
**Best First Film:** *This I Wish and Nothing More* (Kornél Mundruczó).
**Special Prizes:** actor József Szarvas (*We Live Only Once* and *A Matter of Life and Death*); director Krisztina Deák, director of photography Gábor

Balogh, art director József Romvári, costume designer Györgyi Szakács (*Jadviga's Pillow*); director Tibor Klöpfler (*El Niño*); actress Ildiko Toth (*Jadviga's Pillow* and *El Niño*).
**Gene Moskowitz Prize (foreign critics):** *Sunshine* (István Szabó).
**Best Experimental Film:** *Pannonian Hill* (József Szolnoki).
**Best Sound:** György Kovács (*Glamour* and *We Live Only Once*).
**Best Editor:** Eva Szentandrási (*Our Love*).
**Best Documentary:** *More Than Love* (Tamás Almási).
**Best Documentary Director:** Csaba Szekeres (*Ruin and Flower*).
**Audience Award:** *Le petit voyage* (Mihály Buzás).
**National Radio & TV Prize:** *Glamour*.

# Producers

**Béla Balázs Studio**
Bajcsy-Zsilinszky ut 36-38
1054 Budapest
Tel/Fax: (36 1) 111 2809

**Budapest Film Studio**
Róna utca 174

1045 Budapest
Tel: (36 1) 251 8568
Fax: (36 1) 251 0478

**Focus Film**
Pasaréti út 122
1026 Budapest
Tel: (36 1) 176 7484
Fax: (36 1) 176 7493

**Forum Film**
Róna utca 174
1145 Budapest
Tel/Fax: (36 1) 220 5413

**Hunnia Studio**
Róna utca 174
1145 Budapest
Tel: (36 1) 252 3170

Fax: (36 1) 251 6269

**InterPannonia**
(animation, also distribution)
Gyarmat utca 36
1145 Budapest
Tel: (36 1) 267 6514, 267 6515
Fax: (36 1) 267 6516

**Magic Media**
Róna utca 174
1145 Budapest
Tel: (36 1) 163 3479
Fax: (36 1) 263 3479

**Movie Innovation Partnership (MIP)**
Kinizsi utca 28
1092 Budapest
Tel: (36 1) 218 3600, 218 0983
Fax: (36 1) 216 3601

**Novofilm**
(also services)
Hajógyárisziget 131
1033 Budapest
Tel: (36 1) 188 9304
Fax: (36 1) 155 9177

**Objektiv Film Studio**
Róna utca 174
1145 Budapest
Tel: (36 1) 252 5359
Fax: (36 1) 251 7269

**Pannonia Film**
(animation)
Hüvösvölgyi út 64
1021 Budapest
Tel: (36 1) 176 3333
Fax: (36 1) 176 3409
ALSO
Róna utca 174
1145 Budapest
Tel/Fax: (36 1) 183 5930

**Varga Studio**
(animation, F/X)
Raktár utca 25-31
1035 Budapest
Tel: (36 1) 168 8296
Fax: (36 1) 168 6418

# Distributors

**Budapest Film**
Báthori utca 10
1054 Budapest
Tel: (36 1) 132 8198
Fax: (36 1) 111 2687

**Flamex**
Labanc utca 22B
1021 Budapest
Tel: (36 1) 176 1534
Fax: (36 1) 176 0596

**Hungarofilm**
(also production services)
Báthori utca 10
1054 Budapest
Tel: (36 1) 111 0020, 131 4746
Fax: (36 1) 153 1850

**InterCom**
Bácskai utca 28-36
1145 Budapest
Tel: (36 1) 467 1400
Fax: (36 1) 252 2736

**UIP-Dunafilm**
Hüvosvolgyi ut 54
1021 Budapest
Tel: (36 1) 274 2180
Fax: (36 1) 274 2177

# Useful Addresses

**Assoc. of Hungarian Film Distributors**
Karolina út 65
1135 Budapest
Tel/Fax: (36 1) 295 5001

**Filmunio Hungary**
(festivals, foreign promo)
Városligeti fasor 38
1068 Budapest
Tel: (36 1) 351 7760 351 7761
Fax: (36 1) 268 0070 351 7766

**Motion Picture Foundation of Hungary (MMA)**
Városligeti fasor 38
1068 Budapest
Tel: (36 1) 351 7696
Fax: (36 1) 268 0070

**Mafilm Corp.**
(studio complex)
Róna utca 174
1145 Budapest
Tel: (36 1) 252 2870
Fax: (36 1) 251 1080

**S-media 2000**
Szemlöhegy 28-30
1022 Budapest
Tel/Fax: (36 1) 326 0698

# ICELAND — Ásgrímur Sverrisson

The Icelandic film scene looks very promising in 2000-2001, with lots of ingenious activity across the board. This represents quite a change from the past few years, when film-makers were depressed by a shortage of funding, and other dispiriting factors. The government has positively addressed the financial problems of the Icelandic Film Fund and the television sector has also shown signs of increasing local production. In addition, the digital revolution has spread to Iceland, with five digital films in various stages of production, all shot on digital video (DV) by newcomers with minuscule budgets.

Optimism is in the air, although many in the industry are aware that it is becoming increasingly difficult to finance Icelandic-language movies through international co-production – a situation repeated throughout Europe, whose many languages all seem to be fighting a losing battle against almighty English. This struggle is not new, but, worryingly, it leaves Icelandic and other European film-makers asking how they can accurately represent the diversity of European culture and experience if market forces determine that they must shoot in English, especially when American films continue to dominate the cinemas.

The six films premiered in Iceland over the past year offered a wide range of subject matter and approaches. Haukur M's DV movie **Abnormality** (*Óedli*) premiered in 1999 to mixed reviews and low box-office. The director, who wrote the script and played the lead, did not even bother to transfer it to film, but used a video projector at the cinema. *Abnormality* is about a disturbed youngster who takes out his revenge on the girlfriend who left him for his best friend. The script and direction are adequate, but Haukur's energetic performance has some entertainment value; he has swiftly moved on to a second feature.

In scope and ambition, veteran director Hrafn Gunnlaugsson was at the other end of the film-making scale with **Witchcraft** (*Myrkrahöfdinginn*), an epic tale of sexual obsessions and religious fervour in seventeenth century Iceland. It comes out with all guns blazing – but unfortunately shoots mostly blanks. Gunnlaugsson opts for vulgarity where restraint and discipline are called for, and the result is a sprawling mess, redeemed only by the fine performance of Hilmir Snaer Gudnason in the lead role of a passionate priest who wants to save his flock from the devil, only to find demons raging within himself.

An altogether gentler experience was Gudny Halldórsdóttir's **The Honour of the House** (*Ungfrúin góda og húsid*), based on a short story by her father, the Nobel-prize winner Halldór Laxness. The tragi-comic story tells of a hypocritical and selfish woman who holds power over her younger, unselfish and humanitarian sister by hiding the shame of the younger sister's pregnancy, with the purpose of upholding the aristocratic status of their name and household. This is by far the best work to date by the experienced Halldórsdóttir, though the fine performances and rich atmosphere are slightly marred by unclear structure and underwritten characters. The film went on to win five Edda Awards at the first such ceremony held by the Icelandic Film and Television Academy in November 1999, including Picture, Director and Actress of the year (Tinna Gunnlaugsdóttir).

Fridrik Thór Fridriksson's latest, **Angels of the Universe** (*Englar alheimsins*) was released early in 2000. Based on a popular, Nordic Literature prize-winning book by his long-time collaborator Einar Már Gudmundsson, it turned out to be a gigantic hit, still showing six months after its premiere – and deservedly so. This is a wonderful, moving film about the life and death of a mentally ill man, told in a matter of fact style, with humour and compassion.

Ragnar Bragason's debut film, **Fiasco** (*Fíaskó*), based on his own script, earned a warm reception in March 2000. It is the story of a day in the life of a family in downtown Reykjavík, told in three segments, with each generation of the family getting their own story during one grey, snowy winter day. The grandfather falls in love with a faded beauty and former movie star; the mother dreams of love and spiritual enlightenment in the arms of a narcissistic preacher; the daughter can't decide which one of her two boyfriends is the father of the child she carries. This a lovely and at times touching film with flashes of black humour and told with conviction and wit.

Another film debutant, theatre director

and actor Baltasar Kormákur, gave us **101 Reykjavík**, based on a novel by Hallgrímur Helgason. It's a funny look at the empty life of an aimless, thirty-something who still lives with his mother, stays on the dole and in front of the computer all day, while partying hard at nights. Reality hits him straight on the chin when he discovers that he's the father of the child carried by his mother's pregnant lesbian lover. Energetic, fast and furious, the film has an excellent lead performance by Hilmir Snær Gudnason (who also appeared in *Witchcraft*), aided by a lively turn from Spanish star Victoria Abril as the lesbian lover.

The year 2000 seems to be heralding a generational change in Icelandic cinema, with around ten new directors working on their first films. What sets this new batch apart from their predecessors seems to be their emphasis on the here and now and the travails of modern living, rather than a desire to point their cameras at the past, as has so often been the case in Icelandic films. This is a welcome change of direction.

ÁSGRÍMUR SVERRISSON is a director and writer.

# Recent and Forthcoming Films

**ÓSKABÖRN THJODARINNAR (Plan b – report)**

Script and Dir: Jóhann Sigmarsson. Phot: Gudmundur Bjartmarsson. Players: Grímur Hjartarson, Óttar Proppe. Prod. Sigmarsson/Fridrik Thór Fridriksson.

Petty criminals and drug addicts seek a way out of their seedy underworld.

**IKINGUT**

Script: Jón Steinar Ragnarsson. Dir: Gísli Snaer Erlingsson. Phot: Sigurdur Sverrir Pálsson. Prod: Fridrik Thór Fridriksson/The Icelandic Film Corporation.

In the late seventeenth century, a small eskimo boy drifts on an iceberg from

Greenland to Iceland where the superstitious locals regard him as an evil spirit, apart from young Boas, the priest's son, who befriends him.

**VILLILJÓS (Dramarama)**

Script: Huldar Breidfjörd. Directors: Dagur Kári Pétursson, Inga Lísa Middleton, Ragnar Bragason, Ásgrímur Sverrisson, Einar Thor Gunnlaugsson. Phot: Agust Jakobsson. Prod.: Thorir Snaer Sigurjónsson, Skuli Malmquist/Zik Zak Filmworks.

Five darkly comic stories intertwine into one as Reykjavík suffers a powercut during a cold winter night.

**SÓLON ÍSLANDUS (Solon Leonardo Islandus)**

Dir. and script: Margrét Rún. Prod.: The Icelandic Dream Factory/Edgar Reitz Film-produktiongesellschaft mbH.

A historical drama about the eccentric nineteenth-century painter and philosopher Sölvi Helgason.

**GEMSAR (Cell)**

Script and dir: Mikael Torfason. Phot: Jakob Ingimundarson. Players: Halla Vilhjálmsdóttir, Sigurdur Skúlason, Matthías Freyr Matthíasson. Prod: ZikZak Filmworks.

Coming-of-age story about teenagers coming to terms with parental relationships and love.

**ÍSLENSKI DRAUMURINN (The Icelandic Dream)**

Script and Dir: Róbert I. Douglas. Phot: Júlíus Kemp. Players: Thórhallur Sverrisson, Jón Gnarr, Hafdís Huld, Matt Keeslar. Prod: Júlíus Kemp & Jón Fjörnir Thoroddsen.

A young businessman, weekend dad and fan of one of Iceland's worst football teams in Iceland has to cope with the day-to-day pressures of running his business, raising his child, dealing with his ex-wife, and, most importantly, watching his team loose every game of the season.

**AUSTAN VID MÓNA (East of the Moon)**

Script: Marteinn Thórisson, Ron Marryott & Ásgrímur Sverrisson.

Director: Erik Gustavson. Prod: Pegasus Pictures and ImX Communications.

Iceland. 1944, a group of US Allied Navy Seabee's are sent to build a military installation on a mountain in the East Fjords. They meet resistance from the villagers, who object to their plans, as they believe the elves, known as the "hidden people" inhabit the sacred mountain.

**MONSTER**

Script and Dir: Hal Hartley. Prod: Fridrik Thór Fridriksson/Icelandic Film Corporation

**REGÍNA**

Script: Margrét Örnólfsdóttir. Dir: María Sigurdardóttir. Prod:

Icelandic Film Corporation.

**FÁLKAR (Falcons)**

Script: Einar Kárason. Dir: Fridrik Thór Fridriksson. Prod: Icelandic Film Corporation in co-operation with Filmhuset (Norway), Bridie Films (UK) & Peter Rommel Film Productions (Germany).

**MÁVAHLÁTUR (Laughing Seagulls)**

Script and Dir: Ágúst Gudmundsson. Prod: Kristín Atladóttir. Produced by: Isfilm in co-operation with Archer Street (UK) & Exposed Film Productions (Norway)

# Producers

### The Icelandic Film Corporation
Contacts: Friðrik Thór Friðriksson, Anna María Karlsdóttir
Hverfisgata 46
101 Reykjavík.
Tel: (354) 5512260
Fax: (354) 5525154
e-mail: amk@vortex.is
www.saga.is/ifc

### Pegasus Pictures
Contact: Snorri Thórisson.
Sóltún 24
105 Reykjavík
Tel: (354) 511 4590
Fax: (354) 511 4595
pegasus@pegasus-pictures.com
www.pegasus-pictures.com

### Ísfilm
Contact: Ágúst Gudmundsson
Óðinsgata 20,
101 Reykjavík
Tel: (354) 5613395
Fax: (354) 5523395

### Umbifilm
Contacts: Halldór Thorgeirsson
Gudný Halldórsdóttir.
Melkot
270 Mosfellsbær
Tel: (354) 566-6874
Fax: (354) 566-8002

### ZIK ZAK Filmworks
Engjateigur 19
IS – 105 Reykjavík
Tel: (354) 511 2019/699 7664
Fax: (354) 511 3019
e-mail: sfmzz@itn.is/tsszz@itn.is

### Icelandic Filmcompany
Bankastraeti 11
IS-101 Reykjavík
Tel/Fax: (354) 562 4615
Website:
www.icelandicfilmcompany.com

# Useful Addresses

### Association of Icelandic Film Distributors
Laugarásbíó
Laugarási
104 Reykjavík
Tel: (354) 553 8150
Fax: (354) 568 0910

### Icelandic Film Fund
Contact: Thorfinnur Ómarsson
Túngata 14
101 Reykjavík
Tel: (354) 562-3580
Fax: (354) 562 7171
e-mail: iff@iff.is
www.iff.is

### Association of Icelandic Film Producers
Pósthússtraeti 13
PO Box 476
121 Reykjavík
Tel: (354) 562 8188
Fax: (354) 562 3424

### Ministry of Culture and Education
Sölvhólsgötu 4
101 Reykjavík
Tel: (354) 560 9500
Fax: (354) 562 3068

### The Icelandic Film Makers Association
PO Box 5162
121 Reykjavík
Tel: (354) 5521202
Fax: (354) 562 0958
e-mail: fk@isholf.is

### The Association of Icelandic Film Directors
Laugarnestangi 65
105 Reykjavík
Tel: (354) 588 1706
Fax: (354) 588 1706

### Land & synir
Bi-monthly film magazine
Björn Brynjúlfur Björnsson, editor
e-mail: bjorn@hugsjon.is

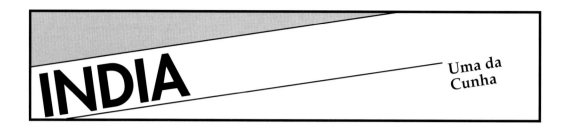

# INDIA

Uma da Cunha

The new millennium brought with it a new spin to 'globalisation', a much-reviled word among some of India's economic planners. For the despairing film industry, world earnings from exported products brought new hope. The business has been spoilt for too long by its reliance on the large national market, and formulaic films were the predictable outcome. By definition, Indian cinema had become stagnant, almost devoid of creative energy. Box-office takings have been studies in red, but now distributors are reaping come considerable overseas earnings.

Conversely, English-language imports have grown sharply, up ten-fold over the past eight years to stand at more than $80m in 2000. There was some local good news, too, in the form of a shining new star in his debut film. Hrithik Roshan is 26, green of eye, boyish of demeanour, twinkle-toed yet well-muscled. Even better, his dad is a producer and film personality in his own right, set on making a star of junior. His debut, **Tell Me You Love Me** (*Kaho Na – Pyar Hai*), opened in early January 2000, and was still filling houses six months later.

Time will tell how closely Roshan will approach the orbit of megastar Amitabh Bachchan. Nearly 60, Bachchan was voted the BBC's 'Star of the Millennium' in a worldwide poll, with Indian votes accounting for a goodly proportion of Bachchan's support. Bachchan plans to launch the career of *his* son, Abhishek, in a blockbuster, *Refugee*.

Overall, the domestic market is depressed, figuratively and in its figures. One major film after another has bombed. Yet negative costs – star salaries, production budgets and exhibition – continue to soar. Films continue to be made in the same numbers, without visible attempts at enonomy. It would be inexplicable were it not for some clues, like the fact that the 'industry' is not really recognised as such, certainly not by reputable banks. It is therefore an attractive piggybank for unaccounted, untaxed cash. Hence perhaps the lack of financial prudence and controls. Hence, also, the industry's secretive stance on money.

After all, there's this endlessly beckoning market created by the insatiable Indian appetite for the filmic fix. Here, films are FMCG (fast moving consumer goods). But there are parts of the silver screen behind a purdah. Government, national and local, continues to treat cinema as the golden goose. It is taxed at every turn. This, despite a film industry going blue in the face proclaiming its losses.

## A dangerous game

The blue mood has begun to stem from another source: fear. Film folk are becoming targets of a ruthless mafia. High profile figures are the victims of extortion and death threats, increasingly and tragically carried out, with several film personalities gunned down in public. In January 2000, a week after the opening of his celebrated *Kaho na – Pyar Hai*, producer Rakesh Roshan was shot and seriously wounded. An abortive murder attempt was made a month earlier on an important lab owner. Just before *Refugee*, the Bachchan biggie opened, a bid on the director's life was thwarted by police. The extortionists, it is said, no longer want cash. They demand overseas rights to films.

The treasure trove in their sights is the

Indian diaspora, affluent, many millions strong and faithful to the home and culture they left for economic reasons. The overseas audience for Indian films is now gaining immigrants from elsewhere too. The younger age groups are paying money for the idiosyncratic escapist fare.

The export market has grown an amazing 80% in the past two years. It is expected to double in the coming year. An expatriate Indian population of 15 million spends some $800m on Indian movies, TV serials and music. In 1998, just two films netted $8.2m in export sales, the equivalent of 60% of their total earnings in India. A favourable rupee/dollar exchange rate helps. *Taal*, not that successful in India, grossed $1.1m in the first ten days of its US release and did no less well in the UK. Director Subhash Ghai relished being told how the mainstream Hindi cinema was bringing back Indian values and customs to children cut off from their country. Parents back home may well think the opposite.

Today, film producers are making music-driven spectaculars tailored to the tastes of Indians and Asians settled abroad. Raj Kapoor, filming the 1950s-set *Sangam*, travelled to Switzerland to film a kissing scene, taboo in India. Today, filming overseas embellishes a story otherwise steeped in Indian culture.

Delegations from Switzerland, England, Australia, New Zealand, Africa and elsewhere have been courting the Indian film industry to use their locations. Hungary and India have a cultural tie-up which resulted in the making of **Straight from the Heart** (*Hum Dil De Chuke Sanam*), a major hit abroad, less so in India. The film was shot in India and Budapest, with the latter presented on screen as Italy. "Who has heard of Budapest in most of India?", asked director Sanjay Leela Bhansali. Italy is better-known.

## Southern star

Quite unexpected is the success of south Indian star Rajnikanth, first in Japan and now in South Korea. His Tamil film **Muthu**, released July 1998 in Tokyo, ran for 178 days, grossing $4m. A Japanese-language book about the film sold well. On June 2, 2000, it opened with Korean subtitles in Seoul to an impressive initial collection. Rajnikanth's latest film, *Padayappa*, was planned to hit Tokyo in July 2000, to coincide with the release of a compilation album of the actor's most famous film songs.

Indian beauty queens are vying for star power. The ethereal Aishwarya Rai, a former Miss World, is in demand after her ravishing appearance in *Straight from the Heart* and *Taal* and Sushmita Sen, a former Miss Universe, is also stealing stellar roles. The concept of the pliant, well-rounded Indian heroine is giving way to the western model: tall, slim, straight, striding, even strident.

India has slightly extended its lead as the world's most prolific film producer. In 1999, 764 films were censored, up 10% on the previous year. The regional break-up stayed the same, with Hindi leading (166 films) followed by the south Indian block with Tamil (153 ), Telugu (132), Kannada (87) and Bengali (51). Interestingly, there were six English releases. Foreign movies dubbed into Indian languages included *Titanic*, *The Sixth Sense*, *The Matrix* and *Star Wars: Episode I*.

With big-budget Indian movies pulling out, more playing time and theatres are being offered to English films. The English import has grown tenfold, from $840,000 in 1992 to $81m in 2000. Admissions, 8 million in 1992, are well over 15 million in mid-2000. American films now arrive in India soon after their international release. In mid-year, in Bombay city, a dozen English films were being screened, including the extremely popular *American Beauty* (which ran for six weeks) and *Erin Brockovich*.

## New movies, expatriate moguls

The regional arthouse movie in India is looking up. From Calcutta, young

Rituparno Ghosh (seen as a Satyajit Ray disciple) is launching three films in a single year. His **Lady of the House** (*Bariwali*) followed the festival trail after it opened at Berlin's Forum. His next, *Utsab*, was scheduled for a summer 2000 premiere in Los Angeles and his third, *Chokher Bali*, should be ready by January 2001. Buddhadeb Dasgupta's latest, *Uttara*, is competing in Venice. Goutam Ghosh has started his *Dhrishtipaat*. In Bombay, Shyam Benegal has two films ready, *Hari Bhari* and *Zubeida* (featuring glamour queen Karishma Kapoor). Govind Nihalani has begun *Deham*, based on Manjula Padmanabhan's prize-winning novel, *Harvest*.

In the south, V. Chandran has been shooting *Susanna* and Mani Ratnam's modest love story **The Waves** ran to full houses. There is fresh talent. From Karnataka, Kavita Lankesh presented her promising debut, **Deveeri**, at the Kerala International Film Festival, where it shared the FIPRESCI award. Newcomer V.K. Prakash showed signs of an innovative style in his debut feature, **Rehabilitation**.

Journalist-scriptwriter Khalid Mohammad is directing his first feature, **Fiza**, with Hrithik Roshan in the lead. Director-cinematographer Santosh Sivans' ground-breaking *The Terrorist* screened at the Toronto and Sundance festivals, and gained distribution in the US, thanks to the support of John Malkovich. Sivan's next is a ritzy historical extravaganza, *Asoka*, his first film in Hindi, with top star Shahrukh Khan in the lead.

Indian entrepreneurs abroad are looking homewards to create a new kind of international cinema. Houston-based telecom expert Sutapa Ghosh has teamed with Calcutta's Tapan Biswas to form Cinemawalla, which aims to fund and promote high-quality Indian cinema. Their first two ventures are films directed by Rituparno Ghosh.

*Still from Rituparno Ghosh's UTSAB*

*Manja, left, and Nandita Das in Kavitha Lankesh's DEVEERI*

In Washingon DC, the partnership of engineer-scientist D.G.Parekh with writer-director Raj Basu has led to the making of *Wings of Hope* starring Roshan Seth. In New York, writer-director Anurag Mehta is launching his mythic comedy, *American Chai*, teaming Indian actor Paresh Raval with locals Ajay Naidu, Aasif Mandvi, Sheetal Seth, Josh Ackeman and Alok Mehta.

A cloud gathered over foreign film shoots in India when Deepa Mehta's *Water* ran headlong into local politics. Her many attempts at resuming the shoot were scuttled despite reassurances. With luck, the film will still be made in India. The indefatigable Ismail Merchant released his **Cotton Mary**, launched James Ivory's *The Golden Bowl* in Cannes and by mid-2000 was working on his fourth film as a director. *The Mystic Masseur*, based on the V.S.Naipaul novel, will feature Sakina Jaffrey, Aasif Mandvi, Ayesha Dharker and Prayag Raj.

Mira Nair has been back on home ground, first with her documentary on the science of yogic laughter, **The Laughing Club of Bombay**. Her next feature, *A Monsoon Wedding*, which was scheduled to begin shooting in August 2000, will be India's first digital video production. The film harks back to Nair's own Punjabi community and their rambunctious, song-driven celebration of marriage.

UMA DA CUNHA heads Medius (India) Services Pvt Ltd, which provides casting, promotional and executive services for films shot in India. She is a freelance journalist and a consultant for festivals in India and abroad. She is preparing to launch her own publication, *India & International Screens*, in print and as a website.

# Recent and Forthcoming Films

## ASOKA

Script: Saket Chowdhury, Santosh Sivan. Dir and Phot: Sivan. Players: Shahrukh Khan, Kareena Kapoor, Danny Denzongpa. Prod: Arcs, Lights and Sound. Lang: Hindi.

After the minimalist *The Terrorist*, Sivan switches to a period extravaganza, featuring top-notch stars and India's traditional song-and-dance style. The film presents Emperor Asoka, whose reign around 260 BC introduced philosophical ideology and humanistic tenets, still revered today, into a warring society.

## UTSAB (Celebration)

Story, Script and Dir: Rituparno Ghosh. Phot: Aveek Mukhopadhaya. Players: Madhabi Mukherjee, Rituparna Sengupta, Pradeep Mukherjee, Alakananda Roy, Arpita Pal, Bodhisattva, Mazumdar, Anuradha Roy, Vinit Ranjan Mitra, Mamata Shankar, Ratul Shankar Ghosh, Prosenjit Chatterjee. Prod: Sutapa Ghosh and Tapan Biswas for Cinemawalla. Lang: Bengali.

An elderly matriarch welcomes family members at her country home for their annual celebration of the four-day Durga Puja festival. As the festivities proceed, their suppressed anxieties, rivalries and greed begin to simmer. Lead player Madhabi Mukherjee gave an unforgettable performance in Satyajit Ray's *Charulata*.

## CHOKHER BALI (Sand in her Eye)

Script and Dir: Rituparno Ghosh. Story: Rabindranath Tagore. Phot: Aveek Mukhopadhaya. Players: Prasenjit Chatterjee, Nandita Das, Raima Sen. Prod: Sutapa Ghosh and Tapan Biswas for Cinemawalla. Lang: Bengali.

Ghosh, an adept observer of psychological interplay, traces a complex and disturbing quadrangular relationship, involving lost opportunities, personal sacrifice and emotional revenge.

## ZUBEIDA

Story and Script: Khalid Mohammad. Dir: Shyam Benegal. Phot: Rajen Kothari. Players: Karisma Kapoor, Manoj Bajpai, Rekha, Amrish Puri, Shakti

Kapoor. Prod: Farouq K Rattonsey for SKR Prods. Lang: Hindi.

A young man, Riyaz, who has set out to uncover the life story of the mother he never knew, discovers the passionate but tragic love story of Zubeida, a daring young woman who flouts convention.

## UTTARA (The Wrestlers)

Script and Dir: Buddhadeb Dasgupta. Story: Samaresh Bose. Phot: Asim Bose. Players: Jaya Seal, Tapas Paul, Shankar Chakravarty, Raisul Islam Asad, Sourav Das. Producer: Dulal Roy. Language: Bengali.

In a distant rustic village, two staunch friends who love to wrestle, along with a Christian pastor and his tribal converts, are all caught in a vortex of violence.

## LAGAAN (Land Tax)

Dir: Ashutosh Gowarikar. Phot: Anil Mehta. Players: Aamir Khan, Gracie Singh, Suhasini Mulay, Om Puri. Prod: Aamir Khan Prods Pvt Ltd. Lang: Hindi.

In Imperial India in the early nineteenth century, a British army base hopes to upstage the simple, gutsy local folk of an adjoining village to prove their might and superiority as rulers. The matter is put to a simple, outrageous test.

## ALAIPAYUTHEY (The Waves)

Script and Dir: Mani Ratnam. Phot: P.C.Sreeram. Players: Madhavan, Shalini, Jayasudha, Swanamalaya, Raviprakash. Prod: G.Srinivasan. Lang: Tamil.

Two medical students fall in love and marry, but marriage is followed by niggling problems which threaten to sever their relationship.

## EK ALAG MAUSAM

Story and Script: Mahesh Dattani. Dir: K.P.Sasi. Phot: Sunny Joseph. Players: Rajat Kapoor, Nandita Das, Anupam Kher, Sally Whittaker, Gargi Vegiraju,Yash Joshi. Prod: Action-Aid. Lang: Hindi

Set in and around a hospice, the film is a love story about HIV-positive adults and children.

*Om Puri, right, in BOLLYWOOD CALLING*

## FIZA

Story, Script and Dir: Khalid Mohammed. Phot: Santosh Sivan. Players: Karisma Kapoor, Hrithik Roshan, Jaya Bachchan, Manoj Bajpai, Sushmita Sen, Nadira, Bikram Saluja. Prod: Pradip Guha. Lang: Hindusthani.

Loosely based on a true story, the film traces a middle-class Muslim girl's search for her brother, who's been missing for six years. She eventually tracks him down in Rajasthan. This is a first feature by a leading film journalist and scriptwriter.

## BOLLYWOOD CALLING

Script and Dir: Nagesh Kukunoor. Phot: Keshav Prakash. Players: Om Puri, Navin Nischol, Patrick Cusick, Perizaad Zorabian. Prod: Satyam Entertainment. Lang: English.

Filming a Bombay masala-musical, producer Ubramaniam plans legendary star Manu Kapur's comeback, pairing him with American B-minus actor Pat Stormore and aspiring starlet Kajal. Stormore arrives to find the producer parading in his home-town, Hyderabad, as a moneyed big-wig.

## BAS YAARI RAKHO (My Little Devil)

Script and Dir: Gopi Desai. Phot: Darshan Dave. Players: Rushab Patni, Om Puri, Pooja Batra, Satyajit Sharma, Firdausi

Jassawalla, Gaffar Modi, Rachit Mehta. Prod: Productions La Fete (Canada)/NFDC (India). Lang: Hindi.

A film about a small boy, Joseph, uprooted from his peaceful village life to live as a boarder at a private Christian school in the city, where he must make a painful adjustment to its strict regime.

## THE MYSTIC MASSEUR

Script: Paul Bradley, based on V.S.Naipaul's novel. Dir: Ismail Merchant. Phot: Larry Pizer. Players: Om Puri, Sakina Jaffrey, Asif Mandvi, Ayesha Dharker. Prod: Merchant-Ivory. Lang: English.

In 1950s Trinidad, where black, white and Indian people form a multi-cultural melting pot, an Indian goes to his village for his father's burial and stays on to be a writer. After his initial failure as an author, he turns into a sought-after healer, which in turn propels him into politics.

## SUSANNA

Dir and Script: T.V.Chandran. Phot: K.G.Jayan. Players: Vani Vishwanath, Bharat Gopi, Nedumudy Venu, Charuhasan, Narendra Prasad. Prod: T.V.Chandran. Lang: Malayalam.

An unmarried mother living in orthodox Kerala in the 1970s is forced to become the mistress of her lover's father. She smokes, drinks and becomes the paramour of five men, all of whom depend on her.

## DEHAM (Harvest)

Script: Manjula Padmanabhan, based on her novel. Dir, Phot and Prod: Govind Nihalani. Players: Kitu Gidwani, Joy Sengupta, Ali Khan, Surekha Sikri, Mohan Kapur, Salone Mehta, Suhita Thatte, Sumant Jaikrishnan. Lang: Hindi and English.

Set in the second decade of the twenty-first century, the film dwells on the undercurrent of conflict between technologically advanced countries and third world nations.

## BAVANDAR (The Sandstorm)

Script: Ashok Mishra and Jag Mundhra. Dir: Jagmohan. Phot: Ashok Kumar. Players: Nandita Das, Rahgubir Yadhav, Rahul Khanna, Gulshan Grover, Govind Namdeo, Ravi Jhankal. Prod: Smriti Pictures Pvt Ltd. Lang: Hindi and English.

When a rural low-caste woman working for a Rajasthan government development scheme speaks out against child

marriage, she is gang-raped by the village's upper-caste men. Seeking justice, she is pitted against a judicial system rife with sexism, chauvinism, feudalism and political chicanery.

## THE LAUGHING CLUB OF BOMBAY

Documentary. Dir: Mira Nair. Phot and Prod: Adam Bartos. Prod: Mirabai Films Inc/LaForest Inc. Lang: English.

A lively documentary on the growing popularity in Bombay of the yogic science of laughter, a novel health practice.

## DHRISIPAAT (Glance)

Script, Story, Dir and Phot: Gautom Ghosh. Players: Soumitra Chatterjee, Debashree Roy. Prod:

Following his documentary on Satyajit Ray, the first to be based on the master's fabled red books, Gautom Ghosh started shooting this new feature in May 2000. It's the story of three people separated by age, class and gender but united by their blindness: one was born blind, another blinded by an accident, the third through old age.

## HARI BHARI (Fertility)

Script: Shama Zaidi. Dir: Shyam Benegal. Phot: Rajen Kothari. Players: Shabana Azmi, Nandita Das, Surekha Sikri, Rajat Kapoor, Shree Vallabh Vyas. Prod: Ministry of Health and Family Welfare. Lang: Hindi.

Illuminated by Benegal's perceptive insights into small-town life, the film examines the plight of women in a male-dominated rural society, dovetailing the lives of five women and their individual struggles as wives and hapless parents.

## DEVEERI

Story: P.Lankesh. Dir: Kavita Lankesh. Phot: S. Ramachandra. Players: Nandita Das, Kyatha, Bhavana, Kashi, Asif Farooqi. Prod: Navajeevana Films. Lang: Kannada.

Debut feature depicting the harshness and humanity of the world, as seen by an impoverished orphan boy whose only driving force is the bond he shares with his elder sister.

# Useful Addresses

## Ministry of Information and Broadcasting
Joint Secretary (Films)
Shastri Bhavan
New Delhi
Fax: (91 11) 338 3513
[for government permissions on shooting feature films in India]

## Film Federation of India
B/3, Everest Building
Tardeo
Mumbai 400 034
Tel/Fax: (91 22) 495 2062
[umbrella body for India's film industry]

## Federation of Indian Chambers of Commerce and Industry
Federation House
Tansen Marg
New Delhi 110 001
Tel: (91 11) 331 6527/373 8770
(ext.323)

Fax: (91 11) 332 0714/372 1504
e-mail: ficcinat@vsnl.com
www.ficci.com

## National Film Development Corporation of India
Discovery of India Building
6th and 7th Floors
Nehru Centre
Dr Annie Besant Road
Worli
Bombay 400 018
Fax: (91 22) 495 9753/0591/1455

## Children's Film Society
c/o Films Division [see below]
Tel: (91 22) 387 6136
Fax: (91 22) 387 5610
[organisers of the International Children's Film Festival of India]

## Films Division
24 Dr G Deshmukh Road
Mumbai 400 026
Tel/Fax: (91 22) 380 1008
Tel: (91 33) 386 1461

[organisers of the Bombay International Film Festival of Documentaries and Shorts]

## Calcutta Film Festival
Director: Ansu Sur
Nandan Festival Complex
1/1 AGC Bose Road
Calcutta 700 020
Fax: (91 33) 223 5744
email: cffcal@cal2.vsnl.net.in

## International Film Festival of Kerala
Director – Shaji N Karun
Kerala State Chalachitra Academy
Elankom Gardens
Vellayambalam
Trivandrum 695 010
Kerala, India
Tel: (91 471) 310 323
Fax: (91 471) 310 322
email: chitram@md3.vsnl.net.in

# INDONESIA

Marselli
Sumarno

Indonesian director Garin Nugroho (b.1962) combined documentary and fiction film techniques in his fifth film, the black-and-white **Unconcealed Poetry** (*Puisi Tak Terkuburkan*). Set against the political turmoil of 1965, it tells the true story of the poet Ibrahim Kadir and a number of other residents from Aceh, North Sumatra, who were thrown behind bars and made to wait their turn to be executed. Nugroho offered a free interpretation of the so-called "Communist 30th September Movement" which mercilessly victimised this innocent poet and his fellow countrymen. Nugroho's previous film, *Leaf on a Pillow,* was one of the ten most popular features of 1998, but *Unconcealed Poetry* was much less commercially successful.

Nevertheless, its release indicated that in the current phase of reform, there is much greater freedom of expression, and film-makers now exempt from the previous policy of script censorship can freely tackle political material. Indonesia has still not recovered from the economic crisis which began in mid-1997 and the socio-political disturbances that come with economic turmoil continue to damage the country's film industry. Riots broke out in the regions, rallies occur almost every day in Jakarta, and the Rupiah has been weakening against the US dollar at an alarming rate.

The Department of Information, which controlled the film industry in the past, has now been dissolved, so the bureaucracy overshadowing the film industry has been cut down a lot, leading to the emergence of new film importers. The film community still has the National Film Advisory Board, but its request for a government fund designed to subsidise some 20 films to be produced in the year 2000 was rejected because of the state's financial problems. Feature investment is so hard to come by that older film producers prefer to do business with the private TV stations (five new stations are set for launch in 2001). The hope must be that younger producers will raise the funds they need from international sources.

New talents are also emerging and they are trying hard to realise their first films. They apply an independent approach, keeping costs as low as possible, including shooting on digital video. Names demonstrating this "independent cinema" spirit include Sentot Sahid and Enison Sinaro. Shanty Harmayn, who at the end of 1999 successfully organised the first Jakarta International Film Festival, has announced plans to try her hand at film production.

## Time for reform

The three-year-old Film Law, a product of the previous regime, must be revised. The number of cinemas is declining, especially in the regions, where many local movie houses have closed because of the drastic shortage of new Indonesian films, as domestic production has dwindled. Non-Hollywood films, including titles from India, are again being imported, but they are only shown in upmarket cinemas belonging to Group 21.

Equally damaging is the flood of pirated VCDs in the big cities and the small towns, selling for $1, whereas the licensed original sells for $5. Illegal reproduction, which is suspected to be the work of a syndicate, is difficult to be eradicated.

Director-producer   Slamet   Rahardjo

*Political prisoners in Garin Nugroho's UNCONCEALED POETRY*

finally released his **Telegram**, a joint-production with a French producer. It took them three years to produce the film. Actress-producer Christine Hakim (43) will be producing **The Dancing Wolf** (*Angin Menari*), to be directed by Nan Triveni Achnas. Mira Lesmana's Miles Production had scheduled a June 2000 release for her children's film, **Sherina's Adventures** (*Petualangan Sherina*). Directed by Riri Riza and starring popular child singer Sherina it seemed certain to become a blockbuster in the domestic market.

MARSELLI SUMARNO is a film director and teaches at the Faculty of Films & Television, Jakarta Institute of the Arts.

# Recent and Forthcoming Films

**PUISI TAK TERKUBURKAN (Unconcealed Poetry)**

Script: Nana Mulyana. Dir: Garin Nugroho. Phot: Winaldha E. Melalatoa. Players: Ibrahim Kadir, Berliana Febrianti, El Manik. Prod: SET Production.

**PETUALANGAN SHERINA (Sherina's Adventures)**

Script: Jujur Prananto. Dir: Riri Riza. Phot: Yadi Sugandhi. Players: Sherina Munaf, Butet Kartaredjasa, Didi Petet. Prod: Miles Productions.

**TELEGRAM**

Script: Putu Wijaya. Dir: Slamet Rahardjo. Phot: Jaques Bouquin. Players: Sujiwo Tejo, Ayu Azhari, Desy Ratnasari. Prod: Eka Praya Tata Cipta Film/Artcam International.

**ANGIN MENARI (The Dancing Wind)**

Script and Dir: Nan T. Achnas. Prod: Christine Hakim Film.

**EPISODA**

Script: Seno Gumira Ajidarma. Dir: Noorman Benny. Player: Sophia Latjuba. Prod: Kem Multimedia.

**GADIS PANTAI (The Beach Girl)**

Script and Dir: Srikaton.

# Producers

**Star Vision**
Jalan Cempaka Putih Raya 116 A–B
Jakarta Pusat 10510
Tel: (62 21) 425 3390
Fax: (62 21) 425 5477

**Diwangkar Citra Film**
Jalan Kayu Putih VI B/28
Jakarta Timur
Tel: (62 21) 489 6434

**Eka Praya Film**
Jalan Pahlawan no. 4
Rempoa
Jakarta Selatan
Tel/Fax: (62 21) 743 0146

**Cinevisi**
Gedung PSKD
Jalan Kramat IV
Jakarta 10330
Tel: (62 21) 334 333/361 824
Fax: (62 21) 310 2133

**Pancaran Indra Cine**
Jalan KS Tubun 75B
Jakarta 10260
Tel: (62 21) 571 0998/571 1003
Fax: (62 21) 573 1636

**Miles Production**
Jalan Pelita 18
Cipete
Jakarta Selatan
Tel: (62 21) 720 7341
Fax: (62 21) 722 6569

**Rapi Film**
Jalan Cikini II/7
Jakarta Pusat
Tel: (62 21) 357 135/332 860

**Parkit Film**
Roxi Mas
Blok C–2, no. 31-34
Jakarta
Tel: (62 21) 386 7315/7316

**Elang Perkasa Film**
Jalan Kayu Putih 4/48
Jakarta Timur
Tel: (62 21) 470 0801
Fax: (62 21) 489 4574

**Prasidi Teta Film**
Jalan Dr. Sahardjo 149 J
Jakarta Selatan

Tel: (62 21) 828 2740/1324

**Bola Dunia Film**
Jalan Pintu Air 51C
Jakarta Pusat
Tel: (62 21) 384 3983/8721

**Sepakat Bahagia Film**
Jalan Mangga Besar Raya 107
Blok D–7
Jakarta Pusat
Tel: (62 21) 649 6657

**Virgo Putra Film**
Jalan KH Hasim Ashari Dalam 111
Jakarta Pusat
Tel: (62 21) 363 308

**Studio 41**
Jalan Kapten P. Tendean 41
Mampang
Tel: (62 21) 520 4356
Fax: (62 21) 520 1493

# Distributors/ Importers

**Satrya Perkasa Estetika**
(European/American importer)
Subentra Building
Jalan Gatot Subroto Kav.21
7th Floor
Jakarta
Tel: (62 21) 522 0022

**Suptan Film**
(Mandarin importer)
Subentra Building
Jalan Gatot Subroto Kav.21
7th Floor
Jakarta
Tel: (62 21) 522 0022

**Buanavista Indah Film**
(Asia non-Mandarin importer)
Jalan Pintu Air 51C
Jakarta
Tel: (62 21) 384 3983/8721

# Useful Addresses

**Faculty of Film and Television –
The Jakarta Institute of the Arts**
Jalan Cikini Raya 73
Jakarta 10330
Tel: (62 21) 316 1258
Fax: (62 21) 323 603

**Directorate for Film and Video
Development**
Ministry of Information
Gedung Film
Jalan MT Haroyono
Kav. 47–48
Jakarta
Tel: (62 21) 7919 6086/6087
Fax: (62 21) 7919 6085

**National Film Advisory Board**
Jalan MT Haryono
Kav. 47–48
Jakarta Selatan
Tel: (62 21) 790 2974/2975
Fax: (62 21) 790 2973

**State Film Production Centre**
Jalan Otto Iskandardinata 125–127
Jakarta Timur
Tel: (62 21) 819 2508
Fax: (62 21) 819 0339

**Indonesian Film Producers
Association**
Pusat Perfilman H. Usmar Ismail
Jalan Rasuna Said
Jakarta 12940
Tel: (62 21) 526 8461
Fax: (62 21) 526 8460

**Association of Film and TV
Technicians**
Pusat Perfilman H. Usmar Ismail
Jalan Rasuna Said
Jakarta 12940
Tel: (62 21)526 8459/8457
Fax: (62 21) 526 8457

**Sinematek Indonesia**
Pusat Perfilman H. Usmar Ismail
Jalan Rasun Said
Jakarta 12940
Tel: (62 21) 526 8455/527 8841
Fax: (62 21) 526 8454

**Inter Pratama Studio & Lab**
Jalan Raya Pasar Ragunan
Jakarta 12550
Tel: (62 21) 780 6030
Fax: (62 21) 780 6230

**Televisi Republic Indonesia**
(TVRI, state-owned TV network)
Jalan Gerbang Pemuda
Senayan
Jakarta
Tel: (62 21) 570 4720/4732
Fax: (62 21) 531 1195

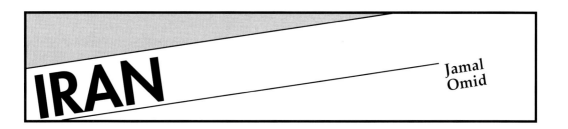

# IRAN

Jamal
Omid

**S**eifollah Daad's constant preoccupation during his three-year tenure as Iran's deputy minister for film affairs has been the methodical transfer of government functions and facilities to the private sector. Film trade guilds now determine their own courses in production and exhibition and to stabilise the new procedures Daad's new policies were adopted by the government early in the Iranian calendar year (March 20, 2000 – March 20, 2001).

The seven key objectives of Daad's policies, which will rely on private sector participation, include the creation of legal foundations for film-making; encouraging foreign production finance; establishing a National Film Organisation, and promoting training. The most significant targets are increasing annual production from 56 titles in the current year to 109 titles by 2004 – 2005, and expanding screening capacity from the current 210,000 seats to 360,000 seats within the same period.

Only 25 new screens have been built in the past year, leaving many districts in Tehran and more than a hundred provincial towns without a cinema. Nonetheless, exhibition revenues in 1999 were still up 50% on 1998, and the upward trend continued in 2000, perhaps reflecting the relative freedom film-makers now enjoy in dealing with relevant, contemporary issues, particularly problems related to the young. This would seem to indicate that Iranian cinema is slowly and successfully emerging from a crisis period.

## A master at work

In Abbas Kiarostami's **The Wind Will Carry Us** (*Bad Ma Ra Khahad Bord*), a group of strangers arrives in a village in

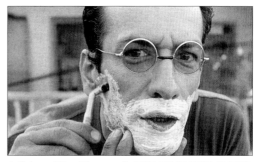

*Still from Abbas Kiarostami's THE WIND WILL CARRY US*

Kurdistan. No one knows what they want, and the head of the group is amused by the villagers' suspicion that they are treasure-hunters. But the leader's attention is mysteriously directed to a room where an old woman is dying. When finally the old woman seems to be passing her last moments, the stranger begins to ponder on the great mystery of life and death. The familiar atmosphere and people of Kiarostami's films are present once again in his boldest, most abstract work to date. After receiving the special Jury Prize at Venice in 1999, he announced that he did not intend to compete at future festivals, and wanted to leave the competition arena to younger film-makers.

After a lapse of 20 years, and several abortive feature projects, Bahman Farmanara created an autobiographical work, **Smell of Camphor, Fragrance of Jasmine** (*Bouye Caphor, Atra-e Yas*), whose protagonist, Bahman Farjami, is a veteran film-maker who has not made a movie for 20 years. All his close director friends like Sohrab Shahid-Saless, Bahram Reypour and Ali Hatami have died, and, believing his own death must be around the corner, he decides to make a film about his own funeral. *Smell of Camphor...* is a highly personal film which nevertheless arouses

PROMOTING
IRANIAN CINEMA

Farabi Cinema Foundation

PRODUCTION ,CO-PRODUCTION
ACQUISITION ,SALES , DISTRIBUTION

55, SIE-TIR AVE., TEHRAN 11358, IRAN
TEL:( 98 21) 6701010,6708156, Fax: 6708155
E-mail:fcf1@dpi.net.ir
Web site :www .fcf-ir.com

great sympathy. It has a pleasant rhythmic flow in which every element falls into its proper place and it won awards at the 18th Fajr International Film Festival (Tehran, February 2000).

In three decades of film-making, Khosro Sinai's many documentaries have been more popular than his few fiction features. **The Bride of Fire** (*Arous-e Atash*), however, is an exception, abandoning documentary techniques in favour of classic narrative cinema which examines a highly contemporary social issue within the framework of a love story. A tribal girl from southern Iran, who is studying at a medical college in Tehran, falls in love with her professor. Tribal traditions, however, have condemned her to marriage with her semi-literate fisherman cousin. For the first time with a Sinai feature, spectators of all age groups and classes were captivated by the story and *The Bride of Fire* won the Fajr festival's prize for Most Popular Film.

## An overdose of rhetoric

In **Born in September** (*Motevaled-e Mahe Mehr*), Ahmad Reza tells the story of the love between Danial, a provincial youth studying at university in Tehran, and Mahtab, his classmate. Subsequent problems cause Danial to give up all his expectations and leave, while Mahtab goes to search everywhere for him. The campus relationship, against a background of political turmoil, and Mahtab's search for Danial at battle fronts do not come together. The film's political relevance, as well as the tender sentiments of the drama are marred by unnecessary political rhetoric.

In Masud Kimia'ie's **The Protest** (*Eteraz*), Amir Khan is released from prison after serving a 12-year-term for a crime he committed to save his family's honour. Disappointed and dissatisfied, Amir finds it increasing difficult to come to terms with the new social environment – very much like Kimia'ie, who has demonstrated in the past two decades that he cannot come to terms with the new circumstances of Iranian cinema. He continues to broach

*Bahman Farmanara in his own SMELL OF CAMPHOR, FRAGRANCE OF JASMINE*

relevant social and political issues intelligently, but abandons them after a cursory examination. *The Protest*, like some of his other films, appears a jerky picture, over-loaded with political rhetoric.

**The Child and the Soldier** (*Kudak va Sarbaz*) is a brilliant debut feature by Seyed Reza Mir Karimi. It's the simple story of a young soldier ordered to take a juvenile delinquent from a station in Sarakhs, Khorasan Province, to a reform school in Tehran on the last day of the year. Their adventures en route create a marvellous humane relationship. *The Child and the Soldier* is an admirable example of a young film-maker treading in the footsteps of Kiarostami, by avoiding a cheap, sentimental approach.

Behruz Afkhami dedicated **The Hemlock** (*Shokaran*) to Jalal Moqaddam, the prominent director of the previous generation whose *The Window* inspired *The Hemlock*; Adrian Lynne's *Fatal Attraction* was surely another influence. Basirat, deputy manager of a factory, married with two children, starts an affair with Sima, a hospital nurse. When he later tries to end the affair Sima creates problems for him and his family. *The Hemlock* is an intelligently-crafted picture. Afkhami was due to begin his duties as a member of the new Islamic parliament in June 2000 and will probably be absent from the film-making scene for some time.

At 20, Samira Makhmalbaf became the youngest director ever to vie for the Palme D'Or when her second feature competed at Cannes 2000; it shared the Jury Prize. **Blackboards** tells the story of a number of school teachers in the Kurdistan province

who go from village to village, trying to find people interested in learning to read and write.

---

JAMAL OMID has worked in Iranian cinema for 35 years, as the author of 15 books, as a screenwriter and as director of the Fajr and Tehran international film festivals.

---

# Recent and Forthcoming Films

**BOUYE CAPHOR, ATRA-E YAS (Smell of Camphor, Fragrance of Jasmine)**

Script and Dir: Bahman Farmanara. Phot: Mahmud Kalari. Players: B. Farmanara, Roya Nonahali, Reza Kianian, Firuz Behjat Mohammadi. Parivash Nazariye. Prod: Morteza Shayesta (Hedayat Film, Fazlolloh Yusefpoor).

**BAD MA RA KHAHAD BORD (The Wind Will Carry Us)**

Script: Abbas Kiarostami, based on a story by Mahmud Aideen. Dir: Kiarostami. Phot: Mahmud Kalari. Players: Behzad Dowrani, and the people of Siah-Darre village. Prod: MK2 (France)/Kiarostami (Iran).

**AROUS-E ATASH (The Bride of Fire)**

Script: Khosro Sinai, Hamid Farrokh-Nezhad. Dir: Sinai. Phot: Ali Loqmani. Players: Saeed Poorsamimi, Ghazal Saremi, H. Farrokh-Nezhad, Salime Rangzan. Prod: Qasem Qolipoor.

**ETERAZ (The Protest)**

Script and Dir: Masud Kimia'ie. Phot: Asghar Rafi'ie Jam. Players: Dariush Arjommand, Mohammud Reza Forutan, Mitra Hajjar, Mahdi Fathi, Bita Farrahi. Prod: Seyed Zia Hashemi.

**MOTEVALED-E MAHE MEHR (Born in September)**

Script and Dir: Ahmad Reza Darvish. Phot: Hassan Puya. Players: Mohammad Reza Forutan, Mitra Hajjar, Mahmud Azizi. Prod: Tamasha Cutural Institute/Soore Cinema Development Organisation.

**SHOKARAN (The Hemlock)**

Script: Minu Farshchi, Behruz Afkhami. Dir: Afkhami. Phot: Nemat Haqiqi. Players: Fariborz Arabnia, Hedye Tehrani, Rosita Ghaffuri, Mohammad Saleh Ala, Manuchehr Sadeqpoor. Prod: Soore Cinema Development Organization, Seyed Zia Hashemi.

**KUDAK VA SARBAZ (The Child and the Soldier)**

Script: Mohammad Rezai Rad. Dir: Seyed Reza Mir Karimi. Phot: Hamid Khozui Abyane. Players: Mahdi Lotfi, Ruhollah Hosseini, Mehran Rajabi. Prod: Vahid Nik-Khan Azad.

**BLACKBOARDS**

Script: Mohsen Makhmalbaf, Samira Makhmalbaf. Dir: Samira Makhmalbaf. Phot: Ebrahim Ghaffuri. Players: Behnaz Jafari, Saeed Mohammadi, Bahman Qobadi. Prod: Makhmalbaf Film Productions.

*Dariush Arjomand, left, and Mohammad Reza Forutan in THE PROTEST*

### UNDER THE SKIN OF THE NIGHT

Script: Farid Mostafavi, Rakhshan Bani-etemad. Dir: R. Bani-etemad. Phot: Hossein Jafarian. Players: Golab Adine, Mohammad Reza Forutan, Baran Kowsari. Prod: Jahangir Kowsari, R. Bani-etemad.

### SEVEN ACTS

Script: Saeed Aqiqi. Dir: Farzad Motamen. Phot: Homayun Pievar. Players: Fariborz Arabnia, Asal Badi'ie, Mahaya Petrossian. Prod: Varahonar Film Company.

### THE RUNAWAY BRIDE

Script: Asghar Abdollahi, Iraj Tahmasb. Dir: Mohammad Hossein Latifi. Phot: Fereydun Masruri. Players: Iraj Tahmasb, Fateme Motamed Aria, Jamile Sheikhi, Turan Mehrzad. Prod: Majid Modarresi, Hamid Aqagolian.

### THE PARTY

Script and Dir: Saman Moghaddam. Phot: Bahram Badakhshani. Players: Hedye Tehrani, Sorush Gudarzi, Mehdi Khayyami. Prod: Morteza Shayeste.

### JOURNEY TO THE ORIENT

Script: Abdolreza Kahani. Dir: Seyed Mahdi Borqei. Phot: Hossein Nazarian. Players: Imanollah Varan, Hassan Rezai, Morteza Zarrabi. Prod: Saeed Hajimiri.

### THE UNFINISHED PIECE

Script: Kambuzia Partovi. Dir: Maziar Miri. Phot: Hassan Puya. Players: Ghogha Bayat, Alireza Anushfar. Prod: Davud Rashidi.

### MARRIAGE BY PROXY

Script: Mohammad Hadi Karimi. Dir: Kazem Masumi. Phot: Mojtaba Rahimi. Players: Ahmad Reza Abedzade, Zia Shojai-Mehr, Marjan Shahi. Prod: Seyed Mohsen Vaziri.

### THE FOOTBALLERS

Script and Dir: Ali Akbar Saqafi. Phot: Maziar Partov. Players: Hamid Stilli, Fateme Gudarzi, Jamshid Esmailkhani. Prod: Habib Allahyari, A. A. Saqafi.

### THE LITTLE PRINCE

Script: Hassan Mehdifar. Dir: Reza Namvari Farid. Phot: Reza Iran-nezhad. Players: Nushin Amjadi, Hamed Kolohdari, Mahmud Basiri. Prod: Naqsh-e Jahan Art – Cultural Institute.

### THE RAIN

Script and Dir: Majid Majidi. Phot:: Mohammad Davudi. Players: Hossein Abedini, Zahra Khorrami, Amir Mohammad Naji. Prod: M. Majidi, Fuad Nahhas.

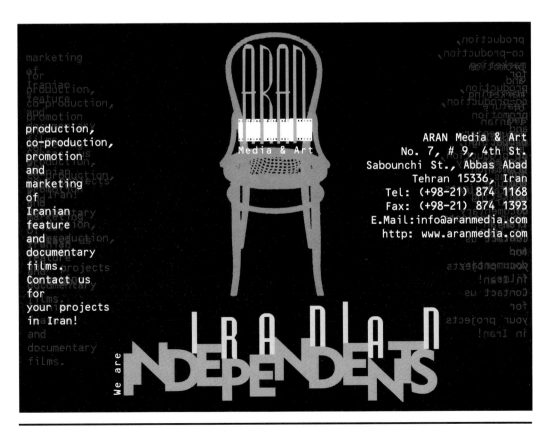

## FIRE AND WATER

Script and Dir: Fereydun Jeyrani. Phot: Mahmud Kalari. Players: Parviz Parastui, Leyla Hatami, Atila Pasiyani, Behnaz Jafari, Farimah Farjami. Prod: Mohammad Reza Takhtkashian.

## THE EPIC OF HURAM

Script and Dir: Farhad Mehranfar. Phot: Nader Masumi. Players: Yusef Moradian, Maryam Moqaddam. Prod: Mohammad Reza Sarhangi.

## THE RICH AND THE POOR

Script and Dir: Fereydun Hossanpoor. Phot: Ebrahim Ghaffuri. Players: Akbar Abdi, Fateme Sadeqi, Ahmad Aqaloo. Prod: Tamasha Cultural Institute.

## KAI

Script and Dir: Abolfazl Jalili. Phot: Mohammad Ahmadi. Players: Ka'iem Alizade, Rahmatollah Ebrahimi, Ebrahim Ebrahimzade. Prod: A. Jalili, Kitano T. Mark (Japan).

*Hedye Tehrani in THE HEMLOCK*

## THE SECRET OF THE RAINY NIGHT

Script and Dir: Siamak Atlasi. Phot: Hossein Maleki. Players: Farhad Mahadian, Shaqayeq Farahani. Prod: S. Atlasi.

## END GAME

Script and Dir: Homayun As'adian. Phot: Bahram Badakhshani. Players: Hamed Behdad, Pupak Goldarre, Shirin Poormokhtar. Prod: Namadin Company.

## THE CHILDREN OF THE RIVER

Script and Dir: Ali Shah-hatami. Phot: Rasul Ahadi. Players: Faramarz Shahni, Nemat Soltani. Prod: Mohtaba Faravarde.

# Producers/ Distributors

## Iran Film Development

(Alireza Raisian)
No. 5 Arbabi Alley, Nesa St
Dastgerdi Ave
Tehran
Tel: (98 21) 222 1600
Fax: (98 21) 225 5621

## Didar Film

(Shabanali Eslami)
No. 24 Behruzi Alley
North Kargar Ave
Tehran
Tel/Fax: (98 21) 928 034

## Basir Film

(Habibollah Bahmani)
No. 12J. St Moqaddas Ardebili
Vali-e Asr Ave
Tehran
Tel/Fax: (98 21) 204 0545

## Abgun Cultural Center

(Ali Akbar Saqafi)
No. 401 Avarez, Shariati Ave
Tehran
Tel: (98 21) 762047

## Dohol Film

(Mohammad Baqer Khosravi)
246 (Opposite Mir Emad St)
Motahari Ave
Tehran
Tel: (98 21) 882 5519

## Ofoq Cinema Organization

(Rasul Mollaqolipoor)
No. 23 Mansur Alley
(Adjacent to Tehran Grand Hotel)
Motahari Ave
Tehran
Tel: (98 21) 872 1871
Fax: (98 21) 872 1781

## Arta Film

(Tahmine Milani, Abolhassan Davudi)

No. 1/1 Etehad Alley
South Shiraz St, Molla Sadra Ave
Tehran
Tel: (98 21) 803 1193

## Arman Film

(Ali Akbar Erfani)
No. 5 Ghaffari Alley, Fajr (Jam) St
Motahhari Ave
Tehran
Tel: (98 21) 882 2117
Fax: (98 21) 884 4025

## Avishan Film

(Naser Shafaq)
2nd Floor, No. 17,
Fath Alley, Baba Taher St
Dr. Fatemi Ave
Tehran
Tel: (98 21) 650 927
Fax: (98 21) 650 975

## Omid Film

(Sirus Taslimi)
No. 23 Tajbakhsh Alley, Nesa St

Mirdamad Ave
Tehran
Tel: (98 21) 227 6746
Fax: (98 21) 227 2310

**Pakhshiran**
(Harun Yashayaie)
No. 8 Somaye St, Bahar St
Tehran
Tel: (98 21) 882 4052
Fax: (98 21) 883 7684

**Varahonar**
(Mehdi Karimi)
No. 168 Avang Alley
Parvin Etesami St
Dr. Fatemi Ave
Tehran
Tel: (98 21) 800 0345
Fax: (98 21) 802 8853

**Purika Film**
1st Floor, No. 105 Somaye St
Tehran
Tel: (98 21) 882 8442

**Film Noor**
(Fuad Noor)
No. 9 Azarshahr Alley, Iranshahr St
Tehran
Tel: (98 21) 834 889
Fax: (98 21) 272 310

**Puya Film**
(Hussein Farahbakhsh,
Abdollah Alikhani)
No. 10 Tavakkol Bldg, Jomhuri Ave
Tehran
Tel: (98 21) 670 3574

**Peyman Film**
(Abdolhassan Sanamari)
No. 11 Mehrzad Alley
South Iranshahr St
Tehran
Tel: (98 21) 883 9163
Fax: (98 21) 883 3789

**Iran Film Development**
(Alireza Raisian)
No. 5 Arbabi Alley, Nesa St
Dastgerdi Ave
Tehran
Tel: (98 21) 222 1600
Fax: (98 21) 225 5621

**Jozan Film**
(Masud Jafari Jozani)
No. 20 Razmandegan Alley
Ghaffari, Fajr (Jam) St, Motahhari

Tehran
Tel: (98 21) 883 7271/8844010
Fax: (98 21) 882 6876

**Ama Medium**
(Mohammad Mehdi Dadgu)
No. 138 Shahid Beheshti Ave
Tehran
Tel: (98 21) 874 4694/874 6275
Fax: (98 21) 875 2976

**Roshan Film**
(Ali Mazinani)
No. 97 Arbab Jamshid, Kushk St
Ferdowsi Ave
Tehran
Tel: (98 21) 671 2975

**Sepahan Film**
(Mohammad and Asghar Banki)
No. 126 Razi Alley, Sheikh Hadi St
Jomhuri Ave
Tehran
Tel: (98 21) 670 3047
Fax: (98 21) 670 6268

**Sahra-Film Cultural Institute**
(Majid Modaresi)
No. 39. corner of 6th Alley,
Eshqyar St.
Khorramshahr Ave
Tehran
Tel: (98 21) 876 5392/876 6110

**Iran-Milad**
(Bizhan Emkanian)
No. 1 Marivan St, South Sohrevardi
Tehran
Tel: (98 21) 831 549
Fax: (98 21) 752 4881

**Mahed Film**
Ground Floor, No. 7. Nasr
Alley, Valiy Asr Sq,,
Tehran
Tel: (98 21) 821 3042
Fax: (98 21) 228 009

**Hamrah Coorperative**
(Hassan Hedayat)
No. 40 Baharmastian Alley
7th of Tir Sq.
Tehran
Tel: (98 21) 883 4612
Fax: (98 21) 840 3212

**Nimruz**
(Mehdi Sabbaghzade)
No. 1 Mohammadi Alley
North Bahar St

Tehran
Tel/Fax: (98 21) 753 6727

**Soore Film Development
Organization**
(Mohammad Ali Hussein-Nezhad)
No. 213 Somaye St
Nejatollahi Ave
Tehran
Tel: (98 21) 881 0270
Fax: (98 21) 889 3530

**Sima Film**
(Mohammad Mehdi Heidarian)
No. 53 Kuhyar Alley, Fereshte St
Tehran
Tel: (98 21) 221 9531
Fax: (98 21) 221 5889

**Atlas Film**
(Mohsen Shayanfar)
No. 26 Khorram Alley, Anari St
Jomhuri Ave
Tehran
Tel: (98 21) 646 6131

**Shahr Film**
(Jalal Qazal-Ayaq)
No. 1/36 Kabkanian (Homa) St
Keshavarz Blvd
Tehran
Tel: (98 21) 658 181
Fax: (98 21) 652 480

**Shiraz Film**
(Mohammad Hashem Sabuki)
No. 1/56 Neauphle-le-Chateau St
Tehran
Tel: (98 21) 670 7952
Fax: (98 21) 670 2985

**Oruj Film**
(Mohammad Shariati)
No. 335 Darband, Tajrish
Tehran
Tel: (98 21) 801 8414
Fax: (98 21) 602 2193

**Fanus Khiyal**
(Gholamreza Azadi)
No. 75 Bakhtyar St, 7th of Tir Sq
Tehran
Tel: (98 21) 883 4678
Fax: (98 21) 884 7795

**Andishe Film Workshop**
(Seyed Mohsen Vaziri)
No. 728 Shariati Ave
Tehran
Tel: (98 21) 840 5398

**Fajr Cinema Organization**
(Abdolreza Sa'atchifard)
No. 52 Shahin Alley, Shoa Sq
Qaem Maqam Farahani St
Tehran
Tel: (98 21) 882 5650
Fax: (98 21) 883 7991

**Kowsar Cinema Organization**
(Ruhollah Khoshkam)
No. 363 Motahhari Ave
Tehran
Tel/Fax: (98 21) 872 5809

**Gol Film**
(Majid Ashtianipoor)
No. 2 Maraghe St, Villa St
Tehran
Tel: (98 21) 880 2151
Fax: (98 21) 881 0150

**Lale Film**
(Gholamhasan Bolurian)
No. 41 Amir Soleimani, Enqelab Ave
Tehran
Tel: (98 21) 649 4562
Fax: (98 21) 671 5518

**Mehrab Film**
(Jamal Shurje)
No. 86, 25th St, Jahan-Ara
Shahid Gomnam Express Way
Tehran
Tel/Fax: (98 21) 800 0076

**Institute of Film Affairs of Mostazafan Foundation**
(Alireza Sarbakhsh)
Bldg. No. 343, Shahid Beheshti Ave
Tehran
Tel: (98 21) 871 6666

**Film Baharan**
(Akbar Sadeqi)
No. 101 Baharmastian Alley
7th of Tir Sq
Jami St
Tehran
Tel: (98 21) 670 6473

**Mahab Film**
(Seyed Zia Hashemi)
No. 85 Bakhtyar Alley, 7th of Tir Sq
Tehran
Tel: (98 21) 837 547
Fax: (98 21) 883 4332

**Misaq Film**
(Hussein Yaryar)
No. 101 North Sohrevardi Ave

Tehran
Tel: (98 21) 875 7517

**Milad Film**
(Rasul Sadr-Ameli)
No. 3 Fourth St, Asadabadi Ave
Tehran
Tel: (98 21) 872 7673
Fax: (98 21) 885 7119

**Mina Film**
(Mohammad Reza Alipayam)
No. 9, 11, Bldg. No. 1317, Vanak Sq
Tehran
Tel: (98 21) 887 9314
Fax: (98 21) 879 9803

**Nahid Film**
(Hojjatollah Seifi)
No. 27 Sharif Alley, Sheikh Hadi St
Jami St
Tehran
Tel: (98 21) 670 6473

**Novin Film**
(Hushang Nurollahi)
No. 15 48th Passage, Jomhuri Ave
Tehran
Tel/Fax: (98 21) 640 3697

**Yaran Film**
(Samuel Khachikian)
No. 78, 1st Haeri, Shahid Adibi St
Shariati Ave
Tehran
Tel: (98 21) 870 2552

**Afaq Film**
(Amir Hussein Sharifi)
No. 23 Shahid Amini
(Farahbod) St Vali-e Asr Ave
Tehran
Tel: (98 21) 879 8588
Fax: (98 21) 884 5141

**Shekufa Film**
(Dariush Babaiyan)
No. 18 Amir Parviz, Abureyhan St
Enqelab Ave
Tehran
Tel: (98 21) 641 6939
Fax: (98 21) 640 2202

**Hedayat Film**
(Morteza Shayeste)
No.75 7th St
Khaled Eslamboli Ave
Tehran
Tel: (98 21) 872 7188/9
Fax: (98 21) 871 4220

**Sobhan Film**
(Saeed Hajimiri)
No. 45, Nuri Cul-de-sac,
Valiye Asr Ave
Tehran
Tel: (98 21) 641 016
Fax: (98 21) 641 5098

**Resane Filmsazan**
(Seyed Gholamreza Musavi)
No. 7, Ghaffari Alley
Baharmastian St, 7th of Tir Sq
Tehran
Tel: (98 21) 830 676/883 2839

**Film Emruz**
(Davud Rashidi Haeri)
No. 27, Sohrevardi Ave
Tehran
Tel: (98 21) 866 639

**Nemayesh Film Co.**
(Habibollah Sahranavard)
No. 2, Mirmotahari, Seyed Khandan
Bridge, Shariati Ave
Tehran
Tel: (98 21) 868 703/866 638

**Tuba Film Co.**
(Ruhollah Braderi)
No. 505, Corner of 51st Alley
Asadabadi Ave
Tehran
Tel: (98 21) 878 7515/878 7516

**7th Art Cultural Institute**
(Karim Atashi)
No. 334, Khaje Nasir Tusi St
Shariati Ave
Tehran
Tel: (98 21) 750 3797

**Tamasha Cultural Institute**
(Taqi Aliqolizade)
No. 1, 14th Alley, Eshqyar St,
Khorramshar Ave
Tehran
Tel: (98 21) 873 3843/873 3844

**Negin Film Production Cooperative**
(Farlborz Arabnia)
Unit 103, 2nd Block, Chehelstun Bldg.
South Bahar St
Tehran
Tel: (98 21) 753 1961

# IRELAND — Michael Dwyer

Summer ought to be the busiest period of the year for film production in Ireland, given such benefits as the extended daylight hours available for location shooting and the prospects of good weather. However, the summer of 1999 was a dismal period of inactivity, with no productions on location in Ireland apart from the BBC television series *Ballykissangel*.

A year later it was a different story, and at Cannes in May 2000, Roger Greene, chief executive of the Screen Commission of Ireland, announced that 18 feature projects were awaiting certification from the Department of Arts and Heritage. All of these productions had applied to make use of the tax incentive scheme under Section 481 of the Finance Act, and all were set to shoot before the end of 2000.

This very significant upsurge in production can be attributed to the decision of the Minister of Finance to renew the Section 481 scheme for another five years. In 1998 it had been renewed for just one year, which clearly did not inspire confidence in potential investors or producers planning more than 12 months ahead. A further boost to the industry has been the weakness of the euro in relation to the US dollar and to sterling. Greene commented at Cannes: "You cannot base a film industry on the exchange rate. However, the present stability of the tax incentive certainly will benefit the Irish industry in the long term."

Among the projects scheduled for the second half of 2000 were the $40m Spyglass Entertainment production, *The Count of Monte Cristo*, starring Guy Pearce, and directed by Kevin Reynolds; a new version of *The Magnificent Ambersons* from veteran film-maker Herbert Ross; and new features from Irish directors Paddy Breathnach, Conor McPherson, Johnny Gogan and Shimmy Marcus.

## Beckett 19 – McCourt 1

A particularly ambitious endeavour has been the Beckett Film Project, which will bring all of Samuel Beckett's 19 stage plays to cinema and television screens. The producers are Michael Colgan, artistic director of Dublin's Gate Theatre, and Alan Moloney of Parallel Films, who set up Blue Light Films to film the Beckett canon. The $6m budget was raised from Ireland's RTE Television, Britain's Channel 4, Section 481 investment and some American investors. Colgan and Moloney have attracted a range of internationally renowned film-makers, among them Anthony Minghella, David Mamet, Neil Jordan, Atom Egoyan, Patricia Rozema, Richard Eyre and Karel Reisz; along with young Irish directors such as Damien O'Donnell, Conor McPherson, Kieron J. Walsh and Enda Hughes.

The wealth of international acting talent assembled for the Beckett films includes Julianne Moore, Kristin Scott Thomas, Juliet Stevenson, Alan Rickman, Jeremy Irons, Rosaleen Linehan, Stephen Brennan, Susan Fitzgerald, Barry McGovern, Sean McGinley, Michael Gambon, David Thewlis and, in his last screen appearance, the late Sir John Gielgud. The first of the films to appear has been Jordan's film of *Not I*, featuring Julianne Moore and shown in Critics' Week at Cannes.

Meanwhile, the newly established Irish Film and Television Academy held its first awards ceremony in Dublin in late 1999, honouring productions which had been particularly successful at Irish cinemas.

*Emily Watson and Robert Carlyle in ANGELA'S ASHES
photo: David Applebey/Angelus Films*

*Susan Lynch and Ewan McGregor in NORA
photo: Alliance-Atlantis*

John Boorman's *The General* won Best Film and Best Actor (Brendan Gleeson). *I Went Down* took the awards for Best Screenplay (Conor McPherson) and Best Craft Contribution (director of photography Cian De Buitlear), and Brid Brennan was named Best Actress for *Dancing at Lughnasa*.

By far the most commercially successful Irish-made film at the national box-office in recent years has been **Angela's Ashes**, Alan Parker's admirably restrained and unsentimental film of Frank McCourt's Pulitzer Prize winning best-seller. It follows a boy's upbringing in a poverty-stricken Limerick family in the 1940s. In an exemplary cast, young Frank is played at different ages by three remarkable youngsters: Joe Breen, Ciaran Owens and Michael Legge – who appear together briefly in a magical scene.

For all the horrors and abject poverty it unflinchingly addresses, Parker's film is shot through with humour – and with the great humanity which has marked out the most honest and socially-concerned features in international cinema, the Italian neo-realist classics in particular.

## When James met Nora

Three recent Irish period movies based on books and directed by women included writer-director Pat Murphy's return to feature films after 15 years with **Nora**. Her compelling, visually striking film dramatises the first eight years in the often turbulent relationship between James

Joyce (a remarkably understated Ewan McGregor) and Nora Barnacle (the wonderfully vibrant Susan Lynch), beginning with their first meeting in Dublin in 1904. The drama persuasively catches the passion of their relationship and the changes which this ostensibly incompatible couple undergo. In this economically told story, which wisely eschews voice-over narration, Murphy refreshingly chooses to go where few Irish films have ventured before – depicting a full-blooded sexual relationship between Irish partners.

The acclaimed English theatre director Deborah Warner made a confident crossover into cinema with **The Last September**. Elegantly adapted by John Banville from Elizabeth Bowen's novel, it is set in County Cork in 1920, and acutely observes the dying days of the Anglo-Irish aristocracy known as the Ascendancy. Keeley Hawes brings a beguiling freshness to the pivotal role of the free-spirited young Lois Farquar who lives with her uncle (Michael Gambon) and aunt (Maggie Smith). The parallel themes of the nationalist struggle for independence and Lois' own yearnings for freedom eventually merge in this assured and involving study of a collective state of mind.

However, the most popular of these three period pictures at the Irish box-office was the least accomplished: Anjelica Huston's **Agnes Browne**, based on Irish comedian Brendan O'Carroll's novel, *The Mammy*. Set in what is purportedly Dublin in 1967, Huston's film is permeated by, and sinks under, crude attempts at humour, an air of forced jollity and a distinct whiff of 'Oirish' phoniness. Huston herself takes the title role, as a street trader who manages to look remarkably radiant for someone struggling to raise seven children after the death of her husband. Singer Tom Jones makes a cameo appearance as himself, looking a great deal older than he actually was back in 1967.

## Waste of Spacey

There was an even greater disappointment in Thaddeus O'Sullivan's **Ordinary Decent Criminal**, which features an uncomfortably miscast Kevin Spacey as a Dublin criminal clearly inspired by the real-life crook, Martin Cahill, who had already been the subject of two recent productions, *The General* and the TV film *Vicious Circle*. O'Sullivan's movie adds few fresh perspectives, and adheres so closely to the outline of the Cahill story that it merely registers as a dull case of déjà vu.

The two Irish directors who fared best on the awards circuit this year were fêted for films made outside Ireland. Neil Jordan added to his trophies with a BAFTA screenplay award for his Graham Greene adaptation, *The End of the Affair*, which also received two Oscar nominations. Damien O'Donnell's auspicious feature debut, *East Is East*, put a distinctive young talent on the world map and collected the BAFTA for best British Film.

A substantial box-office success in Britain, *East Is East* also fared very well at Irish cinemas, which enjoyed another remarkably strong year in 1999. Admissions rose from 12.39 million in 1998 to 16.39 in 1999. The good news continues, with figures for the first quarter of 2000 registering 4.2 million admissions, a dramatic 38% increase over attendances in the corresponding period of 1999. The figures were boosted by hits such as *Toy Story 2*, *American Beauty* and *Angela's Ashes*.

The next Irish movie likely to make a major impact at home is Gerard Stembridge's **About Adam**, which had its world premiere at the 2000 Sundance

*Anjelica Huston in her own AGNES BROWNE*

festival. This exuberant, immensely entertaining romantic comedy features Kate Hudson as a young Dubliner longing for a fresh face in her life. He turns up in the form of Adam (Stuart Townsend), who effortlessly charms his way into her bed before going on to seduce both her sisters (Frances O'Connor and Charlotte Brady), and in one of the movie's wittiest sequences, looks like he is about to add their only brother (Alan Maher) to his conquests. Stembridge's screenplay is cleverly devised to show key events from the perspectives of the different characters, and he generates sparkling, intoxicating comedy.

*Keeley Hawes in THE LAST SEPTEMBER*

# Recent and Forthcoming Films

## ABOUT ADAM

Script and Dir: Gerard Stembridge. Phot: Bruno De Keyser. Players: Stuart Townsend, Frances O'Connor, Kate Hudson, Charlotte Bradley, Rosaleen Linhean. Prod: Venus Film & Television

## ACCELERATOR

Script: Mark Stewart, Vinny Murphy. Dir: Murphy. Phot: Seamus Deasy. Players: Mark Dunne, Gavin Kielty, Aisling O'Neill, Suart Sinclair Blyth. Prod: Two For the Show.

## AGNES BROWNE

Script: John Goldsmith, Brendan O'Carroll. Dir: Anjelica Huston. Phot: Tony Redmond. Players: Huston, Marion O'Dwyer, Arno Chevrier, Ray Winstone, Tom Jones. Prod: Hell's Kitchen.

## ANGELA'S ASHES

Script: Laura Jones, Frank McCourt. Dir: Alan Parker. Phot: Michael Seresin. Players: Emily Watson, Robert Carlyle, Ciaran Owens, Joe Breen, Michael Legge. Prod: Dirty Hands.

## THE BORSTAL BOY

Script: Nye Heron, Peter Sheridan. Dir: Sheridan. Phot: Ciaran Tanham. Players: Shawn Hatosy, Danny Dyer, Michael York, Eva Birthistle. Prod: Hell's Kitchen.

## CONAMARA

Script: Greg Brennan. Dir: Eoin Moore. Phot: Michael Hammon. Players: Andreas Schmidt, Ellen Ten Damme, Darragh Kelly. Prod: Boje Buck Produktion.

## COUNTRY

Script and Dir: Kevin Liddy. Phot: Donal Gilligan. Players: Dean Pritchard, Des Cave, Lisa Harrow, Pat Laffan. Prod: Indi Films.

## DISCO PIGS

Script: Enda Walsh. Dir: Kirsten Sheridan. Phot: Igor Jadue-Lillo. Players: Cillian Murphy, Elaine Cassidy, Brian F. O'Byrne, Geraldine O'Rawe, Eleanor Methven. Prod: Temple Films.

## AN EVERLASTING PIECE

Script: Barry McEvoy. Dir: Barry Levinson. Phot: Seamus Deasy. Players: Barry McEvoy, Brian F.O'Byrne, Anna Friel, Billy Connolly, Pauline McLynn. Prod: Everlasting Productions/DreamWorks.

## FLICK

Script and Dir: Fintan Connolly. Phot: Owen McPolin. Players: David Murray, Isabelle Menke, David Wilmot. Prod: Fubar.

## I COULD READ THE SKY

Script: Nichola Bruce, Steve Pyke. Dir: Bruce. Phot: Seamus McGarvey. Players: Dermor Healy, Stephen Rea, Maria Doyle Kennedy, Brendan Coyle. Prod: Liquid Films.

## THE LAST SEPTEMBER

Script: John Banville, from Elizabeth Bowen's novel. Dir: Deborah Warner. Phot: Slawomir Idziak. Players: Keeley Hawes, Maggie Smith, Fiona Shaw, Michael Gambon, Lambert Wilson, Jaen Birkin. Prod: Scala/Thunder Films.

## THE MOST FERTILE MAN IN IRELAND

Script: Jim Keeble. Dir: Dudi Appleton. Phot: Ronan Fox. Players: Kris Marshall, James Nesbitt, Bronagh Gallagher, Kathy Kiera Clarke. Prod: Samson Films.

## NIGHT TRAIN

Script: Aodhan Madden. Dir: John Lynch. Phot: Seamus Deasy. Players: John Hurt, Brenda Bleythn. Prod: Subotica Films.

## NORA

Script: Pat Murphy, Gerard Stembridge. Dir: Pat Murphy. Phot: Jean-Francois Robin. Players: Susan Lynch, Ewan McGregor, Peter McDonald. Prod: Volta/Natural Nylon.

## NOT AFRAID, NOT AFRAID

Script: Annette Carducci, Barry

*Stuart Townsend as a serial seducer in ABOUT ADAM*

Devlin. Dir: Annette Carducci. Phot: Seamus Deasy. Players: Dianne Wiest, Jack Davenport, Elsa Zylverstein, Michael Weir. Prod: World 2000/Metropolitan Films.

## ON THE NOSE

Script: Tony Philpott. Dir: David Caffrey. Phot: Paul Sarossy. Players: Dan Aykroyd, Brenda Blethyn, Robbie Coltrane, Eanna MacLiam. Prod: Subotica Films.

## ORDINARY DECENT CRIMINAL

Script: Gerard Stembridge. Dir: Thaddeus O'Sullivan. Phot: Andrew Dunn. Players: Kevin Spacey, Linda Fiorentino, Peter Mullan, Stephen Dillane. Prod: Little Bird/Icon.

## PEACHES

Script and Dir: Nick Grosso. Phot: Brendan Galvin. Players: Matthew Rhys, Kelly Reilly, Justin Salinger. Prod: Stone Ridge Entertainment.

## RAT

Script: Wesley Burrowes. Dir: Steve Barron. Phot: Brendan Galvin. Players: Pete Postlethwaite, Imelda Staunton, Frank Kelly, David Wilmot. Prod: Jim Henson Company/Ruby Films/Samson Films.

## SALTWATER

Script and Dir: Conor McPherson. Phot: Oliver Curtis. Players: Peter McDonald, Brendan Gleeson, Brian Cox, Conor Mullen. Prod: Treasure Films.

## THE SMILING SUICIDE CLUB

Script: Daniel James, John Carney. Dir: Carney. Phot: Eric Edwards. Players: Cillian Murphy, Jonathan Jackson, Tricia Vesey, Stephen Rea, Gerard McSorley. Prod: Hell's Kitchen.

## THE TAILOR OF PANAMA

Script: John Boorman, from John

Le Carré's novel. Dir: Boorman. Phot: Seamus Deasy. Players: Pierce Brosnan, Jamie Lee Curtis, Geoffrey Rush, Brendan Gleeson. Prod: Merlin Films.

## WHEN BRENDAN MET TRUDY

Script: Roddy Doyle. Dir: Kieron J. Walsh. Phot: Ashley Rowe. Players: Peter McDonald, Flora Montgomery, Maynard Eziashi, Eileen Walsh. Prod: Deadly Films 2.

## WHEN THE SKY FALLS

Script: Michael Sheridan, Colum McCann, Ronan Gallagher. Dir: John MacKenzie. Phot: Seamus Deasy. Players: Joan Allen, Patrick Bergin, Pete Postlethwaite, Liam Cunningham, Kevin McNally. Prod: Irish Screen.

# Producers

### Ferndale Films
4 Harcourt Terrace
Dublin 2
Tel: (353 1) 676 8890
Fax: (353 1) 676 8874

### Hell's Kitchen Productions
92 Merrion Road
Ballsbridge
Dublin 4
Tel: (353 1) 667 5599
Fax: (353 1) 667 5592

### Irish Screen
34 Lower Baggot Street
Dublin 2
Tel: (353 1) 662 3505
Fax: (353 1) 662 3507

### Little Bird Productions
122 Lower Baggot Street
Dublin 2
Tel: (353 1) 661 4245
Fax: (353 1) 660 0351

### Merlin Films Group
16 Upper Pembroke Street

Dublin 2
Tel: (353 1) 676 4373
Fax: (353 1) 676 4368

### Parallel Film Productions
14-15 Sir John Rogersons Quay
Dublin 2
Tel: (353 1) 671 85-55
Fax: (353 1) 671 8242

### Samson Films
The Barracks
76 Irishtown Road
Dublin 4
Tel: (353 1) 667 0533
Fax: (353 1) 667 0537

### Temple Films
4 Windmill Lane
Dublin 2
Tel: (353 1) 671 9313
Fax: (353 1) 671 9323

### Treasure Films
Shamrock Chambers
Dame St
Dublin 2
Tel: (353 1) 670 9609

Fax: (353 1) 670 9612

### World 2000 Productions
Ardmore Studios
Bray
Co. Wicklow.
Tel: (353 1) 286 2971
Fax: (353 1) 286 6810

# Distributors

### Abbey Films
35 Upper Abbey Street
Dublin 1
Tel: (353 1) 872 3422
Fax: (353 1) 872 3687

### Buena Vista International
12 Parliament Street
Dublin 2
Tel: (353 1) 677 3484
Fax: (353 1) 671 0098

### Clarence Pictures
13 Denzille Lane
Dublin 2
Tel: 661 4022
Fax: 661 4186

**Columbia TriStar Films**
Seagrave House
20 Earlsfort Terrace
Dublin 2
Tel: (353 1) 616 3200
Fax: (353 1) 616 3210

**20th Century Fox**
14/15 Kildare Street
Dublin 2
Tel: 661 7171
Fax: 661 7228

**Warner Bros**
9 Townyard Lane
Malahide
Co Dublin
Tel: (353 1) 845 1844
Fax: (353 1) 845 1858

**United International Pictures**
D'Olier Chambers
D'Olier Street
Dublin 2
Tel: (353 1) 679 2433
Fax: (353 1) 679 8801

# Useful Addresses

**Ardmore Studios**
Herbert Road
Bray
Co Wicklow
Tel: (353 404) 286 2971
Fax: (353 404) 286 1894

**The Arts Council**
70 Merrion Square
Dublin 2
Tel: (353 1) 661 1840
Fax: (353 1) 676 0436

**Espace Video Européen**
(EVE)
6 Eustace Street
Dublin 2
Tel: (353 1) 679 5744
Fax: (353 1) 679 9657

**Film Institute of Ireland**
6 Eustace Street
Dublin 2
Tel: (353 1) 679 5744
Fax: (353 1) 679 9657

**Film Makers Ireland**
The Studio Building
Meeting House Square
Temple Bar
Dublin 2
Tel: (353 1) 671 3525
Fax: (353 1) 671 4292

**Irish Film & Television Academy**
43/44 Temple Bar
Dublin 2
Tel: (353 1) 670 7535
Fax: (353 1) 670 7168

**Irish Film Board**
Rockfort House
St Augustine Street
Galway
Co Galway
Tel: (353 91) 561398
Fax: (353 91) 561405

**Irish Film Centre**
6 Eustace Street
Dublin 2
Tel: (353 1) 679 5744
Fax: (353 1) 679 9657

**Radio Telefis Eireann**
(RTE)
Donnybrook
Dublin 4
Tel: (353 1) 208 3111
Fax: (353 1) 208 3080

**Screen Commission of Ireland**
16 Eustace Street
Dublin 2
Tel: (353 1) 672 7252
Fax: (353 1) 672 7251

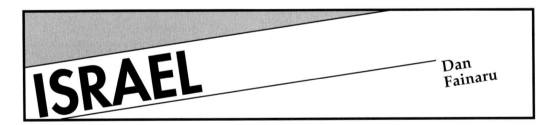

# ISRAEL

Dan Fainaru

The good news in 2000 is that Israel finally has a Cinema Law. After countless ups and downs, the much-discussed legislation, first touted as the magic wand that would save the ailing industry from inevitable demise, then vilified when half its resources were about to be cut, was cleared by parliament in its original form. As of September 1, 2000, half the taxes paid by all Israel's commercial TV broadcasters will be diverted to subsidise Israeli cinema. Altogether, approximately $15m a year will be allocated not only to production but also every other type of film activity, including archives, festivals, and schools.

A Film Commission, recently created amid a flurry of public protest contesting its professional capacity, is in charge of distributing the money and finding solutions for the many loopholes left by the lawmakers. The commission can only advise, however, and the final decisions on funding allocation rest with the Ministry of Culture.

That was the good news. The bad news was that Israeli cinema, judging by last year's crop, including the titles unveiled at the Jerusalem Film Festival in July 2000, is going through one of its worst crises. Hardly any films managed to emulate *Yana's Friends* and *Kadosh*, both released in 1999, by holding the attention of media and audiences – a strange plight in a country whose daily crises cry out for dramatic treatment. The less said about most of the year's new films, the better.

The uncertainty which hovered over the industry goes a long way towards explaining these thin pickings. The Cinema Law might dispel some of the anxiety, but if there is any long-term hope it lies with the quickly expanding new media, and television in particular. A third terrestrial television network is already in the works, the battle raging between cable and satellite channels has already claimed

hundreds of millions of dollars. For the time being, the only types of domestic product these channels want are sitcoms, soaps, sports events and game-shows. But if they exhaust these options, one dares to hope they may turn to more serious business, and fund domestic feature films.

## Wartime horrors

By far the most distinguished Israeli film of the year, still awaiting a domestic release in August 2000, was Amos Gitai's harrowing war drama **Kippur**. After establishing his career abroad, Gitai came back home several years ago, working here intensively but using funds from European sources. His work has never been considered mass entertainment and he is the Israeli film-maker most concerned with film form and language; his output has been often almost experimental.

The Israeli Film Fund, the organisation whose financial help is essential for all Israeli features, turned down Gitai's

*Kadosh*, which went on to worldwide praise, and they also misguidedly rejected *Kippur*, even though the film had the benefit of massive help from the Israeli Army, which supplied all the necessary military hardware.

Enthusiastically received at Cannes, *Kippur* is probably Gitai's most powerful film to date, based on his own experiences in the Yom Kippur War in October 1973, when he was attached to a helicopter unit flying rescue missions over the Syrian front. Refraining from the preaching, militant stance he has adopted in the past, he simply allows his images to speak for themselves. War has never looked grimmer, more horrible or less heroic than it does in *Kippur*'s depiction of a series of rescue operations.

A handful of faceless young men try to pull out other, equally unrecognisable young men, burned, shot and crushed, from the smoking carcasses of their armoured cars, tanks and jeeps. It's a nightmarish experience: relentless, numb-ing and deafening. There is no story here, no individual characters, no discussion about right or wrong. Survival is such an enormous task that nothing else really matters. A pity, then, that Gitai opens and closes the picture with a long, virtuoso shot of a love scene, probingly shot by his cameraman Renato Berta. Impressive as they are on their own, these bookends, obviously intended as a hymn to life in contrast to the terrible devastation contained between them, look far too precious and calculated within a major condemnation of war.

## Hippy trips

Dedicated to all drop-outs in search of themselves, Gur Bentwich's **Total Love** is a freakish road movie catering to a young, hip audience, familiar with the drug culture. Shot over a number of years by a tiny crew on a non-existent budget, this is a truly independent venture, exuberant and sometimes imaginative, though often awkwardly amateurish. Its very loose plot follows several characters from Israel to the

*The rescue crew in action in Amos Gitai's harrowing war drama, KIPPUR*

Netherlands, then India and back to Israel, as they search for a potent, love-inducing drug which works only when the 'right' people take it. Bentwich's *The Blue Planet* (1996), an equally hallucinatory effort, is still an attraction at midnight screenings, and he has a good chance of achieving similar status with *Total Love*.

Dan Wolman's ultra low-budget **Foreign Sister** was well-intentioned but terribly didactic in its portrait of foreign workers in Israel. Two crime stories, Marek Rozenbaum's noir-ish **The Investigation** and Josef Pitchhadze's timid tribute to Tarantino, **Besame Mucho**, both suffered from under-developed characters, manipulative plots and limp climaxes. **Vulcan Junction**, Eran Riklis' attempt to recreate the mood which gave birth to Israeli rock music on the eve of the Yom Kippur War, was neither as zany as it sometimes tried to appear, nor sufficiently realistic; at least it was the first Israeli production whose marketing campaign matched international standards.

Documentaries are still, for the time being, the best element of domestic production, though some of the bloom has worn off, since it is now pretty obvious that the subjects of these films are often more enticing than the film-making itself, with too many projects resembling overlong television reports. This year's hands-down winner was **Love Inventory**, made by David Fisher about his own close-knit family and their search for a lost sister who had mysteriously disappeared at birth. It reveals five siblings, the children of immigrant Holocaust survivors, who are very different from each other in their choice of careers and lifestyles, and yet so close emotionally that even their spouses find it difficult to wedge their way into the family.

DAN FAINARU is an Israeli film critic and journalist, and Editor-in-Chief of *European Film Review*. A former director of the Israeli Film Institute, he is a familiar face at the world's major and minor festivals.

# Recent and Forthcoming Films

### KIPPUR

Script: Amos Gitai, Marie-Josee Sanselme. Dir: Gitai. Phot: Renato Berta. Players: Liron Levo, Tomer Russo, Uri Ran, Yoram Hatav, Guy Amir, Juliano Mer. Prod: MP Productions.

### HABOLESHET HOKERETH (The Investigation)

Script: Haim Merin. Dir: Marek Rozenbaum. Phot: Valentin Belogonov. Players: Moshe Ivgi, Aki Avni. Prod: Marek Rozenbaum (Transfax Productions).

### HATUNA ME'UCHERET (Belated Wedding)

Script and Dir: Dover Kosashvili. Phot: Danny Schneur. Players: Lior Ashkenazi, Ronit Elkabetz, Moni Moshonov, Livia Hachmon. Prod: Marek Rozenbaum

(Transfax Productions).

### ISH HAHASHMAL (Electricity Man)

Script: Yaron Zelig (based on idea by Ruth Lev-Ari). Dir: Eli Cohen. Phot: David Gurfinkel. Players: Menashe Noy, Ayeleth Zorer, Lior Ashkenazi, Amnon Wolf. Prod: Omri Maron, Ruth Lev Ari (April Communications).

### AHOT ZARA (Foreign Sister)

Script, Dir and Prod: Dan Wolman. Phot: Itamar Hadar. Playerst: Tamar Yerushalmi, Askala Makos, Zwi Salton, Miriam Nevo, Neli Tagar.

### GIRAFOT (Giraffes)

Script and Dir: Tzahi Grad. Phot: Giora Bejach. Players: Meital Duan, Tinkerbell, Liat Gluck,

Micha Selekatar. Prod: Isaac Shani, Tzahi Grad (C-Shell Ltd).

### HAHESDER

Script and Dir: Joseph Ceder. Phot: Ofer Inov. Players: Aki Avni, Tinkerbell, Assi Dayan, Idan Alterman, Amnon Wolf. Prod: David Mandil, Eyal Shirai (Cinema Factory).

### BESAME MUCHO

Script and Dir: Joseph Pitchadze. Phot: Shai Goldman. Players: Moni Moshonov, Lalla Malcos, Carmel Beto, Shira Ferber, Ezra Kafri. Prod: Mosh Dannon, Shai Goldman, Joseph Pitchadze, Dov Steuer.

### KIKAR AMEYU'ASHIM (Square of Despair)

Script and Dir: Benny Torati.

Phot: Dror Morel. Players: Yossi Shiloach, Yona Elian, Muhammad Bakri, Uri Gavriel, Sharon Reginiano, Nir Levi. Prod: Amir Harel, Haim Manor (TMH Ltd).

## ASPHALT TZAHOV (Yellow Ashphalt: A Trilogy of Dessert Stories)

Script, Dir and Prod: Danny Verete. Phot: Yoram Milo.

## Producers

**Screen Entertainment**
Eitan Even and Effi Atad
Merkaz Baalei Melacha 40
Tel Aviv 63824
Tel: (972 3) 528 1191
Fax: (972 3) 528 1192

**Parlite Productions**
Uri Sabbag and Einat Bikel
57 Nahmani St
Tel Aviv
Tel: (972 3) 560 8217
Fax: (972 3) 560 7947

**Cinema Factory**
11 Hayei Adam St
Tel Aviv
Tel: (972 3) 691 4279
Fax: (972 3) 691 3982

## Distributors

**Globus Group (UIP, Warner)**
10 Glickson St
Tel Aviv
Tel: (972 3) 526 6333
Fax: (972 3) 526 6373

**A.D.Matalon & Co. (Columbia, TriStar, Fox)**
13 Yona Hanavi St
Tel Aviv
Tel: (972 3) 5162020
Fax: (972 3) 5161888

**Forum/Israeil Theatres (Buena Vista)**
91 Medinath Hayehudim
PO Box 12598
Herzlyia Pituakh
Tel: (972 9) 952 6200
Fax: (972 9) 956 1581

**Shapira Films**
34 Allenby St

Players: Moshe Ivgi, Tatiana Blacher, Abd Zuabi, Sami Samir, Matti Katz, Raida Adun.

## LEHATCHIL ME'HADASH (Starting Over)

Script: Gallia Ron-Feder-Amit. Dir: Yohanan (Jorge) Weller. Phot: Claudio Steinberg. Players: Galia Albin, Nir Levy, Shmeel Ben-Ari, Sharon Zadok, Josie

*Still from Gur Bentwich's road movie, TOTAL LOVE*

Tel Aviv
Tel: (972 3) 517 2923
Fax: (972 3) 510 1370

**Shani Films**
Lev Cinemas
Dizengoff Center
Tel Aviv
Tel: (972 3) 528 8282
Fax: (972 3) 620 4749

## Useful Addresses

**Israeli Film Center**
Ministry of Industry and Trade
PO Box 299
Jerusalem
Tel: (972 2) 622 0608
Fax: (972 2) 623 6303

**Israeli Film & TV Producers Association**
PO Box 20486
Tel Aviv
Tel: (972 3) 561 3919
Fax: (972 3) 561 2529

Katz. Prod: Galia Albin (Almedia Ltd).

## ODOT HAMONITIN (A Matter of Reputation)

Script and Dir: Yoram Kislev. Phot: Nimrod Hiram. Players: Assi Dayan, Nir Levy, Efrat Ben Zur, Alon Dahan. Prod: Haim Mecklenberg, Haim Avni (HLS Film Productions).

**Jerusalem Cinematheque and Israeli Film Archive**
11 Hebron Rd
Jerusalem
Tel: (972 2) 672 4131
Fax: (Fax: (972 2) 671 3044

**Tel Aviv Cinematheque**
2 Shprintzak St
PO Box 20370
Tel Aviv 61203
Tel: (972 3) 691 7181
Fax: (972 3) 696 2841

**Israeli Film Fund**
12 Judith Blvd.
Tel Aviv 61203
Tel: (972 3) 562 8180
Fax: (972 3) 562 5992

**The New Fund for Cinema and Television**
113 Hashmonaim St
Tel Aviv
Tel: (972 3) 561 5786
Fax: (972 3) 562 7991

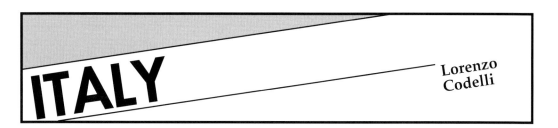

# ITALY

Lorenzo
Codelli

**W**hy is it that Italian customers no longer give a damn about Italian movies? A frightful 11% slump in 1999, pushing the market share for domestic features down to only 16.3% of the total gross, compared to 63.5% for US imports, cannot be explained away solely because most of the new Italian films were low-grade fare, nor by superstar Roberto Benigni's overlong break after *Life is Beautiful*.

More persuasive explanations can be found on the small screen. National television series about middle- and working-class characters are getting much higher ratings than in the past; even young people are staying home more, either to watch endless soaps, or the soccer matches aired day and night. Cable and satellite channels are playing a growing role too, offering an avalanche of recent movies. Furthermore scores of potential ticket buyers were discouraged by lame Italian pictures in competition at Venice and Berlin, and none at all in competition at Cannes.

Surefire comedians such as Leonardo Pieraccioni and Carlo Verdone look puzzled by their sudden drop in popularity. True, neither Pieraccioni's **A Fish in Love** (*Il pesce innamora*), nor Verdone's **There Was a Chinaman in a Coma** (*C'era un cinese in coma*) can be counted among their best achievements, since Pieraccioni, the Tuscan beau, was lazily reworking his former hits, while Verdone, the Roman idol, was taking embittered pot-shots at showbiz.

Two of the three Italian moneyspinners which made the year's top 20 list, **Christmas Holidays 2000** (*Vacanze di Natale 2000*) and **Soccer Fans** (*Tifosi*), belong to producer-distributor-exhibitor

*Licia Maglietta and Bruno Ganz in BREAD AND TULIPS*

Aurelio De Laurentiis' farcical factory, exploiting his regular team. Comedy is still the most profitable way for TV entertainers to get a chance on the big screen; and yet unamusing debuts by surrealist Gialappa's Band with **All the Idiot's Men** (*Tutti gli uomini del deficiente*), as well as by Roman rude boy 'Er Piotta' in **The Secret of the Jaguar** (*Il segreto del giaguaro*), were dismissed even by their worshippers.

## Romance versus romps

Out of the blue, Silvio Soldini's **Bread and Tulips** (*Pane e tulipani*) became a sleeper, defying the curse upon state-financed artsy efforts, which normally are scorned by audiences. This first comedy from an austere Swiss/Italian auteur concerns a frustrated housewife finding new life and love in a still Goldonian Venice; over half a million dreamers relished such a pleasant escape, which was awarded nine David di Donatello prizes.

Pupi Avati evoked his late mother's youthful ardour in the picaresque romp **The Way of the Angels** (*La via degli angeli*). This elegy set in the Fascist era, over never-neverland Emilian hills, starring Avati's off-beat gang together with ethereal Valentina Cervi, marks another milestone in his impressive career.

Explicit sex is cool again, as a kind of exorcism against the repressive Vatican Jubilee. Davide Ferrario's hip **Look at Me** (*Guardami*) traces the painful illness of late porn-queen Moana Pozzi's (embodied by plump Elisabetta Cavallotti). Tinto Brass' **Betrayals** (*Tra(sgre)dire*) does not betray his voyeur fans, dwelling on blonde Yuliya Mayarchuk's urges. Salvatore Piscicelli's **The Body of the Soul** (*Il corpo dell'anima*) dares a hot physical confrontation, Italo Svevo-style, between a wealthy old writer and his gorgeous proletarian maid (Roberto Herlitzka and Raffaella Ponzo, both excellent). Loredana Cannata's lupine nakedness makes Aurelio Grimaldi's **The She-Wolf** (*La donna lupo*) almost biting. In her directorial debut, a delirious self-portrait aptly entitled **Scarlet Diva**, actress Asia Argento enjoys intercourse with some horny partners.

A far tamer trend is enhancing romantic heartbeats, as personified by half-a-dozen dramas. Salvatore Maira's **Love in the Mirror** (*Amor nello specchio*) was a classy tribute to eighteenth-century travelling stage companies; in **Lost Love** (*L'amante perduto*), Roberto Faenza delivered an over-reverent adaptation of Abraham B. Yehoshua's novel, set in Israel; the hero of Neapolitan jester Vincenzo Salemme's **Love at First Sight** (*Amore a prima vista*) was a blind macho man getting a pair of female eyes.

Tonino De Bernardi's **Passionate Women** (*Appassionate*) was a colourful but rather stingy round-up of Neapolitan folk ballads. With **Making Love** (*Canone inverso*), Ricky Tognazzi orchestrated a flat, English-speaking, Middle European sonata, striving to conquer foreign markets – as is Giacomo Campiotti's multinational hotchpotch **Time for Love** (*Il tempo dell'amore*).

### The teen scene

Gianni Zanasi's provincial teenagers in **See You Tomorrow** (*A Domani*) are regressing

*High school rebels in NOBODY LIKE YOU*

to hyperbourgeois values, whereas Gabriele Muccino's high-school rebels are assaulting their once revolutionary parents in **Nobody Like You** (*Come te nessuno mai*), a top-speed *tour de force* revealing a brilliant talent. Alessandro Piva's **La Capagira** pokes fun at Bari's misfits and drug dealers using strict local lingo, subtitled into Italian!

Social disparities between Northern and Southern youngsters are trivialised by Mimmo Calopresti's **I Prefer the Sound of the Sea** (*Preferisco il rumore del mare*). Backed by producer Giuseppe Tornatore, Roberto Andò's **The Prince's Manuscript** (*Il manoscritto del principe*) relates the kinship between Sicilian prince Tomasi di Lampedusa (author of *The Leopard*) and his pupils.

Among the best new film books published in 1999-2000, infamous censorship cuts are documented by Tatti Sanguineti's diptych, *Italia taglia* and *Totò e Carolina* (both published by Transeuropa). Gianfranco Mingozzi, who was Fellini's assistant, remembers the Maestro at work in *Dolce dolce vita*, in words and rare pictures (Giorgio Menna Editore). Veteran director Luigi Comencini gives us a compelling autobiography, *Infanzia, adolescenza e esperienze di un regista* (Baldini

& Castoldi). Circolo del Cinema of Mantua has been celebrating the fiftieth instalment of its outstanding collection of illustrated scripts, which covers classic movies as well as unproduced projects by Zurlini, Emmer, Monicelli, Rosi, Germi, Taviani, Martone, Zavattini and others.

LORENZO CODELLI has written for many periodicals, including *Positif*. He is a member of the boards of the Cineteca del Friuli, the Pordenone Silent Film Festival and Udine Incontri Cinema.

# Recent Films

### A DOMANI (See You Tomorrow)

Script and Dir: Gianni Zanasi. Phot: Giulio Pietromarchi. Players: Stefania Rivi, Andrea Corneti. Prod: Tangram Film/Istituto Luce/RAI.

### L'AMANTE PERDUTO (Lost Love)

Script: Sandro Petraglia, Roberto Faenza, from the novel by Abraham B. Yehoshua. Dir: Faenza. Phot: José Luis Alcaine. Players: Ciaran Hinds, Juliet Aubrey. Prod: Jean Vigo/Mikado/RAI/Tele+(Italy)/Steel Pictures

(UK)/British Screen/British Sky Broadcasting.

### AMOR NELLO SPECCHIO (Love in the Mirror)

Script and Dir: Salvatore Maira. Phot: Maurizio Calvesi. Players: Anna Galiena, Peter Stormare, Simona Cavallari. Prod: Factory/Genial Movies Financing.

### AMORE A PRIMA VISTA (Love at First Sight)

Script and Dir: Vincenzo Salemme.

Phot: Mauro Marchetti. Players: Salemme, Mandala Tayde. Prod: Cecchi Gori Group.

### APPASSIONATE (Passionate Women)

Script: Tonino De Bernardi, Mario Sesti. Dir: De Bernardi. Phot: Tommaso Borgstrom. Players: Anna Bonaiuto, Iaia Forte, Galatea Renzi. Prod: A.S.P.

### CANONE INVERSO (Making Love)

Script: Graziano Diana, Simona Izzo, Ricky Tognazzi, from Paolo Maurensig's novel. Dir: Tognazzi. Phot: Fabio Cianchetti. Players: Hans Matheson, Melanie Thierry. Prod: Pacific Pictures.

### LA CAPAGIRA

Script: Andrea Piva. Dir: Alessandro Piva. Phot: Gianenrico Bianchi. Players: Dino Abbrescia, Mino Barbarese. Prod: KublaKhan/Munbut.

### LA CARBONARA

Script and Dir: Luigi Magni. Phot: Danilo Desideri. Players: Lucrezia Lante della Rovere, Nino Manfredi. Prod: Letizia Cinematografica.

### C'ERA UN CINESE IN COMA (There Was a Chinaman in a Coma)

Script: Carlo Verdone, Giovanni Veronesi, Pasquale Plastino. Dir: Verdone. Phot: Danilo Desideri. Players: Verdone, Beppe Fiorello. Prod: Cecchi Gori Group.

### COME TE NESSUNO MAI (Nobody Like You)

Script: Gabriele Muccino, Silvio Muccino, from a story by Marco Valerio Fusco. Dir: Gabriele Muccino. Phot: Arnaldo Catinari. Players: Muccino, Giulia Steigerwalt. Prod: Fandango/Mikado/RAI.

### IL CORPO DELL'ANIMA (The Body of the Soul)

Script: Carla Apuzzo, Salvatore Piscicelli. Dir: Piscicelli. Phot: Saverio Guarna. Players: Raffaella Ponzo, Roberto Herlitzka. Prod: Metropolis Film.

### IL DOLCE RUMORE DELLA VITA (The Sweet Noise of Life)

Script: Mimmo Rafele, Lidia Ravera, Giuseppe Bertolucci. Dir: Bertolucci. Phot: Fabio Cianchetti. Players: Francesca Neri, Alida Valli. Prod: Letizia Cinematografica.

### LA DONNA LUPO (The She-Wolf)

Script: Aurelio Grimaldi, Michele Lo Foco. Dir: Grimaldi. Phot: Massimo Intoppa. Players: Loredana Cannata, Arturo Paglia. Prod: Arancia Cinema.

### E ALLORA MAMBO (Let's Mambo)

Script: Fabio Bonifacci, Lucio Pellegrini. Dir: Pellegrini. Phot: Fabio Cianchetti. Players: Luca Bizzarri, Luciana Litizzetto. Prod: Medusa Film/Tele+.

### FANTOZZI 2000 – LA CLONAZIONE (Fantozzi 2000 – The Cloning)

Script: Alessandro Bencivenni, Domenico Saverni. Dir: Saverni. Phot: Marco Onorato. Players: Paolo Villaggio, Milena Vukotic. Prod: Italian International Film/Cecchi Gori Group.

### IL GRANDE BOTTO (The Big One)

Script: Gennaro Nunziante, Paolo Rossi, Leone Pompucci. Dir: Pompucci. Phot: Massimo Pau. Players: Carlo Buccirosso, Emilio Solfrizzi, Francesca Nunzi. Prod: Videomaura/Cecchi Gori Group.

### GUARDAMI (Look at Me)

Script and Dir: Davide Ferrario. Phot: Giovanni Cavallini. Players: Elisabetta Cavallotti, Stefania Orsola Garello. Prod: Trio Film.

### IO AMO ANDREA (I Love Andrea)

Script: Carla Giulia Casalini, Ugo Chiti, Francesco Nuti. Dir: Nuti. Phot: Maurizio Calvesi. Players: Nuti, Francesca Neri. Prod: FrancescAndrea.

### LIBERATE I PESCI (Free the Fishes)

Script: Cristina Comencini, Enzo Monteleone, Gennaro Nunziante. Dir: Comencini. Phot: Roberto Forza. Players: Michele Placido, Francesco Paolantoni, Emilio Solfrizzi. Prod: Cattleya/Cineritmo.

### IL MANOSCRITTO DEL PRINCIPE (The Prince's Manuscript)

Script: Roberto Andò, Salvatore Marcarelli. Dir: Andò. Phot: Enrico Lucidi. Players: Michel Bouquet, Jeanne Moreau. Prod: Sciarlò/RAI.

### METRONOTTE (Nightwatchman)

Script: Francesco Calogero, Umberto Contarello, from a story by Vincenzo Pardini. Dir: Calogero. Players: Diego Abatantuono, Anna Safroncik. Prod: Digital Film/RAI/Tele+.

### PANE E TULIPANI (Bread and Tulips)

Script: Doriana Leondeff, Silvio Soldini. Dir: Soldini. Phot: Luca Bigazzi. Players: Licia Maglietta, Bruno Ganz, Giuseppe Battiston. Prod: Monogatari/Istituto Luce/RAI (Italy)/Amka Films/TSI (Switzerland).

### IL PESCE INNAMORATO (A Fish in Love)

Script: Leonardo Pieraccioni, Giovanni Veronesi. Dir: Pieraccioni. Phot: Arnaldo Catinari. Players: Pieraccioni, Yamila Diaz. Prod: Cecchi Gori Group.

### PREFERISCO IL RUMORE DEL MARE (I Prefer the Sound of the Sea)

Script: Mimmo Calopresti, Francesco Bruni, from a story by Calopresti, Bruni, Heidrun Schleef. Dir: Calopresti. Phot: Luca Bigazzi. Players: Silvio Orlando, Michele Raso, Paolo Cirio. Prod: Bianca Film/Mikado/RAI (Rome)/Arcapix/Canal+ (Paris).

### PRIME LUCI DELL'ALBA (First Lights at Dawn)

Script: Nicola Molino. Dir: Lucio Gaudino. Phot: Felice De Maria. Players: Gianmarco Tognazzi, Laura Morante. Prod: Caviar.

### QUESTO É IL GIARDINO (This is the Garden)

Script: Carolina Freschi, Giovanni Davide Maderna. Dir: Maderna. Phot: Luca Bigazzi. Players: Carolina Freschi, Denis Fasolo. Prod: Lucky Red.

## SCARLET DIVA

Script and Dir: Asia Argento. Phot: Frederic Fasano. Players: Argento, Jean Shepherd, Daria Nicolodi. Prod: Opera Film.

## IL SEGRETO DEL GIAGUARO (The Secret of the Jaguar)

Script: Piotta, Manetti Bros, Fabio Zanello, Herbert Simone Paragnani, Antonello Fassari. Dir: Fassari. Phot: Massimo Intoppa. Players: Piotta, Fassari, Lando Buzzanca. Prod: Italian International Film.

*Rural life in THE WAY OF THE ANGELS*

## IL TEMPO DELL'AMORE (Time for Love)

Script: Giacomo Campiotti, Alexandre Abadachian. Dir: Campiotti. Phot: Blasco Giurato. Players: Juliet Aubrey, Natacha Regnier. Prod: Emme Cinematografica (Rome)/Noé Films (Paris)/British Screen.

## TERRA BRUCIATA (Burnt Earth)

Script: Fabio Segatori, Ugo Sani. Dir: Segatori. Phot: Bruno Cascio, Giancarlo Ferrando. Players: Giancarlo Giannini, Raoul Bova. Prod: Globe Films/Istituto Luce/ Dean Films.

## TIFOSI (Soccer Fans)

Script: Neri Parenti, Marco Martani, Fausto Brizzi, Enrico Vanzina. Dir: Parenti. Phot: Gianlorenzo Battaglia. Players: Massimo Boldi, Diego Abatantuono, Christian De Sica. Prod: Filmauro.

## TRA(SGRE)DIRE (Betrayal)

Script: Tinto Brass, Carla Cipriani, Nicolaj Pennestri, Silvia Rossi, Massimiliano Zanin. Dir: Brass. Phot: Massimo Di Venanzo. Players: Yuliya Mayarchuk, Jarno Berardi, Francesca Nunzi. Prod: C.R.C.

## TUTTI GLI UOMINI DEL DEFICIENTE (All the Idiot's Men)

Script: Gialappa's Band, Andrea Salvadore, Enzo Santin, Paolo Costella. Dir: Costella. Phot: Fabrizio Lucci. Players: Claudia Gerini, Paolo Hendel, Marina Massironi. Prod: Palomar/ Gialappa's Band/Medusa Film.

## TUTTO L'AMORE CHE C'É (All the Love There Is)

Script: Domenico Starnone, Sergio Rubini. Dir: Rubini. Phot: Paolo Carnera. Players: Damiano Russo, Margherita Buy, Vittoria Puccini. Prod: Cecchi Gori Group.

## UN UOMO PERBENE (A Respectable Man)

Script: Maurizio Zaccaro, Umberto Contarello, from a story by Silvia Tortora. Dir: Zaccaro. Phot: Pasquale Rachini. Prod: Clemi Cinematografica.

## VACANZE DI NATALE 2000 (Winter Holidays 2000)

Script: Enrico Vanzina, Carlo Vanzina. Dir: Carlo Vanzina. Phot: Gianlorenzo Battglia. Players: Massimo Boldi, Christian De Sica, Megan Gale. Prod: Filmauro.

## LA VIA DEGLI ANGELI (The Way of the Angels)

Script: Antonio Avati, Pupi Avati, from a story by Ines Vigetti and Marco Bernardini. Dir: Pupi Avati. Phot: Cesare Bastelli. Players: Valentina Cervi, Carlo Delle Piane, Gianni Cavina. Prod: DueA Film/Medusa Film.

# Useful Addresses

**Adriana Chiesa Enterprises**
Via Barnaba Oriani, 24/A
00197 Roma
Tel: (39 06) 808 6052
Fax: (39 06) 8068 7855

**Agis**
Via di villa Patrizi, 10
00161 Roma
Tel: (39 06) 884 731
Fax: (39 06) 4423 1838

**Anica**
[Main Italian producers association]
Viale Regina Margherita, 286
00198 Roma
Tel: (39 06) 442 5961
Fax: (39 06) 440 4128

**Banca Nazionale del Lavoro –
Sezione Credito**
Cinematografico
Via degli Scipioni, 297
00192 Roma
Tel: (39 06) 4702 0940
Fax: (39 06) 4702 0970

**CAM**
Via Cola di Rienzo, 152
00192 Roma
Tel: (39 06) 687 4220
Fax: (39 06) 687 4046

**Carol Levi Company**
Via Pisanelli, 2
00196 Roma
Tel: (39 06) 3600 2430
Fax: (39 06) 3600 2438
e-mail: clevi@ntt.it

**Cecchi Gori Group**
Via Valadier, 42
00193 Roma
Tel: (39 06) 324 721
Fax: (39 06) 3247 2303
www.cecchigori.com

**Cinecittà Holding**
Via Tuscolana, 1055
00173 Roma
Tel: (39 06) 722 861
Fax: (39 06) 722 1883

**Clemi Cinematografica**
Via Salaria, 292
00198 Roma
Tel: (39 06) 854 8821
Fax: (39 06) 841 9749

**Dipartimento dello Spettacolo –
Presidenza del Consiglio dei
Ministri**
Via della Ferratella in Laterano, 45/51
00184 Roma
Tel: (39 06) 77321

**DueA Film**
Piazza Cola di Rienzo, 69
00192 Roma
Tel: (39 06) 321 4851
Fax: (39 06) 321 5108

**Eagle Pictures**
Via Buonarroti, 5
20149 Milano
Tel: (39 02) 438 5091
Fax: (39 02) 481 3389
e-mail: eagle.pictures@gpa.it
www.eaglepictures.gpa.it

**Filmalbatros**
Via di Villa Ada, 10
00199 Roma
Tel: (39 06) 855 4700
Fax: (39 06) 855 5280

**Filmexport Group**
Via Polonia, 7/9
00198 Roma
Tel: (39 06) 855 4266
Fax: (39 06) 855 0248

**Fininvest/Mediaset/Rete Italia**
Mediaset
viale Europa 44/48
20093 Cologno Monzese
Tel: (39 02) 25141

Mediaset
Largo del Nazareno 8
00187 Roma
Tel: (39 06) 673 831
www.mediaset.it

**Filmauro**
Via XXIV Maggio, 14
00187 Roma
Tel: (39 06) 699 581
Fax: (39 06) 6995 8410
e-mail: filmauro@colosseum.it

**International Recording**
Via Urbana, 172
00184 Roma
Tel: (39 06) 476 701
Fax: (39 06) 474 5246

**Istituto Luce**
Via Tuscolana, 1055
00173 Roma
Tel: (39 06) 729 921
Fax: (39 06) 722 1127
www.luce.it

**Italia Cinema**
Via Aureliana, 63
00187 Roma
Tel: (39 06) 4201 2539
Fax: (39 06) 4200 3530
www.italiacinema.org

**Key Films**
Via Tartaglia, 16
00197 Roma
Tel: (39 06) 8069 2052
Fax: (39 06) 8069 1676
e-mail: keyfilms@tin.it
www.keyfilms.it

**Lucky Red**
Via Baiaonti, 10
00195 Roma
Tel: (39 06) 3735 2296
Fax: (39 06) 3735 2310
e-mail: luckyred@mclink.it

**Magica**
Master Europeo in Gestione di
Impresa
Cinematografica e Audiovisiva
Via Lucullo 7, int. 8
00187 Rome
Tel: (39 06) 420 0651
Fax: (39 06) 4201 0898

**Medusa Film**
Via Aurelia Antica, 422/424
00165 Roma
Tel: (39 06) 663 901
Fax: (39 06) 6639 0450
www.medusa.it

**Mikado Cinematografica**
Via Gianturco, 4
00196 Roma
Tel: (39 06) 324 4989
Fax: (39 06) 321 9489
e-mail: mikado@tin.it

**Rai – Radiotelevisione Italiana**
Viale Mazzini, 14
00195 Roma
Tel: (39 06) 3878
Fax: (39 06) 372 5680
www.rai.it

**Rai Trade**
Via Novaro, 18
00195 Rome
Tel: (39 06) 374 981
Fax: (39 06) 372 3492

**Sacher Film**
Via Annia Faustina, 25
00153 Roma
Tel (39 06) 574 5353
Fax: (39 06) 574 0483

**Tele+**
Via Piranesi, 46
20137 Milan
Tel: (39 02) 700 271
Fax (39 02) 7002 7201

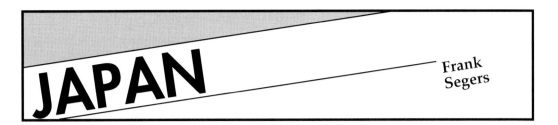

# JAPAN

Frank
Segers

Japanese cinema, much like the country's economy, moved largely in fits and starts in 1999, making little net progress. Theatre attendance (144.7 million) retreated a bit from 1998's lofty level, but still qualified 1999 as a respectable year commercially, with total box-office of $1.7 billion (at $1/Y108).

Good news for foreign distributors was the drop in market share for domestic films; the 169 Japanese titles released in 1999 (excluding pornographic films) accounted for 32% of the overall gross – well below the domestic share snared back in 1980, when Japanese titles took more than 50%. As a result, Japan continues to be one of the two most lucrative foreign markets for Hollywood films, and of the 246 foreign titles released in Japan in 1999, 136 originated in the US.

While that statistic brought joy for exhibition executives at Japan's major studios – Toho, Toei and Shochiku – it brought cold comfort for their colleagues in production, who were trimming in-house slates in favour of co-productions and acquisitions. While these companies are stabilising or reducing output to between roughly 18 to 27 features per year, smaller distributors are picking up the tempo, channelling more than 100 releases – more than tripling 1998's total – into the theatrical marketplace.

Toho emerged as the top distributor of 1999, grabbing $155m in revenue by relying heavily on tried and tested formulae. Its biggest hits included the usual animation (the *Doraemon* series, and the **Pokémon** phenomenon), plus Masahiro Shinoda's period ninja action movie **Castle of the Owl**, and well-established horror items, led by director Hideo Nakata's **Ring 2**, the latest in a series of highly successful

*Ken Takakura, right, as POPPOYA - RAILROAD MAN*

screamers derived from Koji Suzuki's horror novels.

Toei, the second-ranked major, had a big winner with Yasuo Furuhata's **Poppoya – Railroad Man**, starring that stern-faced stalwart, Ken Takakura. He portrays an overly-dutiful station master working a branch line in northern Japan which has been closed for economic reasons. The railroad veteran habitually waits in vain for trains that never arrive. A wistful treatment of a lonely man coping with loss (a widower, his daughter died suddenly while he was working), *Poppoya* was a substantial box-office success in Japan (some $20m in film rentals) and in Korea. It also swept the Japan Academy Awards ceremony in March, winning prizes in 13 categories, including Best Actor (for Takakura), Best Director and Best Actress

(Shinobu Otake as a young girl the stationmaster briefly encounters).

## A family misfortune

Third-ranked Shochiku, battling back from a series of setbacks over the last two years, was not quite as fortunate with its big, prestige releases. Hoping to cash in on the afterglow of Studio Ghibli's enormous 1997 animation hit, *Princess Mononoke*, Shochiku distributed Ghibli's **My Neighbours, The Yamadas** in the summer of 1999. *The Yamadas* is based on a comic strip by Hisaichi Ishii about a middle-aged Japanese businessman and his family. The film version is a gentle exposition of family values, Japanese style, rendered in water-colours and pastels. Audiences were disappointed by this animation style, strikingly different from the pointed, hard-line techniques of previous Studio Ghibli output, which has been dominated by action-adventure and fantasy titles. The result? The *Yamadas* was the most surprising flop of 1999, proving that animation is not necessarily a surefire bet in Japan.

Shochiku had better luck with its big year-end release of Nagisa Oshima's gay samurai drama, **Taboo** (*Gohatto*). Set in the nineteenth century, in the last days of the Edo era, the film directly addresses homosexual liaisons within an elite group of samurai swordsmen. The excellent cast includes "Beat" Takeshi (known as Takeshi Kitano when he directs) and Ryuhei Matsuda, the 16-year-old son of a genuine screen legend, the late actor Yusaku Matsuda.

While skilfully lensed by Toyomichi Kurita, *Taboo* is a rather static exercise, focused on the sensationalism of its limited subject at the expense of genuine suspense and drama. Oshima enjoys taking on taboo subjects, but homo-eroticism among samurai hardly qualifies as such amid the 'anything goes' ethos of contemporary cinema. The $6m production performed respectably at the box-office in Japan before moving on to compete at Cannes 2000, where it left critics underwhelmed.

Shochiku seems to be pinning its hopes on George Iida's **Another Heaven**, a police suspense drama which, its creator insists, incorporates "the essence of a horror film". The film hopes to partake of the current mini boom in horror titles, which started in 1998 with the original *The Ring* (produced to compete with such Hollywood items as *Seven* and *Scream*). Shochiku promises an all-out media blitz including, inevitably, internet exposure. Produced by Shinya Kawai, who started the *Ring* cycle, *Another Heaven* was reported to be the centrepiece of a campaign that would also include an 11-part television drama and a computer game.

## Bus tale and Beat's return

The remarkable Japanese entry that won two awards in Cannes – the International Critics Prize (FIPRESCI) and the Ecumenical Jury Award – is Shinji Aoyama's **Eureka**. Running at three hours and 37 minutes and shot in black-and-white CinemaScope (with heavy use of sepia), the film assesses the traumatic aftermath of a bus hijacking in Kyushu, focusing on the driver and two surviving passengers, a schoolgirl and her older brother. *Eureka* has a strong cast, led by Koji Yakusho, one of Japan's busiest leading men; he starred in the highly successful *Shall We Dance?*, as well as Shohei Imamura's Palme D'Or winner *The Eel*.

Critics gave a deferential but unenthusiastic response to **Kikujiro**, Takeshi Kitano's endearing road movie about a

*Still from George Iida's crime drama, ANOTHER HEAVEN*

loudmouthed blowhard (Takeshi) who befriends a lonesome boy who is looking for the mother he's never met (searches for missing parents featured in several Japanese titles in 1999). Since then, the director has gone back to basics and his upcoming **Brother** marks a return to familiar crime territory: the story of a gangster's bodyguard (Takeshi) forced to flee Japan for Los Angeles when his boss is murdered. This is Kitano's first film shot largely in English, and partially in Los Angeles. A co-producer is Jeremy Thomas, who backed Oshima's *Merry Christmas, Mr Lawrence*, the 1983 film which firmly established Takeshi's international reputation as an actor to be reckoned with.

Director Shinji Somai came up with **Wait and See** (*Ah, Haru*), an endearing drama about a young salaryman (Koichi Sato, an exceptionally likeable actor) who reassesses his comfortable life after locating the father he never knew. The film won first place in the 1999 *Kinema Junpo* magazine's Best Picture poll.

A welcome surprise was Shinobu Yaguchi's **Adrenaline Drive**, a clever road comedy about a young couple's efforts to outwit a boisterous yakuza gang's quest for a small fortune in cash. Initially depicted as pathetic losers – the husband (Masanobu Ando) is a meek car rental clerk, the wife (Hikari Ishida) is a shy nurse at a city hospital – both characters are neatly transformed into glamorous victors. Ishida (widely known for her television work) beautifully handles the on-screen transformation into a feisty sexpot. Not

surprisingly, *Adrenaline Drive* was acquired for US distribution.

The monster film genre continued to flourish. Toho resurrected the Godzilla series after a four-year lapse, with **Godzilla 2000: Millennium**, and Daiei Co. contributed **Gamera 3 – The Revenge of Iris**, permitting the mighty, fanged turtle to take to the Tokyo skies once more.

FRANK SEGERS is a freelance writer who for many years specialised in Far Eastern entertainment issues for *Variety*.

*Still from Shinji Somai's WAIT AND SEE*

# Recent and Forthcoming Films

### RING 0 – 'BIRTHDAY'

Script: Hiroshi Takahashi. Dir: Norio Tsuruta. Players: Yukie Nakama, Seiichi Tanabe, Kimiko Aso. Prod: Asmik Ace Entertainment.

The fourth and final title in the *Ring* series of horror dramas involving a mysterious heroine, Sadako. In this episode, she tries her hand at a theatre acting career in Tokyo, falls for a

production technician and has deadly skirmishes with a director and other cast members.

### DORA-HEITA

Script: Akira Kurosawa, Keisuke Kinoshita, Kon Ichikawa, Masaki Kobayashi. Dir: Kon Ichikawa. Players: Koji Yakusho, Yuko Asano. Prod: Nikkatsu Corp.

Samurai film, co-written years ago by

Kurosawa and resurrected by co-scripter-director Ichikawa, about a small-town magistrate investigating three local crime bosses. This is the 85-year-old Ichikawa's 74th feature as a director.

### KURAYAMI NO REQUIEM (Requiem of Darkness)

Script and Dir: Toshiyuki Morioka. Players: Kazunari Aizawa, Kanako Kojima, Tomomi Kuribayashi. Prod:

Straydog/Hot Entertainment/Valis.

Scripter Morioka's directoral debut, this action-packed melodrama concerns a motley array of characters inside a ragged movie theatre showing vintage films. A group of Yakuza pay an unwelcome visit, stirring up animosities and violence among the audience, including a tired businessman, a prostitute, a cancer-stricken man and a nurse.

## TENSHI NO RAKUEN (Looking for Angel)

Dir: Akihiro Suzuki. Players: Hotaru Hazuki, Akira Suehiro. Prod: Piss Factory.

Director Suzuki's feature debut is a self-syled "anti-heterosexual movie" about a sexually-confused young man who finds himself at a "party" for a deceased porn actor. Flashback plot charts previous, ambiguous encounters between the young man and the porn performer.

## SEMI-MATSURI NO SHIMA (The Island of Cicada Festival)

Dir: Hiroyuki Yokoyama. Players: Kumiko Tsuchiya, Kazuki Kitamura, Naoto Takenaka. Prod: Japan Art/ Urban Times/Saison Corp.

Yokoyama's debut feature describes itself as a modern version of Japan's first colour film, Keisuke Kinoshita's *Carmen Comes Home* (1951). A pregnant stripper's dead-beat husband is hit by a car and dies. The woman visits Nokoto, a small island famous for a traditional cicada festival, where the late husband's mother runs an inn. Mistaken identity involving the young wife ensues, as does the notion that islanders killed off-shore return in the form of a cicada.

# Producers/ Distributors

**Daiei Co. Ltd.**
Tokuma Shoten Honsha Bldg.
1-1-16 Higashi Shimbashi
Minato-ku
Tokyo 105-8055
Tel: (81 3) 3573 8716
Fax: (81 3) 3573 8720

**Nikkatsu Corp.**
3-28-12 Hongo
Bunkyo-ku
Tokyo 113-0033

## JIKKEN EIGA (Experimental Film)

Dir: Makoto Tezka. Players: Masatoshi Nagase, Reika Hashimoto. Prod: Media Factory/ Neotetra Film.

Director Tezka, 39, took just seven days to shoot this film about the relationship between a film-maker and a young girl – who are making a film in seven days.

## FREEZE ME

Script and Dir: Takashi Ishii. Players: Harumi Inoue, Shingo Tsurumi, Kazuki Kitamura. Prod: KSS Inc./Nikkatsu Corp.

Young woman exacts unusual revenge on three rapists, using a freezer unit. Suspense item from the director of *A Night In The Nude* and *Gonin*.

## GENJITSU NO TSUZUKI, YUME NO OWARI (A Chance To Die)

Script: Su Chao Pin, Chen Yi Wen. Dir: Chen Yi Wen. Prod: Burning Prod/Nikkatsu Corp.

Kung-fu actioner shot in Japan and Taiwan about a Taiwanese gangland attack on Japanese yakuza.

## UNCHAIN

Dir: Toshiaki Toyoda. Prod: Film-Makers Inc./Little More Co.

Documentary shot over a five-year period about a down-and-out boxer who storms a workers' centre in Osaka before being institutionalised. From the director of gritty, streetwise *Pornostar* (1998).

## SUZURAN – SHOJOKI NO

Tel: (81 3) 5689 1026
Fax: (81 3) 5689 1043
e-mail: nobu@nikkatsu.co.jp.

**Shochiku Co. Ltd.**
4-1-1 Tsukiji
Togeki Bldg., 16th Fl.
Chuo-ku
Tokyo 104-8422
Tel: (81 3) 5550 1623
Fax: (81 3) 5550 1654
e-mail: mkoga@shochiku.co.jp

## MONOGATARI (Return of Happiness)

Dir: Rintaro Mayuzumi. Players: Isao Hashizume, Hiroyuki Ikeuchi, Hitomi Kuroki. Prod: Shochiku Co./NHK Enterprise 21.

Spin-off from the hit NHK television series, *Suzuran*; focuses on the girlhood of heroine Moe and her relations with her biological mother. Melodrama from the director of 1994's *Rampo*.

## TENGOKU MADENO HYAKU-MILES (100 Miles To Heaven)

Dir: Sho Igarashi. Players: Saburo Tokio, Kaoru Yachigusa, Shinobu Otake. Prod: Team Okuyama Corp.

Put-upon middle-aged man intensifies his relationship with his mother following severe business reversals. Based on the best-selling novel by Jiro Asada.

## SALARY MAN KINTARO

Dir: Takashi Miike. Players: Katsunori Takahashi, Michiko Hada. Distributor: Toho Co.

Based on a manga comic hero who quits a motorcycle gang to become a salaried worker. Problems within the firm make his erstwhile gangland life seem idyllic.

## SPACE TRAVELLERS

Dir: Katsuyuki Motohiro. Players: Takeshi Kaneshiro, Eri Fukatsu, Masanobu Ando. Prod: Fuji Television Network/Toei Co./ Robott.

Detective actioner starring Takeshi Kaneshiro, who has worked in Hollywood. Follow-up to the 1998 hit *Bayside Shakedown*.

**Toei Co.**
2-17, 3-chome
Ginza, Chuo-ku
Tokyo
Tel: (81 3) 3535 7621
Fax: (81 3) 3535 7622

**Toho International Co.**
Hibiya Park Building
8-1 Yukucho, 1-chome
Chiyoda-ku
Tokyo
Tel: (81 3) 3213 6821
Fax: (81 3) 3213 6825

# Distributors/ Sales Agents

**Asmik Ace Entertainment, Inc.**
5-24-5 Hongo
Bunkyo-ku
Tokyo 113
Tel: (81 3) 3817 6717
Fax: (81 3) 3817 6718

**GAGA Communications Inc.**
East Roppongi Building
3-16-35 Roppongi
Minato-ku
Tokyo 106
Tel: (81 3) 3589 7503
Fax: (81 3) 3589 7499

**Nippon Herald Films Inc.**
5-11-1 Ginza
Chuo-ku
Tokyo 104
Tel: (81 3) 3248 1162
Fax: (81 3) 3248 1169

**Pony Canyon Inc.**
2-5-10 Toranomon, Minato-ku
Tokyo 105-8487
Tel: (81 3) 5521 8024
Fax: (81 3) 5521 8122
e-mail: sakoda@ponycanyon.co.jp

**Shibata Organisation Inc.**
(France Eigasha)
2-10-8 Ginza
Chuo-ku
Tokyo
Tel: (81 3) 3545 3411
Fax: (81 3) 3545 3519
e-mail: dze0200@nifty.ne.jp

**Studio Ghibli**
1-4-25 Kajino-cho
Koganei-shi
Tokyo 184-0002
Tel: (81 4) 2253 2961
Fax: (81 4) 2253 5891

**Tohokushinsha Film Co. Ltd.**
4-17-7 Akasaka
Minato-ku
Tokyo 107
Tel: (81 3) 3582 0211
Fax: (81 3) 3584 2824

**Toho-Towa Co. Ltd.**
Playguide Building 3F
2-6-4 Ginza
Chuo-ku
Tokyo
Tel: (81 3) 3562 0109
Fax: (81 3) 3535 3656

**UniJapan Film**
Ginza 1-6-5, Chuo-ku
Tokyo 104–0061
Tel: (81 3) 3538 0621
Fax: (81 3) 3538 0622

# KAZAKHSTAN — Eugene Zykov

Though five Kazakh features were scheduled for release in 2000, compared to six in 1999, there is optimism amongst the industry's major players. In early 2000, President Nazarbaev launched a national campaign to support domestic culture and under a new law the government started funding the film and television industries. Tax privileges gave a strong boost to a major domestic producer, Kazakh Film Studios (KFS), which also won a Japanese grant of nearly $500,000 to upgrade its facilities with new Japanese equipment.

**Three Brothers**, director Serik Aprymov's lyrical memoir about youngsters growing up on the outskirts of a Kazakh city, enjoyed a successful world premiere at the Rotterdam Festival in 2000, and the Children's Festival in Berlin. Another Aprymov film, **Aksuat**, also lensed at KFS and became a local box-office hit. This is the story of a young man who visits his elder brother in their home village; he has adopted a city lifestyle, while his brother has stuck to rural tradition.

In the summer of 2000 **Paratroopers**, which might be termed the first Kazakh *Rambo* was finally released. Based on real-life events, it features four teenage friends who join the Army together and later become part of an elite force of border guards, fighting drug and ammunition smugglers and running peace-keeping missions to ethnic conflicts. KFS also released a historical drama, **The Youth Of Zhambul**, directed by Kano Kasymbekov, about a prominent Kazakh poet, Zhambul

Zhabaev. He is remembered for 'To My People Of Leningrad', a poem which was on the leaflets dropped from Soviet planes into the city during the 900-day siege by the Nazis.

Many independent producers are struggling, but some keep afloat. Gala-TV has won numerous festival awards and generally finds international markets for its features and documentaries. Scheduled for release in the last quarter of 2000 was the Gala-TV/KFS co-production **Ompa 2**, a sequel to the hit comedy *Ompa*, charting the further adventures of two pilots who shuttle across Kazakhstan in their vintage plane. Writer-director Rustam Khamdamov, a talented and controversial figure whose *Anna Karamazoff* was in competition at Cannes in 1991 is slowly developing his new feature, said to be an allegorical tale exploring the human search for truth and perfection in the modern world.

Another successful independent company is Khabar, which specialises in productions for the largest Kazakh television channel. In the past five years

*Still from historical drama THE YOUTH OF ZHAMBUL*

Khabar has produced more than 500 episodes of the top-rating Kazakh soap *The Crossroad* and recently started shooting a new crime series, *Locust*, intended for combined distribution in the domestic video and theatrical markets.

EUGENE ZYKOV is a Moscow-based freelance writer for Variety Media Publications and *Channel 21 International*.

# Recent and Forthcoming Films

**YOUNOST DZHAMBULA (The Youth of Zhambul)**

Script: Marzatai Zholdasbekov. Dir: Kano Kasymbekov. Phot: Bulat and Abybakir Suleev. Players: Mukhamedzhan Mukhamedzhanov, Renat Yesimgaliev. Prod: Kazakh Film Studios.

**DESANT (Paratroopers )**

Script: Alexander Baranov, Rafad Samigullin. Dir: Leila Oranysheva. Players: Bolot Beishenaliev,

## Useful Addresses

**Firm-Kino**
16 Al-Farabi Ave
480067 Almaty
Tel: (7 32 72) 482 606
Fax: (7 32 72) 630 901

**Gala-TV**

Bopesh Zhandayev, Dimash Akimov. Phot: Valerii Mulgaut. Prod: Firma Kino Studios/Kazakh Film Studios.

**AKSUAT**

Script and Dir: Serik Aprymov. Phot: Boris Troshev. Players: Sabid Kurmanbekov, Inessa Rodionova, Nurzhuman Ihtynbayev. Prod: Kazakh Film Studios/Firma Kino Studios.

**TRI BRATA (Three Brothers)**

23A Tole Bi St
480100 Almaty
Tel: (7 32 72) 617 031
Fax: (7 32 72) 616 816
e-mail: galatv@galatv.almaty.kz

**Kazakh Film Studios**
16 Al-Farabi Ave
480067 Almaty

Script and Dir: Serik Aprymov. Phot: Boris Troshev. Players: Farkhad Abdraimov, Bolot Piyshenalyev, Nurzhuman Ihtynbayev. Prod: Kazakh Film Studios.

**OMPA 2**

Script and Dir: Saty-Baldy Narymbetov. Phot: Alexei Berkovich. Players: Alexander Pankratov-Chernyi, Doskhan Zholzhaksymov. Prod: Gala-TV/ Kazakh Film Studios.

Tel: (7 32 72) 482 211
Fax: (7 32 72) 480 909

**Khabar Agency**
13 Republic Sq
Almaty 480013
Tel: (7 32 72) 625 526
Tel/Fax: (7 32 72) 506 344
e-mail: tan@khabar.almaty.kz

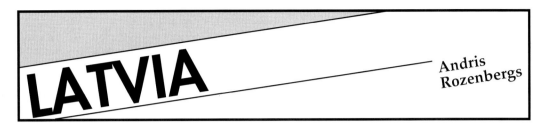

# LATVIA

Andris
Rozenbergs

More than 60 films, including those produced for television, were screened at the biannual national film festival, Lielais Kristaps. Having served on the selection committee, I can testify that Latvia's production output during the last two years has provided an exciting panorama. Given that state support amounts to about 37% of the industry's production overheads, the number of films completed is quite astonishing, proving that production companies have fully adapted to the demands of a market economy. They have had little choice.

One of the most recurrent themes in Latvian cinema in this time of globalisation has been the notion of 'borders'. Stories no longer take place on an isolated patch of land between the Baltic Sea and the Russian border, as used to be the case. Now there is a sense of the wider, contemporary world. In **Follow Me** (*Seko Man*), for example, director Una Celma and scriptwriter Lauris Gundars tell a simple story of a young Latvian woman who responds to a marriage invitation from Sweden. It is a piquant, sometimes ironic exploration of the national and social prejudices of two neighbouring peoples. However, there are moments when Celma loses confidence and makes her message too obvious, instead of knitting a subtle web of relationships between her characters.

Romualds Pipars investigates a somewhat similar situation in his documentary *Liberty Live* (referred to in *IFG* 2000 as *Shocking Aija*), which was still awaiting completion at the time of the festival. It is the story of a Latvian woman who has married a Serb composer. Though accepted, she is still a foreigner in the Serb community, working for Radio Liberty during the Balkan wars, first in Bosnia then in Kosovo. In this conflicting situation the main character is trying to maintain her professional and human integrity.

In **New Times in Crossroad Street**, director and cinematographer Ivars Seleckis together with scriptwriter Talis Margevics return to the Latvian community they explored ten years ago in their prize-winning documentary, *Crossroad Street*. They discover, with a kind of bitterness and irony, that instead of the solidarity of the late 1980s, a strange fashion of fence- and hedge-building has developed. Surrounded by the miniature borders they have built themselves, lured by private property for the first time in their humble lives, the residents believe that by defending their possessions they are protecting their identities, but instead have alienated themselves from their neighbours.

## Invisible borders

Another group of films addresses intangible social divisions. In **Man at the End of a Side Road,** director Dace Pakule, a recent graduate from the Academy of Culture, joins the 'shopping bus' drivers who travel over bleak terrain to reach old

*Samuel Froler, left, and Baiba Broka in FOLLOW ME*

people nobody cares about, in a place where their meagre pensions are useless because there are no shops. Once or twice a week, in rundown Soviet jalopies, the travelling salesmen supply bread, salt and cheap sweets – and the old people's only link to the outside world. Astonishingly, despite their awful situation, the film shows the elderly people to be full of wit and an unshakeable desire to live.

Other film-makers are concerned with the borders in history and tradition. Aigars Grauba, a musician and showman with a passion for cinema, dramatised the disastrous days in June 1940 when the Red Army occupied Latvia in his second film, **The Summer of Terror** (*Baiga Vasara*, previously mentioned in *IFG* 2000 as *The Gruesome Summer*). He sets a simple love story against a rich historical background and the film triggered heated discussions about how such painful moments in the past should be treated by artists. Unfortunately, Grauba could not quite fuse together the personal and historical elements of his film.

The festival's main prize went to **Wedding**, the half-hour-long debut of theatre director Viesturs Kairiss. It is a boisterous, frantically-paced spectacle about a present-day wedding that is supposed to unfold according to centuries-old tradition, but develops into a surreal

*Arturs Skrastins in THE SUMMER OF TERROR*

show, with fantastic visions of the main characters, in which traditional figures from folklore suddenly take on the shape of Nosferatu the vampire.

While none of these films can be classed as 'great' on an international scale, they represent great promise. Despite its chronic shortage of finance, Latvian cinema is working hard to re-establish its identity within a fast-changing world.

ANDRIS ROZENBERGS has directed seven fiction films and a dozen documentaries. He is Deputy Director of Latvia's National Film Centre, in charge of International Relations.

# Recent and Forthcoming Films

**SEKO MAN (Follow Me)**

Script: Lauris Gundars. Director: Una Celma. Phot: Robert Nordström. Players: Baiba Broka, Samuel Froler, Juris Zagars, Eva Lena Bjorkman. Production: KAUPO Filma/ Bjorking Produktion AG (Sweden).

**JAUNIE LAIKI SKERSIELA (New Times in Crossroad Street)**

Documentary. Script: Talivaldis Margevics. Dir and Phot: Ivars Seleckis. Production: Eiropas Dokumentala kino simpoziji.

**BAIGA VASARA (The Summer of Terror)**

Script: Aigars Grauba, Andrejs Ekis, Pauls Bankovskis. Director: Grauba. Phot: Gints Berzins. Players: Uldis Dumpis, Arturs Skrastins, Inese Caune, Janis Reinis. Production: PLATFORMA Filma.

**BRIVIBA TIESAJA ETERA (Liberty Live)**

Documentary. Script: Romualds Pipars, Baiba Steina. Dir: Pipars. Phot: Pipers, Olegs Kotovics. Production: Gilde.

# Useful Addresses

**National Film Centre of Latvia**
Elizabetes 49
Riga LV-1010
Tel: (371) 750 5074
Fax: (371) 750 5077
e-mail: nfc@nfc.gov.lv
www.latfilma.lv/nfc

**Film-Makers Union of Latvia**
Elizabetes 49
Riga LV-1010
Tel: (371) 728 8536
Fax: (371) 724 0543

# MALAYSIA — Baharudin A. Latif

*Aziz M. Osman, third from left, directing LT. ADNAN*

At the start of the new millennium hopes are high for better times within a film industry devastated by the economic downturn that struck in mid-1997, a downturn that looks set to end soon. The Central Bank of Malaysia has predicted an economic growth of around 5% for 2000 and there has been a corresponding jump in film production.

Grand Brilliance is feeling confident enough to schedule five new productions annually. In 1999, the company released **Scenario** (*Senario*), a madcap comedy à la The Three Stooges. Starring the ever popular television comedy group Scenario, it grossed $1.4m (RM5.3m), and the team were sure to pull in huge crowds with even sillier goings-on in the sequel *More Scenario* (*Senario Lagi*), which was scheduled for the summer 2000 season. Both films were directed by Aziz M. Osman, whose two previous features, youth-oriented romantic comedies *Dream Princess* and *Dream Princess 2*, were the top-grossers of 1998 and 1999. Osman is now justifiably known as 'King of the Box-Office'.

Grand Brilliance started operating in 1994 as the feature film production arm of TV3, the first private television station, and has churned out a coterie of modest-budgeted, mainstream films. There have been duds as well as hits, but the company has emerged as a role model within the Malaysian industry and in summer 2000 was filming its most ambitious production to date, *Lt. Adnan*, a large-scale war film, again under Osman's direction.

Further cause for optimism within the industry came when the Information Ministry pledged to provide financing for up to 12 films a year, with an investment limit of $500,000 for each film. Details have not been made available, however, on how it plans to implement this ambitious objective. FINAS, the National Film Development Corporation, has applied to the Treasury to be the official dispenser of the $26.3m grant that was supposedly approved by the Cabinet under the 1999 Budget. When the money will ever be released, or if it has even been allocated to the proper agency, are questions that no official sources will readily answer.

## Mind your language

Shuhaimi Baba tried to be innovative by using English dialogue for her latest, **Moon's Dream** (*Mimpi Moon*), a comedy of sorts, but it flopped badly. Its failure indicated that film-makers who think they can increase box-office revenue by attracting a wider cross-section of the diverse Malaysian society through the use of English are in for a shock. The film was obviously aimed at the educated higher-income group, but this segment of society has long shunned locally-made films, opting instead for imported ones.

Likewise, imported films dubbed into Bahasa Melayu, the national language, have never fared well, as in the recent case of Disney's *Tarzan*; the dubbed version was a dismal failure. The Shaw Brothers learned this lesson in the early 1970s when, to fill a vacuum for Malay language films after their Singapore studio collapsed in 1967, they experimented by dubbing one of their Hong Kong-produced Chinese sword epics, *The New One-Armed Swordsman*, into Malay and it flopped badly. Malaysian audiences prefer films in their original language, with Bahasa Melayu and Chinese subtitles.

The exhibition sector was boosted with the opening of a new 18-screen multiplex owned by Golden Screen Cinema in Kuala Lumpur. The market is expanding and a new exhibition consortium, Mega Pavilion, operating multiplexes in Penang, on the northern tip of the peninsula, has plans to expand to Kuala Lumpur, with 25 screens set to open over the next five years.

Meanwhile, plans to set up the Entertainment Village on a 485 hectare site in Cyberjaya, Malaysia's new electronics growth area, are on schedule. The first phase, costing around $100m, was set for completion in September 2000, involving the construction of a "Studio Precinct" containing eight state-of-the-art studios and sound-stages, one of which will be the tallest in the world, at nine-storeys. The Studio Precinct should eventually also house an academy and production support services.

BAHARUDIN A. LATIFF is a professional film buff and historian who has written extensively on Malaysian cinema since the mid-1960s for more than 100 publications, including *Variety*, *Asia Magazine* and *Asiaweek*.

# Recent and Forthcoming Films

### SENARIO LAGI (More Scenario)

Script and Dir: Aziz M. Osman. Phot: Badaruddin Ami. Players: Azlee Jaafar, Wahid Senario, Lan Pet Pet, Saiful Apek, Yassin, Umie Aida. Prod: Grand Brilliance.

### PASRAH (Surrender)

Script and Dir: Yusof Haslam. Phot: Omar Ismail and Omar Man. Players: Erra Fazira, Norma

Hakim. Prod: Skop Productions/ Grand Brilliance.

### SOAL HATI (Heart's Desire)

Script: Habsah Hassan. Dir: Othman Hafsham. Phot: Khalid Zakaria. Players: Erra Fazira, Afdlin Shauki, Zaibo, Khatijah Tan. Prod: Serangkai Productions.

### SPINNING GASING (Spinning

Top)

Script and Dir: Teck Tan. Phot: Teoh Gay Hin. Players: Ellie Suriaty Omar, Craig Robert Fong.

### LT. ADNAN

Script and Dir: Aziz M. Osman. Phot: Badaruddin Azmi. Players: Hairie Othman, Umie Aida, Faizal Hussein, Rosdi Ramli. Prod: Grand Brilliance.

## Producers, Importers and Exhibitors

**Grand Brilliance Sdn. Bhd.**
991 Jalan Tandak, off Jalan Bangsar
59100 Bangsar
Kuala Lumpur
Tel: (603) 284 6900
Fax: (603) 284 6864

**Golden Screen Cinemas Sdn. Bhd.**
1 Jalan SS22/19
Damansara Jaya
47400 Petaling Jaya
Selangor DE
Tel:(603) 719 5666
Fax: (603) 712 1655

*The comedy group Scenario in their hit sequel, MORE SCENARIO*

**Eurofine Sdn. Bhd.**
#A-03-10, Block A
Third Floor
PJ Industrial Park
Section 13
Jalan Kemajuan
46200 Petaling Jaya
Selangor DE.
Tel: (603) 750 6634
Fax: (603) 750 6449

**Tanjung Golden Village Sdn. Bhd.**
Level 27, Menara Maxis
Kuala Lumpur City Centre
50088 Kuala Lumpur
Tel: (603) 381 3535
Fax: (603) 381 3139

**Smile-UA Complex (Holdings) Sdn. Bhd.**
7C, Jalan 1/57D, off Jalan
Segambut
51200 Kuala Lumpur
Tel: (603) 623 1840
Fax: (603) 623 2189

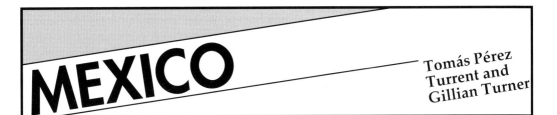

# MEXICO — Tomás Pérez Turrent and Gillian Turner

Levels of national film production in 1999 were similar to those in recent years, and we are still a long way from the massive output of the 1950s (an average of 125 films per year), or even the 1980s (an average of 52 films per year). In 1999, just nine Mexican features were made, and yet in terms of quality this was an excellent year for domestic film exhibition.

A good example was the partner-swapping comedy, **Sex, Shame and Tears** (*Sexo, pudor y lagrimas*), by Antonio Serrano, which filled movie theatres for six months, competing with the Aztec-era drama, **The Other Conquest** (*La otra conquista*), by Salvador Carrasco (both were distributed by 20th Century Fox), and box-office successes from Hollywood. **Santitos**, by Alejandro Springall, a comedy about a deeply religious widow, was also very well received.

The magical, reflective **Bajo California, el limite del tiempo** was a complete revelation, and **Nobody Writes To The Colonel** (*El coronel no tiene quien le escriba*), from Arturo Ripstein was more commercially successful than is usual for Ripstein's films. The success of these features meant that in 1999, for the first time in many years, there was a period when four domestic films were running concurrently, all attracting good audiences.

The trend was similar early in 2000. Luis Estrada's bloodthirsty farce about political corruption, **Herod's Law** (*La ley de Herodes*), was very popular in the first quarter; the scandal provoked by the censor's attempt to have it banned worked to its advantage. Its success also demonstrated that audiences want to see films which reflect contemporary Mexican reality.

Blending elements of thriller and comedy, Fernando Sari–ana's **Gimme Power** (*Todo el poder*), the story of a young film-maker exposing police corruption in Mexico City, drew a massive response from middle-class audiences, attracted by its arresting treatment of Hollywood film-making rules and the lack of security in permanently crisis-hit Mexican society.

*Still from HEROD'S LAW*

Arturo Ripstein was invited to Cannes for the third consecutive year (this time to Un Certain Regard). What is most interesting about his new film, **That's Life** (*Asi es la vida*), is that it was made on Digital Video, transferred to 35 mm; the first use of this process by a Mexican director. Ripstein was very satisfied with the speed and economy this allowed him (he made the film in three weeks) and the hope must be that such a relatively inexpensive approach may facilitate increased Mexican film production, since the greatest obstacle within the industry remains financing.

---

TOMÁS PÉREZ TURRENT was awarded the Salvador Toscano Medal for Cinematographic Merit, 1999, in recognition of his 33 years as a scriptwriter, critic, historian and researcher. In December 1999 his work as a scriptwriter was honoured during the Festival des Trois Continents in Nantes.

---

# Recent and Forthcoming Films

## LAS ALAS DEL CORAZON/SEXO POR COMPASION (Heavenly Whore)

Script and Dir: Laura Mañá. Phot: Henner Hoffman. Players: Elizabeth Margoni, José Sancho, Juan Carlos Colombo, Ana Ofelia Murguía, Pilar Bardem, Max Kerlow. Prod: Miguel Torrente, Fernando Cámara, Salvador de la Fuente. Visual Grup-Resonancia Productora Mexico-Spain.

First full length film directed by the Spanish actress Laura Mañá. Dolores, a mature woman whose husband has left her, remains kind and optimistic. One day she decides to 'sin' for the first time by having sex with another man, but as she ends up saving his life, what began as a sin ends up as charity. Good works and bad actions blend together and Dolores surrenders to her saintly vocation.

## CRONICA DE UN DESAYUNO (The Breakfast Chronicles)

Script: Sergio Schmucler, based on the stage play by Jesus Gonzalez Davila. Dir: Benjamín Cann. Phot: Serguei Saldivar Tanaka. Players: María Rojo, Bruno Bichir, Fabiana Perzabal, José Alonso. Prod: Bruno Bichir/Imcine-Escarabajo-Tabasco Films-Argos.

Mexican family life at the end of the twentieth century. A father returns home after a long absence, wishing he were elsewhere. A daughter suffers from a secret sorrow. The son is full of guilt and complaints. The youngest child is a small boy who sponges up all the tensions of the home while the self-effacing mother would rather get up and leave it all. Fine third film from theatre director Cann.

## DE IDA Y VUELTA (To and Fro)

Script: Salvador Aguirre, Alejandro Lubezki, Gerónimo Denti. Dir: Aguirre. Phot: Gerónimo Denti. Players: Gerardo Taracena, Tiaré Scanda, Ricardo Esquerra, Alejandro Parodi. Prod: Angeles Castro, Hugo Rodriguez/CCC-Imcine-Foprocine-Estudios Churubusco-Azteca.

First feature from young graduate of the Centro de Capacitación Cinematográfica (Film Training Centre). A man returns to his home town after working in the US and is overcome by his own ambition. Betrayed and lovelorn, he becomes involved in violent events.

## EN EL PAÍS DE NO PASA NADA (In The Country Where Nothing Happens)

Script: Maricarmen Lara, Laura Sosa. Dir: Lara. Phot: Arturo de la Rosa. Players: Fernando Luján, Julieta Egurrola, María Isasi, Alvaro Guerrero. Prod: Laura Imperiale, Alvaro Garnica, Jorge Sánchez/Filmania-Foprocine-Calacas/Palomas-Altavista Films-Imcine-Cartel (Mexico/Spain).

Enrique, a government official involved in the distribution of polluted milk, is kidnapped. A video is delivered to his wife showing her husband with his mistress. The man's treachery and double life, the inexperience of his kidnappers and the fantasy world inhabited by his wife, spark off one another in this comedy set against the backdrop of everyday Mexican life. Good debut from a young film-maker who specialises in stories told from a woman's perspective.

## EN UN CLAROSCURO DE LA LUNA (Moonlight Shadow)

Script: Sergio Olhovich, Vladimir Valutsky, Sergio Molina, based on a story by Edith Jiménez. Dir: Olhovich. Phot: Anatoli Mucassei. Players: Arcelia Ramírez, Jorge Sanz, Petr Veliaminov, Tiaré Scanda. Prod: Roberto Gómez Bolaños, Sergei Zhigonov/Televicine, S.A. de C.V./Center TV (Mexico-Russia).

A Russian immigrant has two daughters. One of them marries a militant ecologist who is murdered on their honeymoon. The girl falls into a state of shock from which it seems she will never recover. When the immigrant's wife dies he returns to his homeland with his comatose daughter. This is veteran film-maker Sergio Olhovich's twelfth film, and it won him the Audience Award at the Guadalajara Year 2000 Film Show.

## ENTRE LA TARDE Y LA NOCHE (Minerva's Quest)

Script: Oscar Blancarte, Avlaro del Amo. Dir: Blancarte. Phot: Arturo de la Rosa, Jorge Suárez. Players: Angélica Aragón, Francisco Gattorno, Lumi Cavazos, Claudia Pezzuto. Prod: Angel Flores Marini/Foprocine-Imcine-Flores/Roffiel/Senyal y Asociados, S.A.-Cooperativa de Cine Séptimo Arte, S.C.L.

A middle-aged woman decides to abandon the everyday life which has prevented her from writing the novel she has always wanted to create. She returns to her homeland looking for a past full of phantoms. What begins as escape turns into a quest for self-knowledge and she writes the story of her life.

### LA LEY DE HERODES (Herod's Law)

Script: Luis Estrada, Jaime Sampietro, Fernando León, Vicente Leñero. Dir: Estrada. Phot: Norman Christianson. Players: Damián Alcazar, Pedro Armendáriz, Isela Vega, Leticia Huijara. Prod: Luis Estrada, Bandido Films.

When a corrupt mayor is lynched by the townsfolk, Juan Vargas, an obedient militant member of the PRI political party, which has ruled since 1927, is named as the new Mayor. Vargas begins his work with the best of intentions but is soon overcome by corruption and ambition, while the law, instead of punishing him, rewards him.

This is a bloodthirsty farce and a cruel political fable which was attacked by the censor (which did not want the film shown until after the Mexican Presidential Elections of July 2, 2000). But the film defeated its opponents and has enjoyed a resounding box-office success, also winning the prize for the Best Latin American Film at the Sundance Film Festival, 2000.

### RITO TERMINAL (Last Rite)

Script and Dir: Oscar Urrutia Lazo. Phot: Ciro Cabello. Players: Guillermo Larrea, Soledad Ruiz, Fabiana Perzábal, Ignacio Guadalupe. Prod: Mitl Valdés/CUEC-UNAM/Imcine-Foprocine.

The celebration of the Patron Saint's Day in a native community results in a photographer losing his shadow. In order to get it back he must leave on a journey of initiation, together with the local inhabi-

*Alejandro Gamboa directing* THE SECOND NIGHT

tants, thereby penetrating the indigenous world in a very singular manner.

### LA SEGUNDA NOCHE (The Second Night)

Script: Alejandro Gamboa, Gabriela Ortigoza. Dir: Gamboa. Phot: Alfredo Kassem. Players: Iran Castillo, Mariana Avila, Francesca Guillén, Sherlyn González, Osvaldo Benavides. Prod: Eckehardt von Damm/Videocine-Warner Bros.

The story of four teenage girls, aged 13 to 19, who live out their dreams, desires, fears, illusions and disappointments, experimenting with new emotions as their sexuality awakens. This is a partial sequel to its successful predecessor *La primera noche* (*The First Night*), this time with a story told from the girls' viewpoint, rather than the boys'.

### TODO EL PODER (Gimme Power)

Script: Fernando Sariñana, Enrique Rentería, Carolina Rivera. Dir: Sariñana. Phot: Eduardo Martínez Solares. Players: Demián Bichir, Cecilia Suárez, Luis Felipe Tovar, Claudia Lobo. Prod: Francisco González Compean, Fernando Sariñana/Altavista Films.

A young, divorced video director finds himself in an extreme situation in Mexico City. The van lent him by his ex-wife is stolen and he is confronted by the passivity of the police – and their complicity with delinquents. He decides to stop being a victim and to uncover the network of criminals, police and government officials, all involved in the traffic of stolen vehicles. Treating a serious theme very effectively in comic terms, the film was very well received by Mexican audiences.

# Producers

### Alameda Films
Av. Division del Norte 2462-501
03300 Mexico D.F.
Tel: (52 5) 688 0330/5085/7318
Fax: (52 5) 605 8911
www.alamedafilms.com

### Amaranta Films
Atletas 2
Edificio Pedro Infante
Piso 3
Col. Country Club
04220 Mexico, D.F.
Tel: (52 5) 544 5425

Tel/Fax: (52 5) 549 2119
e-mail: mailto:amaranta@acnet.net

### Argos Producciones, S.A. de C.V.
Rousseau No.22
Col. Anzures
11590 Mexico D.F.
Tel: (52 5) 250 1700
Fax: (52 5) 203 8394

### Cinematografica Filmex, S.A. de C.V.
Av. Div. Del Norte 2462-901
03300 Mexico D.F.
Tel: (52 5) 688 8092/7551
Fax: (52 5) 688 7221

### Cinematografica Macondo, S.A. de C.V.
Atletas No.2-2° Piso
Col. Country Club
04220 Mexico D.F.
Tel: (52 5) 689 1142/1190
Fax: (52 5) 554 9075

### Cineproducciones Internacionales, S.S.
Av. Div. Del Norte No. 2462-403
03300 Mexico D.F.
Tel: (52 5) 688 7022/7223
Fax: (52 5) 688 7044

**Cortometraje** [formerly Didecine]

Av. Division del Norte 2462
3 piso
03300 Mexico D.F.
Tel: (52 5) 688 7614/7079
Fax: (52 5) 688 7611

**Estudio Mexico/Altavista**
CIE Palmas 1005
Col. Lomas de Chapultepec
11000 Mexico D.F.
Tel: (52 5) 201 9000
Fax: (52 5) 201 9384

**IMCINE**
Tepic 40
Col. Roma Sur
06760 Mexico D.F.
Tel: (52 5) 574 2144/3155
Fax: (52 5) 574 1705/0712

**Producciones Rosas Priego, S.A.**
Av. Div. Del Norte No. 2462-402
Col. Portales
03300 Mexico D.F.
Tel: (52 5) 688 7022/7385/7223
Fax: (52 5) 688 7044

**Rio Mixcoac, S.C.L.**
Morelos 33-4
Col. Torriello Guerra, Tlalpan
14060 Mexico D.F.
Tel: (52 5) 665 6417/8998
Fax: (52 5) 665 9123

**Tabasco Films**
Cuernavaca 17
Col. Condesa
06140 Mexico D.F.
Tel: (52 5) 286 1860/1890
Fax: (52 5) 286 2063

**Tamarindo Films, S.A. de C.V.**
Homero No.1824-501
Col. Los Morales Chapultepec
11510 Mexico D.F.
Tel: (52 5) 207 7223
Fax: (52 5) 207 9666

**Televicine, S.A. de C.V.**
Benito Juarez No.7
Col. Del Carmen Coyoacan
04100 Mexico D.F.
Tel: (52 5) 659 2961/658 2699
Fax: (52 5) 659 7964

**Tequila Gang, S.A. de C.V.**
Av. Palmas 2030
Col. Lomas de Chapultepec
11000 Mexico D.F.
Tel: (52 5) 245 2023

**Triana Films, S.A. de C.V.**
Paseo de las Palmas 731-1er Piso
Col. Lomas de Chapultepec
11000 Mexico D.F.
Tel: (52 5) 520 2779/0526
Fax: (52 5) 202 7068

# Distributors

**Buena Vista Columbia Tristar Films de Mexico S.A. de C.V.**
Av. Prolf. Paseo de la Reforma 600
Col. Santa Fe Pea Blanca
01210 Mexico D.F.
Tel: (52 5) 258 2717/2518

**Cine Alternativo**
Periferico Sur No.4121
Col. Fuentes del Pedregal
14141 Mexico D.F.
Tel: (52 5) 420 1309/645 4080
Fax: (52 5) 645 5704

**Columbia TriStar/Buena Vista**
Edif. Plaza Reforma
Prolg. Paseo de la Reforma No.600
PH 331
Col. Santa Fe Peña Blanca
01210 Mexico D.F.
Tel: (52 5) 258 2700/2702
Fax: (52 5) 570 1012/0957

**Geminis Films, S.A. de C.V.**
Guanajuato No.131-203
Col. Roma
06700 Mexico, D.F.
Tel: (52 5) 564 0294

**Gussi (Artecinema/Videomax)**
Gob. Ignacio Esteva No.70
Col. San Miguel Chapultepec
Mexico D.F.
Tel: (52 5) 277 8999/0955
Fax: (52 5) 516 5729

**Latina, S.A. de C.V.**
Atletas No.2, Edificio Pedro Infante
Col. Country Club
04220 Mexico D.F.
Tel: (52 5) 689 3850/549 3060 ext. 176

**Twentieth Century Fox Film de Mexico, S.A.**
Blvd. Manuel Avila Camacho No.40
Piso 12
Col. Lomas de Chapultepec
11000 Mexico, D.F.
Tel: (52 5) 201 4200

**United International Pictures, S. De R.L.**
Fuente de Trevi No.23-3ª 5° Piso
Col. Lomas de Tecamachalco
53950 Mexico
Tel: (52 5) 589 9657/9658/9660/9664

**VideoVisa**
Av. Acoxpa 444
Col. Vergel del Sur
14340 Mexico D.F.
Tel: (52 5) 229 3100/3110
Fax: (52 5) 230 3332

# Useful Addresses

**Asociacion de Productores y Distribuidores de Peliculas Mexicanas**
Av. Div. Del Norte 2462-8° Piso
03300 Mexico D.F.
Tel: (52 5) 688 7251/8705
Fax: (52 5) 688 7378

**Camara Nacional de Cine (CANACINE)**
Gen. Anaya 198
Col. San Diego Churubusco
04120 Mexico D.F.
Tel: (52 5) 688 0442/3258
Fax: (52 5) 688 8810

**Cinemex**
Montes Urales No.723
Col. Lomas de Chapultepec
11000 Mexico, D.F.
Tel: (52 5) 540 6954/520 5184

**Direccion General de Actividades Cinematograficas UNAM**
San Ildefonso 43
Col. Centro
06020 Mexico, D.F.
Tel: (52 5) 704 3700/702 4454
Fax: (52 5) 702 4503

# MOROCCO — Roy Armes

**M**orocco currently has the only coherent system of state support for film-makers in North Africa. As a result, the country has emerged as the region's leading producer, with 40 features, and a similar number of shorts, completed in the 1990s – almost all thanks to government funding. A further dozen feature projects have received funding, six of them scheduled for release in the year 2000.

Initially, the government scheme seemed to be aimed at older directors, such as 58-year-old producer Mohamed Lotfi (making his feature directing debut), 56-year-old Abdallah Zerouali (completing a feature left unfinished 15 years earlier) and 50-year-old Mohamed Abbazi (making a second feature, 16 years after his first). There was even limited funding for 90-year-old French veteran Jean Delannoy (best-known for 1946's *La Symphonie pastorale*, with Michèle Morgan) to complete his final project, *Marie de Nazareth*, on location in Morocco. But more recently, state funding has been used to encourage younger film-makers – such as Nabil Ayouch and Daoud Aloued Syad – to make their feature debuts after completing two or three shorts.

After the Fifth National Film Festival in Casablanca, held in November 1998, three new features were released in 1999. The first was *Keid Ensa* (reviewed in *IFG* 2000), an impressive fairytale made by one of north Africa's few female writer-directors, Farida Benlyazid. The second was Moumen Smihi's **Moroccan Chronicles** (*Chroniques Marocaines*), shown at the Milan 2000 African Film Festival. Smihi's career dates back to *El Chergui* in 1975 and he is one of the veterans of Moroccan cinema. His fifth feature received no state

*Still from Moumen Smihi's MOROCCAN CHRONICLES*

funding support and took five years to complete because of financial problems.

Shot on 16mm early in the 1990s, *Moroccan Chronicles* comprises three stories shot in disparate parts of the country. The first shows the punishment of three boys who misbehave on Jma el Fnaa square in Marrakech, the second depicts the flirtation of a pair of lovers on the walls of the seaside town of Essaouira (one of the locations for Orson Welles' *Othello*), while the third is the tale of an old fisherman who talks of catching a mythical great white whale off the coast of Tangier, but instead suicidally confronts a huge white ferry.

The three stories – all beginning 'Once upon a time...' – are told by a mother to comfort her son who has been frightened and hurt by his (late) circumcision. But he rejects them all and the film ends with his voice-over letter to his mother, explaining that he has set off for Europe to try to find his father, an emigrant worker.

## Never the twain...

The third film of 1999 was **Mabrouk**, the debut of Driss Chouika (b. 1953), who had previously worked in television. This is the humorous tale of the clash of two worlds, one inhabited by a rich and beautiful young European woman, Lycénia, and the other by humble Moroccan workman Miloud and his faithful donkey Mabrouk.

Morocco has made an even stronger start to the new millennium, with six features announced for distribution in 2000 alone, three of them by debutant directors. This means that with 49 feature directors, Morocco can for the first time claim to have the largest roster of film directors of all the cinemas of North Africa.

Among the established names, Said Souda returns after 15 years with *From Heaven to Hell* (*Du paradis à l'enfer*), Jillali Ferhati has made *Tresses*, and Hakim Noury has confirmed his status as the

Maghreb's most prolific director – and earned an unofficial prize for the longest film title – with *She is Diabetic and Hypertensive and She Refuses to Die* (*Elle est diabétique et hypertendue et elle refuse de crever*).

Among new directors, Abdelmajid Rchich (b. 1942) is a veteran with more than 30 years' work behind him in documentary and short films. His first fictional feature, *The Story of a Rose* (*L'histoire d'une rose*), is co-scripted by Farida Benlyazid. The other two new-comers have graduated to feature work through the state system, after completing two or three fictional shorts: Ahmed Boulane (b. 1956) completing *Ali, Raabia and the Others* (*Ali, Raabia y les autres*), while Jamal Belmajdoub (b. 1956) has made *Yacout*.

## Recent Films

**MABROUK**

Script: Driss Chouika and Ali Smali. Dir: Chouika. Phot: Kamal Derkaoui. Players: Abdellah Ferkous, Touria Alarin, Nezha Regaoui, Omar Said. Prod: Zawaya Communication (Morocco)/Free Artists (Norway).

**CHRONIQUES MAROCAINES (Moroccan Chronicles)**

Script and Dir: Moumen Smihi. Phot: Hélène Delale. Players: Aicha Mahmah, Tarik Jamil, Miloud Habachi, Soumaya Akaboun, Ahmed Soussi. Prod: Art Cam (France)/Femis (France) /Imago Films (Morocco).

## Useful Addresses

**Centre Cinématographique Marocain**
Quartier industriel
avenue al-Majd
BP 421
Rabat
Tel: (212 7) 798 110
Fax: (212 7) 798 108

**Chambre Marocaine des Distributeurs de Films**
36 boulevard d'Anfa
Casablanca
Tel: (212 5) 272 081

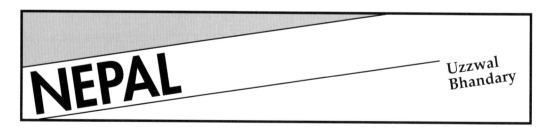

# NEPAL

Uzzwal Bhandary

**F**ilm-making is a boom industry in Nepal, and in 1999-20 (the year 2056 in the Nepalese calendar) about 30 films were released. However, as in the previous year, few were especially memorable, or successful at cinemas, not least because most of the producers investing in the new

productions have minimal knowledge of film-making.

French director Eric Valli's **Caravan** made the greatest impact on Nepalese and international audiences and was the most popular film of the year in Kathmandu.

*Still from Eric Valli's Oscar-nominated CARAVAN*

The second film Valli has made in Nepal, following *Honey Hunter*, *Caravan* was nominated for the Best Foreign Language Film Oscar. Its setting is a remote village in the Dolpo region of the north-western Himalayas, at an altitude of 5,000 metres, and it focuses on Tinle, an elderly, charismatic Buddhist chieftain whose eldest son has just died. Tinle refuses to allow the young man whom he accuses of being responsible for the death of his son to lead the village's yak caravan.

The sentimental drama **Blood Relative** (*Nata Ragatko*) has been popular, attracting largely female audiences. Actress Niruta plays the heroine who, after her mother's death, is ill-treated by her father and new stepmother. Suddenly her father falls seriously ill and the daughter is the only person willing and able to donate one of her kidneys to save his life – and bring about a tearful reconciliation with the stepmother. *Blood Relative* was directed by the vastly experienced Prakash Thapa, aged 70, who started his film career in Bombay in 1958 as an actor and has since directed more than a dozen features. *Blood Relative* won him Best Director and Best Film at the third annual Nepal Film Awards, but sadly it might be his last feature, as he has been in poor health.

The lavish love story **Zidagani** [literally, *Course of Life*] did good business in 2000. This is the second film from director Ujol Ghimire, who recouped his personal investment in the production from the

Kathmandu box-office gross and stood to make a healthy profit from takings in the rest of the country.

As suggested in *IFG* 2000, **Bhanubhakta: First Poet**, about the life of Nepal's first great literary figure, was aimed squarely at intellectual audiences and schools. Its producer-director, Yadav Kharel, is now working on a similar project: *Great Poet* (*Maha Kavi Laxmi Prasad Devkota*) about a Nepalese writer who has written more than 40 novels and hundreds of poems. Finally, National Studio Ltd has high hopes for its forthcoming historical drama, *Basanti*, based on a popular novel by Nepalese writer Diamond Shamsher.

UZZWAL BHANDARY has been an actor in Nepalese film and television for 17 years. He also works as a tour guide and travel consultant.

*Still from the historical drama, BASANTI*

# NETHERLANDS — Pieter van Lierop

The Dutch film industry is attracting attention from big business. Dutch government measures to channel private funds into investment in celluloid have proved a success, both through FINE, the agency created to bring investors and film producers together, but also through the many banks who have discovered a whole range of options for investing cash in production companies.

Thanks to new tax incentives, the banks can achieve a considerable return on their investment, from films that do not even have to break even. In just 18 months, approximately $160m (350m guilders) has been generated in this way. That figure makes the resources of the Nederlands Fonds Voor De Film (Netherlands Film Fund), with an annual budget of just $8m (17.5 million guilders), pale into insignificance, even after Dutch secretary of state for culture, Rick van der Ploeg, freed up an additional $1.6m to bring the total for the year 2000 to $9.6m.

How long this boom can last, while interest in Dutch films is in the doldrums, is the key question. Early in 2000, van der Ploeg revealed that the share of Dutch films in the total of some 19 million annual cinema admissions in 1998 and 1999 was just 5.5%. And this figure would have been even more depressing had it not been for the enormous success of two children's films, each of which drew more than a million visitors.

The mass enthusiasm at the end of 1998 for *Abeltje* (*The Flying Liftboy*) was followed in December 1999 by the success of **Little Crumb** (*Kruimeltje*), which performed even better. A Christmas film in the classic mould – an orphan with a cute dog, a lot of snow and poverty in scenic 1920s Rotterdam – its concept may not have been

*Ruud Feltkamp as LITTLE CRUMB*

devastatingly original, but the realisation by director Maria Peters was highly inventive.

It was not only at the box-office that audiences in the Netherlands expressed a preference for children's films. At the national festival in Utrecht in September 1999, *Abeltje* took the Golden Calf for best full-length feature film; *Missing Link* (by Ger Poppelaars) won best screenplay; Rijk de Gooijer took the best actor award for his role in *Scratches On The Table* (by Ineke Houtman), a film that also topped the audience poll. All three were children's films. It is to be hoped that the enthusiasm will continue in December 2000 with the medieval children's films *Mariken* and *Minoes*, directed by André van Duren and produced by Burny Bos, the man behind *Abeltje*.

## Flop follows flop

All Dutch films aimed at an adult audience have been consistently failing, even those that deserved to succeed, such as Eddy Terstall's **Rent-A-Friend**, a jaunty comedy of manners about an artist who sets up an agency renting out 'friends'. The agency does fabulous business; unfortunately for Terstall, the same could not be said of the film, which attracted only 15,000 admissions. Interest in films such as Lodewijk Crijns' *Jezus Is A Palestinian* (26,000 tickets sold), Roel Reiné's *The Delivery* (27,000), Jos Stelling's *No Trains No Planes* (6,000), Frans Weisz's *A Woman of the North* (3,000), and Dana Nechustan's *Total Loss* (2,600) was equally lukewarm, and well below pre-release expectations.

The spectacular English-language thriller **Do Not Disturb**, given an exceptionally wide, 79-print release, could only sell 66,000 tickets – a stark contrast to the combined five million admissions its director Dick Maas previously achieved with his three *Flodder* films. In *Do Not Disturb* a mute 10-year-old girl visits the Netherlands with her parents (William Hurt and Jennifer Tilly), witnesses an underworld killing and becomes a target for the murderers, who pursue the child through the alleys and canals of sinful Amsterdam. The film is competently made, but having taken the trouble to hire Hurt and Tilly, it would have been better to give them more to do than just shuttle desperately between the reception desks of hotels, police stations and hospitals.

This spring, Jean van de Velde came up with a decent thriller, **Leak** (*Lek*). Cas Jansen plays a simple beat cop who comes across an old friend from his youth, now involved in drug dealing. The cop has to turn his friend into a police informer. However, it soon appears that the drugs gang has a spy inside the Amsterdam police, and this runs the whole operation

*Thomas Acda, left, and Cas Jansen in the crime thriller,* LEAK

aground. With a pistol in each hand, Cas sets out to avenge himself on the gangsters who beat his pregnant girlfriend so badly she has a miscarriage. Van de Velde offers honest, Dutch-scale entertainment with a few neat tricks, and too many clichés.

In **The Delivery**, two young, cash-strapped men take a package to Spain for a drugs baron, phoning five times while en route to receive new instructions. The plot is nonsense, as other criminals muscle in on the deal and the gangster double-crosses them, but with the help of raw, modern violence and a certain flair, debut director Roel Reiné created such a convincing copy of American pulp that *The Delivery* was picked up for distribution in the States.

## Language barrier?

The trend among Dutch producers to look abroad is set to continue, with Jeroen Krabbé and Léon de Winter choosing not to shoot their new films in Dutch. De

Winter produced *The Hollywood Sign*, based on one of his own novels, in Los Angeles, with Burt Reynolds and Tom Berenger, directed by the German Sönke Wortmann.

However, the latest films by Michael Apted (*Enigma*) and John Badham (*Ocean Warrior*) are both taking advantage of the special investment climate in the Netherlands by means of a Dutch co-producer, an empty shed for a few interior shots and some Dutch bit-part actors. Take the money and run!

In short, it seems that the Dutch government's measures are serving economic rather than cultural interests and are likely to have a negative impact on a specifically Dutch film culture. A culture that is in enough trouble already considering the state of ticket sales, whereby it should be taken into account that the films concerned hardly receive tremendous screening opportunities. The latter problem is the result of an acute shortage of cinemas, a dire situation alleviated somewhat in Amsterdam with the opening in April 2000 of Pathé Arena, a 14-screen megaplex.

Since Dutch films are attracting so little credit at home, we should be doubly pleased when they succeed at international festivals, as happened in 1998 with Karim Traïdia's *The Polish Bride*. The warmth and lyricism of that film is lacking, however, in **Les Diseurs de Vérité**, Traïdia's new opus, about an Algerian journalist who is forced during a visit to the Netherlands to choose between return to his homeland or an application for asylum. In Algeria, he has to fear for his life, while in the Netherlands he is confronted by a demeaning bureaucratic machine, cultural isolation and homesickness. *Les Diseurs de Vérité* is an honest, harrowing drama, though it would have made a greater impact with a less rigid structure.

The lot of immigrants in the Netherlands is interestingly demonstrated in the debut film by Fow Pyng Hu and Brat Ljatifi, **Jacky**. We see how the rootlessness of Chinese who have lived for many decades by the North Sea leads to lethargy; without any plans for assimilation, but equally unable to live meaningfully according to their own culture. *Jacky*, which was shown in Un Certain Regard at Cannes, does not rely on storytelling in the traditional sense, but rather on the sober but inventive creation of atmosphere.

**And the winners are...**

In Utrecht, Roel Reiné took the award for best director for *The Delivery* and the Golden Calf for best actress went to Nadja Hüpscher for her role in *Based On The Novel* (by Eddy Terstal). A Golden Calf for cameraman Rogier Stoffers recognised the element that had lent such quality to **Unter Den Palmen**, by Miriam Kruishoop. In the film, Rotterdam is depicted as an unsettling metropolis in which Helmut Berger, Udo Kier and Thom Hoffman demonstrate the hedonism and egoism of today's world citizens.

Sonia Herman Dolz emphasised her exceptional talent with **Yo Soy Asi**, a documentary about ageing transvestites in a Barcelona nightclub. In **The Long Vacation**, Johan van der Keuken made a report on his globetrotting and, it seems, successful search for a cure for his cancer. The film picked up four international awards within as many months. The best documentary was **She Believes In Me**, the portrait by John Appel of Dutch torch song artist André Hazes. The film conquered the International Documentary Filmfestival in Amsterdam in November, and attracted 170,000 cinemagoers.

The best animated film was Paul Driessen's **3 Misses**, about three heroically inspired attempts to save a trio of damsels in distress. The comic nature of the film and the wispy style of the drawing is characteristic of Driessen's work, and it earned him the first Oscar nomination of a distinguished career.

PIETER VAN LIEROP has written about film since 1974 and is film editor of the Netherlands Press Association GPD (18 syndicated daily papers). He has been a correspondent for *IFG* since 1981.

# Recent and Forthcoming Films

### THE DELIVERY

Script: David Hilton. Dir: Roel Reiné. Phot: Jan van den Nieuwenhuijzen. Players: Fedja van Huêt, Freddy Douglas, Aurelie Meriel, Esmee de la Bretonière, Jonathan Harvey, Rik Launspach. Prod: Thijs Bayens and Roel Reiné for Two Independent Film BV.

### LES DISEURS DE VÉRITÉ

Script and Dir: Karim Traïdia. Phot: Jacques Laureys. Players: Sid Ahmed Agoumi, Monic Hendrickx, Jaap Spijkers. Prod: Frans van Gestel and Jeroen Beker for Motel Films.

### DO NOT DISTURB

Script and Dir: Dick Maas. Phot: Marc Felperlaan. Players: William Hurt, Francesca Brown, Jennifer Tilly. Prod: Laurens Geels for First Floor Features.

### JACKY

Script and Dir: Fow Pyng Hu and Brat Ljatifi. Phot: Benito Strangio. Players: Fow Pyng Hu, Eveline Wu, Gary Guo, Ad van Kempen. Prod: Frans van Gestel and Jeroen Beker for Motel Films.

### IK OOK VAN JOU

Script: Karina van Tol. Dir: Ruud van Hemert. Phot: Tom Erisman. Players: Anthonie Kamerling, Angela Schijf, Beau van Erven Dorens. Prod: Frank Bak for Theorema Films.

### KRUIMELTJE (Little Crumb)

Script and Dir: Maria Peters. Phot: Hein Groot. Players: Ruud Feltkamp, Thekla Reuten, Rick Engelkes, Hugo Haenen. Prod: Hans Pos, Dave Schram and Maria Peters for Shooting Star Filmcompany.

### LEK (Leak)

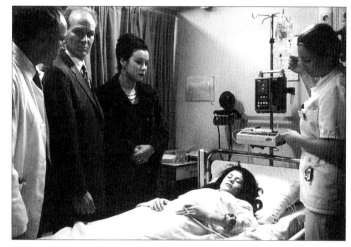

*William Hurt, second left, and Jennifer Tilly, centre, in DO NOT DISTURB*

Script: Jean van de Velde and Simon de Waal. Dir: van de Velde. Phot: Jules van den Steenhoven. Players: Cas Jansen, Victor Löw, Ricky Koole, Thomas Acda. Prod: Rolf Koot for All Yours FilmVoF.

### LEF (Guts)

Script and Dir: Ron Termaat. Phot: Maarten Kramer. Players: Viggo Waas, Alice Reys, Rick Engelkens, Cees Geel. Prod: Ron Termaat for C.V. Lef.

### MARIKEN

Script: Peter van Gestel and Kim van Kooten. Dir: André van Duren. Phot: Steve Walker. Players: Jan Decleir, Kim van Kooten, Willeke van Ammelrooy, Johanna ter Steege. Prod: Hans de Weers for Egmond Film and Television.

### MET GROTE BLIJDSCHAP

Script: Kim van Kooten and Lodewijk Crijns. Dir: Crijns. Phot: Joos van Gelder. Players: Renée Soutendijk, Jaap Spijkers, Jack Wouterse, Camilla Siegertsz. Prod: Frans van Gestel and Jeroen Beker for Motel Films

### DE OMWEG (The Detour)

Script and Dir: Frouke Fokkema. Phot: Wolfgang Simon. Players: Tamar van den Dop, Thom Hoffman, Jan Decleir, Willeke van Ammelrooy. Prod: Matthijs van Heijningen for Sigma Pictures Productions.

### RENT-A-FRIEND

Script and Dir: Eddy Terstall. Phot: Stefan Bijnen. Players: Marc van Uchelen, Rifka Lodeizen, Nadja Hüpscher, Huub Stapel. Prod: Marc Heijdeman for Jordaan Film.

### TOTAL LOSS

Script: Marco van Geffen. Dir: Dana Nechustan. Phot: Bert Pot. Players: Franky Ribbens, Roef Ragas. Prod: Leontine Petit and Joost de Vries for Lemming Film.

### UNTER DEN PALMEN

Script and Dir: Miriam Kruishoop. Phot: Rogier Stoffers. Players: Helmut Berger, Sheri Hagen, Udo Kier, Thom Hoffman. Prod: Erik Schut and Peter van Vogelpoel for Argus Film Production.

**EEN VROUW VAN HET NOORDEN (A Woman of the North)**

Script: Ger Thijs and Angelo Pasquini. Dir: Frans Weisz. Phot: Goert Giltay. Players: Johanna Ter Steege, Massimo Ghini, Anthony Calf, Alessandro Haber. Prod: Ren Seegers for Hungry Eye Lowland, and Enzo Porcelli for Alia Film.

**WILDE MOSSELS (Wild Mussels)**

Script and Dir: Erik de Bruyn. Phot: Joost van Gelder. Players: Fedja van Huêt, Frank Lammers, Freek Brom, Will van Kralingen. Prod: Erik Schut and Peter van Vogelpoel for Argus Film Production.

**DE ZWARTE METEOOR (The Black Meteor)**

Script: Kees van Beijnum. Dir: Guido Pieters. Phot: Wouter Suyderhoud. Players: Erik van der Horst, Peter Tuinman. Prod; Matthijs van Heijningen for Sigma Pictures Productions.

# Producers

**Argus Film Productions**
Peter van Vogelpoel/
Erik Schut
PO Box 58188
1040 HD Amsterdam
Tel: (31 20) 686 8013
Fax: (31 20) 686 8093
e-mail: argusfpr@xs4all.nl

**Bos Bros**
Film & TV Productions
Burny Bos/Michiel de Rooji
PO Box 2282
1200 CG Hilversum
Tel: (31 35) 625 5777
Fax: (31 45) 625 5700
e-mail: info@bosbros.a2000.nl

**Egmond Film and Television**
Hans de Weers/
Hans de Wolf
Potgieterstraat 38
1053 XX Amsterdam
Tel: (31 20) 589 0909
Fa: (31 20) 589 0901
e-mail: egmondnl@xs4all.nl

**First Floor Features**
Laurens Geels/
Dick Maas
Czaar Petersstraat 213
0181 PL Amsterdam
Tel: (31 20) 330 2222
Fax: (31 20) 622 7282
e-mail:
first.floor.features@worldonline.nl

**Fu Works**
San Fu Maltha
Koudelaan 3
3723 ME Bilthoven
Tel: (31 55) 666 8776
Fax: (31 55) 666 8963
e-mail: fuworkds@wxs.nl

**Graniet Film**
Marc van Warmerdam/
Alex van Warmerdam/
Tom Schippers
PO Box 57121
1040 BA Amsterdam
Tel: (31 20) 606 0633
Fax: (31 20) 606 0616
e-mail: graniet@orkater.nl

**Hungry Eye Lowland Services BV & Hungry Eye Film BV**
Rene Seegers
Cleem Calis
Stadhouderskade 6
1054 ES Amsterdam
Tel: (31 20) 668 0492
Fax: (31 20) 694 1018
e-mail: info@hungry-eye.nl

**Jordaan Film**
Marc Heijdeman
Ruyschstraat 9-11
1091 BP Amsterdam
Tel: (31 20) 463 1771/634 5150
Fax: (31 20) 468 0388/634 5157
e-mail:
101461.2107@Compuserve.com

**The Kasander Film Company**
Kees Kasander
PO Box 14510
1001 LA Amsterdam/
Duivendrechtsekade 80
1096 Amsterdam
Tel: (31 20) 684 0499
Fax: (31 20) 684 0922
e-mail: kasandra@worldonline.nl

**Lagestee Film BV**
Martin Lagestee
Haarlemmer Houttuinen 305
1013 GM Amsterdam
Tel: (31 20) 627 3374
Fax: (31 20) 626 1049
e-mail: lbv@lagesteefilm.nl

**Lucid Eye Films**
Johan van der Keuken/
Noshka van der Lely
Oude Schans 69-A
1011 KW Amsterdam
Tel: (31 20) 623 0354
Fax: (31 20) 638 2986
e-mail: lucid@dds.nl

**M&B Film BV/All Yours Film**
Rolf Koot/
Jean van de Velde
Konenginneweg 141-bv
1075 CM Amsterdam
Tel: (31 20) 471 1147
Fax: (31 20) 471 1148
e-mail: mbflim@wxs.nl

**Motel Films**
Frans van Gestel/
Joel Beker
Keizersgracht 651
1017 DT Amsterdam
Tel: (31 20) 638 6095
Fax: (31 20) 622 1212
e-mail: motelf@xs4all.nl

**Movie Masters**
Bob Hubar/ Denis Wigman
PS Hooftstraat 154
1071 CG Amsterdam
Tel: (31 20) 675 8821
Fax: (31 20) 675 7596
e-mail: dwigman@attglobal.net

**MGS Film Amsterdam BV**
Taiga Films BV
George Luizer/Anne Lordon
Singel 64
1015 AC Amsterdam
Tel: (31 20) 623 1593/662 9960
Fax: (31 20) 624 3181

**Oduesseia Films**
Eddy Wijingaarde
Muntplein 10
1012 WR Amsterdam

Tel: (31 20) 530 4777
Fax: (31 20) 530 4774
e-mail: films@odusseia.com

**Pieter van Huystee Film & TV
Productions BV**
Pieter van Huystee
Keizersgracht 784
1017 EC Amsterdam
Tel: (31 20) 421 0606
Fax: (31 20) 638 6255
e-mail: bigpete@euronet.nl

**Rotterdam Fioms**
Dirk Rijneker/
Mildred van leev Waarden
Provenienssins el33
3033 EG Rotterdam
Tel: (3110) 465 8565
Fax: (3110) 465 8392
e-mail: info@rotterdamfilms.nl

**Shooting Star Film Company**
Hans Pos/Dave Schram/
Maria Peters
Prinsengracht 546
1017 KK Amsterdam
Tel: (31 20) 624 7272
Fax: (31 20) 626 8533
e-mail: shooting@xs4all.nl

**Sigma Pictures Productions BV**
Matthijs van Heijningen
Singel 132
1015 AG Amsterdam
Tel: (31 20) 535 3320
Fax: (31 20) 535 3329

**Stichting de Toekomst/Isabella
Films BV**
Els Vandevorst/
Wilfried Depeweg
Singel 272
1016 AC Amsterdam
PO Box 10433
1001 EK Amsterdam
Tel: (31 20) 638 7476/422 7964
Fax: (31 20) 428 3096
e-mail: st.toekomst@wxs.nl

**Jos Stelling Films BV**
Jos Stelling
Springweg 50-52
3511 VS Utrecht
Tel: (3130) 231 3789
Fax: (3130) 231 0968
e-mail: Stelling@Knoware.nl

**Studi Nieuwe Gronden**
Rene Scholten

Van Hallstraat 52
1051 HH Amsterdam
Tel: (31 20) 686 7837
Fax: (31 20) 682 4367

**Theorema Films**
Frank Bak/Rene Huybrechtse
Van Hallstraat 52
1051 HH Amsterdam
Tel: (31 20) 688 1843
Fax: (31 20) 686 3574
e-mail: mail@theoremafilms.nl

**Unlimited Brains Productions**
Ate de Jong
Keizersgracht 649
1017 DT Amsterdam
Tel: (31 20) 627 4339
Fax: (31 20) 624 9697

**Verenigde Nederlands Film**
Televisiecompagnie BV
an Luykenstraat 5
1071 CJ Amsterdam
Tel: (31 20) 675 7774
Fax: (31 20) 675 7754
e-mail: film comp@euronet.nl

**Ijswater Films**
Marc Bary & Ilana Netiv
Kromme Mijdrechtstraat 110 IV
1079 LD Amsterdam
Tel: (31 20) 442 1760
Fax: (31 20) 442 1725
e-mail: icewater@xs4all.nl
www.xs4all.nl/~icewater

# Distributors

**A-Film Distribution**
PO Box 12107
1100 AC Amsterdam
Tel: (31 20) 430 4033/4034
Fax: (31 20) 430 4055
e-mail: office@a-film.nl

**Buena Vista International
(Netherlands) BV**
Windestraat 9
PO Box 349
1170 AH Badhoevedorp
Tel: (31 20) 658 0303
Fax: (31 20) 659 3349
e-mail:
eline_danker@studio.disney.com

**Cinemien**
Entrepotdok 66
1018 AD Amsterdam

Tel: (31 20) 627 9501/623 8152
Fax: (31 20) 620 9857
e-mail: info@cinemien.nl

**Columbia TriStar Films (Holland)**
Gebouw Autumn
Overschiestraat 184-L
1062 XK Amsterdam
Tel: (31 20) 346 2060
Fax: (31 20) 346 2061

**Contact Film Cinematheek**
PO Box 3100
680-2 DC Arnhem
Tel: (31 26) 443 4949
Fax: (31 26) 351 1316

**Filmmuseum Distribution**
Vondelpark 3
PO Box 74782
1070 BT Amsterdam
Tel: (31 20) 589 1423
Fax: (31 20) 683 3401
e-mail:filmmuseum@nfm.nl

**Hungry Eye Pictures BV**
Stadhouderskade 6
1054 Amsterdam
Tel: (31 20) 669 6126
Fax: (31 20) 694 1018

**Indies Film Distribution**
Regentesselaan 20-26
1217 EG Hilversum
Tel: (3135) 538 5300
Fax: (3135) 538 5304
e-mail: jean@indies.nl

**RCV Film Distribution**
Oscar Romerolaan 10
PO Box 142
1200 AC Hilversum
Tel: (3135) 625 1200
Fax: (3135) 625 1256
e-mail: nancy@rcv.nl

**Paradiso Entertainment
Netherlands BV**
Anthony Fokkeweg 1
1059 CM Amsterdam
Tel: (31 20) 615 9222
Fax: (31 20) 614 2027
e-mail: penfilm@wxs.nl

**Shooting Star Film Distribution**
Prinsengracht 546
1017 KK Amsterdam
Tel: (31 20) 624 7272
Fax: (31 20) 626 8533
e-mail: shooting@xs4all.nl

**Three Lines Pictures**
Mauritslaan 53
1211 JZ Jilversum
Tel: (3135) 623 0555
Fax: (3135) 623 9966

**20th Century Fox**
Postesweg 175
PO Box 90205
1006 BE Amsterdam
Tel: (31 20) 510 6988
Fax: (31 20) 669 4818
e-mail: margueritef@foxinc.com

**United International Pictures
(Netherlands)**
Willemsparkweg 112
1071 HN Amsterdam
Tel: (31 20) 662 2991
Fax: (31 20) 662 3240

**Warner Bros (Holland) BV**
De Boelelaan 16
1083 HJ Amsterdam
Tel: (31 20) 541 1211
Fax: (31 20) 642 7738

# Useful Addresses

**Ministry of Education, Culture
and Science Department of Film**
Europaweg 4
PO Box 25000
2700 LZ Zoetermeer
Tel: (31 79) 323 4321
Fax: (31 79) 323 4959

**Dutch Film Fund**
yclef Rienstra
Jan Luykenstraat 2
1071 CM Amsterdam
Tel: (31 20) 570 7676
Fax: (31 20) 570 7689
e-mail: film fund@hollandfilm.nl

**Fine Film Investors Netherlands
BV**
Drs. Gamila Ylstra
Sarphatikade 12
1017 WV Amsterdam
Tel: (31 20) 530 4700
Fax: (31 20) 530 4701
e-mail: g.ylstra@fine.nl

**Netherlands Cinematographic
Federation (NFC)**
Jan Luykenstraat 2
1071 CM Amsterdam
Tel: (31 20) 679 9261
Fax: (31 20) 675 0398

**Rotterdam Film Fund**
Jacques van Heijningen
Rochussenstraat 3C
3015 EA Rotterdam
Tel: (31 10) 436 0747
Fax: (31 10) 436 0553

**Netherlands Institute for
Animation Film (NIAF)**
Willem straat 47
PO Box 9358
5000 HJ Tilburg
Tel: (31 13) 535 4555
Fax: (31 13) 580 057

**Circle of Dutch Film Critics**
Prinsengracht 770
1017 LE Amsterdam
Tel: (31 20) 623 0121
Fax: (31 20) 627 5923

# NEW ZEALAND — Peter Calder

Peter Jackson makes an unlikely messiah. Chubby and cheerful, he dresses like an indigent university student, but he was looking mighty like an industry saviour as he started spending $130m of New Line's money on a trilogy based on J.R.R. Tolkien's fantasy classic *The Lord of the Rings*.

Cameras started rolling in locations in the country's rugged rural hinterland late in 1999 on the most expensive production ever undertaken south of the equator, and star sightings became commonplace in the capital, Wellington, where Jackson is based, since Ian McKellen, Ian Holm, Christopher Lee and Liv Tyler head the cast. The back-to-back shooting of three full-length features is expected to wrap by the end of 2000 and post-production –

undertaken at Jackson's own state-of-the-art digital effects studio – will take most of 2001.

Jackson's determination to remain on home soil, rather than follow other expat Kiwis like Roger Donaldson and Lee Tamahori to Hollywood, is a huge confidence boost for the local industry. The budget is a good deal larger than the combined budget for every 35mm New Zealand-produced feature in history, and a triumphant vindication of the New Zealand Film Commission, a state- and lottery-funded film bank which has been the major production kickstarter for the past 25 years.

The commission, though not directly involved in *Lord of the Rings* has said for years that state funding of the movie industry is not so much a subsidy as an investment in the future. It invested barely $2.5m in Jackson's early films – three no-budget cult splatter pictures and the sublime factually-based drama of matricide, *Heavenly Creatures*. He's paying that contribution back with interest now, and the Tolkien epic will have earned New Zealand more in 2000-2002 than its celebrated wine industry.

This positive message seemed to have reached the corridors of power as well. A change of government in November 1999 brought in a centre-left coalition whose leader is a devoted arts enthusiast, and within a few months the government had announced increased funding for film, including a $10m cash injection. The commission had hitherto devoted its limited budget to funding first-timers, with mixed results, but this extra money will be used to fund directors' second efforts.

### Location, location, location

In the past year, expatriate Kiwi producer Lloyd Phillips and director Martin Campbell (*The Mask of Zorro*) hung Chris O'Donnell off precipices in the spectacular mountains of South Island, for the high-altitude thriller *The Vertical Limit*, for Columbia TriStar. American productions – including long-running shoots of small-screen hits like *Xena: Warrior Princess* – have injected cash and energy into an industry whose technicians often work for small change on low-budget local productions. Bollywood came down under, too: more than a dozen Indian features were shot here in 1999-2000.

But it's been a big year for the local industry as well. Seven features were released in 1999 and nine are slated for 2000. And although some industry observers say the downmarket and often dark tone of indigenous movies chases audiences away, commission chief executive Ruth Harley is upbeat. "You're not going to succeed every time," she declared. "But the more horses you have at the starting line the more will make it to the finish."

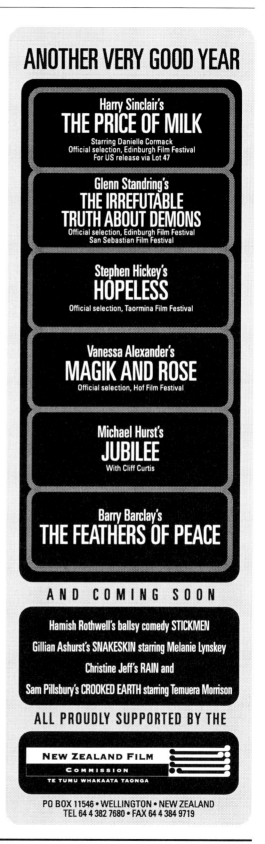

Two local pics definitely struck a chord. **What Becomes of the Broken-Hearted**, the redemptive sequel to the gritty 1994 urban drama *Once Were Warriors*, was the work of a different writer-director team, but Temuera Morrison reprised his star turn as the volcanically violent Jake Heke. Meanwhile **Scarfies**, a *Shallow Grave*-style comedy thriller set in the southern city of Dunedin (the title is the local term for university students) was about a bunch of youngsters who find a massive marijuana crop in the basement of the house they are squatting in. Both did well (the former came in fifth in the local box office chart) and the latter, voted film of the year by local critics, made the top 30 and matched the local gross of the much-hyped *Eyes Wide Shut*.

Others movies met with less applause from critics and public. **Savage Honeymoon**, a comedy about a family of hard-drinking working-class bikers, attracted a flurry of attention when the censor imposed, and withdrew on appeal, an 'R18' rating (equivalent to America's 'NC-17', and therefore a commercial kiss-of-death), partly because of a scene in which a gas cylinder is thrown into a bonfire. **Jubilee**, the feature debut as director of Michael Hurst, who starred in and directed some episodes of the *Hercules* TV series, was a genial comedy about a small-town loser organising a school reunion. Even the presence of Cliff Curtis who has had roles in American movies (*Three Kings*, and Martin Scorsese's *Bringing Out the Dead*) failed to pull in the crowds.

Upcoming releases include *Wild Blue*, in which Judge Reinhold plays a crop-dusting pilot who falls in love with a farmer's daughter (Dale Bradley directs) and a new film from Harry Sinclair, who made the intriguingly titled *Topless Women Talk About Their Lives*. Premiered at Cannes, *The Price of Milk* is a rural, contemporary fairytale, billed as "a magical romance about a man, a woman and a herd of dairy cows".

Meanwhile *Warriors* producer Robin Scholes signed LA-based Kiwi Sam Pillsbury (*Zandalee*) to direct *Crooked Earth*, a Maori story about two brothers fighting for leadership of their tribe. Starring Cliff Curtis and Temuera Morrison, it was in post-production when this article went to press. Scholes is also producing the feature debut of Christine Jeffs, one of the country's top commercials directors.

On the exhibition side, admissions have flattened out after a multiplex building boom had spawned years of double-digit growth. In 1991 there were 6.1 million admissions at 140 screens, and in 1999 16.75 million at 315 screens (slightly down on a per-screen basis from 1998's 16.26 million on 290 screens). New Zealanders are still (behind Singapore and Iceland) the world's most enthusiastic cinemagoers outside the US.

Virtually every city suburb and large town is now served by a good multiplex, and the centre of Auckland has been brightened by the completion of a $40m, 12-screen development, incorporating an IMAX cinema, a Planet Hollywood and an impressive refurbishment of the Civic, one of the hemisphere's finest art deco picture palaces.

PETER CALDER has been a film critic for the *New Zealand Herald* since 1984.

# Recent and Forthcoming Films

**SAVAGE HONEYMOON**

Script and Dir: Mark Beesley. Players: Nicholas Eadie, Perry Piercy, Sophia Hawthorne. Prod: Steve Sachs.

Mayhem hits a beachside camping ground when a biker couple go on a second honeymoon.

**WHAT BECOMES OF THE BROKEN-HEARTED**

Script: Alan Duff. Dir: Ian Mune. Players: Temuera Morrison, Rena Owen, Nancy Brunning. Prod: Bill Gavin.

The violent Jake Heke is forced to confront the cost of his actions.

**SCARFIES**

Script: Robert Sarkies, Duncan Sarkies. Dir: Robert Sarkies. Players: Willa O'Neill, Neill Rea. Prod: Lisa Chatfield.

Black comedy about university students who discover a marijuana crop in their basement.

## HOPELESS

Script and Dir: Stephen Hickey. Players: Sally Stockwell, Phil Pinner, Adam Gardiner. Prod: Larry Parr.

Slacker comedy about a hopeless romantic searching for true love.

## STICKMEN

Script: Nick Ward. Dir: Hamish Rothwell. Players: Robbie Magasiva, Scott Wills, Paolo Rotondo. Prod: Michelle Turner.

'Serious comedy' about three guys up to their necks in pool-playing.

## SNAKESKIN

Script and Dir: Gillian Ashurst. Players: Melanie Lynskey, Dean O'Gorman. Prod: Debra Kelleher-Smith.

Supernatural road movie.

## MAGIK AND ROSE

Script and Dir: Vanessa Alexander. Players: Alison Bruce, Nicola Murphy. Prod: Larry Parr.

*Still from the slacker comedy, HOPELESS*

Set in a small town, this is a female buddy picture about two women, Magik and Rose, both desperate to have babies.

## THE PRICE OF MILK

Script and Dir: Harry Sinclair. Prod: Fiona Copland. Players: Danielle Cormack, Karl Urban.

## THE FEATHERS OF PEACE

Script and Dir: Barry Barclay. Prod: Ruth Kaupua-Panapa.

Excellent dramatised documentary on the genocide of the native people of the Chatham Islands by invading Maori in the 1830s.

# Producers

**Fiona Copland**
PO Box 47632
Ponsonby
Auckland
Tel: (64 9) 413 8405
Fax: (64 9) 413 8403
e-mail: fcopland@ibm.net

**Communicado Ltd**
PO Box 5779
Wellesley Street
Auckland
Tel: (64 9) 379 3734
Fax: (64 9) 377 7419

**Essential Productions Ltd**
45A Crummer Road
Ponsonby
Auckland1002
Tel: (64 9) 378 9754
Fax: (64 9) 303 1630
e-mail: jonathan@esspro.co.nz

**Gibson Group**
PO Box 6185
Te Aro

Wellington
Tel: (64 4) 384 7789
Fax: (64 4) 384 4727

**He Taonga Films**
72 Williamson Avenue
Grey Lynn
Auckland
Tel: (64 9) 376 0332
Fax: (64 9) 376 0332

**Kahukura Productions**
PO Box 31444
Lower Hutt
Wellington
Tel: (64 4) 619 0759
Fax: (64 4) 619 0944
e-mail:
100351.2475@compuserve.com

**Pacific Films**
PO Box 6249
Wellington
Tel: (64 4) 938 7526
Fax: (64 4) 382 9916

**Preston Laing Productions**
PO Box 9175

Wellington
Tel: (64 4) 384 6405
Fax: (64 4) 384 7406

**South Pacific Pictures**
PO Box 35 656
Browns Bay
Auckland
Tel: (64 9) 444 3000
Fax: (64 9) 443 5900

# Distributors

**Buena Vista International (NZ)**
PO Box 37524
Parnell
Auckland
Tel: (64 9) 302 7565
Fax: (64 9) 302 0201

**Columbia Tristar (New Zealand) Ltd**
PO Box 68 041
Newton
Auckland
Tel: (64 9) 366 9499
Fax: (64 9) 366 9488

**Essential Films**
PO Box 47045
Ponsonby
Auckland
Tel: (64 9) 376 3682
Fax: (64 9) 376 3293
e-mail: kellyrogers@rialto.co.nz

**REP Film Distributors**
30 Prosford Street
Ponsonby
Auckland
Tel: (64 9) 360 2360
Fax: (64 9) 360 2920

**Roadshow Film Distributors**
PO Box 68 246
Newton
Auckland
Tel: (64 9) 377 9669
Fax: (64 9) 377 9449

**Twentieth Century Fox**
PO Box 6923
Auckland
Tel: (64 9) 309 0955
Fax: (64 9) 309 0967

**United International Pictures**
PO Box 105 263
Auckland
Tel: (64 9) 379 6269
Fax: (64 9) 379 6271

# Useful Addresses

**Screen Producers and Directors Association**
PO Box 9567
Wellington
Tel: (64 4) 802 4931
Fax: (64 4) 385 8755
e-mail: info@spada.co.nz

**New Zealand Film Archive**
PO Box 11449
Wellington
Tel: (64 4) 384 7647
Fax: (64 4) 382 9595
e-mail: nzfa@actrix.gen.nz

**New Zealand Film Archive Auckland**
PO Box 68 747
Newton
Auckland
Tel: (64 9) 379 0688
Fax: (64 9) 379 0688
e-mail: nzfaauck@iprolink.co.nz

**New Zealand Film Commission**
PO Box 11546
Wellington
Tel: (64 4) 382 7680
Fax: (64 4) 384 9719
e-mail: marketing@nzfilm.co.nz

**NZ On Air**
PO Box 9744
Wellington
Tel: (64 4) 382 9524
Fax: (64 4) 382 9546

**Film New Zealand**
[assists visiting productions]
PO Box 24 142
Wellington
Tel: (64 4) 802 4594
Fax: (64 4) 385 8755
e-mail: info@filmnz.org.nz

**NZ Federation of Film Societies**
PO Box 9544
Wellington
Tel: (64 4) 385 0162
Fax: (64 4) 801 7304
e-mail: enzedff@actrix.gen.nz

# NORWAY — Trond Olav Svendsen

Cinema managers and distributors seem moderately optimistic after an encouraging rise in total ticket sales in 1999. The list of box-office hits offered some surprises, with four animated features in the top ten, and a Swedish low-budget slice-of-life film by a first-time director, *Fucking Åmål*, doing better than *Star Wars*. Not surprisingly, the one Norwegian feature in the chart was **The Olsen Gang – Final Mission**, the last instalment in the popular Olsen Gang series (actually remakes of Danish originals).

In 1999 a management consultancy firm hired by the Department of Culture proposed major changes in the way film is produced in Norway. Then there was a change of government, from a Christian Democrat coalition to Labour and the new Minister of Culture, Ellen Horn, an actress known from the National Theatre and films, decided to put the plans on ice. Her message was not a thumbs down, more a case of 'let's not rush things'.

The turmoil surrounding the proposed changes has yielded some results, such as the fact that Norwegian films have been discussed more often and more extensively than usual in the media. A group of younger directors have formed a lobbying organisation and there is probably increased pressure on the government production company Norsk Film (which the proposal threatens to close down) to make films which perform better at the box-office.

As far as Norwegian films are concerned, the 1999-2000 season was neither a success nor a failure – average in both quality and commercial performance. Eight features were released, most of them targeted at one specific audience or another. Interestingly, after a lengthy spell which had produced many directorial debuts, only two films were helmed by first-time directors, and one of these was already well-established in theatre.

## A philosophical grand tour

The season began with **Sophie's World** (*Sofies verden*), based on Jostein Gaarder's worldwide best-seller, which certainly seemed like an opportunity to reach a wide audience. It was directed by Erik Gustavson, one of the most experienced Norwegian directors, and starred young newcomer Silje Storstein and the popular Swedish actor Tomas von Brömssen.

As it turned out, the book's catalogue structure, with Sophie confronting the thoughts of one famous philosopher after another, was rather less effective on film than on the page. For most of the time, the film did not seem to be going in any particular direction, merely providing potted lessons on the history of ideas in chronological order. Although both Storstein and Brömssen were good, the digital work used to recreate historical periods and cities was uneven.

**Misery Harbour**, directed by Nils Gaup of *Pathfinder* fame, was a biopic about the early life of Aksel Sandemose, the well-known Norwegian (though Danish-born) novelist who died in 1965. Sandemose was known for being ferociously critical of the

kind of small community where he grew up, and which was rife with cruelty, deep-rooted envy, intolerance and gossip. His writings also suggest that he once killed a man while working as a seaman and lumberjack in Canada. The film contrasts the uncivilised Canadian environment with the pseudo-sophisticated, equally intolerant literary milieu in 1930s Oslo. Perhaps surprisingly, the depiction of the latter is more successful than the Canadian segment.

Berit Nesheim, who was Oscar-nominated in 1996 with *The Other Side of Sunday*, came up with a potential box-office success in the crime story **Eva's Eye** (*Evas øye*), about a young woman connected to several murders, which are investigated by a sympathetic police detective. The film is nicely shot and acted, and Andrine Sæther, who plays the central part (as she did in the celebrated *Junk Mail*) has in some modest way become Norway's first lady of film. However, in the final analysis the story, with its rather thin characterisations, taken from a best-seller by crime writer Karin Fossum, does not prove substantial enough for the big screen.

## Double vision

Knut Erik Jensen's **Passing Darkness** (*Når mørket er forbi*) was a disappointment. Jensen, whose films speak up for the people of Arctic Norway, has a proven talent, but his semi-documentary, semi-experimental style is now wearing thin. This time it unsuccessfully camouflages a lack of substance in the story of a man who leaves Oslo to return his roots in the North.

A fresher view of modern Norway was presented by first-time director Catrine Telle, with **Eye Ball** (*Ballen i Øyet*), an absurdist tale of a young woman who after being hurt while playing soccer, sees everything in pairs. The film sometimes sounds and looks like a children's feature, but is nonetheless thought-provoking, thanks to recognisable characters and funny details. Telle's 'day job' as a director at the National Theatre is very much in evidence, particularly in the way she makes the actors enjoy their parts.

*Eva´s Eye*
director Berit Otto Nesheim

*Aberdeen*
director Hans Petter Moland

*Passing Darkness*
director Knut Erik Jensen

Norwegian Film Institute presents
feature films worldwide

*Odd Little Man*
director Stein Leikanger

*Detector*
director Pål Jackman

NORWEGIAN
FILM INSTITUTE

For further information please contact Stine Oppegaard.
Department of Production and International Relations P.O.Box 482 Sentrum, N-0105 Oslo
Tel: +47 22 47 45 75/71 or +47 90 85 96 38 Fax: +47 22 47 45 97
E-mail: filmavd@nfi.no  www.nfi.no

*Mads Ousdal, left, and Susan Badrkhan in Leidulv Risan's THE WEDDING*

Eventually, however, *Eye Ball*'s messy visuals conform too strictly to the kind of staging favoured by today's Norwegian theatre directors.

The last film of the season was Leidulv Risan's **The Wedding** (*Bryllupet*), a level-headed look at a relationship between a Norwegian man and an Iraqi woman: a

decent, but rather ordinary film to round off a decent, but rather ordinary season.

TROND OLAV SVENDSEN has a history degree from the University of Oslo. He works as a critic and film historian, and has published a *Theatre and Film Encyclopaedia*, and other books on film.

# Recent and Forthcoming Films

**SOFIES VERDEN (Sophie's World)**

Script: Petter Skavlan and Erik Gustavson, from the book by Jostein Gaarder. Dir: Gustavson. Phot: Kjell Vassdal. Players: Silje Storstein, Tomas von Brömssen, Andrine Sæther, Bjørn Floberg. Prod: Filmkameratene AS (John M. Jacobsen)/Norwegian Broadcasting Corporation (Oddvar Bull Tuhus).

**MISERY HARBOUR**

Script: Sigve Endresen and Kenny Sanders, based on the writings of Aksel Sandemose. Dir: Nils Gaup. Phot: Erling

Thurmann-Andersen. Players: Nikolaj Coster Waldau, Anneke von der Lippe, Stuart Graham, Graham Greene, Bjørn Floberg. Prod: Motlys AS (Sigve Endresen).

**S.O.S.**

Script and Dir: Thomas Robsahm. Phot: Gaute Gunnari. Players: Gianmarco Tognazzi, Jacqueline Lustig, Kjersti Holmen. Prod: Speranza Film AS (Thomas Robsahm).

**EVAS ØYE (Eva's Eye)**

Script: Berit Nesheim, based on a

novel by Karin Fossum. Dir: Nesheim. Phot: Erling Thurmann-Andersen. Players: Andrine Sæther, Bjørn Sundquist, Gisken Armand, Sverre Anker Ousdal. Prod: Northern Lights AS (Axel Helgeland).

**FOMLESEN I KATTEPINE (Fumblebody in a Cat's Jam)**

Script: Arthur Johansen. Dir: Petter A. Fastvold. Phot: Philip Øgaard. Players: Lars Vik, Sverre Anker Ousdal, Henriette Steenstrup. Prod: Yellow Cottage AS (Aage Aaberge).

**NÅR MØRKET ER FORBI (Passing**

Darkness)

Script: Alf R. Jacobsen and Knut Erik Jensen, based on a novel by Jacobsen. Dir: Jensen. Phot: Svein Krøvel. Players: Stig Henrik Hoff, Gørild Mauseth, Snorre Tindberg, Gunnel Lindblom, Nicholas Hope. Prod: Barentsfilm AS (Jan-Erik Gammleng).

## BALLEN I ØYET (Eye Ball)

Script: Beate Grimsrud. Dir: Catrine Telle. Phot: Peter Mokrosinski. Players: Laila Goody, Bjørnar Teigen, Marit A. Andreassen, Kristin Kajander, Kjersti Holmen, Anne Krigsvoll, Tom Tellefsen. Prod: Norsk Film AS (Tom Remlov).

*Still from Catrina Teller's EYE BALL*

## BRYLLUPET (The Wedding)

Script: Leidulv Risan and Bjørn Skaar. Dir: Risan. Phot: Helge Semb. Players: Susan Badrkhan, Mads Ousdal, Benaissa Ahssain, Samir Ibrahim Zedan, Naama Alward. Prod: Norwegian Broadcasting Corporation (Oddvar Bull Tuhus).

## ABERDEEN

Script: Kristin Amundsen and Hans Petter Moland. Dir: Moland. Phot: Philip Øgaard. Players: Stellan Skarsgård, Lena Headey, Ian Hart, Charlotte Rampling. Prod: Norsk Film AS (Tom Remlov).

## DETEKTOR (Detector)

Script: Erlend Loe. Dir: Pål Jackman. Phot: Bo Tengberg. Players: Mads Ousdal, Hildegunn Riise, Allan Svensson, Harald Eia. Prod: Christiania Film AS (Edward A. Dreyer).

## DA JEG TRAFF JESUS... MED SPRETTERT (Odd Little Man)

Script: Stein Leikanger, based on a novel by Odd Børretzen. Dir: Leikanger. Phot: John Christian Rosenlund. Players: Fredrik Stenberg Ditlev-Simonsen, Martin Jonny Raaen Eidissen, Fredrik Stengaard Paasche, Gjertrud

Jynge, Gard Eidsvold. Prod: Nordic Screen (Petter J. Borgli, Tomas Backstrøm).

## NÅR NETTENE BLIR LANGE (When the Nights Grow Longer)

Script and Dir: Mona J. Hoel. Phot: Robert Nordstrøm. Players: Kari Simonsen, Svein Scharffenberg, Gørild Mauseth, Benedikte Lindbeck, Bjarte Hjelmeland. Prod: Dis Film AS (Malte Forsell).

## "UNTITLED"

Script: Bibbi Moslet, based on a novel by Anne B. Ragde. Dir: Nathilde Overrein Rapp. Phot: Svein Krøvel. Prod: Norsk Film AS (Tom Remlov).

## HEFTIG OG BEGEISTRET (Strong and Excited)

Documentary. Dir: Knut Erik Jensen. Phot: Svein Krøvel. Prod: Norsk Film AS (Tom Remlov).

## PIAS VERDEN (Pia's World)

Script and Dir: Margreth Olin. Phot: Aslaug Holm. Prod: Speranza Film AS (Thomas Robsahm).

## "PROJECT 3"

Script: Pål Sletaune and Jonny

Halberg. Dir: Sletaune. Phot: Kjell Vassdal. Players: Robert Skjærstad, Trond Høvik, Philip Zandén, Bjørn Sundquist, Andrine Sæther. Prod: 4 Production (Turid Øversveen).

## FACTOTUM

Script: Bent Hamer and Jim Stark, based on a novel by Charles Bukowski. Dir: Hamer. Phot: Philip Øgaard. Prod: Stark Sales (Jim Stark), BulBul Film AS (Bent Hamer).

## DET STØRSTE I VERDEN (The Greatest Thing)

Script: Siri Senje, based on a novel by Bjørnstjerne Bjørnson. Dir: Thomas Robsahm. Phot: Gaute Gunnari. Prod: Norsk Film AS (Tom Remlov).

## IL NORVEGESE – A ROMANTIC COMEDY

Script: Lars Saabye Christensen. Dir: Erik Gustavson. Prod: Norsk Film AS (Tom Remlov).

## KARLSSON PÅ TAKET (Karlsson on the Roof)

Script: Vibeke Idsø, based on the writings of Astrid Lindgren. Dir: Nille Tystad and Waldemar Bergendahl. Prod: Filmkameratene AS (John M. Jacobsen).

# Producers

**Barentsfilm AS**
Wedel Jarlsbergsv. 36
N-1319 Bekkestua
Tel: (47) 8800 3230
Fax: (47) 8800 3234
Contact: Jan-Erik Gammleng

**BulBul Film AS**
Helgerødvn. 171
N-3233 Sandefjord
Tel: (47) 3346 4895
Fax: (47) 3346 4895
Contact: Bent Hamer

**Christiania Film AS**
Sagvn. 17
N-0459 Oslo
Tel: (47) 2322 8340
Fax: (47) 2322 8347
Contact: Edward A. Deyer

**Dis Film AS**
Parkvn. 47 B
N-0256 Oslo
Tel: (47) 2244 2688
Fax: (47) 2255 7845
Contact: Mona J. Hoel

**Filmhuset AS**
President Harbitz gt. 22 A
N-0259 Oslo
Tel: (47) 2256 2100
Fax: (47) 2255 1540
Contact: Egil Ødegård

**Filmkameratene AS**
PO Box 6868
St. Olavs plass
N-0130 Oslo
Tel: (47) 2335 5300
Fax: (47) 2335 5301
Contact: John M. Jacobsen

**Motlys AS**
Islandsgt. 6
N-0658 Oslo
Tel: (47) 2322 8360
Fax: (47) 2303 5561
Contact: Sigve Endresen

**MovieMakers AS**
PO Box 6868 St. Olavs plass
N-0130 Oslo
Tel: (47) 2246 3200
Fax: (47) 2246 3201
Contact: Dag Nordahl

**Nordic Screen Production AS**
PO Box 271
N-1319 Bekkestua
Tel: (47) 6752 5460
Fax: (47) 6712 3773
Contact: Petter J. Borgli

**Norsk Film AS**
PO Box 270
N-1319 Bekkestua
Tel: (47) 6752 5300
Fax: (47) 6712 5108
Contact: Tom Remlov

**Northern Lights AS**
PO Box 276
N-1319 Bekkestua
Tel: (47) 6752 5330
Fax: (47) 6752 5340
Contact: Axel Helgeland

**Speranza Film AS**
PO Box 619 Sentrum
N-0106 Oslo
Tel: (47) 2282 2470
Fax: (47) 2282 2471
Contact: Thomas Robsahm

**Unni Straume Filmproduksjon AS**
Via Santi Quattro 45
I-04019 Terracina
Italy
Tel: (39) 0773 70 0183
Fax: (39) 0773 70 4366
Contact: Unni Straume

**Yellow Cottage AS**
PO Box 274
N-1319 Bekkestua
Tel: (47) 6752 5345
Fax (47) 6752 5349
Contact: Aage Aaberge

# Distributors

**Arthaus**
Dronningens gt. 16
N-0152 Oslo
Tel: (47) 2247 4685
Fax: (47) 2247 4692
Contact: Svend B. Jensen

**BV Film AS**
PO Box 17
N-4299 Avaldsnes
Tel: (47) 5284 6470
Fax: (47) 5284 6471
Contact: Irmelin Nordahl

**Egmont Columbia Tristar
Filmdristributors AS**
PO Box 7064 Majorstuen
N-0306 Oslo
Tel: (47) 2336 6680
Fax: (47) 2336 6681
Contact: Bjørn Hoenvoll

**Europafilm AS**
Stortingsgt. 30
N-0161 Oslo
Tel: (47) 2283 4290
Fax: (47) 2283 4151
Contact: Åge Hoffart

**AS Fidalgo**
PO Box 2054 Posebyen
N-4668 Kristiansand
Tel: (47) 3802 4004
Fax: (47) 3802 2354
Contact: Arild Frøyseth

**Kommunenes Filmcentral AS**
PO Box 411 Sentrum
N-0103 Oslo
Tel: (47) 2236 9530
Fax: (47) 2242 1469
Contact: Bjørn Jacobsen

**Sandrew Metronome Norge AS**
PO Box 411 Sentrum
N-0103 Oslo
Tel: (47) 2235 8200
Fax: (47) 2235 8220
Contact: Frida Ohrvik

**Scandinavian Entertainment
Group AS**
President Harbitz gt. 22 A
N-0259 Oslo
Tel: (47) 2256 2100
Fax: (47) 2255 1540
Contact: Tore Erlandsen

**SF Norge**
PO Box 6868
St. Olavs plass
N-0130 Oslo
Tel: (47) 2200 7800
Fax: (47) 2200 7801
Contact: Guttorm Petterson

**United International Pictures AS**
PO Box 7134 Majorstua
N-0307 Oslo
Tel: (47) 2285 3737
Fax: (47) 2285 3738
Contact: Liv Jacobsen

## Useful Addresses

**Foundation for Audiovisual Production**
Dronningens gt. 16
N-0152 Oslo
Tel: (47) 2247 4650
Fax: (47) 2247 46 91
Contact: Elin Erichsen

**National Association of Municipal Cinemas**
Dronningens gt. 16
N-0152 Oslo
Tel: (47) 2247 4610
Fax: (47) 2247 4699
Contact: Lene Løken

**National Centre for Screen Studies**
PO Box 904 Sentrum

N-0104 Oslo
Tel: (47) 2282 2400
Fax: (47) 2282 2422
Contact: Kjersti Alver

**Norwegian Film Distributors Association**
Øvre Slottsgt. 12
N-0157 Oslo
Tel: (47) 2242 4844
Fax: (47) 2242 3093
Contact: Kristin Hoenvoll

**Norwegian Film Institute**
PO Box 482 Sentrum
N-0105 Oslo
Tel: (47) 2247 4571
Fax: (47) 2247 4597
Contact: Jan Erik Holst

**Norwegian Film and TV-**

**Producers Association**
Dronningens gt. 16
N-0152 Oslo
Tel: (47) 2311 9311
Fax: (47) 3211 9316
Contact: Tom G. Eilertsen

**Norwegian Film Workers Association**
Dronningens gt. 16
N-0152 Oslo
Tel: (47) 2247 4640
Fax: (47) 2247 4689
Contact: Kjersti Paulsen

**Norwegian International Film Festival**
PO Box 145
N-5501 Haugesund
Tel: (47) 5273 4430
Fax: (47) 5273 4420
Contact: Gunnar Johan Løvik

# PAKISTAN — Aijaz Gul

Wall-to-wall television coverage of the Cricket World Cup from England, in May-June 1999, followed by further one-day cricket matches, practically crippled the film business. No new films were released for almost two months during the World Cup – maybe it is time to make a film about a cricket match! A rise in cinema admission prices to $1 (50 rupees), ordered by the provincial governments, was the wrong decision at the wrong time and theatres lost a sizeable segment of their audience because of the hike.

Producer-distributors are also shying away from saturation pre-release TV advertising, following the closure of Network Television Marketing, which used to offer dirt cheap rates for film publicity. The box-office performance of good films like *Lost Paradise* (*Jannat Ki Talash*), *Repentance* (*Jazba*) and even *Moon* (*Mujhey Chand Chahiye*) all suffered due to lack of pre-release TV publicity.

Among 50 features released in 1999 (Urdu: 28, Pushto: 16, Punjabi: 6), director Syed Noor's calculated **Bandit** (*Daku Rani*) was the top rental. Hassan Askari's **Lost Paradise** addressed a meaningful social subject but was a nationwide box-office disaster. With Shan and Resham in the leads, the film revolved around a poet and his lost love; the heroine is tortured and humiliated as she finds herself trapped in the tragedy of Partition in 1947. Askari also directed **Repentance**, a good revenge drama in which the villain Shahid chain-smoked too much. This was another title which suffered because of poor marketing and insufficient TV publicity.

Askari's third film of the year, **Landlady** (*Chaudhrani*), gave Anjuman, an enormously buxom heart-throb from Punjabi films of the 1980s, a brief but successful comeback as an elder sister. She also made some quickies in which she danced and romanced with heroes young enough to be her son.

## Noor hits a bump

Among 15 features released in the first quarter of 2000, director Syed Noor tarnished his reputation and bankable image, first with **Flames** (*Angarey*), then with *Jungle Queen*. *Flames*, a tale of urban gangsters, ran for over three hours, at a snail's pace. **Jungle Queen** was about the vengeance of a wild woman in the jungles of Sri Lanka. It was a hackneyed rehash of any number of earlier jungle movies, had an intolerable musical score and even the seductive Saima, dressed in a lion skin, could not save it from utter failure; the strangest, most disastrous film of the year. With a dozen titles in various stages of production, it seemed Noor might have taken on too much, but there were better hopes for his *Collector* (*Dil Diwana Hai*), a loose remake of William Wyler's 1965 film of the same name.

Director Iqbal Kashmiri's **Return** (*Ghar Kab Aao Gey*) was a slick action movie, with Dolby sound and impressive underwater photography, shot in the Philippines. It played extremely well for two months. Actor-director Shan's long-awaited **Moon** was absolutely charming, spanning two generations of love, mistrust, betrayal and finally repentance. Charming Atiqa Odho plays a single mother who must raise Shan alone. In the end, his father (Javaid Shaikh) seeks forgiveness with a musical encore and the family is reunited. Gripping direction, subtle performances from Atiqa, Shan, Moammar, Reema and a smashing score made *Moon* brilliant entertainment. Shan is fully in command as director after his lukewarm debut last year with *Guns'n'Roses*; and *Moon*'s moderate commercial performance could again be attributed in part to poor marketing. Saima and Shan were the most bankable superstars of 2000. Newcomer Noor impressed in *Return* and *Moon*.

The National Film Development

*Atiqa Odho as a single mother in MOON*

Corporation Limited (NAFDEC) bestowed Pakistan's National Film Awards in December 1999. *Bangles* (*Choorian*) grabbed 11 out of 19 awards, including Best Film, Director (Syed Noor), Actress (Saima), Supporting Actor (Shafqat Cheema) and Composer (Zulfiqar Ali). NAFDEC also arranged successful film festivals from Iran, China, Japan and an "Old is Gold" retrospective of Pakistani films from the 1950s and early 1960s. Amongst imported titles *The Mummy* and *The Matrix* were especially successful. *Jinnah*, a US/UK co-production about the founder of Pakistan, also did good business.

AIJAZ GUL has an MA in cinema from the University of Southern California, Los Angeles, and has written three books and numerous articles on film. He represents the Pakistan chapter of the Network for the Promotion of Asian Cinema and currently works for the National Film Development Corporation.

# Useful Addresses

**National Film Development Corp.**
NAFDEC Complex
56-F Jinnah Avenue
Islamabad
Tel: (92 51) 920 3853
Fax: (92 51) 922 1863

**Pakistan Film Producers Association**
Regal Cinema Building
Shahrah-e-Quaid-e-Azam
Lahore
Tel: (92 42) 732 2904
Fax: (92 42) 724 1264

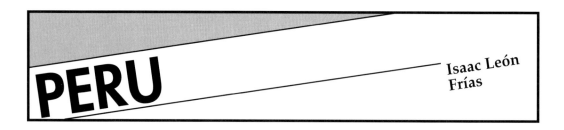

**PERU** — Isaac León Frías

Despite the difficult conditions facing the film industry in Peru, production has continued, with three new features released in 1999: the magical realist drama *The Bait* (*La carnada*), directed by Marianne Eyde and reviewed in *IFG 2000*; *Pantaleón and the Visitors* (*Pantaleón y las visitadoras*), directed by Francisco Lombardi, and *At Half Past Midnight* (*A la medianoche y media*), a Peruvian-Venezuelan co-production directed by Peru's Marité Ugaz and Venezuela's Mariana Rondón.

**Pantaleón and the Visitors** was the biggest hit of 1999, which meant that for the first time a Peruvian film had beaten Hollywood blockbusters to the top spot, relegating *Star Wars: Episode I* into second place. A co-production between Inca Films and América Televisión, *Pantaleón* was also the most expensive local film ever made, and was sold to more foreign territories than any other Peruvian feature.

Based on Mario Vargas Llosa's novel of the same name, *Pantaleón*, though not a great film, is far superior to the first, disappointing screen version of the book, co-directed by Vargas Llosa in 1976. The story relates the attempts of Captain Pantaleón Pantoja to establish a service of "visitadoras" (whores) in the military camps of the Peruvian jungle. The first part shows well-timed humour but the tale becomes unconvincing in the latter stages.

**At Half Past Midnight** is an experimental feature about a mysterious woman in a town menaced by a tidal wave. It tries to create an odd atmosphere by mixing up two levels of narrative – the external 'reality' and fantasy. However, the approach might have worked better in a short film; at feature length, the atmosphere loses its suggestive quality.

*Still from AT HALF PAST MIDNIGHT*

Four new films have been completed and scheduled for release before the end of 2000: Felipe Degregori's *City of M* (*Ciudad de M*), Edgardo Guerra's *Death of Love* (*Muerto de amor*), Augusto Tamayo's *The Elusive Good* (*El bien esquivo*) and Armando Robles Godoy's *Impossible Love* (*Imposible amor*). In April 2000, Francisco Lombardi began filming *Red Ink* (*Tinta roja*), based on the novel by Chile's Alberto Fuguet.

However, during 1999 no contest for feature film projects was organised by CONACINE (Consejo Nacional de Cinematografía), as there are no public funds available for new Peruvian film production, only outstanding payments for projects previously awarded finance by the CONACINE juries.

CONACINE invited applications from directors in the first months of 2000 for a new contest, not in order to give money from public funds but in the hope of financing new projects through co-production, especially the IBERMEDIA project. CONACINE will act as a mediator, seeking economic support for distinguished feature film ideas, while state subsidy remains in short supply. In the meantime, Peruvian film-makers keep trying to look for other sources of finance at home and abroad.

---

ISAAC LÉON FRÍAS is a film critic and Professor of Language and Film History at the University of Lima. From 1965 to 1985 he was director of *Hablemos de Cine* magazine and is now a member of the editorial council of *La gran ilusión* magazine, and director of Filmoteca de Lima.

# Recent and Forthcoming Films

### PANTALEON Y LAS VISITADORAS (Pantaleon and the Visitors)

Script: Giovanna Pollarolo and Enrique Moncloa. Dir: Francisco J.Lombardi. Phot: Teo Delgado. Players: Salvador del Solar, Angie Cepeda, Mónica Sánchez, Pilar Bardem. Prod: América Televisión/Inca Films/Tornasol Film (Spain)/Televisión Española.

### LA CARNADA (The Bait)

Script and Dir: Marianne Eyde. Phot: Cesar Pérez. Players: Mónica Sánchez, Orlando Felioces, Miguel Medina, Cecilia Natteri. Prod: Cusi Films.

### A LA MEDIA NOCHE Y MEDIA (At Half Past Midnight)

Script and Dir: Marité Ugaz and Mariana Rondón. Phot: MIcaela Cajahuaringa. Players: Salvador del Solar, María Fernanda Ferro, Constanza Morales. Prod: Imagen Latina (Perú)/Sudaca Films (Venezuela).

### EL BIEN ESQUIVO (The Elusive Good)

Script: Augusto Tamayo and Alejandro Rossi. Dir: Tamayo. Phot: Juan Durán. Players: Jimena Lindo, Diego Bertie, Orlando Sacha. Prod: Argos Interactiva.

### CIUDAD DE M (City of M)

Script: Giovanna Pollarolo. Dir: Felipe Degregori. Phot: Micaela Cajahuaringa. Players: Christian Meier, Santiago Magill, Gianela Neyra, Jorge Madueño. Prod: Inca Films/Torre de Bebel Producciones/Producciones UVK.

### MUERTO DE AMOR (Death of Love)

Script and Dir: Edgardo Guerra. Phot: Alberto Arévalo. Players: Diego Bertie, Vanessa Robbiano, Karina Calmet. Prod: Sur Producciones.

### IMPOSIBLE AMOR (Impossible Love)

Script and Dir: Armando Robles Godoy. Phot: Luciano Talledo. Players: Vanessa Robbiano, Mónica Sánchez, Orlando Sacha. Prod: Películas del Pacífico.

### TINTA ROJA (Red Ink)

Script: Giovanna Pollarolo. Dir: Francisco J. Lombardi. Phot: Teo Delgado. Players: Giovanni Ciccia, Lucía Jiménez, Fele Martínez. Prod: Inca Films (Peru)/Tornasol Films (Spain).

# Useful Addresses

**Asociación de Cineastas del Perú**
Calle Manco Capac 236
Lima -18
Tel: (51 14) 461 829
e-mail: cineperu@chavin.rcp.net.pe

**Casablanca Films**
Malecón Grau 967
Chorrillos
Lima
Fax: (51 14) 300 603/408 550

**CONACINE**
Museo de la Nación
Av. Javier Prado 2465
Lima
Tel/Fax: (51 14) 225 6479

**Filmoteca de Lima**
Paseo Colón 125
Lima-1
Fax: (51 14) 331 0126
e-mail: filmolima@terra.com.pe

**Kusi Films**
Godofredo García 140
Lima-27
Tel: (51 14) 226 005

**Producciones Inca Films**
Francisco de Paula Ugarriza 271
Lima-18
Fax: (51 14) 241 6941
e-mail: incafilms@clabsperu

**Peliculas del Padifico**
Manuel A. Fuentes 671
Lima-27
Tel/Fax: (51 14) 221 3746

**Sociedad Peruana de Productores y Directores Cinematográficos (SOCINE)**
Manuel A. Fuentes 671
Lima-27
Tel/Fax: (51 14) 221 3746

# PHILIPPINES — Agustín Sotto

With production down by half in the first six months of 2000, and June's annual Manila Film Festival cancelled because of the shortage of new local movies, Filipino cinema faces a bleak future. Attacks by the Muslim separatist movement, previously restricted to the southern provinces, had spread to the metropolis by May 2000, discouraging cinemagoing and leading to the postponement of new local and foreign movie openings.

Ironically, 1999 was a great year for Filipino movies at the box-office, albeit thanks to the screening of a number of highly profitable sex-driven films. The censors had lifted the taboos on frontal nudity and that allowed some studios teetering on bankruptcy to clamber back into the black. This liberalisation was too much for a conservative Christian society: nationwide rallies were held, forcing the censors to wield the scissors once again. Chief censor Armida Sigiuon-Reyna was the target of criticism, but hung on to her position, largely, it was suggested, because she is a close associate of the Filipino president, movie actor Joseph Estrada.

Movie industry leaders had already figured in attempts to muzzle anti-Estrada elements within the media, particularly the *Philippines Daily Inquirer*, the country's leading newspaper. By pulling out movie advertisements from this broadsheet, under the guise of a cost-cutting measure, producers and distributors hoped to protect their favourite son from criticism.

The film year was not without distinction. Jeffrey Jeturian's **Fetch a Pail of Water** (*Pila-Balde*), a powerful snapshot of life amongst slum dwellers, won the Gold Medal at the Houston International Film Festival. Raymond Red's *Shadow* (*Anino*) was named Best Short at Cannes 2000. It follows a member of a dying breed: the itinerant photographers who used to congregate in large numbers around churches and carnivals, to scrape together an income by taking pictures of the public. The down-and-out photographer, practitioner of a dying craft, struggles to maintain a modicum of artistic integrity by taking shots of urban decay.

Also impressive was Mike de Leon's **Third World Hero** (*Bayaning Third World*), a probe into the 'National Hero' status of Jose Rizal, the novelist who in the late nineteenth century inspired the Philippines to rise up against colonial occupation by Spain. Rizal's name is on practically every main street in the Philippines, and on all kinds of merchandise and businesses, from matchboxes to funeral parlours; yet to most people he is nothing more than a distant figure on countless stone monuments, and his life and achievements are poorly understood. The film deconstructs the process by which a mere mortal becomes a national hero and the third world tendency to elevate anything and everything – people, animals, trees – to 'national' status.

AGUSTÍN SOTTO is an archivist and film critic who chairs Manunuri ng Pelikulang Pilipino, the Phillipine film critics' circle.

*Joel Torre, left, and Lara Fabregas in THIRD WORLD HERO*

# Useful Addresses

**Cultural Center of the Philippines (Film Division)**
Roxas Blvd
Pasay City
Tel: (632) 832 5120
Fax: (632) 833 0267

**Film Academy of the Philippines**
Sampaguita Compound
Gilmore
Quezon City
Tel/Fax: (632) 726 2325

**Film Development Foundation of the Philippines**
Production Design Bldg
CCP Complex
Roxas Blvd
Quezon City
Tel/Fax: (632) 831 1465

**Mowelfund Film Institute**
66 Rosario Drive
Quezon City
Tel: (632) 727 1915
Fax: (632) 722 8628

**National Commission on Culture and the Arts**
633 General Luna
Intramuros
Manila
Tel/Fax: (632) 527 2194

**Philippine Information Agency (Film Division)**
Visayas Ave
Quezon City
Tel/Fax: (632) 920 4395

**Regal Films**
38 Valencia
Quezon City
Tel/Fax: (632) 410 6494

**Society of Film Archivists**
C63A Gueventville II
Libertad Mandaluyong
Manila
Tel/Fax: (632) 531 2235

**Star Cinema**
41 Scout Borromeo
Quezon City
Tel: (632) 924 4101
Fax: (632) 415 2272

**University of the Philippines Film Center**
Diliman
Quezon City
Tel: (632) 922 2722

# POLAND

Rick Richardson

Epic fever has gripped Poland. Following the huge success of two costume adventures in 1999 – Jerzy Hoffman's $8m *With Fire and Sword*, based on the book by Nobel scribe Henryk Sienkiewicz, and Andrzej Wajda's $3.5m *Pan Tadeusz*, adapted from the vast eighteenth-century poem by Polish national poet, Adam Mickiewicz, the epic has become the genre of choice. Both films set box-office records and combined to snare nearly 40% of local admissions last year, leaving American imports impotently rattling their sabres. *With Fire and Sword* drew 7.1 million admissions and *Pan Tadeusz* 5.5 million – unprecedented totals for Polish films in modern times.

Although *Pan Tadeusz* was not nominated for the Best Foreign Language Film Oscar, Wajda – whose career might be regarded as a personal epic – received a Lifetime Achievement Oscar in 2000 and despite the diminution of his powers over the last ten years he remains the dean of Polish directors.

The phenomenal figures for these two films have inevitably prompted others to jump on the epic bandwagon. As of summer 2000, two more Sienkiewicz books were being filmed: *In Desert and Wilderness* and *Quo Vadis*. Popular director Maciej Dutkiewicz was in South Africa to shoot *In Desert and Wilderness*, which follows the journey through Africa of a teenage Pole and his English girlfriend, who are kidnapped during the Mahdi uprising of 1883-85. The film promises to appeal to a public who long for historical portraits of Polish heroes winning against impossible odds.

The Roman saga, *Quo Vadis*, has been filmed many times before, most famously by MGM in 1951. Veteran director Jerzy Kawalerowicz's $12m version boasts Poland's biggest star, Boguslaw Linda, as Petronius, and newcomer Magdalena Mielcarz as Ligia. Filmed in Tunisia, Provence and on a massive set in the Warsaw suburbs, the love story set against the backdrop of nascent Christianity looks set to be another hit for its numerous investors, including Polish state television and the State Commitee of Cinematography.

For Kawalerowicz, this is the realisation of a longstanding dream. In 1967, when his film *Pharaoh* was nominated for an Oscar, he started talks about an adaptation of *Quo Vadis* in Los Angeles. In 1981 he met with MGM representatives, but their talks were interrupted by the declaration of Martial Law in Poland. Kawalerowicz expresses an intense Polish identification with *Quo Vadis*, because of the story's message of faith overcoming tyranny. The Poland in which Sienkiewicz wrote at the end of the eighteenth century had suffered partition and occupation at the hands of the Russians, Austrians and Prussians for 100 years. Poles saw Nero, the insane dictator of *Quo Vadis*, as a representative of contemporary Polish enemies, and the suffering of the Christians as an allegory of Poland's threatened identity under occupation.

## Polanski's return

While homegrown films are sating the appetite for rousing historical spectacle, most foreign-backed films still seek Poland as a location for disturbing, downbeat subjects from the more recent past. Roman Polanski is returning to Poland in 2001 to film on home turf for the first time since the early 1960s. He will team up again with Gene Gutowski, who produced *Repulsion* and *Cul de Sac*, for *The Pianist*, scripted by Ronald Harwood (*The Dresser*), from the bestselling novel by Wladyslaw Szpilman about a Jewish artist struggling to survive in the Warsaw Ghetto under the Nazis.

*Rafal Kubacki as Ursus and Magdalena Mielcarz as Ligia in Jerzy Kawalerowicz's lavish new screen version of QUO VADIS*
*photo: Piotr Bujnowicz/Chronos Film*

Another recent Second World War story filmed in Poland was *Edges of the Lord*, set during the German occupation of Poland during 1944-45 and starring *The Sixth Sense*'s Haley Joel Osment and Willem Dafoe. It is directed by Polish Hollywood exile Yurek Bogayevicz, who calls the picture a "children's view of the apocalypse". Poland substituted for Chechnya for Taylor Hackford's *White Nights*, starring Russell Crowe, and Oliver Stone was scheduled to use Polish mountain scenery for his movie about Chechnya.

Huge cinema complexes continue to be built in Poland, with a new multiplex opening its doors every two to three months. In 1999, five multiplexes in Poland accounted for 30% of the national gross, and cinema owners and distributors are confident that the only obstacle to Poland becoming a major European box-office market is the number of screens (currently around 800). They are working to push the total back towards its pre-1989 peak of 1,600.

RICK RICHARDSON, who has written about Poland for *Variety* for seven years, is a screenwriter and film-maker.

# Recent and Forthcoming Films

### DUZE ZWIERZE (The Big Animal)

Script: Krzysztof Kieślowski. Dir: Jerzy Stuhr. Phot: Pawel Edelman. Players: Jerzy Stuhr, Anna Dymna.

A man's best friend is his camel.

### DEBT (Debt)

Script: Krzysztof Krauze, Jerzy Morawski. Dir: Krauze. Phot: Bratosz Prokopowicz. Players: Robert Gonera, Jacek Borcuch.

Two debtors decide to kill their egregious moneylender.

### LIFE AS A FATAL SEXUALLY TRANSMITTED DISEASE

Script and Dir: Krzysztof Zanussi. Phot: Deward Klosinski. Players: Krystyna Janda, Zbigniew Zapasiewicz.

A doctor comes to terms with cancer in a classic Zanussi navel-gazer.

### WOJACZEK (Life Hurts)

Script: Lech Majewski, Maciej Mielecki. Dir: Majewski. Phot: Adam Sikora.

Legendary anti-communist poet commits suicide.

### TYDZIEN Z ZYCIA MECZYZNY (A Week in the Life of a Man)

Script and Dir: Jerzy Stuhr. Phot: Edward Klosinski. Player: Jerzy Stuhr.

Lucky prosecutor suffers twist of fate in seven-day saga. Winner of the OCIC Prize at Venice in 1999.

### CHLOPAKI NIE PLACZA (Boys Don't Cry)

Script: Mikolai Korzynski. Dir: Olaf Lubaszenko. Phot: Martin Strba. Players: Maciej Stuhr, Cezary Pazura.

Provincial bumpkin gets up to monkey business with the Warsaw mob.

### FUKS (Lucky Strike)

Script: Robert Brutter, Maciej Dutkiewicz. Director: Dutkiewicz. Phot: Andrzej Jarosiewicz. Players: Janusz Gajos, Agnieszka Krukowna, Maciej Stuhr.

Computer geek robs businessman; cheeky cop gives chase.

### PAN TADEUSZ

Script: Andrzej Wajda, Piotr Weresniak, Jan Zarzyckiir. Dir: Wajda. Phot: Pawel Edelman. Players: Boguslaw Linda, Daniel Olbrychski, Andrzej Seweryn, Michal Zebrowski

Inspired by Napoleon, Poles battle Russians. Based on epic poem by Adam Mickiewicz

### QUO VADIS

Script and Dir: Jerzy Kawalerowicz. Phot: Andrzej Jarosiewicz. Players: Boguslaw Linda, Pawel Delag, Magdelena Mielcarz.

Polish adaptation of Sienkiewicz epic: Christians yearn, Rome burns.

### TO JA ZLODZIEJ (Thief)

Script: Jacek Bromski, based on an idea by Piotr Weresniak. Dir: Bromski. Phot: Witold Adamek. Players: Jan Urbanski, Janusz Gajos.

Kids steal car from a Mafia boss and face consequences.

# Producers

**Film Studio Dom**
Puławska 61
02595 Warsaw
Tel: (48 22) 455 065

**Film Studio Kadr**
Puławska 61
02595 Warsaw
Tel: (48 22) 454 923

**Film Studio Oko**
Puławska 61
02595 Warsaw
Tel: (48 22) 454 041, ext. 222

**Film Studio Perspektywa**
Puławski 61
02595 Warsaw
Tel: (48 22) 455 494

**Film Studio Tor**
Puławska 61
02595 Warsaw
Tel/Fax: (48 22) 455 303

**Film Studio Zebra**
Puławska 61
02595 Warsaw
Tel/Fax: (48 22) 455 484

**Film Studio Zodiak**
Puławska 61
02595 Warsaw
Tel: (48 22) 452 047

**Karol Irzykowski Film Studio**
Mazowiecka 11
02595 Warsaw
Tel: (48 22) 276 653, 276 656

**Film Studio Kronika**

Chełska 21
00724 Warsaw
Tel/Fax: (48 22) 416 221

**S.F. Semafor**
Pabianicka 34
93513 Łódź
Tel/Fax: (48 42) 814120

**Studio Indeks**
Targowa 61/63
90323 Łódź
Tel: (48 42) 205 126

**Łódź Film Centre**
Łąkowa 29
90554 Łódź
Tel: (48 42) 367 500
Fax: (48 42) 360 487

**WFDiF (Wytwórnia Filmów Dokumentalnych i Fabularnych)**

Chełmska 21
00724 Warsaw
Tel: (48 22) 411 211
Fax: (48 22) 415 891

# Independent Producers

**Apple Film Production Ltd**
Pl. Konstytucji 3/10
00647 Warsaw
Tel/Fax: (48 22) 290 754

**Ekran Bis**
Łąkowa 29
90554 Łódź
Tel: (48 42) 372 577
Fax: (48 42) 362 046

**Feniks Film**
Chełmska 21
00724 Warsaw
Tel/Fax: (48 22) 413 821

**Figaro**
Chełmska 21
00724 Warsaw
Tel/Fax: (48 22) 635 6130

**Focus Producers Ltd**
Ryżowa 42
02495 Warsaw
Tel: (48 22) 662 7586
Fax: (48 22) 662 7083

**Fokus Film Ltd**
Okrąg 4/45
Łódź
Tel: (48 42) 297 003

**Gambit Productions**
Przemysłowa 7
02496 Warsaw
Tel/Fax: (48 22) 667 4596

**Heritage Films**
Marsałkowska 2/6
00581 Warsaw
Tel: (48 22) 625 2601
Fax: (48 22) 625 2693

**Marek Nowowiejski Film Productions**
Chełmska 21
00740 Warsaw
Tel/Fax: (48 22) 644 3400

**MS Film**
Chełmska 21

00724 Warsaw
Tel: (48 22) 405 056
Fax: (48 22) 405 935

**N (Independent Studio "Niezalezni")**
Lajkonika 5
04110 Łódź
Tel: (48 42) 861 394

**Pleograf Ltd**
pl. Mirowski 18
00138 Warsaw
Tel/Fax: (48 22) 208 342

**MM Potocka Productions**
Puzonistów 4
02876 Warsaw
Tel: (48 22) 643 9556
Fax: (48 22) 643 9553

**Skorpion Film**
Chełmska 21
00724 Warsaw
Tel/Fax: (48 22) 416 171

# Distributors

**Film Agency Silesia-Film**
Kościuszki 88
40519 Katowice
Tel/Fax: (48 832) 512 284
*and*
al. Ujazdowskie 20/10
00478 Warsaw
Tel/Fax: (48 22) 628 4518

**Gentrum Filmowe Graffiti Ltd**
Sw. Gertrudy 5
31046 Krakow
Tel: (48 12) 211 628
Fax: (48 12) 211 402

**Fundacja Sztuki Filmowej**
Andersa 1
00174 Warsaw
Tel: (48 22) 311 636
Fax: (48 22) 635 2001

**MAF – Mlodziezowa Akademia Filmowa**
Marsałkowska 28
00639 Warsaw
Tel/Fax: (48 22) 628 9698

**Black Cat**
Magnoliowa 2
20208 Lublin
Tel/Fax: (48 81) 774 654

**Iti Cinema**
Marsałkowska 138
00004 Warsaw
Tel: (48 22) 826 9862
Fax: (48 22) 826 8552

**Solopan Film Centrum**
Krakówskie Przedmiescie 21/23
00071 Warsaw
Tel/Fax: (48 22) 635 0044

**Syrena Entertainment Group**
Marsałkowska 115
00102 Warsaw
Tel: (48 22) 273 503
Fax: (48 22) 275 648

**Vision**
Rydygiera 7
01793 Warsaw
Tel: (48 22) 390 753
Fax: (48 22) 391 367

**Imp Poland**
Hoża 66/68
00950 Warsaw
Tel/Fax: (48 22) 628 7691

**Imperial Entertainment**
Kolska 12
01045 Warsaw
Tel: (48 22) 472 052
Fax: (48 22) 430 585

**Artvision**
Jerolimskie 125/127
01017 Warsaw
Tel: (48 22) 628 9315
Fax: (48 22) 467 239

# Useful Addresses

**Committee for Cinema**
Krakowskie Przedmiescie 21/23
00071 Warsaw
Tel: (48 22) 826 7489
Fax: (48 22) 276 233

**Film Polski**
Mazowiecka 6/8
00048 Warsaw
Tel: (48 22) 826 8455
Fax: (48 22) 826 2370

# PORTUGAL — Martin Dale

There's no more room for excuses. We no longer need to shout furiously against the Americans who inundate us with their products. Portuguese cinema will never be the same again." With these bold words, Portugal's leading broadcaster, SIC, launched an ambitious slate of ten 'telefilms' for 2000, instantly doubling the number of feature-length films produced in Portugal, and providing opportunities to 11 new screenwriters and seven new directors.

The Portuguese audio-visual landscape has been profoundly altered by this scheme, which was initially strongly contested by the 'Old Guard' auteur school. Telefilms have been produced in the past in Portugal, but the real significance of this new slate is the wider context of historical change in the Portuguese industry, including the emergence of new talent, multiplication of funding sources and decision centres, greater emphasis on the rigours of screenwriting, acting and distribution, and new private sector initiatives, which have energised a previously rather moribund environment, that relied heavily on state subsidies and lobbying.

The six telefilms broadcast before July 2000 have been varied in theme, style and achievement. They are all straightforward "true-life" stories that can appeal to a mainstream audience, with strong emphasis on national stars, steady camerawork and realism. Their main weakness is lack of character development and dramatic tension.

Perhaps the most creatively satisfying films to date have been the first, **I Love You, Teresa** (*Amo-te Teresa*), directed by Cristina Boavida and Ricardo Espírito

*Ana Padrão and Diogo Morgado in I LOVE YOU, TERESA*

Santo, and *Knives and Angels* (*Facas e Anjos*), directed by Eduardo Guedes. *I Love You, Teresa* tells the story an underage teenager who falls in love with a thirtysomething doctor in a small rural village in Portugal. The local population is outraged by this "abuse of a minor", and the couple are forced to flee. Engaging, solid performances and an effective soundtrack cannot mask the very superficial depiction of the central relationship. However, assisted by the massive television marketing campaign which promoted all the telefilms, *I Love You, Teresa* was watched by almost a third of the Portuguese population, the highest rating for a film in Portuguese television history.

## Big top and bright future

**Knives and Angels** follows a young man brought up in a strict military environment who one day quarrels with his father and flees to join the circus. He becomes a clown and falls in love with a trapeze artist, with whom he has a child. Their relationship ends tragically, but father, son and grandson are reunited. The film is well directed and acted, with a particularly good performance by Carla Bolito. Screenwriter Vicente Alves do Ó has been a revelation, having co-written *Knives and Angels* and another telefilm, as well as *The Immortals (Os Imortais)*, the forthcoming film from António Pedro Vasconcelos.

The longer term impact of the telefilms is likely to be felt in the cinema, as these new directors expand their horizons. SIC will inevitably play a leading role in this "Second Wave" of talent that should pump fresh blood into Portuguese Cinema. Far from heralding the death of auteur cinema in Portugal, telefilms are likely to highlight the differences between cinema and television film-making, and encourage greater audacity for the big screen.

In the short term, telefilms may, however, have a negative impact on theatrical audiences for more mainstream Portuguese films. Perhaps a small indication of this trend was the relative failure of Joaquim Leitão's Christmas 1999 release, **Inferno**, which opened on more than 40 screens – a record for a Portuguese film – but clocked up less than 100,000 admissions, a disappointing figure, given that Leitão had previously directed record box-office hits such as *Adam and Eve* and *Temptation*. *Inferno* is a more intimate work, following a group of ex-comrades from the colonial war, on a long night's reunion. Marketed as Portugal's first "action thriller", the film's real interest lies in its subdued portrayal of middle-aged men trying to recapture some of the glory of their 1970s youth.

## Talking about a revolution

The most hyped release in the last year was Maria de Medeiros' **Captains of April**, which recreates the day of Portugal's 1974 revolution. Selected for Un Certain Regard at Cannes 2000, it has enjoyed a mixed response in both the Portuguese and international press. The film's main appeal is its successful recreation of the flower-power atmosphere of the April revolution, and its whimsical humour. Medeiros suggests that the army captains who forged the military overthrow were actually bit-players in a much wider shift of power. This insight is valuable, but leaves the audience feeling they are not seeing the true "revolution", either in terms of power players, or the impact on ordinary people.

Other recent Portuguese films of note, include **Evil** (*Mal*), by Alberto Seixas Santos, which was included in the official selection at Venice 1999. A slow-moving, labyrinthine journey through modern Lisbon, it aims to present a cold, gritty portrayal of hopeless lives. **Too Late** (*Tarde de Mais*), by José Nascimento, recreates the moving true story of a group of fishermen who drowned on the Tagus river in Lisbon. Upcoming films of interest include Manoel de Oliveira's latest, *Word and Utopia (Palavra e Utopia)*, based on the teachings of a seventeenth-century priest, Father Antonio Vieira, and Paulo Rocha's *The Roots of the Heart (Raiz do Coração)*, an extravagant tale of transvestites and corrupt politicians.

Alongside SIC's telefilms, another important breeding ground for new talent has been the state's increased funding commitment to short films, creating what has been called the "Shorts Generation". Names such as Antonio Ferreira, Pedro Caldas, António Borges Correia, Miguel Gomes, João Figueiras, Sandro Aguilar and Raquel Freire have directed fine shorts and are likely soon to make feature debuts. Animation is also booming in Portugal, in particular with the acclaimed *The Suspect (A Suspeita)*, by José Miguel Ribeiro.

On the institutional level, there had been relative calm after the turbulent departure of the former ICAM president, José Costa Ramos, in 1999, but in July 2000 there was renewed turmoil following the sudden resignation of the Minister of Culture, Maria Manuel Carrilho. The main hopes of the independent production sector are now fixed on the government's promise to establish a production fund for independent television producers, due to be in place by 2001.

MARTIN DALE has lived in Lisbon since 1994 and is currently working as an independent media consultant. He has written several books on the film industry, including *The Movie Game* (Cassell, 1997).

# Recent and Forthcoming Films

### PALAVRA E UTOPIA (Word and Utopia)

Script and Dir: Manoel de Oliveira. Phot: Emmanuel Machuel. Players: Ricardo Trêpa, Luis Miguel Cintra, Lima Duarte. Prod: Madragoa Filmes (Portugal)/ Gemini Films (France).

### AS BODAS DE DEUS (God's Wedding)

Script and Dir: João Cesar Monteiro. Phot: Mário Barroso. Players: João Cesar Monteiro, Luis Miguel Cintra, Joana Azevedo, Rita Durão. Prod: Madragoa Filmes.

### TARDE DE MAIS (Too Late)

Script: João Canijo. Dir: José Nascimento. Phot: Mario Castanheira. Players: Vitor Norte, Adriano Luz, Rita Blanco. Prod: Madragoa Filmes.

### PEIXE LUA

Script and Dir: José Alvaro Morais. Players: Luis Miguel Cintra, Beatriz Batarda, Marcello Urgeghe. Prod: Madragoa Filmes.

### O MAL (Evil)

Script and Dir: Alberto Seixas Santos. Players: Rui Morrison, Pauline Cadell, Alexandre Pinto. Prod: Rosa Filmes.

### INFERNO

Script and Dir: Joaquim Leitão. Phot: David Carretero. Players: Joaquim de Almeida, Nicolau Breyner, Ana Bustorff. Prod: MGN Filmes

### AMO-TE TERESA (I Love You, Teresa)

Script: Cristina Boavida. Dir: Ricardo Espirito Santo, Cristina Boavida. Phot: José António Loureiro. Players: Ana Padrão, Diogo Morgado, José Wallenstein. Prod: SIC Filmes.

### FACAS E ANJOS (Knives and Angels)

Script: Vicente Alves do Ó, João Alfacinha da Silva. Dir: Eduardo Guedes. Phot: José António Loureiro. Players: Miguel Moreira, Carla Bolito, Raul Solnado, Ana Bustorff. Prod: SIC Filmes.

### THE WINDOW IS NOT THE LANDSCAPE

Script and Dir: Edgar Pêra. Phot: Luís Branquinho. Players: Lúcia Sigalho, José Wallenstein, Nuno Melo. Prod: Akademya Lusoh Galaktika.

### CAPTAINS OF APRIL

Script: Maria de Medeiros, Eve Duboise. Phot: Michel Abramowitz. Dir: de Medeiros. Players: Stefano Accorsi, Joaquim de Almeida, Emmanuel Salinger. Prod: JBA Production.

# Producers

**Akademya Lusoh-Galaktika**
Beco de Galheta, 26
1200–676 Lisbon
Tel: (351) 1 395 22 10
Fax: (351) 1 395 22 09

**Animanostra**
Av. Cinco Outubro, 10, 7°, sala 2
1000 Lisbon
Tel: (351 1) 315 7692
Fax: (351 1) 353 4194

**Animatógrafo**
Rua de Rosa, 252, 2º

1200 Lisbon
Tel: (351 1) 347 5372
Fax: (351 1) 347 3252

**AS Produções**
Rua Jacinto Nunes, 18–1 E
1170 Lisbon
Tel: (351 1) 813 20 90
Fax: (351 1) 812 44 04

**David & Golias**
Rua da Madalena 91, 3ºD
1100 Lisbon
Tel: (351 1) 888 2028
Fax: (351 1) 888 2046

**Fábrica de Imagens**
Largo do Contador Mor, 3
1100 Lisbon
Tel: (351 1) 888 1102
Fax: (351 1) 886 0 23

**Filmógrafo**
Rua Duque de Loulé, 141 R/C
4000 Oporto
Tel: (351 2) 208 6780
Fax: (351 2) 208 6861

**Madragoa Filmes**
Av. D. Manuel 1, nº 3
2890 Alcochete

Lisbon
Tel: (351 1) 234 2185/2225/2233
Fax: (351 1) 234 2202

**MGN Filmes**
Rua de S. Bento, 644, 4º Esq.
1200 Lisbon
Tel: (351 1) 388 7497
Fax: (351 1) 388 7281

**Mutante Filmes**
Rua Imprensa Nacional, 48, 3'E
1250 Lisbon
Tel: (351 1) 395 2975
Fax: (351 1) 395 2975

**Produções Off/Rosi Burguete**
Rua da Barroca, 72-3'
1200 Lisbon
Tel: (351 1) 347 0378
Fax: (351 1) 347 0370

**Rosa Filmes**
Campo de Cebolas, 17, 2º, Esqº
1100 Lisbon
Tel: (351 1) 882 0160
Fax: (351 1) 882 0169

**S.P. Filmes**
Rúa Das Pracas, 60, 1º DTº
Lisbon
Tel: (351 1) 396 4222
Fax: (351 1) 397 1352

**Virtual Audiovisuais**
Avenida de Roma, 72, 8 D
1700 Lisboa
Tel: (351) 846 3891
Fax: (351) 846 3898

# Distributors

**Filmes Castelo Lopes**
Rua de Sto Amaro à Estrêla, 17A
1200 Lisbon
Tel: (351 1) 392 9750
Fax: (351 1) 395 5924

**Filmes Lusomundo**
Av. Liberdade, 266
1250 Lisbon
Tel: (351 1) 318 7300
Fax: (351 1) 352 3568

**Atalanta Filmes**
Rua Tomás Ribeiro 8, 2º
1050 Lisbon
Tel: (351 1) 353 1585/9
Fax: (351 1) 353 1636

# Useful Addresses

**Cinemateca Portuguesa**
Rua Barata Salgueiro, 39
1250 Lisbon
Tel: (351 1) 354 6279
Fax: (351 1) 352 3180

**IPACA/ICAM – Instituto da Cinema, Audiovisual e Multimedia**
Rua São Pedro de Alcântara, 45-1'
1250 Lisbon
Tel: (351 1) 323 0800
Fax: (351 1) 343 1952

**Media Desk, Portugal**
Rua S. Pedro de Alcântara, 45, 1º

1200 Lisbon
Tel: (351 1) 347 8644
Fax: (351 1) 347 8643

**Radiotelevisao Comercial (RTC)**
Av. Fontes Pereira de Melo, 17-19, 2º-3º
1050 Lisbon
Tel: (351 1) 352 8835
Fax: (351 1) 355 7076

**Radiotelevisao Portuguesa (RTP)**
Av. 5 de Outubro, 197
1094 Lisbon Codex
Tel: (351 1) 757 5070/793 1774
Fax: (351 1) 796 6227

**Sociedade Independente de Comunicaçao (SIC)**
Estrada da Outurela, 119
Linda-A-Velha
2795 Carnaxide
Tel: (351 1) 417 3138/71
Fax: (351 1) 417 3119/20

**Televisão Independente (TVI)**
Rua Mário Castelhano, 40
Queluz de Baixo
2745 Queluz
Tel: (351 1) 435 5181
Fax: (351 1) 435 8747

**Tobis Portuguesa**
Praça Bernardino Machado
1700 Lisbon
Tel: (351 1) 759 5425
Fax: (351 1) 758 9622

# PUERTO RICO
José Artemio Torres

The big news for Puerto Rican film-makers at the moment is not cinema but television. Lower production costs and a large, eager audience have prompted local directors to make TV movies. The trend started with *The Night Toño Bicicleta Appeared* (*La noche que apareció Toño Bicicleta*), a thriller about a local criminal, produced by theatre director Vicente Castro and actor Jorge Luis Ramos. Their XCL-TV production company has been the most prolific, with eight films in 18 months, but their style owes more to the traditional *telenovela* (soap operas) than to cinema.

There was also *Impacto mortal*, a mediocre detective yarn by a group of recently-graduated film students. Their second outing, *Complot*, was a spy saga, and a step up on the technical side, but the improvements could not hide the fact that they were just young people trying to play at James Bond.

*Los Díaz de Doris*, produced and directed by Abdiel Colberg, is the best of the small-screen films. Shot in 16mm and transferred to video, it chronicles with feeling and humour the travails of Doris Díaz, a divorced working mother of two who finally finds true love. Colberg is a veteran director of commercials and drama who a few years ago made *Miracle in Yauco* (*Milagro en Yauco*), one of the first Puerto Rican TV movies.

This trend has given directing opportunities to a group of women. Actress Elia Enid Cadilla made a cross between a mini-series and a *telenovela* with *After the Farewell* (*Después del adiós*). Also completed are *The Kiss* (*El beso*), a romantic suspense drama directed by Sonia Fritz, who has made documentaries and three dramatic shorts, and the comedy about bigamy, *'What if Cristobal awakens?'* (*¿Y si Cristóbal despierta?*), by newcomer Sonia Valentín, with the help of a Mexican screenwriter, Bernardo Romero, and star, Angélica Aragón.

Most of these films are shot on video or 16mm, and are funded in several ways: by the government, through the Film Commission and the Labour Department (which pays half the salaries of cast and crew); through product placements and through payments by the TV stations.

## Crash landings

In contrast to the small screen activity, only one Puerto Rican feature film premiered in the fiscal year 1999-2000. **Flight of Fancy**, about a boy who befriends an American pilot (Dean Cain) after he crashes his biplane in a mountain town, collected mixed reviews and did not fare well at the box-office, maybe because of its lack of cultural identity. The film was shot in English with a largely Hispanic cast, but there is no real sense of Puerto Rican time and place to the story; everything revolves

*Director Abdiel Colberg, centre, on the set of LOS DÍAZ DE DORIS*

around the three principal characters, with the locals a mere backdrop.

*Flight of Fancy* was financed in part by the Puerto Rico Investors' Tax Credit Enhanced Film Fund (PRITCEFFF), which took a beating with the failure of *The Dream Team*. This television series, a mix of *Charlie's Angels* and *Mission:Impossible*, was pulled after two episodes, leaving a long list of creditors. An auction of the series' assets was held in Los Angeles under the auspices of the Screen Actors' Guild and PRITCEFFF in an attempt to recover some of the losses.

Production finance has become scarce because of the failure of productions backed by the film funds in recent years. Banco Popular, the biggest player, has closed its Motion Pictures and Allied Services Department. This development, and dissatisfaction with the tax credits offered by a new film law, prompted the Puerto Rican Producers Association to propose that the government established a $15m fund exclusively for local feature production, with the money to come from individuals' and corporations' tax contributions. A new bill was drafted, public meetings were held and the hope must be that after elections in November, 2000, the new administration which takes office in January 2001 will mark a new beginning for Puerto Rican film-makers.

JOSÉ ARTEMIO TORRES is a film-maker and writer. He heads La Linterna Mágica, a film and video production and distribution company, and is also Executive Director of the San Juan Cinemafest.

# Forthcoming Films

**EL BESO (The Kiss)**
Script: Eliseo Alberto, based on a novel by Stella Soto. Dir: Sonia Fritz. Phot: Agustín Cubano. Players: Maricarmen Avils, Jimmy Navarro, Carola García, René Monclova. Prod: Producciones Nuevo Siglo, S. E. 2000.

Romance and suspense mix in the story of a TV reporter whose son is kidnapped by her husband.

**¿Y SI CRISTÓBAL DESPIERTA? (What if Cristobal awakens?)**
Script: Bernado Romero, Juan Camilo Jaramillo. Dir: Sonia Valentín. Phot: Carlos Marrero. Players: Angélica Aragón, Alba Nydia Díaz, Sonia Valentín, Braulio Castillo, hijo. Prod: Producciones COPELAR.

Comedy in which the title character suffers a heart attack. While he lies unconscious his three wives decide what to do with him.

# Producers

**A.C. Produccioines**
Estancias Reales
83 Príncipe Guillermo St
Guaynabo
Puerto Rico 00969
Tel. (1 787) 287 1073

**Tropical Visions Entertainment Group**
954 Ponce de León Ave.
Suite 208
San Juan
Puerto Rico 00907
Tel. (1 787) 725 3565
Fax: (1 787) 724 4333
e-mail: tvegsjpr@prtc.net

**XCL-TV**
709 Unión Street
Suite 501
San Juan
Puerto Rico 00907
Tel/Fax: (1 787) 725 8956

# Distributors

**Premiere Films**
PO Box 8598
San Juan
Puerto Rico 00910-8598
Tel: (1 787) 724 0762
Fax: (1 787) 723 4562
e-mail: premiere@caribe.net

**La Linterna Mágica, Inc.**
667 Ponce de León Ave.
Box 132
San Juan
Puerto Rico 00907
Tel: (1 787) 723 2362
Fax: (1 787) 723 6412
e-mail: llmagica@tld.net

# Useful Addresses

**Corporación para el Desarrollo del Cine en Puerto Rico** [film commission]
PO Box 2350
San Juan
Puerto Rico 00936-2350
Tel: (1 787) 754 7110
Fax: (1 787) 756 5806

**Asociación de Productores** [producers' association]
PO Box 190399
San Juan
Puerto Rico 00919-0399
Tel: (1 787) 764 1589
Fax: (1 787) 764 1204

**Archivo de Imàgenes en Movimiento** [film archive]
Archivo General de Puerto Rico
PO Box 4184
San Juan
Puerto Rico 00902
Tel. (1 787) 722 2113/0331
Fax: (1 787) 722 9097

**Puerto Rico Investors' Tax Credit Enhanced Film Fund**
Banco Popular Center
Suite 1414
San Juan
Puerto Rico 00917
Tel. (1 787) 759 8080
Fax: ( 787) 753 75 10

**Muvi Films** [film fund]
El Caribe Building
Suite 1103
53 Palmeras Street
San Juan
Puerto Rico 00901-2415
Tel: (1 787) 729 9180
Fax: (1 787) 729 9183

**San Juan Cinemafest**
PO Box 9020079
San Juan
Puerto Rico 00902
Tel (1 787) 721 6125
Fax: (1 787) 722 4187
November 2001

**Puerto Rico International Film Festival**
Calle Mayagüez 17
Suite B-1
San Juan
Puerto Rico 00918
Tel: (1 787) 763 4997
Fax: (1 787) 753 5367
Director: Juan Gerard González
February 2001

# ROMANIA

Cristina
Corciovescu

The long-awaited revival of the Romanian film industry still seems a long way off, and expectations concerning the new law which reorganised state film finance are proving to have been unrealistically optimistic. In 1999, only two Romanian movies were launched: *The Famous Paparazzo*, a tale of political sleaze, directed by Nicolae Margineanu, and Sergiu Nicolaescu's First World War drama *Deadly Triangle*; both were moderately successful. Another 11 titles are in various stages of production, but the myriad financial problems they face mean it is impossible to say when they will be completed and released.

The new director of the National Film Office, Stere Gulea, is calling for the film law to be amended, and there is talk of bringing the cinema industry back under the Ministry of Culture's jurisdiction, where it logically belongs. While the state-funded cinema is in trouble, however, Romania's private studios remain very active. Filmex, the first private studio established in this country after the 1989 revolution, co-produced (with France's MK2) Michael Haneke's *Unknown Code* (*Code Inconnu*). One of the drama's main characters is a peasant woman from northern Romania, who has ended up as a beggar in the streets of Paris.

Castel Film, established in 1992, has become the largest full-service private film studio in Romania, with four well-equipped sound stages, able to accommodate between 10 and 15 features a year. In the spring of 2000, Castel finished work on the $20m English-language *Vlad the Impaler* (*Vlad Tepes*). Directed by Joel Chapelle, this is an epic depiction (5,000 extras) of the life of Romania's notorious fifteenth-century ruler, whose name is closely connected to the Dracula legend.

While Castel Film mainly works with US studios such as Paramount and Miramax, Atlantis Film makes movies in collaboration with French companies: full-length features for the M6 television channel (four in 1999) and for the large screen. In May 2000, Atlantis finished shooting *Crazy and Co.* (*Les Percutées*), directed by Gérard Cuq, a tragi-comic thriller about an accidental hold-up whose perpetrators end up in an asylum.

Even though many of these films will not be released in Romanian cinemas, they are vitally important to the local industry, providing work for technicians and crafts-people and ensuring the survival of a broad skills base. It is good to see that the abilities of men such as cinematographers Vlad Paunescu (Castel Film) and Ion Marinescu (Atlantis Film), and director Constantin Popescu (Filmex) are in demand on international productions.

Romania is also faced by an alarming decrease in cinema attendance, as many people struggle to afford nights out at the movies. The cinemas are still administered

*Still from* VLAD THE IMPALER

by the state, but discussion has recently begun about privatising them, not least because Bucharest's old theatres must now compete with Romania's first multiplex, which opened in summer 2000. This 10-screen venue, in the middle of Bucharest's first shopping mall, is run by InterCom, a Hungarian firm which through its recent merger with Guild Film Romania has become one of the country's leading distributors.

All those involved in distribution and

exhibition expect great things from this multiplex as a first step to luring people away from their televisions and back to the big screen. However, let us not forget that 2000 is the year of local, parliamentary and presidential elections in Romania; broadcast on all the TV channels, these offers audiences a 'show' just as entertaining as many feature films.

CRISTINA CORCIOVESCU is a film critic and author of several cinema dictionaries.

# Forthcoming Films

**IN FIECARE ZI DUMNEZEU NE SARUTA PE GURA (Every Day God Kisses Us on the Mouth)**

Script and Dir: Sinisa Dragin. Players: Dan Condurache, Ana Ciontea.

Released after ten years in prison for murder, Dumitru kills again, repeatedly and with impunity. He wants to die, but cannot, and realises that God has plans for him.

**MARFA SI BANII (Stuff & Dough)**

Dir: Cristi Puiu.

A young man is paid a large sum of money to take a small consignment of medicine from a provincial town to Bucharest, but he is pursued by violent assailants, proving that the package is not what it seems to be.

**MANIPULAREA (The Manipulation)**

Script: Mihai Creanga. Dir: Nicolae Opritescu. Players: Florin Zamfirescu, Ilinca Goia, Ion Haiduc, Dorel Visan, Dan Condurache.

After the December 1989 Revolution, a French woman comes to Timisoara, the town where the uprising started, to

investigate the circumstances of her journalist friend's death during those troubled days.

**TAXI CONTRA LIMUZINA (Taxi vs. Limo)**

Script and Dir: Titus Muntean. Players: Gheorghe Dinica, Marcel Iures, Marius Stanescu,

Ioana Macarie.

Bucharest, 1977. An 18-year old provincial girl is murdered, and parts of her body are scattered in public toilets. A taxi driver is wrongfully gaoled for the crime but after three years in prison he is released when the real murderer is caught. Finding reintegration into society impossible, he resolves to seek out the truth behind his imprisonment.

*Still from the comedy-thriller, CRAZY AND CO.*

# Producers

**Atlantis Film**
Str. Vasile Gherghel nr. 90
Bucharest
Tel/Fax: (401) 230 5644

**Castel Film**
Str. Episcop Timus nr. 25
Sector 1
Bucharest
Tel: (401) 231 5532/33
Fax: (401) 231 5531
e-mail: mailto:castel@dial.roknet.ro

**Domino Film**
Str. Dr. Felix nr. 59, et. 1
Sector 1
Bucharest
Tel: (401) 210 3713/223 4669
Fax: (401) 312 9609
e-mail: dominofilm@xnet.ro

**Filmex**
Str. Pictor Verona nr. 2
Sector 1
Bucharest
Tel: (401) 615 8913/615 9038
Fax: (401) 312 1388

**SC. Rofilm SA**
Bd. M. Kogalniceanu nr. 11
Sector 5
Bucharest
Tel: (401) 311 2710
Fax: (401) 311 3080

# Distributors

**Glob Com Media**
Str. Brezoianu nr. 57A, et. 2
Sector 1
Bucharest
Tel: (401) 315 4707
Fax: (401) 315 4506
e-mail: globcom@fx.ro

**InterComFilm**
Str. Arcului nr. 14A, et.1, ap.7
Sector 2
Bucharest 70221
e-mail: gfrm@dial.kappa.ro

**Independenta Film**
Str. Vasile Lascar nr. 35, ap.3
Sector 2
Bucharest
Tel/Fax: (401) 211 1126
e-mail: indep@opensys.ro

**RolMAGE 2000**
Sos. Mihai Bravu nr. 85093
bl. C16, sc. C, ap. 8
sector 2
Bucharest
Tel: (401) 252 6066
Tel/Fax: (401) 252 7661
e-mail: roimage@pcnet.ro

**Vision PM**
Sos. Cotroceni nr. 7-9
Bucharest
Tel: (401) 638 4045
Fax: (401) 222 1551

# Useful Addresses

**Oficiul National al
Cinematografiei**
Str. Dem I. Dobrescu nr. 4-6
Bucharest
Tel: (401) 310 4301
Fax: (401) 310 4300

**Romania Film**
Str. Thomas Massaryk nr. 25
Bucharest 70231
Tel: (401) 210 7398 / 7835
Fax: (401) 611 7660

**Uniunea Cineastilor**
Str. Mendeleev nr. 28-30
Sector 1
Bucharest 70169
Tel: (401) 650 4265
Fax (401) 311 1246

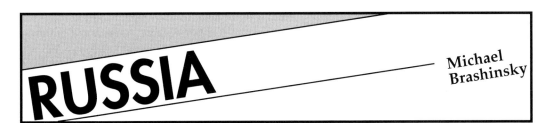

# RUSSIA — Michael Brashinsky

In 1999, Goskino, the Russian Ministry of Film, completed its three-year economic development programme. Then, in May 2000, the ministry was abruptly abolished by newly-elected president Vladimir Putin and its functions transferred to the Ministry of Culture. In a business so heavily dependent on state support, the move was met with a wave of protest and self-pity. Film-makers feared that federal funding would decrease even further. But they failed to recognise that this change may signal the beginning of a new era, and should be welcomed. In August 1998, the economic collapse had dramatically altered the new Russian cinema's upward progress. Now, the post-crisis stage could begin, the stage of new solitude and responsibility.

The preceding year had brought nothing but decline and stagnation, with extremely low production output and even lower morale. According to Goskino statistics, printed by the leading trade bulletin *Kinoprotsess*, only 17 state-supported features were released in 1999. In total, only 37 features were registered for theatrical distribution. The state boasted that it fulfilled its financial obligations, without pointing out that these obligations consisted of just under $250,000 for the whole industry. Many productions, stalled in 1998, were simply abandoned in 1999. The rest remained without much hope of reaching the screen.

But by summer 2000, it was obvious that the paralysing effects of the crisis were waning. Something began to shift. One industry branch that paradoxically never slowed down during the crisis, was exhibition: by mid-2000, Russia had 60-plus cinemas equipped with up-to-date projection and Dolby Stereo. This promised encouraging prospects to the fledging film-makers who suddenly turned out to be all young and ready to work, although we will have to wait for their films.

## A shocking showcase

The quality of the majority of the year's output, showcased in June 2000 at the annual Kinotaur National Film Festival in Sochi, was quite appalling. The air of bewilderment at the rollercoaster of social change that made the bad Russian films of the 1990s at least somewhat appealing, had gone. What remained was an air of helpless narcissism that united the vets with their nominal and actual children.

Oscar-winner Vladimir Menshov (*Moscow Does Not Believe in Tears*), now in his sixties, showed **Gods' Envy** (*Zavist bogov*), an inept, thoroughly fake melodrama about the love affair between a Russian woman and a French man. The young were not much livelier. Yegor Konchalovsky, son of Hollywood-based director Andrei Konchalovsky, made **The Recluse** (*Zatvornik*), a ludicrous, identical-twins thriller that tried too hard to put on a Brian De Palma smirk. Ilya Khotinenko, the son of a well-established director, Vladimir Khotinenko, produced a "Russian-soul" comedy, **A Person of French Descent** (*Litso frantsuzskoi natsionalnosti*), that made one blush for the makers much more often than smile.

The eagerly-anticipated thriller **The Fan** (*Poklonnik*), by sophomore director Nikolai Lebedev, proved that the expectations aroused by his debut, *The Snake Spring*, two years ago may have been greatly exaggerated. All these jumbled efforts made only one thing clear: their makers had nothing to say and did not even know how to say it.

It was not entirely their fault. All

*Still from Vladimir Menshov's GOD'S ENVY*

cinematic attempts to capture contemporary Russian reality were doomed from the outset. The reality remained too fluid and shapeless to offer itself to film. Its meanings continued to slip away from the camera. Film-makers sensed that, and very few of them dared to face the situation directly.

The brightest was Vassily Pichul, the talented maker of *Little Vera* (1988) who has finally completed the long-awaited **The Sky of Diamonds** (*Nebo v almazakh*). Within a loose, criminal narrative framework, he attempted a grotesque vision of the new Russia as a mix of the unmixable. The result was a deliberately chaotic and crazy film that had to sacrifice depth and structure to stay true to life.

## The Soviet revival

Other film-makers, sensing life's unfriendliness to the camera, looked for detours. One was found in simply retreating from the "new Russian" into the safety of the "Soviet". During the past decade Russians have learned to long for the old regime as for a firm but fair parent who took away all the pain of responsibility for making choices. The most vivid example of this approach was Valery Ogorodnikov's **The Ward** (*Barak*) that justly compared Soviet life to living in a "communal" apartment, or a ward, but made no conclusions, except that people remain people wherever they are. This conservative picture, both aesthetically and ideologically, received the second prize at Locarno.

Even more spectacularly than by dealing with the times past, the "Soviet" quality presented itself in dealing with the times present. Eldar Ryazanov, the mammoth of Soviet comic melodrama, made a frenzied satire, **Old Nags** (*Starye klyachi*). Georgy Danelia, the mammoth of Soviet romantic comedy, made a *L'Atalante*-esque fairy tale, **Fortune** (*Fortuna*). And Yevgeny Matveev, mammoth of the Soviet social drama, made a typical Soviet social drama, **To Love, the Russian Way 3** (*Lyubit' po-russski-3*). All three films by these veteran directors were different in their degrees of failure, but exactly the same in the way they applied the 1970s Soviet film language to the present. The age of the film-makers was not the only reason for this; the new Russian cinema has yet to come up with a language to describe post-Soviet reality. All it had was the Soviet one.

## Men with guns

Another distraction from bumping head-first into unshaped reality was to use a genre, the thriller, as protective gear. Many of the year's productions, including **24 Hours** (*24 chasa*), **The Good and the Bad** (*Khoroshiye i plokhiye*), **The Cheque** (*Chek*) and **Fourteen Colours of Rainbow** (*Chetyrnadtsat tsvetov radugi*), all featured multiple gunplay, lots of bullet-ridden Mercedes and romantic killers, trying to cope with the new "one-against-all" scenario. The criminal context, indeed, remained urgent in Russia. What for Americans is pulp fiction, for Russians is still everyday life. The films, however, looked unconvincing, as they attempted to recreate one reality by borrowing clichés from another. Russia in them looked vaguely foreign, but really, faceless.

The only success here was the prolific Alexei Balabanov's **The Brother 2** (*Brat-2*), the sequel to his 1997 hit *The Brother*. Balabanov made a witty choice that saved his film from feeling second-hand: in order to avoid borrowing from the American movies he sent his hero to America. The simplistic though energetic film, featuring the new star Sergei Bodrov Jr. (*Prisoner of the Mountains*) and a soundtrack featuring virtually every popular Russian band of the moment, was made to succeed with the audiences, and did so.

*The Brother 2*, produced by the leading St. Petersburg independent film company STV, made one thing clear: the Russian independents have started to shift from arthouse and festival fare towards the commercial mainstream. This was also true for NTV-Profit, the country's leading producer. Aside from supplying seven features to Kinotaur (twice as many as any other studio) it has a number of low- and medium-budget genre films in production to support its claim to populism.

## Not Russian enough?

Despite the year's poor output, a small number of productions represented Russia internationally to considerable success. In Venice 1999, it was Bakhtier Khudoinazarov's *Luna Papa* (*Lunnyi papa*), in Cannes 2000, Pavel Loungine's *The Wedding* (*Svadba/La noce*), and in Karlovy Vary, Alexei Uchitel's *His Wife's Diary* (*Dnevnik ego zheny*). At Kinotaur, *Luna Papa* took the first prize, and *His Wife's Diary* the second.

The striking similarity between these unlikely neighbours was in how "un-Russian" they were. **The Wedding** was purely a French production, though done by a Russian-born director in Russia. **Luna Papa** was a German-Austrian-Swiss co-production (with the participation of NTV-Profit), directed from a Georgian script about Uzbeks by a Tadjik director, based in Germany.

**His Wife's Diary**, though financed locally, was about the "French period" in the life of Ivan Bunin, the first Russian Nobel laureate in literature. But these (location and finance) were just signs of the deeper qualities. The "un-Russianness" of these films showed in how little they were concerned with the local context and how much with the global one. Luna Papa, like *The Wedding*, exploited the trendy (thanks to Kusturica and the Iranians) aesthetic of the "new provincialism", that blended two extremely marketable commodities: ethnic exoticism and "magic realism".

*His Wife's Diary* was more complex. It presented an explosive web of relationships (Bunin at one stage shared a house with his wife, his lover and her lesbian girlfriend) without ever betraying its clarity of vision and subtlety of the tone. Like the best European productions of the year, it was a substantially post-postmodern film – not only deliberately old-fashioned, but also telling a story after the end of History, when all that is left is relationships and, therefore, stories. So it

was proven, once again, that Russia can be quite modern in the most uncompromising international context. All she has to do is stop feeling sorry for herself and start feeling like a citizen of the world.

MICHAEL BRASHINSKY is a columnist for *Afisha* magazine in Moscow. He is co-author of *The Zero Hour: Glasnost and Soviet Cinema in Transition*, and co-editor of *Russian Critics on the Cinema of Glasnost* (both with Andrew Horton). He divides his time between St. Petersburg, Moscow and New York.

# Recent and Forthcoming Films

**24 CHASA (24 Hours)**

Script: Natalya Koretskaya. Dir: Alexander Atanesian. Phot: Alexei Rodionov, Masha Solovyova. Players: Maxim Sukhanov, Andrei Panin, Sergei Novikov, Mikhail Kozakov, Igor Starygin. Prod: NTV-Profit/ Media-Park.

**BARAK (The Ward)**

Script and Dir: Valery Ogorodnikov. Phot: Yuri Klimenko. Players: Yevgeny Sidikhin, Yulia Svezhakova, Irina Senotova, Leonid Yarmolnik, Nina Usatova, Alexei Devotchenko. Prod: Lenfilm.

**BRAT-2 (The Brother 2)**

Script and Dir: Alexei Balabanov. Phot: Sergei Astakhov. Players: Sergei Bodrov, Jr., Victor Sukhorukov, Sergei Makovetsky, Irina Saltykova, Konstantin Pirogov, Konstantin Murzenko. Prod: STV/RTR.

**CHEK (The Cheque)**

Script and Dir: Boris Giller, Alexander Borodyansky. Phot: Pavel Lebeshev. Players: Alexei Makarov, Yerzhan Berkimbayev, Alexandra Tverdohlib, Nikolai Rastorguyev, Nikolai Fomenko, Yuliya Rutberg. Prod: BAG/ Courrier.

**CHETYRNADTSAT TSVETOV RADUGI (Fourteen Colours of the Rainbow)**

Script: Igor Ageev, Dmitry Svetozarov. Dir: Svetozarov. Phot: Alexander Ustinov. Players: Sergei Bekhterev, Igor Lifanov, Svetlana Smirnova. Prod: Pan-Terra.

**DMB (Draftees)**

Script: Ivan Okhlobystin, Roman Kachanov. Dir: Kachanov. Phot: Anatoly Susekov. Players: Petr Korshunkov, Mikhail Petrovsky, Stanislav Duzhnikov, Sergei Artsybashev, Victor Pavlov, Alexander Belyavsky, Yuozas Budraitis, Vladimir Shainsky. Prod: Poligon/Soyuz-video.

**MYSTERII (Mysteries)**

Script: Mikhail Kalatozishvili, Roustam Ibragimbekov. Dir: Kalatozishvili. Phot: Archil Akhvlediani. Players: Tolstyi, Nodar Kalanadze, Zurab Kipshidzee, Nato Murvanidze, Felix Kogan, Alexander Bolshakov. Prod: Lenfilm/ Barmaley/Goskino.

**NEBO V ALMAZAKH (The Sky of Diamonds)**

Script: Maria Khmelik. Dir: Vassily Pichul. Players: Nikolai Fomenko, Angelika Varum, Alla

Sigalova, Valentin Gaft, Anna Mikhalkova. Prod: Soyuzkino/ InterCinema/Parnasse Internation (France).

**POKLONNIK (The Fan)**

Script: Nikolai Lebedev, Olga Nagdaseva. Dir: Lebedev. Phot: Sergei Machilsky. Players: Marina Cherepukhina, Yelena Safonova, Rergei Garmash, Nina Usatova, Boris Shcherbakov, Yekaterina Durova, Svetlana Toma. Prod: NTV-Profit/Rekun-Film.

**RANGER IZ ATOMNOI ZONY (Ranger from the Atomic Zone)**

Script: Valentin Chernykh. Dir: Vyacheslav Nikiforov. Phot: Players: Alexei Kravchenko, Vladimir Samoilov, Tatyana Mescherkina. Prod: Slovo.

**STARYE KLYACHI (Old Nags)**

Script: Vladimir Moiseenko, Yuri Fedorov, Eldar Ryazanov. Dir: Ryazanov. Phot: Players: Lyudmila Gurchenko, Svetlana Kryuchkova, Lia Akhedjakova, Irina Kupchenko, Nikolai Fomenko, Valentin Gaft. Prod: Kinomost/Luch.

**SVADBA (The Wedding)**

Script: Pavel Loungin, Alexander

Galin. Dir: Loungin. Phot: Alexander Burov. Players: Marat Basharov, Maria Mironova, Maria Golubkina, Andrei Panin, Natalya Kolyakanova, Vladimir Kashpur. Prod: CDP Films (France)/Mosfilm-Service.

### TONKAYA SHTUCHKA (Subtle Thing)

Script: Arkady Inin. Dir: Alexander Polynnikov. Phot: Sergei Lando. Players: Alexandra Zakharova, Igor Bochkin, Dmitry Pevtsov, Nikita Djigurda, Alexei Serebryakov, Ilya Oleinikov. Prod: Miko-Film/Mavr.

### VMESTO MENYA (Instead of Me)

Script: Vladimir Basov, Valery Todorovsky. Dir: Basov, Olga Basova. Phot: Yury Lyubshin. Players: Oleg Strizhenov, Sergei Bezrukov, Irina Apeksimova, Vsevolod Abdulov, Sergei Shkalikov, Alexandra Skachkova. Prod: Akter Kino, Goskino.

### VRATA EVY (Eve's Gates)

Script: Vat Koreshi, Pavel Finn. Dir: Albert Minga. Phot: Vladimir Shevtzik. Players: Magdalena Vuichik, Irina Nizina, Ndrichim Azhepa. Prod: 12a Studio (Albania)/Albanian Radiotelevidenie/Goskino.

### ZATVORNIK (The Recluse)

Script: Maxim Stishov. Dir: Yegor Konchalovsky. Phot: Mikhail Agranovich. Players: Amalia Mordvinova, Alexander Baluyev.

### ZAVIST BOGOV (Gods' Envy)

Script: Marina Mareeva, Vladimir Menshov. Dir: Menshov. Phot: Vadim Alisov. Players: Vera Alentova, Anatoly Lobotsky, Alexander Feklistov, Larisa Udovichenko, Irina Skobtseva, Vladlen Davydov, Gérard Depardieu. Prod: Genre.

### ZHENSHSCHIN OBIZHATI NE REKOMENDUYTESYA (Mistreating Women is Not Recommended)

Script: Valentin Chernykh. Dir: Valery Akhadov. Phot: Valentin Piganov. Players: Vera Glagoleva, Maxim Sukhanov, Valery Garkalin, Alexander Potapov, Alexander Porokhovschikov, Irina Feofanova, Galina Polskikh. Prod: NTV-Profit.

### DNEVIK EGO ZHENY (His Wife's Diary)

Script: Dunya Smirnova. Dir: Alexei Uchitel. Phot: Yuri Klimenko. Players: Andrei Smirnov, Galina Tyunina, Olga Budina, Yelena Morozova, Yevgeny Mironov, Sergei Vinogradov, Tatyana Moskvina, Koni Kogan. Prod: Rock Studio/Lenfilm/AM-Studio (Bulgaria)/Goskino.

### LUNNYI PAPA (Luna Papa)

Script: Irakly Kvirikadze with Bakhtier Khudoinazarov. Dir: Khudoinazarov. Phot: Martin Schlacht, Rostislav Pirumov, Dusan Eksimovich, Raly Ralyshev. Players: Chulpan Khamatova, Moritz Bleibtreu, Ato Mukhamedjanov, Nikolai Fomenko, Merab Ninidze. Prod: Pandora Film (Germany)/Prisma (Austria)/Thomas Koefer Films (Switzerland)/Vvys (Tadjikistan)/NTV-Profit/Eurospace (Japan)/Les Films de L'Observatoire (France).

### LYUBIT PO-RUSSKI – 3. GUBERNATOR (To Love, the Russian Way 3: The Governor)

Script: Valentin Chernykh. Dir: Yevgeny Matveev. Players: Yevgeny Matveev, Galina Polskaya, Nikita Djigurda. Prod: Slovo.

### MOSKVA (Moscow)

Script: Vladimir Sorokin. Dir: Alexander Zeldovich. Players: Tatyana Drubich, Ingeborga Dapkunaite, Natalya Kolyakanova, Alexander Baluyev, Viktor Gvozditsky, Stanislav Pavlov. Prod: Telekino/Goskino.

### MUZHSKOI KHARAKTER, ILI TANGO NAD PROPASTYU – 2 (Male Ego or, Tango Over the Abyss 2)

Script: Igor Talpa, Nikolai Shumeiko. Dir: Talpa. Phot: Yuri Zenin, Vladimir Burlachenko. Players: Yulia Rutberg, Yevgeny Sidikhin, Lev Durov, Timofei Fedorov, Igor Guzun, Vasile Zubku. Prod: Profilm Company/Moldova-Film/Teleraddio-Moldova.

# Useful Addresses

### Afisha Magazine
14/2 Bolshaya Nikitskaya St
Str. 7
Moscow
Tel/Fax: (7 095) 788 0686
[*Time Out*-type publication]

### Cosmopol Film Distribution
Contact: Anton Mazurov
Tel: (7 095) 915 5741
e-mail: mazurov@crosswinds.net

### East-West
[Distributor]
9 Voznesensky Per
Str. 4
Moscow 103009
Tel: (7 095) 229 6991
Fax: (7 095) 200 4249

### Filmmakers' Union
13 Vassilyevskaya St
Moscow 123825
Tel: (7 095) 251 5106

### The Gorky Film Studio
8 Sergei Eisenstein St
Moscow 129226
Tel: (7 095) 181 0434/1418
Fax: (7 095) 188 9871

### Gosfilmofond
[Central film archives]
Belye Stolby
District 6
Moscow 142050
Tel: (7 095) 546 0505/0513
Fax: (7 095) 546 0525

**Goskino**
7 Malyi Gnezdnikovsky per.
Moscow 103877
Tel: (7 095) 229 3704/4522
Fax: (7 095) 229 2248

**Higher Courses of Screenwriters and Directors**
12 Bolshoy
Tishinsky Per
Moscow123557
Tel: (7 095) 253 6488
Fax: (7 095) 253 8709

**Intercinema**
[distribution, production]
15 Druzhinnikovskaya ul.
Moscow 123242
Tel/Fax: (7 095) 255 9052
Contact: Raissa Fomina

**Iskusstvo Kino Film Magazine**
9 Ussievicha St
Moscow 125319
Tel: (7 095) 151 5651
Fax: (7 095) 151 0272
e-mail: kinoart@glasnet.ru

**Kinotaur Film Festival**
[domestic and international]
35 Arbat
Suite 533
Moscow 121835
Tel: (7 095) 248 3498
Fax: (7 095) 248 0966
[Also: Faces of Love Festival; films about love]

**Lenfilm**
[Production, distribution]
10 Kamennoostrovsky Pr.
St. Petersburg 197101
Tel: (812) 232 8359
Fax: (812) 232 8881

**Message To Man**
Tel/Fax: (7 095) 310 9992
[Non-fiction International Film Festival held in St. Petersburg]

**Moscow International Film Festival**
10 Khokhlovski Per.
Str. 1
Moscow 109028
Tel: (7 095) 917 2486
Fax: (7 095) 916 0107

**Mosfilm**
1 Mosfilmovskaya St
Moscow 119858
Tel: (7 095) 143 9100
Fax: (7 095) 143 9290

**Museum of Film**
15 Druzhinnikovskaya St
Moscow 123242
Tel: (7 095) 255 9886/9189
Fax: (7 095) 255 9096

**NTV-Profit**
[Production, distribution]
4 Pereyaslavsky Per.
Moscow 129110
Tel: (7 095) 284 1338
Fax: (7 095) 971 1279

**Premiere Film Magazine**
35 Myasnitskaya St
Suite 742
Moscow 101959
Tel: (7 095) 204 1787
Fax: (7 095) 204 1583.
e-mail: premiere@hfm.ru

**Seance Film Magazine**
10 Kamennoostrovsky Pr.
St. Petersburg 197101
Tel: (7 812) 237 0842
Fax: (7 812) 232 4925
e-mail: seans@peterlink.ru

**Slovo Production Company**
1 Mosfilmovskaya St
Moscow 119858
Tel/Fax: (7 095) 143 4917
e-mail: slovo@cyberax.ru

**STV Studio**
[Production, distribution]
10 Kamennoostrovsky Pr.
St. Petersburg 197101
Tel: (7 812) 326 8330/31

**Tri-T Studio**
11 Maly Kozikhinsky Per.
Moscow 103001
Tel/Fax: (7 095) 299 4068/3102

**VGIK (Film School)**
3 Wilhelm Pik St
Moscow 129226
Tel: (7 095) 181 0605
Fax: (7 095) 187 7174

# SERBIA & MONTENEGRO

Goran
Gočić

NATO's bombing of Yugoslavia left a strong impression on Serbia's film-makers, since almost every film screened at the most recent Belgrade Documentary Festival focused on the dramatic events of March-June 1999, while the Austrian-made documentary on the NATO campaign, **The Punishment**, directed by Goran Rebić, shared the top prize at the documentary festival in Graz.

Several Serbian features deal with the same subject.

Even in these depressing times, when film crews are willing to work for profit-share only, and producers cannot rely on state subsidies, small, private companies in Belgrade somehow find strength, inspiration and, miraculously, money, to make interesting films. Serbian cinema is actually flourishing, and admissions were up in 1999.

One of these Belgrade companies, Sinema Dizajn, produced two of the year's four new features: *Wheels* (*Toćkovi*) and *Sky Hook* (*Nebeska udica*). Sinema Dizajn is owned by actor Ljubiša Samardžić, who is fondly remembered for, amongst other lively portrayals, his performance in Puriša Djordjević's *Morning*, which earned him the Best Actor award at Venice in 1967.

He made his directorial debut at 63 with the enjoyable **Sky Hook**. The only two things that Serbs remain good at are cinema and basketball and *Sky Hook*'s screenwriters Srdjan Koljević and Djordje Milosavljević combine the two in a story of boys from the Belgrade 'hood who clear bombed-out basketball courts and spitefully pursue their hoop dreams in the midst of the NATO air raids. This small film strikes all the right emotional and political chords and was premiered in the official programme at Berlin 2000.

In **Wheels**, Samardžić stuck to acting, while Milosavljević made his debut as a director, as well as supplying a dark screenplay set on one day at a roadhouse bar, where a newly-arrived stranger is instantly suspected of a series of murders. *Wheels* is an adequate attempt at a Tarantino-style thriller, still a virtually non-existent genre in Serbian cinema. Milosavljević was already shooting his second feature in summer 2000, *The Mechanism* (*Mehanizam*), from a script by the prolific Gordan Mihić, whose daughter, actress Ivana Mihić, is the film's star and producer.

## The man in *The White Suit*

Lazar Ristovski, best known internationally for his high-powered performance as Blacky in Emir Kusturica's award-winning *Underground*, wrote, directed, produced and took two starring roles in **The White Suit** (*Belo odelo*) and even put his own money into it, with British Screen helping

*The defiant basketball team in SKY HOOK*

to complete the $1.8m budget, a decent sum for a Serbian film.

Ristovski applies a distinctively Eastern European, slightly surreal touch to this Balkan tale of a grieving officer who encounters fatal Russian hookers, over-worked blue-collar employees, gross drunkards, professional bridegrooms and underwater striptease – all on the same train trip. Ristovski should perhaps have let somebody else write the film, because his screenplay – a collection of running, mostly banal gags – is the weakest point. However, *The White Suit* broke into the box-office top ten.

After a lot of hesitation and re-editing, Želimir Žilnik's **Where is this Ship Going?** (*Kud Plovi Ovaj Brod*) was finally released, and the result is a confused picture which falls short in comparison to the justly famous wit and political edge of his earlier works. Like some of these, the whole of *Where is this Ship Going?* relies heavily on the charisma of its protagonist. This time, with the aged Giuzeppe Pastorchich revisiting the states of the former Austro-Hungarian Empire, and his memories, the formula just did not work.

**Family Treasure** (*Porodicno blago*), a spin-off sequel from the popular TV series of the same name, in which a suitcase full of money unexpectedly changes hands – and destinies – passed the magic 300,000 admissions mark. Directed by Miroslav Lekić, **Dagger** (*Noz*) was seen by more than half a million people in 1999, and the audiences' favourite was also probably the best film of the season. *Dagger* is a belated adaptation of Vuk Drašković's best-selling novel of the same title, depicting the futile animosities between Serbs and Muslims in Bosnia-Herzegovina from the Second World War onwards. A baby boy is spared when Muslims kill a Serbian family during the Second World War. When the Serb Army comes for revenge, they recover the wrong boy, so both boys grow up paying a heavy price for their nationalist illusions. They discover their mistaken identities only when it is too late.

*Lazar Ristovski, director and star of THE WHITE SUIT*

One of the most harrowing measures introduced by Serbia, a country crippled by a decade-long economic blockade, has been the similar blockade it imposed against Montenegro, so the recent wartime drama from Montenegro, **In the Name of the Father and the Son** (*U ime oca i sina*), could be seen at festivals, but not on commercial release at Serbian cinemas. On the other hand, after an almost two-year delay, Goran Paskaljević's *The Powder Keg* has been distributed in Croatia; *Sky Hook* has been released in Slovenia and a selection of recent Croatian films have been premiered in Belgrade. Could these developments signal the beginning of a beautiful Balkan friendship?

GORAN GOCIĆ is a freelance journalist who contributes to various publications in Yugoslavia and abroad. He is the author of a monograph, *Andy Warhol and Strategies of Pop*, and his monograph on Emir Kusturica is scheduled for publication in 2001.

# Recent and Forthcoming Films

### DORĆOL-MENHETN (Dorcol-Manhattan)

Script and Dir: Isidora Bjelica. Phot: Milorad Glušica. Players: Katarina Žutic, Gru. Prod: Paj-kitsch & Son (Belgrade).

### MEHANIZAM (The Mechanism)

Script: Gordan Mihić. Dir: Djordje Milosavljević. Players: Ivana Mihič, Nikola Kojo. Prod: Horizont 2000 (Belgrade).

### NEBESKA UDICA (Sky Hook)

Script: Djordje Milosavljević, Srdjan Koljević. Dir: Ljubiša Samardzić. Phot: Radoslav Vladić. Players: Nebojsa Glogovac, Ana Sofrenović. Prod: Sinema Dizajn (Belgrade)/Cine Enterprise Viareggio (Italy).

### PORODICNO BLAGO (Family Treasure)

Script: Siniša and Ljiljana Pavić. Dir: Aleksandar Djordjević, Misa Vukobratović. Players: Nebojsa Glogovac, Bata Živojinović. Prod: Komuna (Belgrade).

### RANJENA ZEMLJA (Wounded Land)

Script: Gordan Mihić. Dir: Dragoslav Lazić. Phot: Zoran Jovanović. Players: Vera Čukić, Petar Kralj. Prod: Studio Čaplin (Belgrade).

### RAT UŽIVO (The War – Live)

Script: Stevan Koprivica, Igor Bojović. Dir: Darko Bajić. Players: Dragan Bjelogrlić, Dubravka Mijatović. Prod: Cobra Film (Belgrade).

### TT SINDROM (TT Syndrome)

Script and Dir: Dejan Zecević. Phot: Vlada Obradović. Players: Nebojsa Glogovac, Sonja Damjanović.

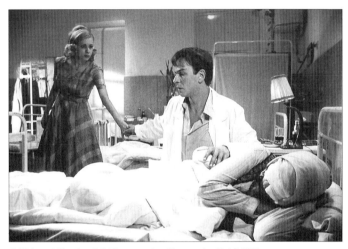

*Still from Miroslav Lekić's exceptionally popular DAGGER*

# Producers

**Sinema Dizajn**
Ustanicka 125/1
11000 Beograd
Tel: (381 11) 488 2377
Fax: (381 11) 488 8011

**Monte Royal Pictures**
Skerliceva 30
11000 Beograd
Tel: (381 11) 431 726
Fax: (381 11) 444 1951

**VANS**
(also distributor)
Njegoseva 84
11000 Beograd
Tel: (381 11) 432 492
Fax: (381 11) 434 226

**Metrofilm International**
(also distributor)
Trg Nikole Pasica 8
11000 Beograd
Tel: (381 11) 334 0318
Fax: (381 11) 323 5221

# Distributors

**First Production**
Kumodraska 176/6
11000 Beograd
Tel: (381 11) 471 403
Fax: (381 11) 473 207

**Tuck**
Velikomoravska 11-15
11000 Beograd
Tel: (381 11) 42 46
Fax: (381 11) 41 31 77

# Useful Address

**Yugoslav Film Institute**
Cika Ljubina 15
11000 Beograd
Tel: (381 11) 625 131
Fax: (381 11) 634 253

# SINGAPORE

Yvonne Ng

The past few years have seen distributors and exhibitors in Singapore operating under a cloud of gloom, as cinema attendance has continued to fall steadily. The main culprit has been the widespread Video CD (VCD) piracy which Singapore's exhibitors claim cuts box-office profits by 25-30%. Other factors include competition from newer leisure options such as the internet.

To bring back viewers, new multiplexes have been built, with state-of-the-art projection technology and plush interiors, while older cinemas are being upgraded (there are now more than 180 screens on the island). In a move to check costs and consolidate resources, Golden Village Pictures and Warner Bros announced a merger in December 1999 to form Warner-Golden Village, the city's largest distributor.

The pace of local production has also slowed. Instead of the dozen features expected in 1999, only eight materialised. Among them were **The Truth about Jane and Sam**, written and directed by Hong Kong's Derek Yee. A co-production between Singapore's Raintree Pictures and Yee's Film Unlimited, the film stars Fann Wong, a popular Singapore TV actress, and Taiwanese singer Peter Ho in a story focusing on the romance between two mismatched characters whose relationship is put to the test by their contrasting backgrounds and parental objections. Solid performances and witty dialogue are marred by sentimentality, but this $800,000 production still took a relatively decent $1.06 million.

Locally produced by Act Venture, the $1m **Street Angels** is another feature by a Hong Kong director, David Lam. The story revolves around five teenage girls from dysfunctional families, one played by Hong Kong's Grace Ip, the other four by Singapore actresses: Melody Chen, Justine Liow, Sherlin Ho and Rosalind Pho. Although the film makes a laudable attempt to address the problem of teenage female delinquency, its plot weakens in the second half. *Street Angels* managed only $100,000 in ticket sales.

## Coming up for *Air*

First-time directors Kelvin Tong, a local film critic, and Jasmine Ng, a film editor, declined the Singapore Film Commission's offer of an investment loan after they found private funding for their first feature, **Eating Air** (*Chi Feng*). This follows the exploits of a group of teenage motorbike fans and blends drama, romance, comedy and tragedy. There were natural performances by the cast of young first-timers, who were recruited off the street. The dialogue is mostly in Hokkien, with a mix of Mandarin, English and Malay and the soundtrack combines electronic scores, punk and industrial rock as well as ballads, in a fusion of languages and dialects.

*Eating Air* was produced by Ng's Multi-Story Complex for $800,000 but recouped only $350,000. Nevertheless, it looks set for a healthy life on the festival circuit after being nominated for the Tiger Award at the Rotterdam Film Festival in January 2000. It was also shown at the Hong Kong Festival and won the Singapore Film Commission Young Cinema Award at the 13th Singapore International Film Festival (SIFF).

The first local movie of the new century was **2000 AD**, a co-production between

Raintree Pictures and Hong Kong's Media Asia Films. Directed by Hong Kong's Gordon Chan, the $6.3m action thriller features computer-generated effects and a mixed cast from Hong Kong, Taiwan and Singapore, with star power provided by Hong Kong's Aaron Kwok. Unfortunately, the plot – capitalising on fears surrounding the over-hyped Y2K bug – was dated by the time the film opened on the island in February, and it took just $900,000.

## A digital dawn

Increasingly, Singapore film-makers are countering rising production costs and declining ticket sales by switching to digital video. This economical medium enabled a group of students at the National University of Singapore to make a feature-length comedy about hostel life for just $18,000. Scripted and directed by 26-year-old Mano Ramakrishnan, **Stamford Hall** may eventually enjoy a commercial release.

*Still from STORIES ABOUT LOVE*

Singapore's most renowned auteur, Eric Khoo, has also gone digital. **Stories about Love**, produced by Khoo's Zhao Wei Films, comprises three episodes, each written and directed by a different film-maker: *The Music Teacher*, by James Toh, tells the story of a beautiful, thirtysomething violinist who becomes attracted to a 17-year-old boy; *Haura*, by Abdul Nizam, is about a young woman looking for true love; *Click*, by Cheah Chee Kong (also known as CheeK) portrays a drab computer worker who dreams of becoming the most successful 'technopreneur' in Singapore. Made for under $300,000, *Stories about Love* is financed by Geoffrey Malone, founder of the SIFF, and hotelier Andrew Yap.

In another low-budget digital effort, writer-director Ong Lay Jinn has revived the immensely popular Malay *pontianak* (female vampire) genre of the 1950s and 1960s. Made for $180,000 by Vacant Films, his 'horror-misadventure', **Return to Pontianak**, features a group of city dwellers who venture into the jungle in search of a lost Malay village. The film stars Vietnamese actress Hiep Thi Le, star of Oliver Stone's *Heaven and Earth* (1993), but most of the cast are non-professionals.

YVONNE NG was born in Singapore and graduated in film studies from the University of Waterloo, Ontario. She has written on Asian cinema and is on the editorial board of *KINEMA* (published at the University of Waterloo). She is the co-author of *Latent Images: Film in Singapore* (Oxford University Press, Singapore).

# Recent and Forthcoming Films

**GONGYUAN 2000 NIAN (2000 AD)**

Script and Dir: Gordon Chan (from an original English screenplay by Stu Zicherman). Players: Aaron Kwok, Phyllis Quek, James Lye, Damiel Wu. Prod: Media Asia Films Ltd/ Raintree Pictures.

**CHI FENG (Eating Air)**

Script and Dir: Kelvin Tong,

Jasmine Ng. Phot: Lucas Jodogne, Marijke Van Kets. Players: Joseph Cheong, Benjamin Heng, Alvina Toh, Ferris Yeo, Andy Chng. Prod: Multi-Story Complex.

**RETURN TO PONTIANAK**

Script and Dir: Ong Lay Jinn. Phot: Minh Nguyen. Players: Hiep Thi Le, Fadali, Eleanor Lee, Fadzlinda, Steven Banks, Victor

Khong. Prod: Vacant Films.

**STORIES ABOUT LOVE**

Script and Dir: James Toh, Abdul Nkizam, Cheah Chee Kong. Phot: Daniel Low, Chew Tze Chuan, Ryan Seet. Players: Beatrice Chia, Mark Richmond, Amy Cheng, Andrea D'Cruz, Gerald Chew Prod: Zhao Wei Films.

# Producers

**Monster Films**
53B Boat Quay
Singapore 049842
Tel: (65) 536 9140
Fax: (65) 536 9154
e-mail: monster@monsterfilms.com
www.monsterfilms.com

**The Moving Visuals Company**
10-A Loke Yew Street
Singapore 179229
Tel: (65) 333 3051/2
Fax: (65) 339 6329
e-mail: galenyeo@singnet.com.sg
www.movingvisuals.com

**Oak 3 Films**
73A Pagoda St.
Singapore 059232
Tel: (65) 226 2338
Fax: (65) 226 2339
e-mail: oak3films@pacific.net.sg

**Raintree Pictures**
Caldecott Broadcast Centre
Andrew Rd
Singapore 299939
e-mail: davidlgh@raintree.com.sg

**Sunnez**
106B Amoy St.
Singapore 069926
Tel: (65) 221 1488
Fax: (65) 221 1955

**Zhao Wei Films**
22 Scotts Rd, Unit 01–28
Singapore 228221
Tel: (65) 730 1809
Fax: (65) 737 8195
e-mail: zhaowei@pacific.net.sg
www.zhaowei.com

# Distributors and Exhibitors

**Cathay Organisation Holdings**
#02-04, 11 Unity St
Robertson Walk
Singapore 237995
Tel: (65) 337 8181
Fax: (65) 334 3373
www.cathay.com.sg

**Eng Wah Organisation**
400 Orchard Road
#16–06 Orchard Towers
Singapore 238875
Tel: (65) 734 0028
Fax: (65) 235 4897

**Golden Village Multiplex Pte Ltd**
68 Orchard Rd
#07-10/14 Plaza Singapura
Singapore 238839
Tel: (65) 334 3766
Fax: (65) 334 8397
www.goldenvillage.com.sg

**Overseas Movie Pte Ltd**
1 Park Rd
#04-21, People's Park Complex
Singapore 059108
Tel: (65) 535 0555
Fax: (65) 535 0783
e-mail: oegroup@pacific.net.sg

**Shaw Organisation**
1 Scotts Rd
#14–01, Shaw Centre
Singapore 228208
Tel: (65) 235 2077
Fax: (65) 235 2860
www.shaw.com.sg

**United International Pictures**
1 Scotts Rd
#15–05, Shaw Centre
Singapore 228208
Tel: (65) 737 2484
Fax: (65) 235 3667
e-mail: roger_pollock@uipham.com

# Useful Addresses

**Centre for Film and Media Studies**
Ngee Ann Polytechnic
Block 23, #01–01
535 Clementi Rd
Singapore 599489
Tel: (65) 460 6992
Fax: (65) 462 5617
e-mail: vtv@np.edu.sg
www.np.edu.sg

**Singapore Film Commission**
140 Hill St.
Mita Bldg #05-01
Singapore 179369
Tel: (65) 837 9891
Fax: (65) 837 9848
www.sfc.org.sg

**Singapore Film Society**
Golden Village Marina
5-A Raffles Avenue
#03–01 Marina Leisureplex
Singapore 039801
Fax: (65) 737 1543
e-mail: ktan@sfs.org.sg
www.sfs.org.sg

**Singapore International Film Festival**
45A Keong Saik Rd
Singapore 089 136
Tel: (65) 738 7567
Fax: (65) 738 7578
e-mail: filmfest@pacific.net.sg
www.filmfest.org.sg

Hana
Cielová

Almost ten years after the break-up of Czechoslovakia, Slovakia looks like a Cinderella nation beside the neighbouring Czech Republic. The Czech Republic (population: ten million) produces around 20 films a year; Slovakia (population five million) saw just one new domestic film in distribution in 1999: the teen drama sequel **Fountain for Susannah 3** (*Fontána pre Zuzanu 3*). Admittedly *Fountain* was one of the year's most successful titles, but with only 100,000 viewers, a small figure compared to *Cosy Dens*, the Czech film which achieved one million admissions in the Republic.

Slovak distribution suffers from a shortage of modern cinemas (the first multiplex in Slovakia was scheduled to open in December 2000) and the state cannot afford adequately to subsidise production. Fortunately, there is more optimism within the industry in 2000, with two new features (both co-productions) completed by June and three or perhaps four more likely to be ready by the end of the year.

The first new release is a traditional fairytale, **King of Falcons** (*Sokoliar Tomáš*), made with finance from Slovakia, the Czech Republic, Germany, France and Poland, shot in beautiful Slovakian locations and directed by the veteran Czech director Václav Vorlícek. Written by the experienced Ondrej Šulaj, this a romantic adventure story about a 15-year old boy, Tomáš (talented Brano Holíček), growing up in the mountains among wild animals. He falls in love with the beautiful Formína, only to find himself framed for a crime. As always in fairytales, truth eventually wins the day.

The co-production between prolific Slovak producer Rudolf Biermann and Czech Television, **Magnificent Six** (*Šest' statočných*), is a series of short films by young Slovak and Czech directors, who prove there are enough talented film-makers in both countries who deserve opportunities to make features. Most of the sextet are students or recent graduates of the Slovak and Czech Film academies, VSMU and FAMU, and the Slovak press appreciated their unconventional approach, playfulness and fresh ideas, while the three excellent animation shorts within the film proved that the animation industry for which Czechoslovakia was once so famous is still alive and well.

Another Biermann production, *Little Country* (*Krajinka*), is eagerly awaited as it is the new film from talented Slovak director Martin Šulík (*The Garden*), which was scheduled for an autumn 2000 premiere. Šulík has worked again with his usual team, except for the scriptwriter – instead of Ondrej Šulaj this time it is Dušan Dušek. But the recipe for the project, set against momentous historical events, looks very similar to Sulík's previous films: bizarre characters, countryside, poetry and humour arising from the Slovak mentality, and even a couple of miracles.

### Graduating to the big league

Recent VSMU graduate Vladimír Adásek will make his feature debut with the poetical comedy *Hannah and Her Brothers* (*Hana a jej bratia*), a low-budget co-production between the academy and two small production companies, which might prove an increasingly viable partnership in future. Also due for completion by the end of 2000 is *As Wild Geese* (*Ako divé husy*), based on the book of Milan Ferko which looks back into Slovak history, and is

*Some of the bizarre characters from Martin Šulík's LITTLE COUNTRY*

directed by the veteran Martin Ťapák. It is co-financed by Slovak Television (STV), which also invested in *King of Falcons* and *Little Country*.

Still in development when this article went to press was *Fatigue* (*Únava*), written by the young VSMU graduate Tina Diosi, who plans to co-direct her script with Martin Štrba, cinematographer for Martin Šulík's films. Štrba moved to Prague recently, because he finds feature work with young directors of his generation more easy to come by there than at home. *Fatigue* received a grant from the Czech state cinema fund, and will be produced by the young, dynamic Czech production company Negativ, but may still be a Slovak language production.

While the economic situation for the Slovak industry remains bleak, the above films demonstrate that there is certainly no shortage of local talent, and further evidence comes from the fact that films by VSMU students travelled to no less than 70 international festivals between April 1999 and April 2000. Let us hope their skills have a chance to blossom in future.

HANA CIELOVA is a freelance writer who works for Czech Television (on a monthly program about film, *Filmopolis*). She is also a programmer of "Forum of Independents" at the Karlovy Vary International Film Festival.

# Recent and Forthcoming Films

**SEST STATOCNÝCH (Magnificent Six)**

Portmanteau film comprising six shorts: three animation and three live-action. Scripts: Vladimír Král; Vojtěch Mašek; Tereza Kučerová; Laura Siváková and Jaroslav Vojtek; Dušan Dušek; Aurel Klimt. Directors: Král, Mašek, Kučerová; Vojtek; Martin Repka; Klimt. Phot: Peter Hudák; Tomás Sysel; Zdeněk Kovář; Martin Kollár; Peter Bencsik; Zdeněk Pospíšil. Prod: Charlie's/CT/In film.

**SOKOLIAR TOMÁŠ (King of Falcons)**

Script: Ondrej Šulaj. Dir: Václav Vorlíček. Phot: Emil Sirotek. Players: Braňo Holíček, Juraj

## Producers

**Alef Film and Media Group**
Tekovská 7
821 02 Bratislava 2
Tel: (421 7) 4445 8511
Fax: (421 7) 4445 8510
e-mail: unfilm@webdesign.sk
urbanmarian@webdesign.sk

**Ars Media**
Odeská 13
813 01 Bratislava 1
Tel: (421 7) 4552 3492
Fax: (421 7) 4552 3600
e-mail: arsmedia@ba.Telecom.sk

**Charlie's**
Spitálska 4
811 01 Bratislava 1
Tel: (421 7) 5296 3430
Fax: (421 7) 5292 3678
e-mail: norma_charlies @ics.sk

**Film Factory**
Mudronova 59
811 03 Bratislava 1
Tel: (421 7) 5443 0121
Fax: (421 7) 5443 0179
e-mail: filmfactory@ba.entry.sk

**K2 Studio**
Guothova 2
831 01 Bratislava 3

Kukura, Klára Jandová. Prod: AG Studio, Bamac, Golem Film Prague/CT/STV/Schwarzwald Film/Focus Film Paris/Oko Film Warsaw.

**KRAJINKA (Little Country)**

Script: Dušan Dušek, Martin Šulík. Dir: Šulík. Phot: Martin Štrba. Players: Ivan Gontko, Jana Segešová, Anton Vaculík, Vilma Cibulková, Csongor Kassai, Jirí Pecha. Prod: Rudolf Biermann/ Charlie's/Titanic/In Film Praha/ STV/CT.

**HANA A JEJ BRATIA (Hannah and Her Brothers)**

Script and Dir: Vladimír Adásek.

Tel: (421 7) 5477 3429
Fax: (421 7) 5477 3468
e-mail: k2@k2studio.sk

**Partners Production Ltd.**
Fialkové údolie 5
81101 Bratislava
Tel: (421 7) 5441 0637/4318
Fax: (421 7) 5441 0674
e-mail: partners@ba.sunnet.sk

## Distributors

**Continental Film**
PO Box 124
811 09 Bratislava
Tel/Fax: (421 7) 5441 2383
e-mail: cofilm@ba.pubnet.sk
<cofilm@ba.pubnet.sk

**Intersonic Taunus Productions**
PO Box 44
840 00 Bratislava
Tel: (421 7) 6542 1005/2070
Fax: (421 7) 6542 4977
e-mail: baisova@intersonic.sk
www.intersonic.sk

**Ita Slovakia**
Priemyselná 1
821 09 Bratislava
Tel: (421 7) 5556 6071
Tel/Fax: (421 7) 5556 6072
e-mail: Italsovakia@nextra.sk

Phot: Juraj Chlpík. Players: Martin Keder, Marta Źuchová, Lucia Hurajová, Patrícia Jariabková, Rudo Kratochvíl, Juraj Mojžis. Prod: Saint Anthony/ VSMU/Trigon Production.

**AKO DIVÉ HUSY (As Wild Geese)**

Script: Milan Ferko. Dir: Martin Ťapák. Phot: Ján Ďuriš. Players: Leopold Haverl, Zlatica Gillová, Lubomír Paulovič, Ján Greššo. Prod: Pedard Film, STV

**NAVA (Fatigue)**

Script: Tina Diosi. Dir: Diosi, Martin Štrba. Phot: Martin Strba. Prod: Negativ.

**Saturn Entertainment**
Senická 17
811 04 Bratislava
Tel: (421 7) 5479 1935
Fax: (421 7) 5479 1939
e-mail: dusan_hajek@saturn.sk
www.saturn.sk

**Tatra Film**
Priemyselná 1
821 09 Bratislava
Tel: (421 7) 5557 3311
Fax: (421 7) 5556 1051
e-mail: tatrafilm@tatrafilm.sk

**Walter Nittnaus – WN Danubius Film**
Júnová 10
831 01 Bratislava
Tel: (421 7) 5556 8901
Fax: (421 7) 5557 2044
e-mail: walter.nittnaus@atlas.cz
www.viapvt.sk/wndf

## Useful Addresses

**ASFK**
(Film-makers association)
Grösslingová 32
811 09 Bratislava
Tel: (421 7) 5273 3213
Fax: (421 7) 5292 5533

e-mail: asfk@max.sknet.sk
film.gratex.sk/ASFK

**SFTA**
(Film and Television Academy)
Grösslingová 32
811 09 Bratislava
Tel: (421 7) 5292 2929/5296 1232
Fax: (421 7) 5273 32 14

**UFD**
(Union of Film Distributors)

Priemyselná 1
821 09 Bratislava
Tel: (421 7) 5557 3311
Fax: (421 7) 5556 1051

**VSMU**
(Film school)
Ventúrska 3
813 01 Bratislava
Tel/Fax: (421 7) 5443 2182

**International Film Festival
Bratislava**
Fialkové údolie 5
81101 Bratislava
Tel: (421 7) 5441 0673/5310
Fax: (421 7) 5441 0674
e-mail: iffbratislava@ba.sunnet.sk
www.iffbratislava.sk

# SOUTH AFRICA — Martin P. Botha

The year 1999 saw international acclaim for South African short films, with victory at the Venice Film Festival for Teboho Mahlatsi's grim account of redemption in a township, *Portrait of a Young Man Drowning*. But it was also a year in which even the best homegrown features failed to reach domestic audiences. The delightful comedy, *Chikin Biznis – The Whole Story* (reviewed in *IFG* 2000), failed miserably at the South African box-office, and even the slapstick comedy about the Rugby World Cup, **Heel Against the Head**, could not reach the crucial $1.2m (8m rands) benchmark figure. It only grossed about $500,000, despite a wide release of 70 prints.

Another feature which underperformed commercially was Gavin Hood's **A Reasonable Man,** which won a Special Jury Award at the Karlovy Vary Film Festival. This is a powerful courtroom drama about the trial of a rural herd boy who has killed a baby because he believed it to be an evil spirit. The director himself plays a city lawyer defending the boy and having to confront the multicultural complexities of South African society.

These three disappointments were bad news within an industry which has been 'up-and-coming', albeit slowly, for several years. Many factors still inhibit progress. These include a long history of badly-directed and managed funding schemes; limited access to funding to stimulate South African made productions; insufficient distribution and exhibition of South African content, as well as limited access to distribution and exhibition facilities.

The South African National Film and Video Foundation (NFVF), established in 1999, will also have to address problems such as the shortage of cinemas in the townships, a lack of commitment by exhibitors and distributors to South African content and the corresponding domination of American movies on local screens, as well as insufficient audience development. There is inadequate co-ordination and an absence of standards in training provision; underdeveloped scripts; as well as insufficient representation and participation in the industry by previously disadvantaged groups, who need incentives and encouragement to facilitate their involvement.

The NFVF will be the most important vehicle for government assistance to the film and television industry. Apart from providing and encouraging the provision of opportunities for people, especially from disadvantaged communities, to get involved in the film and video industry, it will also encourage the development and distribution of local film and video products. It will also support the nurturing and development of the film and video industry, and address historical imbalances in the infrastructure and distribution of skills and resources.

This is an awesome task for a commission with an annual budget of just $1.4m! During 1999 about $1.3m was allocated by the NFVF to 151 projects ranging from training institutions to the development and production of short films, documentaries and features. Seven features, 37 documentaries and seven short films received production grants, while grants for development went to 22 documentaries, 23 features, six short films and two animation projects. Fourteen film-training initiatives were also supported, as well as a film festival in Soweto and the annual Southern African International Film and Television Market (Sithengi).

## A part imitating life

Despite these limitations local film-makers are still productive. Oliver Schmitz, who directed arguably the most acclaimed local feature of the 1980s, *Mapantsula*, returned to film directing after a 13-year break. **Hi Jack** is a gangster comedy about a young middle-class black actor living in traditionally white suburbs who has to audition for a role as a hijacker in a movie. He knows nothing about the lifestyle so he travels to Soweto where he undergoes some kind of method training with a real-life gangster and a kind of role reversal takes place. Funding came from Germany, France and the United Kingdom.

Another prominent South African director, Ross Devenish, who left South Africa almost two decades ago, returned to the country during the Sithengi market in

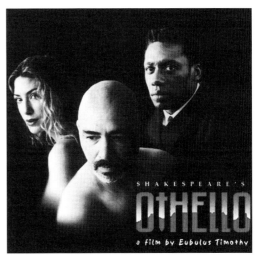

*A publicity poster for Eubulus Timothy's adaptation of* OTHELLO

November 1999. It was announced that Devenish would direct Deon Mayer's acclaimed first novel, *Feniks*, about a tough Cape Town policeman. Devenish became internationally known for three outstanding South African films: *The Guest*, *Marigolds in August* and *Boesman and Lena* (based on the play by Athol Fugard). American director John Berry died soon after filming a new version of Fugard's play during 1999, with Angela Bassett and Danny Glover in the main roles. Another exciting project is Eubulus Timothy's post-modernist version of Shakespeare's *Othello*. The first 18 minutes of a work in progress were screened to some acclaim at Sithengi.

The lack of locally made features was clearly visible at Sithengi 1999. Short films and documentaries, mostly made for television, dominated the market. John Badenhorst's TV melodrama about slavery in colonial Cape Town, *Slavery of Love*, won the market's Best New Feature Award and will be best remembered for Sven Vosloo's outstanding cinematography – each interior resembles a painting by Rembrandt or Vermeer; while the exteriors are bathed in rich impressionistic colours.

Two of the most innovative film-makers in South Africa presently are Jack Lewis and Luiz De Barros. Lewis chronicled oral

*Production shot from HOT LEGS*

noted for a few ground-breaking short films on gay experiences, including *Hot Legs*. The trio are working on their first feature, **Pressure**, South Africa's first full-length fictional account of male homosexuality.

histories of gay and lesbian lives in this country in powerful documentaries such as *Apostles of Civilised Vice*, while De Barros and his producer, Marc Schwinges, were

Dr MARTIN BOTHA is a member of the Council of the South African National Film and Video Foundation, as well as the Board of the Cape Film Commission. He teaches international film history and theory at CityVarsity Film & Television School in Cape Town. His latest book, published in Europe, examines the depiction of gays and lesbians in African, Asian and Latin American cinema.

# Recent and Forthcoming Films

**APOSTLES OF CIVILISED VICE**

Documentary Dir: Zackie Achmat. Prod: Jack Lewis, Idol Pictures.

**A REASONABLE MAN**

Script and Dir: Gavin Hood. Players: Gavin Hood, Nigel Hawthorne, Janine Eser, Nandi Nyembe, Ian Roberts. Prod: Pandora Cinema/Moviworld Production/African Media Entertainment.

**ASSASSIN OF APARTHEID**

Documentary. Dir and Prod: Guy Spiller.

**BANDIT HOUSE**

Script: John Greyson, Jack Lewis. Dir: Greyson. Prod: Big World Cinema/Idol Pictures and Pluck Inc.

**BOESMAN AND LENA**

Script and Dir: John Berry. Players: Angela Bassett, Danny Glover, Willie Johan. Prod: Pathé

Image/Primedia Pictures.

**HEEL AGAINST THE HEAD**

Script: Paul Slabolepszy, Bill Flynn. Dir and Phot: Rod Stewart. Players: Bill Flynn, Paul Slabolepszy, Shirley Johnson. Prod: Thorntree.

**HI JACK**

Dir: Oliver Schmitz. Players: Tony Kgoroge, Rapulana Seiphemo. Prod: Philippe Guez.

**MAIN REEF ROAD**

Documentary. Dir: Nicolaas Hofmeyr.

**OTHELLO**

Script and Dir: Eubulus Timothy. Players: Haheem Hae-Hazim, Royston Stoffels, Brian O'Shaunessy, Susan Oosthuizen. Prod: Eubulus Timothy.

**PORTRAIT OF A YOUNG MAN DROWNING**

Script and Dir: Teboho Mahlatsi.

Players: Ronnie Nyakale. Prod: Pierre Hinch, Lesego Majatladi, Primedia.

**PRESSURE**

Script and Dir: Luiz De Barros. Prod: Underdog Productions, Marc Schwinges.

**RANDOM FIRE**

Script: Bernard Stone. Dir: Yossi Wein. Prod: Malow de Mardt, Brigid Olen.

**SHOPPING IN HELL**

Script and Dir: Luiz De Barros. Prod: Underdog Productions, Marc Schwinges.

**SLAVERY OF LOVE**

Script and Dir: John Badenhorst. Players: Chantell Stander, Zorina Malick, Joanie Combrink, Mark Bible, Aldin Hendrickse. Prod: Three Worlds Films/African Connection Productions/SABC3.

# Producers

### African Media Entertainment
Roberta Durrant
PO Box 3189
Parklands 2121
Johannesburg
Tel: (27 11) 483 2006
Fax: (27 11) 483 2037
e-mail: penguin@icon.co.za

### African Mirror
Wynand Dreyer
PO Box 226
Cape Town 8000
Tel/Fax: (27 21) 928 673

### Beulah Films
Mark Gevisser
PO Box 28938
Kensington 2101
Tel/Fax: (27 11) 614 8047
e-mail: gevisser@wn.apc.org

### Endemol Entertainment International/ Endemol Productions
Carl Fischer
PO Box 71917
Bryanston 2021
Tel: (27 11) 799 2200
Fax: (27 11) 465 6001
e-mail: endemol.sa@iafrica.com

### M-Net
New Directions
Richard Green
PO Box 1237
Ferndale
Randburg 2160
Tel: (27 11) 329 5279
Fax: (27 11) 329 5474
e-mail: newdirections@mnet.co.za

### Naked Grail Productions
Naas Ferreira
PO Box 12402
Elspark 1418
e-mail: ngrailpro@gem.co.za

### Primedia Pictures
Jeremy Nathan
PO Box 652110
Benmore 2010
Johannesburg
Tel: (27 11) 784 3466
Fax: (27 11) 884 1707
e-mail: pictures@primedia.co.za
www.primepix.com

### SABC
Molefe Mokgatle
Chief Executive: Television
Private Bag x 41
Auckland Park 2006
Johannesburg
Tel: (27 11) 714 2414
Fax: (27 11) 714 3341
e-mail: swartes@sabc.co.za

### Underdog Productions
Marc Schwinges
PO Box 78965
Sandton 2146
Tel: (27 11) 325 5252
Fax: (27 11) 325 6252
e-mail: info@underdog.co.za
www.underdog.co.za

### Videovision Enterprises
Sanjeev Singh
134 Essenwood Road
Berea
Durban 4001
Tel: (27 31) 204 6000
Fax: (27 31) 202 5000
e-mail: info@videovision.co.za

# Distributors

### Nu-Metro Entertainment
Sid Morris
PO Box 392026
Bramley 2018
Johannesburg
Tel: (27 11) 880 7040
Fax: (27 11) 442 7030
e-mail: sid@numetro.co.za

### Ster-Kinekor
Mike Ross
PO Box 76461
Wendywood 2144
Tel: (27 11) 455 7700
Fax: (27 11) 444 0659

### UIP Warner
7 Junction Avenue
Castrol House
Parktown
Johannesburg 2000
Tel: (27 11) 484 4215
Fax: (27 11) 484 3339

# Useful Addresses

### The Camera Guild
Antoinette Steinhobel
11 Frenschhoek Bergbron
Northcliff x.19
1709
Tel/Fax: (27 11) 706 0775

### Cape Film Commission
Kevin Hosking
22nd floor
2 Long Street
Cape Town 8001
Tel: (27 21) 418 6464
Fax: (27 21) 418 2323
e-mail: capefilm@wesgro.org.za

### Cape Film Office
Film Coordinator
PO Box 4511
Cape Town 8000
Tel: (27 21) 400 3205
Fax: (27 21) 400 5932
e-mail: mailto:cdelcie@cct.org.za
www.cct.org.za

### Cape Town International Film Festival
Trevor Steele Taylor
University of Cape Town
Private Bag
Rondebosch
Cape Town 7700
Tel: (27 21) 238 257
Fax: (27 21) 242 355
e-mail: filmfest@hiddingh.uct.ac.za

### Commercial Producers Association of SA (CPA)
Bobby Amm
PO Box 678
Parklands 2121

### Department of Arts, Culture, Science and Technology
(for information on the National Film and Video Foundation)
Themba Wakashe
Private Bag x894
Pretoria 0001
Tel: (27 12) 337 8132
Fax: (27 12) 324 2720

### Film Resource Unit
Mike Dearham
Training, Distribution and Resource Centre
Gate 2, Newtown Cultural Precinct

1 President Street
Newtown
Johannesburg 2001
Tel: (27 11) 838 4280/1/2
Fax: (27 11) 838 4451
e-mail: fru@wn.apc.org

**Independent Producers'
Organisation of South Africa**
Qetello Zeka
PO Box 2631
Saxonwold 2132
Tel/Fax: (27 11) 482 2187
e-mail: ipo@yebo.co.za
www.ipo.org.za

**National Film, Video and Sound
Archives**
Brenda Kotze
Private Bag x236
Pretoria 0001
Tel: (27 12) 343 9767/323 5300
ext 204
Fax: (27 12) 344 5143

**National Film and Video
Foundation (NFVF)**
347 Main Avenue
1st Floor,
Ferndale 2194
Tel: (27 11) 789 6387/8/9
Fax: (27 11) 886 2465
e-mail: prime.time@mega.co.za

**National Television and Video
Association of Southern Africa
(NTVA)**
Glynn O'Leary
Western Cape
Tel: (27 21) 480 3100
Fax: (27 21) 424 7580
e-mail: ntva@iafrica.com

www.ntva.org.za

**Out in Africa: Gay and Lesbian
Film Festival**
Nodi Murphy
808 Dumbarton House
1 Church Street
Cape Town
Tel: (27 21) 424 1532
www.oia.co.za

**Performing Arts Workers' Equity
(PAWE)**
Ramolao Makhene
PO Box 30802
Braamfontein 2017
Tel: (27 11) 403 6234/5/6
Fax: (27 11) 403 1681

**Screen Africa**
Angela van Schalkwyk
PO Box 706
Strathavon
Sandton 2031
Tel: (27 11) 884 3162
Fax: (27 11) 883 9281

**Showdata**
Alan Hammond: Showdata
Webmaster
PO Box 15756
Vlaeberg
Cape Town 8018
Tel: (27 21) 683 7280
e-mail: admin@showdata.org.za
www.showdata.org.za

**South African Guild of Editors**
Micki Stroucken
PO Box 66105
Broadway
Kensington

Johannesburg 2020

**South African Society of
Cinematographers**
Duane Rogers
PO Box 81251
Parkhurst 2120
Tel/Fax: (27 11) 788 0802
e-mail: sasc@mweb.co.za

**Southern African International
Film & Television Market
(Sithengi)**
Richard Ishmael
PO Box 1176
Auckland Park 2006
Tel: (27 21) 430 8160
Fax: (27 11) 430 8186
e-mail: md@sithengi.co.za
www.sithengi.com

**South African Screenwriter's
Laboratory**
Liza Key
Tel: (27 11) 442 6379
Fax: (27 11) 442 6391
e-mail: scrawl@iafrica.com

**South African Scriptwriters'
Association**
Etienne van den Heever
PO Box 91937
Auckland Park 2006
Tel/Fax: (27 11) 482 7171

**Women in Film**
Merrilee Kick
PO Box 130982
Bryanston 2021
Tel: (27 11) 483 2006
Fax: (27 11) 483 2037
e-mail: homekey@icon.co.za

# SOUTH KOREA — Frank Segers

**A**fter a remarkable 1999, commercially and artistically, South Korea has reshaped its image as a mildly interesting cinematic backwater in Asia, and can now claim parity with Japan, and, arguably, even with the more traditional film nations of Europe.

What brought about this transformation? A combination of several key developments. New directors and scriptwriters, many tutored in the West, and well-versed in the latest film techniques, have emerged onto the scene. Enterprising, deep-pocketed investment sources have replaced the big, family-run conglomerates which quit the movie business amid the economic trauma of 1997-98. A newly reconstituted Korean Film Commission has, for all its internal turmoil, broken new ground on behalf of producers and directors. Long overdue multiplexes have been built in Seoul.

In terms of actual output, little changed in 1999: 49 South Korean features were released, up a mere six titles from 1998. But here's the big difference: domestic titles cornered 36% of total box-office – one of the highest domestic market shares in the world (leapfrogging Japan's 1999 share of 32%), and the highest in South Korea since the early 1980s, when there was a national embargo on foreign films.

Cinema attendance for 1999 jumped 26% from 1998, to 63.1 million, and since South Korea's average ticket price remained at the $5 mark (6,000 won), total box-office revenue rose by a similar percentage, to $271m. The 80 South Korean films exported last year generated $5.7m in sales, up twelve-fold from 1991. Box-office returns for the first quarter of 2000 indicate that this upsurge in market share and exports is likely to continue, or even expand.

## King Kang

The one title which can claim the largest share of credit for all this is Kang Je-gyu's **Shiri**. Released in February 1999, this sleek, $6m espionage thriller became a national phenomenon, selling 2.5 million tickets in Seoul alone (South Korea's total population is 46.8 million), and grossing $25m nationwide to oust *Titanic* as the nation's most popular film ever. *Shiri* went on to successful runs in Japan, Hong Kong and Taiwan and after appearing in the 2000 Cannes market may well wind up as the first South Korean title to gain wide distribution throughout Asia and Europe.

*Shiri* is a fast-paced yarn about a terrorist doomsday plot, hatched by a female North Korean agent (codename Shiri) and her crazed male counterpart, who plan to set off a bomb during an inter-Korean soccer

*Still from Kang Je-gyu's THE LEGEND OF GINKO*

match. Drawing on Hollywood and Hong Kong action techniques, while remaining essentially Korean and melodramatic at heart, *Shiri* is 38-year-old Kang's second feature and second major success (his drama *The Ginko Bed* was 1996's sixth-ranked box-office hit, outgrossing such Hollywood fare as *Ransom* and *Twister*).

Kang has established himself as a significant commercial force, operating his own production/sales company and planning an ambitious slate of new titles – as many as 10 over the next year. When this article went to press, Kang was producing a $4.5m sequel, *The Legend of Ginko*, and planning his next outing as a director. This as yet untitled feature, budgeted at $20m and set in the future, will, he has promised, be "very different" from *Shiri*.

While relative newcomer Kang led the way commercially, veteran Im Kwon-taek, 65-year-old godfather of modern South Korean cinema, set the pace artistically. Im is the creator of 97 films since 1962. The titles made before 1973, he says, are hackwork. His latest title, **Chunhyang**, is definitely not in that category. This is (at least) the fifteenth screen adaptation of a classic story, set in the thirteenth century, charting the star-crossed romance between a regional governor's son and the winsome daughter of a former courtesan. Im's version became the first South Korean feature to be invited to compete at Cannes in the main competition.

The invitation could not have come at a better time for Im, whose career of late has been in the doldrums. He was disappointed at *Chunhyang*'s box-office reception in Seoul and, to make matters worse, was berated by a civic group complaining about the sex scenes involving the title character, played by a 16-year-old neophyte actress. The film's Cannes invite was considered vindication of Im in South Korea, and although *Chunhyang* won no prizes at the festival, critics were intrigued by its use of *pansori* – solo operatic performances by a male singer, accompanied by a percussionist – to move the narrative forward. Im had incorporated *pansori* into his 1993 hit, *Sopyonje*, but the form played a more integral part in his story-telling in *Chunhyang*.

### Sex and lies

Also at Cannes 2000, in the Critics Week, was 32-year-old Jung Ji-woo's extraordinary debut feature, **Happy End**, about the misfortunes of a genial, out-of-work banker and his wife, who is having an intense affair with a former college flame; the sex scenes are bracingly graphic. *Happy End* boasts excellent performances from Chun Do-yeon as the wife, and Choi Min-sik as the mild-mannered cuckold, displaying his remarkable versatility after playing the macho, violently deranged North Korean terrorist in *Shiri*.

After opening the 1999 Pusan International Film Festival, **Peppermint Candy**, the second film from director Lee Chang-dong, played the Cannes Directors Fortnight section. This is the personal history of an unhinged, 40-year-old man whose life and experiences parallel South Korea's development from dictatorship to democracy. It went on to dominate the Grand Bell awards, winning four major categories.

On a lighter note, Hong Sang-soo's **Virgin Stripped Bare By Her Bachelors** (*Oh! Su-Jeong*), the saga of a young woman's musings about future lovers, also turned up at Cannes in Un Certain Regard. The 18-year-old protagonist of Jang Sun-woo's **Lies** takes a far bolder approach to sex. She loses her virginity to a sculptor 20 years her senior, and embarks on an intense affair with the older man which leads them into stranger and ever more exotic sexual territory. *Lies* created a stir in South Korea after the local censorship board refused permission to have it shown in theatres uncut. After protracted negotiations between Jang and the board in late 1999, *Lies* finally opened in censored form in January 2000, with more than five minutes of the spicier material missing.

# 37th Grand Bell Awards

**Best Film:** *Peppermint Candy.*
**Best Director:** Lee, Chang-dong for *Peppermint Candy.*
**Best Screenplay:** Lee, Chang-dong for *Peppermint Candy.*
**Best Actor:** Choi, Minn-soo for *Ghost – The Submarine.*
**Best Actress:** Jeon, Do-yeon for *Harmonium in My Memory.*
**Best Supporting Actor:** Joo, Jin-mo for *Happy End.*
**Best Supporting Actress:** Kim, Yeo-jin for *Peppermint Candy.*
**Best Cinematography:** Chung, Kwang-suk for *Nowhere To Hide.*
**Best New Director:** Min, Byung-chun for *Ghost – The Submarine.*

# Forthcoming Films

## BICHUNMOO

Script: Jung Yong-gi, Kim Young-jun. Dir: Kim Young-jun. Phot: Byun Hee-sung. Players: Shin Hyun-jun, Kim Hee-sun, Jung Jin-young, Jang Dong-jik. Prod: Taewon Entertainment.

Expensive ($3.3m) martial arts melodrama set in fourteenth-century China, at the end of the Yuan dynasty. Only son of a Korean nobleman falls for the daughter of the Mongolian commander responsible for the murder of the boy's parents. Mayhem ensues.

## BLOODY BEACH

Script: Shim Hae-won, Park Mi-young, Sohn Kwang-su, Baek Seung-jae, Noh Jin-soo. Dir: Kim In-soo. Phot: Kim Yoon-soo. Players: Lee Hyun-gyun, Lee Jung-jin, Kim Hyun-jung, Kim Min-sun, Lee Se-eun, Lee Seung-chae. Prod: Koo & Film.

Slasher-horror involving nasty e-mails sent to eight members of an internet community summering on the beach.

## COOL

Script and Dir: Kim Yong-gyun. Prod: Chung-Nyun Films.

Romantic melodrama involving an animator, 26, who lives with her scriptwriter boyfriend, 27, but becomes sexually involved with her half-brother. The emotional anguish leads her to produce some unusually creative animation.

## THE GINKO BED 2

Script: Kim Sun-mee. Dir: Park Je-hyun. Phot: Kim Young-chul. Players: Lee Mee-sook, Choi Jin-shil, Kim Yoon-jin, Kim Suck-hoon. Prod: Kangjegyu Film.

Red-hot producer (also *Shiri* director) Kang Je-gyu's sequel to his 1996 debut feature hit. A costume melodrama with Wagnerian overtones, the film tells of rival tribes, an angry Mountain God and a plot-turning eclipse.

## JASON LEE – 2000

Script: Richard Park. Dir: Park Woo-sang. Phot: Richard Park. Players: Yoo Seung-jun, Shin Hyun-june. Prod: Dong-A Cinema Corp.

Pop star Yoo Seung-jin stars in this $4m action movie about the true-life adventures of a Korean gangster who becomes an organised crime boss in 1920s San Francisco.

## JOINT SECURITY AREA/JSA

Script: Kim Hyun-seok, Jung Sung-san. Dir: Park Chan-wook. Phot: Kim Sung-bok. Players: Lee Young-aeh, Lee Byung-hyun, Song Kang-ho. Prod: Myung Film Co. Ltd.

A $4m drama about the murder of two North Korean soldiers in the Demilitarised Zone. The female investigator heroine, of Swiss-Korean ancestry, finds that things are not what they seem.

## LOVE BEYOND TIME

Script: Yeo Jina. Dir: Lee Hyun-seung. Phot: Hong Kyung-po. Players: Lee Jung-jae, Jeon Ji-hyun. Prod: Sidus.

Romantic melodrama about a young man who receives strange letters from a woman, post-dated two years in the future.

## NIGHTMARE

Script and Dir: Ahn Byung-ki. Phot: Lee Seok-hyun. Players: Yoo Ji-tae, Kim Kyu-ri, Ha Ji-won, Yoo Jun-sang. Prod: Mythos.

Horror movie about a female graduate student trying to unravel murderous goings-on involving women members of a group called 'A Few Good Men'.

## URINE NATION

Script and Dir: E J-yong. Prod: Koo & Film.

Drama about a young man who becomes involved with a woman via a porn website. The two wind up heading for Alaska.

*Still from Hong Sangsoo's VIRGIN STRIPPED BARE BY HER BACHELORS*

# Producers

**Ahn's World Production**
5th Fl., Sambo Bldg.
88-10 Cheongdam-dong
Kangnam-gu
Seoul 135-100
Tel: (82 2) 3443 9427-9
Fax: (82 2) 3443 9420
e-mail: ahsworld@netsgo.com

**Cinema Service**
3d Fl., Heunggook Bldg.
43-1 Chuja-dong
Chung-gu
Seoul 100-240
Tel: (82 2) 2264 2181-6
Fax: (82 2) 2264 2180
e-mail: cineserv@netsgo.com

**Cineworld Entertainment**
# 603 Younghan Bldg.
59-23 Chungmuro 3-ga
Chung-gu
Seoul 100013
Tel: (82 2) 2264 2946
Fax: (82 2) 2264 2949
e-mail: CNWD@unitel.co.kr

**CK Pictures**
84-1 Dongsun-dong 1-ga
Sunbuk-gu
Seoul 136-051
Tel: (82 2) 921 2282
Fax: (82 2) 921 2283
e-mail: ckstars@netsgo.com

**Ilshin Investment Co. Ltd. (Tube Entertainment)**
10th Fl., CCMM Bldg.
12 Yoido-dong
Youngdeungpo-gu
Seoul 150-010
Tel: (82 2) 784 9371
Fax: (82 2) 784 9372
e-mail: garden71@tube.co.kr

**Kang Je-gyu Film**
4th Fl., Bingre Bldg.
518 Apgujung-dong
Kangnam-gu
Seoul 135-110
Tel:(82 2) 3444 4700
Fax: (82 2) 3444 4701
e-mail: kangfilm@unitel.co.kr

**Myung Film**
36-5 Myungryun-dong 1-ga
Chongo-gu
Seoul 110-521

Tel: (82 2) 766 7406
Fax: (82 2) 3673 3286
e-mail: hoggie@myungfilm.co.kr

**Shincine Communications**
2nd Fl., Miseung Bldg.
609-1 Sinsa-dong
Kangnam-gu
Seoul 135-120
Tel: (82 2) 3446 2370
Fax: (82 2) 3445 6230
e-mail: shincine@netian.com

**Taehung Pictures**
3-1 Hannam-dong
Yongsan-gu
Seoul 140-210
Tel: (82 2) 797 5121
Fax: (82 2) 797 5125
e-mail: taehung@chollian.net

**Taewon Entertainment**
6th Fl. Kinema Bldg.
86 Cheongdam-dong
Kangnam-gu
Seoul 135-100
Tel: (82 2) 541 0266
Fax: (82 2) 541 0268
e-mail: twent@unitel.co.kr

**Unikorea**
80-19 Chungdam-dong
Kangnam-gu
Seoul 135-100
Tel: (82 2) 3446 5100
Fax: (82 2) 3446 0511
e-mail: unicinema@netsgo.com

# Distributors/ Sales Companies

**Cineclick Asia**
B1 Sukchon Bldg. 10-38
Yangjaw-dong
Sepcho-gu
Seoul
Tel: (82 2) 577 6694
Fax: (82 2) 3462 3482
e-mail: yjsuh@cineclick.co.kr

**CJ Entertainment**
12th Fl., Cheiljedang Bldg.
500 Namdaemunro 5-ga
Chung-gu

Seoul 100-095
Tel: (82 2) 726 8484
Fax: (82 2) 726 8291

**Media Film International**
47 Yangpyung-dong 3-ga
Youngdeungpo-gu.
Seoul 150-103
Tel: (82 2) 2635 3800
Fax: (82 2) 2637 7283
e-mail: mfico@chollian.net

**Mirae Asset Capital Co. Ltd.**
3d Fl., Mirae Asset Bldg.
45-1 Yoido-dong
Youngdeungpo-gu
Seoul 150-010
Tel: (82 2) 786 5930
Fax: (82 2) 780 6065

**Mirovision**
7th Fl., Garden Yesikjang Bldg.
45-18 Yoido-dong
Youngdeungpo-gu
Seoul 150-010
Tel: (82 2) 737 1185
Fax: (82 2) 737 1184
e-mail: mirovision@channeli.net

**Sidus**
1st Fl., Hansung Bldg.
88 Samsungdong
Kangnamku
Seoul 130-090
Tel: (82 2) 6005 6000
Fax: (82 2) 6005 6599
e-mail: hwlee@sidus.net

# Useful Addresses

**Korean Film Commission (KOFIC)**
206-46 Chongnyangni-dong
Tongdaemun-gu
Seoul 130-010
Tel: (82 2) 958 7584-6
Fax: (82 2) 958 7592
e-mail: dustinyu@hanmail.net

**Pusan International Film Festival**
Rm. 208 Yachting Center
1393 Woo 1-dong
Haeundai-gu
Pusan 612-021
Tel: (82 51) 747 3010-1
Fax: (82 51) 747 3012

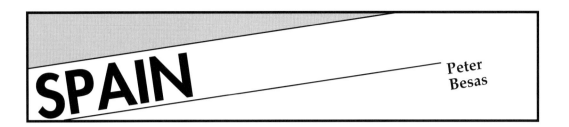

Peter
Besas

The film scene in Spain has been booming as seldom before. A new vitality, stemming in part from widened financing sources and the flowering of a generation of younger film-makers, is boosting not only the number of features produced, but the scope of the projects.

Spain's brightest directorial star continues to be Pedro Almodóvar, especially after his *All About My Mother* swept film prizes worldwide, culminating in the Oscar for Best Foreign Language Film. The Almodóvar phenomenon, now a decade-old, is almost unrelated to the rest of what is happening in Spain – namely the emergence of new talents and the finance needed to bring their work to the screen.

In 1999, 83 features were produced in Spain, and the market share of national films rose to nearly 14%, double the usual figure from the late-1990s. Moreover, a wide spectrum of films caught the attention of critics and theatre audiences. **Die Laughing** (*Muertos de risa*) was a local comedy directed by Alex de la Iglesia, who had formerly brought in the crowds with way-out spoofs such as *The Day Of The Beast*. With a bumptious screenplay (co-written by the director and Jorge Guerricaechevarría) set in the early days of Spanish TV, de la Iglesia in his fourth film spins a yarn about a pair of comics whose hugely successful, 25-year career comes to a tragic conclusion on a New Year's Eve programme. Stars Santiago Segura and El Gran Wyoming made their antics howlingly funny.

On a different tack is Alvaro Fernandez Armero's sci-fi thriller **The Art of Dying** (*El arte de morir*), with Fele Matinez, María Esteve and Gustavo Salmerón. The story revolves around a young artist who has been missing for four years, presumed dead. The artist had been obsessed with death and particularly the works of Hieronymous Bosch. However, a new clue about his disappearance induces the police to reopen the case, and four of his friends are brought together again, and found to have murdered him.

## Under the skin

Less commercial than Armero's film, but much commented-upon, was Gerardo Vera's gay-themed **Second Skin** (*Segunda piel*), with Ariadna Gil, Jordi Mollà, Javier Bardem and Cecilia Roth. A marriage on the rocks degenerates into a steamy triangle of passions, when the couple interact individually with a gay doctor.

Mateo Gil's **Nobody Knows Anybody** (*Nadie conoce a nadie*) featured two of Spain's hottest male actors, Eduardo Noriega and Jordi Mollà. Using Holy Week in Seville as the backdrop, novice director Gil limns a fast-moving thriller that earned him excellent reviews. The story concerns an aspiring writer who makes a living compiling crossword puzzles for a newspaper. After receiving a threatening phone call ordering him to include the word 'adversary' in the crossword puzzle for Palm Sunday, he is drawn into a complex plot in which he eventually becomes the scapegoat for a series of crimes.

Younger writer-directors such as de la Iglesia, Juanma Bajo Ulloa, Gerardo Vera, Alejandro Almenabar, Jaume Balaguero and others of an older generation, such as Bigas Luna, Carlos Saura and Luis Garcia Berlanga are revitalising what films are in Spain. Instrumental to this change is the huge expansion of film financing.

EL DESEO, S.A. - TEQUILA GANG - OML ENTERTAINMENT
present

MARISA PAREDES   EDUARDO NORIEGA   FEDERICO LUPPI

# THE DEVIL'S BACKBONE
("EL ESPINAZO DEL DIABLO")

a film by GUILLERMO DEL TORO

EL DESEO S.A.  Ruiz Perelló 15 - 28028 Madrid
Tfno: 3491-7250107     Fax: 3491-3557467
eldeseo@eldeseo.es

*Still from Alvaro Fernandez Armero's thriller, THE ART OF DYING*

The producers' association (FAPAE) has signed deals with five of Spain's TV networks for an investment of over $130m in feature production over the next three years. Spain's telecom giant, Telefonica, is pouring millions into Lolafilms, which plans to produce 30 new features by 2004. Print media groups, such as PRISA and El Mundo and Planeta, are all jumping on the financing bandwagon to produce bigger and, they hope, better films.

One Barcelona-based company, Filmax, is revving up production with a whole slew of new fantasy/horror films, a project co-ordinated by American film-maker Brian Yuzna, who directed the first of these titles, **Faust**. At the same time, Filmax is preparing a major film based on the Spanish comic book character Captain Thunder, to be directed by Juanma Bajo Ulloa.

Meanwhile, Lolafilms, via its London-based subsidiary, is launching into an ambitious programme of English-language films. Other key producers such as Aurum, Cartel and Araba are being challenged by relatively new companies such as Juan Gordon's Manga Films, or José Antonio Romero's Rioja Films, some with a background in advertising, and thus more commercial-minded than the traditional "auteur" producers.

## Buñuel, Dali and Malkovich

Rioja Films is producing Carlos Saura's *Buñuel and King Solomon's Table*. It promises to be a highly idiosyncratic film with unknown actors, a sort of *cinéma vérité* piece set in 1927 Madrid, whose three main characters are Luis Buñuel, Salvador Dalí and Federico García Lorca; it will mark the centenary of Buñuel's birth.

Another title raising expectations is *The Dancer Upstairs*, the directorial debut of John Malkovich, based on an English-language script by Nicholas Shakespeare, but starring Spanish talent, which includes Javier Bardem, Juan Diego Botto and Elvira Minguiz. Shot in Portugal, Spain and South America, it focuses on the activities of Peru's Shining Path revolutionary movement.

*Still from Mateo Gil's NOBODY KNOWS ANYBODY*
*photo: Sogepaq*

Juan Diego Botto, as more Spanish films are seen abroad.

The expansion in talent and production has been accompanied by a huge growth in exhibition. New multiplexes are springing up around the country, many built with foreign investment capital. On the distribution side, the US majors continue to hold the lion's share of the market, while films from other European countries continue to be of scant interest to Spanish audiences, culling only about 7% of market share at the box-office.

Spanish screen talent is also starting to go international. First it was Antonio Banderas, then Penélope Cruz. Now other Spanish actors and actresses may be on the international threshold, such as Javier Bardem, Carmelo Gómez, Jordi Mollà,

PETER BESAS has lived in Madrid since the mid-1960s and for over 25 years was chief of *Variety*'s Madrid bureau. He has written various books, including *Behind the Spanish Lens*, a history of Spanish cinema. He is now bureau chief in Madrid for the British trade publication *Moving Pictures*.

# Recent and Forthcoming Films

**EL ARTE DE MORIR (The Art of Dying)**

Script: Juan Vicente Pozuelo and Francisco Javier Royo. Dir: Alvaro Fernández Armero. Phot: Javier Salmones. Players: Fele Martinez, María Esteve, Gustavo Salmerón. Prod: Aurum.

**ESA CHICA DE RIO (That Girl from Rio)**

Script and Dir: Christopher Monger. Phot: José Luis Alcaine. Players: Hugh Laurie, Vanessa Nunes, Santiago Segura. Prod: Lolafilms.

**GAUDI AFTERNOON**

Script: James Myhre. Dir: Susan Seidelman. Phot: José María Civit. Players: Judy Davis, Lili Taylor, Marcia Gay Harden. Prod: Lolafilms.

**LA COMUNIDAD (The Community)**

Script: Jorge Guerricaecheverria

and Alex de la Iglesia. Dir: De la Iglesia. Phot: Players: Carmen Maura, Emilio Gutiérrez Caba, Eduardo Antuña. Prod: Lolafilms.

**THE DANCER UPSTAIRS (Pasos de Baile)**

Script: Nicholas Shakespeare. Dir: John Malkovich. Phot: José Luis Alcaine. Players: Javier Bardem, Juan Diego Botto, Elvira Mínguiz. Prod: Lolafilms.

**LOS SIN NOMBRE (The Nameless)**

Script and Dir: Jaume Balaguero. Phot: Xavi Giménez. Players: Emma Vilasarau, Karra Elejalde, Tristán Ulloa. Prod: Filmax.

**NADIE CONOCE A NADIE (Nobody Knows Anybody)**

Script and Dir: Mateo Gil. Phot: Javier Salmonés. Players: Eduardo Noriega, Jordi Mollà, Natalia Verbeke. Prod: Sogetel.

**PUNTO DE MIRA (One of the Hollywood Ten)**

Script and Dir: Karl Francis. Phot: Nigel Walters. Players: Jeff Goldblum, Greta Scacchi, Angela Molina. Prod. Morena Films (Spain)/Bloomstreet (UK)/Saltire Entertainment (US).

**PLENILUNIO**

Script: Elvira Lindo, based on the novel by Antonio Muñoz-Molina. Dir: Imanol Uribe. Phot: Gonzalo Berridi. Players: Juan Diego Botto, Charo López, Miguel Angel Solá. Prod: Aiete and Ariana Films/Sogetel.

**MUERTOS DE RISA (Die Laughing)**

Script: Jorge Guerricaechevarría and Alex de la Iglesia. Dir: De la Iglesia. Phot: Flavio Martinez Labiano. Players: Santiago Segura, El Gran Wyoming, Alex Angulo. Prod: Lolafilms.

## LAZARO DE TORMES

Script: Fernando Fernán-Gómez. Dir: Fernán-Gómez and J. Luis García Sánchez. Phot: Javier Salmones. Players: Rafael Alvarez "El Brujo", Karra Elejalde, Beatriz Rico. Prod: Lolafilms.

## BUÑUEL Y LA MESA DEL REY SOLOMON (Buñuel and King Solomon's Table)

Script: Carlos Saura, Agustín Sánchez Vidal. Dir: Saura. Phot: Javier Aguirresarobe. Players: Non professionals. Prod: Rioja Films/Centre Promotor de la Imatge.

*Still from Fernando Fernán-Gómez's LAZARO DE TORMES*

# Goya Awards 1999

**Best Film:** *All About My Mother.*
**Best Director:** Pedro Almodóvar.
**Best Original Screenplay:** Benito Zambrano *(Solas).*
**Best Adapted Screenplay:** Rafael Azcona (*The Tongue of the Butterfly*).
**Best Actor:** Francisco Rabal (*Goya in Bordeaux*).
**Best Actress:** Cecilia Roth (*All About My Mother*).
**Best Supporting Actor:** Juan Diego (*Paris – Tombuctú*).
**Best Supporting Actress:** María Galiana (*Solas*).
**Best Cinematography:** Vittorio Storaro (*Goya in Bordeaux*).

# Producers

**Araba Films**
Prudencio 13
01005 Vitoria
Tel: (34 945) 140 126
Fax: (34 945) 143 256

**Aurum Films**
Avda. de Burgos, 12
Madrid 28036
Tel: (34 91) 768 4800
Fax: (34 91) 302 5764

**Bailando en la Luna**
Plaza de España 18, piso 13, Of.11
28008 Madrid
Tel: (34 91) 548 3090
Fax: (34 91) 547 9821

**Boca a Boca Producciones**
Marqués de Valdeiglesias 5, 2 Izqa
28004 Madrid
Tel: (34 91) 701 4580
Fax: (34 91) 701 4581

**Cartel**
Lanzarote 4

Polígono Ind. "Los Alamillos"
San Sebastián de los Reyes
28700 Madrid
Tel: (34 91) 654 2857
Fax: (34 91) 654 3390

**El Deseo SA**
Ruiz Perelló, 15, bajo centro
28028 Madrid
Tel: (34 91) 725 0106/7
Fax: (34 91) 355 7467

**Elías Querejeta PC**
Maestro Lasalle 21
28016 Madrid
Tel: (34 91) 345 7139
Fax: (34 91) 345 2811

**Els Films de la Rambla**
Casp, 59, 3er, 2°
08010 Barcelona
Tel: (34 93) 265 3026
Fax: (34 93) 232 2870

**Enrique Cerezo PC**
Ferrán González 28
28009 Madrid
Tel: (34 91) 431 4790

Fax: (34 91) 431 7555

**Esicma**
Maestro Lasalle 15
28016 Madrid
Tel: (34 91) 345 8708
Fax: (34 91) 359 6683

**Fernando Colomo PC**
Genova 5 -5°, escalera interior
28004 Madrid
Tel: (34 91) 310 3834
Fax: (34 91) 310 4613

**Fernando Trueba PC**
Antonio Cavero, 37
28043 Madrid
Tel: (34 91) 759 6264
Fax: (34 91) 300 0104

**Filmax**
Miguel Hernández 81-87
Poligno Pedrosa
08908 L'Hospitalet de Llobregat
Barcelona
Tel: (34 93) 336 855
Fax (34 93) 263-4778

**Igeldo Komunikazioa**
Aldamar 9, 5° izda.
20003 San Sebastián
Tel: (34 43) 431 252/3
Fax: (34 43) 427 794

**Lolafilms**
Velázquez 12, 7°
28001 Madrid
Tel: (34 91) 431 4246
Fax: (34 91) 435 5994

**Mate Producciones**
Hortaleza 59, 1A
28004 Madrid
Tel: (34 91) 532 0225
Fax: (34 91) 532 9450

**Morena Films**
Orellana 6 – 4° izq.
28004 Madrid
Tel: (34 91) 700 2780
Fax: (34 91) 319 4432

**Rioja Films**
La Pedriza,10
28002 Madrid
Tel: (34 91) 416 0232
Fax (34 91) 415 4323

**Sogetel**
Gran Vía 5
28013 Madrid
Tel: (34 91) 524 7200
Fax: (34 91) 522 2297

**Tornasol**
Plaza Emilio Jiménez Millás, 2, 1°B
Veneras, 9
28013 Madrid
Tel: (34 91) 542 9564
Fax: (34 91) 542 8710

# Distributors

**Alta Films**
Cuesta de San Vicente, 4
28008 Madrid
Tel: (34 91) 542 2702
Fax: (34 91) 542 8777

**Araba Films**
Avenice del Doctor Arce, 13
28002 Madrid
Tel: (34 91) 564 9498
Fax: (34 91) 564 5738

**Buena Vista International (BVI)**
José Bardasano Baos, 9.

(Edif. Gorbea 3)
28016 Madrid
Tel: (34 91) 384 9460
Fax: (34 91) 766 9241

**Columbia TriStar Films de España**
Hernández de Tejada, 3
28027 Madrid
Tel: (34 91) 377 7100
Fax: (34 91) 377 7129

**Cine Company**
Zurbano 74, 2 dcha
28010 Madrid
Tel: (34 91) 442 2944
Fax: (34 91) 441 0098

**Cine Mussy**
Quintana 1 – 2° B
28008 Madrid
Tel: (34 91) 542 0036
Fax: (34 91) 559 9069

**Filmax**
Miguel Hernández 81–87
Pol. Pedrosa
L'Hospitalet de Llobregat
Barcelona 08908
Tel: (34 93) 336 8555
Fax: (34 93) 263 4778

**Filmayer**
Edificio Bronce
Avda. de Burgos, 8A, 10°-1
28036 Madrid
Tel: (34 91) 383 1572
Fax: (34 91) 383 0845

**Golem Distribución**
Corazón de María 56 – 9° A
Madrid 28002
Tel: (34 91) 519 1737
Fax: (34 91) 416 3626

**Lauren Films**
Balmes 87, principal
08008 Barcelona
Tel: (34 93) 496 3800
Fax: (34 93) 323 6155

**Lider Films**
Avda. de Burgos, 12
Madrid 28036
Tel: (34 91) 768 4800
Fax: (34 91) 302 5764

**Musidora Films**
Quintana 1 – 2a
28008 Madrid

Tel: (34 91) 542 0036
Fax (34 91) 559 9069

**Sogepaq**
Gran Via 32, 1°
28013 Madrid
Tel: (34 91) 524 7220
Fax: (34 91) 521 0875

**Tripictures**
Doce de Octubre, 28
28009 Madrid
Tel: (34 91) 400 9920
Fax: (34 91) 574 9005

**20th Century Fox Films**
Avda. de Burgos, 8A, Pl.11
28036 Madrid
Tel: (34 91) 343 4640
Fax: (34 91) 343 4655

**United International Pictures (UIP)**
Plaza Callao 4, 6°
28013 Madrid
Tel: (34 91) 522 7261
Fax: (34 91) 532 2384

**Vertigo**
Silva 2, 4°, officina 4
28013 Madrid
Tel: (34 91) 542 2225
Fax: (34 91) 541 6985

**Wanda Films**
Avda. Europa 9, Portal 3 bajo
Pozuelo 28224
Tel: (34 91) 352 8376
Fax: (34 91) 352 8371

**Warner Sogefilms**
Cardenal Marcelo Spinola, 8
Madrid 28016
Tel: (34 91) 768 8800
Fax: (34 91) 768 8829

# Useful Addresses

**Academia de Artes y Ciencias Cinematográficas**
Sagasta 20 – 3° dcha.
Madrid 28004
Tel: (34 91) 593 4648
Fax: (34 91) 593 1492

**Catalan Films & TV**
Portal Santa Madrona 6 – 8
08001 Barcelona
Tel: (34 93) 316 2780
Fax: (34 93) 316 2781

**Federación de Asociaciones de Productores Audiovisuales Espanoles (FAPAE)**
Capitán Haya, 50, 6° D
28020 Madrid
Tel: (34 91) 571 1682
Fax: (34 91) 571 1841

**Filmoteca Nacional**
Ctra. Dehesa de la Villa s/n
Madrid 28040
Tel: (34 91) 549 0011
Fax: (34 91) 549 7348

**Instituto de la Cinematografia y de las Artes Audiovisuales (ICAA)**
Plaza del Rey, 1
28004 Madrid
Tel: (34 91) 701 7000
Fax (34 91) 332 3940

# SRI LANKA — Amarnath Jayatilaka

The past year was one of multiple achievements for Sri Lanka's oldest and youngest film-makers. Lester James Peries, now in his eighties, received a Lifetime Achievement Award from the Indian government for his outstanding contribution to Asian cinema, and was admitted to France's Légion d'Honneur. One of his classic movies, *Nidhanaya* (1975), was unanimously adjudged the best in the 50-year history of Sri Lankan cinema in a poll of the country's film critics, and a book of his collected essays was published.

Sri Lanka's youngest director, Prasanna Vithanage, with **Death on a Full Moon Night** (*Purasanda Kaluwara*), entirely financed by NHK of Japan, won the Grand Prix award at Amiens. Its star, Joe Abeywickrema, one of Sri Lanka's finest older actors, won Best Actor at the Singapore International Film Festival. The film tells the story of Wannihamy (Abeywickrema), an old, blind peasant from a distant village in the dry zone, whose soldier son is killed by the Tamil Tigers. They deliver the body in a sealed coffin at the old man's hut – an all-too common occurrence today in the context of the ongoing civil war – but he refuses to accept that his son is dead.

Another film that movingly and realistically portrays the human horrors of the battle against the LTTE terrorists is **Saroja**, by first-time writer-director Somaratna Dissanayake. It follows a Tamil girl, Saroja, who is stranded with her wounded father after her mother is brutally murdered by an LTTE group, on whose side the father had been fighting. The pair are rescued by a six-year-old Sinhala girl and nursed back to health. The two child actors, one Tamil, the other Sinhalese, both act for the first time and give sterling performances. *Saroja* enjoyed a successful run at the box-office.

Of the 20 Sinhala films released in 1999, seven were essentially sex films. For the last five years, movies bordering on the pornographic have been the mainstay of commercial cinema, as producers took advantage of the liberal censorship policy of the Public Performance Board. But now the trend is dying a natural death and only a couple of the 1999 'erotic' releases were successful. The most popular film of the year was Udayakanta Warnasuriya's low-brow comedy, **Two Wives** (*Bahu Bharya*).

## Praise for the new broom

Following the announcement of its new film policy in the middle of 1999, the government replaced the entire board of directors of the National Film Corporation (NFC) and for the first time in its 25-year history, it now has a chairman and CEO who is a highly-qualified film professional: Tissa Abeysekara, an award-winning writer, director and actor. Abeysekara has transformed the NFC to meet the demands of the present open market, achieving in barely eight months what the corporation had failed to achieve in the last 10 years.

The corporation is set to become the regulatory body for the film industry and, most importantly, Abeysekara has obtained government support for tax concessions on film production, the modernisation and construction of cinemas and the establishment of three Film Equipment Units to update existing studios. He has also established plans for a serious, quarterly film magazine, film festivals and seminars.

After the government ended the NFC's monopoly on film imports, and allowed the private sector to distribute foreign movies, major Hollywood movies have begun to be screened locally for the first time in six years. The first to be released was *Titanic*, which promptly smashed all existing box-office records, despite the fact that pirated and licensed video copies had been available for two years.

Finally, the first English-language book on the history of Sri Lankan Cinema has been published. *Profiling Sri Lankan Cinema* was written by Professor Wimal

*Still from Somaratna Dissanayake's SAROJA*

Dissanayaka, a film scholar at the East-West Center, Hawaii, and Ashley Rantavibhushana, a critic who heads the Asian Film Center in Colombo.

AMARNATH JAYATILAKA is a filmologist and one of the leading personalities in Sri Lankan cinema. He has been the country's *IFG* correspondent for the last 27 years.

# Useful Addresses

**Ceylon Entertainment Ltd**
Liberty Cinemas Ltd
35 Sri Anagarika Dharmapala
Mawata
Colombo 7
Tel: (94 1) 325 764
(Importer/exhibitors)

**Ceylon Theatres Ltd**
8 Sir C. Gardner Mawata
Colombo 2
Tel: (94 1) 431 243/431 109
(Producer/importer/exhibitor)

**EAP Films & Theatres Ltd**
122 Ward Place
Colombo 7
Tel: (94 1) 694 517/694 608
Fax: (94 1) 694 845
(Producer/importer/exhibitor)

**Film Location Services Ltd**
Taprobane Pictures Ltd
790 Kotte Road, Etul Kotte
Tel: (94 1) 864 928/875 120
Fax: (94 1) 875 119
(Producer/importer/services)

**National Film Corporation**
224 Bauddhaloka Mawata
Colombo-07
Tel: (94 1) 580 247
Fax: (94 1) 585 526

# SWEDEN — Bengt Forslund

The critics were not very satisfied with the new Swedish movies of 1999, but commercially it was a very good year, with nationally-produced features capturing 21.5% of the market, up from 16% in 1998, and three films on the Top Ten list.

The hit of the year was a local comedy, the long-awaited new film from Lasse Åberg, **The Health Farm** (*Hälsoresan*). This is the seventh in a series from Åberg, a kind of Swedish Tati who has become very popular since his first film in 1979. All seven have featured the shy, awkward character Stig Helmer and *The Health Farm*, like its six predecessors, attracted about one million spectators in Sweden. Åberg's sole success abroad has come in Norway, as Stig Helmer's permanent buddy is a popular Norwegian comedian.

The children's film **Tsatsiki, Mum and the Policeman** (*Tsatsiki, morsan och polisen*), the third feature from Ella Lemhagen, and Kjell Sundwall's relationship comedy **In Bed with Santa** (*Tomten är far till alla barnen*), both reached an audience of half a million, a very good figure for a movie, with further exposure ahead on video and television ahead. *Tsatsiki...* was most liked by the critics, winning their award for best film of 1999 and no less than four Golden Bugs. Adapted from two popular novels, it's the tale of a boy called Tsatsiki because his father was a Greek fisherman whom his mother met on holiday in Greece but never saw again. The boy thinks of his absent dad often and they finally meet in Greece. It is nice, very nice, and the kid is charming, very charming, but not really deserving of so much critical praise.

Sundvall's *In Bed with Santa*, based on an original screenplay, is certainly a more personal film. It's a black, salty comedy, centred on a Christmas party at which a

*Samuel Haus, child star of TSATSIKI, MUM, AND THE POLICEMAN*

*photo: Eric Nilsson*

wife has invited her two former husbands and their new wives so that all three sets of kids can be together for once. Sundvall does not call himself an artist; rather, he is proud to be a good craftsman, and with *Santa* he demonstrates his versatility (a few years ago he made the action movie *The Hunters*, a fair international success whose script was sold to Hollywood). *Santa* was the most original example so far in a genre which has became very popular in Sweden lately. **Adult Behaviour... it's All in the Mind** (*Vuxna människor*) was another

*Still from Kjell Sundwall's IN BED WITH SANTA*

*photo: Åke Ottosson*

example, a twisty first film by stand-up comedians Felix Herngren and Fredrik Lindström.

## A captive audience

**Breaking Out** (*Vägen ut*) was another promising debut, by television director Daniel Lind Lagerlöf, a captivating comedy about a young unemployed actor staging a play in a prison with prisoners acting all the parts. The police movie of the year was **Zero Tolerance** (*Noll tolerans*), by action director Anders Nilsson, dealing with the danger of just being a witness to a crime. The film collected no less than five nominations for the Golden Bugs, but, inexplicably, came away empty-handed.

Richard Hobert's impressive under-taking, a film series about the seven deadly sins, written, produced and directed in seven years, came to an end with **Where the Rainbow Ends** (*Där regnbågen slutar*) and **The Birthday** (*Födelsedagen*). Some critics have been lukewarm, finding the project a bit pretentious, and the films have certainly been uneven, but personally I have enjoyed his games with different genres, his skilful scriptwriting and his excellent handling of actors. He has never won a Golden Bug, but there have been several for his actors over the years, and former Cannes award winner Pernilla August won for her part in *Where the Rainbow Ends*.

While Swedish movies have not been seen much abroad lately, Swedish actors like August (appearing in *Star Wars: Episode I*) have been more fortunate. Marie Richardson, who played the imperilled witness in *Zero Tolerance*, had a small but expressive part in Kubrick's *Eyes Wide Shut*, and Lena Olin acted with Johnny Depp in Polanski's *The Ninth Gate*. Colin Nutley's wife and star, Helena Bergström, got her first international part in Brian Gibson's British comedy *Still Crazy*, and the Academy Award nomination as Best Foreign Language Film for Nutley's *Under the Sun* (*Under solen*; reviewed in *IFG* 2000), may bring her further international offers.

Meanwhile Stellan Skarsgård and Peter

*Jakob Eklund in ZERO TOLERANCE*

Stormare seem indefinitely lost to American and international films, Skarsgård lately appearing in films by John Frankenheimer and Renny Harlin, while Stormare has been working with the Coen Brothers, Joel Schumacher and Wim Wenders. Max von Sydow is still in demand, lately playing an attorney in Scott Hicks' *Snow Falling on Cedars*.

## Contrasting futures

*Under the Sun* will, one hopes, not be the only Swedish film observed abroad in 2000, since for the first time Sweden had two films in competition in Cannes. Liv Ullmann's adultery drama, **Faithless** (*Trolösa*), with an autobiographical script by Ingmar Bergman and a devastating performance from Lena Endre, was sold to 40 countries. The other entry, Roy Andersson's long expected comeback, **Songs from the Second Floor** (*Sånger från andra våningen*), described by the director as an "episodic slice-of-life pastiche of modern urban society", earned a joint share of the Jury Prize. A new film by Jan Troell was scheduled for an autumn 2000 release.

The Swedish Film Institute has finally settled a promising new agreement with the state, providing for additional funding, a new board of directors who are genuinely interested in film *and* a new, strong leader, former Norwegian culture secretary Åse Kleveland. Mrs Kleveland is half-Swedish, fluent in both languages, but most important of all, she loves film and makes her fellow workers, as well as ordinary people and reluctant politicians, enthusiastic about the work of the Film Institute.

Less promising is the future of Svensk Filmindustri (SF), the leading Swedish Film company for the past 90 years, now under the so far relatively anonymous leadership of another Norwegian, Rasmus Ramstad. Last year, SF closed down their new studios and in 2001 they will move their cinema and distribution offices to a 'new' location, Filmstaden in Solna. In fact, SF built their first studios at Solna in 1920 all its famous silents and, later, the Bergman films, were shot there over a 50-year period. Now they will be back on historical ground, but with very few productions of their own. The old studios

at Filmstaden had been torn down and in 1999-2000 SF produced only one major film. Has the most important chapter of Swedish film production come to an end? Let us hope not.

# The Golden Bugs 1999

**Best Film:** *Tsatsiki, Mum and the Policeman.*
**Best Direction:** Ella Lemhagen *(Tsatsiki).*
**Best Actress:** Katarina Ewerlöf *(In Bed with Santa).*
**Best Actor:** Björn Kjellman *(Breaking Out).*
**Best Script:** Ulf Stark *(Tsatsiki).*
**Best Camera:** Anders Bohman *(Tsatsiki).*
**Best Supporting Acress:** Pernilla August *(Where the Rainbow Ends).*
**Best Supporting Actor:** Shanti Roney *(Breaking Out).*
**Best Foreign Film:** *All About My Mother* (Spain).

# Recent and Forthcoming Films

### DEN BÄSTA SOMMAREN (A Summer Tale)

Script: Ulf Malmros, Lars Johansson. Dir: Malmros. Phot: Mats Olofsson. Players: Kjell Bergqvist, Rebecca Scheja, Stasse Soulis, Cecilia Nilsson, Brasse Brännström. Prod: Memfis Film/Zentropa/Swedish Film Institute/Film i Väst/SVT Göteborg/DFI/Nordic Film & TV-Fund.

### DET BLIR ALDRIG SOM MAN TÄNKT SIG (Shit Happens)

Script and Dir: Måns Herngren, Hannes Holm. Phot: Mats Olofsson. Players: Bibi Andersson, Gösta Ekman, Josefin Nilsson, Marie Richardson. Prod: S/S Fladen/SVT Drama/Swedish Film Institute/Nordic Film & TV-Fund.

### DUBBEL-8 (Double 8)

Script: Gunnar Andersson, Daniel Fridell, Jimmy Karlsson, Håkan Bjerking. Dir: Fridell. Phot: Esa Vuorinen. Players: Francisco Jacob, Jenny Ulving. Prod: Bjerking Prod/ Swedish Film Institute/Film i Väst/ Film i Dalarna/Nordic Film & TV-Fund.

### DÄR REGNBÅGEN SLUTAR (Where the Rainbow Ends)

Script and Dir: Richard Hobert. Phot: Lars Crépin. Players: Rolf Lassgård, Camilla Lundén, Göran Stangertz, Pernilla August Prod: Cimbria Film/SVT Drama Malmö/ Swedish Film Institute/ Sonet/ Film på Österlen.

### FÖDELSEDAGEN (The Birthday)

Script and Dir: Richard Hobert. Phot: Lars Crépin. Players: Camilla Lundén, Göran Stangertz, Lena Endre, Pernilla August, Sven Lindberg. Prod: Cimbria Film/SVT Drama Malmö/Swedish Film Institute/Sonet/Film på Österlen.

*Rolf Lassgård and Göran Stangertz in WHERE THE RAINBOW ENDS*

## HÄLSORESAN (The Health Farm)

Script: Lasse Åberg, Bo Jonsson. Dir: Åberg. Phot: Dan Myrman. Players: Lasse Åberg, Jan Skolmen, Anna Norberg, Ia Langhammar. Prod: Viking Film/ Smart Egg Pictures/Svensk Filmindustri.

## EN HÄXA I FAMILJEN (A Witch in the Family)

Script: Johan Bogaeus, based on a novel by Ulf Stark. Dir: Harald Hamrell. Phot: Olof Johnson. Players: Margret Weivers, Karin Bogaeus, Rebecca Scheja, Johan Rheborg. Prod: Filmlance Int./Chimney Pot/Sonet/Yellow Cottage/Swedish Film Institute/ Nordic Film & TV-Fund.

## JÄRNGÄNGET (White Water)

Script: Mats Gustavsson, Rita Holst, Jon Lindström. Dir: Lindström. Phot: Jens Fischer. Players: Emil Forselius, Alexander Skarsgård, Marika Lagercrantz, Per Oscarsson. Prod: Cinetofon/ Swedish Film Institute/Filmpool Nord/Joson/Scanbox.

## KNOCK OUT (Knockout)

Script: Peter Birro. Dir: Agneta Fagerström-Olsson. Phot: John O. Olsson. Players: Örjan Landström, Reine Brynolfsson, Igor Chernevich. Prod: Giraff Film/Svensk Filmindustri/Swedish Film Institute/Filmpool Nord/SVT Drama/SF Norge/Nordic Film & TV-Fund.

## NOLL TOLERANS (Zero Tolerance)

Script: Anders Nilsson, Joakim Hansson. Dir: Nilsson. Phot: Jacob Jorgensen. Players: Jacob Eklund, Marie Richardsson, Peter Andersson. Prod: Sonet Film/Film i Väst/Sandrew Metronome/TV4/ TV 1000/Nordic Film & TV-Fund.

## RÄDD (Fear)

Script: Mikael Bengtssons, Reza Parsa. Dir: Parsa. Phot: Eigil Bryld. Players: Per Graffman, Tintin Anderzon, Maria Lundqvist. Prod: Illusion Film/Film i Väst/ Swedish Film Institute/Felicia Film/ Per Holst Film/Norsk Film/SVT Drama/DFI/TV 1000/ Eurimages/ Nordic Film & TV-Fund.

## SÅ VIT SOM EN SNÖ (As White as in Snow)

Script: Jacques Werup, Jan Troell, Jimmy Karlsson, Carl-Eric Olsson. Dir and Phot: Troell. Players: Amanda Ooms, Björn Granath, Stina Ekblad, Björn Kjellman, Rikard Wolf. Prod: Nordisk Film/SVT Drama/Svensk Filmindustri/Swedish Film Institute/ DFI/Eurimages/Nordic Film & TV-Fund.

## SÅNGER FRÅN ANDRA VÅNINGEN (Songs from the Second Floor)

Script and Dir: Roy Andersson. Phot: István Berbas. Players: Lars Nord, Stefan Larsson, Lucio Vucinaa. Prod: Studio 24/Swedish Film Institute/SVT Drama/Arte/ Nordic Film & TV-Fund.

## TILLSAMMANS (Together)

Script and Dir: Lukas Moodysson. Phot: Ulf Brantås. Players: Lisa Lindgren, Gustav Hammarsten, Mikael Nyqvist, Emma Samuelsson. Prod: Memfis Film/ Zentropa/Film i Väst/Swedish Film Institute/SVT Drama Göteborg/DFI/Nordic Film & TV-Fund.

## TOMTEN ÄR FAR TILL ALLA BARNEN (In Bed with Santa)

Script: Monica Rolfner. Dir: Kjell Sundwall. Phot: John Christian Rosenlund. Players: Peter Haber, Katarina Ewerlöf, Dan Ekborg, Jessica Zandén. Prod: Filmlance Int/Swedish Film Institute/ Yellow Cottage/Kinoprod/Sandrew Metronome/Sonet/Chimnet Pot.

## TROLÖSA (Faithless)

Script: Ingmar Bergman. Dir: Liv Ullmann. Phot: Jörgen Persson. Players: Lena Endre, Erland Josephson, Krister Henriksson, Thomas Hanzon. Prod: SVT Drama/Svensk Filmindustri/ Swedish Film Institute/NRK/YLE/ ZDF/RAI/Nordic Film & TV-Fund.

## TSATSIKI, MORSAN OCH POLISEN (Tsatsiki, Mum and the Policeman)

Script: Ulf Stark, based on two novels by Moni Nilsson-Brännström. Dir: Ella Lemhagen. Phot: Anders Bohman. Players: Samuel Haus, Alexandra Rapaport, Jacob Ericksson, Jonas Karlsson. Prod: Felicia Film/Per Holst Film/ Swedish Film Institute/DR/RUV/ TV 1000/Eurimages/Nordic Film & TV-Fund.

## VUXNA MÄNNISKOR (Adult Behaviour... it's All in the Mind)

Script: Fredrik Lindström. Dir: Felix Herngren, Fredrik Lindström. Phot: Göran Hallberg. Players: Felix Herngren, Fredrik Lindström, Karin Bjurström, Cecilia Ljung.

## VÄGEN UT (Breaking Out)

Script: Malin Lagerlöf. Dir: Daniel Lind Lagerlöf. Phot: Jens Fischer. Players: Björn Kjellman, Peter Haber, Shanti Roney.

# Producers

**Cimbria Film**
Östra Parkskolan
S-272 31 Simrishamn
Tel: (46) 4141 6660
Fax: (46) 4141 6661

**FilmLance International**
Box 27156
S-102 52 Stockholm
Tel: (46) 8665 1100
Fax: (46) 8662 0444

**Cinema Art Productions**
Box 20105
S-161 02 Bromma
Tel: (46) 8555 24860
Fax: (46) 898 1005

**Memfis Film & Television**
Upplandsgatan 35
S-113 28 Stockholm
Tel: (46) 833 5576
Fax: (46) 830 9934

**MovieMakers Sweden**
Råsundavägen 150
S-171 30 Solna
Tel: (46) 8730 2850
Fax: (46) 8730 2853

**Moviola Film**
Box 20102
S-161 02 Bromma
Tel: (46) 8799 6900
Fax: (46) 829 1386

**Omega Film & Television**
Box 20105
S-16102 Bromma
Tel: (46) 8555 24800
Fax: (46) 8555 24810

**Sandrew Metronome**
Box 5612
S-114 86 Stockholm
Tel: (46) 8762 1700
Fax: (46) 810 3850

**Spice Produktion**
Box 20105
S-161 02 Bromma
Tel: (46) 8555 24000
Fax: (46) 890 3002

**Svensk Filmindustri**
(also distributors)
S-127 83 Stockholm
Tel: (46) 8680 3500
Fax: (46) 8710 4460

**Sveriges Television/Drama**
S-105 10 Stockholm
Tel: (46) 8784 0000
Fax: (46) 8664 5418

**Sweetwater**
Grev Turegatan 21
S-114 38 Stockholm
Tel: (46) 8662 1470
Fax: (46) 8662 1471

**Viking Film**
Sturegatan 8
S-114 35 Stockholm
Tel: (46) 8679 9115
Fax: (46) 8679 9120

# Distributors

**Atlantic Film**
Box 21112
S-100 31 Stockholm
Tel: (46) 830 5230
Fax: (46) 830 5280

**Buena Vista International**
Box 181
S-10220 Stockholm
Tel: (46) 8555 44500
Fax: (46) 8555 44580

**Columbia TriStar Films**
Box 9501
S-102 74 Stockholm
Tel: (46) 8555 79000
Fax: (46) 8555 79050

**Folkets Bio**
Box 2068
S-103 12 Stockholm
Tel: (46) 8566 26100
Fax: (46) 8566 26149

**Fox Film**
S-127 83 Stockholm
Tel: (46) 8680 3500
Fax: (46) 8710 4460

**Novemberfilm**
Nidarosgatan 4, 2tr.
S-164 34 Kista
Tel: (46) 8751 5144
Fax: (46) 8632 0185

**Polfilm**
Östra Rönneholmsvägen 4
S-211 47 Malmö
Tel: (46) 4012 4044
Fax: (46) 4012 4044

**Sandrew Film**
Box 5612
S-114 86 Stockholm
Tel: (46) 8762 1700
Fax: (46) 810 3850

**Scanbox Sweden**
Box 1447
S-17128 Solna
Tel: (46) 8444 7600
Fax: (46) 8444 7610

**Sonet Film**
Box 20105
161 02 Bromma
Tel: (46) 8555 248 00
Fax: (46)828 58 34

**Triangel film**
Box 285
S-201 22 Malmö
Tel: (46) 4012 5547
Fax: (46) 4012 9099

**United International Pictures**
Box 9502
S-102 74 Stockholm
Tel: (46) 8616 7400
Fax: (46) 884 3870

**Warner Bros**
Box 9503
S-102 74 Stockholm
Tel: (46) 8658 1050
Fax: (46) 8658 6482

**Willmar Andersson Film**
Box 5612
S-114 86 Stockholm
Tel: (46) 823 4700
Fax: (46) 810 3850

# Useful Addresses

**The National Archive of Recorded Sound and Moving Image**
Box 27890
S-115 93 Stockholm
Tel: (46) 8783 3700
Fax: (46) 8663 1811

**The Swedish Film Distributors' Association**
Box 23021
S-10435 Stockholm
Tel: (46) 8441 5570
Fax: (46) 8343 810

**Swedish Film Institute**
Box 27126
S-102 52 Stockholm
Tel: (46) 8665 1100
Fax: (46) 8661 1820

**Swedish Film Producers' Association**
Blasieholmsg. 4B
S-10329 Stockholm
Tel: (46) 8762 7798
Fax: (46) 8762 7760

**The Swedish Institute**
Cultural Film Events
Box 7434
S-103 91 Stockholm
Tel: (46) 8789 2000
Fax: (46) 820 72 48

# SWITZERLAND

Michael Sennhauser

Enthusiasm for films remains unfalteringly high in Switzerland. In 1999, the country's seven million inhabitants again bought more than 15.5 million cinema tickets between them. All over the country, multiplexes are being built, adding to the current total of more than 370 cinemas. The main attractions, as in every other European country, were the 225 American films released in Switzerland last year, but arthouse films, screened by independent cinemas and film clubs, were more successful than in many other parts of the continent. The arthouse circuit is very important for Swiss films, which only achieved a market share of 2.5% (1998: 2.1%). In 1999, Daniel Schmid's mildly political comedy *Beresina* was the only domestic title to notch more than 100,000 admissions; by comparison, *Notting Hill*, the year's biggest hit, attracted 670,000.

Florian Froschmayer's superficial but very slick thriller **Exclusive** (*Exklusiv*), about an investigative yellow-press reporter who gets too close to a bizarre series of murders, was the second most successful Swiss film, with only 28,000 admissions. Veteran director Alain Tanner's **Jonas et Lila, à demain**, the

Still from Alain Tanner's JONAS ET LILA, A DEMAIN

sequel to Tanner's 1976 success, *Jonas qui aura vingt-cinq ans en l'an 2000*, could not even muster 10,000 patrons. In the sequel, Jonas, now 25, has completed his studies at a film school and married Lila, a young African woman. Jonas and Lila, in their relationship with one another and with a disenchanted film-maker, Anziano, try to cope with the instability of modern life, and Tanner's film reflects on this theme in a series of everyday scenes, rather than through a conventional story.

There are some positive stirrings on the Swiss film scene. For one, "succès cinéma"

a box-office-success-dependent system of subsidies established in 1997, appears to be working. Even if the public is yet not very hot on Swiss features, exhibitors claim that without the system they would hardly be able to show any Swiss titles. Presently, the federal law regulating the national subsidy system for film is being revised to adapt to the changing needs of film-makers and exhibitors; the federal film office hopes to increase public funding.

On the production side, 1999 also saw the founding of Film Location Switzerland, a new film commission which promotes Switzerland's locations and production centres. The third annual "Swiss Film Awards" were presented in January 2000, and the event has undoubtedly caught the public's imagination.

### Twenty-first century hits

In the first three months of 2000, **Komiker**, a strictly commercial comedy directed by Markus Imboden in Swiss-German, about a hapless wanna-be stand-up comedian who secretly finds shelter in his mother's room in an old people's home, sold more than 127,000 tickets. Two new features by young film-makers from the French-speaking part of Switzerland have enjoyed some critical as well as a mild public success: François-Christophe Marzal's **Beware of the Dogs** (*Attention aux chiens*), a crime comedy reminiscent of Godard, and Romed Wyder's **No coffee, no TV, no sex** (*Pas de café, pas de télé, pas de sexe*), a squatter-story.

*Still from the popular documentary, ID SWISS*

The main strength of Swiss cinema remains its co-productions and documentaries. Léa Pool's *Emporte-moi*, a Swiss-Canadian co-production was not only successful at festivals all over the world, but also Canada's official entry for the foreign-language Oscar. Silvio Soldoni's *Bread and Tulips* (*Pane e tulipani*), an Italian comedy co-produced by Switzerland, proved a box-office hit not only in Italy but later also in Switzerland and was invited to the Directors Fortnight at Cannes.

The documentaries remain the "pièces de résistance". Of the 23 documentaries produced in 1999, 17 had a theatrical release. One of the finest was **ID Swiss**, a humorous and innovative piece, consisting of seven episodes by the younger generation of Swiss film-makers, offering highly personal views of their homeland as a place made up of a fascinating kaleidoscope of several different cultures.

*ID Swiss* struck a strong chord with the public, as did **A Synagogue in the Hills**, a labour of love built up over several years by Franz Rickenbach, which reveals the fate of the synagogue in the last Jewish community in Delémont, in the French-speaking Swiss countryside, a community which has been slowly, inexorably dying. Also impressive, and picked up by several international distributors, was **Berlin Cinema** (working title only), by Samira Gloor-Fadel, a black-and-white meditation on Berlin as (among other things) a film-makers' city, including comments by Wim Wenders, Jean-Luc Godard and the architect Jean Nouvel.

---

MICHAEL SENNHAUSER is chief editor of the German edition of the Swiss monthly *FILM* (formerly *Zoom*), and co-editor of Switzerland's monthly bilingual trade-paper, *Ciné-Bulletin*.

# Recent and Forthcoming Films

### ATTENTION (AUX CHIENS)
Script and Dir: François Christophe Marzal. Phot: Séverine Barde. Players: Jacques Roman, Christian Gregori, Délphine Lanza, Sacha Bourdo, Ania Temler. Prod: Light Night Production.

### BEGINNING ANEW
Documentary. Script, Dir and Phot: Thomas Lüchinger. Prod: roses for you/Beat Curti.

### BERLIN-CINEMA
Documentary. Script and Dir: Samira Gloor-Fadel. Phot: Philippe Bonnier, Patrice Cologne, Denis Jutzeler. Prod: Les Films de la Terrasse/La Sept-arte.

### ELOGE DE L'AMOUR
Script and Dir: Jean-Luc Godard. Phot: Christophe Pollock. Players: Bruno Putzulu, Cécile Camp, Philippe Loyrette, Claude Baignères. Prod: Avventura Films/Périphéria/Vega Film.

### EXKLUSIV
Script: Tobias Kunz, Florian Froschmayer. Dir: Froschmayer. Phot: Pascal Walder. Players: Martin Rapold, Daniel Bill, Stefan Gubser, Beat Schlatter, Sabrina Steinmetz, Judith Wiprächtiger,

*Still from Markus Imboden's hit comedy, KOMIKER*

Stefan Kollmuss, Barbara Azzi. Prod: Paparazzi Pictures

### GRIPSHOLM
Script: Stefan Kolditz. Dir: Xavier Koller. Phot: Pio Corradi. Players: Ulrich Noethen, Heike Makatsch, Jasmin Tabatabai, Marcus Thomas, Kol Simcha. Prod: Catpics/Thomas Wilkening Filmgesellschaft/Dor Film.

### ID SWISS
Documentary. Dir: Fulvio Bernasconi, Christian Davi, Nadia Fares, Wageh George, Kamal Musale, Thomas Thümena,

Stina Werenfels. Prod: Dschoint Ventschr Filmproduktion for SRG SSR idée suisse.

### JONAS ET LILA, A DEMAIN
Script: Bernard Comment, Alain Tanner. Dir: Tanner. Phot:Denis Jutzeler. Players: Jérôme Robart, Aïssa Maïga, Marisa Peredes, Heinz Bennent, Cécile Tanner. Prod: CAB Productions/Filmograph/Gemini.

### KOMIKER
Script: Walter Bretscher, Beat Schlatter. Dir: Markus Imboden. Phot: Rainer Klausmann. Players:

Beat Schlatter, Patrick Frey, Stephanie Glaser, Brigitte Beyeler, Pinkas Braun, Walo Lüönd, Mathias Gnädinger. Prod: Vega Film.

### DER ONKEL VOM MEER

Script and Dir: Marie-Louise Bless. Phot: Jörg Schmidt-Reitwein. Players: Ana Xandry, Robin Dreja, Agnes Dünneisen, Giselle Vesco, Ueli Jäggi. Prod: Silvia Filmproduktion/Tiger TV.

### PAS DE CAFE, PAS DE TELE, PAS DE SEXE

Script and Dir: Romed Wyder. Phot: Stéphane Kuthy. Players:

## Producers

### Alhena Films SA
8, rue des Moraines
CH-1227 Carouge GE
Tel: (41 22) 823 0303
Fax: (41 22) 823 0304

### Ascot Elite Entertainment Group
Molkenstrasse 21, PO Box
CH-8026 Zürich
Tel: (41 1) 298 8181
Fax: (41 1) 298 8170
e-mail: info@ascot-elite.ch

### Balzli & Fahrer GmbH Filmproduktion
Altenbergstrasse 16
CH-3013 Bern
Tel: (41 31) 332 9438
Fax: (41 31) 332 9438

### CAB Productions SA
17, rue du Port-Franc
CH-1003 Lausanne
Tel: (41 21) 321 1500
Fax: (41 21) 321 1509
e-mail: cabprod@vtx.ch

### Carac Film AG
Zinggstrasse 16
CH-3007 Bern
Tel: (41 31) 372 0040
Fax: (41 31) 372 0481
e-mail: info@carac.ch

### Catpics Coproductions AG
Steinstrasse 21

Vincent Coppey, Alexandra Tiedemann, Pietro Musillo, Nalini Selvadoray. Prod: Laïka Films.

### SCHLAGEN UND ABTUN

Documentary. Script and Dir: Norbert Wiedmer. Phot: Peter Guyer. Prod: Biograph Film.

### A SYNAGOGUE IN THE HILLS

Documentary. Script and Dir: Franz Rickenbach. Phot: Pio Corradi. Prod: I-Magus Filmproduktion.

### WERANGSTWOLF

Script, Dir and Phot: Clemens

CH-8003 Zürich
Tel: (41 1) 451 2358
Fax: (41 1) 462 0112
e-mail: catpics@bluewin.ch

### Ciné Manufacture SA
11, rue des Vieux-Grenadiers
CH-1205 Genève
Tel: (41 22) 800 2022
Fax: (41 22) 800 2021
e-mail: info@cinemanufacture.ch

### Climage
Maupas 8
CH-1004 Lausanne
Tel: (41 21) 648 3561
Fax: (41 21) 646 2787
e-mail: climage@worldcom.ch

### Arthur Cohn
Gellertstrasse 18
CH-4052 Basel
Tel: (41 61) 312 1242
Fax: (41 61) 312 0717

### C-Films AG
Hallenstrasse 10, PO Box
CH-8032 Zürich
Tel: (41 1) 253 6555
Fax: (41 1) 251 5253
e-mail: c-films@c-films.ch

### Dschoint Ventschr Filmproduktion AG
Zentralstrasse 156
CH-8003 Zürich
Tel: (41 1) 456 3020
Fax: (41 1) 456 3025

Klopfenstein. Players: Bruno Ganz, Tina Engel, Mathias Gnädinger, Stefan Kurt, Caroline Redl, George Meyer-Goll, Jeanet Haufler, Norbert Klaasen, Doraine Green. Prod: Ombra Films.

### ZORNIGE KÜSSE

Script: Judith Kennel, Markus Imhoof. Dir: Kennel. Phot: Sophie Maintigneux. Players: Jürgen Vogel, Maria Simon, Julia Jentsch, Adina Vetter, Katharina Quast, Lydia Schönfeld, Verena Zimmermann, Gudrun Gabriel, Bernadette Vonlanthen, Roswitha Dost, Verena Buss. Prod: Triluna Film/Vox/Colibri.

e-mail: dvfilm@dschointventschr.ch

### Fama Film AG
Balthasarstrasse 11
PO Box 243
CH-3027 Bern
Tel: (41 31) 992 9280
Fax: (41 31) 992 6404
e-mail: info@famafilm.ch

### JMH Distribution SA
4, rue de la Cassarde
PO Box 58
CH-2005 Neuchâtel 5
Tel: (41 32) 729 0020
Fax: (41 32) 729 0029

### Lang Filmverleih
[production and distribution]
Dorfstrasse 14d
CH-8427 Rorbas-Freienstein
Tel: (41 1) 865 6627
Fax: (41 1) 865 6629
e-mail: langfilm@kino.ch

### Maximage
Neugasse 6
CH-8005 Zürich
Tel: (41 1) 272 6677
Fax: (41 1) 272 7550
e-mail: maximage@access.ch

### PCT cinéma & télévision s.a.
Les Rappes
CH-1921 Martigny-Croix
Tel: (41 87) 880 2810
Fax: (41 87) 880 2811
e-mail: pat@cortex.ch

**T&C Film AG**
Seestrasse 41a
CH-8002 Zürich
Tel: (41 1) 202 3622
Fax: (41 1) 202 3005
e-mail: tcemail@tcfilm.ch

**Thelma Film AG**
Josefstrasse 106
PO Box 258
CH-8031 Zürich
Tel: (41 1) 271 8124
Fax: (41 1) 271 3350
e-mail: thelmafilm@access.ch

**Triluna Film AG**
Neugasse 6
CH-8005 Zürich
Tel: (41 1) 273 0053
Fax: (41 1) 273 0106
e-mail: trilunafilm@access.ch

**Vega Film AG**
Seefeldstrasse 115
PO Box
CH-8034 Zürich
Tel: (41 1) 384 8090
Fax: (41 1) 384 8099
e-mail: info@vegafilm.com

# Distributors

**Agora Films Distribution**
8, rue des Moraines
CH-1227 Carouge GE
Tel: (41 22) 823 0303
Fax: (41 22) 823 0304
e-mail: jmbuhler@alhena.ch

**Buena Vista International Ltd.**
Am Schanzengraben 27
CH-8002 Zürich
Tel: (41 1) 289 2200
Fax: (41 1) 289 2222

**Columbus Film AG**
Steinstrasse 21
CH-8036 Zürich
Tel: (41 1) 462 7366
Fax: (41 1) 462 0112
e-mail: info@columbusfilm.ch

**Elite Film AG**
Molkenstrasse 21, PO Box
CH-8026 Zürich
Tel: (41 1) 298 8181
Fax: (41 1) 298 8189
e-mail: elite@active.ch

**Fama Film**
[see address under Producers]

**Filmcooperative**
Heinrichstrasse 114
PO Box 1366
CH-8031 Zürich
Tel: (41 1) 448 4422
Fax: (41 1) 448 4428
e-mail: filmcoopi@filmcoopi.ch

**Focus Film AG**
Mittelstrasse 14, PO Box
CH-8034 Zürich
Tel: (41 1) 382 3388
Fax: (41 1) 382 3389

**Frenetic Films**
Bachstrasse 9, PO Box
CH-8038 Zürich
Tel: (41 1) 483 0660
Fax: (41 1) 483 0661
e-mail: mail@frenetic.ch

**Lang Filmverleih**
[see address under Producers]

**Look Now!**
Staffelstrasse 10
CH-8045 Zürich
Tel: (41 1) 201 2440
Fax: (41 1) 201 2442
e-mail: looknow@kino.ch

**Monopole Pathé Films SA**
Neugasse 6, PO Box 1827
CH-8031 Zürich
Tel: (41 1) 277 7080
Fax: (41 1) 277 7089

**Praesens Film AG**
Münchhaldenstrasse 10
PO Box 919
CH-8034 Zürich
Tel: (41 1) 422 3832
Fax: (41 1) 422 3793
e-mail: info@praesens.com

**Rialto Film AG**
Neugasse 6
CH-8005 Zürich
Tel: (41 1) 444 2277
Fax: (41 1) 444 2280
e-mail: info@rialto.ch

**Sadfi SA**
8, rue de Hesse, PO Box
CH-1211 Genève 11
Tel: (41 22) 311 7766/67
Fax: (41 22) 781 3119

**Stamm Film AG**
Löwenstrasse 20, PO Box
CH-8023 Zürich
Tel: (41 1) 211 6615
Fax: (41 1) 212 0369

**trigon-film**
Klosterstrasse 42, PO Box
CH-5430 Wettingen 1
Tel: (41 56) 430 1230
Fax: (41 56) 430 1231
e-mail: info@trigon-film.org

**UIP (Schweiz) GmbH**
Signaustrasse 6, PO Box 295
CH-8032 Zürich
Tel: (41 1) 383 8550
Fax: (41 1) 383 6112

**Vega Distribution AG**
Seefeldstrasse 115, PO Box
CH-8034 Zürich
Tel: (41 1) 384 8060
Fax: (41 1) 384 8069
e-mail: distribution@vegafilm.com

**Warner Bros. (Transatlantic), Inc.**
Baslerstrasse 52, PO Box
CH-8066 Zürich
Tel: (41 1) 495 7777
Fax: (41 1) 495 7795

# Useful Addresses

**Federal Office of Culture**
Film Department
Hallwylstrasse 15
CH-3003 Bern
Tel: (41 31) 322 9271
Fax: (41 31) 322 5771
e-mail: cinema.film@bak.admin.ch

**Film Location Switzerland**
PO Box 2743
CH-1002 Lausanne
Tel: (41 21) 312 05 50
Fax: (41 21) 312 05 51
e-mail: info@filmlocation.ch

**Pro Helvetia**
Arts Council of Switzerland
Film Department
Hirschengraben 22, PO Box
CH-8024 Zürich
Tel: (41 1) 267 7171
Fax: (41 1) 267 7106
e-mail: phmail@pro-helvetia.ch

**Swiss Film Center**
Neugasse 6, PO Box
CH-8031 Zürich
Tel: (41 1) 272 5330
Fax: (41 1) 272 5350
e-mail: info@swissfilms.ch
www.swissfilms.ch

**Swiss Film and Video Producers**
Weinbergstrasse 31

CH-8006 Zürich
Tel: (41 1) 266 6446
Fax: (41 1) 262 2996
e-mail: info@filmproducers.ch

**Swiss Film Producers'
Association SFP**
Zinggstrasse 16
CH-3007 Bern
Tel: (41 31) 372 4001
Fax: (41 31) 372 4053

e-mail: advocomplex@bluewin.ch

**Swiss Short Film Agency**
Maupas 2
CH-1004 Lausanne
Tel: (41 21) 311 0906
Fax: (41 21) 311 0325
e-mail: agency@filmnet.ch

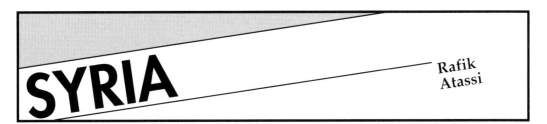

# SYRIA — Rafik Atassi

The last 18 months have been the worst period in the 30-plus year history of Syrian cinema. Not a single film was produced by the National Film Organisation (NFO), although in spring 2000 there were high hopes that the long-awaited new film by Osama Mohammad, *Box of the Globe* (*Sandouk Al-Dunia*), was finally going to begin shooting. Other projects in pre-production include Ghassan Shumeit's *Zahr Al-Rumman*, Abdullatif Abdulhamid's *Two Moons and an Olive*, and Mohammad Malas' *Cinema Al-Dunia*, which like his two previous features, *City Dreams* and *Night*, is based on his own memories. There was at least some small-scale activity from Syrian TV's cinema department. Newcomer Firas Dehni made his feature debut with **Tale of a Dream**, about a young man disappointed by the consumerism of present-day Damascus.

*Still from Firas Dehni's TALE OF A DREAM*

There was much concern within the industry over the appointment of Dr Maha Kanout as the new minister of culture, replacing Dr Najah Attar, who was in the post for 25 years and can claim much of the credit for the achievements of Syrian cinema in that period. Following Dr Kanout's appointment, the director of the NFO, Marwan Haddad, was abruptly sent into retirement, and was not replaced. Veteran film-maker and former NFO director Mohammad Shain (*Sun on a Cloudy Day*) is in temporary charge.

This uncertain situation brought production to a standstill, with everyone waiting to find out what the new minister, who has yet to show any interest in film-making, will do. This may oblige film-makers to seek alternative means of finance, resurrecting independent production, or it could signal the end of the hopes and dreams of a Syrian film industry whose productions are still gaining acclaim at Arabic festivals. The inaugural Bahrain festival in March 2000 saw the most recent Syrian films, Samir Zekra's *Land of Strangers* and Abdullatif Abdulhamid's *Breeze of the Soul*, win three major prizes, two years after they were completed.

RAFIK ATASSI is a Syrian film critic and author of a book about Syrian and Arabic cinema. A member of the organising committee of the Damascus Film Festival, he is head of programmes for the Syrian Satellite Channel.

# Recent and Forthcoming Films

**SANDOUK AL-DUNIA (Box of the Globe)**
Script and Dir: Osama Mohammad. Phot: Abdou Hamza. Players: Zuheir Ramadan, Maha Saleh, Leena Hawarneh. Prod: National Film Organisation.

**AL-TWAIBI**
Script: Nabeel Suleiman. Dir: Basel Khateeb. Phot: Hisham Maleh. Players: Ayman Zeidan, Norman Asaad, Khaled Taja. Prod: Cham Aldawlia.

**TALE OF A DREAM**
Script: Rafi Wahbe. Dir: Firas Dehni. Phot: Nader Koussa. Players: Wael Ramadan, Karees Bashar. Prod: Syrian TV.

## Producers

**National Film Organisation**
Rawda
Damascus
Tel: (963 11) 333 4200

**Haya for Artistic Production**
Bashir Ghaiah
Salheia
Damascus
Tel: (963 11) 221 8144

**Nader Atassi**
Fardous St
Damascus
Tel: (963 11) 221 6009

**Tahseen Kawadri**
Tigheez St
Damascus
Tel: (963 11) 223 6767

**Ghanem Films**
Malki
Damascus
Tel: (963 11) 333 6279

**Al-Nejm**
Baramkeh
Damascus
Tel: (963 11) 222 3730

**Igraa Films**
Khateeb St
Damascus
Tel: (963 11) 444 1446

**Cham Al-Dawkia**
Mezz
Damascus
Tel: (963 11) 613 3382

**Al-Tawam**
Kafr Sousa
Damascus
Tel: (963 11) 212 4040

**Ara Films**
Fine Arts Square
Damascus
Tel: (963 11) 442 0083

**Mak for TV and Cinema**
Abou Rummaneh
Damascus
Tel: (963 11) 332 1000

**Al-Surriah**
Mezza
Damascus
Tel: (963 11) 613 4020

**Aleppo Al-Dawlia**
Sabeel
Aleppo
Tel: (963 21) 331 2752

**Syrian TV**
Omayad Square
Damascus
Tel: (963 11) 221 2000
Fax: (963 11) 222 5374

**Momen Mulla**
Rokn El-deen
Damascus
Tel: (963 11) 512 284

**Ara for Artistic Production**
Fine Arts Square
Damascus
Tel: (963 11) 442 008

## Distributors

**Tiba and Abboud**
Fardous St
Damascus
Tel: (963 11) 222 1096

**Mamoun Serri**
Fardous St
Damascus
Tel: (963 11) 221 1188

**Shamra**
Mezza
Damascus
Tel: (963 11) 666 5601

**Ibrahim Nejma**
Aleppo St
Damascus
Tel: (963 11) 331 2193

**Venus**
Mezza
Damascus
Tel: (963 11) 611 5433

## Useful Addresses

**Cham Cinemas**
Maysaloun St
Damascus
Tel: (963 11) 223 2300

**Syndicate of Artists**
Baghdad St
Damascus
Tel: (963 11) 444 5809

Derek
Elley

In a year that has seen a Taiwanese win the Best Director palm at Cannes for the first time (Edward Yang for *A One and a Two...*), and a Taiwanese co-production looking set for worldwide box-office success (Ang Lee's *Crouching Tiger, Hidden Dragon*), it is ironic that the island's film industry remains between a rock and a hard place.

On the one hand, acclaim at international film festivals and 10 years of government subsidies have simply encouraged auteurist directors to ignore audiences and make pictures which satisfy only themselves. On the other, Taiwan's government, eager not to offend the US and jeopardise eventual membership of the World Trade Organisation, has rolled over and relaxed restrictions on imported films, to the point where they are meaningless. Whatever theatrical market remains between these extremes – self-indulgent local features or mainstream Hollywood product – is swallowed by Hong Kong movies.

The plain facts of the past five years make grim reading: Taiwan films have on average secured 5% of the local market by number of releases, and around 1% by box-office revenues. For 1999 the figures are starker still: 16 movies released (4%), against 129 (27%) from Hong Kong (reflecting its recent revival) and 327 (69%) from other countries (i.e. North America). By box-office revenue, the split is even more dramatic: Taiwan 0.4%, Hong Kong 3%, other countries 96.6%. Local movies earned a mere $360,000 (NT$11 million), out of total annual revenue of $83m.

Unlike neighbouring South Korea, which has so far valiantly fought off US attempts to scrap its domestic quota, Taiwan has none. Instead, it has a limit on the number of prints for a foreign title, but since 1997 this has risen from 31 prints to 58 – effectively meaningless in a small territory. Even films into which the government has put subsidies sometimes cannot find screens on which to play as they are all occupied by Hollywood product.

As other countries have found, building more (and better) cinemas will not ease the shortage of screens playing local movies . Warner Village Cinemas plans 10 more multiplexes in Taiwan's main cities by 2003, but without some sort of government-imposed quota these will simply provide more revenue for Hollywood fare.

### Blame America?

In late 1999, the Motion Picture Committee proposed an amendment to the Motion Picture Law (which has governed the production and exhibition of local films for the past 17 years), by which tax relief could be given to potential investors. The proposal was over-ruled by the Finance Ministry, fearful that the amendment might affect Taiwan's entry into the WTO – for which it requires US backing. In May 2000, legislators met to discuss changes to the Law, but no one in the Taiwan film community is holding their breath for a positive outcome.

Not everything can be blamed on US pressure. In many respects the island's film-makers have only themselves to blame. Ten years of Government Information Office subsidies, currently totalling around $3.3m a year, have resulted only in a string of movies that please critics but not the public. With a maximum subsidy of $330,000 per title, and the minimum cost of a feature being around $530,000 (rising to around $650,000 if local stars are cast), Taiwan's film-makers can often go into production with scant regard for the need to recoup via the local theatrical market.

It is not, as is often claimed by Taiwanese film-makers, that no one is interested in funding movies: Taiwanese capital has continued to go into Hong Kong productions, Mainland-shot movies and the like. They just aren't interested in funding purely home-grown fare by auteurs.

Yang's **A One and a Two...** was financed from a variety of sources (including venture capital) all over East Asia, including Japan. Its considerable merits are discussed on p.47, and, though difficult in terms of length, at almost three hours, it is undoubtedly a major work.

## Enter the *Dragon*

Lee's **Crouching Tiger, Hidden Dragon** (*Wo hu cang long*) is a conundrum. In the works for some five years, and technically a Taiwan/Hong Kong co-production, the $15m movie was mostly financed and packaged by Columbia Pictures Film Production Asia, the Hong Kong arm of the US major. Its international marketing has already benefited from the full force of Columbia's muscle, though as a pure movie it is highly problematical. Baptised by an out-of-competition screening at Cannes, and with Lee's name attached, it was received by many western critics (especially Americans) in gushing terms, especially as the film's veteran martial arts director, Yuen Woo-ping, had been previously "discovered" by them through his work on *The Matrix*.

In the broader history of Chinese swordplay movies, Lee's film is nothing special or innovative. Adapted from a little-known 1920s pulp novel, about a swordsman searching for a magic sword stolen by his long-time nemesis, it is an uneasy mixture of action set-pieces – several of them very striking, but no better

*Chang Chen, left, and Zhang Ziyi in CROUCHING TIGER, HIDDEN DRAGON*
*photo: Columbia TriStar*

than their equivalents in many other movies – and static conversation scenes in which both Hong Kong star Chow Yun-fat and Malaysian-born Michelle Yeoh are evidently ill-at-ease acting in Mandarin (Chow's native dialect is Cantonese and Yeoh was English-educated). The movie does, however, reveal a striking new star in young Mainland-born actress Zhang Ziyi (from Zhang Yimou's *The Road Home*) and provide a fine showcase for veteran actress Taiwanese Cheng Pei-pei (a King Hu discovery from the 1960s). A sequel is already being discussed.

## Two play a waiting game

The island's other name directors – Hou Hsiao-hsien and Tsai Ming-liang – were quiet during the past year. Shooting on Hou's *Millennium Mambo* (*Qianxi manbo*) was delayed in 1999 because stars Maggie Cheung and Tony Leung Chiu-wai were tied up in Wong Kar-wai's marathon, on-off production of *In the Mood for Love*. Hou started shooting for a while with actress Shu Qi but then halted for script revisions. With Wong now embarking on *2046* (with the same actors), the future of his film looks equally vague.

A handful of other films have made appearances at festivals during the past year. Maverick Huang Ming-chuan's third feature, **Flat Tyre** (*Po luntai*), though highly specialised, proved to be his liveliest work so far, and at only 73 minutes one that didn't outstay its welcome. Centred on a documentary film-maker and his actress lover, the film is an acerbic and often witty commentary on Taiwan's own cinematic and political bankruptcy.

**Hidden Whisper** (*Xiao Bai wu jinji*), shown in the Cannes Critics' Week, is an interesting debut by Vivian Chang (Chang Hui-lan), a former assistant to Sylvia Chang and Tsai Ming-liang, but a film that will not travel very far. A three-part portmanteau movie, united by its description of female emotions at various ages, it is best in its first and last sections (the latter featuring Shu Qi and veteran Elaine Jin as her dying mother). Quietly atmospheric and moody, it represents a solid calling card.

*Hidden Whisper* is certainly more coherent than **Woman Soup** (*Nü tang*) by Emily Liu (Liu Yi-ming), a nicely shot but weakly written tale of four Taipei women

with man problems. As in *Kangaroo Man* (1995), her earlier rip-off of the Schwarzenegger comedy *Junior*, Liu ironically shows she has the talent and interest to produce quality mainstream fare, but here her scriptwriting abilities fail her, despite an interesting cast including May Chin (from *The Wedding Banquet*) and local sexpot Tien Hsin.

The surprise local hit of early 2000 – the kind of success that sends market observers into a flat spin – was a Taiwanese glove-puppet movie, **Legend of the Sacred Stone** (*Sheng shi chuanshuo*). Topping the February box-office, and beating *Toy Story 2*, it grossed some $3.3m (NT$100m) in its first month alone, equivalent to about a third of its budget. The first feature to use this traditional local form (already familiar from TV), it tells a traditional tale of wisdom and fighting, and was directed by 44-year-old Chris Huang (Huang Wen-tse), whose family has been devoted to the craft for generations. An English-dubbed version is already in the works.

*Still from Huang Ming-chuan's FLAT TYRE*

# 36th Golden Horse Awards

The following awards were presented in Taipei on December 12, 1999:
**Best Film:** *Ordinary Heroes**.
**Grand Jury Prize:** *Darkness and Light.*
**Best Director:** Ann Hui (*Ordinary Heroes*).
**Best Actor:** Ko Chun-hsiung (*Generation Pendragon*).
**Best Actress:** Rachel Lee (*Ordinary Heroes*).
**Best Supporting Actor:** Leon Dai (*A Chance to Die*).
**Best Supporting Actress:** Deanie Ip (*Crying Heart*)*.
**Best Original Script:** Chang Tso-chi (*Darkness and Light*).
**Best Photography:** Arthur Wong (*Purple Storm*)*.

**Best Visual Effects:** Centro Digital Pictures (*A Man Called Hero*)*.
**Best Art Direction:** Elbut Poon, Ringo Fung (*Ordinary Heroes*).
**Best Production Design:** Elbut Poon (*Ordinary Heroes*).
**Best Action Direction:** Tung Wai (*Purple Storm*).
**Best Original Music:** Peter Kam (*Purple Storm*).
**Best Original Song:** March of Happiness.
**Best Editing:** Chen Po-wen (*Darkness and Light*).
**Best Sound Effects:** Kinson Tsang (*Purple Storm*).
**Best Documentary:** Hsiao Chu-chen (*The Legend of Red Leaf*).
**Special Jury Prize:** Huang Ming-chuan (*Flat Tyre*).
**People's Choice Award:** *Darkness and Light.*
**Posthumous Life Achievement Award:** Pai Ching-jui.
**Life Achievement Award:** Kung Hung.
* Hong Kong production.

# Useful Addresses

**Central Motion Picture Corp. (CMPC)**
8/F 116 Hanchung St
Taipei
Tel: (886 2) 371 5191
Fax: (886 2) 331 0681

**Chang-Hong Channel Film & Video Co.**
3/F, No. 9, Alley 6, Lane 166
Section 3, Hsinyi Rd
Taipei
Tel: (886 2) 705 2603
Fax: (886 2) 709 0334

**Long Shong Pictures**
2/F, 113 Hankou St
Section 2
Taipei
Tel: (886 2) 311 0249
Fax: (886 2) 314 5157

**Scholar Films Co.**
10/F, 88 Omei St
Taipei
Tel: (886 2) 361 5850
Fax: (886 2) 311 9692

**3-H Films**
3/F, No. 19, Lane 2
Wanli St
Taipei
Tel: (886 2) 230 0136

**Taiwan Film Centre**
4/F, No. 19, Lane 2
Wanli St
Taipei
Tel: (886 2) 239 6026
Fax: (886 2) 239 6501

**Zoom Hunt Intl. Prods. Co.**
Tel: (886 2) 2761 7879
Fax: (886 2) 2761 6876

# THAILAND

Anchalee
Chaiworaporn

Although domestic feature production dropped significantly in 1999, with only nine features completed, compared to 13 in 1998, the industry was excited by the enormous success of **Mrs Nak** (*Nang Nak*), which out-grossed even *The Phantom Menace* to become the year's biggest hit.

The second feature from Nonsee Nimitbutr, whose 1997 debut, *Daeng Bailey and Young Gangsters*, established the previous record for the top-grossing Thai film, *Mrs Nak* is a remake of an oft-filmed Thai story about a female ghost who defies death and destiny to continue living with her husband. Using Hollywood-style visual spectacle, and adding some new twists to a familiar tale, it not only won over the mass audience, but also captured numerous domestic awards. Nevertheless, Hollywood blockbusters and other US titles continue to dominate, accounting for 223 of the 285 movies released in Thailand in 1999.

With forecasters starting to predict economic recovery, Thailand has been joining the multiplex revolution, thanks to Entertain Golden Village, Thailand's first multiplexing investor, which opened the seven-screen Grand EGV in Bangkok. Its two gold-class theatres have just 40 seats each and offer an elaborate refreshment service – a luxurious arrangement never previously offered in Thailand.

Most of the Thai films released in the first few months of 2000 flopped, with the exception of the surprise hit, **Iron Ladies** (*Satree Lex*), a fact-based sports comedy about the transvestite volleyball team that won a national championship in 1996. The feature debut of commercial TV director Youngyoot Thongkongthun, it became a sleeper hit, grossing a magnificent $2.7m, despite not boasting any big stars.

## Royal approval

Directed by veteran Prince Chatreechalerm Yugala, historical epic **Suriyothai** is set to become the most expensive film in Thai history. The story of an heroic Thai queen from the sixteenth century, its production has constantly hit the headlines, not least

*The transvestite volleyball team in IRON LADIES*

*Still from the historical epic, SURIYOTHAI*

because the proposed two-year production schedule is longer than for any other domestic feature. The cast has more famous stars than any previous Thai production, real-life political figures will be taking minor roles, the director has a royal background and part of the $5m-plus budget is reported to have come directly from a royal fund. Queen Sirikit and the Crown Prince even appeared at a gala event celebrating the production and the hope within the industry is that in 2001 *Suriyothai* might become the first Thai film to go to Cannes.

Another major development has been the launch of new production company Film Bangkok, a joint venture between two leading entertainment companies: BEC World, the operator of Channel 3 television, and Tero Entertainment, the record company and music promoter. Film Bangkok announced a slate of ten movies to be directed by both experienced directors and relative newcomers. The experienced ones included Adirak Wattaleela, Thanit Jitnukul, Kittikorn Liawsakul, Suthep Tannirat, Nonsee Nimitbutr, Oxide and Danny Pang and Chalerm Wongphim. The newcomers are those with track records in TV series, music video direction and scriptwriting: Suphon Wichianchai, Heman Khetmee and Wisit Sasanathiang. Directors have been signed for one project each.

When this article went to press, Film Bangkok was preparing to release its first two movies. *Fah Talai Jone*, directed by former scriptwriter Wisit Sassanathiangis, is a story of love and betrayal amongst a group of friends during the Second World War, and *Bangkok Dangerous* is an action film about a deaf hitman, directed by Hong Kong twins Danny and Oxide Pang.

Finally, several well-known directors have returned after long breaks. Internationally-acclaimed Cherd Songsri filmed a classic novel, **Behind the Painting**, a tale of forbidden love between a couple whose age difference leads to sorrow. Euthana Mukdasanit came up with **Youth Soldiers** (*Yuwachon Tahan*), the story of a group of high-school students who volunteered during the Second World War. Bandit Ritthakol had also started shooting his heritage film, *Satang*, a satire juxtaposing Thai attitudes to life and money since the 1997 economic crisis, with scenes showing the previous downturn during the Second World War.

---

ANCHALEE CHAIWORAPORN is a freelance film writer and critic for Thai and international periodicals, and one of the Thai contributors to the recently-published book, *Film in South East Asia – Indigenous Views*.

# Recent and Forthcoming Films

### BANGKOK DANGEROUS

Dir: Oxide and Danny Pang. Players: Pawaris Mongkolpisit, Pattarawarin Timkul. Prod: Film Bangkok.

### BEHIND THE PAINTING

Script and Dir: Cherd Songsri. Players: Kara Pholasit, Theeradej Wongphuaphan. Prod: Cherdchai Production.

### FAH TALAI JONE

Dir: Wisit Sassanathiang. Players: Chatchai Ngamsan, Stella Maluki. Prod: Film Bangkok.

### SATANG

Dir: Bandit Ritthakol. Players: Jintara Sukphat, Saranyoo Wongkrajang, Jetsadaporn Pholdee. Prod: Five Star Production/BEC Film.

### SATREE LEX

Dir: Yongyoot Thongkongthun. Players: Jetsadaporn Pholdee. Prod: Tai Entertainment.

### SURIYOTHAI

Script and Dir: Prince Chatreechalerm Yugala. Photo: Igor Luther. Players: Chatchai Plengphanij, Johnny Anfone, Mai Charoenpura. Prod: Phrommitr Production.

## Producers

### Cherdchai Production
523-5 Sutthisarn Road
Dindaeng
Bangkok 10400
Fax: (662) 275 4840

### Film Bangkok
622 Emporium Bldg. 16th Floor.
Sukhumvit
Bangkok 10110
fax: (662) 262 3831
email: filmbangkok@mail.com

### Film Factory Ltd
95 Soi Sukhumvit 99
Bangchak, Phrakanong
Bangkok 10250
email: penek@loxinfo.co.th

### Five Star Productions Co. Ltd.
157/9 Soi Areesamphan 2
Bangkok 10310
Fax: (662) 246 2105
hal@loxinfo.co.th
alvyannie@hotmail.com

### Grammy Film
209/1 CMIC Tower B
Sukhumvit 21
Bangkok 10110
Fax: (662) 664 0246

### Phrommitr Production
52/25 Moo 8
Siwalee Village
Srinakarin Road
Bangkok 10250
Fax: (662) 736 2304

### RS Film
419/1 Ladphrao 15
Jatujak, Bangkok 10900
Fax: (662) 511 2324

### Tai Entertainment
79/23 Srinakarin Rd
Pravej, Bangkok 10260
Fax: (662) 366 0377
email: tai-e@usa.net

## Useful Address

### Thai Film Foundation
21/1 Sukhumvit 61
Klong Toey
Bangkok 10110
Fax: (662) 437 9818
email: thaifilm@ji-net.com

# TUNISIA

Roy Armes

In Tunisia, where state support for cinema is minimal and only about two features a year were made during the 1990s, film still has a key role in popular consciousness, as demonstrated by the success of the biennial film festival, the Journées Cinématographiques de Carthage. Every major Tunisian film-maker currently has a project: *The Time of the Rats* for Ridha Behi, *The Prince Who Studied his Soul* for Naceur Khemir, *Odyssey* for Brahim Babai, *The Bitter Taste of Pink Laurel* for Ahmed Djemai, *Noria* for Abdellatif Ben Ammar, amongst many others.

*Still from Mahmoud Ben Mahmoud's THE POMEGRANATE SIESTA*

Film Festival in Milan at its tenth session in 2000.

The one Tunisian feature film to be released in 1999, and shown at Milan, was Mahmoud Ben Mahmoud's **The Pomegranate Siesta** (*Les Siestes Grenadine*). Ben Mahmoud first achieved international acclaim with his debut film, *Crossing Over*, in 1982 and has since co-directed a second feature, *Chich Khan*, with Fadhel Jaibi, and made a number of documentaries, some of them on video.

*The Pomegranate Siesta* (the title refers to the season when the pomegranate ripens) is carefully shaped as a narrative, and impeccably shot. The fundamental issue is that of Tunisia caught between two forces, Europe and Sub-Saharan Africa, but the film raises many other issues too: immigration, emigration and the rural exodus, the clash of generations, the discovery of old roots and the creation of new fusions.

The good news is that Moufida Tlatli, whose first feature, looking at the struggles of women, *The Silences of the Palace*, was such an international success, is currently completing her second film, which shows a shift in focus: *The Season of Men*. However, Tunisian cinema is mostly represented at international festivals by shorts, made by young film-makers with close links to Europe. Recent examples include *Across the Way* (*En face*) by two young script readers for Canal Plus Cinéma, Mehdi Ben Attia and Zina Modiano, *First Christmas* (*Premier Noel*), by the Paris-born Kamel Cherif, and the video, *Cafichanta*, by poet and film enthusiast Hichem Ben Ammar, all of which were shown at the African

The heroine, Soufiya, returns with her father from Senegal, where they have been living since her parents' divorce, but she finds it impossible to reintegrate into contemporary Tunisian society. Equally significant is the role of her father, Wahid, who had taken his daughter South to keep her from the influence of her French mother. It is his prejudices, silences and past lies which lead directly to the film's unhappy outcome.

# Recent Film

## LES SIESTES GRENADINE (The Pomegranate Siesta)

Script: Mahmoud Ben Mahmoud, Maryse Léon Garcia and Moncef Dhouib. Dir: Ben Mahmoud. Phot: Gilberto Azevedo. Players: Yasmine Bahri, Hichem Rostom, Loubna Azabaal, Nadir Fardi. Prod: Les Films du Fleuve (Belgium)/Touza Productions (France)/Touza Films (Tunisia).

# Useful Addresses

**Carthage Image** [Formerly SATPEC: Film Laboratory]
20 avenue Taieb
Mehri
Gammarth 2003
Tel: (21 61) 740 944

**Canal Horizons Tunisie** [television company]
rue de la Monnaie
Tunisia 1000
Tel: (21 61) 333 100
Fax: (21 61) 333 104

**Journées Cinématographiques de Carthage** [biennial film festival]
5 rue Ali Belhouane
2070 La Marsa
Tel: (21 61) 745 355
Fax: (21 61) 745 564

**SeptièmeArt** [film journal]
B.P. 992 - 1045
Tunis R. P.
Tel: (21 61) 256 904

**International du Film Amateur de Kelibia (FIFAK)** [film festival]
B.P. 116
1015 Tunis
Tel: (21 61) 280 298

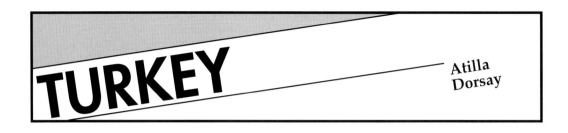

# TURKEY

Atilla Dorsay

There was a generally optimistic outlook in Turkey at the start of the new millennium. Alongside a booming economy and progress towards membership of the EU, cinema was also in very good health. So much so that the all-time Turkish blockbuster, *The Bandit* (*Eşkiya*) saw its record of three millions tickets seriously challenged by **Byzance the Whore** (*Kahpe Bizans*), an unsophisticated but ultimately quite effective historical satire on Ottoman-Byzantine relations, written and directed by a first-timer, the columnist Gani Müjde. By the time this article went to press, his film had reached 2.5 million admissions much faster than *The Bandit*, and the total was sure to rise further.

After years of decline, during which the number of cinemas in Turkey fell from several thousand to just a few hundred, the opening of new cinemas, mainly multiplexes, has brought the total close to 1,000 screens. This prompted an increase in attendance of about 25%. In total, 180 films were released, with the American majors dominating the market as usual. Thanks to local distributor Özen Film, however, there has been an increase in the number of independent American releases.

There was a remarkable comeback from veteran Zeki Ökten, acclaimed director of films written by Yilmaz Güney, such as *The Herd* (*Sürü*) and *The Enemy* (*Düşman*). His first feature for almost ten years was an old-fashioned tearjerker, **Goodbye** (*Güle Güle*), a story of long-lasting love and friendship. It sold almost 1.5 million tickets. Another veteran, Atif Yilmaz also made a comeback with a small-scale film, **After the Fall** (*Eylul Firtinasi*), an understated depiction of left-wing Turkish intellectuals living on a small Aegean island immediately after the military coup of September 1980, their lives viewed through the eyes of a small boy.

## The new generation

Young directors continued to work hard. Zeki Demirkubuz, after his acclaimed *Innocence* (*Masumiyet*), again depicted the miserable lives of society's underclass with deep compassion and an unsentimental psychological approach in **The Third Page** (*Üçüncü Sayfa*). The second feature from Nuri Bilge Ceylan, after his much talked-about *The Town* (*Kasaba*), was **Clouds of May** (*Mayis Sikintisi*), which saw him once again putting on the screen his own family, who had acted in *The Town*.

He takes an almost Kiarostami-like approach to the relationship between life and fiction, and beautifully captures the rhythm of passing days, and the way our souls are affected by them. At the Istanbul festival in 2000, *Clouds of May* won four awards (given by four different juries). The festival gave its Lifetime Achievement Awards to Youssef Chahine and Theo Angelopoulos.

Reha Erdem, years after his cult movie *Aaayy*, returned with a film that retained his trademarks of style, but in more accessible form, **Run, Money, Run** (*Kaç Para Kaç*). It told the intriguing story of a young man whose life is transformed when he finds a large sum of cash in a taxi. An extremely cinematic piece, making wonderful use of locations in Istanbul, it had no chance of gaining domestic awards or international recognition, because the director categorically refuses to participate in any festivals.

Mustafa Altioklar, with two big hits

behind him in *Istanbul Beneath my Wings* and *Cholera Street,* did not make much impact with **The Lift** (*Asansör*), the curious, unconvincing story of a man held prisoner by a mysterious woman inside the lift of an old building. Newcomer Yalçin Yelence fared no better with his attempt to make a popular comedy satirising Turkish traditions in **The Trial** (*Duruşma*).

İsmail Ateş' **Where the Rose Ends** (*Gülün Bittiği Yer*) bravely dealt with a taboo topic, the torture of political prisoners in Turkey in the days of military rule, but deserved greater credit for its ambition than its achievement. Directed by two young people, **The Border** (*Sinir*) tried to shed light on the ongoing Kurdish issue in Turkey but was so inept as to lose all credibility.

### Female perspectives

On of the year's two women directors, the experienced Tomris Giritlioğlu, made the beautiful **Salkim Hanim's Necklace** (*Salkim Hanimin Taneleri*), which explored a shameful episode in Turkish history, which official records have always concealed. Set during the Second World War, the film looks at how a very unjust, even inhuman tax was imposed on Istanbul's traders, mainly the ethnic minorities, many of whom were then forced into exile because they could not pay the tax. It won an award at the local Antalya festival. The other woman director, İlhan Biket, was less successful with **The Boatman** (*Kayikçi*), a muddled effort about the love affair between a Turkish fisherman and a beautiful Greek girl.

**Journey to the Sun** (*Güneşe Yolculuk*), made by young female director Yeşim Ustaoğlu and reviewed in *IFG* 2000, was an important film which sensitively handled a controversial subject: the present-day friendship between a Turkish boy and a Kurdish boy. Contrary to expectations, the film was commercially released in Turkey, with no censorship problems. However, its box-office results were poor, proving that Turks are no longer attracted to political films.

ATILLA DORSAY has been a film critic since 1966. He is the author of 15 books on cinema, is president of SIYAD, the Turkish film critics' association, and a member of the organising committee of the Istanbul Film Festival.

# Recent and Forthcoming Awards

### ASANSÖR (The Lift)

Script and Dir : Mustafa Altioklar. Players: Mustafa Uğurlu, Arzu Yanardağ. Prod: Özen Film (Istanbul).

### EYLUL FIRTINASI (After the Fall)

Script: Gaye Boralioğlu. Dir: Atif Yilmaz. Players: Tarik Akan, Zara, Kutay Özcan. Prod: Delta Film (Istanbul).

### FASULYE (The Bean)

Script: Haluk Özenç. Dir: Bora Tekay. Players: Bülent Kayabaş, Haluk Bilginer, Burak Sergen. Prod: Konsey Film (Istanbul).

### GÜLE GÜLE (Goodbye)

Script: Fatih Altinok. Dir: Zeki Ökten. Players: Zeki Alasya, Metin Akpinar,Yildiz Kenter. Prod: United Film (Istanbul).

### GüLÜN BİTTİĞİ YER (Where the Rose Wilted)

Script: Ömer Lütfi Mete, İsmail Güneş. Dir: Güneş. Players: Cüneyt Arkin, Tulga Tibet, Yağmur Kaşifoğlu. Prod: Mavi Film (Istanbul).

### KAÇ PARA KAÇ (Run Money Run)

Script and Dir: Reha Erdem. Players: Taner Birsel, Zuhal Gencer. Prod: Atlantik Film (Istanbul).

### KAHPE BİZANS (Byzance the Whore)

Script and Dir: Gani Müjde. Players: Mehmet Ali Erbil, Hande Ataizi, Yilmaz Köksal. Prod : Özen Film (Istanbul).

### MAYIS SIKINTISI (Clouds of May)

Script and Dir: Nuri Bilge Ceylan. Players: M. Emin Ceylan, Muzaffer Özdemir, Fatma Ceylan. Prod: NBC Film (Istanbul).

## Producers/ Distributors

**Umut Sanat**
**Halaskargazi Caddesi**
Gezi Ethem Pasa Sitesi, 214/7
80220 Sisli
Istanbul
Tel: (90 212) 230 4041
Fax: (90 212) 232 3583

**Özen Film**
Sakizagaci Caddesi, 21
Beyoglu/Istanbul
Tel: (90 212) 7070/71
Fax: (90 212) 244 5851

**Plato Film**
Akyol Caddesi
Visne Sokak
14/2 Cihangir
Istanbul
Tel:(90 212) 252 4583
Fax: (90 212) 249 3584
e-mail: plato1@platofilm.com
www.platofilm.com

**Warner Bros**
Topcu Cad. Uygun Is Merkezi. No 2/6

80090 Taksim
Istanbul
Tel: (90 212) 237 2000
Fax: (90 212) 237 2600

## Useful Addresses

**CASOD (The Association of Actors)**
Istiklal Caddesi
Atlas Sinemasi Pasaji–C Blok 53/3
Beyoglu
Istanbul
Tel: (90 212) 251 9775
Fax (90 212) 251 9779

**FILM-YÖN (The Association of Directors)**
Ayhan Isik Sokak, 28/1
Beyoglu
Istanbul
Tel: (90 212) 244 0138
Fax: (90 212) 245 7194

**Istanbul Kültür ve Sanat Vakfi**
(The Istanbul Culture and Arts Foundation)
Istiklal Caddesi, Louvre Apt. 146
800070 Beyoglu
Istanbul
Tel: (90 212) 293 3133
Fax (90 212) 249 7771
e-mail: film.fest@istfest-tr.org

**SİYAD (The Association of Film Critics)**
Mr Atilla Dorsay
Hakki Şehithan Sokak
Barlas Apt. 33/13
Ulus
Istanbul
Tel: (90 212) 279 5998
Fax: (90 212) 269 8284
e-mail: al.dorsay@superonline.com

**TÜRSAK (The Turkish Cinema and Audiovisual Culture Foundation)**
Gazeteci Erol Dernek Sokak
11/2 Hanif Han
Beyoglu
Istanbul
Tel: (90 212) 244 5251
Fax (90 212) 251 6770

# UNITED KINGDOM
Philip Kemp

Deploring the latest wretched home-grown movie to hit the nation's screens, The *Observer*'s veteran film critic Philip French wrote in May 2000: "You can hardly see the coffin of the current British cinema for all the nails that have recently been driven into it." In terms of quantity, British cinema is riding high; in terms of overall quality it's scraping the depths. Guy Ritchie's 1998 smash hit, *Lock, Stock and Two Smoking Barrels*, has a lot to answer for. Almost every week, it seems, another jokey, slapdash, self-indulgent British gangster movie – *Fast Food, Rancid Aluminium, You're Dead, Love, Honour & Obey, Circus, Honest* – lurches into view and clogs the cinemas for a week or two, before

being shovelled off into well-deserved oblivion. Crime movies aren't the only offenders: a spate of witless comedies such as *Mad Cows, Guest House Paradiso* and *Brothers* have proved equally dispiriting.

Judging purely from the statistics, everything looks healthy: 112 wholly or partly British films were produced in 1999, as against only 78 the previous year. Wholly UK-funded films were up from 42 to 58; UK-US co-productions all but doubled, from 13 to 24, as did UK-European collaborations, up from 11 to 21. True, the number of high-budget US films shot in the UK dropped from 11 to five, but this was thanks partly to *The World Is Not*

*Enough* taking over Pinewood for six months, while Leavesden, where the previous Bond outing was shot, closed for refurbishment. Britain also lost *Mission: Impossible 2* and the next two *Star Wars* prequels to Australia. But there was no shortage of other shoots to take their place, and the major British studios remain booked up well in advance.

Overall funding is at an all-time high, with the combined budgets of 1999's UK productions totalling $804m. FilmFour consolidated its position as the most consistent of UK backers, with annual spending now nudging $50m. The BBC, which had long hesitated to follow its rival wholeheartedly into film production, at last took the plunge. Under the Corporation's new Director-General, Greg Dyke, BBC Films becomes a virtually independent entity under David Thompson, with a forecast doubled budget of some $33m and a brief to concentrate on cinematic rather than small-screen fare. Among a shoal of new and revitalised production outfits announcing ambitious slates of films, one famous name from the past stands out: if current plans come to fruition, Hammer Films will rise again from the grave.

UK cinema admissions resumed their 15-year rise, making up for 1998's slight fall, to stand at 140 million (compared to 64 million in 1984). One new multiplex opens, on average, every two weeks, although the arthouse sector is still sparsely served. A further 500 new screens are scheduled to open in 2000, including Warner Village's 30-screen megaplex in Birmingham. Rank, completing its long, slow withdrawal from the industry, sold off both Pinewood and the Odeon cinema circuit; the latter was snapped up by Cinven, which already controls the ABC circuit, making it the UK's largest exhibitor, with more than 600 screens. France's UGC acquired the Virgin Cinemas chain.

## New century, new money

On the distribution side, the dominance of a handful of Hollywood-linked majors that

*AN IDEAL HUSBAND, one of the UK's few Lottery-funded successes*

*photo: Pathé*

for years has skewed the UK distribution market could soon be challenged by a bunch of new, hungry British and European outfits such as Redbus, Momentum (backed by Germany's Kinowelt and Canada's Alliance Atlantis), Mel Gibson's Icon, Metrodome, as well as the longer-established Entertainment, the UK's leading independent distributor.

After a couple of decades when memories of the collapse of Goldcrest scared off City investors, financial institutions seem to be regaining confidence in the industry. Several respected companies, including leading insurance house Ernst & Young, are actively putting money behind productions. However, private cash is by nature precarious, and can vanish overnight if there's a glitch in the markets. In October 1999 the London-based finance company Flashpoint pledged $250m over five years to the newly-formed production house Alchymie. In March 2000, three weeks before the start of principal photography on Alchymie's *Born Romantic*, Flashpoint abruptly withdrew its funding. Luckily, alternative backing was secured from Harvest Films.

Despite such ominous portents, the government approved the move by investment house WhiteCliff to buy into The Film Consortium, one of the three Lottery-funded consortia. Here, as so often, private funding was attracted by the seedcorn of public subsidy. But widespread criticism, sparked by the abysmal quality of so many recent British movies, has focused on Lottery funding. Public money, it's alleged, is being spent not only on trash, but unprofitable trash at that. One independent producer has calculated that of the 130 Lottery-funded features, 121 have been commercial failures. None of the three consortia (the other two being Pathé and DNA Films) has met industry expectations, and only one Lottery-backed film, Pathé's Oscar Wilde adaptation *An Ideal Husband*, has come anywhere near recouping its grant.

### From Gilbert to Glasgow

To be fair, just as not all the bad films were Lottery-funded, by no means all Lottery movies could be described as trashy. Among those that have scored critical if not commercial successes were Mike Leigh's Gilbert and Sullivan biopic **Topsy-Turvy**, and Lynne Ramsay's poignant, poetic *Ratcatcher*. Leigh's film is far from conventional. While respecting the historical facts, he gives events a distinctly personal spin, stripping away the complacent accretions of D'Oyly Carte tradition to concentrate on the toil and anguish of theatrical creation.

The film covers a year or so in the lives of G&S, from the disappointment of *Princess Ida* to the premiere of their greatest triumph, *The Mikado*, in 1885. The irascible Gilbert is congenitally dissatisfied with his own work, while Sullivan, convinced his talents fit him for higher things, wants to dissolve the partnership. The backstage scenes, where Leigh draws on his own

lifelong experience of working with actors, are the best in the film, and there are relishable performances. But it's as if the director, in love with his own recreation of Victorian stagecraft (complete with Oscar-winning costumes by Lindy Hemming), can't bear to lose a second of it, and at more than two-and-a-half hours, the film is way too long.

Ramsay's debut, **Ratcatcher**, is set in 1970s Glasgow during a refuse collectors' strike. Vermin swarm, festering bags of garbage pile up everywhere and in the putrid canal 12-year-old James, horsing about with a young friend, inadvertently causes the other lad to drown. It's taken as a solo accident, but guilt eats into James' bony frame and pinched features. Telling her story almost entirely from the boy's point of view, Ramsay convincingly creates the texture of a child's world, edgy and opportunistic, full of unuttered fears and dreams. This is a patient, compassionate film, but the boy's ultimate fate feels over-determined, and the cramped tenements are in danger of becoming a latterday cliché of British cinema.

*William Eadie and Leanne Mullen in RATCATCHER*
*photo: Pathé*

## A hit from up North

Recent critically acclaimed releases such as Peter Mullan's searing black comedy, *Orphans*, and Jazmin Dizdar's Cannes-acclaimed comedy, *Beautiful People*, have suffered from a kind of Gresham's Law of exhibition, whereby bad movies drive out good ones. With such a vast glut of relatively low-budget British films competing for a woefully limited share of screen-time, good and bad films are pushed out on release for a week or two with minimal publicity support, and then vanish or are shunted on to video.

One film, though, that against all expectations did gain widespread distribution was Damien O'Donnell's lively comedy **East Is East**, triumphantly defying conventional wisdom, which states that films set in the British Asian community can never achieve mainstream success. Set in Salford, 1971, it features the familiar comic figure of the heavy father trying to browbeat his offspring into conforming with old traditions. George

Khan (known to his kids, inevitably, as Genghis) lives with his English wife Ella and their mixed-race children. George, proudly Pakistani, demands unquestioning obedience, insists that his six sons and one daughter learn Urdu, study at the mosque and enter into arranged marriages. The children feel more English than Pakistani, and eagerly find various paths to revolt.

Skilfully adapted from his own stage play by Ayub Khan-Din and sparkily directed by O'Donnell, the film draws on a wealth of period detail – space hoppers, flares, Enoch Powell's racially inflammatory speeches. Rich in culture-clash jokes, at times it overplays its comic hand: a randy Dalmatian shows up at least once too often. But it boasts a sharp script, spirited ensemble playing (especially from Linda Bassett as the stoic, put-upon Ella) and a towering central performance from the great Indian actor Om Puri, who penetrates behind the monstrous figure of George to reveal a bewildered, beleaguered man desperately clinging to ancient

*Linda Bassett and Om Puri in Damien O'Donnell's EAST IS EAST*

*photo: Jaap Buitendijk/FilmFour*

certainties as his world disintegrates around him.

*East Is East* was initially offered to BBC Films, who turned it down as lacking in box-office potential – a lapse in judgement that may have been a prime reason behind Greg Dyke's initiative to increase BBC Films' punching power. The producers went to FilmFour instead, who gave the film the promotional backing it needed to build good word-of-mouth, and were rewarded when it became the company's biggest money-spinner of the year, grossing more than $10m.

*John Gordon-Sinclair, centre, in GREGORY'S 2 GIRLS*
*photo: Nick Wall/FilmFour*

The increasingly bullish FilmFour is moving into big-budget international productions, having signed a three-way deal with the French company TF1 and America's Regency Enterprises. At the same time the company is keen to remain involved in low-budget British projects, encouraging new talents and fresh ideas. According to FilmFour's chief executive, Paul Webster, the trouble with British cinema at the moment is that "writers are very complacent in this country. They tend to repackage something that was originally written for TV."

This lack of originality seems to have affected some unexpected figures. Stephen Poliakoff's Lottery-funded **Food of Love**, finally released more than a year after it was completed, came across as a drab retread of Kenneth Branagh's *In the Bleak Midwinter*, while Bill Forsyth's long-awaited comeback movie, **Gregory's 2 Girls**, felt as wearily second-hand as its title implied. Even so, recycling of ideas needn't necessarily entail box-office disaster: witness the international smash hit scored by **Notting Hill**, which with shameless calculation rejigged all the favourite elements from its predecessor, *Four Weddings and a Funeral*.

### Fiennes romance, low-budget gems

*Notting Hill*'s success was an exception, though, in a year when tried-and-true formulas seemed to be losing their magic – that reliable old British staple, the classic

literary adaptation, included. Branagh's attempt to turn **Love's Labours Lost** into a musical, and Patricia Rozema's injection of modish feminist and lesbian elements into **Mansfield Park** both fell between two stools, pleasing neither purists nor more youthful audiences.

An adaptation that was less gimmicky than these two, but nonetheless did fairly poor business, was Martha Fiennes' feature debut, **Onegin**, based on the same Pushkin narrative poem from which Tchaikovsky drew his finest opera. A powerful, handsomely-mounted drama, it's filmed with lively intelligence and an overwhelming emotional sweep. It's also a Fiennes family affair: Martha's brother, Ralph, takes the title role, while their younger brother, Magnus, contributes the music score. The film looks unfailingly superb, making stunning use of its

*Still from Kenneth Branagh's musical version of LOVE'S LABOUR'S LOST*
*photo: Pathé*

*Ralph Fiennes as the hero of ONEGIN, directed by his sister, Martha*

*photo: Entertainment*

St. Petersburg locations and meticulously designed sets, and carries a strong sense of historical context, as Russia, fascinated but uneasy, opens up to outside influences. Onegin himself is a cross-cultural figure, half world-weary Byronic dandy, half doomy Russian fatalist.

Tiring of fashion-mad St. Petersburg, Onegin moves to his newly-inherited country estate. When his neighbour's daughter, the idealistic young Tatyana, declares her love for him he coolly rejects her, and instead flirts with her sister, engaged to his friend, Lensky. Lensky demands a duel, and Onegin kills him. Six years later, he meets Tatyana again, now married to his cousin, and realises too late the value of what he so casually threw away. Fiennes, a master of poignant nuance, conveys all the anguish of a man ambushed by his emotions, and he's well matched by the rest of the cast, including Liv Tyler's innocently sensual Tatyana.

Not for the first time, true originality and risk-taking were to be found within the confines of the tiniest budgets. Shane Meadows, recovering from the commercial failure of his over-hyped and formulaic *TwentyFourSeven*, took us confidently back into the mean streets of Nottingham with **A Room for Romeo Brass**, a vividly observed, disquietingly off-kilter study of misdirected social attraction. Meadows drew utterly truthful performances from his unknown cast – especially from Paddy Considine, whose seamless transition from pitiable twerp to violent sociopath was chillingly credible.

An even more remarkable use of minimal resources was **Following**, a labyrinthine, noirish thriller written, directed, shot and co-edited by first-time feature-maker Christopher Nolan. Shot in 16mm black-and-white and running a lean 69 minutes, the film plays sophisticated games with perception and exposition, keeping us guessing as to just who's doing what to whom until the final reel.

A young would-be novelist takes to following people in the street until one of them confronts him, announcing himself as a professional burglar. Fascinated by his activities, the young man becomes increasingly complicit, only realising too late that there are levels to the relationship he never suspected. Nolan cunningly fragments his narrative, flipping back and forth in time as the various pieces in the jigsaw drop into place, and making evocative use of anonymous London streets. *Following* is an astonishingly assured first film, and it's depressing to know that on the strength of it Nolan has already relocated to Los Angeles.

## Wise Council?

The crisis of creativity facing British cinema is to be addressed – or so it's hoped – by the newly constituted, publicly-funded Film Council (FC). Launched on April 1, 2000 (the inevitable jokes were made), and headed by film director Alan Parker, the new body will oversee all public support for the film sector. With an annual budget of $88m, it takes under its umbrella the British Film Institute, the British Film Commission, financing body British Screen and all of the Lottery funding previously administered by the Arts Council. The FC's immediate aim has been summed up by Parker thus: "to establish a substantial industry producing stronger films."

The Council plans to take a wider, longer-term view than any of its constituent bodies could. It will be able to solicit projects and sign first-look deals with producers, widen the range of films it can support, initiate links with European and US production companies, and generally take a far more proactive, commercially savvy role. As part of its long-term strategy, the FC intends to tackle the industry's structural problems, not least the vexed question of distribution.

It's an ambitious programme, and already sceptical murmurs have been heard. But before all else, the Film Council must do all it can to raise the overall standard of British movies and stem the current flood of schlock. Already a promising start has been made with the announcement that the FC will not only set aside $7.8m for innovative film-making, but will fund Terry Gilliam's latest project, *The Man Who Killed Don Quixote*, to the substantial tune of $3.1m.

PHILIP KEMP is a freelance writer on film, contributing regularly to *Film Comment* and *Sight and Sound*. He has recently completed a book about the Coen Brothers.

# Recent and Forthcoming Films

### BIRTHDAY GIRL
Script: Tom Butterworth, Jez Butterworth. Dir: Jez Butterworth. Phot: Oliver Stapleton. Players: Nicole Kidman, Ben Chaplin, Vincent Cassel, Mathieu Kassovitz. Prod: Portobello.

### BORN ROMANTIC
Script and Dir: David Kane. Phot: Robert Alzaraki. Players: Craig Ferguson, Jane Horrocks, Catherine McCormack, David Morrissey. Prod: Kismet.

### BREAD AND ROSES
Script: Paul Laverty. Dir: Ken Loach. Phot: Barry Ackroyd. Players: Pilar Padilla, Adrien

Brody, Elpidia Carillo. Prod: Parallax.

### CHICKEN RUN
Animation. Script: Karey Kirkpatrick, Jack Rosenthal. Dir: Nick Park, Peter Lord. Phot: Tristan Oliver, Frank Passingham. Voices: Mel Gibson, Julia Sawalha, Miranda Richardson, Timothy Spall. Prod: Aardman/DreamWorks/Pathé.

### BILLY ELLIOT
Original title: 'Dancer'. Script: Lee Hall. Dir: Stephen Daldry. Phot: Brian Tufano. Players: Julie Walters, Jamie Bell, Jamie Draven, Gary Lewis. Prod: Working Title.

### THE DARKEST LIGHT
Script: Simon Beaufoy. Dir: Beaufoy, Billie Eltringham. Phot: Mary Farebrother. Players: Stephen Dillane, Kerry Fox, Keri Arnold. Prod: Footprints.

### DUST
Script and Dir: Micho Manchevski. Phot: Barry Ackroyd. Players: Joseph Fiennes, David Wentham, Adrian Lester, Anne Brochet. Prod: Film Consortium/History Dreams/ena/Fandango.

### ENIGMA
Script: Tom Stoppard, from the novel by Robert Harris. Dir:

Michael Apted. Players: Dougray Scott, Kate Winslet, Jeremy Northam, Saffron Burrows. Prod: Jagged/Broadway.

## GANGSTER NO.1

Script: Johnny Ferguson. Dir: Paul McGuigan. Phot: Peter Sova. Players: Malcolm McDowell, David Thewlis, Paul Bettany. Prod:Pagoda/Road Movies/Film Four.

## GAUDI AFTERNOON

Script: Joaquin Oristrell, James Myhre. Dir: Susan Seidelman. Phot: José Maria Civit. Players: Judy Davis, Marcia Gay Harden, Lili Taylor, Juliette Lewis. Prod: Lolafilms UK.

## THE GOLDEN BOWL

Script: Ruth Prawer Jhabvala, from the novel by Henry James. Dir: James Ivory. Phot: Tony Pierce-Roberts. Players: Uma Thurman, Nick Nolte, Jeremy Northam, Kate Beckinsale. Prod: Merchant Ivory.

## THE HOUSE OF MIRTH

Script and Dir: Terence Davies. Phot: Remi Adefarasin. Players: Gillian Anderson, Eric Stoltz, Dan Aykroyd, Laura Linney. Prod: Three Rivers.

## IT WAS AN ACCIDENT

Script: Ol Parker. Dir: Metin Huseyin. Phot: Guy Dufaux. Players: Chiwetel Ejiofor, Thandie Newton, Max Beesley, Hugh Quarshie. Prod: Litmus.

## KINGDOM COME

Script: Frank Cottrell Boyce. Dir: Michael Winterbottom. Players: Wes Bentley, Natassia Kinski, Peter Mullan, Sarah Polley. Prod: Pathe/UA/BBC Films.

## LAVA

Script and Dir: Joe Tucker. Phot: Sam McCurdy. Players: Tom Bell, Nicola Stapleton, Joe Tucker, James Holmes. Prod: Sterling/ Orangetop/Walking Point.

## LONDINIUM

Script and Dir: Mike Binder. Phot: Sue Gibson. Players: Mike Binder, Mariel Hemingway, Irène Jacob, Colin Firth. Prod: Sun Lite.

## LOVE'S LABOURS LOST

Script and Dir: Kenneth Branagh. Phot: Alex Thompson. Players: Branagh, Alicia Silverstone, Natascha McElhone, Nathan Lane. Prod: Shakespeare Film Co/Intermedia/Pathé.

## THE LUZHIN DEFENCE

Script: Peter Berry. Dir: Marleen Gorris. Phot: Bernard Lutic. Players: John Turturro, Emily Watson, Geraldine James, Stuart Wilson. Prod: Renaissance.

## MAYBE BABY

Script and Dir: Ben Elton. Phot: Roger Lanser. Players: Hugh Laurie, Joely Richardson, James Purefoy. Prod: Pandora/BBC Films.

## ONE DAY IN SEPTEMBER

Documentary. Script and Dir: Kevin Macdonald. Phot: Alwin Küchler, Neve Cunningham. Prod: Cohn/Passion.

## PANDEMONIUM

Script: Frank Cottrell-Boyce. Dir: Julien Temple. Phot: John Lynch. Players: Linus Roache, John Hannah, Emily Woof, Samantha Morton. Prod: Mariner/BBC Films.

## PLATO'S BREAKING POINT

Script and Dir: Nigel Braker. Phot: Miles Cook. Players: Joe Ferrera, William Halliday, Delphine Lanson, Melodi Boreland. Prod: Robark.

## A ROOM FOR ROMEO BRASS

Script: Paul Fraser, Shane Meadows. Dir: Meadows. Phot: Ashley Rowe. Players: Andrew Shim, Ben Marshall, Paddy Considine, Vicky McClure. Prod: Company/Big Arty.

## SAVING GRACE

Script: Craig Ferguson, Mark Crowdy. Dir: Nigel Cole. Phot: John de Borman. Players: Brenda Blethyn, Craig Ferguson, Martin Clunes. Prod: Homerun/ Sky/Fox.

*Still from Shane Meadows' A ROOM FOR ROMEO BRASS*
*photo: Momentum Pictures*

## SHINER

Script: Scott Cherry. Dir: John Irvin. Phot: Mike Molloy. Players: Michael Caine, Martin Landau, Frances Barber. Prod: Wisecroft.

## SIMON MAGUS

Script and Dir: Ben Hopkins. Phot: Nic Knowland. Players: Noah Taylor, Embeth Davidtz, Stuart Townsend. Prod: FilmFour/ Lucky Red/ARP/Hollywood Partners.

## TOPSY-TURVY

Script and Dir: Mike Leigh. Phot: Dick Pope. Players: Jim Broadbent, Allan Corduner, Timothy Spall. Prod: Canning Williams.

## UP AT THE VILLA

Script: Belina Haas. Dir: Philip Haas. Phot: Maurizio Calvesi. Players: Kristin Scott Thomas, Sean Penn, Anne Bancroft, James Fox. Prod: Mirage/

Buchtal/Intermedia/October.

## WONDERLAND

Script: Laurence Coriat. Dir: Michael Winterbottom. Phot: Sean Bobbitt. Players: Ian Hart, Gina McKee, Molly Parker, Jack Shepherd. Prod: Kismet/ Revolution.

# Producers

**Alibi Films**
12 Maiden Lane
London WC2E 7NA
Tel: (44 20) 7845 0410
Fax: (44 20) 7836 6776
e-mail: afi@alibifilms.co.uk
www.alibifilms.co.uk

**Arcane Pictures**
46 Wetherby Mansions
Earl's Court Square
London SW5 9DJ
Tel: (44 20) 7244 6590
Fax: (44 20) 7565 4495
e-mail: thomson@dircon.co.uk
www.arcanepictures.com

**BBC Films**
56 Wood Lane
London W12 7SB
Tel: (44 20) 8743 8000
Fax: (44 20) 8749 7520

**Celador Productions**
39 Long Acre
London WC2E 9JT
Tel: (44 20) 240 8101
Fax: (44 20) 497 9541
e-mail: tvhits@celador.co.uk
www.whowantstobeamillionaire.co.uk

**Company Pictures**
Suffolk House
1-8 Whitfield Place, 2nd Floor
London W1P 5SF
Tel: (44 20) 7380 3900
Fax: (44 20) 7380 1166
e-mail:
reception@companypictures.co.uk

**DNA Films**
75-77 Margaret St, 3rd Floor
London W1N 7HB
Tel: (44 20) 7291 8010
e-mail: info@dnafilms.com

**Ecosse Films**
12 Quayside Lodge
Watermeadow Lane
London SW6 2UZ
Tel: (44 20) 7371 0290
Fax: (44 20) 7736 3436
e-mail: info@ecossefilms.com
www.ecossefilms.com

**Figment Films**
75-77 Margaret St, 3rd Floor
London W1N 7HB
Tel: (44 20) 7291 8030
Fax: (44 20) 7291 8040
e-mail: figment@globalnet.co.uk
www.figmentfilms.com

**FilmFour Ltd**
76-78 Charlotte St
London W1P 1LX
Tel: (44 20) 7868 7700
Fax: (44 20) 7868 7766
www.filmfour.com

**Flashlight Films Ltd**
10 Golden Square
London W1R 3AF
Tel: (44 20) 7287 4252
Fax: (44 20) 7287 4232
e-mail:
flashlightfilms@compuserve.com
www.flashlightfilms.com

**Granada Film**
London Television Centre, 16th Floor

Upper Ground,
London SE1 9LT
Tel: (44 20) 7737 8681
Fax: (44 20) 7737 8682
e-mail:
granada.film@granadamedia.com

**Gruber Films**
74 Margaret St
London W1N 7HA
Tel: (44 20) 7436 3413
Fax: (44 20) 7436 3402
e-mail: office@gruberfilms.com

**Heyday Films**
5 Denmark St
London WC2H 8LP
Tel: (44 20) 7836 6333
Fax: (44 20) 7836 6444

**Little Bird Co.**
9 Grafton Mews
London W1P 5LG
Tel: (44 20) 7380 3980
Fax: (44 20) 7380 3981
e-mail: info@littlebird.co.uk
www.littlebird.ie

**Merchant Ivory Productions**
46 Lexington St
London W1R 3LH
Tel: (44 20) 7437 1200
Fax: (44 20) 7734 1579
e-mail:
miplondon@merchantivory.demon.
co.uk

**Miramax Films**
Elsley House
24-30 Great Titchfield St
London W1P 7AD
Tel: (44 20) 7535 8300

Fax: (44 20) 7535 8301

**Pagoda Film & TV Corp**
20th Century House
31-32 Soho Square
London W1V 6AP
Tel: (44 20) 7534 3500
Fax: (44 20) 7534 3501
e-mail: pag@pagodafilm.co.uk

**Parallax Pictures**
7 Denmark St
London WC2H 8LS
Tel: (44 20) 7836 1478
Fax: (44 20) 7497 8062

**Pathé Pictures**
Kent House, 4th Floor
14-17 Market Place
Great Titchfield St
London W1N 8AR
Tel: (44 20) 7323 5151
Fax: (44 20) 7631 3568
www.pathe.co.uk

**Rafford Films**
26-27 Oxendon St
London SW1Y 4LT
Tel: (44 20) 7839 1800
Fax: (44 20) 7839 3600
e-mail: algscott@aol.com

**Rocket Pictures**
1 Blythe Road
London W14 0HG
Tel: (44 20) 7603 9530
Fax: (44 20) 7348 4830
e-mail:
caroline@rocketpictures.co.uk

**Samuelson Productions**
13 Minett St
London W1V 5LB
Tel: (44 20) 7439 4900
Fax: (44 20) 7439 4901
e-mail: samuelsonp@aol.com

**Sarah Radclyffe Productions**
83-84 Berwick St, 5th Floor
London W1V 3PJ
Tel: (44 20) 7437 3128
Fax: (44 20) 7437 3129
e-mail: srpltd@globalnet.co.uk

**Scala Productions**
15 Frith St
London W1V 5TS
Tel: (44 20) 7734 7060
Fax: (44 20) 7437 3248
e-mail: scalaprods@aol.com

**Scott Free**
42-44 Beak St
London W1R 3DA
Tel: (44 20) 7437 3163
Fax: (44 20) 7439 2478

**The Film Consortium**
6 Flitcroft St
London WC2H 8DJ
Tel: (44 20) 7691 4440
Fax: (44 20) 7691 4445

**Toledo Films**
30 Oval Rd
London NW1 7DE
Tel: (44 20) 7291 8050
Fax: (44 20) 7485 4422
e-mail:
adam.tudhope@dnafilms.com

**Tony Kaye Productions**
33 Tottenham St
London W1P 9PE
Tel: (44 20) 7323 1511
Fax: (44 20) 7323 1711
e-mail: tonykltd@yahoo.com

**Trademark Films**
5 Sherwood St
London W1V 7RA
Tel: (44 20) 7287 5944
Fax: (44 20) 7287 1786
e-mail: mail@trademarkfilms.co.uk

**Working Title Films**
Oxford House, 76 Oxford St
London W1N 9FD
Tel: (44 20) 7307 3000
Fax: (44 20) 7307 3001

# Distributors

**Artificial Eye Film Ltd**
14 King St
London WC2E 8HM
Tel: (44 20) 7240 5353
Fax: (44 20) 7240 5242
e-mail: email@artificial-eye.com

**Blue Dolphin Film & Video Ltd**
40 Langham St
London W1N 5RG
Tel: (44 20) 7255 2494
Fax: (44 20) 7580 7670

**Buena Vista International**
Centre West
3 Queen Caroline St
London W6 9PE

Tel: (44 20) 8222 1000
Fax: (44 20) 8222 2795
www.bvimovies.co.uk

**Columbia TriStar Film Distributors**
Sony Pictures Europe House
25 Golden Square
London W1R 6LU
Tel: (44 20) 7533 1111
Fax: (44 20) 7533 1015
www.spe.sony.com

**Entertainment Film Distributors**
27 Soho Square,
London W1V 6HU
Tel: (44 20) 7439 1606
Fax: (44 20) 7734 2483

**Feature Film Co.**
68-70 Wardour St
London W1V 3HP
Tel: (44 20) 7734 2266
Fax: (44 20) 7494 0309
e-mail: mail@featurefilm.co.uk
www.featurefilm.co.uk

**Film Four Distributors**
(see details under Producers)

**Gala Film Distributors**
26 Danbury St
London N1 8JU
Tel: (44 20) 7226 5085
Fax: (44 20) 7226 5897

**ICA Projects**
12 Carlton House Terrace,
London SW1Y 5AH
Tel: (44 20) 7930 0493
Fax: (44 20) 7873 0051
www.ica.org.uk

**Metrodome Films**
110 Park St
London W1Y 5LG
Tel: (44 20) 7408 2121
Fax: (44 20) 7409 1935
www.metrodomegroup.com

**Metro Tartan**
Atlantic House
5 Wardour St
London W1V 3HE
Tel: (44 20) 7494 1400
Fax: (44 20) 7439 1922
e-mail: info@metro-tartan.co.uk

**Momentum Pictures**
184-192 Drummond St, 2nd Floor

London NW1 3HP
Tel: (44 20) 7391 6900
Fax: (44 20) 7383 0404
www.momentumpictures.co.uk

**Pathé Distributions**
Kent House, 4th Floor
14-17 Market Place
Great Titchfield St
London W1N 8AR
Tel: (44 20) 7323 5151
Fax: (44 20) 7631 3568
www.pathe.co.uk

**Twentieth Century Fox**
20th Century House
31-32 Soho Square
London W1V 6AP
Tel: (44 20) 7437 7766
Fax: (44 20) 7434 2170

**U.I.P.**
UIP House
45 Beadon Road
London W6 OEG
Tel: (44 20) 8741 9041
Fax: (44 20) 8748 8990
www.uip.com

**Warner Bros.**
98 Theobalds Road
London WC1X 8WB
Tel: (44 20) 7984 5000
Fax: (44 20) 7984 5551
www.warnerbrothers@warner
brothers.com

# Sales Companies

**Alibi Films**
12 Maiden Lane
London WC2E 7NA
Tel: (44 20) 7845 0410
Fax: (44 20) 7836 6919
e-mail: afi@alibifilms.co.uk
www.alibifilms.co.uk

**Capitol Films**
23 Queensdale Place
London W11 4SQ
Tel: (44 20) 7471 6000
Fax: (44 20) 7471 6012
e-mail: films@capitolfilms.com

**Goldcrest Film International**
65-66 Dean St
London W1V 6PL
Tel: (44 20) 7437 8696
Fax: (44 20) 7437 4448

**IAC Film & TV**
Greencoat House
15 Francis St
London SW1P 1DH
Tel: (44 20) 7592 1620
Fax: (44 20) 7592 1621
e-mail: general@iacholdings.co.uk
www.iacfilm.co.uk

**Icon Films**
4 West End
Somerset Street
Bristol BS2 8NE
Tel: (117) 7924 8535
Fax: (117) 7942 0386
e-mail: info@iconfilms.co.uk
www.iconfilms.co.uk

**Intermedia**
9-13 Grosvenor St
London W1X 9FB
Tel: (44 20) 7495 3322
Fax: (44 20) 7495 3993
www.intermedia.com

**J&M Entertainment**
2 Dorset Square
London NW1 6PU
Tel: (44 20) 7723 6544
Fax: (44 20) 7724 7541
e-mail: sales@jmnet.com
www.jmnet.com

**Portman Entertainment Group Ltd.**
167 Wardour St
London W1V 3TA
Tel: (44 20) 7468 3400
Fax: (44 20) 7468 3469
e-mail: annie.protheroe@
port-ent.co.uk

**The Sales Company**
62 Shaftesbury Ave
London W1V 7DE
Tel: (44 20) 7434 9061
Fax: (44 20) 7494 3293
e-mail: thesalesco@btinternet.com

**Summit Entertainment**
118-120 Wardour St
London W1V 3LA
Tel: (44 20) 7494 1724
Fax: (44 20) 7494 1725

**United Artists Int'l**
10 Stephen Mews, Office 718
London W1P 1PP
Tel: (44 20) 7333 8877

Fax: (44 20) 7333 8878
www.mgm.com

**Universal Pictures International**
4th Floor, Oxford House
76 Oxford St
London W1N 0HQ
Tel: (44 20) 7307 1300
Fax: (44 20) 7307 1301
www.unistudios.com

**Victor Film Co.**
39-43 Brewer St
London W1R 3FD
Tel: (44 20) 7494 4477
Fax: (44 20) 7494 4488
e-mail: post@victor-film-
co.demon.co.uk
www.victor-film-co.demon.co.uk

**Vine International Pictures**
VIP House, Greenacres
New Road Hill, Downe Orpington
Kent, BR6 7JA
Tel: (44 1689) 854 123
Fax: (44 1689) 850 990
e-mail: vine@easynet.co.uk
www.vine-international.co.uk

**Winchester Film & TV Sales**
19 Heddon St
London W1R 7LF
Tel: (44 20) 7851 6500
Fax: (44 20) 7851 6505
e-mail: mail@winchesternet.co.uk
www.winchesterfilms.com

# Useful Addresses

**British Academy of Film and Television Arts (BAFTA)**
195 Piccadilly
London W1V 0LN
Tel: (44 20) 7734 0022
Fax: (44 20) 7734 1792
www.bafta.org

**British Board of Film Classification (BBFC)**
3 Soho Square
London W1V 6HD
Tel: (44 20) 7439 7961
Fax: (44 20) 7287 0141
e-mail: webmaster@bbfc.co.uk
www.bbfc.co.uk

**British Actors Equity Association**
Guild House
Upper St. Martins Lane
London WC2H 9EG
Tel: (44 20) 7379 6000
Fax: (44 20) 7379 7001
e-mail: abaxter@equity.org.uk
www.equity.org.uk

**The British Council**
Films, Television, & Video Dept.
11 Portland Place
London W1N 4EJ
Tel: (44 20) 7389 3065
Fax: (44 20) 7389 3041
www.britfilms.com

**British Film Commission**
Queens Yard
179a Tottenham Court Road
London W1P 0BE
Tel: (44 20) 7224 5000

Fax: (44 20) 7224 1013
e-mail: info@britfilmcom.co.uk
www.britfilmcom.co.uk

**British Film Institute**
21 Stephen St
London W1P 1PL
Tel: (44 20) 7255 1444
Fax: (44 20) 7436 7950

**Cinema Exhibitors' Association**
22 Golden Square
London W1R 3PA
Tel: (44 20) 7734 9551
Fax: (44 20) 7734 6147
e-mail: cea@cinemauk.ftech.co.uk

**Directors' Guild of Great Britain**
15-19 Great Titchfield St
London W1P 7FB
Tel: (44 20) 7436 8626
Fax: (44 20) 7438 8646

www.dggb.co.uk

**London Film Commission**
20 Euston Centre
Regent's Place
London NW1 3JH
Tel: (44 20) 7387 8787
Fax: (44 20) 7387 8788
e-mail: lfc@london-film.co.uk
www.london-film.co.uk

**PACT**
45 Mortimer St
London W1N 7TD
Tel: (44 20) 7331 6000
Fax: (44 20) 7331 6700
e-mail: inquires@pact.co.uk

**Scottish Screen**
249 West George Street, 2nd Floor
Glasgow G2 4QE
Tel: (44 141) 7302 1700
Fax: (44 141) 7302 1711

# UNITED STATES

Eddie
Cockrell

**M**ovies are better than ever. That was the advertising slogan crafted decades ago to bolster film industry enthusiasm in the face of a new technology: television. That sense of determined optimism might also describe the current mood of Hollywood as it grapples with the meteoric rise of extras-laden DVDs, movie websites, digital production and projection, online piracy (with resulting lawsuits) and an audience inundated with new, confusing and perpetually mutating entertainment choices.

While only beginning to affect how movies are seen, these new wrinkles in how they are made and distributed have had an immediate impact on film aesthetics, with digital film-making becoming increasingly common in the mainstream, and the look of some high-profile 35mm titles reflecting the more energetic, fragmented and visually diverse (read grainy) nature of the 'Do-It-Yourself' credo of independent film-makers.

But nothing has yet arrived to dampen people's enthusiasm for the tactile experience of actually going to the movies. Admissions rose by an aggregate of nearly 25% during the 1990s, and when it comes to Hollywood apprehensions over pre-serving its slice of the entertainment pie in the face of digital piracy, the official year-end tallies for 1999, and good results for the first half of 2000, reveal that both the pie itself and the individual slices grow ever bigger, suggesting either an ongoing satisfaction with the diversity of the product, or the continued efficiency of the corporate publicity machine. Probably a bit of both.

For the eighth consecutive year, America's cumulative box-office gross for 1999 set yet another record, with *Variety* reporting a record 1.48 billion admissions – the highest level in decades – and a jump in domestic ticket sales to $7.4 billion (up 8% on 1998's $6.95 billion). This increase was achieved with fewer films in release (461, against 509 in 1998, according to the Motion Picture Association of America), and was credited by the MPAA to an 8.3% increase in the average ticket cost, from $4.69 to $5.08. This, in turn, discreetly reflected a kind of controlled panic within studio gates and multiplexes, as staffs and overheads were cut to streamline the production and exhibition machines. Factor in the usual boardroom shuffles and two high-profile mergers (AOL/Time-Warner and Vivendi/Seagram/Canal +) and the increase seems downright restrained.

## An animated year

Many year-end summaries seized on the title of Mike Leigh's most recent film, *Topsy-Turvy*, to describe American cinema in 1999. Yet it is this very diversity that makes the industry strong, as for every critically drubbed title such as **Eyes Wide Shut** (domestic gross: $55m), there was a breakout hit from left field, a *Sixth Sense* ($276m) or **American Pie** ($101m) that seemed at once to conform to the idea of Hollywood genre product, while simultaneously subverting the cookie cutter mentality assumed to be at the core of popular entertainment.

To no one's surprise, **Star Wars: Episode I – The Phantom Menace** overcame tepid reviews – as did many of the year's 'event' pictures – to lead the year in domestic revenues, and land in second place on the all-time top grossing list, with $927m worldwide (still a long way behind *Titanic's* scarcely credible $1.8 billion). *Phantom Menace* resembled nothing so much as *The Empire Strikes Back*, which

*AMERICAN PIE was one of the year's surprise hits*
*photo: Vivian Zink/Universal*

sacrificed much of its entertainment value in favour of narrative connective tissue, setting up future conflicts in its increasingly eccentric and oddly quaint universe.

Some 16 other films passed the still magic (but now somehow paltry) $100m benchmark in 1999. The year's second biggest hit, **The Sixth Sense**, was an intelligent and crafty parlour trick of a movie which dumbfounded audiences with its genuinely unsettling final twist, and confirmed Bruce Willis as a shrewd – and perhaps lucky – judge of scripts (his streak of moppet-themed successes continued in summer 2000 with the unexpectedly strong debut of *Disney's The Kid*). Although *The Sixth Sense* garnered six Oscar nominations, it failed to win even one award, joining fellow Buena Vista release **The Insider** ($26m; seven nominations, no wins) as the big and unfortunate losers at the 1999 Academy Awards.

*Bruce Willis, left, and M. Night Shayamalam, star and director of THE SIXTH SENSE*
*photo: Buena Vista Int'l/Kobal Collection*

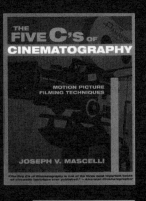

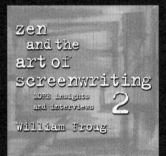

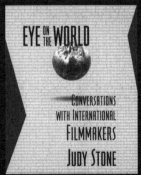

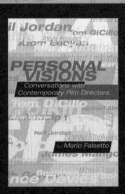

# Silman-James Press

Publishers of books on

**Film, Filmmaking,
the Motion Picture Industry,
and the Performing Arts**

## Comic Insights: The Art of Stand-up Comedy

Franklyn Ajaye, 280 PAGES, 6 X 9, 1-879505-54-1, $18.95 PAPER
*"Franklyn Ajaye is the Miles Davis of comedy."* —Keenen Ivory Wayans
*"Ajaye has Pryor's insights, Cosby's cool!"* —San Francisco Chronicle
*Comic Insights* combines essential advice about the fundamentals of stand-up comedy with candid, insightful interviews with today's top comedians: Louie Anderson, Richard Belzer, Elayne Boosler, George Carlin, Ellen DeGeneres, Rich Jeni, Jay Leno, Richard Lewis, Bill Maher, Roseanne, Paul Reiser, Chris Rock, Jerry Seinfeld, Garry Shandling, Sinbad, George Wallace, Jonathan Winters. **Franklyn Ajaye** is an Emmy-nominated writer-producer-actor. Among his many television writing and producing credits are *The Parent'Hood, In Living Color, Roc, NYPD Blue*, and *Politically Incorrect*. Among his acting credits are *Hollywood Shuffle, The Burbs*, and *Stir Crazy*.

## Why We Write: Personal Statements and Photographic: Portraits of 25 Top Screenwriters

Ed. by Lorian Tamara Elbert, 233 PAGES, 9x8, 25 B&W PORTRAITS, 1-879505-45-2, $22.95 PAPER
The screenwriters in this collection offer personal essays about why they write, what inspires them, and how they cope with Hollywood. Each essay is accompanied by a photographic portrait. Includes: Scott Alexander and Larry Karaszewski, Jeff Arch, John Briley, Pen Densham , Patrick S. Duncan , Trey Ellis, Michael Ferris and John Brancato , Michael Grais, James V. Hart, Velina Hasu Houston, Lawrence Konner and Mark Rosenthal , Dale Launer , Kasi Lemmons, Angelo Pizzo, Gary Ross, Tom Schulman, Ed Solomon , Dana Stevens, Joan Tewkesbury, Michael Tolkin, Randall Wallace, Daniel Waters.

## Zen and the Art of Screenwriting 2: More Insights and Interviews

William Froug, 332 PAGES, 8x8, 1-879505-56-8, $21.95 PAPER
*Three cheers for Bill Froug, who supports the creative act of screenwriting and . . . encourages writers to express ther own visions, instead of recycling tired old outlines.* —Roger Ebert
This collection of new thought-provoking essays and informative interviews with some of Hollywood's top filmmakers is a sequel to Froug's popular *Zen and the Art of Screenwriting*. The interviewees are Richard Donner (*Lethal Weapon,*), Scott Frank (*Get Shorty*), Brian Helgeland (*L.A. Confidential*), Nicholas Kazan (*Reversal of Fortune*), Frank Pierson (*Dog Day Afternoon*), Eric Roth (*Forrest Gump*), Lauren Shuler-Donner (*Bulworth*), Aaron Sorkin (*A Few Good Men*), Robin Swicord (*Little Women*). **William Froug** is an Emmy-winning writer-producer whose television credits include *Playhouse 90* and *The Twilight Zone* .

## Zen and the Art of Screenwriting: Insights and Interviews

William Froug, 332 PAGES, 8x8, 1-879505-31-2, $20.95 PAPER
A tapestry of short essays and interviews with top screenwriters. Froug's essays cover such topics as avoiding the obvious, the birth of ideas, the process of rewriting, dealing with writer's block, creativity and spontaneity, handling rejection, and breaking the screenwriting "rules." The interviewees are Frank Darabont, Callie Khourie, Eric Roth, Ruth Prawer Jhabvala, David Peoples, Janet Peoples, Bo Goldman, Laurence Dworet, Stuart Kaminsky, and Larry Gelbart.

## Screenwriting Tricks of the Trade

William Froug, 150 PAGES, 5½x8½, 1-879505-13-4, $10.95 PAPER,
*"I wish every studio executive, director, producer and agent in town would read this book... it is a book of wisdom and good, sound advice about the <u>process</u> of screenwriting."*
—Jeffrey Boam, screenwriter, *Indian Jones and the Last Crusade, Lethal Weapon 2*
Froug distills his many years of teaching at USC and UCLA into a concise and witty primer that is both fresh and timeless. Froug doesn't rehash the time-worn formulas promoted in many other screenwriting books. Instead, he presents a practical approach to following one's own muse. Abundant with examples from films, this popular book will take the reader from the first urge to write through the completion of a well-wrought script.

## The New Screenwriter Looks at the New Screenwriter

William Froug, 369 PAGES, 6x9, 1-879505-04-5, $15.95 PAPER
Interviews with Jeffrey Boam, Ronald Bass, Jack Epps & Jim Cash, Gregory Widen, Dan Pyne, Anna Hamilton Phelan, Diane Frolov, Bill Bryan, Fay Kanin , Laurence Dworet, Dan O'Bannon, Joe Eszterhas, Bill Haber and Roland Perkins.

SILMAN JAMES

## The Screenwriter Looks at the Screenwriter

William Froug, 362 PAGES, 6x9, 1-879505-01-0, $16.95 PAPER

Interviews with Nunnally Johnson, I.A.L. Diamond, Buck Henry, Fay Kanin Ring Lardner, Jr., Walter Brown Newman, Edward Anhalt, Stirling Silliphant, Lewis John Carlino, David Giler, William Bowers, and Jonathan Axelrod.

## African-American Screenwriters Now:
## Conversations with Hollywood's Black Pack

Erich Leon Harris, 273 PAGES, 6x9, ILLUS., 1-879505-28-2, $16.95 PAPER

A vivid picture of the opportunities and obstacles that face today's black filmmakers. Interviewed are Robert Townsend, Charles Burnett, Lawrence Andries, Rusty Cundieff, Eric Daniel, Michael Dinwiddie, Carl Franklin, Julie Dash, Dwayne Johnson-Cochran, Yvette Lee-Bowser, Tim Reid, Carol Munday Lawrence, and Jeanne Williams.

## Making a Good Writer Great:
## A Creativity Workbook for Screenwriters

Linda Seger, 233 PAGES, 5½x8½, 1-879505-49-5, $14.95 PAPER

*"Linda's technique is a light to see by."* —Ray Bradbury

Designed not just to awaken creativity, but to teach the writer the process of being creative within the context of screenwriting, this addition to Seger's popular collection of books combines the tools necessary to learn how to think and work creatively with indispensable screenwriting know-how. *Making a Good Writer Great* provides both novice and experienced writers with the means to expand their creativity and write at a higher artistic level. **Linda Seger** is the author of five popular books on screenwriting including *Making a Good Script Great, Creating Unforgettable Characters*, and *The Art of Adaptation.* Seger created and defined the job of script consultant and has consulted on more than 2,000 film and television projects.

## The Screenwriter's Bible:
## A Complete Guide to Writing, Formatting, and Selling Your
## Script • 3rd Edition • Expanded and Updated

David Trottier, 314 PAGES, 8½x11, INDEX, 1-879505-44-4, $19.95 PAPER

*"Whether you are a rank beginner who needs instruction, or an old pro who needs reminding, you could not do better than David Trottier's book. A brilliant effort by a first-class, dedicated teacher."*
—William Kelly, Academy Award-winning Writer, *Witness*

*The Screenwriter's Bible,* one of the most popular and useful books on screenwriting, is divided into six major sections: **How to Write a Screenplay**—A Primer (A concise presentation of screenwriting basics); **Correct Format for Screenplays and Teleplays**—A Style Guide for Spec Scripts (The industry-accepted format); **Writing Your Breakthrough Spec Script**—A Script Consultant's View (This dissects and analyzes sample scenes and revisions of those same scenes, drawing the reader through the process of self-criticism); **Steps to a Stunning Script**—A Workbook (A step-by-step guide to the screenwriting process—from nascent idea through revisions); **How to Sell Your Script**—A Marketing Plan (Marketing and sales strategies, and up-to-date information about today's screenplay and teleplay marketplaces); **Resources** (Industry contacts, guilds, schools, publications, support groups and services, contests, etc.).

## The Comic Toolbox: How To Be Funny Even If You're Not

John Vorhaus, 250 PAGES, 6x9, 1-879505-21-5, $14.95 PAPER

*"A funny idea is worthless until you understand the mechanics of its construction and execution. Meet Mr. Goodwrench."* —Russ Woody, Producer, *Murphy Brown*

*The Comic Toolbox* is a straightforward, workbook approach to creative problem solving. Vorhaus offers writers and comics the tools of the trade—"clash of context," "tension and release," "the law of comic opposites," "the wildly inappropriate response," and more.

## Creativity Rules! A Writer's Workbook

John Vorhaus, 271 PAGES, 6x9, 1-879505-50-9, $15.95 PAPER

Beginning or completing any writing project can be highly daunting work. Faced with the often terrifying blank page, many writers find themselves frozen by indecision and doubt. *Creativity Rules!* addresses these anxieties—and the whole writing process—through an extensive series of exercises that allow the writer to break down a project into a collection of not-so-daunting "tasks" and step directly and quickly into the act of writing.

SILMAN·JAMES

## Movie Money:
## Understanding Hollywood's (Creative) Accounting Practices

Bill Daniels, David Leedy, and Steven D. Sills, 299 PAGES, 7X9, 1-879505-33-9, $19.95 PAPER

The distribution of a motion picture's "profits" is a murky, labyrinthine domain ruled by studio/distributor accountants and lawyers. *Movie Money* unravels and clearly explains the film industry's unique, arcane, "creative" accounting practices. It presents numerous film-industry definitions of "gross" and "net" profits, examines a film's various revenue-generating and revenue-consuming components, and provides discussion of the various aspects of profit participation—terminology, deal practices, audits and claims, and negotiating tips and tricks.

## Clearance and Copyright:
## Everything the Independent Filmmaker Needs to Know

Michael C. Donaldson, 250 PAGES, 7X9, 1-879505-30-4, $26.95 PAPER

*"Donaldson provides an indispensable guided tour of an area of law—filled with landmines—which filmmakers cannot afford to ignore. A wealth of information is presented in a clear, accessible, even friendly manner. Read it once for background and then keep it for reference."* —Marcie Bloom, Sony Picture Classics

This legalese-free guide provides filmmakers with essential advice on almost every conceivable rights issue that they might encounter—from the initial acquisition of material through the situations encountered in pre-production, production, post-production, and final release.

## Marketing and Selling Your Film Around the World:
## A Guide for Independent Filmmakers

John Durie, Annika Pham, and Neil Watson, 165 PAGES, 7X9, 1-879505-43-6, $19.95 PAPER

The overseas film markets are financially important outlets for American films. This manual guides the independent filmmaker through the demographics and business practices of film markets around the world and gives essential information on how to secure a sales agent, what types of deals one can expect from international distributors, and much more.

## Dealmaking in the Film and Television Industry:
## From Negotiations Through Final Contracts

Mark Litwak, 406 PAGES, 7X9, 1-879505-15-0, $26.95 PAPER

*"This book breaks the secret code attorneys use, explaining the fine print and why it's necessary . . . Litwak explains in a few hours what it took me years to learn."* —Dale Launer, screenwriter, *My Cousin Vinny*

This "self-defense" book for everyone working in the film industry, addresses a general, non-attorney readership. It is an accessible (no impenetrable legalese) guide to entertainment law's peculiarities and practical applications. Armed with this book, filmmakers can save thousands of dollars in legal fees as they navigate the shark-infested waters of the industry.

## Contracts for the Film and Television Industry—2nd Ed.

Mark Litwak, 460 PAGES, 8½X11, 1-879505-46-0, $35.00 PAPER

An invaluable collection of sample entertainment contracts. Includes contracts covering: Depiction—release, option, purchase; Literary submission and sale—release, option, purchase; Artist employment—writer, director, actor; Collaboration—writer, joint venture, co-production; Music—television rights license, soundtrack, composer; Financing—finder, limited partnership, prospectus; Distribution—theatrical, video; and much more.

## Reel Power:
## The Struggle for Influence and Success in the New Hollywood

Mark Litwak, 336 PAGES, 5½x8½, ILLUS., 1-879505-19-3, $14.95 PAPER

*"Such books as McClintick's* Indecent Exposure *and Bach's* Final Cut *have given us glimpses of the beast, but Litwak's* REEL POWER *is the first that lets us look the monster in the face . . . a chilling study of that frightening creature that is the new Hollywood."* —Chicago Tribune

## Movie Marketing: Opening the Picture and Giving It Legs

Tiiu Lukk, 274 PAGES, 6X9, 1-879505-38-X, $19.95 PAPER

*Movie Marketing* makes complex marketing issues simple, tracing marketing strategies for successful films through the words of those responsible for developing and implementing these strategies. Among the films profiled are *Four Weddings and a Funeral*, *Pulp Fiction*, *GoldenEye*, *Hoop Dreams*, *Welcome to the Dollhouse*, *Howard's End*, *Crumb*, *Carnosaur*, and *Brother's Keeper*.

## The Biz: The Basic Business, Legal and Financial Aspects of the Film Industry

Schuyler M. Moore, 365 PAGES, 7X9, 1-879505-53-3, $26.95 PAPER

Today's film industry is a legal and financial obstacle course that independent filmmakers must learn to master. This comprehensive guide to negotiating that ostacle course is an accessible overview of the industry's important business, legal, and financial aspects. Filled with industry-savvy advice, it clearly explains raising financing; business structuring; securities laws; budgeting essentials; dealing with the guilds; loans; completion guarantees; the legal and financial ramifications of distribution deals; calculating net profits; screen credits; talent demands; film-industry accounting practices and contingent payments; copyright, publicity, and trademark laws; litigation problems; bankruptcy; taxation of film companies; the internet distribution of film; film-industry business jargon; and much more.

## Film Finance and Distribution: A Dictionary of Terms

John W. Cones, 638 pages, 6x9, 1-879505-12-6, $24.95 paper

This dictionary defines thorny legal and financial terms that often elude novice filmmakers and impede their attempts to secure financing and distribution.

## Grammar of the Film Language

Daniel Arijon, 640 PAGES, 5½X8½, ILLUS., 1-879505-07-X, $24.95 PAPER

This unique magnum opus (640 pages/1,500 illustrations) covering the visual narrative techniques that form the "language" of filmmaking has found an avid audience among filmmakers—including students, producers, directors, writers, and cinematographers. This "language" is basic to the very positioning and moving of players and cameras, as well as the sequencing and pacing of images, and does not date as new technologies appear. Arijon presents visual narrative formulas basic to the very scripting of a scene or planning of a shoot.

## Getting the Best Score for Your Film: A Filmmakers' Guide to Music Scoring

David Bell, 130 PAGES, 6x9, ILLUS., 1-879505-20-7, $12.95 PAPER

One of the greatest challenges faced by filmmakers is dealing with the music score. This book directly addresses filmmakers about such film-scoring basics as the functions of underscore, choosing and communicating with a composer, the spotting session, the composing process, time and budget requirements, the personnel involved, and more.

## Making Movies Work: Thinking Like a Filmmaker

Jon Boorstin, 228 PAGES, 7X9, ILLUS., 1-879505-27-4 , $19.95 PAPER

The first question that filmmakers ask themselves isn't "Is this brilliant?" but "Does this work?" *Making Movies Work* is about how filmmakers think about film. To this end, the author identifies three ways in which we, both filmmakers and audience, watch movies. Then, through practical examples, he demonstrates how, at any given moment, the way we watch dictates its own rules of time and space and demands its own set of film techniques to address them. Contains over 100 illustrations, which include film stills and storyboards.

## Filmmaking: Narrative and Structural Techniques

Bob Foss, 224 PAGES, 6x9, ILLUS., 1-879505-14-2, $15.95 PAPER

A unique, illustrated guide to and appraisal of the basic narrative and structural techniques employed, either consciously or intuitively, by all successful filmmakers. The author seamlessly joins theory and practice in an accessible approach to filmmaking that should find an eager audience among filmmakers (directors, editors, cinematographers, producers, and screenwriters).

## Micro-Budget Hollywood: Budgeting (and Making) Feature Films for $50,000 to $500,000

Philip Gaines and David J. Rhodes, 220 PAGES, 7X9, ILLUS., 1-879505-22-3, $17.95 PAPER

*Micro-Budget Hollywood* offers filmmakers a fully-explained, line-by-line budget geared specifically to their economic bracket. This straight-forward, common-sense approach to shoestring budgeting is an invaluable aid to understanding how to keep a film on track and within budget. It also includes interviews with eleven successful micro-budget filmmakers.

FILM PRODUCTION, DIRECTING, ETC.

SILMAN·JAMES

## What a Producer Does: The Art of Moviemaking (Not the Business)

Buck Houghton, 200 PAGES, 6x9, ILLUS., 1-879505-05-3, $14.95 PAPER

*"...a lucid and comprehensive manual of filmmaking from the producer's point of view. Buck Houghton clarifies many confusing issues...I found myself nodding in agreement as I wandered through many familiar situations. It would be helpful to anyone interested in film production."* —Francis Coppola

Houghton delves into movie production and addresses the job's creative concerns rather than its fund-raising aspects. His insights into the whole of the moviemaking process should set any film, television, or even music-video producer onto the right tracks. **Buck Houghton** is most readily known as the producer of the first one hundred-plus episodes of the *Twilight Zone*.

## The Five C's of Cinematography: Motion Picture Filming Techniques

Joseph V. Mascelli, 252 PAGES, 8½x11, ILLUS., INDEX, 1-879505-41-X, $29.95 PAPER

*'The Five C's of Cinematography is one of the three most important books on cinematic technique ever published."* —American Cinematographer

With the aid of hundreds of photographs and diagrams, *The Five C's* clearly and concisely presents all of the essential concepts and techniques of motion picture camerawork. The five C's are; **Camera Angles** (Objective, Subjective, Point-of-View, Subject Size, Subject Angle, Camera Height); **Continuity** (Cinematic Time and Space, Filming Action, Master Scenes,Screen Direction, Transitional Devices); **Cutting** (Types of Editing, Cross-Cutting, Cutting on Action); **Close-ups** (Over-the-Shoulder, Cut-in, Cut-Away); **Composition** (Compositional Rules, Compositional Language, Attracting or Switching the Center of Interest).

## The Digital What?: A Filmmaker's Non-Technical Guide to Digital Effects

Shilo T. McClean, 132 PAGES, 5½x8½, 1-879505-55-X, $12.95 PAPER

Today's cutting-edge digital technologies are no longer completely cost-prohibitive for the independent filmmaker. *The Digital What?* is a concise and entertaining overview of the basic concepts and processes behind today's digital effects. With this book, filmmakers can painlessly learn about such basic effects as blue/green-screen composites, crowd replication, image manipulation, digital effects planning, pricing, and use during both production and postproduction, and much more.

## In the Blink of an Eye: A Perspective on Film Editing

Walter Murch, 108 PAGES, 6x9, 1-879505-23-1, $12.95 PAPER

*"An incredibly lucid trek into the formidable craft of film editing, which in my opinion is the core of the cinematic art form. Walter Murch's depth of insight into this subject is astonishing, and the book is a must for anyone who is interested in truly understanding the filmmaking process."* —George Lucas

Murch's vivid, multifaceted, thought-provoking essay on film editing starts with the most basic question—"Why do cuts work?"—and then treats the reader to a marvelous "ride" through the esthetics and practical concerns of cutting film. Murch offers his insights on continuity and discontinuity; the blink of the eye as both an analog to and an emotional cue for the cut; non-linear digital editing; and more. **Walter Murch** is an Oscar-winning editor, sound designer, director and screenwriter. Among the films he has edited are *The Conversation*, *American Graffiti*, *Apocalypse Now*, *The Godfather (Part II & III)*, and *The English Patient*.

## What an Art Director Does: An Introduction to Motion Picture Production Design

Ward Preston, 190 PAGES, 7x9, ILLUS. (8 PAGES OF FULL-COLOR), 1-879505-18-5, $21.95 PAPER

In this comprehensive introduction to film and television art direction and production design, Preston leads the reader through all the responsibilities and duties that fall on the art director's shoulders. Includes information on preparing script breakdowns, research, design and presentation, scouting and working on locations, set construction and design, and much more.

## The Film Director's Team

Alain Silver and Elizabeth Ward, 250 PAGES, 6x9, 1-879505-11-8, $19.95 PAPER

The assistant director and the production manager are essential elements in the smooth operation of any film as they oversee and regulate the ever-shifting, day-to-day production activities. This thorough study is a must-read for all who contemplate working in these jobs, as well as for all students of film directing and production. Includes detailed, practical discussions of cost reporting, script breakdown, production boards, scheduling, production reports, and more.

## The Complete Postproduction Handbook for Independent Filmmakers

Sallie Estes Seltzer, 280 PAGES, 8½×11, 1-879505-57-6, $26.95 PAPER

*The Complete Postproduction Handbook* guides the filmmaker through the complete, often labyrinthine, process of taking a film from raw footage to a properly delivered print. It provides filmmakers with an easy-to-follow game plan for making all important postproduction decisions, regardless of a film's budget or chosen format. It includes an overview of the many paths postproduction can take; explanations of the postproduction crafts and processes; advice about hiring the principal postproduction personnel and facilities; and many invaluable forms, checklists, charts, and timelines.

## The Avid® Digital Editing Room Handbook:
## 2nd Edition • Expanded and Updated

Tony Solomons, 233 PAGES, 8½×11, ILLUS., 1-879505-48-7, $26.95 PAPER

Today, most feature films and television projects are edited digitally. And the most widely used digital editing system is the Avid, which is in place in an estimated 90% of all professional digital editing rooms. In this up-to-date manual, which was written to meet the needs of both novice and seasoned digital editors and assistant digital editors, Solomons presents a thorough and clear guide to the Avid system and to the whole process of digital editing in general—from the basics of digitized images and time code through the specific operation of Avid equipment.

## Actors Turned Directors: On Eliciting the Best Performance from an Actor and Other Secrets of Successful Directing

Jon Stevens, 300 PAGES, 6×9, ILLUS., 1-879505-34-7, $19.95 PAPER

Directors whose careers began in front of the cameras offer their insights into the subject of directing actors. Includes tips on casting, rehearsing, communicating and working with actors. The interviewees are Jodie Foster, Mel Gibson, Kevin Bacon, Sydney Pollack, Leonard Nimoy, Ron Maxwell, Richard Benjamin, Melanie Mayron, Kevin Hooks, and Paul Mazursky.

## Personal Visions: Conversations With Contemporary Film Directors

Mario Falsetto, 320 PAGES, 6×9, 1-879505-51-7, $19.95 PAPER

In this collection, seventeen of this today's most creative filmmakers candidly discuss their creative visions, their careers, and today's film industry: Neil Jordan, Michael Radford, Tom DiCillo, Nicholas Hytner, Atom Egoyan, Alan Rudolph, Richard Linklater, Michael Tolkin, Terence Davies, Anna Campion, Philip Ridley, John McNaughton, Benjamin Ross, Keith Gordon, Michael Almereyda, Lynne Stopkewich, Alison Maclean.

## Eye on the World: Conversations with International Filmmakers

Judy Stone, 826 PAGES, 8×10, ILLUS., 1-879505-36-3, $35.00 PAPER

*"Judy Stone knows about movies, she knows about politics, she knows about life. Here, in this informative and entertaining book, she brings it all together."* —Jules Feiffer

214 filmmakers from 40 countries are included in this engrossing look at cinema from around the world. Among the filmmakers profiled in discussions with Ms. Stone are Babenco, Bertolucci, Branagh, Buñuel, Coppola, Fassbinder, Forman, Kaige, Jordan, Klimov, Kurosawa, Lee, Lucas, Menzel, Nair, Szabó, Tavernier, Varda, Weir, Wenders, Wertmuller, and Yimou. Stone has been writing for the *San Francisco Chronicle*, *The New York Times* and other publications for forty years.

## Raymond Chandler in Hollywood

Al Clark, 229 PAGES, 8×9, ILLUS. (OVER 100 STILLS), 1-879505-29-0, $19.95 PAPER

A comprehensive assessment of Chandler's turbulent association with Hollywood, both as a screenwriter (*Double Indemnity*, *The Blue Dahlia*, and *Strangers on a Train*) and provider of source material—his six filmed novels have yielded ten movies.

## David Lean and His Films

Alain Silver and James Ursini, 265 PAGES, 6×9, ILLUS., 1-879505-00-2, $14.95 PAPER

A film-by-film accounting of the work of the Academy Award-winning director.

## Robert Wise on His Films: From Editing Room to Director's Chair

Sergio Leemann, 224 PAGES, 8×11, ILLUS. (270 B&W PHOTOS), 1-879505-24-X, $24.95 PAPER

Each film is presented with photos, cast/credits, story synopsis, and Wise's own comments.

Disney/Pixar's beguiling **Toy Story 2**, in tandem with Disney's **Tarzan**, returned the company to huge profitability with its core audience. Yet the most resonant and notorious animated picture of the year was way down at 46 on the box-office chart: **South Park: Bigger, Longer & Uncut** ($52m). If exuberant excess is a reliable yardstick of satire, then this big-screen version of the popular but primitive cable TV hit towers above the year's releases (animated or live-action) for sheer inventive tastelessness. Working with popular composer Marc Shaiman (the *Sister Act* franchise), director Trey Parker and co-creator Matt Stone wrote 15 howlingly funny, breathtakingly obscene songs to punctuate the new adventures of foul-mouthed school kids Cartman, Kenny, Kyle and Stan. Parker and Stone's Swiftian satire held a mirror up to the contradictions of pop culture and the importance of free speech.

**The Iron Giant** ($23.1m) was another animated feature which in 1999 reached out for an adult audience under the guise

*Al Pacino, left, and Russell Crowe in THE INSIDER*
*photo: Touchstone*

of family entertainment and by presstime, 2000 had seen its share of animated successes and failures: Disney's *Dinosaur* ($126m), *Fantasia 2000* ($55m) and *The Tigger Movie* ($45m) were joined by the poorly-reviewed but doggedly publicised **The Road to El Dorado** (DreamWorks, $50m) in the win column, while veteran animator Don Bluth's **Titan A.E.** (Fox, $21m) could not overcome bad reviews and poor word-of-mouth.

*SOUTH PARK: BIGGER, LONGER, & UNCUT - the year's most inventively tasteless film*
*photo: Paramount/Kobal Collection*

## Reality: virtual and video

The year's fifth-ranked movie, **The Matrix**, tapped into a new realm of eye-catching special effects, made all the more believable by their logic within the narrative framework of the virtual reality universe entered by perpetually wide-eyed, incredulous hero Keanu Reeves. In a final surprise, the film won four technical Oscars – thus denying *The Phantom Menace* a single statuette in a contest it was expected to dominate. Inevitably, Warners has scrambled to capitalise on *The Matrix*'s franchise potential by putting two sequels into back-to-back production in Australia (where the next *Star Wars* episode is being shot completely digitally).

The poster child for breakout independent successes was **The Blair Witch Project**, which took $140m on a budget so murkily minuscule (most reports place it below $100,000) that its profits-to-cost ratio outstripped every other film in history. Though sold as a low-budget psycho-logical horror film, pieced together from footage shot by three student film-makers lost in the Maryland woods as they search for a title entity that seems to toy with them, the film is also very much about the stubborn sense of entitlement and deep self-absorption endemic to its target audience, traits which doom these fledgling film-makers as surely as the most determined demonic force.

Credit should go to young directors Daniel Myrick and Eduardo Sanchez for

*Keanu Reeves and Carrie-Ann Moss in THE MATRIX*
*photo: Jasin Boland/Warners*

having the discipline to jettison extraneous mockumentary material and focus on the real drama of poor, dumb, bratty Heather and her two increasingly petulant crew members, Joshua and Michael, as they flail around the forest. Even though exit polls revealed a huge dissatisfaction with the movie itself, *Blair Witch* will also go down in the history books as the first movie to have a wildly successful website, which fuelled business to a phenomenal degree – and sent studio honchos scrambling to launch custom websites for every new release (of these, only the sites amplifying the themes of *The Matrix* and *Being John Malkovich* rose above the clutter).

### Altman heir and Mendes magic

Featured on many year-end 'Ten Best' lists was Paul Thomas Anderson's third feature, **Magnolia** ($18m). His much-anticipated follow-up to 1997's *Boogie Nights* was nothing less than a *Nashville* for the late 1990s (complete with two major

*THE BLAIR WITCH PROJECT became the most profitable film in history*

*Philip Seymour Hoffman as a nurse in Paul Thomas Anderson's sprawling MAGNOLIA*

*photo: Peter Sorel/New Line*

players from that landmark film in minor roles), with the action shifted to Southern California's San Fernando Valley and the style amplified to reflect the cacophony of modern living.

Alongside the labyrinthine relationships among the characters, the across-the-board emotional accuracy of the ensemble cast (Tom Cruise had never been as commanding) and the extraordinary use of Aimee Mann's Oscar-nominated music, the most talked-about element will always be that out-of-nowhere biblical climax, predicted throughout the film by references, both veiled and overt, to a single verse, Exodus 8:2. *Magnolia* confirms Anderson's status as among America's most promising young film-makers. Coincidentally, at presstime the DVD of Altman's long-unseen *Nashville* was scheduled for release only a few weeks prior to the *Magnolia* disc, inviting the public to judge the two side-by-side.

The history of Hollywood is studded with examples of seemingly complacent suburban living given new vigour through the gaze of an outsider (Alfred Hitchcock's

*Shadow of a Doubt* is but a single example), so British stage director Sam Mendes' extraordinary film debut, **American Beauty**, is not without precedent. From the echoes of *Sunset Boulevard* in the mischievously macabre narration of protagonist Lester Burnham (Kevin Spacey), to the magnificent photography of Hollywood veteran Conrad L. Hall, *American Beauty* seems at once reassuringly familiar and bewilderingly strange, as if aliens were masquerading as an average family. This is precisely the point: the heartaches in the Burnhams' dream home are no different from those felt by untold numbers of people. Where *American Beauty* excels is in the details of Alan Ball's audacious script, scored to Thomas Newman's perfectly calibrated, spell-inducing music, at once respectful of and spoofy towards the New Age tropes it mimics.

## Jonze at the double

A solid, if financially unspectacular favourite with both critics and audiences, **Being John Malkovich** ($18m)

*Left to right: Wes Bentley, Thora Birch and Mena Suvari in AMERICAN BEAUTY*

*photo: Lorey Sebastian/DreamWorks*

demonstrates the fresh, music video-fuelled views of directing newcomer Spike Jonze and sells the wild idea of average people climbing inside the head of one of America's most intense and enigmatic actors. Part of this success comes from the clean logic behind the patently absurd idea in Charlie Kaufman's script, and much of it arises from John Cusack's typically selfless performance as Craig Schwartz, the frustrated, idealistic puppeteer whose filing job (he's got fast fingers) leads him to the aforementioned portal.

*Catherine Keener in BEING JOHN MALKOVICH*
*photo: John P. Johnson/Universal*

Many critics have pointed out how much less successful the film might have been with any actor other than the at once approachable and off-kilter Malkovich, but the true inspiration on view here is the casting against respective types of American Indie queen Catherine Keener as the vampy Maxine and a virtually unrecognisable Cameron Diaz as Craig's frumpy, spaced-out wife, Lotte. These are just the most obvious gambles in a movie filled with brave choices, off-the-wall charm and subtle profundity.

Along with *Being John Malkovich* and the much-maligned **Fight Club** ($36m), one of the most dramatic examples of cutting-edge aesthetics on view in mainstream American cinema during 1999 was David O.Russell's irreverent, anti-war comedy-adventure **Three Kings** ($59m), which stretched the movie form like taffy, and did for the Gulf War what Mike Nichols' *Catch-22* did for the Second World War and Robert Altman's *M\*A\*S\*H* for Korea. Improbably reminiscent of the giddy clash of greed and glory in Clint Eastwood's cult 1970 movie, *Kelly's Heroes*, *Three Kings* spreads its cynicism thicker than most entries in the genre, but tempers it with a cheerful streak of absurdist panache that keeps the irony from overwhelming the drama.

Little in Russell's previous two features (*Spanking the Monkey* and *Flirting With Disaster*) indicated his leanings towards this kind of epic sweep, yet the picture struts along for three-quarters of its 105 minutes on the sheer brio of its conceit: with a map plucked from the ass of a dead Iraqi soldier, four unlikely compatriots chase down a cache of gold ingots, and discover the flaws of the military action and the strengths of their individual characters. In the lead, George Clooney finally shows the charm and authority he is capable of, while Mark Wahlberg, Ice Cube and *Being John Malkovich*'s Spike Jonze are precise in support. Special mention to cinematographer Newton Thomas Sigel for one of the year's most unorthodox visual styles and composer Carter Burwell for a memorable score.

## A critic-proof sequel

Mainstream genre cinema was not without its titles of interest, headed by the final part of the emblematic teen horror franchise, **Scream 3** ($89m). This managed to, shall we say, flesh out the fates of its characters without stretching credulity. Putting the overly-complicated but shrewdly funny plot aside for a moment (the faithful know it, newcomers are advised to see the films sequentially), the film's makers made themselves critic-proof by deriding the movie's very existence before it opened. Yet for all the meddling that apparently went on behind the scenes, director Wes Craven made a movie that succeeds both as mindless entertainment and a sly meditation on personal growth, remorse and the need to face up to individual and group demons. *Scream 3* proved a surprisingly fun conclusion to a unique cycle of horror films that were just as surely the products of their decade as the 1990s cycle of mindless teen comedy-romances.

High-profile misfires in 1999-2000

*Left to right: Mark Wahlberg, George Clooney and Ice Cube in* THREE KINGS
*photo: Buena Vista Int'l/Kobal Collection*

included Jan De Bont's ill-advised remake of Robert Wise's **The Haunting** ($91m), a desultory and suspense-free special effects extravaganza which rode the popularity of co-stars Liam Neeson (who hated the experience so much he threatened in one interview to quit acting altogether) and Catherine Zeta-Jones; and the John Travolta-driven sci-fi hoot, **Battlefield Earth**, which on a budget of around $70m

*Neve Campbell and David Arquette in* SCREAM 3
*photo: Buena Vista Int'l*

fell off the radar after making only $20m; it was, by critical consensus, the most misguided and worst movie of the millennium to date.

The first few months of 2000 saw Julia Roberts receive her best notices in years for Steven Soderbergh's **Erin Brockovich** (discussed by Emanuel Levy on p.40). Russell Crowe pulled off a physically demanding chameleon act by transforming himself from doughy whistleblower Jeffrey Wigand in Michael Mann's *The Insider* to 'buff' fighting machine in the sword'n'sandal epic, **Gladiator** (a pleasing return to form for director Ridley Scott); and Tom Cruise resurfaced from his multi-year hiatus with Kubrick with box-office appeal intact, as **Mission: Impossible 2** became the first popcorn movie of the millennium to break the $200m barrier.

Although highly-anticipated for its subject matter and convoluted production history, Mary Harron's **American Psycho** failed to become an obsession with moviegoers and was emblematic of the short shrift often afforded ambitious projects in a hectic marketplace. The profile

(or lack thereof) afforded specialty and foreign films continued to be problematic. For every **Dogma** ($28.9m) or *Run Lola, Run* ($7.2m), titles which entered the fringe of public consciousness through controversy and visual brio, respectively, there are dozens – if not hundreds – of deserving works which either receive token urban releases or never attract domestic distribution at all, only seeing the light of day on the admittedly over-congested festival circuit.

What is to become of such films, many of which are on par with the titles that do find playdates and reviews? In the end, it will be up to those same festivals, distributors and exhibitors to make room in the system for unheralded work, ploughing some of those hard-won profits back into the talent pool from which their popular successes emanate.

EDDIE COCKRELL is a Maryland-based film critic and programming consultant who reviews for *Variety* from festivals in Europe and North America. He is the east coast editor of Nitrate Online.

*Christian Bale in Mary Harron's AMERICAN PSYCHO*

*photo: Entertainment*

# Forthcoming Films

### 13 DAYS

Script: David Self. Dir: Roger Donaldson. Phot: Roger Deakins. Players: Kevin Costner, Bruce Greenwood, Steven Culp. Prod: Armyan Bernstein, Kevin Costner, Peter Almond.

### 15 MINUTES

Script and Dir: John Herzfeld. Players: Robert De Niro, Edward Burns. Prod: Herzfeld, David Blocker, Keith Addis, Nick Wechsler.

### 102 DALMATIANS

Script: Kristen Buckley. Dir: Kevin Lima. Players: Glenn Close, Gérard Depardieu, Ioan Gruffudd, Tim McInnerney. Prod: Edward S. Feldman, Patricia Carr.

### ALL THE PRETTY HORSES

Script: Ted Tally. Dir: Billy Bob Thornton. Phot: Barry Markowitz. Players: Matt Damon, Henry Thomas, Lucas Black, Penélope Cruz, Ruben Blades, Bruce Dern, Robert Patrick. Prod: Mike Nichols.

### ALONG CAME A SPIDER

Script: Marc Moss, James Patterson, from Patterson's novel. Dir: Lee Tamahori. Players: Morgan Freeman. Prod: Joe Wizan, David Brown.

### ANTITURST

Script: Howard Franklin. Dir: Peter Howitt. Players: Tim Robbins, Ryan Phillippe. Prod: Keith Addis, Nick Wechsler, David Nicksay.

### AUTUMN IN NEW YORK

Script: Allison Burnett. Dir: Joan Chen. Players: Richard Gere, Winona Ryder, Anthony LaPaglia, Elaine Stritch. Prod: Amy Robinson, Gary Lucchesi, Tom Rosenberg.

### CAST AWAY

Script: William Broyles Jr. Dir: Robert Zemeckis. Phot: Don Burgess. Players: Tom Hanks, Helen Hunt. Prod: Tom Hanks, Jack Rapke, Steve Starkey.

### GET CARTER

Script: David McKenna. Dir: Stephen Kaye. Phot: Players: Sylvester Stallone, Miranda Richardson, Rachel Leigh Cooke, Michael Caine. Prod: Mark Canton, Elie Samaha, Neil Canton.

### FINDING FORRESTOR

Script: Michael Rich. Dir: Gus Van Sant. Players: Sean Connery. Prod: Laurence Mark.

### THE LEGEND OF BAGGER VANCE

Script: Jeremy Leven, Richard LaGravenese. Dir: Robert Redford. Players: Will

*Matthew Broderick and Reece Witherspoon in ELECTION, one of the year's most original independent movies*
*photo: Bob Akester/Paramount*

Smith, Matt Damon, Charlize Theron, Jack Lemmon. Prod: Robert Redford, Michael Nozik, Jake Eberts.

### THE LORD OF THE RINGS

Script: Fran Walsh, Philippa Boyens, Stephen Sinclair, Peter Jackson. Dir: Peter Jackson. Players: Ian Holm, Ian McKellen, Viggo Mortensen, Sean Bean, Liv Tyler, Christopher Lee, Cate Blanchett. Prod: Tim Sanders, Barrie M. Osborne, Peter Jackson.

### THE MAN WHO CRIED

Script and Dir: Sally Potter. Players: Robert De Niro, Christina Ricci, Johnny Depp, John Turturro, Cate Blanchett. Prod: Sally Potter, Christopher Sheppard.

### MEET THE PARENTS

Script: Jim Herzfeld, John Hamburg. Dir: Jay Roach.

Players: Robert De Niro, Ben Stiller, Blythe Danner. Prod: Jane Rosenthal, Nancy Tenenbaum.

### NUMBERS

Script: Adam Resnick. Dir: Nora Ephron. Players: John Travolta, Lisa Kudrow, Ed O'Neill, Tim Roth. Prod: Jonathan Krane, Andrew Lazar, Sean Daniel.

### PAY IT FORWARD

Script: Leslie Dixon. Dir: Mimi Leder. Phot: Players: Kevin Spacey, Helen Hunt, Haley Joel Osment. Prod: Steven Reuther, Peter Abrams, Robert L.Levy.

### RED PLANET

Script: Chuck Pfarrer, Jonathan Lemkin. Dir: Anthony Hoffman. Players: Val Kilmer, Carrie-Anne Moss, Tom Sizemore, Terence Stamp. Prod: Mark Canton, Bruce Berman, Jorge Saralegui.

### REMEMBER THE TITANS

Script: Gregory Allen Howard. Dir: Boaz Yakin. Players: Denzel Washington, Will Patton, Ethan Suplee. Prod: Jerry Bruckheimer, Chad Oman.

### THE SIXTH DAY

Script: Cormac Wibberley, Marianne Wibberly. Dir: Roger Spottiswoode. Phot: Pierre Mignot. Players: Arnold Schwarzenegger, Tony Goldwyn. Prod: Jon Davison, Arnold Schwarzenegger, Mike Medavoy.

### STATE AND MAINE

Script and Dir: David Mamet. Phot: Oliver Stapleton. Players: Alec Baldwin, Charles Durning, Patti Lupone, William H. Macy. Prod: Sarah Green, Maggi Renzi.

### UNCONDITIONAL LOVE

Script: P.J. Hogan, Jocelyn Moorhouse. Dir: Hogan. Phot: Remi Adefarasin. Players: Kathy Bates, Rupert Everett. Prod: Jerry Zucker, Jocelyn Moorhouse, Patty Whitcher.

*Joaquin Phoenix, left, and Russell Crowe in GLADIATOR*

photo: Jaap Buitendijk/DreamWorks

# Producers

**Alliance Atlantis**
808 Wilshire Blvd
Ste 321
Santa Monica, CA 90401
Tel: (1 310) 899 8000
Fax: (1 310) 899 8100

**American Zoetrope**
916 Kearny St
San Francisco, CA 94133
Tel: (1 415) 788 7500
Fax: (1 415) 989 7910
www.zoetrope.com

**Brillstein-Grey Entertainment**
9150 Wilshire Blvd, #350
Beverly Hills, CA 90212
Tel: (1 310) 275 6135
Fax: (1 310) 275 6180

**Cappa Production**
(Martin Scorsese)
445 Park Ave, 7th Floor
New York, NY 10022
Tel: (1 212) 906 8800
Fax: (1 212) 906 8891

**Castle Rock Entertainment**
335 N. Maple Drive, #135
Beverly Hills, CA 90210
Tel: (1 310) 285 2300
Fax: (1 310) 285 2345
www.castle-rock.com

**Cinergi Pictures Entertainment**
2308 Broadway
Santa Monica, CA 90404
Tel: (1 310) 315 6000
Fax: (1 310) 828 0443

**Donner Productions**
Warner Bros.
4000 Warner Blvd.
Burbank, CA 91522
Tel: (1 818) 954 4437
Fax: (1 818) 954 4908

**DreamWorks SKG**
100 Universal City Plaza
Building 10
Universal City, CA 91608
Tel: (1 818) 733 7000
Fax: (1 818) 733 6131

**The Robert Evans Company**
The Lubitsch Bldg, #117
5555 Melrose Ave

Hollywood, CA 90038
Tel: (1 323) 956 8800
Fax: (1 323) 862 0070

**40 Acres & a Mule Filmworks**
(Spike Lee)
124 Dekalb Ave
Brooklyn, NY 11217
Tel: (1 718) 624 3703
Fax: (1 718) 625 0169
www.40acres.com

**Fox Filmed Entertainment**
10201 W. Pico Blvd
Los Angeles, CA 90035
Tel: (1 310) 369 1000
Fax: (1 310) 369 3155
www.fox.com

**Hanna Barbera Productions**
15303 Ventura Blvd
Sherman Oaks, CA 91403
Hollywood, CA 90068
Tel: (1 818) 977 7500
Fax: (1 818) 977 7510

**Hollywood Pictures**
(distributed through Buena Vista)
500 South Buena Vista St
Burbank, CA 91521
Tel: (1 818) 560 1000
Fax: (1 818) 562 6920

**Imagine Entertainment**
9465 Wilshire Blvd, 7th Floor
Beverly Hills, CA 90212
Tel: (1 310) 858 2000
Fax: (1 310) 858 2020
www.imagine-entertainment.com

**King World Productions**
12400 Wilshire Blvd. #1200
Los Angeles, CA 90025
Tel: (1 310) 826 1108
Fax: (1 310) 207 2179
www.kingworld.com

**Kopelson Entertainment**
2121 Avenue of the Stars, #1400
Los Angeles, CA 90067
Tel: (1 310) 369 7500
Fax: (1 310) 369 7501

**Kushner-Locke Intl**
11601 Wilshire Blvd, 21st Floor
Los Angeles, CA 90025
Tel: (1 310) 481 2000
Fax: (1 310) 481 2100
kl@kushner-locke.com
www.kushner-locke.com

**MGM/UA**
2500 Broadway St, #E-2029
Santa Monica, CA 90404
Tel: (1 310) 449 3000
Fax: (1 310) 449 3069
www.mgmua.com

**Miramax Films**
7966 Beverly Blvd
Los Angeles, CA 90048
Tel: (1 323) 951 4200
Fax: (1 323) 951 4216
www.miramax.com

**Morgan Creek Productions**
4000 Warner Blvd, Bldg. 76
Burbank, CA 91522
Tel: (1 818) 954 4800
Fax: (1 818) 954 4811
www.morgancreekproductions.com

**New Line Cinema Corp**
(Distributor/Producer)
116 North Robertson Blvd. #200
Los Angeles, CA 90048
Tel: (1 310) 854 5811
Fax: (1 310) 854 1824
www.newline.com

**New Regency Productions Inc**
10201 W. Pico Blvd, Bldg. 12
Los Angeles, CA90035
Tel: (1 310) 369 8300
Fax: (1 310) 969 0470
www.newregency.com

**Peters Entertainment**
4000 Warner Blvd., Bldg 15
Burbank, CA 91522
Tel: (1 818) 954 2441
Fax: (1 818) 954 4976

**Red Wagon Productions**
Hepburn Bldg W
10202 W. Washington Blvd
Culver City, CA 90232
Tel: (1 310) 244 4466
Fax: (1 310) 244 1480

**Ruddy-Morgan Organization**
9300 Wilshire Blvd, #508
Beverly Hills, CA 90212.
Tel: (1 310) 271 7698
Fax: (1 310) 278 9978
ruddymorgan@earthlink.net

**Saban Entertainment**
10960 Wilshire Blvd
Ste. 500
Los Angeles, CA 90024

Tel: (1 310) 235 5100
Fax: (1 310) 235 5102
www.foxfamilychannel.com

**Silver Pictures**
4000 Warner Blvd, Bldg. 90
Burbank, CA 91522
Tel: (1 818) 954 4490
Fax: (1 818) 954 3237

**Spelling Entertainment Group Inc**
5700 Wilshire Blvd., #575
Los Angeles, CA 90036
Tel: (1 213) 965 5700
Fax: (1 213) 965 5895

**Tisch Company**
3815 Hughes Ave
Culver City, CA 90232
Tel: (1 310) 838 2500
Fax: (1 310) 204 2713

**Trimark Pictures**
(Distributor/Producer)
4553 Glencoe Ave, #200
Marina del Rey, CA 90292
Tel: (1 310) 399 8877
Fax: (1 310) 392 0252
www.trimarkpictures.com

**Warner Bros. Studio**
4000 Warner Blvd
Burbank, CA 91522
Tel: (1 818) 954 3000
Fax: (1 818) 954 2677
wbsf@warnerbros.com
www. wbsf.com

**Wildwood Enterprises Inc.**
(Robert Redford)
1101 Montana Ave, #E
Santa Monica, CA 90403
Tel: (1 310) 395 5155
Fax: (1 310) 395 3975

**Wind Dancer Films**
1040 North Las Palmas, Bldg 2,
Hollywood, CA 90038
Burbank, CA 91521
Tel: (1 323) 645 1200
Fax: (1 323) 645 1255

**Winkler Films Inc**
211 S. Beverly Drive, #200
Beverly Hills, CA 90212
Tel: (1 310) 858 5780
Fax: (1 310) 858 5799

# Distributors

**Buena Vista Pictures**
(Disney)
500 South Buena Vista St
Burbank, CA 91521
Tel: (1 818) 560 5900
Fax: (1 818) 841 6847
www.disney.com

**Columbia TriStar**
10202 West Washington Blvd
Culver City, CA 90232
Tel: (1 310) 244 5187
Fax: (1 310) 244 0932

**Miramax Films**
Tribeca Film Center
375 Greenwich Street
New York, NY 10013-2338
Tel: (1 212) 941 3800
Fax: (1 212) 941 3949
www.miramax.com

**Paramount Pictures**
5555 Melrose Ave
Hollywood, CA 90038
Tel: (1 323) 956 5000
Fax: (1 323) 862 1703
www.paramount.com

**Sony Pictures Entertainment Inc**
10202 West Washington Blvd
Culver City, CA 90232
Tel: (1 310) 244 4000
Fax: (1 310) 244 2626
www.spe.sony.com

**Twentieth Century Fox**
10201 West Pico Blvd.
Los Angeles, CA 90035
Tel: (1 310) 369 1000
Fax: (1 310) 369 2735
www.fox.com

**Universal Pictures Inc**
100 Universal Plaza
Universal City, CA 91608
Tel: (1 818) 777 1000
www.universalstudios.com

**USA Films**
65 Bleecker St, 2nd Floor
New York, NY 10012
Tel: (1 212) 539 4000
Fax: (1 212) 539 4099
www.octoberfilms.com

**Warner Bros. Studios**
4000 Warner Blvd

Burbank, CA 91522
Tel: (1 818) 954 3000
Fax: (1 818) 954 2677

# Useful Addresses

**Academy of Motion Picture Arts and Sciences**
8949 Wilshire Blvd
Beverly Hills, CA 90211
Tel: (1 310) 247 3000
Fax: (1 310) 859 9619

**American Film Institute**
John F. Kennedy Center for
the Performing Arts
Washington D.C. 20566
Tel: (1 202) 416 7815
Fax: (1 202) 659 1970

**The Directors Guild of America**
7920 Sunset Blvd
Los Angeles, CA 90046
Tel: (1 310) 289 2000
Fax: (1 310) 289 2029
www.dga.org

**Independent Feature Project**
104 W. 29th St, 12th Floor
New York, NY 10001
Tel: (1 212) 465 8200
Fax: (1 212) 465 8525
ifpny@ifp.org
www.ifp.org

**International Documentary Association**
1201 West 5th St, #M320
Los Angeles
CA 90017-1461
Tel: (1 213) 534 3600
Fax: (1 213) 534 3610
e-mail: info@documentary.org
www.documentary.org

**Motion Picture Association of America**
15503 Ventura Blvd
Encino, CA 91436
Tel: (1 818) 995 6600
Fax: (1 818) 382 1784
www.mpaa.org

**ShoWest**
116 North Robertson Blvd, #708
Los Angeles, CA 90048
Tel: (1 310) 657 7724
Fax: (1 310) 657 4758
showest@aol.com

# VENEZUELA — Andreína Lairet Morreo

With politics dominating the nation's thoughts since late 1998, the Venezuelan film industry continues to struggle against the odds for finance and prestige. The Autonomous National Center for Cinematography (CNAC) still has not recovered from the 60% budget cut imposed at the beginning of President Hugo Chavez's first year of government in 1999, and its slim budget for 2000 has led it to seek financial aid from international organisations such as UNESCO and the World Bank. In the first quarter of 2000, the institution could only afford to grant funds for the production of one feature and three shorts.

Three new Venezuelan features which found their budgets elsewhere were released in 1999. Ciro Duran's **Ship of Dreams** (*La Nave de los Sueños*), about six Venezuelan stowaways on a ship bound for New York, was a Venezuelan-Mexican-Colombian co-production and participated in important festivals such as Huelva and San Sebastián in Spain, as well as the Latin Festival in London.

Reminiscent of 1960s European cinema was Julio Soza Pietri's **Curl** (*Rizo*), a drama about a famous playwright, his women and his artistic and moral principles. The story of carnal passions and aesthetic obsessions has a hostile edge. Elia Schneider's **Glue Sniffer** (*Huelepega*), a grim drama about the lives of homeless Latin American children, screened at the Chicago Latin Film Festival in April 2000 and ran for four months at Venezuelan cinemas, grossing almost $1m, a record for national productions.

The first domestic release of 2000 was Pablo De la Barra's **Before Dying** (*Antes de Morir*), a thriller inspired by the tragic Chilean experience of crime and torture.

Unfortunately, the film died in cinemas after a couple of weeks, largely because of poor support from distributors and exhibitors.

More positively, there are 17 varied titles in production or awaiting release, including several debuts: *Three nights* (*Tres noches*) by Fernando Venturini, *Florentino and the Devil* (*Florentino y el diablo*) by Michael New, and *The Valley* (*El Valle*) by Gustavo Balza. Historical productions will include *Games Under the Moon* by Mauricio Walerstein, based on Carlos Noguera's novel about the Venezuelan political struggles of the 1950s.

Also in the pipeline is Leonardo Henríquez's third feature, *Bleeder* (*Sangrador*), an audacious attempt to adapt *Macbeth* to the contemporary Venezuelan Andes. *Oscar's Magic Adventure* (*La mágica aventura de Oscar*), a debut feature by Diana Sánchez, stands out as the only children's film: the tale of an eight-year-old boy who sets out to rescue his kidnapped mother from the evil Mr Black. Finally, José Ramón Novoa's second film, *Garimpeiros*, could be the most commercially successful of all. A co-production with Spain, it tells the tale of how far men will go in their search for gold in a poverty-stricken mining village in the depths of the Amazon jungle.

ANDREÍNA LAIRET MORREO is a Venezuelan journalist with experience in short film direction and production. She is now Content and Product Co-ordinator for a leading Latin American internet company.

# Recent and Forthcoming Films

**LA NAVE DE LOS SUEÑOS (The Ship of Dreams)**

Dir: Ciro Durán. Players: Gledys Ibarra, Frank Spano, Lourdes Elizarraras, Luis Felipe Tovar, Oscar Borda, Ramiro Meneses, Claude Pimont.

**RIZO (Curl)**

Script and Dir: Julio Sosa Pietri. Players: Jean Carlo Simancas, Arcelia Ramírez, Luly Ramírez, Luly Bossa, Claudio Obregón, Julio Medina, Daisy Granados.

**HUELEPEGA (Glue Sniffer)**

Script: Néstor Caballero, Elia Schneider, Santiago Tabernero. Dir: Schneider. Phot: Oscar Pérez. Players: José Gregorio Rivas, Luis Campos, Alfredo Medina, Pedro Lander. Prod: Joel Films.

**ANTES DE MORIR (Before Dying)**

Script: David Suárez, Pablo De La Barra. Dir: De La Barra. Players: Rolando Padilla, Hielen Abad, Manuel Escolano, Flor Elena González, Bettina Grand.

**EL VALLE (The Valley)**

Script: Armando Coll, Gustavo Balza. Dir: Gustavo Balza. Players: Eliana López, Luke Grande, Iván Tamayo, Luis Fernández, Pedro Durán.

**FLORENTINO Y EL DIABLO (Florentino and the Devil)**

Script: Edilio Peña, Michael New. Dir: New. Players: Pastor González, Juana New, José Mantilla, Ben Mantilla.

**JUEGOS BAJO LA LUNA (Games Under the Moon)**

Script: Claudia Nazoa, Mauricio Walerstein, adapted from Carlos Noguera's novel). Dir: Walerstein. Players: Alberto Alifa, Arcelia Ramírez, Juana Acosta, Vicente Tepedino.

**SANGRADOR (Bleeder)**

Script: Leonardo Henríquez, based on Shakespeare's *Macbeth*. Dir: Henríquez. Players: Daniel Alvarado, Karina Gómez, Francisco Alfaro, Alfonso Rivas.

**LA MÁGICA AVENTURA DE OSCAR (Oscar's Magic Adventure)**

Script: Yutzil Martínez, Diana Sánchez, Hilda De Luca. Dir: Sánchez. Players: Javier Vidal, Julie Restifo, Carolina Espada, Samantha Dagnino. Prod: Tango

*Manuel Escolano, left, and Roland Padilla in BEFORE DYING*

*Still from the forthcoming GARIMPEIROS, a drama about gold-hunters in the Amazon jungle*

Bravo Producciones/Philippe Toledano.

### GARIMPEIROS

Script: Sonia Chocrón. Dir: José Ramón Novoa. Players: Rocío Miranda, Laureano Olivares, Roberto Hernández, Jenny Hernández.

### TRES NOCHES (Three Nights)

Script and Dir: Fernando

Venturini. Players: Víctor Mayo, Juan Carlos Vellido, Adriana Velásquez, Frank Spano.

### BORRÓN Y CUENTA NUEVA (Let's Start Over)

Script: Ana María Uslar. Dir: Henrique Lazo. Players: Gustavo Peraza, Mimi Lazo, Elba Escobar, Marcelo Cezán, Carolina Perpetuo.

### LUNES DE CARNAVAL (Carnival

Monday)

Script: Claudia Nazoa, Malena Ronayolo. Dir: Roncayolo. Players: Mimí Lazo, Armando Gutiérrez, Luis Felipe Tovar, Abril Schneider, Antonio Cuevas.

### TOSCA

Dir: Iván Feo. Players: María Alejandra Martín, Eduardo Serrano, Miguel Angel Suárez.

# Producers

**Alter Producciones**
Ave. Diego de Losada
Qta. Alter
San Bernardino
Caracas
Tel: (58 2) 527 197/511 923
Fax: (58 2) 552 7297

**Bolivar Films**
Av. Luis Guillermo Villegas Blanco
Edif. Bolívar Films. Sta
Eduvigis
Caracas
Tel: (58 2) 283 8455
Fax: (58 2) 284 1011
www.bolivarfilms.com

**Caral Cine**
2da transversal
Qta. El Laurel
Sta. Eduvigis
Caracas
Tel: (58 2) 283 9944
Fax: (58 2) 285 9056

**Centro de cinematografía de La**

**Universidad de los Andes**
Altos Comedor
Universitario
Entrada Vía Chorros de Milla
Mérida
Tel: (58 74) 401 725/401 720/441 514

**Cine Marte**
Calle Santa Ana con Calle Lecuna
Boleíta Sur
Caracas
Tel: (58 2) 239 5376
Fax: (58 2) 239 2073

**Cine Sur C. A.**
Av. Principal de San Marino
Qta. Siboney
Chacao
Caracas
Tel: (58 2) 261 8685/266 7667
Fax: (58 2) 266 7667

**Pablo de la Barra Producciones**
3era transversal con 4ta avenida
Edificio Elite
Apto. 105, Los Palos Grandes
Caracas
Tel: (58 2) 283 4990/284 3484
Fax: (58 2) 149 355 057
e-mail: amaru@truevision.net

**Premiere Producciones**
Primera Av. De los Palos Grandes
Edif. Roxul
piso 3. Ofc. 31
Caracas
Tel: (58 2) 286 1291/6967
Fax: (58 2) 284 338
e-mail: alopezsojo@cantv.net

*Still from Enríque Lazo's LET'S START OVER*

photo: Juan Toro

**Producciones 800**
Edifcio Torre Financiera
Oficina Mezanina M-O
Ave. Beethonven (al lado de Maxy's)
Urbanización Bello Monte
Caracas 1060
Tel: (58 2) 751 7076/752 1821

**Producciones Doble Ele**
Avenida Principal de Prados
del Este
Residencias los Copigües
piso 7, apto. 7-4
Lomas de Prados del Este
Caracas
Tel: (58 2) 976 8273/261 8685
Fax: (58 2) 266 7667

**Producciones Tango Bravo**
4ta Avenida entre 9na
Y 10ma. Transversal
Qta. Turandot
Los Palos Grandes
Caracas
Tel: (58 2) 283 4829/285 9237
Fax: (58 2) 285 9213
e-mail: tango.bravo@cantv.net

**T&M Films**
Ave. Luis Guillermo Villegas Blanco
Edif. Rivera, Piso 1
oficina 11, Santa Eduvigis
Caracas
Tel: (58 2) 283 4653/285 4747
Fax: (58 2) 283 4653
e-mail: tymfilms@facilnet.com

**TVA**
Av. El Retiro
Qta. 34, El Rosal
Caracas 1060
Tel: (58 2) 952 5727
Fax: (58 2) 953 0778

# Distributors

**Blancica**
3era Av. Las Delicias
Sabana Grande
Edif. Las Delicias PB
Caracas
Tel: (58 2) 762 9781
Fax: (58 2) 762 4264

**Cineven 2.000**
Alberto Benaim
4ta Avenida entre 9na
Y 10ma.
Transversal
Qta. Turandot
Los Palos Grandes
Caracas
Tel: (58 2) 283 4829/283 7156
Fax: (58 2) 285 9237

**Di Fox**
Av. Las Palmas
Edif. Las Palmas
Piso 3
Caracas
Tel: (58 2) 781 7511
Fax: (58 2) 782 5087

**Korda Films**
Ed. Teatro Altamira PH
Altamira Sur
Caracas
Tel: (58 2) 762 6030

**Movie Movie Asesoramientos**
Av. Libertador, cruce con
Av. Las Palmas
Edif. Teatro Las Palmas
Sótano 1. Of. 7
Caracas
Tel: (58 2) 793 7158

**Roraimex**
Av. Las Palmas
Ed. Las Palmas
Mezzanina
Caracas
Tel: (58 2) 793 7377

**Tepuy Films**
Av. Libertador
Torre EXA, PH 1

El Rosal
Caracas 1060
Tel: (58 2) 953 3363/0942
Fax: (58 2) 953 6880
e-mail: tepuy@hdq.true.net

**Venefilms**
Av. Rómulo Gallegos
Esq. El Carmen
Ed. Torre Samán, piso 1
of. 11, Los Dos Caminos
Caracas
Tel: (58 2) 762 9781/239 6417

# Useful Addresses

**Asociación Nacional de Autores Cinematográficos (ANAC)**
Urb. Avila, Av
San Gabriel
Qta. Primavera
Alta Florida
Tel: (58 2) 740 366/741 954

**Asociación Nacional de Exhibidores**
Av. Rómulo Gallegos
Esq. El Carmen
Ed. Torre Samán
psio, 1, of. 11
Los Dos Caminos
Caracas
Tel: (58 2) 237 0397/1262
Fax: (58 2) 239 6417

**Cámara de la Industria del Cine y del Video**
Tel: (58 2) 283 4829/7156
Fax: (58 2) 285 9237

**Cámara Venezolana de Productores de Largometrajes (CAVEPROL)**
4ta Avenida entre 9na Y 10ma
Transversal
Qta. Turandot
Los Palos Grandes
Caracas.
Tel: (58 2) 283 4829/7156
Fax: (58 2) 285 9237

**Centro Nacional Autónomo de Cinematografía (CNAC)**
Av. Ppal de Los Ruices
Edificio Centro Monaca
Ala Sur, Piso 2
Los Ruices
Caracas
Tel: (58 2) 238 6494/1050
Fax: (58 2) 237 4942
e-mail: presidencnac@true.net

**Venezuela Film Commission**
Av. Ppal de Los Ruices, Edificio
Centro Monaca
Ala Sur
Piso 2. Los Ruices
Caracas
Tel: (58 2) 238 6494/1050
Fax: (58 2) 237 4942
e-mail: venefilmcomis@true.net

**Sindicato Profesional de Trabajadores de Radio, Cine, TV y Afines del**
Distrito Federal y Estado Miranda
Av. Nivaldo
Qta. San Joseph
no. 175, La Florida
Caracas
Tel: (58 2) 744 444
Fax: (58 2) 731 0976

# ZIMBABWE — Roy Armes

**Z**imbabwe's rich and varied land-scapes made it a popular location for major films in the 1980s, from Richard Attenborough's *Cry Freedom*, through Euzhan Palcy's *A Dry White Season*, to Clint Eastwood's *White Hunter, Black Heart*. But over the past decade a range of initiatives has been taken to give Zimbabwe a real filmic identity of its own.

The UNESCO-Zimbabwe Film Training scheme has proved a useful initiative, as has the African Script Development Fund. Three years ago, Zimbabwe participated, through Framework International, in the production of Idrissa Ouedraogo's first English-language film, *Kini and Adams*, and the Southern African Film Festival has been established in Harare, with the aim of becoming a prime regional film event and a showcase for African film-making.

A modest national feature output began in the 1990s, with films like Godwin Mawura's *Neria*, Isaac Meli Mabhikwa's *More Time*, Tsiti Dangarembga's *Everyone's Child* and Ingrid Sinclair's *Flame*, and a basic infrastructure of personnel and facilities has been established.

It is ironic therefore that the most recent feature by a Zimbabwean film-maker, Michael Raeburn's **Home Sweet Home**, needed none of these domestic resources. Raeburn has worked in a number of contexts and formats since he made his debut with the 16mm militant docu-mentary, *Rhodesia Countdown*, 30 years ago.

Though he has done much of his work in the UK, he also shot one of the first Zimbabwean 35mm feature films, *Jit*, a light comedy about a young country boy, nicknamed UK because his friends think he 'will go far', who struggles to raise the 'bride money' needed to marry the girl he has instantly fallen in love with on arrival in the big city.

Raeburn made *Home Sweet Home* with his partner, the US documentarist Heidi Draper, and the film explores their mutual differences and similarities as they face a Thanksgiving Day family reunion in Boston. Like so many other current African films, it was made from a production base in Paris, where Raeburn currently lives. The novelty of the film lies in the particular results achieved by shooting with a small digital camera – which allows the whole notion of a film crew to be dispensed with – and then afterwards finding the finance to transfer the edited result to 35mm film for international screening.

Though it was criticised by some for its lack of a specific African identity, *Home Sweet Home* won third prize at the Milan 2000 African Film Festival. Raeburn's work undoubtedly points to the increasing difficulty, in these days of co-productions by film-makers living abroad for long periods, of attributing a genuine national identity to films which proclaim them-selves 'African'.

## Useful Addresses

**Z Promotions Pvt Ltd** [publisher]
PO Box 6109
Harare
Tel: (263 4) 726 795
Fax: (263 4) 726 796

**The Southern African Film Festival**
Box CY 724
The Causeway
Harare
Tel/Fax: (263 4) 704 227

**The African Script Development Fund**
36 McChlery Avenue
Eastlea
Harare
Tel/Fax: (263 4) 733 404

# THE WORLD OF VARIETY

## VARIETY
Published weekly
•
Provides essential entertainment business news
•
News coverage and analysis to global
industry leaders in 84 countries

## DAILY VARIETY
Published every weekday
•
This leading business publication
delivers breaking entertainment news in
Hollywood and around the world

## DAILY VARIETY GOTHAM
Published every weekday
•
Global show business news with a
focus on New York's entertainment,
financial and media-related industries

## eV
Published monthly
•
This unique monthly is focused on the business
of entertainment and the digital economy,
featuring in-depth coverage and analysis of technology's
impact on the global entertainment industry

*AROUND THE WORLD IN 80 DAYS (above), and KERABAN'S FANTASTIC JOURNEY (below), both adapted as full-length animated films by Manfred Durniok Productions of Berlin, from the books by Jules Verne*

# FESTIVALS

## The Karlovy Vary International Film Festival's First 35 Years

By Michael Wellner-Pospíšil

During the late eighteenth and early nineteenth centuries, the town of Karlovy Vary, lying just over a hundred kilometres west of Prague, on the Czech-German border, became celebrated for its medicinal springs (under its German name of Carlsbad). Since 1946, it has become internationally recognised as home to the Karlovy Vary International Film Festival.

The festival founders' original idea – to facilitate a free international exchange of cultural values – was dampened by the Communist take-over of Czechoslovakia and the gradual isolation of the Eastern bloc from Western Europe, culminating in the closure of the borders. In the spirit of Communist propaganda, particularly during the early 1950s, the festival programme contained only films originating from the Eastern bloc (USSR, GDR, Poland, Hungary, China), or imported works which "mirrored rotten Western society and American imperialism".

The titles of the prizes, at that time copiously awarded, so that no film would be the loser, speak for themselves: The Peace Award, the Friendship Among Nations Award, the Fight for Social Progress Award, the Fight for Freedom Award, the Fight for a Better World Award, the Fight for the New Man Award, the awards presented by the Czechoslovak Committee for Defenders of Peace and the magazine *Issues of Peace and Socialism*.

*Gina Lollobrigida arrives to receive the award for her contribution to world cinema in 1995*

From the mid-1950s the festival's appeal grew as it began to orient itself towards films from the Third World, which at that time were only marginally represented at other large festivals. The temporary easing of international tension, as well as competent organisation and hospitality, lured eminent film personalities to Karlovy Vary from Western Europe, particularly Italy and France, but also West Germany, Spain, Greece and Scandinavia. Around this time, the festival's guests included Giuseppe de Santis, Mario Monicelli, Carlo Lizzani, Virna Lisi, Claudia Cardinale, Giovanna Ralli, Luis Buñuel, Yves Ciampi, Jules Dassin, Françoise Rosay, Christian Jaque, Andrzej Munk, Ousmane Sembene,

*The Grand Hotel Pupp, the Festival's principal venue*

Raj Kapoor, Glauber Rocha, Nelson Pereira dos Santos, Gabriel Figueroa.

The prestige of the festival was also enhanced with the recognition of the International Federation of Film Producers' Associations (FIAPF) which included it in 1956 among "non-specialised festivals with an international competition of feature-length films", otherwise known as "A grade festivals".

**Bad news from Moscow**

In 1958, the organisers discovered that a film festival was to be established in Moscow in 1959 and that, based on a political decision, it would alternate with the Karlovy Vary event. During the 1960s, Karlovy Vary still had an excellent reputation, mostly because of the political and cultural development in Czechoslovakia, which after a temporary sharpening of ideological censorship had moved towards endeavours to reform Socialism – the phenomenon which culminated in the "Prague Spring".

Soon after the tanks of the "friendly armies" had suppressed these attempts at political reform, the festival returned to the early 1950s era of propagandist slogans. It occasionally hosted important film-makers from the West, who sometimes even won awards; nevertheless, the majority of prizes went to bombastic Soviet films, whose prevalence gradually discouraged audiences.

In 1978 the festival was moved from its original location in the former Grand Hotel Pupp (then re-christened the Moscow Hotel) to the Great Hall of the Thermal Hotel, which became increasingly devoid of cinemagoers. It was no surprise that under these circumstances, the call was made to transfer the festival to Prague, where it would potentially have had a greater audience.

The idea of moving the festival to Prague found its supporters even after the fundamental political changes of late 1989. Originally organised by the state, the festival found itself under the admin-

*Lord Mayor Josef Pavel, centre, leads the toast to the 34th Festival, with (left to right) Culture Minister Pavel Dostál, Václav Klaus, speaker of the House of Deputies, Festival President Jiří Bartoška, and Programme Director Eva Zaoralová*

istration of an independent foundation at the close of 1993, established by the Czech Ministry of Culture, Karlovy Vary town council and the Grand Hotel Pupp. The foundation was headed by Jiří Bartoska, a popular Czech actor whose charismatic personality and talent as an organiser created the pre-requisites for the financial security of the festival, which was still cut off from state funding and forced to raise 94% of its budget from sponsors.

## The Turning Point

The 29th festival, in 1994, was the first organised by the Karlovy Vary Film Festival Foundation, and it immediately proved that the event should remain in its original location. Thanks to its intimate character, its position on the western border of the Czech Republic and its unique atmosphere as a spa town, Karlovy Vary is a much more suitable site than a metropolis like Prague, which is already saturated with myriad cultural events.

Moreover, the organisation was in the hands of a team of enthusiasts with a firm knowledge of the field, who would guarantee audiences a worthwhile programme and take into account the media's hunger for visiting celebrities. Apart from directors John Schlesinger, Irvin Kershner and Bruce Beresford, in 1994 Karlovy Vary also hosted Max von Sydow, Philippe Noiret and Leonardo DiCaprio, at that time a 19-year-old lad riding about undisturbed on his bicycle.

The inclination to terminate the Karlovy Vary IFF nevertheless persisted in some quarters, culminating in 1995 with the founding of a new competitive festival in Prague. This folded after two years and not only did the Karlovy Vary festival emerge victorious, its popularity at home and abroad began to increase significantly from its thirtieth year (1995), since the event was now being held annually.

The thirtieth anniversary event saw the arrival of film critic Eva Zaoralová-Hepnerová as artistic director. She had been editor for many years of the most

*Julian Sands with Programme Director Eva Zaoralová in 2000*

*photo: Radovan Subín*

important Czech specialist film magazine, *Film a doba*. In her new role she was able to make use not only of her expert knowledge but also her experience from regularly attending important international festivals,

her work in the FIPRESCI bureau and as a lecturer at FAMU, the Prague Film School. With a small circle of colleagues and advisers Mrs Zaoralová puts together a programme enjoyed every year by audiences and critics.

## The Competitions

Naturally, the main part of the festival is the competition which, in accordance with the FIAPF statutes, is only open to feature films which have not been entered in official competition at other international festivals. A number of world famous personalities have sat on the international jury, including Ivan Passer, Robert Wise, Ellen Burstyn, Régis Wargnier, Jerzy Stuhr, Jerzy Skolimowski, Gila Almagor, Julia Ormond, Vera Belmont, Yves Boisset, Brian Gilbert, Karen Shakhnazarov, Nanna Dyordyadze, Irakly Kvirikadze, Márta Mészaros, André Delvaux, Arnost Lustig, Jiří Menzel, Terry Rawlings, Teresa Villaverde, Pavel Kohout, Beki Probst, Abbas Kiarostami and Jutta Bruckner.

*Gregory Peck with Czech President Václav Havel in 1996*

The jury presents the Grand Prix (the Crystal Globe) for Best Film, which carries a $20,000 prize, also the Special Jury Award, and the awards for Best Director, Best Actor and Actress; on exceptional occasions it may decide to award an honourable mention. Between 1994 and 1999 the Crystal Globe went to the following films: *Mi hermano de alma* (*My Soul Brother*, Dir: Mariano Barroso, Spain), *Jízda* (*The Ride*, Dir: Jan Sverák, Czech Republic), *Kavkazsky Plennik* (*Prisoner of the Mountains*, Dir: Sergei Bodrov, Kazakhstan/ Russia), *Ma vie en rose* (Dir: Alain Berliner, Belgium/France), *Le cœur au poing* (*Streetheart*, Dir: Charles Binamé, Canada) and *Hachaverim shel Yana* (*Yana's Friends*, Dir: Arik Kaplun, Israel). With a few exceptions, these films were all screened as world or international premieres, and several have later become candidates for the Best Foreign-Language Film Oscar; this was the case with *Ma vie en rose* and *Yana's Friends*, while *Prisoner of the Mountains* was nominated.

The introduction of a competition for documentaries, judged by a separate international jury, was well-received both by film-makers and viewers, and after a temporary break in 1999, this strand has continued. A number of new documentaries have appeared in this section, despite the fact that the works selected need not observe the rule that they cannot previously have competed at other festivals.

## Special Sections

The informative "Horizons" presents works which attracted attention during the previous season, many of them winning awards at major festivals. Over the last five years "Horizons" acquainted its audiences with new films by the likes of David Lynch, Wim Wenders, Woody Allen, Pedro Almodóvar, Abel Ferrara, Tsai Ming-liang, Won Kar-wai, Joel Coen, Jim Jarmusch, Aki Kaurismaki, Paul Thomas Anderson, Mike Figgis, Bruno Dumont, Luc and Jean-Pierre Dardenne, Frédéric Fonteyne, Alexander Rogozhkin, Ilya Averbach, Tom DiCillo, Alexei Balabanov, Michael Haneke, Alan Parker, Mike Leigh, Abbas Kiarostami,

*Milos Forman, a regular guest*

*Saul Zaentz after a panel discussion*

*The Variety Critics' Choice has been part of the agenda since the 33rd Festival*

Lars von Trier, Scott Hicks and Takeshi Kitano.

New discoveries, films with unusual themes and so-called independent productions are included in "Another View", which has featured, among others, films by Shinya Tsukamoto, Zhang Yuan, Fruit Chan, Nuri Bilge Yeylan, Ko I-cheng, Sabu, Carlos Markovich, Oskar Roehler, Ben van Lieshout, Jean-Michel Carré and Robert Jan Westdijk.

The similarly oriented independent section "Forum of Independents", programmed by Hana Cielová and Stefan Uhrík, always generates huge interest. Its profiles of film-makers such as Ulrich Seidel, Steve Buscemi, Bruce McDonald, Errol Morris, Mohsen Makhmalbaf, Amir Naderi, Olivier Assayas and Robert Lepage, and presentations by independent companies such as Good Machine, find devotees among students, in particular.

"East of the West" is a special feature which each year brings together between 20 and 30 of the latest films from the former

Eastern Bloc, including titles from the former Soviet republics of Central Asia: Kazakhstan, Uzbekistan, Turkmenistan, Tadzhikistan and Azerbaijan. A special jury has been awarding the Philip Morris Freedom Prize since 1999 to films in this section which are a director's first, second or third feature. Last year this $5,000 prize was presented to Russia's Pyotr Lutzyk for *Okraina*.

A special section of the festival focuses on the Czech or Slovak film industry, whose numerous followers are able to see practically the entire output from the previous year. Each year the festival showcases a specific cinema's industry; after screenings devoted to directors from the former Yugoslavia who had studied in Prague (Lordan Zafranović, Srdjan Karanović, Goran Paskaljević, Goran Marković and Rajko Grlić), the festival then presented a profile of Australian film over the last two decades, new Spanish film, Canadian animation and French regional film.

The unique "Focus on Kazakhstan" was

*The Czech First Lady, Dagmar Havlová, presents Hilmar Thate with his Best Actor Award for PATHS IN THE NIGHT in 1999*

*Franco Zeffirelli presenting Israel's Arik Kaplun with the Crystal Globe for YANA'S FRIENDS at the 34th Festival*

followed by a project on the cinema industry of Bosnia & Herzegovina. The programme also always includes tributes to individual film-makers: Pedro Almodóvar, Maurizio Nichetti, Jan Svankmajer, Alexander Sokurov, Ilya Averbach, Milos Forman, Dusan Vukotić and Károly Makk are among the names selected in the past.

## Retrospectives and Restoration

The official programme also commemo-

rates the history of film: retrospectives on the Czech avant-garde, Jean Epstein, the films of Antonin Artaud and Belgian Surrealism were valued by film specialists as a unique opportunity to become better acquainted with some of the less familiar aspects of film history.

This part of the festival also showcases restoration work undertaken by European film archives. The premiere in 1999 of the restored copy of Georg Wilhelm Pabst's first film, *Der Schatz* (*The Treasure*), from

*Alan Alda and his wife enjoying a coach ride in 1997*

*photo: Luzana Mináčová*

*Lauren Bacall in conversation with Eva Zaoralová, centre, and Gila Almagor, Jury President at the 33rd Festival*

*Woody Harrelson signing autographs*

1923, accompanied by a live orchestra, was a very special event. The screening took place in the historical, newly reconstructed municipal theatre and was organised in co-operation with the Munich-based company Kirchgruppe.

The huge success of this screening led to a similar performance in 2000, this time the premiere of the restored *Menschen am Sonntag (People on Sunday)*, the German semi-documentary directed by Robert Siodmak in 1929 and co-written by Billy Wilder; a live orchestra was again used on this occasion. Specialists in film history and the general public are also being treated to screenings of restored films from the Italian series *The Seven Deadly Sins*, with original piano accompaniment by Czech composer Stepán Konícek; the project is organised in co-operation with the National Film Archive in Prague.

Seminars are a regular feature of the festival, organised in co-operation with the Association of Czech Film Employees (FITES), the Association of Czech Producers and the Union of Czech Distributors. International organisations are customarily involved in their preparation (Eureka Audiovisuel, Eurimages, Media, FIPRESCI), with the participation of Czech and foreign specialists.

The colourful and well-balanced line-up of films, which takes into account the more discerning audience, is also designed to appeal to the general public, attracting increasing numbers each year. Ticket prices are low and the organisers offer generous discounts to students, senior citizens and film professionals. In 1995, the festival hosted 80,000 visitors, but by 1999 this figure had soared to almost 120,000.

Over the last two years the number of accredited visitors has reached 7,000, of which approximately 800 were media representatives. Each year brings more foreign television crews to Karlovy Vary and Czech Television closely follows the build-up and the event itself. The closing ceremony, including the award presentations, is broadcast live and enjoys outstanding audience ratings.

## Secrets of Success

Several factors are attributed to the success of the festival under the direction of Jiří Bartoska and Eva Zaoralová, with whom prominent Slovak producer Rudolf Biermann also worked for several years in a managerial position. Undoubtedly, one is the understanding shown by certain sponsors and their faith in the beneficial value of a large film festival to the cultural reputation of the Czech Republic. Although this fact was finally also recognised by the state when it contributed a more substantial sum to the 2000 festival than in previous years, its financial share, together with the share from Karlovy Vary's town council, has thus far not exceeded 20% of the overall budget.

Another established factor is the above-mentioned symmetry of the programme. Thanks to highly efficient collaboration with Czech and Slovak distribution companies, apart from specifically original, "modest" films attracting perhaps a more initiated film audience, it also offers advance screenings of major distribution films for which the festival succeeds in securing the presence of famous faces and renowned names.

The podium of the Great Hall in the Thermal Hotel, the festival centre, has been host to a number of well-known figures since 1995: Gregory Peck, Michael Douglas, Alan Alda, Olympia Dukakis, Jason Robards, Lauren Bacall, Rod Steiger, Tim Roth, Mia Farrow, Maruschka Detmers, Geoffrey Wright, Woody Harrelson, Pierre Richard, Klaus Maria Brandauer, Matti Pellonpää, Ornella Muti, Maggie Cheung, Saul Williams, Anne Thompson, John Landis, Louise Fletcher, Christopher Walken, Salma Hayek, Matt Day, Robert Forster, Lou Reed, Tom Wilkinson, Boguslaw Linda, Olaf Lubaszenko, Katarzyna Figura, Philip Seymour Hoffman and, naturally, a number of directors beginning with Milos Forman, who remembers visiting Karlovy Vary early on in his career, when he was

*Carlos Saura arriving to collect his award for contribution to world cinema in 2000*

*photo: Radovan Subín*

still living in what was then Czechoslovakia.

Forman is also one of the film-makers to whom the festival has presented the special Crystal Globe for outstanding achievement in world film. The president of the festival has also bestowed this honour on Gina Lollobrigida, Michael Douglas, Saul Zaentz, Lauren Bacall, Franco Zeffirelli and Carlos Saura.

The festival is equally important for

*Edward Norton in conversation with Festival President Jiří Bartoška in 2000*

film-makers whose works endure a tough ride to the cinemas. Many films have been purchased by Czech distributors for cinema and television screening precisely because they have appeared at Karlovy Vary. The festival is thus not only an important social event, satisfying the needs of the media and sponsors, but it also admirably fulfils the worthwhile cultural goals it set itself: to become a kind of alternative distribution circuit, where audiences can gain an insight into the cinemas of the East and West, new world artistic trends, changes in film expression and opinion, and where they can trace the human destinies of their fellow men, whether neighbours or inhabitants of a distant continent.

The interest generated by the Karlovy Vary IFF, particularly from young visitors arriving each year with rucksacks on their backs, proves that an international public appreciates these goals – and that is the ultimate reward for the event's organisers.

# Guide to Leading Festivals

## Amiens

November 9-18, 2001

A competitive festival in northern France for shorts, features, fiction and documentaries. There are also retrospectives, tributes and the "Le monde comme il va" series, which includes works from Africa, Latin America and Asia. *Inquiries to:* Amiens International Film Festival, MCA, Place Léon Gontier, 80000 Amiens, France. Tel: (33 3) 2271 3570. Fax: (33 3) 2292 5304. e-mail: amiensfilmfestival@burotec.fr

## Austin Film Festival

October 4-11, 2001

The original film festival dedicated to recognising the screenwriter's contribution to the motion picture and television industry. Austin holds the Heart of Film Screenplay Competition, the four-day Heart of Film Screenwriter's Conference, which features more than 40 panels on the art, craft and business of screenwriting, conducted by over 80 industry professionals. The festival includes a competition for Best Narrative Film, Best Feature, Best Short, Best Student Short. *Inquiries to:* Austin Film Festival, 1604 Nueces, Austin, TX 78701, USA. Tel: (1 512) 478 4795. Fax: (1 512) 478 6205. e-mail: austinfilm@aol.com. Website: www.austinfilmfestival.org.

## Bergen

October 2001

Norway's beautiful capital of the fjords is launching an annual film festival to coincide with Bergen's EU appointment as one of the "European Culture Cities". There will be a main programme and sidebars, focusing on arthouse films and new media. There will be a Jury Prize and an Audience Award. Inquires to: Bergen Int'l Film Festival, Georgernes verft 3, N-5011 Bergen, Norway. Tel: (47) 5532 2590. Fax: (47) 5532 3740. e-mail: biff@bgnett.no.

## Berlin

February 7-18, 2001

Having celebrated its Golden Jubilee, and moved to the spectacularly modernist Potsdamerplatz, Berlin is generally regarded as the most efficiently-organised of the world's festivals, although arrangements should be made as far in advance as possible. In addition to the competitive programme (with its Golden Bears and Silver Bears, dispensed by an international jury) and information section, there are screenings of all new German films, a retrospective and the Forum of Young Cinema. *Inquiries to:* Berlin International Film Festival, Potsdamer Str. 5, D-10787 Berlin, Germany. Tel: (49 30) 259 20202. Fax: (49 30) 259 200299. e-mail: info@berlinale.de. Website: www.berlinale.de.

### AWARDS 2000

*Golden Bear:* **Magnolia** (US), Anderson.
*Jury Grand Prix:* **The Road Home** (China), Zhang Yimou.
*Best Director:* Milos Forman for **Man on the Moon** (US).
*Best Actor:* Denzel Washington for **The Hurricane**.
*Best Actress:* Bibiana Beglau and Nadja Uhl for **The Legends of Rita** (Germany).
*Best Short:* **Hommage à Alfred Lepetit**, Jean Rousselot.

## Brisbane

July-August 2001

Now in its ninth year, Brisbane screens shorts, fiction features and documentaries on film and video. There is also the

**21st Amiens International Film Festival**

*November, 9th - 18th 2001*

*Information/ accreditation form:*

Tel: +33 3 22 71 35 70
Fax: +33 3 22 92 53 04
e-mail: amiensfilmfestival@burotec.fr

Chauvel Award for a distinguished contribution to Australian feature film-making, retrospectives and an Asia Pacific Focus. *Inquiries to:* Brisbane International Film Festival, PO BOX 94, Brisbane Albert Street Q. 4002, Australia. Tel: (61 7) 3224 4114. Fax: (61 7) 3224 6717. e-mail: pftc@pftc.com.au Website: www.pftc.com.au

# Cannes

May 9-20, 2001

Cannes remains the world's top festival,

attracting key American independents and personalities, and entries and industry personnel from all over the globe. Cannes includes two official sections: the Competition and "Un Certain Regard". There are also the Directors' Fortnight, as well as the much-improved Market (MIF), whose facilities were extended and improved in 2000, the Critics' Week, and innumerable other useful screenings (e.g. Australian, New Zealand and Scandinavian films. *Inquiries to:* Festival International du Film, 99 boulevard Malesherbes, 75008 Paris, France. Tel: (33 1) 4561 6600. Fax: (33 1) 4561 9760. Website: www.cannes-fest.com. e-mail: festival@cannes.bull.net

**AWARDS 2000**
*Palme d'Or:* **Dancer in the Dark** (Denmark),Von Trier.
*Grand Prix:* **Guizi lai le** (China), Jiang Wen.
*Best Actor:* Tony Leung for **In the Mood for Love**.
*Best Actress:* Björk for **Dancer in the Dark**.
*Best Direction:* Edward Yang for **A One and a Two**.
*Best Screenplay:* John C. Richards & James Flamberg for **Nurse Betty** (US).
*Jury Prize:* Samira Makhmalbaf for **Blackboards** (Iran), Roy Andersson for **Songs from the Second Floor** (Sweden).
*Technical Prize:* Christopher Doyle, Mark Li Ping Bing, William Chang Suk-Ping for **In the Mood for Love** (China).
*Caméra d'Or:* **Un temps pour l'ivresse des chevaux**, Bahman Ghobadi.

# Cartagena

March 2-9, 2001

Ibero-Latin American films, including features, shorts, documentaries, tributes to Latin American directors and a film and TV market. A competitive section for Colombian films was added in 2000. *Inquiries to*: Cartagena International Film Festival, Apartado Aereo 1834, Baluarte

San Francisco Javier, Calle San Juan de Dios, Cartagena, Colombia. Tel: (57 5) 660 0966/664 2345. Fax: (57 5) 660 0970/660 1037.

## Centro Espressioni Cinematografiche

April 20-28, 2001

The third edition of "Far East Film" (Udineincontri Xiii), held in the Teatro Nuovo cultural centre in Udine, north-eastern Italy, will continue to dwell on the best of popular cinema from across the Orient. The 2001 programme will also embrace Japan and other countries from Southeast Asia. Personal tributes, archive restorations and genre surveys are included. *Inquires to:* Centro Espressioni cinematografiche, Via Villalta 24, 33100 Udine, Italy. Tel: (39 04) 3229 9545. Fax: (39 04) 3222 9815. e-mail: fareastfilm@cecudine.org. Website: www.udineincontri.it

*Hong Kong actor Simon Yam at the Centro Espressioni Cinematografiche in Udine*

*photo: Paolo Jacob*

## Chicago

October 4-18, 2001

Now in its fourth decade, the Chicago International Film Festival is the oldest competitive event in North America. It spotlights the latest work by established international directors and seeks out work by new directors. The festival bestows its highest honour, the Gold Hugo, on the best feature film in its International Competition, with separate prizes for documentaries, student films and shorts. Chicago is the only US site to award the FIPRESCI prize for first- and second-time directors, judged by a jury of top international film critics. *Inquiries to:* Michael Kutza (founder & artistic director), Chicago International Film Festival, 32 W. Randolph St., Suite 600, Chicago, IL 60601, USA. Tel: (1 312) 425 9400. Fax: (1 312) 425 0944. e-mail: filmfest@wwa.com. Website: www.chicago.ddbn.com/filmfest/

### AWARDS 1999

*Gold Hugo:* **La Maladie de Sachs** (France), Michel Deville.
*Best Director.* Lynne Ramsay for **Ratcatcher** (UK)
*FIPRESCI prize:* **The Love of Three Oranges** (Taiwan), Hung Hung.
*Best Actress:* Hilary Swank for **Boys Don't Cry** (US).
*Best Actor:* Benoit Poelvoorde for **The Carriers Are Waiting** (Belgium/France).

**CLERMONT-FERRAND SHORT FILM FESTIVAL**

January 26 February 3, 2001

13th International Competition
23rd French Competition
16th Short Film Market

ADDITIONAL PROGRAMMES :
Korean Panorama
S & M and Fetish Films
Hitchcock, Spain...

**NEW ADDRESS:**
La Jetée, 6 place Michel-de-L'Hospital
63058 Clermont-Ferrand Cedex 1 - France

Tel: (33) 473.91.65.73 - Fax: (33) 473.92.11.93
**E-mail :** info@clermont-filmfest.com
**Web:** http://www.clermont-filmfest.com

*Best Documentary:* **American Hollow**, Rory Kennedy (US).
*Best Short Narrative:* **Acide Anime**, Guillame Breaud (France).

## Cinéma Tout Ecran

October 29-November 4, 2001

The first and, until recently, the only festival to devote its programme to films of artistic quality produced by television. The main criteria for selection are the film-maker's distinctive view of the world and story-telling style. Highlights include the International Competition (three major prizes), New TV Series, Retrospective, Thematic Night, an international selection of shorts, and professional seminars. *Inquiries to:* Cinéma Tout Ecran, Maison des Arts du Grütli, 16 rue du Général Dufour, Case postale 5305, CH-1211 Genève 11, Switzerland. Tel: (41 2) 2800 1554. Fax: (41 2) 2329 3747. e-mail: info@cinema-tout-ecran.ch. Website: www.cinema-tout-ecran.ch.

## Clermont-Ferrand

January 26-February 3, 2001

The ideal destination for anyone who wants to explore over 200 of the year's best short films, the volcanoes of the Auvergne and the region's exquisite cuisine. Now in its 23rd year, this major event for shorts (entries from 76 countries, 125,000 spectators and 2,000 professionals attended in 2000) offers both national and international competitions alongside retrospectives, children's and African programmes, debates and an accessible

marketplace for shorts. *Inquiries to:* Clermont-Ferrand Short Film Festival, La Jetée, 6 place Michel-de-L'Hospital, 63058 Clermont-Ferrand Cedex 1, France. Tel: (33 4) 7391 6573. Fax: (33 4) 7392 1193. e-mail: info@clermont-filmfest.com Website: www. clermont-filmfest.com.

**AWARDS 2000**
*International Festival*
*Grand Prix:* Babami Hirsizlar **Caldi** (Switzerland), Isik.
*Prix spécial du jury:* **Salam** (France), El-Bouhati.
*Prix Recherche:* **In Loving Memory** (Ireland), O'Reilly.
*Prix du Public:* **La Comtesse de Castiglione** (UK) Lodge.
*National Festival*
*Grand Prix (ex aequo):* **Salam**, El-Bouhati.
*Prix spécial du jury:* **Beau comme un camion**, Cordier.

*Former French Culture Minister Catherine Trautmann visiting Clermont-Ferrand in 2000*

# Denver

October 11-20, 2001

The Denver International Film Festival, an invitation event, presents approximately 150 films and plays host to more than 60 film artists over eight days. New international feature releases, cutting-edge independen fiction films and docu- mentaries, animation, experimental works, children's programmes and short subjects are included. The festival presents a Lifetime Achievement Award, the John Cassavetes Award, the Krzysztof Kieślowski Award for Best European Film, the Starz! Cinema Award to the best independent film without US distribution and the Encore People's Choice Award for the most popular fiction feature and feature-length documentary. Entry fee: $30 ($20 for students). The Denver Film Society also produces the Aurora Asian Film Festival in June and the Denver Jewish Film Festival in August. *Inquiries to:* Denver Film Festival, Starz Encore Film Center at the Tivoli, 900 Auraria Parkway, Denver, Colorado 80204 USA. Tel: (1 303) 595 3456. Fax: (1 303) 595 0956. e-mail: dfs@denverfilm.org. Website: www.denverfilm.org

# Edinburgh

August 12-26, 2001

The oldest continually-running film festival in the world, Edinburgh is also one of the most accessible. Emphasis on new films, innovation and excellence in film-making world-wide, UK films and young directors, with retrospectives and seminars particularly well-chosen by Lizzie Francke. There's an off-beat sparkle to the Edinburgh mix of local audiences and visitors. The event also features the New British Expo, a unique showcase of British film production. Now aided by Film Four as a major sponsor. *Inquiries:* Edinburgh International Film Festival, 88 Lothian Road, Eduinburgh EH3 9BZ, Scotland. Tel: (44 131) 228 4051. Fax: (44 131) 229 5501. e-mail: info@edfilmfest.aug.uk. Website: www.edfilmfest.aug.uk.

# Espoo Ciné

August 21-26, 2001

Espoo Ciné has established itself as *the* annual showcase of contemporary European – primarily long feature – cinema in Finland. The traditional section should appeal to every movie buff in Finland, and the ever-growing fantasy film selection should attract all those hungry for stimulation of the imagination. Espoo Ciné is a member of the European Fantasy Film Festivals' Federation and organises every year a Méliès d'Argent fantasy film competition. Other treats include US indies, new films from other continents, the best of contemporary Finnish cinema, outdoor screenings, retrospectives, sneak previews, seminars and distinguished guests of honour. *Inquiries to:* Espoo Ciné. PO Box 95, FIN-02101 Espoo, Finland. Tel: (358 9) 466 599. Fax: (358 9) 466 458. e-mail: espoocine@cultnet.fi. Website: www.espoo.fi/cine.

**24th Denver International Film Festival**
**OCTOBER 11-20, 2001**

*Inquiries to:*
Denver International Film Festival
Starz Encore Film Center at the Tivoli
900 Auraria Parkway
Denver, Colorado 80204 U.S.A.

Phone 303.595.3456
Fax 303.595.0956
e-mail dfs@denverfilm.org
www.denverfilm.org

## Fajr International Film Festival

January 31-February 10, 2001

The Fajr Festival has flourished as a competitive event and aims to provide a bridge between Eastern and Western cinemas. Fajr focuses mainly on Iranian films but, since 1999, has incorporated an international competition section. *Inquiries to:* Fajr International Film Festival, Farhang Cinema, Dr. Shariati Ave., Gholhak, Tehran 19139, Iran. Tel: (98 21) 200 2088-90. Fax: (98 21) 267 082.

### AWARDS 2000
*Best Film:* **The Emperor and the Assassin** (China), Chen Kaige.
*Best Director:* Hans-Christian Schmid for **23** (Germany).
*Best Actor:* Richard Farnsworth for **The Straight Story** (US), David Lynch.
*Best Screenplay:* Bahman Farmanara for **Smell of Camphor, Fragrance of Jasmine** (Iran), Farmanara.
*Special Jury Prize:* **The Eleventh Child** (Vietnam/Canada), Doi Sijie.

## Fantasporto

February 23-March 4, 2001

The Oporto International Film Festival, now going into its 21st edition, specialises in fantasy and science-fiction films in its Official Competitive section. It also includes the 11th New Directors Week with an official competition, a Fantasia section dedicated to Korean films and a Panorama section. There is a programme of Portuguese cinema for the benefit of foreign guests. The festival runs now in eight theatres (2,700 seats in total) and screens nearly 300 feature films each year. The leading Portuguese newspapers, radio stations and television networks all cover the festival. Attendance hovers around the 100,000 mark. *Inquiries to:* Fantasporto/ Oporto International Film Festival, Rua Anibal Cunha 84, Sala 1.6, 4050-048 Porto, Portugal. Tel: (351 2) 2207 6050. Fax: (351 2) 2207 6059. e-mail: info@fantasporto. online.pt. Website: www.caleida.pt/ fantasporto

### AWARDS 2000
*Best Film:* **Siam Sunset** (Australia), John Polson.
*Best Director:* Jaume Balagueró for **The Nameless** (Spain), and Ben Hopkins for **The Nine Lives of Thomas Katz** (UK).
*Best Actor:* Thomas Fisher for **The Nine Lives of Thomas Katz** (UK) and Konstantin Prochorowski for **Halgi** (Germany).
*Best Actress:* Danielle Cormack for **Siam Sunset** (Australia).
*Best Screenplay:* Max Dann & Andrew Knight for **Siam Sunset** (Australia).
*Best Special Effects:* Jim Henson's Creature Shop, Sue Rowe & Jonathan Privett for **Animal Farm** (US).
*Best Short:* **The Periwig Maker** (Germany), Stephen Schaeffler.

## Festival Des 3 Continents

November 20-27, 2001

The only annual competitive festival in the world for films originating solely from Africa, Asia and Latin and Black America. The 23-year-old festival aims to present the cultural values of these groups in a non-paternalistic and objective way. One of the few festivals where genuine discoveries may still be made. *Inquiries to:* Alain and Philippe Jalladeau, Directors, Festival des 3 Continents, B.P. 43302, 44033 Nantes Cedex 1, France. Tel: (33 2) 4069 7414. Fax: (33 2) 4073 5522. e-mail: f3c@franceplus.com.

## Filmfest Hamburg

### September 24-30, 2001

Held every September, Filmfest Hamburg is Germany's premiere springboard for independent productions. It focuses on young cinema from around the world, with special attention given to indies from the US and Asia. In total it screens 80-100 full length films (including documentaries) and up to 40 shorts. It previews some Hollywood productions and includes a section for home-grown TV movies. The Douglas Sirk Prize is presented every year to honour outstanding contributions to film culture and business, while the Golden Tesafilm Award – worth DM30,000 – goes to the best first film of the festival, as judged by the audience. With more than 30,000 admissions and about 1,000 industry professionals attending, *Moving Pictures* calls Filmfest Hamburg "an excellent platform to launch independent product". *Inquiries to:* Friedensalee 44, D-22765 Hamburg , Germany. Tel: (49 40) 399 19000. Fax: (49 40) 399 190010. e-mail: filmfesthamburg@t-online.de. Website: www.filmfesthamburg.de.

## Flanders International Film Festival (Ghent)

### October 9-20, 2001

Belgium's most prominent annual film event, which celebrated its Silver Jubilee in 1998 and attracts an annual attendance of more than 90,000, with the prime focus on "The Impact of Music on Film". The competitive Ghent Festival awards grants worth up to $130,000 and screens around

*Jim Jarmusch receiving the Douglas Sirk Prize from Krista Sager, Deputy Mayor of Hamburg, at FilmFest Hamburg in 1999*

Sept 24 - 30, 2001
Germany's No.1 Event For
Young And Independent Cinema

**FILMFEST** HAMBURG

tesa film festival

fon +49-700FILMFEST / fax +49-40-399 19 00-10
e-mail: filmfest-hamburg@t-online.de ...
web: www.filmfesthamburg.de

*Stanley Donen, Sandra Bullock and Irwin Winkler at the Flanders International Film Festival*

*photo: Luk Mousaert*

150 features and 80 shorts, most without a Belgian distributor. Outside the competitive section, screenings include Country Focus, a Film Spectrum of international titles receiving their world, European or Benelux premieres, film music concerts, seminars and workshops, a Digiforum on the future of moving picutres in the digital age, as well as a tribute to an important film-maker. The Joseph Plateau Awards are the highest film honours in Benelux. Deadline for entry forms: August 10. *Inquiries to:* Flanders International Film Festival-Ghent, 1104 Kortrijksesteenweg,

B-9051 Ghent, Belgium. Tel: (32 9) 221 8946/242 8060. Fax: (32 9) 221 9074. e-mail: info@filmfestival.be. Website: www.filmfestival.be.

**AWARDS 1999**
*Best Film:* **Caravan** (France/UK/Switzerland), Valli.
*Best Director:* **Haut les coeurs** (France/Belgium), Anspach.
*Best Composer:* **Ratcatcher** (UK), music by Rachel Portman.

## Fort Lauderdale

October 2001

Screens more than 100 films from around

the world, including features, documentaries, shorts and student films. The festival will present Lifetime Achievement Awards to outstanding industry leaders in the fields of acting, directing, producing, writing and composing. The popular event (65,000 admissions in 1998) also offers film competition with cash prizes and a host of gala events on the beaches and waterways of South Florida. *Inquiries to:* The Fort Lauderdale International Film Festival, 1402 East Las Olas Blvd., Fort Lauderdale, FL 33301, USA. Tel: (1 954) 760 9898. Fax: (1 954) 760 9099. e-mail: brofilm@aol.com. Website: www.fliff.com

**AWARDS 1999**
*Best Film:* **Rien sur Robert** (France), **When the Dead Start Singing** (Croatia), Papić.
*People Choice:* **All About My Mother** (Spain)
*Best Director:* Tim Roth for **The War Zone** (UK).
*Best Actor:* Richard Farnsworth for **The Straight Story** (US).
*Best Actress:* Janet McTeer for **Tumbleweeds** (US).

# Freedom Film Festival
Feb/March 2001

Founded in 1997 by the American Cinema Foundation, this showcase of films from Eastern and Central Europe is dedicated to illuminating Eastern Europe's history, and creating opportunities for its film-makers. Films screened represent the cutting edge of the struggle for many kinds of freedom: personal, political, economic and artistic. The festival coincides with the American Film Market in Los Angeles, and is reprised overseas, participating at Berlin, Karlovy Vary, Moscow and Baku. *Inquiries to:* American Cinema Foundation, 9911 W. Pico Blvd., Suite 510, Los Angeles, CA 90035, USA. Tel: (1 310) 286 9420. Fax: (1 310) 286 7914. e-mail: acinema@cinemafoundation.com. Website: www.cinemafoundation.com.

# Fribourg
March 11-18, 2001

Features, shorts and documentaries from Asia, Africa and Latin America unspool at this Swiss event. There is a competitive section. Inquiries to: Fribourg Film Festival, Rue de Locarno 8, 1700 Fribourg,

FILMS FROM EASTERN EUROPE AND CIS COUNTRIES
THEMES: FREEDOM AND LIVING HISTORY
PRESENTED AND CURATED BY THE AMERICAN CINEMA FOUNDATION

A showcase of new and classic films from Eastern Europe and the CIS countries which contribute to our understanding of political freedom, memorialize the victims of tyranny, and celebrate the priceless gift of a free and pluralistic culture. This initiative supports and promotes a film culture of enduring, humanistic values.

**In Berlin in February:** gala presentation of the Andrzej Wajda/Philip Morris Freedom Prize to a filmmaker at the height of their powers. The third Berlin Freedom Film Showcase screens new films and retrospectives from the Stalinist era to the present.

**In Los Angeles in February/March:** the fourth Freedom Film Festival is Hollywood's annual remembrance of the human rights abuses caused by decades of Communist rule in Europe, reminding our own filmmakers that from time to time history will make profound and unexpected demands on their courage.

**At the Karlovy Vary International Film Festival in July:** the ACF celebrates the "East Of The West" section of the festival, which presents films from Eastern and Central Europe.

**At the Moscow International Film Festival in July:** the ACF supports the Cinema Forum of the CIS and Baltic Countries.

**At the Baku Film Festival in October:** the Freedom Film Festival presents new films from Eastern Europe at one of the leading festivals in Central Asia.

American Cinema Foundation
Contact: Gary McVey, executive director
9911 W. Pico Boulevard, Suite 510
Los Angeles, California 90035 USA
(310) 286-9420 phone   (310) 286-7914 fax
on the web at www.cinemafoundation.com
email: acinema@cinemafoundation.com

**The 25th Hong Kong International Film Festival**

**6~21.4.2001**

A FIPRESCI Award for
Young Asian Cinema
has been installed for the event

For Information, please write to:
Hong Kong International Film Festival,
Film Programmes Office,
Level 7, Administration Building,
Hong Kong Cultural Centre,
Hong Kong SAR, China

Tel : (852) 2734 2903
Fax : (852) 2366 5206
Email : hkiff@hkiff.org.hk
Web-site : www.hkiff.org.hk

Switzerland. Tel: (41 26) 322 2232. Fax: (41 26) 322 7950. e-mail: info@fiff.ch.

## Gijón International Film Festival

November, 2001

One of the oldest festivals in Spain (in its 38th edition in 2000), Gijón is now at the peak of its popularity. Having firmly established itself as a barometer of new film trends worldwide, it draws a large and enthusiastic public. Gijón has built on its niche as a festival for young people, programming innovative and independent films made by and for the young, including retrospectives, panoramas, exhibitions and concerts. As well as a lively Official Section there are sidebars celebrating directors who forged new paths in film-making. Titles which had their Spanish premieres in 1999 included: Majid Majidi's *The Color of Paradise* and Kimberly Peirce's *Boys Don't Cry*. Inquiries to: José Luis Cienfuegos, Director, Gijón International Film Festival, Paseo de Begoña 24, Entresuelo, PO box 76, 33205 Gijón, Spain. Tel: (34) 98 534 3739. Fax: (34) 98 535 4152. e-mail: festcine@las.es. Website: www.las.es/gijonfilmfestival.

## Göteborg

January 26-February 4, 2001

Now in its 23rd year, Göteborg has established itself as one of the best film festivals in Scandinavia and one of the key events in Europe, with an attendance of almost 105,000 enthusiastic spectators always ready to give spontaneous applause. Hotels and cinemas are conveniently close to one another. Swedish TV broadcasts live from the festival and selects a couple of films to screen each year. *Inquiries to:* Göteborg Film Festival, PO Box 7079, S-402 32 Göteborg, Sweden. Tel: (46

31) 410 546. Fax: (46 31) 410 063. e-mail: goteborg@filmfestival.org. Website: www. goteborg.filmfestival.org.

## Haugesund-Norwegian International Film Festival

August 25-September 2, 2001

Held in the west coast region of Haugesund every summer, the Norwegian International Film Festival has become one of the country's major film events, attended by many international visitors and over 1,000 representatives from the Norwegian and Scandinavian film industries. Award-winning films receive Amanda Statuettes and the New Nordic Film market runs in parallel to the Festival. Festival Director: Gunnar Johan Løvvik. Programme Director: Christin Berg. Honorary President: Liv Ullmann. *Inquiries to:* P.O. Box 145, N-5501 Haugesund, Norway. Tel: (47 52) 734 430. Fax: (47 52) 734 420. e-mail: info@filmfestivalen.no. Website: www.filmfestivalen.no.

## Helsinki Film Festival – Love & Anarchy

September 2001

An important film festival in Finland, now in its 12th year, Helsinki promotes daring, high-quality international film-making to Finnish audiences and distributors. True to its subtitle, "Love and Anarchy", the event uncompromisingly challenges limits of cinematic expression and experience. Non-competitive. *Inquiries to:* Helsinki Film Festival, PO BOX 889, FIN-00101 Helsinki, Finland. Tel: (358 9) 684 35230. Fax: (358 9) 684 35232. e-mail: office@hiff.fi. Website: www.hiff.fi.

## Hong Kong

April 6-21, 2001

Regularly includes a selection of Asian product and a Hong Kong Cinema Retrospective among 200 films and videos shown at various venues. The festival has been recognised as a valuable showcase for Asian works that allows the West to discover the riches of Chinese cinema.

*Inquiries to:* Senior Manager, Festivals Office, Urban Services Department, Level 7, Administration Building, Hong Kong Cultural Centre, 10 Salisbury Road, Tsimshatsui, Kowloon, Hong Kong. Tel: (852) 2734 2903. Fax: (852) 2366 5206. e-mail: hkiff@hkiff.org.hk/fpo@lcsd.gov.hk. Website: www.hkiff.org.hk.

*Andrzej Wajda presents Kira Muratova with the first Andrzej Wajda/Philip Morris Freedom Prize at the Berlin Town Hall*

## Huelva

November, 2001

The main aim of the Ibero-American Film Festival in Huelva, Spain, is to show and promote films of artistic quality which contribute to a better knowledge of Ibero-American production, including works from the Hispanic US. Huelva has become a key rendezvous for anyone connected to Latin American movies, enabling European buyers and film buffs to catch up with the latest developments from across the Atlantic. Includes a competition for films from Ibero-America and the Hispanic US, tributes and round table discussions. Inquiries to: Casa Colón, Plaza del Punto s/n, 21003 Huelva, Spain. Tel: (34) 959 210 170/1. Fax: (34) 959 210 173. e-mail: festival@festicinehuelva.com. Website: www.festicinehuelva.com.

**AWARDS 1999**
*Best Film:* **Garage Olimpo** (Argentina).
*Best Director:* Marco Bechis, **Garage Olimpo** (Argentina).
*Best Actor:* Carlos Valencia for **Ratas, ratones, rateros** (Ecuador).
*Best Actress:* Evelina Fernández for **Luminarias** (US).
*Special Jury Prize – Best First Film:* **Ratas, ratones, rateros** (Ecuador), Sebastián Cordero.
*Career Achievement Award:* José Luis Ruíz, Gerardo Herrero, Angela Molina, Miguel Littín.

## Independent Feature Film Market

September, 2001

The Independent Feature Film Market (IFFM) is the original and longest-running market devoted to new, emerging American independent film talent. Since 1979, IFFM has presented the industry with its first look at films such as *American Dream, Blood Simple, The Brothers McMullen, Clerks, Poison, Roger & Me, Stranger Than Paradise* and *Welcome to the Dollhouse.* IFFM screens nearly 300 film projects annually, including Works-in-Progress, and presents over 100 copy-righted feature-length scripts. Deadline: mid-May. *Inquiries to:* Independent Feature Project, 104 West 29th Street, 12th Floor, New York, NY, 10001, USA. Tel: (1 212) 465 8200. Fax: (1 212) 465 8525. e-mail: marketinfo@ifp.org. Website: www.ifp.org.

## India

January 10-20, 2000

Annual, non-competitive event recognised by IFFPA. There is a substantial information section, a new competition for features made by Asian women, a comprehensive "Cinema of the World" section, foreign and Indian retrospectives and a film market, as well as a valuable panorama of the best Indian films of the year, subtitled in English. The event alternates between the major city venues of India, north and south. Inquiries to: International Film Festival of India, 4th Floor, Lok Nayak Bhavan, Khan Market, New Delhi 110 003, India. Tel: (91 11) 461 5953, 469 7167. Fax: (91 11) 462 3430.

## Internationale Hofer Filmtage

October 24-28, 2001

Dubbed "the Home of Films" by Wim Wenders, Hof is famous for its thoughtful selection of some 50 features. Founded by the directors of the New German Cinema, Hof enjoys a high reputation among German film-makers and American cult figures like Roger Corman, Monte Hellman and Henry Jaglom. Directed by one of the most respected German film enthusiasts, Heinz Badewitz, Hof has enjoyed a rising reputation these past 33 years. A screening here often results in a distribution deal. *Inquiries to:* Postfach 1146, D-95010 Hof, Germany: or Heinz Badewitz, Lothstr. 30, D-80335 Munich, Germany. Tel: (49 89) 129 7422. Fax: (49 89) 123 6868. e-mail: info@hofer-filmtage.de. Website: www.hofer-filmtage.de.

## Istanbul

April 14-29, 2001

The only film festival which takes place in a city where two continents meet, the

Istanbul International Film Festival, recognised as a specialised competitive event by IFFPA, acts as a valuable showcase for distributors internationally. Attendance reaches 100,000 every year. Now in its 20th edition, this dynamic event focuses on features dealing with the arts (literature, music, cinema, dance etc.) with other thematic sections such as tributes, selections from World Festivals, "A Country – A Cinema", and a panorama of Turkish cinema. *Inquiries to:* Ms. Hülya Uçansu, Istanbul Kültür ve Sanat Vakfi, Istiklal Cad. Luvr Apt. No. 146, Beyoglu 80070, Istanbul, Turkey. Tel: (90 212) 293 3133/34/35. Fax: (90 212) 249 5575. e-mail: press.pr@istfest-tr.org. Website: www.istfest.org.

## Jerusalem International Film Festival

July 2001

One of Israel's most prestigious cinematic events, which brings to Jerusalem over 150

*Marianne Sägebrecht at the Internationale Hofer Filmtage in 1999*

*photo: Dieter Neidhardt*

# ENCOUNTERS IN İSTANBUL

**14-29 APRIL 2001**

İSTANBUL FOUNDATION FOR CULTURE AND ARTS | 20ᵗʰ INTERNATIONAL İSTANBUL FILM FESTIVAL

**FILM**

**Contact:** Mrs. Hülya Uçansu, Director
**Address:** İstiklal Caddesi, 146 Beyoğlu 80070, İstanbul - Turkey
**Phone:**+ 90 212 293 31 33 ext: 20 21
http://www.istfest.org **e-mail:** film.fest@istfest-tr.org

Corporate Sponsors

KOÇBANK   BAYTUR İNŞAAT TAAHHÜT A.Ş.   MARMARA HOTELS & RESIDENCES   RENAULT   DHL WORLDWIDE EXPRESS

films covering a wide spectrum of themes and categories: Best of International Cinema, Documentaries, Israeli Cinema, Mediterranean Cinema, Animation, Short Films, American Independents, Avant Garde, New Directors, Jewish Themes, Classics and Restorations and Special Tributes. Prize categories include the Wolgin Awards for Israeli Cinema, Lipper Award for Best Israeli Screenplay, international awards like the Wim van Leer "In the Spirit of Freedom" for films focusing on human rights, the Mediterranean Cinema Award and the Films on Jewish Themes Award. *Inquiries to:* Jerusalem Film Festival, PO Box 8561, Jerusalem 91083. Tel: (972 2) 671 5117. Fax: (972 2) 673 3076. e-mail: festival@jer-cin.org.il. Website: www.jer-cin.org.il.

## Karlovy Vary

July 5-14, 2001

Since 1994 an annual event, Karlovy Vary is one of the oldest film festivals in the

*Jury President Mrinal Sen presenting director Nuri Bilge Ceylan with his award for CLOUDS OF MAY at the 19th Istanbul Festival*

world. Its programme includes international competitions of features and documentaries with international juries awarding prizes for the Best Film (Crystal Globe), Director, Actor/Actress and a Jury Award. There is a major focus on Czech features and those from the former Communist countries. The 2000 event featured the *Variety* "Ten to Watch" Programme, a retrospective, Twenty Centuries Anno Domini, a tribute to Károly Makk, a focus on Bosnia & Herzegovina, a programme dedicated to French women film-makers and The Treasures of European Film Archives. *Inquiries to:* Film Servis Festival Karlovy Vary, Panská 1, CZ 11000 Prague 1, Czech Republic. Tel: (420 2) 2423 5412. Fax: (420 2) 2423 3408. e-mail: program@iffkv.cz. Website: www.tlp.cz.

### AWARDS 1999
*Grand Prix:* **Yana's Friends** (Israel), Kaplun.
*Jury Award :* **Fucking Åmål** (Sweden) Moodysson.
*Best Director:* Alexander Rogozhkin for **Blockpost** (Russia).
*Best Actress:* Evlyn Kaplun for **Yana's Friends** (Israel).
*Best Actor:* Hilmar Thate for **Paths in the Night** (Germany).

## La Rochelle

June 29-July 9, 2001

Fighting against the inroads of television, that cinematic polymath Jean-Loup Passek builds a bridge between past and future cinema with his popular and distinguished festival held in this French resort. The event includes a profusion of new features and thematic programmes, sometimes with magnificent discoveries (the Francesca

Bertini retrospective in 1993, and Arne Skouen in 1999, for example). *Inquiries to:* Festival International du Film de La Rochelle, 16 rue Saint Sabin, Paris 75011, France. Tel: (33 1) 4806 1666. Fax: (33 1) 4806 1540. e-mail: festival.de.la.rochelle@wanadoo.fr. Website: www.fiflr.org.

## Le Giornate del Cinema Muto (Sacile)

October 2001

This unique event last year moved from Pordenone, following the demolition of Cinema Verdi, the festival's venue for 17 years. Its new home is the enchanting town of Sacile, 15km from Pordenone. Now, for one week each autumn, this little Italian town is overrun by a devoted band of scholars, collectors, archivists and enthusiasts who travel from around the world for the "Giornate del Cinema Muto", established in 1982 and dedicated to silent films. The Griffith Project, a long-term commitment to show every extant film by

D.W. Griffith started in 1997. These are screened alongside a wealth of other rarities and rediscoveries, all presented with live musical accompaniment. There's also a Film Fair devoted to scripts and books on the cinema. Director: David Robinson. *Inquiries to:* Le Giornate del Cinema Muto c/o La Cineteca del Friuli, Palazzo Gurisatti, Via Bini 33013 Gemona (UD), Italy. Tel: (39 04) 3298 0458. Fax: (39 04) 3297 0542. e-mail: gcm@cinetecadelfriuli.org. Website: www.cinetecadelfriuli.org.

## Leeds

October 2001

Leeds is the UK's largest regional film festival, based in the city at the heart of Yorkshire in the North of England. Competitive for debut features, short films and animation, Leeds also presents pioneering sidebars including 'evolution', which looks at the convergence of film, TV and interactive entertainment; Eureka, a major spotlight on new and archive

**20th Pordenone Silent Film Festival**

LE GIORNATE
DEL CINEMA
MUTO

October 13-20, 2001

Japanese
Silent
Cinema

*For further information:*
Le Giornate del Cinema Muto          Tel: +39-0432-980458
c/o La Cineteca del Friuli               Fax: +39-0432-970542
Palazzo Gurisatti, Via Bini 50          E-mail: info.gcm@cinetecadelfriuli.org
33013 Gemona (UD) Italia               Web: cinetecadelfriuli.org/gcm/

European film; Voices of Cinemas, featuring interviews with personalities from both sides of the camera; and the Fringe, where cutting-edge work is screened in the city's cafes and bars. *Inquiries to*: Leeds International Film Festival, The Town Hall, The Headrow, Leeds, LS1 3AD, UK. Tel: (44 113) 247 8398. Fax: (44 113) 247 8397. e-mail: filmfestival@leeds.gov.uk. Website: www.leedsfilm.com.

## Locarno

### August 8-18, 2001

Under director Marco Müller, Locarno has become a place where world and European premieres are regular occasions, and where serious buyers go to discover creative film-makers. More than 1,000 accredited journalists from over 30 countries are surrounded by an international attendance of 180,000. Every night 7,000 people sit in front of the giant screen in Piazza Grande to discover the lively and varied programmes. The departing Müller can justifiably claim that Locarno is now one of the world's top half-dozen festivals. *Inquiries to:* Festival Internazionale del Film, Via Luini 3a, CH-6601 Locarno, Switzerland. Tel: (41 91) 756 2121. Fax: (41 91) 756 2149. e-mail: info@pardo.ch. Website: www.pardo.ch.

LEEDS CITY COUNCIL PRESENTS
**leeds international**
**FILM FESTIVAL 2001**
**T:** +44 (0)113 247 8398
**E:** filmfestival@leeds.gov.uk
**W:** www.leedsfilm.com

## London

### November 2001

Presented at the National Film Theatre and at cinemas throughout the capital, the programme comprises around 180 features and documentaries, as well as a showcase for shorts. Aside from the British section there is a very strong international selection including the *Evening Standard* Film on the Square, Asia, Africa and Latin America, as well as Europe's largest and most influential selection of US independents. The festival attracts over 400 UK and international press representatives and provides a buyers/sellers liaison office. *Inquiries to:* London Film Festival, South Bank, London SE1 8XT, UK. Tel: (44 20) 7815 1322. Fax (44 20) 7633 0786. e-mail: sarah.lutton@bfi.org.uk. Website: www.lff.org.uk.

## Málaga Spanish Film Festival

### May/June 2001

After three editions, the Málaga Film Festival is firmly established as the key showcase in Spain for Spanish films. Used as a springboard for early Summer releases in Spain, Málaga enjoys large turnouts from both local audiences and Spanish actors, producers and directors. Beyond a competition for features and shorts, tributes and retrospectives, the festival has a documentary sidebar, exhibitions, round tables and a look at local video production. Cash prizes, in the form of distribution aid, run to some $170,000. *Inquiries to:* Salomon Castiel, Director, Málaga Spanish Film Festival, Ramos Marin 2-1c, 29012 Málaga, Spain. Tel: (34 95) 222 8242. Fax: (34 95) 222 7760. e-mail: festcinea@festcinemalaga.com. Website: www.festcinemalaga.com.

**AWARDS 2000**
*Best Film:* **Sex out of Compassion** (Spain), Manná.
*Special Jury Prize:* **Leo** (Spain), Borau.
*Best Director:* Cesc Gay for **Krampack** (Spain).
*Best Actress:* Thaimi Alvariño for **Waiting List** (Spain/Cuba/France/Mexico/Germany).
*Best Actor:* Juan Luis Galiardo for **Goodbye with All My Heart**.
*Audience Prize:* **Sex out of Compassion** (Spain).

## First Light

**A Place for Newcomers
A Competition of Premieres
Quality Films at a Decent Price
And a Lively Co-Production Market**

8.-17. Nov. 2001

Internationales **Filmfestival** Mannheim-Heidelberg

For more information, please contact:
International Filmfestival Mannheim-Heidelberg
Collini-Center, Galerie
D-68161 Mannheim, Germany
phone: +49-(0)621-10 29 43
fax: +49-(0)621-29 15 64
e-mail: ifmh@mannheim-filmfestival.com
web: www.mannheim-filmfestival.com

## Mannheim-Heidelberg

November 8-17, 2001

A festival for young independent film-makers from all over the world. The event which gave early recognition to Truffaut, Fassbinder, Kiéslowski, Jarmusch, and more recently Bryan Singer and Thomas Vinterberg, presents features, shorts and documentaries in competition, with cash prizes for the best film in each category (entry deadline: August 25). Films in the Official Programme are also shown in the "New Film Market", reserved for international buyers and distributors. The "Mannheim Meetings", a market for film projects, runs in parallel to the main event (entry deadline: July 31). *Inquiries to:* Dr. Michael Koetz, International Filmfestival Mannheim-Heidelberg, Collini-Center, Galerie, D-68161 Mannheim, Germany. Tel: (49 621) 102 943. Fax: (49 621) 291 564. e-mail: ifmh@mannheim-filmfestival.com. Website: www.mannheim-filmfestival.com.

### AWARDS 1999

*Best Fiction Film:* **Understanding Jane** (UK), Lindsay.
*Best Documentary:* **A Black Cat on the Snow** (Finland), Kuivalainen.
*Best Short:* **Quand j'etais photographe** (France), Polge & Perreau.
*Rainer Werner Fassbinder Prize:* **My Father's Angel** (Canada), Davor Marjanovic[ac].
Special Award of the Jury: **Les 4 saisons d'Espigoule** (France), Philibert.

## MIFED (Milan)

Late October, 2001

Long-established film market held in the expansive Milan Fair, particularly well-attended by buyers and sellers from all over the world. Third on the annual calendar after the American Film Market and Cannes, Mifed's atmosphere is more sober and business-like. Rivalry with the London Screenings has provoked MIFED to start its own "special screenings" slightly ahead of the main gathering. *Inquiries to:* Mrs Elena Lloyd, E.A. Fiera Internationale di Milano, Largo Domodossola 1, 20145 Milano, Italy.

Málaga Spanish Film Festival

June 2001

Contact address: Ramos Marín, 2, 1° C, (29012) Málaga, SPAIN. Tel.:34 95 222 82 42. Fax.: 34 95 222 77 60.

# WORLD FILM FESTIVAL
# MONTRÉAL 2001

## Keep your agenda open
## at the end of August

**Montreal World Film Festival**
1432 de Bleury St.
Montréal (Québec) H3A 2J1
**Tel. :** (514) 848-3883 / **Fax :** (514) 848-3886
**E-mail :** ffm@qc.aira.com / **Web site :** http://www.ffm-montreal.org

Tel: (39 02) 4801 2912/4801 2920. Fax: (39 02) 4997 7020. e-mail: mifed@fmd.it. Website: www.fmd.it/mifed.

## Mill Valley

October 4-14, 2001

The Mill Valley Film Festival presents a wide variety of international programming, shaped by a commitment to cultural and artistic excellence. This intimate and welcoming event of unusually high calibre and dedication is set in a beautiful small town just north of San Francisco. The 11-day, non-competitive festival includes the prestigious New Media/Videofest, as well as the Children's Film Fest, tributes, seminars and special events. *Inquiries to:* Mill Valley Film Festival, 38 Miller Avenue, Suite 6, Mill Valley, CA 94941, USA. Tel: (1 415) 383 5256. Fax: (1 415) 383 8606. e-mail: info@finc.org. Website: www.mvff.com.

## Montréal World Film Festival

August 24-September 3, 2001

Serge Losique has established a major competitive festival in Montreal in late summer, and it is the only such event recognised by IFFPA in America. There are several categories and a market, public attendance is the highest in North America, and the number of foreign personalities swells each year. Montreal is the ideal location for such an event, with its bilingual facilities and proximity to major North American outlets. *Inquiries to:* World Film Festival (International Film Festival of Montreal), 1432 de Bleury St., Montreal, Quebec, Canada H3A 2J1. Tel: (1 514) 848-3883. Fax: (1 514) 848 3886. e-mail: ffm@qc.aira.com. Website: www.ffm. montreal.org.

### AWARDS 1999

*Grand Prix of the Americas (Best Film):* **The Colour of Paradise** (Iran), Majidi.
*Special Grand Prix of the Jury:* **Fuori dal mondo** (Italy), Piccioni.
*Best Director:* Louis Bélanger for **Post Mortem** (Canada).
*Best Actress:* Nina Hoss for **Der Vulkan** (Germany).
*Best Actor:* Ken Takakura for **Poppoya – Railroad Man** (Japan).
*Best Screenplay:* **Ma petite entreprise**, by Pierre Jolivet and Simon Michaël (France).

*Left to right: Mark Fishkin, Richard Peterson and Ray Harryhausen at the San Rafael Film Center in 2000*

## Netherlands Film Festival

September 19-28, 2001

Since 1981, Holland's only event presenting an overview of the year's entire output of Dutch film-making. A selection of Dutch features, shorts, documentaries and television dramas are screened and judged, with about 150 titles in competition in total, including more than 60 premieres, all completed in the 12 months preceding the festival. The Grand Prix of the Dutch Film, the Golden Calf Award, is presented in 12 categories. Retrospectives on the history of Dutch cinema and special programmes address various aspects of Dutch film. The Holland Film Meeting, the international sidebar, includes a Market Programme. The Netherlands Production Platform, for Dutch and European producers with a project-in-progress, is an initiative to encourage Dutch film talent. In 2000, the festival incorporated for the first time The

FILM INSTITUTE OF NORTHERN CALIFORNIA

## MILL VALLEY FILM FESTIVAL

OCT. 5 - 15, 2000  OCT. 4 - 14, 2001
*and*
The Rafael Film Center

Netherlands Internet Film Festival, from June 29-September 29. *Inquiries to:* Nederlands Film Festival, PO Box 1581, 3500 BN Utrecht, The Netherlands. Tel: (31 30) 232 2684. Fax: (31 30) 231 3200. e-mail: info@filmfestival.nl. Website: www.filmfestival.nl.

**AWARDS 1999**
*Golden Calf for Best Full-Length Feature:* **Abeltje - The Flying Liftboy**, Ben Sombogaart.
*Golden Calf for Best Director:* **The Delivery**, Roel Reiné.
*Golden Calf for Best Actor:* Rijk de Gooijer for **Scratches in the Table**.
*Golden Calf for Best Actress:* Nadja Hüpscher for **Based on the Novel**.
*Golden Calf for Best Short Film:* **Metro**, Eric Steegstra.

## New York
September 2001

The event has resisted the temptation to grow into a major market offering hundreds of films, remaining a small (under 30 total) selection of features and shorts culled from more than 1,000 international entries. The presentation is non-competitive and designed for the public, not just industry insiders. Attendance has been well over 95 per cent for the past decade, and each selection receives extensive local, national and international media coverage. *Inquiries to:* Film Society of Lincoln Center, 70 Lincoln Center Plaza, New York, NY 10023-6595, USA. Tel: (1 212) 875 5638/5610. Fax: (1 212) 875 5636. e-mail: webmaster@filmlinc.com. Website: www.filmlinc.com.

## Nordische Filmtage Lübeck
November 1-4, 2001

Annual event held in the charming medieval town of Lübeck, north of Hamburg, the festival throws a spotlight on Scandinavian and Baltic cinema, enabling members of the trade, critics and other film-goers to see the best new productions. It also features a large documentary section. Celebrates its 42nd anniversary in 2000. *Inquiries to:* Nordische Filmtage Lübeck, Schild Strasse 12, D-23539 Lübeck, Germany. Tel: (49 451) 122 4105. Fax: (49 451) 122 4106. e-mail: info@filmtage.luebeck.de. Website: filmtage.luebeck.de.

## Nyon

April 23-29, 2001

Specialising in creative documentaries, this recently rejuvenated event, entitled "Visions du Réel", includes two competitions, forums and market screenings, attended by film-makers, spectators and buyers, and is a stimulating source of ideas for new projects. *Inquiries to:* Visions du Réel, case postale 593, CH-1260 Nyon, Switzerland. Tel: (41 22) 361 6060. Fax: (41 22) 361 7071. e-mail: docnyon@ visionsdureel.ch.

## Oberhausen

May 3-8, 2001

Now in its 47th year, the International Short Film Festival, Oberhausen, remains one of the world's premiere short film events. It includes a wide selection of international and German issues in the media field. *Inquiries to:* Oberhausen International Short Film Festival, Grillostrasse 34, D-46045 Oberhausen, Germany. Tel: (49 208) 825 2652/2318. Fax: (49 208) 825 5413. e-mail: info@kurzfilmtage.de. Website: www.kurzfilmtage. de.

## Odense

August 2001

Denmark's only international short film festival invites unusual films that display an original and delightful sense of imagination – along the lines of the fairytales of Hans Christian Andersen. All

16mm and 35mm films can participate. Maximum length: 45 minutes. *Inquiries to:* Odense Film Festival, Vindegade 18, DK-5000 Odense C, Denmark. Tel: (45) 6613 1372, ext. 4044. Fax: (45) 6591 4318. e-mail: off.ksf@odense.dk. Website: www. filmfestival.dk.

### AWARDS 1999
*Grand Prix:* **Silence** (Sweden), Yadin and Bringas/ **Patterns** (Ireland), Sheridan
*Most Imaginative Film:* **In My Car** (Canada), Hoolboom.
*Most Surprising Film:* **Todo dia todo** (Brazil), Frederico.

## Oulu International Children's Film Festival

November 19-25, 2001

An annual, competitive festival of full-length feature films for children, it screens both recent titles and retrospectives. Oulu is set in northern Finland on the coast of the Gulf of Bothania. *Inquiries to:* Oulu International Children's Film Festival, Torikatu 8, FIN-90100 Oulu, Finland. Tel: (358 8) 881 1293. Fax: (358 8) 881 1290.

*The children's jury at the Oulu International Children's Film Festival in 1999*

e-mail: oek@oufilmcenter.inet.fi Website: www.ouka.fi.oek.

## Out Of Sight

June 2001

International Film and Television Archive Festival, Nottingham. This festival celebrates the very best in film and television, including new restorations and classics from the world archives and many special events. *Inquiries to:* Out of Sight, Broadway, 14-18 Broad Street, Nottingham, NG1 3 AL. UK Tel: (44 115) 952 6600. Fax: (44 115) 952 6622. e-mail: enquiries@ broadway.org.uk. Website: www.broadway. org.uk.

## Pesaro

Mid-June 2001

Focuses on the work of new directors and emergent, innovative cinemas, including non-fiction, animation, shorts and videos. For the past 35 years, this Mediterranean resort has been the centre for lively screenings and debates. In recent seasons, the programme has been devoted in part to

a specific country or culture. The main festival is coupled each year with a special retrospective of Italian cinema. In addition, each October the festival organises a five-day themed retrospective. *Inquiries to:* Mostra Internazionale del Nuovo Cinema (Pesaro Film Festival), Via Villafranca 20, 00185 Rome, Italy. Tel: (39 06) 445 6643/491 156. Fax: (39 06) 491 163. e-mail: pesarofilmfest@mclink.it. Website: www. pesarofilmfest.it.

## Portland

February 9-25, 2001

The 24th Portland International Film Festival is an invitational event presenting more than 100 films from some two dozen countries. New international features, documentaries and shorts are seen by audiences in excess of 35,000 from throughout the Northwest. Special programmes include classic silents with live orchestra performances, visiting artists, children's programming, an annual Pacific Rim Showcase and short films from around the world. *Inquiries to:* Portland International Film Festival. Northwest

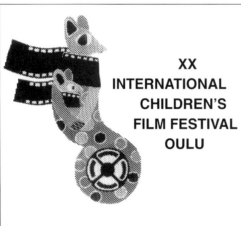

**XX
INTERNATIONAL
CHILDREN'S
FILM FESTIVAL
OULU**

**19-25 NOV 2001**
15 new feature films in competition

Torikatu 8,
SF-90100 Oulu, Finland
Tel: +358 8 8811293, 1294
Fax: + 358 8 8811290
E-mail:oek@oufilmcenter.inet.fi

Film Center, 1219 S.W. Park Avenue, Portland, OR 97205, USA. Tel: (1 503) 221 1156. Fax: (1 503) 294 0874. e-mail: info@nwfilm.org. Website: www.nwfilm. org.

# Raindance
October 2001

Held during the important Pre-MIFED Screenings, Raindance targets international film acquisition executives in London prior to the Milan market, and attracts an eclectic audience of leading industry professionals and genuine film fans. Raindance also aims to reflect the cultural, visual and narrative diversity of international independent film-making, by screening fiction, documentary and experimental feature-length and short films, children's films and pop promos. *Inquiries to*: Raindance, 81 Berwick Street, London W1V 3PF. Tel: (44 20) 7287 3833. Fax: (44 20) 7439 2243, Website: www.raindance.co.uk.

# Rio International Film Festival
October 2001

Formed in 1999 by the merger of Mostra Rio and Rio Cine, the Rio International Film Festival boasts a spectacular backdrop, an eclectic programme and ambition to become a key springboard for film sales to and from Latin America. Admissions at this popular event, which includes screenings on Copacabana, ran at 120,000 for 1999. Key sections in the festival include Premiere Brazil, World Panorama, Expectations 2000, Midnight

Movie, Gay World, a panorama of national cinema (films from the UK in 2000) and various tributes to directors. *Inquiries to*: Iafa Britz, Rio International Film Festival, Rua Fernandes Guimarães, 39-4th floor, 22290 000 Botafogo, Rio de Janeiro, Brasil. Tel: (55 21) 543 4968. Fax: (55 21) 295 4599. e-mail: cima@visualnet.com.br.

# Rotterdam
January 24-Feburary 4, 2001

The largest film festival in Benelux, now into its 30th edition, the Rotterdam International Film Festival has a reputation for programming innovative, independent new work alongside more commercial productions. New film talents from all over the world compete for three Tiger Awards (10,000 Euros, plus guaranteed theatrical and television release in the Netherlands). More than 200 features – including 60 international or European premieres – offer an overview of contemporary world cinema. The festival also hosts CineMart, the leading co-production market for independent film-makers, producers, sales agents, distributors and financiers. Rotterdam's Hubert Bals Fund supports film-makers from developing countries. *Inquiries to:* Rotterdam Film Festival, P.O. Box 21696, 3001 AR Rotterdam, Netherlands. Tel: (31 10) 890 9090. Fax: (31 10) 890 9091. E-mail: tiger@iffrotterdam.nl. Website: www.filmfestivalrotterdam.com.

# San Francisco
April 29-May 3, 2001

The oldest film festival in the Americas, in

*DONOSTIA - SAN SEBASTIÁN*
*INTERNATIONAL FILM FESTIVAL*

*THE SEPTEMBER FESTIVAL*

Apartado de correos, 397
Tel: (34) 943 48 12 12
Fax: (34) 943 48 12 18
Internet: http://www.sansebastianfestival.com
E-mail: ssiff@sansebastianfestival.com
20080 DONOSTIA - SAN SEBASTIAN (Spain)

Collaborator
*IBERIA*

Official Sponsor
**CANAL+**
*SPAIN*

its 44th year, the San Francisco International Film Festival continues to rise in importance and popularity. The 1999 event broke box-office records for the sixteenth year in a row, attracting 77,000 filmgoers. The festival presents over 100 features and 70 shorts from around the world. Special awards include the recently-established SKYY Prize, a $10,000 cash award designed to launch an emerging film-maker into the US marketplace. Attendees at last year's event included festival honoree Sean Penn, Robin Wright Penn, Jeremy Northam and directors Jonathan Demme, David Mamet and Arturo Ripstein. *Inquiries to*: San Francisco International Film Festival, San Francisco Film Society, 39 Mesa Street, Suite 110, San Francisco, CA 94129, USA. Tel: (1 415)561 5022. Fax: (1 415) 921 5099. e-mail: sfiff@sfiff.org. Website: www.stiff.org.

## San Sebastian

### September 2001

Held in an elegant Basque seaside city, the Donostia-San Sebastian Festival remains one of the most important film festivals in Spain in terms of glamour, competition, attendance, facilities, partying and number of films. Events include the Official Competitive section, Zabaltegi and a variety of meticulous retrospectives. The city is known for its superb gastronomy, beautiful beaches and quaint streets. The festival usually attracts a large number of international celebrities, national and international press, talent and film buffs. A special jury awards the New Director's Prize to a first- or second-time producer and director, worth 25 million pesetas (approximately $145,000). Director: Diego Galan. *Inquiries to:* San Sebastian International Film Festival, Apartado de Correos 397, 20080 Donostia, San Sebastian 20080, Spain. Tel: (34 943) 481 212. Fax: (34 943) 481 218. e-mail: ssiff@ sansebastianfestival.com. Website: www. sansebastianfestival.com.

### AWARDS 1999

*Golden Shell:* **C'est quoi la vie?** (France), Dupeyron.
*Special Jury Award:* **Jaime** (Portugal/Luxembourg/ Brazil), Vasconcelos.
*Best Director:* Zhang Yang for **Shower** (China) and Michel Deville for **La Maladie de Sachs** (France).

*Best Actress:* Aitana Sánchez-Gijón for **Volavérunt** (Spain/France).
*Best Actor:* Jacques Dufilho for **C'est quoi la vie?** (France).
*Best Photography:* Alfredo Mayo for **By My Side Again** (Spain).
*New Directors Award.* **Human Resources** (France), Cantet.

## Seattle International Film Festival

### May 17-June 10, 2001

Seattle hosts one of the largest and most highly-attended festivals in the U.S., with over 280 films representing 56 countries presented to an audience exceeding 140,000 at the 2000 event. Awards include the Golden Space Needles (audience awards) for feature, documentary and short films, director, actor and actress; and Jury awards for new Directors Showcase, Documentaries, Contemporary World Cinema, New American Cinema, Midnights, Films4Families, Archival Treasures, the Secret Festival, Emerging Masters, and the Short Film Showcase, as well as weekend galas and panels, master classes and seminars. *Inquiries to*: SIFF c/o Cinema Seattle 911 Pine Street, 6th floor, Seattle, Washington 98101-1818, USA. Tel: (1 206) 464 5830. Fax: (1 206) 264 7919. E-mail: mail@seattlefilm.com. Website: www. seattlefilm.com.

*Festival Director Darryl Macdonald with honoree Peter Weir at the 2000 Seattle event*

## Sitges Festival Internacional de Cinema de Catalunya

October 4-13, 2001

The 33rd edition of Sitges 2000 Festival Internacional de Cinema de Catalunya presents films from all over the world in its usual sections: Fantàstic, the festival's core competitive section devoted to fantasy; Gran Angular, for non-fantasy films; a selection of the most recent international productions; Seven Chances, seven films with little chance of being commercially distributed, chosen by seven critics; Anima't, a selection of the latest animation trends; Audiovisual Català, an encounter with the entire Catalan audiovisual production; Retrospectiva, a selection of classics from the history of cinema; Segundo de Chomón, a recovery of his work; Brigadoon, an alternative space with projections in new formats. *Inquiries to:* Sitges Festival Internacional de Cinema de Catalunya, Av. Josep Tarradellas 135, Esc. A 3 2, 08029 Barcelona, Spain. Tel: (34 93) 419 3635. Fax: (34 93) 439 7380. e-mail: cinsit@sitgestur.com. Website: www.sitges. com/cinema.

## Solothurn Film Festival

January 21-28, 2001

Held every year since 1966, the festival is a source of up-to-date information and gives a representative survey of all forms of creative film and video in Switzerland over the preceding year. It presents a selection of films and videos by Swiss directors and foreign directors resident in Switzerland, as well as Swiss-financed international co-productions. The event is covered by the Swiss and foreign media. This year there will be a special programme for international short fiction films. *Inquiries to:* Solothurn Film Festival, Postfach 140, CH 4504, Solothurn, Switzerland. Tel: (41 32) 625 8080. Fax: (41 32) 623 6410. e-mail: filmtage@cuenet.ch. Website: www.filmtage-solothurn.ch.

*Dino De Laurentiis receiving a lifetime achievement award at Cinema Expo in Amsterdam in June 2000*
*photo: Sigurd Moe Hetland*

## Southern African International Film & TV Market

November 2001

Sithengi (the South African International Film and Television Market) will mark its sixth year in 2001. Held in the exquisite city of Cape Town, Sithengi has become Africa's leading media and entertainment event, featuring a TV programme Market, the Co-Production Forum, and Africa's only Locations Expo. Business conducted at Sithengi exceeds $75m, and is well-attended by broadcasters from all over Africa. *Inquiries to*: Sithengi, PO Box 52120, Waterfront 8002, Cape Town, South Africa. Tel: (27 21) 430 8427. Fax: (27 21) 430 8160. e-mail: info@sithengi.co.za. Website: www.sithengi.co.za.

## Stockholm

November 8-18, 2001

The Stockholm International Film Festival is in its 11th year as the leading, fastest-growing competitive film event in Northern Europe. The only Scandinavian festival recognised by FIAPF, it hosts a FIPRESCI jury and is also a member of European Coordination of Film Festivals. Quentin Tarantino, Joel and Ethan Coen,

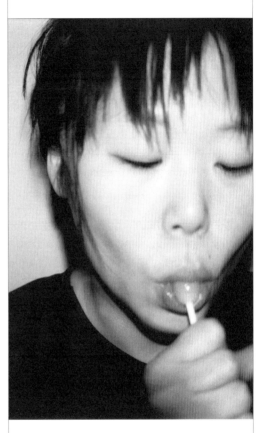

# 12th STOCKHOLM INTERNATIONAL FILM FESTIVAL

[ 8-18 NOVEMBER 2001 ]

Tel +46 8 677 50 00
www.filmfestivalen.se
program@cinema.se

Lars von Trier, Gena Rowlands, Neil Jordan, Elia Kazan and Dennis Hopper are among the personalities who have enjoyed the only festival in the world that operates 24 hours a day. On leaving Stockholm, Hopper stated: "I just wish my whole life was like this festival." Some 80 films have gained distribution in connection with the Stockholm International Film Festival. *Inquiries to:* The Stockholm International Film Festival, PO Box 3136 S-103 62 Stockholm, Sweden. Tel: (46 8) 677 5000. Fax: (46 8) 200 590. e-mail: program@ cinema.se. Website: www.filmfestivalen.se.

### AWARDS 1999
*Best Film:* **The Carriers Are Waiting** (Belgium/ France), Mariage.
*Best First Feature Film:* **Northern Skirts**, Albert.
*Best Actress:* Hilary Swank for **Boys Don't Cry** (US).
*Best Actor:* Ricky Tomlinson for **Nasty Neighbours** (US).
*Best Screenplay:* Kimberly Peirce for **Boys Don't Cry** (US).
*Lifetime Achievement Award:* Roman Polanski.
*Audience Award:* **Boys Don't Cry** (US).

## Sundance Film Festival
January 18-28, 2001

Sponsored by Robert Redford's Sundance Institute, this winter festival ranks among America's most respected displays of American independent cinema. Between 120 and 140 dramatic and documentary films are presented in the annual Independent Feature Film Competition, serving as indicators of the current trends. Between 58 and 70 shorts are also screened. *Inquiries to:* Sundance Film Festival, POBox 16450, Salt Lake City, UT 84116, USA. Tel: (1 801) 328 3456. Fax: (1 801) 575 5175.

### AWARDS 2000
*Grand Jury Prize (Dramatic):* **Girlfight**, Kusama/**You Can Count on Me**, Lonergan.
*Grand Jury Prize (Documentary):* **Long Night's Journey into Day**, Reid, Hoffmann.
*Directing Award (Dramatic):* Karyn Kusama for **Girlfight**.
*Directing Award (Documentary):* Rob Epstein and Jeffrey Friedman for **Paragraph 175**.

## Tampere
March 7-11, 2001

The 31st year of one of the leading short

Tampere International Short Film Festival march 7 -11, 2001

Tampere Film Festival
BOX 305  33100 Tampere
Finland

tel +358 3 213 0034
fax +358 3 223 0121
office@tamperefilmfestival.fi
w w w . t a m p e r e f i l m f e s t i v a l . f i

film festivals in the world. Famous for its international sauna party, the event attracts entries from over 60 countries. The 700 professionals and more than 25,000 spectators can see over 400 shorts in some 100 screenings during five days and nights. The International competition has awards for the best documentary, fiction and animation. The programme offers an interesting collection of top-quality retrospectives and tributes from all over the world. There is also an extensive series of open debates and training seminars for professionals. The market includes shorts and documentaries from northern and eastern Europe. *Inquiries to:* Tampere Film Festival, PO Box 305, 33101 Tampere, Finland. Tel: (358 3) 213 0034. Fax: (358 3) 223 0121. e-mail: film.festival@tt. tampere.fi. Website: www.tampere.fi/ festival/film.

### AWARDS 2000
*Grand Prix International:* **Four Corners** (Canada), Toews.
*Special Prize of the Jury:* **Ferment** (UK), Macmillan.
*Audience Award :* **Kovat Miehet** (Finland), Lalli.

## Telluride
September 2001

A truly unique, friendly gathering in the historic mining town of Telluride, a spectacular location in the mountains of Colorado. The festival continues to be one of the world's most influential, as famous directors, players and critics descend on the Sheridan Opera House and other theatres. The dedication of organisers and participants to the art of cinema gives Telluride a sincere, authentic feel – not forgetting the "surprise" element, with the programme only announced on the first day! *Inquiries to:* The Telluride Film Festival, 379 State Street, Portsmouth, NH 03801, USA. Tel: (1 603) 433 9202. Fax: (1 603) 433 9206. e-mail: Tellufilm@aol.com. Website: www.telluridefilmfestival.com.

# Thessaloniki International Film Festival

## November 2001

In its 40th year, the oldest and one of the most important film events in Greece. Thessaloniki targets a new generation of film-makers as well as high-quality independent films made by established directors. The International competition (for first or second features) awards the Golden Alexander (approx. $38,000) and the Silver Alexander (approx. $23,000). Other sections include the Greek film panorama, retrospectives, Balkan survey, New Horizons and a number of special galas and exhibitions. *Inquiries to:* International Thessaloniki Film Festival, 40

Paparigopoulou street, 114 73 Athens, Greece. Tel: (30 1) 645 3669. Fax: (30 1) 644 8143. e-mail: info@filmfestival.gr. Website: www.filmfestival.gr.

### AWARDS 1999

*Best Full Length Film – Golden Alexander:* **Shower** (China), Zhang Yang.
*Special Jury – Silver Alexander:* **Garage Olimpo** (Italy/France/Argentina), Bechis.
*Best Director:* Justin Kerrigan for **Human Traffic** (UK).
*Best Screenplay:* Atef Hetata for **Closed Doors** (Egypt/France) and Laurent Cantet, Gilles Marchand for **Human Resources** (France).
*Best Actress:* Sawson Badr for **Closed Doors** (Egypt/France).
*Best Actor:* Jean-Pierre Darroussin for **Qui plume la lune** (France).
*Artistic Achievement Award:* **Return of the Idiot** (Czech Republic).
*Special Mention:* Paddy Connor, actor, and Terry Stacey, cinematographer, for **Dream Catcher** (US).

# Torino Film Festival

## November 2001

Well-organised annual event (formerly known as the Festival Internazionale

**THESSALONIKI DOCUMENTARY FESTIVAL IMAGES OF THE 21st CENTURY**

March 2001

Greece's major world documentary event
Doc Market, Seminars,
Round Table Discussions
A showcase of Balkan Documentaries

Contact: Dimitri Eipides
40. Paparigopoulou str. 114, 73 Athens, Greece • Tel: (30.1) 64 53 669
Fax: (30.1) 64 48 143 • e-mail: newhorizons@filmfestival.gr

INTERNATIONAL
THESSALONIKI FILM FESTIVAL
www.filmfestival.gr
NOVEMBER 10-19, 2000

Cinema Giovani) which focuses exclusively on films made by new directors. There are competitive sections for shorts, features and Italian independents, as well as retrospectives, spotlights and premieres. The festival has been recognised as a top showcase for hot new international talent and dubbed second only to Venice on the crowded Italian festival circuit. *Inquiries to:* Torino Film Festival, Via Monte di Pietà 1, 10121 Torino, Italy. Tel: (39 011) 562 3309. Fax: (39 011) 562 9796. e-mail: info@torinofilmfest.org. Website: www.torinofilmfest.org.

## Toronto International Film Festival

September 6-15, 2001

A rich diversity of world cinema is featured annually, offering more than 250 films in 10 days. The event offers a wide range of international programmes: Galas, Special Presentations, Contemporary World Cinema, Planet Africa, Dialogues, Talking with Pictures, Reel to Reel, Directors Spotlight, Midnight Madness, Perspective Canada Discovery, and Masters. There is also a Rogers Industry Centre that includes a Sales Office and Symposium. *Inquiries to:* Toronto International Film Festival, 2 Carlton St., 16th Floor, Toronto, Ontario, Canada M5B 1J3. Tel: (1 416) 967 7371. Fax: (1 416) 967 9477. Public Box Office: (416) 968-FILM. e-mail: tiff@torfilmfest.ca. Website: www.bell.ca/filmfest.

## Tromsø International Film Festival

January 16-21, 2001

Possibly the world's northernmost film event, far beyond the Arctic Circle, this "Winter Wonderland" festival focuses on contemporary art films and documentaries, 35mm feature-length films from all continents. *Inquiries to:* The Arctic Film Festival, Tromsø, Postbox 285, N – 9253 Tromsø, Norway. Tel: (47 77) 75 30 90. Fax: (47 77) 75 30 99. e-mail: ola@tromsk. Website: www.tromsokino.no/filmfestival.

## Umeå

September 2001

Now in its 16th year. An annual, non-competitive event screening around 100 features and 50 shorts from around the world, including a number of Swedish premieres. The festival has gained considerable standing as a gateway for film distribution in Sweden and the Nordic countries and is the largest film festival in Northern Scandinavia. Director Thom Palmen's lively programme includes an international panorama, innovative, funny shorts, Swedish and Nordic documentaries, and special guests. The popular "Camera Obscura" section features obscure films and restored or neglected classics. Also offers seminars and workshops. *Inquiries to:* Umeå International Film Festival, Box 43, S-901 02 Umeå, Sweden. Tel: (46 90) 133 388/356. Fax: (46 90) 777 961. e-mail: film.festival@ff.umea.com. Website: www.ff.umea.com.

## Valencia

October 2001

Launched in 1979 and organised by the Valencia Municipal Film Foundation, the Valencia Mostra/Cinema del Mediterrani's competitive section focuses on films from Mediterranean countries. The Mostra also has an international panorama, a children's film section, a sidebar for first-time Spanish directors, and numerous retrospectives and tributes (to Visconti, John Waters and Luis Berlanga in 1999). The Mostra has a strong star presence: Sophia Loren, Gérard Depardieu and Kathleen Turner attended in 1999. *Inquiries to:* Valencia Mostra/Cinema del Mediterrani, Plaza de Arzobispo 2, Acc. B, 46003 Valencia, Spain. Tel: (34 96) 392 1506. Fax: (34 96) 391 5156. e-mail: festival@mostravalencia.com. Website: www.mostravalencia.com.

### AWARDS 1999

*Golden Palm Tree:* **Urban Feel** (Israel), Seagall.
*Silver Palm Tree:* **Propaganda** (Turkey), Cetin.
*Bronza Palm Tree:* **Le Derrière** (France), Lemercier.
*Best First Film:* **Solas** (Spain), Zambrano.
*Audience Award:* **Waar bliift het licht?** (Netherlands), Conix.

## Valladolid

### October 26-November 3, 2001

In its 46th year in 2001, this annual Spanish event is one of the oldest and most prestigious festivals in Europe and has an excellent reputation for its organisation, professionalism and hospitality. Features, shorts and documentaries are screened in competition. Also on offer are retrospectives, a look at works from a film school, a selection of recent Spanish productions and an exhibition. The 2000 edition sidebars were dedicated to Mike Leigh, Josefina Molina, "15 x 15 The European Film Heritage", big screen adaptations of the plays of Arthur Miller, and the Sam Spiegel School of Cinema, Jerusalem. *Inquiries to*: Fernando Lara, Director, Teatro Calderon, c/Leopoldo Cano, s/n 4 planta, 47003, Valladolid, Spain. Tel: (34 983) 305 700,77,88. Fax: (34 983) 309 835. e-mail: festvalladolid@seminci.com. Website: www.seminci.com.

**AWARDS 1999**
*Golden Spike:* **East Is East** (UK), O'Donnell.

*Silver Spike:* **The War Zone** (UK), Roth.
*"Pilar Miro" Prize to the Best New Director:* Alexander Payne for **Election** (US) and Andreas Dresen for **Night Shapes** (Germany).
*Best Actor:* Takeshi Kitano for **Kikujiro** (Japan).
*Best Actress:* Linda Bassett for **East Is East** (UK).
*Best Cinematography:* Paul Sarossy for **Felicia's Journey** (UK/Canada/US).
*Audience Award:* **Pídelo cuentas al rey** (Spain), Quirós.

## Vancouver

### September 21-October 4, 2001

Now in its 20th year, this festival has grown into an event of considerable stature. About 140,000 people attend more than 300 films from all parts of the world, and the Canadian city's natural beauty enhances the hospitality on offer. Areas of special focus are East Asia, Canada, Documentaries and the Annual Trade Forum. *Inquiries to:* Alan Franey, 410-1008 Homer Street, Vancouver, B.C., Canada V6B 2X1. Tel: (1 604) 685 0269. Fax: (1 604) 688 8221. e-mail: viff@viff.org. Website: www.viff.org.

## Venice

28 August–8 September 2001

In the hands of Alberto Barbera, year two, the oldest world film festival is trying to speed itself up for the new century. Its Lido facilities need major expansion in order to accommodate a rising flood of features, shorts and experimental works, which are increasingly synchronised with other multimedia branches within the Biennale of Art – Venice's unparalleled international goldmine. *Inquiries to:* La Biennale di Venezia, San Marco, Cà Giustinian, 30124 Venice, Italy. Tel: (39 041) 521 8711. Fax: (39 041) 523 6374. e-mail: das@labiennale.com. Website: www.labiennale.org.

**AWARDS 1999**
*Golden Lion for Best Film:* **Not One Less** (China), Zhang Yimou.
*Jury Grand Prix:* **The Wind Will Carry Us** (France/Iran), Kiarostami.
*Silver Lion for Best Direction:* Zhang Yuan for **Seventeen Years** (China).
*Coppa Volpi for Best Actress:* Nathalie Baye for **Une liaison pornographique** (Belgium/France).
*Coppa Volpi for Best Actor:* Jim Broadbent for **Topsy-Turvy** (UK).
*FIPRESCI Award:* **The Wind Will Carry Us** (France/Iran), Kiarostami.

## Victoria Independent Film and Video Festival

February 2-11, 2001

Set in beautiful Victoria, the 7th annual festival includes nine days of features, documentaries, shorts and a chance to come face to face with a 'who's who' of the film world in a laid-back setting. The festival also features a two-day film forum, discussions, a fun-filled opportunity for the public to try film-making first hand (in one evening), an art exhibition (with a film theme, of course) and video installation. *Inquires to*: Victoria Independent Film and Video Festival, 101-610 Johnson Street,

Victoria, British Columbia, Canada V8W 1M4. Tel: (1 250) 389 0444. Fax: (1 250) 380 1547. e-mail: vifvf@direct.ca. Website: mypage.direct.ca/v/vifvf.

## Wellington

July 2001

This 30-year-old festival screens an invited programme of around 100 features and 50 shorts. Along with its Auckland sibling, the event provides a non-competitive New

*Don McKellar during the Mad Hatter's Croquet Party at the Victoria Independent Film & Video Festival*
*photo: Mike Doerkson*

Zealand premiere showcase for a striking diversity of film and video styles. An archival component also enjoys considerable prominence. Now in its second decade under the direction of the apparently tireless Bill Gosden. *Inquiries to:* Wellington Film Festival, Box 9544, Marion Square, Wellington, New Zealand. Tel: (64 4) 385 0162. Fax: (64 4) 801 7304. e-mail: enzedff@actrix.gen.nz. Website: www. enzedff.co.nz.

## Wine Country Film Festival

July 21-August 14, 2001

Set in the heart of Northern California's premium wine region, the event accepts feature films, shorts, documentaries, animation, student films and videos. The five categories are independent features, international films, films making social comment, films about the arts and films about the environment. Generally non-competitive, but with short film, documentary and new directors' prizes.

Many of the films are shown outdoors in spectacular wine country settings. *Inquiries to:* PO Box 303, Glen Ellen, CA 95442, USA. Tel: (1 707) 996 2536. Fax: (1 707) 996 6964. E-mail: wcfilmfest@aol.com. Website: www.winecountryfilmfest.com.

## WorldFest-Houston

April 20-29, 2001

Celebrating its 34th year, the festival offers competition for independent features, shorts, student films, TV productions and commercials, music videos and screen-plays. WorldFest is the largest film and video competition in the world in terms of the number of entries received. It is the only truly independent festival in North America as it no longer accepts major studio films. Festival Founding Director J. Hunter Todd operates a new Discovery Festival programme which automatically notifies the major 200 international film festivals of the WorldFest winners. The programme co-ordinators also submit all student, short and screenplay winners to the top US agents and agencies. *Inquiries to:* WorldFest-Houston, PO Box 56566, Houston, TX 77256, USA. Tel: (1 713) 965 9955. Fax: (1 713) 965 9960. e-mail: worldfest@aol.com. Website: www. Worldfest.org.

*From left: Fernando Arrabal and Alejandro Jodorowsky join festival director Jean-Loup Passek at the 2000 La Rochelle International Film Festival*

# XXVIIIᵉ FESTIVAL INTERNATIONAL DU FILM DE LA ROCHELLE

**directed by jean-loup passek**         **29 JUNE - 9 JULY, 2001**

**100 LONG FEATURE FILMS    300 SCREENINGS    NON COMPETITIVE**

## 3 MAIN SECTIONS

- Retrospectives devoted to the work of past filmmakers

- Tributes to contemporary directors, in their presence

- Le Monde Tel Qu'il Est (The World As It Is), a selection of unreleased films from all over the world.

**Festival International du Film de la Rochelle
16, rue Saint Sabin, 75011 Paris
Phone: (1) 48 06 16 66 Fax: (1) 48 06 15 40**

# Other Festivals and Markets of Note

*Acapulco French Film Festival*, Crater 215, Col. Jardines del Pedregal 01900 Mexico DF, Mexico. Tel: (52 5) 568 0798/8317. Fax: (52 5) 568 0914. *(Organised by Unifrance Film International, used to promote the profile and sales of French films in Latin America. Non-competitive – Nov.)*

*AFI Los Angeles International Film Festival*, AFI Festivals, 2021 N. Western Avenue, Los Angeles, CA 90027, USA. Tel: (1 323) 856 7709. Fax: (1 323) 462 4049. e-mail: afifest@afionline.org. Website: www.afifest.com. *(L.A.'s most prominent film festival – Oct 19-26.)*

*Alcalá de Henares Film Festival*, Plaza del Empecinado 1, 28801 Alcalá de Henares, Madrid, Spain. Tel: (34 91) 881 3934. Fax: (34 91) 881 3906. *(Competition for Spanish shorts, new directors and Madrid-made videos, plus international shorts and Spanish director sidebars – Nov.)*

*American Film Market*, 10850 Wilshire Blvd., 9th floor, Los Angeles, CA, 90024. USA. Tel: (1 310) 446 1000. Fax: (1 310) 446 1600. *(Efficiently-run market primarily for English-language theatrical films. Buyers must be accredited – Feb. 21-28.)*

*Ann Arbor Film Festival*, PO Box 8232, Ann Arbor, MI 48107, USA. Tel: (1 734) 995 5356. Fax: (1 734) 995 5396. e-mail: vicki@ honeyman.org Website: aafilmfest.org. *(Presenting experimental films from all over the world – March 13-18.)*

*Annecy/MIFA*, Centre International du Cinéma d'Animation, B.P. 399, 74013 Annecy Cedex, France. Tel: (33 4) 5010 0900. Fax: (33 4) 5010 0970. e-mail: info@annecy.org Website: www.annecy.org. *(Long-established international and competi-tive animated film festival with a useful market (MIFA) to further the sale and distribution of animated films – June 4-9.)*

*Art Film Festival (Trencianske Teplice)*, Konventna 8, Bratislava, Slovak Republic, 81103. Tel: (421 7) 5441 9479/81. Fax: (42 17) 5441 1679. Website: www.artfilm.sk. *(The Festival encourages interest in and promotion of art films. – June 22-29.)*

*Asian American International Film Festival*, Asian Cinevision, 37 East Broadway, New York, NY. 10002, USA. Tel: (1 212) 925 8685. Fax: (1 212) 925 8157. *(Showcases works by established and emerging Asian and Asian American film-makers – July.)*

*Aspen Shortfest & Filmfest*, 110 E. Hallam, Ste. 102, Aspen, CO. 81611, USA. Tel: (1 970) 925 6882. Fax: (1 970) 925 1967. e-mail: gswanson@aspenfilm.org. Website: www. aspenfilm.org. *(Feature-length invitational – late Sept. Short subject competition – April.)*

*Atlantic Film Festival*, PO Box 36139, Halifax, NS B3J 3S9 Canada. Tel: (1 902) 422 3456. Fax: (1 902) 422 4006. e-mail: festival@atlanticfilm.com. Website: www. atlanticfilm.com. *(Features, documentaries, shorts. Includes strategic partners-coproduction workshop series – Sept.)*

*Auckland International Film Festival*, PO Box 9544, Wellington 6001, New Zealand. Tel: (64 4) 385 0162. Fax: (64 4) 801 7304. e-mail: festival@enzedff.co.nz. Website: www.enzedff.co.nz. *(A leading showcase of over 100 features and 50 shorts. Twinned annually with the Wellington Film Festival July.)*

*Augsburg Children's Film Festival*, Filmbüro Augsburg, Schroeckstrasse 8, 86152 Augsburg, Germany. Tel: (49 821) 349 1060. Fax: (49 821) 349 5218. e-mail: filmbuero@t-online.de. *(New international feature films for children – Nov.)*

*Banff Mountain Film Festival*, The Banff Centre for Mountain Culture, Box 1020, Stn. 38, Banff, AB, Canada TOL OCO. Tel: (1 800) 298 1229. Fax: (1 403) 762 6277. e-mail: cmc@banffcentre.ab.ca. Website: www.banffcentre.ab.ca/cmc. *(International competition for all films and videos related to mountains and the spirit of adventure – Nov 2-4.)*

*The Bilbao International Documentary and Short Film Festival*, Colon de Larreategui, 37, 4 dcha., 48009 Bilbao. Tel: (34 94) 424 8698. Fax: (34 94) 424 5624. *(Long-running festival in this northern Spanish industrial town – Nov.)*

*Birmingham International Film & Television Festival*, 9 Margaret St., Birmingham B3 3BS, UK. Tel: (44 121) 212 0777. Fax: (44 121) 212 0666. e-mail: info@film-tv-festival.org.uk. Website: www. film-tv-festival.org.uk. (Growing provincial festival which features both film and television – Nov.)

*Left to right: Tom Tykwer, Simon Perry, Til Schweiger and Christina Hoffman discussing the export of German films at a panel during the Cologne Cinema Conference*

*photo: A. Stössel*

**Bite the Mango Film Festival**, National Museum of Photography, Film & TV, Pictureville, Bradford, BD1 NQ West Yorkshire, UK. Tel: (44 1274) 203 317. Fax: (44 1274) 770 217. e-mail: i.ajeeb@ nmsi.ac.uk. Website: www.nmpft.org.uk. *(Annual film festival for South Asian and Black Film and TV – Sept.)*

**Bogotá Film Festival**, Calle 26 No. 4-92, Santafé de Bogotá, Colombia. Tel: (57 1) 337 5326/282 5196/243 1901. Fax: (57 1) 342 2872. e-mail: cidc@coll.telecom.com.co. Website: www.bogocine.org.co. *(Competitions for Colombian films and new directors – Oct. 9-17.)*

**Boston Film Festival**, PO Box 516, Hull, MA. 02045, USA. Tel: (1 781) 925 1373. Fax: (1 781) 925 3132. e-mail: GEMSAD@ aol.com. Website: bostonfilmfestival.org. *(Approximately 50 films, including studio releases, American independents, documentaries and shorts – Sept.)*

**Bradford Film Festival**, National Museum of Photography Film & TV, Bradford, BD1 1NQ West Yorkshire, UK. Tel: (44 1274) 202 030. Fax: (44 1274) 770 217. e-mail: l.kavanagh@nmsi.ac.uk. Website: www.

nmpft.org.uk. *(Features a competitive section for new European film-makers, previews of new releases, sections of unreleased film, retrospectives and Widescreen Weekend – March.)*

**British Short Film Festival**, Room A214-BBC TV Centre, Wood Lane, London W12, UK. Tel: (44 20) 8743 8000 ext. 62222. Fax: (44 20) 8740 8540. e-mail: info@british shortfilmfest.com. Website: www.british shortfilmfest.com. *(Only competitive short film festival in UK – Sept.)*

**Brussels Festival of Cartoons and Animated Films**, Folioscope, rue de la Rhetorique 19, B-1060 Brussels, Belgium. Tel: (32 2) 534 4125. Fax: (32 2) 534 2279. e-mail: info@folioscope.be. Website: www. awn.com/folioscope. *(Showcase for the newest, most interesting works in animation – Feb. 20-March 3.)*

**Brussels International Festival of Fantasy, Thriller and Science Fiction Films**, 144 Avenue de la Reine, 1030 Brussels, Belgium. Tel: (32 2) 201 1713. Fax: 210 1469. e-mail: peymey@skypro.be. Website: www.biff.org. *(Competitive international and European selection. Special side events include the Unusual Fashion Show, a Body Painting*

*Contest and exhibitions – March 9-24.)*
**Brussels International Film Festival**, 30 chaussée de Louvain, 1210 Brussels, Belgium. Tel: (32 2) 227 3980. Fax: (32 2) 218 1860. e-mail: infoffb@netcity.be. *(Competitive festival featuring films from many countries – Jan. 18-28.)*
**Buenos Aires Independent Film Festival**, Teatro General San Martin, Avenida Corrientes 1530, piso 8, oficina 3, Capital Federal 1042, Argentina. Tel/Fax: (54 11) 4374 0320. *(A festival with a strong independent and international flavour, founded in 1999 – April.)*
**Cairo International Film Festival**, 17 Kasr El Nil St., Cairo, Egypt. Tel: (20 2) 392 3562. Fax: (20 2) 393 8979. e-mail: info@ cairofilmfestival99.com. Website: www. cairofilmfest.com. *(Competitive, aimed at showing major international films, otherwise usually not available – Nov.)*
**Cairo International Children's Film Festival**, 17 Kasr El Nil St, Cairo, Egypt. Tel: (20 2) 392 3562. Fax: (20 2) 393 8979. *(Organised by the General Union of Arab Artists. Competitive – March.)*
**Camerimage**, Foundation Tumalt, Rynek Nowomiejski 28, 87 100 Torun, Poland. Tel: (48 56) 621 0079. Fax: (48 56) 621 0019. e-mail: camerimage@ascomp.torun.pl. Website: www.camerimage.ascomp.torun.pl. *(International event celebrating the art of cinematography. Includes a competition, student competition, panorama, TV section, workshops, seminars and equipment presentations – Dec.)*
**Canyonlands Film Festival**, 59 S. Main, Suite 214, Moab, Utah, 84532 USA. e-mail: canyonfilm@hotmail.com. Website: www. moab-utah.com/film. *(Competitive, with awards including Best of Festival, Best Documentary, Best Dramatic Feature etc. – March 6-9.)*
**Cape Town International Film Festival**, University of Cape Town, Private Bag, Rondebosch 7700, South Africa.Tel/fax: (27 21) 423 8257. e-mail: filmfest@hiddingh. uct.ac.za. *(Longest established film festival in South Africa. Non-competitive, transgressive in tone – Nov.)*
**Cartoons on the Bay**, Rai Trade, Via Umberto Novaro 18, 00195 Rome, Italy. Tel: (39 06) 3749 8315. Fax: (39 06)3751 5631. E-mail: cartoonsbay@raitrade.it.

Website: www.raitrade.rai.it/cartoonsbay. *(International Festival and Conference on Television Animation, promoted by RAI Radiotelevisione Italian, organised by RAI Trade – Apr.)*
**Chicago International Children's Film Festival**, Facets Mulimedia, 1517 W. Fullerton, Chicago, IL 60614, USA. Tel: (1 773) 281 9075. Fax: (1 773) 929 0266. e-mail: kidsfest@facets.org. *(Largest competitive festival for children's films in North America, programming over 200 films and videos from 40 countries – Oct 11-21. )*
**Chicago Latino Cinema**, International Latino Cultural Center of Chicago, c/o Columbia College Chiago, 600 S. Michigan Ave., Chicago, IL 60605-1996, USA. Tel: (1 312) 431 1330. Fax: (1 312) 344 8030. e-mail: clc@popmail.colum.edu. Website: www. chicagolatinocinema.org. *(ILCC promotes awareness of Latino culture through the arts, including the Annual Chicago Latino Film Festival – April 20-May 2.)*
**Cinefest: The Sudbury Film Festival**, 90 Elm Street, Sudbury, Ontario P3C 1T2, Canada. Tel: (1 705) 688 1234. Fax: (1 705) 688 1351. e-mail: cinefest@vianet.on.ca. Website: www.cinefest.com. *(Aims to programme the best of Canadian and international cinema – Sept. 18-24.)*
**Cinekid**, Korteleidsedwarstraat 12, NL-1017 RC Amsterdam, The Netherlands. Tel: (31 20) 531 7890. Fax: (31 20) 531 7899. e-mail: info@cinekid.nl. *(International film and TV festival for children and young adults – Oct.)*
**Cinema Jove**, Institut Valencià de la Joventut, c/Hospital, 11, 46001 Valencia, Spain. Tel: (34 96) 331 0592. Fax: (34 96) 331 0805. e-mail: cinemajove@ivaj.gva.es. *(Low-glam, high-fun foray into state-of-the-art youth cinema in balmy Spanish east coast city – June.)*
**Cinéma Méditerranéen Montpellier**, 78 Avenue du Pirée, 34000 Montpellier, France. Tel: (33 4) 9913 7373. Fax: (33 4) 9913 7374. e-mail: cinemed@mnet.fr. Website: www.cinemed.tm.fr. *(A major meeting-place of Mediterranean cinema – Oct.-Nov.)*
**Cinéma Italien Rencontres D'Annecy**, Bonlieu Scène Nationale, 1 rue Jean Jaurès, BP 294, 74007 Annecy Cedex, France. Tel: (33 450) 334 400. Fax: (33 450) 518 209.

e-mail: anecital@cybercable.tm.fr. *(Feature films from Italy, with tributes and retrospectives. Competitive – early Oct.)*

**Cinemagic Independent Film Festival for Young People**, 3rd floor, Fountain House, 17-21 Doneyall Place, Belfast, BT1 5AB, Northern Ireland. Tel: (44 28) 9031 1900. Fax: (44 28) 9031 9709. e-mail: info@cinemagic.org.uk. Website: www. cinemagic.org.uk. *(Children's films in competition – Dec.)*

**Cinemayaat (Arab Film Festival)**, 2 Plaza Avenue, San Francisco, CA 94116, USA. Tel (1 415) 564 1100. Fax: ( 1 415) 642 4780. e-mail: info@aff.org. Website: www.aff.org. *(Arab films featured in a Bay Area location – Sept.)*

**Cinequest San Jose Film Festival**, PO Box 720040, San Jose, CA, USA. Tel: (1 408) 995 5033. Fax: (1 408) 995 5713. e-mail: sjfilmfest@aol.com. Website: www. cinequest.org. *(Competition for features, documentaries and shorts, with accompanying tributes, seminars, entertainment – Feb. 22-March 4.)*

**Cleveland International Film Festival**, 2510 Market Ave., Cleveland, OH 44113-3434, USA. Tel: (1 216) 623 3456. Fax: (1 216) 623 0103. E-mail: cfs@clevelandfilm.org. Website: www.clevefilmfest.org. *(International "World Tour" progamme with specials like family films, American independents and lesbian and gay films – March 15-25.)*

**Cork Film Festival**, 10 Washington Street, Cork, Ireland. Tel: (353 21)427 1711. Fax: (353 21)427 5945. e-mail: info@cork filmfest.org. Website: www.corkfilm fest.org. *(Features documentaries, animation, art films, fiction and sponsored shorts. Competitive for shorts – Oct.)*

**Deauville Festival of American Film**, 40 rue Anatole France, 92300 Levallois, France. Tel: (33-1) 41 34 20 00/32. Fax: (33-1) 41 34 20 77. e-mail: sbataille@le-public-systeme.fr. *(Deauville celebrated its 25th anniversary in 1999. Showcase for US features and independent films – early Sept.)*

**Diagonale**, Mariahilfer str. 113, A-1060 Vienna, Austria. Tel: (43 1) 595 4556. Fax: (43 1) 595 455 620. e-mail: wien@ diagonale.at. Website: www.diagonale.at. *(Festival of Austrian Film – March 19-25.)*

**Dublin Film Festival**, 1 Suffolk Street,

Dublin 2, Ireland. Tel: (353 1) 679 2937. Fax: (353 1) 679 2939. e-mail: dff@iol.ie. Website: www.iol.ie/dff. *(Amicable and amiable Irish festival focusing on quality world cinema – Late March/April.)*

**Duisburg Film Week**, Am König-Heinrich-Platz, D-47049 Duisburg, Germany. Tel: (49 203) 283 4187. Fax: (49 203) 283 4130. e-mail: filmwoche.vhs@duisburg.de. Website: www.duisburg.de/filmwoche. *(Dedicated to German-language documentaries – Nov.)*

**Emden International Film Festival**, Postfach 2343, 26703 Emden, Germany. Tel: (49 4921) 915 531/535. Fax: (49 4921) 915 599. e-mail: filmfest@filmfest-emden.de. Website: www.filmfest-emden.de. *(Focusing on North-Western European films, particularly from Germany and the UK – June 6-13.)*

**European First Film Festival (Premiers Plans), Festival d'Angers**, 54 Rue Beaubourg, F-75003 Paris, France. Tel: (33 1) 4271 5370. Fax: (33 1) 4271 4755. Website: www.premiersplans.org. *(Competitive festival for European first films, including features, shorts and film schools – Jan 19-28.)*

**femme totale International Women's Film Festival Dortmund**, c/o Kulturbüro Stadt Dortmund, Kleppingstr. 21-23, D-44122 Dortmund, Germany. Tel: (49 231) 502 5162. Fax: (49 231) 502 25734. e-mail: info@femmetotale.de. Website: www. femmetotale.de. *(Biennial festival with changing themes highlighting films made by women. Non-competitive – March 28-April 1.)*

**Festival of French Cinema**, PO Box 20370, Tel Aviv, 61203 Israel. Tel: (972 3) 691 7181. Fax: (972 3) 696 2841. *(Screens new French fare, many Israeli premieres, with tributes and retrospectives – March 6-9.)*

**Festival International du Film Francophone de Namur**, 175 rue des Brasseurs, 5000 Namur, Belgium. Tel: (32 81) 241 236. Fax: (32 81) 224 384. e-mail: dany.martin-fiff@skynet.be. Website: www. fiff.namur.be. *(Feature films, shorts and documentaries from the French-speaking world. Recognised by the IFFPA as a competitive festival – Sept.)*

**Festival Dei Popoli**, Borgo Pinti 82r, 50121 Firenze, Italy. Tel: (39 055) 244 778. Fax: (39 055) 241 364. e-mail: fespopol@dada.it. Website: www.festivalpopoli.org. *(The* festival is partly competitive and open to documentaries on social, anthropological, historical and political issues – second week in Nov.)

**Festival du Cinema International en Abitibi-Temscamingue**, 215 Avenue Mercier, Rouyn-Noranda, Quebec J9X 5WB, Canada. Tel: (1 819) 762 6212. Fax: (1 819) 762 6762. e-mail: fciat@sympatico.ca. Website: www.telebec.qc.ca/fciat. (Short and medium length features, from animation to documentary – Oct.-Nov.)

**Figueira da Foz**, Post Box 50 407, 1709 Lisbon Codex, Portugal. Tel: (351 233) 402 820. Fax: (351 233) 402 828. (One of Portugal's most established film events – Sept.)

**Filmfest München**, Sonnenstr. 21, D-80331, Munich, Germany. Tel: (49 89) 381 9040. Fax: (49 89) 381 90426. e-mail: festivalleitung@filmfest-muenchen.de. Website: www.filmfest-muenchen.de. (International screenings, TV movies and retrospectives – June 30-Jul. 7.)

**Filmfestival Max Ophüls Prize**, Mainzerstrasse 8 66111 Saarbrucken, Germany. Tel: (49 681) 936 7421. Fax: (49 681) 936 7429. e-mail: filmfestSB@aol.com. (Competitve event for young directors from German-speaking countries – Jan.16-21.)

**Florida Film Festival**, Enzian Theatre,1300 South Orlando Ave. , Maitland, Florida 32751, USA. Tel: (1 407) 629 1088. Fax: (1 407) 629 6870. e-mail: filmfest@gate.net. Website: www.enzian.org. (Specialises in independent American films, with special sections for features, shorts, documentaries and non-competitive spotlight films – June 8-17.)

**Focus on Asia Fukuoka International Film Festival**, c/o Fukuoka City Hall, 1-8-1, Tenjin, Chuo-ku, Fukuoka 810 8620, Japan. Tel: (81 92) 733 5170. Fax: (81 92) 733 5595. e-mail: info@focus-on-asia.com. Website: www.focus-on-asia.com. (Dedicated to the promotion of Asian Film. Non-competitive – Sept.)

**Future Film Festival**, Via Pietralata 55/a-40122 Bologna, Italy. Tel: (39 051) 520 629. Fax: (39 051) 523 816. e-mail: fff@clarence.com. (The first Italian festival about new technologies in animation cinema – Jan 19-23.)

**Galway Film Fleadh**, Cluain Mhuire, Monivea Road, Galway, Ireland. Tel: (353 91) 751 655. Fax: (353 91) 770 746. e-mail: gafleadh@iol.ie. Website: ireland.iol.ie/galfilm/fleadh. (Screens Irish and international features and premieres. Accompanied by the Galway Film Fair, Ireland's only film market – July.)

**Guadalajara Mexican Film Showcase**, Av. Alemania 1370, Colonia Moderna, 44190 Guadalajara, Mexico. Tel: (52) 3810 1148/1151. Fax: (52) 3810 1146. (Competition for yet-to-be released Mexican features. Films from Latin America also invited out of competition – March 9-16.)

**Haifa International Film Festival**, 142 Hanassi Avenue, Haifa 34 633, Israel. Tel: (972 4) 8353 521/522. Fax: (972 4) 8384 327. e-mail: haifaff@netvision.net.il. Website: www.haifaff.co.il. (Includes a broad spectrum of new films from around the world, special tributes, retrospectives and other events – Oct 2-9.)

**Hawaii International Film Festival**, 1001 Bishop Street, Honolulu, Hawaii 96813, USA. Tel: (1 808) 528 3456. Fax: (1 808) 528 1410. e-mail: info@hiff.org. Website: www.hiff.org. (Seeks to promote cross-cultural understanding – Nov.)

**Heartland Film Festival**, 613 N. East Street, Indianapolis, Indiana 46202, USA. Tel: (1 317) 464 9405. Fax: (1 317) 635 4201. e-mail: hff@pop.iquest.net. Website: www.heartlandfilmfest.org. (Established in 1991 in Indianapolis, to honour and reward film-makers whose work explores the human journey, artistically expressing hope and respect for positive values – Oct 17-25.)

**Hébraïca Montpellier**, 500 Boulevard d'Antigone, 34000 Montpellier, France. Tel: (33 4) 6715 0876. Fax: (33 4) 6715 0872. (Theatre Festival, conferences, showcases Jewish and Israeli films. Competitive – March.)

**Holland Animation Film Festival**, Hoogt 4, 3512 GW Utrecht, Holland. Tel: (31 30) 233 1733. Fax: (31 30) 233 1079. E-mail: haff@knoware.nl/info@haff.nl. Website: www.awn.com/haff. (Animation from all over the world, competition for applied animation – Nov.)

**Hometown Video Festival**, The Alliance for Community Media, 666 11th Street, NW #806, Washington, DC 20001, USA. Tel: (1 202) 393 2650. Fax: (1 202) 393 2653. e-mail: acm@alliancecm.org. (Independent community producers from the US and abroad – July.)

*Huesca Film Festival*, Calle del Parque 1,2, Circulo Oscense, 22002 Huesca, Spain. Tel: (34 974) 212 582. Fax: (34 974) 210 065. e-mail: huescafest@tsai.es. Website: www.huesca-filmfestival.com. (*Competitive festival for Ibero-American and international shorts – June*)

*Hungarian Film Week*, Magyar Filmunió, Városligeti, Fasor 38, 1068 Budapest, Hungary. Tel: (36 1) 351 7760. Fax: (36 1) 352 6734. e-mail: filmunio@elender.hu. (*Competitive national festival showcasing Hungarian production from the previous year – Feb.*)

*Independent Film Days*, Filmbüro Augsburg, Schroeckstrasse 8, 86152 Augsburg, Germany. Tel: (49 821) 349 1060. Fax: (49 821) 349 5218. e-mail: filmbuero@t-online.de. (*International event for documentary and independent features, with retrospectives, national focus and symposium of film students – Nov.*)

*International Animated Film Festival-Cinanima*, Apartado 743, 4500 Espinho Codex, Portugal. Tel: (351) 227 34 4611. Fax: (351) 227 34 6015. e-mail: cinanima@mail.telepac.pt. Website: www.cinanima.pt. (*Competition, retrospectives for animated films – Nov.*)

*International Documentary Film Festival-Amascultura*, Rua Angola, Olival Basto, 2675 Odivelas, Portugal. Tel: (351 1) 938 8407. Fax: (351 1) 938 9347. e-mail: amascultura@mail.telepac.pl. (*International documentaries – Nov.*)

*International Documentary Filmfestival – Amsterdam (IDFA)*, Kleine-Gartmanplantsoen 10, 1017 RR Amsterdam, The Netherlands. Tel: (31 20) 627 3329. Fax: (31 20) 638 5388. e-mail: info@idfa.nl. Website: www.idfa.nl. (*Creative documentary films of all lengths, including numerous awards and a special "Kids & Docs" section. Includes the Forum, a market for international co-financing of documentaries – Nov 21-29.*)

*International Film Camera Festival "Manaki Brothers"*, 8. Mart #4, 91100 Skopje, Republic of Macedonia. Tel/fax: (389 91) 211 811. e-mail: ffmanaki@unet.com.mk. (*Held in Bitola, in remembrance of the brothers Yanaki and Milton Manaki, the first cameramen of the Balkans – Sept.*)

*International Festival of New Latin American Cinema*, Calle 23 No. 1155, Vedado, Havana, Cuba. Tel: (53 7)552 841. Fax: (53 7) 334 273. (*Competitive event and market for Latin American and International Films – Dec.*)

*International Film Festival*, Museumstrasse 31, A-6020 Innsbruck. Austria. Tel: (43 512) 560 470. Fax: (43 512) 581 762. e-mail: ffi.cinematograph@tirolkultur.at. Website: www.a2on.com/iffi. (*Films about Africa, America and Asia, Austrian premieres – June 13-19.*)

*International Film Festival of Uruguay*, Lorenzo Cornelli 1311, Casilla de Correo 1170, 11200 Montevideo, Uruguay. Tel: (59 82) 408 2460. Fax: (59 82) 409 4572. e-mail: cinemuy@chasque.apc.org. Website: www. cinemateca.org.uy. (*Uruguayan event – April 7-22, with a Children's Festival – July 4-18.*)

*International Film Forum "Arsenals"*, PO Box 1626, Marstalu 14, Riga, LV 1050, Latvia. Tel: (371 7) 221 620. Fax: (371 7) 820 445. e-mail: programm@arsenals.lv. Website: www.arsenals.lv. (*Biggest film event in the Baltic countries, dedicated to innovative film-making – Sept.*)

*International Student Film Festival*, Tel Aviv Cinémathèque, 2 Sprintzak Street, Tel Aviv, Israel. Tel: (972 3) 691 7181. Fax: (972 3) 696 2840. (*Workshops, retrospectives, tributes, premieres – June.*)

*The World Animation Celebration*, 30101 Agoura Court, Suite 110, Agoura, CA 91301, USA. Tel: (1 818) 991 2884. Fax: (1 818) 991 3773. e-mail: animag@aol.com. Website: www.animag.com.

*International Women's Film Festival*, Maison des Arts, Palace Salvador Allende, 94000 Créteil, France. Tel: (33 1) 4980 3898. Fax: (33 1) 4399 0410. e-mail: filmsfemmes@wanadoo.fr. Website: www.edebussac.fr/filmfem. (*Features, shorts and animated films all made by women – March 23-April 1.*)

*Israel Film Festival*, Israfest Foundation, 6404 Wilshire Blvd., Suite 1240, Los Angeles, CA. 90048, USA. Tel: (1 213) 966 4166. Fax: (1 213) 658 6346. (*US showcase for Israeli features, shorts, documentaries and TV dramas – Jan 25-Feb 1; in Miami, Feb 22-March 8; in NY, March 27-5; in LA, April; April 28 – May 3 in Chicago.*)

*Junior Dublin Film Festival*, Irish Film Centre, 6 Eustace Street, Dublin 2, Ireland.

Tel: (353 1) 671 4094. Fax: (353 1) 670 3074. e-mail: jrdublin@indigo.ie. *(Showcases the best in world cinema for young people; includes workshops and seminars – Nov-Dec.)*

**Kidfilm Festival, USA**, Film Festival, 6116 N. Central Expressway, Suite 105, Dallas, Texas 75206, USA. Tel: (1 214) 821 6300. Fax: (1 214) 821 6364. e-mail: usafilm. airmail.net. Website: www.usafilm festival.com. *(Showcases new and classic children's films from around the world – Jan.)*

**Kraków International Short Film Festival**, c/o Apollo Film, ul. Pychowicka 7, 30-364 Kraków, Poland. Tel: (48 122) 672 340. Fax: (48 122) 671 552. e-mail: festival@apollo.pl. Website: shortfilm.apollo.pl. *(Poland's oldest international film festival and respected short film showcase – May 29-Jun 2.)*

**Kudzu Film Festival**, PO Box 1461, Athens, GA 30603, USA. Tel: (1 706) 227 6090. Fax: (1 706) 2271083. e-mail: omni@prometheus-x.com. Website: www.prometheus-x.com/kudzu. *(Celebrates emerging talent and cultural diversity through features, shorts and documentaries – Oct.)*

**Kiev International Film Festival "Molodist"**, 6 Saksagansky Street, 252033 Kiev, Ukraine. Tel: (380 44) 246 6798. Fax: (380 44) 227 4557. e-mail: molodist@oldbank.com. Website: www.dkmedia.com/molodist. *(Ukraine's largest international film event and annual competition – Oct.)*

**Latin American Film Festival**, 11 Rupert Street, London W1V 7FS, UK. Tel: (44 20) 7434 3357. Fax: (44 20) 7287 2112. *(Films from Latin American countries, including features, documentaries and shorts – Sept 7-21.)*

**Local Heroes International Film Festival**, National Screen Institute Canada, 10159-108 St, Edmonton, Alberta, Canada T5J 1L1. Tel: (1 780) 421 4084. Fax: (1 780) 425 8089. e-mail: localheroes@nsi-canada.ca. Website: www.nsi-canada.ca/localheroes. *(Independent, non-competitive, seminars etc. – Feb. 25-March 3.)*

**London Lesbian & Gay Film Festival**, National Film Theatre, South Bank, London SE1 8XT. UK. Tel: (44 20) 7815 1323. Fax: (44 20) 7633 0786. e-mail: carol.coombes@bfi.org.uk. *(Films made by or about gays and lesbians – April.)*

**Lucas International Children's and Young People's Film Festival**, Deutsches Filmmuseum, Schaumainkai 41, 60596 Frankfurt/Main, Germany. Tel: (49 69) 21238833. Fax: (49 69) 2123 7881. e-mail: direktion@deutsches-filmmuseum.de. Website: www.deutsches-filmmuseum.de. *(New films for children and young people – Sept.)*

**Mar del Plata International Film Festival**, Lima, 319, 3 piso, 1073 Capital Federal, Argentina. Tel: (54 11) 4381 7582/93. Fax: (54 11) 4379 0915. *(Argentina's "A" level festival. International competition with a strong Ibero-American line-up – Mar.)*

**Margaret Mead Film & Video Festival**, American Museum of Natural History, 79th St. at Central Park West, New York, N.Y. 10024, USA. Tel: (1 212) 769 5305. Fax: (1 212) 769 5329. e-mail: meadfest @amnh.org. *(International documentary and ethnographic festival, includes shorts and features – Nov.)*

**Marseille 2001 Documentary Film Festival**, 3 Square Stalingrad, 13001 Marseilles, France. Tel: (33 4) 9504 4490. Fax: (33 4) 9504 4491. e-mail: vuesurlesdocs@wanadoo.fr Website: filmfestivals.com. *(Specialising in documentaries, the festival offers the best of worldwide documentary production – June.)*

**Melbourne International Film Festival**, Fitzroy Mail Centre 3065, Melbourne, Victoria, Australia. Tel: (61 3) 9417 2011. Fax: (61 3) 9417 3804. e-mail: miff@vicnet.net.au. Website: www.melbourne filmfestival.com.au. *(The prestigious festival celebrates its 50th anniversary in 2001. Screening over 300 features, shorts, documentaries and multimedia works – July 18–Aug 5.)*

**"Message to Man" Film Festival**, Karavannaya 12, 191011, St. Petersburg, Russia. Tel: (7 812) 235 2660. Fax: (7 812) 235 3995. e-mail: centaur@spb.cityline.ru. Website: www.message-to-man.spb.ru *(Programme includes international competition, international debut competition, national documentary competition and special programmes – Jun 15-22.)*

**Miami Film Festival**, Film Society of Miami, 444 Brickell Ave. no.229, Miami, Florida 33131. USA. Tel: (1 305) 377 3456. Fax: (1 305) 577 9768. e-mail: mff@gate.net. Website: www.miamifilmfestival.com. *(Festival emphasis is on Hispanic cinema,* featuring an Audience Award – Feb. 23-March 4.)

**Midnight Sun Film Festival**, Malminkatu 36 B 102, 00100 Helsinki, Finland. Tel: (358 9) 685 2242. Fax: (358 9) 694 5560. *(International and silent films, as well as award-winners from Cannes, Berlin, Locarno and Stockholm film festivals – June 13-17.)*

**Minneapolis/St.Paul International Film Festival**, University Film Society, Minnesota Film Center, 425 Ontario Street SE, Minneapolis, MN 55414. Tel: (1 612) 627 4431. Fax: (1 612) 627 4111 e-mail: filmsoc@tc.umn.edu. Website: www.ufilm.org. *(Event built up over 16 years by the reliable Al Milgrom. Screens scores of foreign films, especially Scandinavian – April 6-21.)*

**Montréal International Festival of New Cinema and New Media**, 3668 Boulevard Saint-Laurent, Montreal, Quebec H2X 2V4, Canada. Tel: (1 514) 847 9272. Fax: (1 514) 847 0732. e-mail: montrealfest@fcmm.com Website: www.fcmm.com. *(Focuses on independent cinema and seeks to explore quality experimental films as an alternative to conventional commercial cinema – Oct 11-21.)*

**Moscow International Film Festival**, 10/1 Khokhlovsky per., Moscow, 109028, Russia. Tel: (7 095) 917 2486. Fax: (7 095) 916 0107. e-mail: miff@cityline.ru. Website: www.miff.ru. *(Competitive only for full-length features – June.)*

**Munich International Festival of Film Schools**, Sonnenstrasse 21, D-80331 Munich, Germany. Tel: (49 89) 3819 040. Fax: (49 89) 3819 0426. *(Competition programme of student film productions from about 35 film schools from 25 countries – June 27-July 5.)*

**NAT-Annual Film Festival of Denmark**, NatFilm Festivalen, Festivalsekretariat, Store Kannikestræde 6, 1169 Copenhagen, Denmark. Tel: (45) 3312 0005. Fax: (45) 3312 7505. e-mail: kim@natfilm.dk. Website: www.natfilm.dk. *(Offers offbeat retrospectives and tributes from various countries – March 30-April 15.)*

**New Directors/New Films**, The Film Society of Lincoln Center, 70 Lincoln Center Plaza, New York, N.Y. 10023, USA. Tel: (1 212) 875 5638. Fax: (1 212) 875 5636. Website: www.filmlinc.com. *(A forum for works by new directors, co-sponsored by the Museum of Modern Art and The Film Society of Lincoln Center – March 23-April 8.)*

**New England Film and Video Festival**, Boston Film/Video Foundation, 1126 Boylston Street, room 201, Boston, MA 02215, USA. Tel: (1 617) 536 1540. Fax: (1 617) 536 3576. e-mail: info@bfvf.org. Website: www.bfvf.org. *(Since 1976, competitive regional festival devoted to new works by professionals and students in New England. Residency required for eligibility – April.)*

**New Orleans Film and Video Festival**, PO Box 50819, New Orleans, LA. 70150, USA. Tel: (1 504) 523 3818. Fax: (1 504) 529 2430. e-mail: neworleansfilmfest@worldnet.att.net. *(Twelweth annual festival includes international features, workshops and indie film competition – Oct.)*

**New York Exposition of Short Film and Video**, New York Expo, 532 LaGuardia Place, Suite 330, New York, NY 10012, USA. Tel: (1 212) 505 7742. e-mail: nyexpo@aol.com. website: www.yrd.com/nyexpo. *(Showcases both traditional, well-crafted work and challenging, experimental productions – Nov.)*

**Northwest Film and Video Festival**, Northwest Film Center, 1219 S.W. Park Ave., Portland, Oregon 97205, USA. Tel: (1 503) 221 1156. Fax: (1 503) 294 0874. e-mail: info@nwfilm.org. Website: www.nwfilm.org. *(Annual survey of new moving-image art produced in the US Northwest; features, shorts and documentaries – Nov 1-9. )*

**Ökomedia**, Ökomedia Institute, Habsburgerstr. 9a, D-79104 Freiburg, Germany. Tel: (49 761) 52 024. Fax: (49 761) 555 724. e-mail: oekomedia@t-online.de. Website: www.oekomedia-institute.de. *(Screenings of international film and television productions which offer an up-to-date review of ecological and environmental issues – Oct.)*

**Open Air Filmfest Weiterstadt**, Film Fest Weiterstadt, c/o Pollitt, Bahnhofstrasse 70, D-64331 Weiterstadt, Germany. Tel: (49 615) 012 185. Fax: (49 615) 014 073. e-mail: filmfest@weiterstadt.de. Website: www.weiteerstadt.de/vereine/koki/filmfest. *(Germany's oldest and largest open air film festival – Aug 16-20.)*

**Oslo Animation Festival**, Box 1405, N-1602 Fredrikstad, Norway. Tel: (47 69) 316 924. Fax: (47 69) 300 934. e-mail:

ad@animertedager.no. Website: www.
aimertedager.no. *(Nordic and international
animation, with retrospectives and student
fims. Competitive – April .)*
**Palm Beach International Film Festival**,
1555 Palm Beach Lakes Blvd., 0403 West
Palm Beach, Florida 33401 USA. Tel: (1 561)
233 1044. Fax: (1 561) 683 6655. e-mail:
pbifilms@aol.com. Website: www.
pbifilms.org. *(Approximately 50 films, which
include studio releases, American independents, documentaries and shorts – April
19-26.)*
**Palm Springs International Short Film
Festival**, 1700 E. Tahquitz Way, #3, Palm
Springs, CA 92262, USA. Tel: (1 760) 322
2930. Fax: (1 760) 322 4087. e-mail:
info@psfilmfest.org. Website: www.
psfilmfest.org. *(Largest competitive short film
festival in North America. Student, animation,
documentary and international competition.
Seminars and workshops – July 31-Aug 6.)*
**Panorama of European Cinema**, Minoos
10-16, 11 743 Athens, Greece. Tel: (30-1) 929
96 001. Fax: (30-1) 864 7730. *(In its 13th year
in 2000, the event includes European
Competition Section – Sept 28-Oct. 11.)*
**Peñíscola International Comedy Festival**,
Plaza del Constitución s/n, 12598
Peñíscola, Spain. Tel: (34 964) 474 901. Fax:
(34 964) 481 521. *(Hugely enjoyable local
comedy festival set in a spectacular
Mediterranean seaside resort – June.)*
**Pia Film Festival**, 5-19 Sanban-cho,
Chiyoda-ku, Tokyo, Japan. Tel: (81 3) 3265
1425. Fax: (81 3) 3265 5659. *(Aims to nurture
new, unique voices and emerging talent.
Competitive for amateurs, with an invitational
showcase – July.)*
**Philadelphia Festival of World Cinema**,
International House, 3701 Chestnut Street,
Philidelphia, PA 19104, USA. Tel: (1 215)
895 6593. Fax: (1 215) 895 6535. *(Screens a
worldwide range of features, documentaries
and shorts – April.)*
**Prix Italia**, Via Monte Santo 52, 00195
Rome, Italy. Tel: (39 06) 372 8708. Fax:
(39 06) 372 3966. e-mail: prixitalia@rai.it.
Website: www.citam.unibo/prixitalia.it.
*(International competition, open only to
member organisations, for radio and television
programmes and Web/Multimedia – 16-23
Sept.)*
**Punta del Este International Film Festival**,

c/o Rafael Pérez del Puerto Y Sarandi,
Dirección General de Cultura, Oficina
dirección de festivales Cinematográficos,
Departamento de Maldonado, Uruguay.
Tel: (598 42) 231 786. Fax: (598 42) 230 989.
*(Special emphasis on European films at event in
exquisite seaside resort – Jan. 18-24.)*
**Pusan International Film Festival**, Room
208, #1393 Woo 1 Dong, Haeundae-Gu,
Pusan, Korea. Tel: (82 51) 747 3010. Fax:
(82 51) 747 3012. e-mail: program@piff.org.
Website: www.piff.org. *(Launched in 1996
PIFF celebrates the best in world cinema, with
the emphasis on Asian films – Oct.)*
**RAI Trade Screenings**, Rai Trade, Via
Umberto Novaro 18, 00195 Rome, Italy. Tel:
(39 06) 3749 8257. Fax: (39 06) 3701 343.
Website: www.raitrade.rai.it. *(Opportunity
for international programming buyers to view
audio-visual material from Rai for broadcast,
home video, music, merchandising and
publishing rights – Oct 2-4.)*
**Rouen, Festival du Cinéma Nordique**, 30
rue da la République, 76000 Rouen, France.
Tel: (33 232) 767322. Fax: (33 232) 767323.
*(Competitive festival of Nordic cinema,
including retrospective and information
sections – March 14-25.)*
**Saint Louis Film Festival**, 55 Maryland
Plaza, Suite A, St. Louis, MO 63108-1501,
USA. Tel: (1 314) 454 0042. Fax: (1 314) 454
0540. e-mail: info@sliff.org. Website:
www.sliff.org. *(Showcases approximately 100
US and international independent films,
including studio specialty titles. Competitive –
Nov.)*
**St. Petersburg Festival of Festivals**, 190
Kamennostrovsky Ave., St. Petersburg
197101, Russia. Tel: (7 812) 237 0072.
Fax: (7 812) 237 0304. Website: www
.festoffest.ru. *(Features international
productions as well as local fare. Non-
competitive – June 23-29.)*
**San Francisco International Asian
American Film Festival**, c/o NAATA, 346
9th Street, San Francisco, CA., 94103, USA.
Tel: (1 415) 863 0814. Fax: (1 415) 863 7428.
e-mail: festival @naatanet. *(Film and video
works by Asian-American and Asian artists –
March 8-14.)*
**San Francisco International Lesbian and
Gay Film Festival**, Frameline, 346 Ninth
Street, San Francisco, CA. 94103, USA. Tel:
(1 415) 703 8650. Fax: (1 415) 861 1404.

e-mail: info@frameline.org. Website: www. frameline.org. *(Focus on gay and lesbian themes – June 14-24.)*

**San Sebastián Horror Film Week**, Teatro Victoria Eugenia, República Argentina 2, 20004 San Sebastián, Spain. Tel: (34 943) 481 153/57. Fax: (34 943) 430 621. e-mail: cinema_cinema@donostia.org. Website: www.donostiakultura.com/ terror. *(Panorama of international horror films and competition for short films, as well as retrospectives – Oct/Nov.)*

**São Paulo International Film Festival**, Alameida Lorena, 937 no. 303, 01424-001 São Paulo, Brazil. Tel: (55 11) 883 5137. Fax: (55 11) 853 7936. e-mail: info@ mostra.org. Website: www.mostra.org. *(Competitive event for new film-makers and international panorama– Oct.)*

**Singapore International Film Festival**, 45A Keong Saik Road, 089149 Singapore. Tel: (65) 738 7567. Fax: (65) 738 7578. e-mail: filmfest@pacific.net.sg. Website: www. filmfest.org.sg. *(Showcases the best of Asian and world cinema. Competitive Asian section – April 12-28.)*

**Sydney Film Festival**, PO Box 950, Glebe, NSW 2037, Australia. Tel: (61 2) 9660 3844. Fax: (61 2) 9692 8793. e-mail: info@sydfilm-fest.com.au. *(Broad-based, non-competitive event screening new international films and Australian features and shorts – June.)*

**Taormina International Film Festival**, Corso Umberto 19, 98039 Taormina, Italy. Tel: (39 094) 221 142. Fax: (39 094) 223 348. e-mail: info@taormina/arte.com. *(Non-competitive event in Sicily, stressing films by English-language directors – early July.)*

**Tokyo International Film Festival**, 3rd floor, Landic Ginza, Bldg. II 1-6-5 Ginza, Chuo-ku, Tokyo 104-0061, Japan. Tel: (81 3) 3563 6305. Fax: (81 3) 3563 6310. e-mail: pr@tokyo-filmfest.or.jp. Website: www. tokyo-filmfest.or.jp. *(Major international event, with competition and sidebars – Oct 27.- Nov 4.)*

**Troia International Film Festival**, Forum Luisa Dodi, 2900-461 Setúbal Codex, Portugal. Tel: (351 265) 525 908. Fax: (351 265) 525 681. e-mail: festroia@ mail.teleweb.pt. Website: www.festroia.pt. *(Held in southern city of Setúbal, near Lisbon. Special focus on small national cinemas. Competitive – June 1-10.)*

**Uppsala International Short Film Festival**, PO Box 1746, S-751 47 Uppsala, Sweden. Tel: (46 18) 120 025. Fax: (46 18) 121 350. e-mail: uppsala@shortfilmfestival.com. Website: www.shortfilmfestival.com. *(The only international short film festival in Sweden. Competitive – Oct.)*

**USA Film Festival**, 6116 N. Central Expwy., Suite 105, Dallas, Texas 75206, USA. Tel: (1 214) 821 6300. Fax: (1 214) 821 6364. E-mail: usafilm@airmail.net. Website: www.usafilmfestival.com. *(Eight-day festival featuring new US and foreign independents. Competition for US shorts, with cash prizes – April 19-26.)*

**Viennale**, Stiftgasse 6, A – 1070 Vienna, Austria. Tel: (43 1) 526 5947. Fax: (43 1) 523 4172. e-mail: office@viennale.at. Website: www.viennale.at. *(Presents a line-up of new international films, independent and new cinema, creative documentaries, shorts, tributes dedicated to directors, actors or producers – Oct.)*

**Vila do Conde Festival Internacional de Curtas Metragens**, Auditório Municipal, Praça de República, 4480-715 Vila do Conde, Portugal. Tel: (351 252) 248 469/646 516. Fax: (351 252) 248 416. e-mail: festival@curtasmetragems.pt. Website: www.curtametragems.pt. *(Short film competitive section and retrospectives – July.)*

**Virginia Film Festival**, Dept. of Drama, Culbreth Road, Charlottesville, VA 22903, USA. Tel: (1 804) 982 5277. Fax: (1 804) 924 1447. Website: www.vafilm.com. *(Annual event dedicated to the study of American cinema in relation to international films, with classics, premieres and discussions – late Oct.)*

**Warsaw Film Festival**, PO Box 816, 00-950 Warsaw 1, Poland. Tel: (48 22) 853 3636. Fax: (48 22) 853 1184. e-mail: festiv@ wff.org.pl. Website: www.wff.org.pl. *(Audience-oriented, 12-day event which has been screening current, invitation-only productions since 1985 – Oct 4-15.)*

**Washington, DC International Film Festival (Filmfest DC)**, PO Box 21396, Washington, DC 20009, USA. Tel: (1 202) 724 5613. Fax: (1 202) 724 6578. e-mail: filmfestdc@filmfestdc.org. *(Celebrates the best in world cinema –April 18-29.)*

# FILM SCHOOLS

## AUSTRALIA

**Australian Film, Television and Radio School**, PO Box 126, North Ryde, NSW 1670.

## AUSTRIA

**Universität für Musik und darstellende Kunst, Abteilung für Film und Fernsehen**, Metternichgasse 12, A-1030 Vienna. Tel (43-1) 713 5212-113. Fax: (43-1) 713 5212-114. Director: Mr. Wolfgang Gluck, member of AMPAS, Director's Branch.

## BELGIUM

**Archimedia**, European Training Network for the Promotion of Cinema Heritage, Royal Film Archive, 23 rue Ravenstein, 1000 Brussels. Tel: (32 2) 507 8403. Fax: (32 2) 513 1272. e-mail: archimedia@ledoux.be.

**Institut des Arts de Diffusion (I.A.D.)**, Rue des Wallons No. 77, B 1348 Louvain-la Neuve.

**Institut National des Arts du Spectacle et Techniques de diffusion (I.N.S.A.S)**, Rue Thérésienne, 8, 1000 Brussels. Tel (32 2) 511 92 86. Fax: (32 2) 511 0279. e-mail: sec@insas.be. Website: www.insas.be.

**Koninklijke Academie voor Schone Kunsten-Gent**, Academiestraat 2, B-9000 Gent.

## CANADA

**Queen's University**, 160 Stuart St, Kingston, Ontario K7L 3N6. Tel: (1 613) 533 2178. Fax: (1 613) 533 2063. e-mail: film@post. queensu.ca. Website: www.film. queensu.ca. In its four-year BA (Honours) degree programme and three-year BA degree programme, the Department of Film Studies provides an integrated approach to film criticism, history and production.

**Sheridan College**, Faculty of Visual Arts, 1430 Trafalgar Road, Oakville, Ontario, L6H 2L1. Tel: (1 905) 845 9430 ext. 2958. Fax: (1 905) 815 4041. Intensive and award-winning diploma programmes in: Classical Animation, International Summer School of Animation, Computer Animation, Computer Graphics and Media Arts. Summer workshops available from May to August.

**Simon Fraser University**, School for the Contemporary Arts, 8888 Univeristy Drive, Burnaby, B.C. V5A 1S6. Tel: (1 604) 291 3363. Fax: (1 604) 291 5907.

**Vancouver Film School**, 400-1168 Hamilton Street, Vancouver B.C. V6B 2S2. Tel: (1 604) 685 5808. Fax: (1 604) 685 5830. A unique training centre that offers five programmes in communication production: Film Production, Multimedia Production, Classical Animation, Computer Animation and Acting for Film and Television. All programmes have been designed with industry consultation and are taught by industry professionals. Specialising in shorter (one year) and intensive formats, students create their own graduate productions.

**University of Manitoba**, Film Studies Program, 367 University College, Winnipeg, Manitoba R3T 2M8. Tel: (1 204) 474 9581. Fax: (1 204) 474 7684. e-mail: film@ umanitoba.ca. Basic and advanced film-making and screenwriting.

**University of Windsor**, Communication Studies, Windsor, Ontario N9B 3P4. Tel: (1 519) 253 3000. Fax: (1 519) 971 3642. e-mail: mggold@uwindsor.ca. Film, radio, TV.

York University, Faculty of Fine Arts, Film & Video Dept., 4700 Keele St, Toronto, Ontario M3J 1P3.

## CZECH REPUBLIC

**FAMU**, Film and Television Faculty, Academy of Performing Arts, Smetanovo nábr. 2, CZ 116 65 Prague 1. Tel: (420 2) 2422 9176. Fax: (420 2) 2423 0285. Dean: Karel Kochman.

## DENMARK

**European Film College**, DK-8400 Ebeltoft. Tel: (45) 8634 0055. Fax: (45) 8634 0535. Principal: Kjeld Veirup. Summer season: international, intensive training courses for professionals of the industry. Sept.-April; eight-month undergraduate courses for students from all over the world. No special qualifications required except English language.

**The National Film School of Denmark**, Theodor Christensen's Plads 1, 1437 Copenhagen K. Tel: (45) 3268 6400. Fax: (45) 3268 6410. e-mail: info@filmskolen.dk.

## FINLAND

**Taideteollinen korkeakoulu, elokuvataiteen osasto**, University of Art and Design Helsinki UIAH, Department of Film and TV, Pursimiehenkatu, 29-31 B, SF-00150 Helsinki.

## FRANCE

**La Femis (École Nationale Supérieure des Métiers de L'Image et du Son)**, 6 rue Francoeur, 75018 Paris. Tel: (33 1) 5341 2100. Fax: 33 1) 5341 2109. President: Alain Auclaire.

Director: Gérard Alaux.

**Conservatoire Libre du Cinéma Français (C.I.C.F.)**, 9 quai de l'Oise, 75019 Paris. Tel: (33 1) 4036 1919. Fax: (33 1) 4036 0102.

**ESEC (Ecole superieure études cinematographique)**, 21 rue de Citeaux, 75012 Paris. Tel: (33 1) 4342 4322. Fax: (33 1) 4341 9521. L'ESEC gives a national diploma.

## GERMANY

**Deutsche Film and Fernsehakademie Berlin GmbH**, DFFB, Heerstrasse 18-20, 14052 Berlin.Tel: (49 30) 300 9040. Fax: (49 30) 300 90461. Four-year course deals with theories of film-making, film history and all aspects of practical film and TV production, scriptwriting, direction, camerawork, editing and special effects.

**Filmakademie Baden-Würtenberg**, Mathildenstrasse 20, 71638 Ludwigsburg, Germany. Tel: (49 7141) 969 235. Fax: (49 7141) 969 297.

**Hochschule für Fernsehen und Film**, Frankenthaler Strasse 23, D-81539 München. Tel: (49 89) 689 570. Fax: (49 89) 689 57189. Website: www.hff-muenchen. mhn.de. Approx. 340 students, 80 staff. Four-year course provides instruction in the theory and practice of film and TV. Facilities provide for work in 16mm and 35mm and video. Studies are free and begin each autumn. Two-stage admission process takes place Jan. each year.

## HONG KONG

**Hong Kong Academy for Performing Arts**, School of Film and Television, 1 Gloucester Road, GPO Box 12288, Wanchai, Hong Kong. Tel: (852) 2584 8626/8679. Fax: (852) 2802 4372.

## HUNGARY

**Szinbáz-es Filmmiivészeti Föiskola**, Vas u. 2/c, 1088 Budapest. Rector: Péter Huszti.

General Secretary: Lászlo Vadäsz.

## INDIA

**Film and Television Institute of India**, Law College Road, Pune 411 004. Tel: (91 20) 331 817. Fax: (91 20) 330 416. e-mail: filminst@ pne. vsnl. net.in.

## IRELAND

**European School of Animation, Senior College**, Ballyfermot Road, Dublin 10. Tel: (353 1) 626 9421. Fax: (353 1) 626 6754. e-mail: infoscb.cdcec.ie

## ISRAEL

**Department of Cinema and Television**, Tel Aviv University, Ramat Aviv, Tel Aviv. Tel: (972 3) 640 8403. Fax: (972 3) 640 9935.

## ITALY

**Magica, Master Europeo in Gestione di Impresa Cinematografica e Audiovisiva**, Via Lucullo 7 int. 8, 00187 Rome, Italy. Tel: (39 06) 420 0651. Fax: (39 06) 420 10898. e-mail: courses@audiovisual.org. Website: www. audiovisual.org. An international organisation offering on-line and in-class audiovisual and multimedia management and creative training for professionals and graduates. Specialisations include: screenwriting, audio-visual law and economics, multimedia studies, co-production, management in all areas of production and distribution. All the programmes are designed and taught by European and US industry professionals.

**Scuola Nazionale di Cinema**, Via Tuscolana 1524, 00173 Rome. Tel: (39 06) 722 941. Fax: (39 06) 721 1619. e-mail: snccn@tin.it.

## JAPAN

**Nihon University College of Art**,

Asahiganoka 2-42, Nerimaku, Tokyo, 176.

## NETHERLANDS

**Maurits Binger Film Institut**, Nieuwezijds Voorburgwal 4-10, 1012 RZ Amsterdam. Tel: (31 20) 530 9630. Fax: (31 20) 530 9631. e-mail: binger@binger.ahk.nl. Website: www.binger.ahk.nl. International centre for film and television, devoted to developing skills for working professionals. Programmes include script development and story editing, coaching for first-time feature directors, and management training for independent producers. Special events for the film community at large.

**Nederlandse Film en Televisie Academie**, Markenplein 1, 1011 MV Amsterdam. Tel: (31 20) 527 7333. Fax: (31 20) 527 7344.

## POLAND

**Panstwowa Wyzsza Szkola Filmowa**, Telewizyina i Teatralna, 61/63 Targowa str., 90 323 Lódz. Tel: (48 42) 674 8088. Fax: (48 42) 674 8139. e-mail: swzfilm@ mazurek.man. Website: www. filmowka.lodz.pl.

## ROMANIA

**Universitatea de Arta Teatrala si Cinematografica "I.L. Caragiale"**, str. Matei Voievod nr. 75-77, sector 2, 73224, Bucharest. Tel: (40 1) 252 8112. Fax: (40 1) 252 5881.

## SPAIN

**University of Valladolid**, Cátedra de Historia y Estética de la Cinematografica, Pza Santa Cruz 5, 47002, Valladolid. Tel: (34 983) 423 611. Fax: (34 983) 423 611.

**ECAM (Escuela de Cinematografia de la Comunidad de Madrid)**, Juan de Orduña 3, Ciudad de la imagen, 28223 Pozuelo de Alarcón, Madrid. Tel: (34 91) 512 1060. Fax: (34 91) 512 1070. e-mail: escuelacine@ ecam.es.

*Ben Gibson, left, of the London International Film School, and Dieter Kosslick, of Filmstiftung Nordrhein-Westfalen, at a panel on the role of film schools within the industry, in Cologne in 2000*

**Centre d'Estudis Cinematogràfics de Catalunya (CECC)**, Caspe 33, pral.08010 Barcelona, Spain. Tel: (34 93) 412 0484. Fax: (34 93) 318 8866. e-mail: info@cecc.es. Website: www.cecc.es. Three-year course run by Hector Faver on the theory and practice of film, including direction, script-writing, montage and sound, camera operation, direction of photography and acting.

**ESCAC (Escola Superior de Cinema Audiovisuals de Catalunya)**, Immaculada 35, 08017 Barcelona. Tel: (34 93) 212 1562. Fax: (34 93) 417 2601. A four-year course approved by the University of Barcelona, split between general theory and specialist courses in screen-writing, direction, editing, cinematography, sound, post-production and art direction.

**SWEDEN**

**Department of Cinema Studies University of Stockholm**, Borgvägen 1-5, Box 27062, S-102 51 Stockholm. Tel: (46 8) 647 7627. Fax: (46 8) 665 0723.

**Dramatiska Institutet (College of Theatre, Film, Radio, and Television)**, Borgvägen, Box 27090, S-102 51 Stockholm. Head of School: Kjell Grede.

**UNITED KINGDOM**

**University of Bristol**, Department of Drama, Film and Television Studies, Cantocks Close, Woodland Road, Bristol BS8 1UP. Tel: (44 117) 928 7838. Fax: (44 117) 928 8251.

**University of Derby**, School of Arts and Design, Britannia Mail, Mackworth Road, Derby DE22 3BL. Tel: (44 13) 3262 2281. Fax: (44 13) 3262 2760. e-mail: s.greenhough@derby.ac.uk. MA/FT/PT in Film with TV studies. BA (Honours) – subject to validation.

**University of Westminster**, Harrow School of Design and Media, Watford Road, Northwick Park, Harrow, HA1 3TP. Tel: (44 20) 7911 5903. Fax: (44 20) 7911 5955.

**London International Film School**, 24 Shelton Street, London WC2H 9HP. Tel: (44 20) 7836 9642. Fax: (44 20) 7497 3718. e-mail: info@lifs.org.uk. Website: www.lifs.org.uk. Principal: Martin M. Amstell. Offers a practical, two-year diploma course to professional levels. About half of each term is devoted to film production and the other half to practical and theoretical tuition. All students work on one or more films each term and are encouraged to experience different skill areas.

Facilities include two cinemas, shooting stages, rehearsal stages, and 15 cutting room. Equipment includes 16mm and 35mm Panavision, ArriFlex and rostrum cameras, Nagra recorders, Steenbeck editing machines and U-matic video. Faculty made up of permanent and visiting professionals. Entrance requirements: a degree or art or technical diploma, with exceptions for special ability or experience. Applicants must submit samples of their work and be proficient in English. New courses commence each Jan., April and Sept.

**Middlesex University**, Faculty of Art and Design, Cat Hill, Barnet, Herts EN4 8HT. Tel: (44 20) 8362 5021. Fax: (44 20) 8362 6339.

**National Film and Television School**, Station Road, Beaconsfield, Bucks, HP9 1LG. Tel: (44 1494) 671 234. Fax: (44 1494) 674 042.

**Newport School of Art and Design**, University of Wales College, Newport, College Crescent, Caerleon, PO BOX 179, Gwent NP18 3YG. Tel: (44 1633) 430 088. BA (Hons) Film and Video, Animation, and Media and Visual Culture.

**University of Westminster**, School of Communication, Watford Road, Nortwick Park, Harrow, Middlesex, HA1 3 TP. Tel: (44 20) 7911 5000. Fax: (44 20) 7911 5943.

**Royal College of Art**, Department of Film and Television, Kensington Gore, London SW7 2EU. Tel: (44 20) 7590 4444. Fax: (44 20) 7590 4500. 35 Students.

**The Surrey Institute of Art and Design**, Farnham Campus, Falkner Road, Farnham, Surrey GU9 7DS. Tel: (44 1252) 722 441. Fax: (44 1252) 892 616. Website: www.surrart.ac.uk.

**University of Stirling**, Film and Media Studies, Stirling FK9 4LA. Tel: 01786 467 520. Fax: 01786 466 855.

## UNITED STATES

Information on the thousands of US film schools and courses available can be obtained in the American Film Institute's *Guide to College Courses in Film and Television*, which can be ordered from Publications, The American Film Institute, 2021 North Western Avenue, Los Angeles, CA 90027.

## URUGUAY

**Escuela de Cinematografia**, Chucarro 1036, CP 11300 Montevideo. Tel: (598 2) 709 7637. Fax: (598 2) 707 6389. e-mail: cinevid@chasque.apc.org.

# FILM ARCHIVES

## ARGENTINA

**Cinemateca Argentina**, Salta 1915, CP 1137 Buenos Aires. Tel: (54 11) 4306 0548/0561. Fax: (54 11) 4306 0592. Executive Director: Mrs. Paulina Fernandez Jurado. Established in 1949. Stock: 12,000 film titles, 6,250 books, collection of film periodicals, 352,000 film stills, 6,600 film posters. The collection of micro-filmed clippings holds files on individual films and on foreign and Argentine film personalities. The library is open to researchers and students. The Cinemateca operates one film theatre with daily screenings.

## AUSTRALIA

**Archives Office of Tasmania**, 77 Murray Street, Hobart, Tasmania, Australia 7000. Tel: (61 3) 6249 9013. Fax: (61 3) 6249 9015.

**State Film Archives**, Library and Information Service of Western Australia, Alexander Library Building, Perth Cultural Centre, Perth, WA 6,000. Tel: (61 8) 9427 3310. Fax: (61 8) 9427 3276. e-mail: gfoley@tom.liswa.wa.gov.au. Stock: 3,800 Western Australian titles.

## AUSTRIA

**Österreichisches Filmarchiv**, Obere Augartenstr. 1, 1020 Vienna. Tel: (43 1) 216 1300. Fax: (43 1) 216 1300100.

**Österreichisches Filmmuseum**, A-1010 Vienna, Augustinerstr. 1. Tel: (43 1) 5337 0540. Fax: (43 1) 5337 05625. Directors: Peter Konlechner and Prof. Peter Kubelka. Stock: approx. 14,000 film titles and an extensive library and collection of stills and photographs.

## BELGIUM

**Royal Film Archive**, 23 rue Ravenstein, 1000 Brussels. Tel: (32 2) 507 8403. Fax: (32 2) 513

1272. Website: www.ledoux.be/adchimedia.

## BRAZIL

**Cinemateca Brasileira**, Caixa Postal 12900, 04092 São Paulo. Tel: (55) 577 4666. Fax: (55) 577 7433.

**Cinemateca do Museu de Arte Moderna**, Caixa Postal 44, CEP 20021-140, Rio de Janeiro, RJ. Tel: (55 21) 210 2188. Tel/fax: (55 21) 220 3113. e-mail: mam@mamrio.com.br.

## BULGARIA

**Bulgarska Nacionalna Filmoteka**, ul. Gourko 36,1000 Sofia. Tel: (359 2) 987 3740, 871 392. Fax: (359 2) 876 004.

## CANADA

**La Cinémathèque Québécoise**, 335 boul de Maisonneuve est. Montréal, Québec H2X 1K1.Tel: (1 514) 842 9763. Fax: (1 514) 842 1816. e-mail: jhamel@cinematheque.qc.ca. Curator: Robert Daudelin.

**Conservatoire d'Art Cinémato-graphique de Montréal**, 1455 de Maisonneuve West, Montréal, Québec. Director: Serge Losique.

**National Archives of Canada**, Visual and Sound Archives, 344 Wellington Street, Room 1036, Ottawa, Ontario, K1A 0N3. Tel: (1 613) 995 7504. Fax: (1 613) 995 6575.

## CHINA

**China Film Archive**, No3, Wen Hui Yuan Road, Xiao Xi Tian, Haidian District, Beijing, 100088. Tel: (86 10) 6225 0916. Fax: (86 10) 225 9315.

## CZECH REPUBLIC

**Národní filmovy archiv**, Malesická 12, 130 00 Praha 3. Tel: (4202) 717 70500. Fax: (4202) 697 3057.

## DENMARK

**Danish Film Institute/Archive & Cinematheque**, Gothersgade 55, DK-1123 Copenhagen K. Tel: (45 33) 74 34 00. Fax: (45 33) 74 35 99. Director: Dan Nissen. Stock: 27,500 film titles, 54,000 books, 350 periodicals subscribed to, 2,300,000 film stills, 18,500 posters, three cinemas (178, 140 and 42 seats) used for daily screenings and for researchers and students. DFI/Archive & Cinematheque also publishes a magazine, *Kosmorama*.

## EGYPT

**National Egyptian Film Archive**, c/o Egyptian Film Centre, City of Arts, Al Ahram Road, Guiza. Tel: (20 2) 585 4801/0897. Fax: (20 2) 585 4701. President: Prof. Dr. Mohamed Kamel El Kalyobi.

## FINLAND

**Suomen elokuva-arkisto**, Pursimiehenkatu 29-31 A, P.O. Box 177, FIN-00151 Helsinki. Tel: (358 9) 615 400. Fax: (358 9) 6154 0242. e-mail: sea@sea.fi. Website: www.sea.fi. Stock: 7,200 feature film titles, 26,000 shorts and advertising film (spots), 20,000 video cassettes, 20,000 books, 160 magazines (currently sub-scribed), 10,500 dialogue lists and scripts, 326,000 different stills, 110,000 posters and 41,000 documentation files. The archive arranges regular screenings in Helsinki and eight other cities.

## FRANCE

**Cinémathèque française**, 4 rue de Longchamp, 75116 Paris. Tel: (33 1) 53 65 74 75. Fax: (33 1) 53 65 74 96. President: Jean Saint Geours.

**Cinémathèque de Toulouse**, rue du Taur, BP 824, 31080 Toulouse Cedex 6. Tel: (33 5) 6230 3010. Fax: (33 5) 6230 3012.

**Cinémathèque Universitaire**, 3 rue Michelet, 75006 Paris. Tel: (33 1) 4586 4853. Fax: (33 1) 4570 8230.

**Institut Lumière**, 25 rue du Premier-Film, 69008 Lyon. Tel: (33 4) 7878 1895. Fax: (33 1) 7801 3662. President: Bertrand Tavernier.

**Musée du Cinéma de Lyon**, 69 rue Jean Jaurès. 69100 Villeurbanne. Tel: (33 4) 7853 2769. Fax: (33 4) 7233 7925. President: Paul Génard. Stock: 1,600 film titles, 1,000 film stills, 50 posters.

**Service des Archives du Film du Centre National de la Cinématographie**, 7 bis rue Alexandre Turpault, 78392 Bois d'Arcy Cedex. Tel: (33 1) 3014 8000. Fax: (33 1) 3460 5225.

## GERMANY

**Arsenal/Kino der Freunde der Deutschen Kinemathek**, Potsdamer Str. 2, 10785 Berlin. Tel: (49 30) 269 55142. Fax: (49 30) 269 5511. e-mail: mg@fdk-berlin.de. Website: www.fdk-berlin.de. The nearest equivalent to Britain's NFT. Programming: Ulrich and Erika Gregor, Milena Gregor. The Freunde also runs a non-commercial distribution of about 800 films, most of them from the International Forum, the independent second main programme of the Berlin Film Festival, organised by the Freunde.

**Bundesarchiv-Filmarchiv**, Fehrbelliner Platz 3, 10707 Berlin. Tel: (49 30) 86811. Fax: (49 30) 868 1310. e-mail: barch@barch-fa.uunet.de.

**Deutsches Filmmuseum Frankfurt am Main**, Schaumainkai 41, D-60596 Frankfurt am Main. Tel: (49 69) 2123 8830. Fax: (49 69) 2123 7881. e-mail: info@deutsches-filmmuseum.de. Director: Prof Walter Schobert. Deputy Director and Head of Archives: Hans-Peter Reichmann.

**Deutsches Filminstitut-DIF**, Schaumainkai 41, 60596 Frankfurt am Main. Tel: (49 69) 961 2200. Telefax: (49 69) 620 060. e-mail: deutsches.filminstitut@em.uni-frankfurt.de. Website: www.

filminstitut.de. Stock: 10,000 film titles, 70,000 books, 260 periodicals, 140,000 programmes, 16,000 dialogue lists, 5,000 scripts, 1.8 million stills, 800,000 newspapers clippings on international film production, advertising material.

**Filmmuseum Berlin Deutsche Kinemathek**, Potsdamer Strasse 2, 10785 Berlin, Germany. Uta Orluc, Chief Librarian.

**Münchner Stadtmuseum/ Filmmuseum**, St. Jakobsplatz 1, D-80331 München. Tel: (49 89) 2332 2348. Fax: (49 89) 2332 3931. e-mail: filmmuseum@ compu-serve.com. Director: Stefan Drössler. Founded in 1963, this municipal film archive runs a daily cinema programme. Film archive holds approx. 5,000 titles, including many restored silent German film classics, New German cinema, and the Orson Welles Collection. Estate holdings from G. W. Pabst, Dr. Arnold Fanck etc. Library holds over 6,000 film books, 10,000 film periodicals.

**Filmmuseum Berlin – Deutsche Kinemathek**, Potsdamer Strasse 2, 10785 Berlin. Tel: (49 30) 300 9030. Fax: (49 30) 300 90313. Director: Hans Helmut Prinzler. Stock: 10,000 film titles, 2,000,000 film stills, 20,000 posters, 15,000 set and costume designs, 60,000 film programmes, 30,000 scripts etc. The library contains about 50,000 books and periodicals.

## HUNGARY

**Magyar Filmintézet**, Budakeszi ut 51b, 1021 Budapest. Tel:and fax: (36 1) 200 8739. Director: Vera Gyürey. Stock: 7,022 feature titles, 8,713 short films, 3,756 newsreels, 13,224 books, 3,710 periodicals, 2,708 scripts, 5,381 manuscripts, 143,159 stills, 15,365 posters. In addition to housing the archive, the institute does research into the history of cinema, particularly Hungarian cinema, and encourages the

development of film culture in Hungary.

**Szinház-és Filmmüvészeti Foiskola**, Vas utca 2/c, Budapest 1088. Tel/Fax: (36 1) 329 4790.

## ICELAND

**Kvikmyndasafn Islands (National Film Archive of Iceland)**, Vesturgötu 11-13, 220 Hafnarfjolgur. Tel: (354) 565 5993. Fax: (354) 565 5994. Nearly 400 titles in the collection, the majority documentaries. Numerous sources of informa-tion regarding Icelandic films and the national film history.

## INDIA

**National Film Archive of India**, Ministry of Information and Broadcasting, Government of India, Law College Road, Pune 411 004. Tel: (91 212) 352 259. Fax: (91 212) 370 027.

## IRAN

**National Iranian Film Archive**, Baharestan Square, Tehran. Tel: (98 21) 324 1601. Director: Mohammad Hassan Khoshnevis.

## ISRAEL

**Israel Film Archive/Jerusalem Cinémathèque**, P.O. Box 8561, Jerusalem 91083. Tel: (972 2) 672 4131. Fax: (972 2) 673 3076. Director: Lia van Leer. Stock: 20,000 prints: international, Israeli, Jewish film collections. Books, periodicals, stills, posters and scripts. Film documentation and educational programme for school children and adults. Permanent exhibition of early cinema apparatus and cinema memorabilia. 6000 members. Screening five films every day in two auditoriums. Organisers of the Jerusalem Film Festival.

**Tel Aviv Cinémathèque (The Doron Cinema Centre)**, 2 Sprintzak Street, Tel Aviv. Postal address: P.O. Box 20370, Tel Aviv 61203. Tel: (972 3) 6917 181-8. Fax: (972 3) 696 2841. Director: Alon

Garbuz. Stock: 20,000 video cassettes, 7,000 books, period-icals, stills, posters, scripts. 1,500 screenings yearly, various activities, lectures and seminars for the general public, and special morning educational programmes for schools. Publishes film magazine *Cinémath`eque.*

## ITALY

**Cineteca del Comune di Bologna**, Via Galliera 8, 40121 Bologna. Tel: (39 051) 228 975. Fax: (39 051) 261 680. e-mail: cineteca@comune. bologna.it. Website: www. cinetecadibologna.it.

**Cineteca del Friuli**, Via Bini, Palazzo Gurisatti, 33013 Gemona del Friuli (Udine). Tel: (39 0432) 980 458. Fax: (39 0432) 970 542. e-mail: cdf@cinetecadelfriuli.org. Website: http://cinetecadelfriuli. org. Established in 1977, this excellent Italian archive con-ceived the idea for the Pordenone Silent Film Festival, and organises regular screen-ings. Stock: 2,000 film titles, 3,000 newsreels, 18,000 books. Director: Livio Jacob.

**Cineteca Nazionale**, Via Tuscolana n. 1524, 00173 Rome. Tel: (39 06) 722 941. Fax: (39 6) 721 1619. Sector of the Foundation Scuola Nazional di Cinema. President: Lino Miccichè. General Manager: Angelo Libertini. Director of the archive: Adriano Aprá. Stock: 37,000 films, 500,000 black-and-white stills and transparencies, 50,000 posters. Viewing service for students and researchers.

**Fondazione Cineteca Italiana**, Via Palestro 16, 20121 Milano. Tel: (39 02) 799 224. Fax: (39 02) 798 289. President: Gianni Comencini.

**Fondazione Federico Fellini**, Via Angherà 22, 47900 Rimini. Tel (39 0541) 50085. Fax: (39 0541) 24885. e-mail: fellini@comune. rimini.it Director: Gainfranco Angelucci.

**Museo Nazionale del Cinema –**

**Fondazione Maria Adriano Prolo**, Via Montebello, 15,1, 10124 Turin. Tel: (39 011) 815 4230. Fax: (39 011) 812 2503. e-mail: museo-cinema@to2000.net President: Mario Ricciardi.

**Museo Internazionale del Cinema e dello Spettacolo**, Via Portuense 101, 00153 Rome. Tel/fax: (39 06) 589 8899. Director: Jose Pantieri. The MICS has organised in Italy and abroad a remarkable number of fairs, exhibitions, conferences, publications, experimental courses etc. Film archives and bank (about 5,000 rare and antique films, mostly silent). Photo library (some two million photos from 1850 to the present, daguerrotypes, etc). Film/TV library (books and publications on film/show, original scripts). Newpaper library (specialised periodcals/magazines). Image restoration laboratory. Museum (optical devices, relics, movie cameras, lenses, projectors, costumes, props, original posters, rarities, historical documents, letters, memorabilia).

## JAPAN

**Kawakita Memorial Film Institute**, 18 Ichibancho, Chiyodaku, Tokyo 102-0082. Tel: (81-3) 3265 3281. Fax: (81-3) 3265 3276. e-mail: kmfi@kawakita-film.or.jp. President: Mrs. Masayo Okada.

**National Film Center**, 3-7-6 Kyobashi, Chuoku, Tokyo.

## LATVIA

**Riga Film Museum**, Smerla str. 3, Riga LV 1006. Tel/Fax: (371 2) 754 5099. e-mail: kinomuz@com.latnet.lv.

## LUXEMBOURG

**Cinémathèque Municipale de la Ville de Luxembourg**, 10 rue Eugene Ruppert, L-2453 Luxembourg. Tel: (352) 4796 2644. Fax: (352) 407 519.

## MEXICO

**Cinemateca Luis Buñuel**, Calle 5, Oriente 5, Apdo. Postal 255, Puebla, Pue.

**Cinemateca Mexicana**, Museo Nacional de Antropologia, Calzada M. Gandhi, México 6, D.F.

**Cineteca Nacional**, Av. Mexico-Coyoacán 389, Col. Xoco, C.P. 03330 Mexico, DF. Tel: (52 5) 688 8814. Fax: (52 5) 688 4211. e-mail: srm@spin.com.mx.

**Direccion General de Actividades Cinematograficas Filmoteca UNAM**, Circuito Exterior Dr. Mario de la Cueva s/n, Ciudad Universitaria, 04510 México, D.F. Tel: (52 5) 622 9594. Fax: (52 5) 622 9585. e-mail: trujillo@servidor.unam.mex.

## NETHERLANDS

**Netherlands Audiovisual Archive**, Department film archive, PO Box 1799, 2280 DT Rijswijk. Tel: (31 70) 356 4109, 390 7200. Fax: (31 70) 364 7756, 307 0428.

**Nederlands Filmmuseum (Stichting)**, Vondelpark 3, 1071 AA Amsterdam. Postal Address: Postbus 747 82, 1070 BT Amsterdam. Tel: (31 20) 589 1400. Fax: (31 20) 683 3401. e-mail: filmmuseum@nfm.nl. Website: www.nfm.nl.

## NORWAY

**Henie-Onstad Art Centre**, 1311 Hovikodden, Oslo. Director: Gavin Jantjens. Tel: (47 67) 804 880. Fax: (47 67) 543 270.

**Norske Film Institut**, P.B. 482 Sentrum, 0105 Oslo. Tel: (47 22) 474 500. Fax: (47 22) 474 599. e-mail: nfi@nfi.no.

## PANAMA

**Cinemateca del GECU**, Universidad de Panamá, Apartado 6-1775, El Dorado. Tel/fax: (507) 223 9324, 264 2737. e-mail: gecu@ancon.up.ac.pa. Stock includes films, books, periodicals, film stills and posters. It has a small theatre with three daily screenings. Director: Roberto Enrique King.

## POLAND

**Filmoteka Narodowa**, ul. Pulawska 61, 00-975 Warszaw. Tel: (48 22) 845 5074.

**Muzeum Kinematografi**, Pl Zwyciestwa 1, 90312 Lódz. Tel: (48 42) 674 0957. Fax: (48 42) 674 9006.

## PORTUGAL

**Cinemateca Portuguesa**, Rua Barata Salgueiro 39-1250 Lisboa. Tel: (351 1) 354 6279. Fax: (351 1) 352 3180.

## ROMANIA

**Arhiva Nationala de Filma**, Str. Dem I Dobrescu nr. 4-6, Bucharest. Tel/Fax: (40 1) 313 4904.

## RUSSIA

**Gosfilmofond of Russia**, Belye Stolby, Moskovskaia oblast 142050. Tel: (7 095) 546 0535. Fax: (7 095) 546 0512. General Director: Vladimir Malyshev. Tel: (7 095) 546 0520.

## SERBIA & MONTENEGRO

**Jugoslovenska Kinoteka**, Knez Mihailova 19, 11000 Belgrade. Tel: (381 11) 622 555, 550 471 (Archive). Fax: (381 11) 622 587, 555 015 (Archive). Director: Radoslav Zelenovic Head of Archive: Stevan Jovici´c. Programme Director: Dinko Tucakovi´c.

## SPAIN

**Filmoteca Española**, Carretera Dehesa de la Villa, s/n. 28040 Madrid. Tel: (34 91) 549 0011. Fax: (34 91) 549 7348. Director: José María Prado.

**Filmoteca de la Generalitat de Catalunya**, Portal de Santa Madrona 6-8, Barcelona 08001.

Tel: (34 93) 316 2780. Fax: (34 93) 419 2765.

**Filmoteca Vasca**, Sancho el Sabio 17, trasera, 20010 Donostia (San Sebastian), Aptdo. postal 1017. Tel: (34 943) 468 484. Fax: (34 943) 469 998.

**Instituto Valenciano de Cinematografía Ricardo Muñoz Suay (La Filmoteca)**, Plaza del Ayuntamiento 17, 46002 Valencia. Tel: (34 96) 351 2336. Fax: (34 96) 352 5079.

## SWEDEN

**Cinemateket**, Svenska Film Institutet, Filmhuset, Box 27126, S-102 52 Stockholm. Tel: (46 8) 665 1100. Fax: (46 8) 661 1820. Stock: 19,000 film titles, 42,000 books, 250 subscriptions to periodicals, 1,500,000 film stills, 31,000 posters, and unpublished script material on 7,650 foreign films and 1,950 Swedish films. The collection of microfilmed clippings holds 53,500 jackets on individual films, 17,000 jackets on film personalities and jackets on general subjects classified by the FIAF scheme. Cinemateket has four daily screenings at two theatres in Stockholm. A selection of the programme is also shown in Göteborg and Malmö.

## SWITZERLAND

**Cinémathèque Suisse**, 3 Allée Ernest Ansermet, 1003 Lausanne (Postal address: PO Box 2512, 1002 Lausanne). Tel: (41 21) 331 0101. Fax: (41 21) 320 4888. Stock: 53,000 titles (1,500,000 reels), 600 apparati, 40,000 posters, 5,000,000 film references, 19,000 books, and 1,500,000 stills. Three projections each day.

## TAIWAN

**Chinese Taipei Film Archive**, 4F, No. 7 Ching-Tao East Road, Taipei, Taiwan, R.O.C. Tel: (886 2) 392 4243, 2396 0760. Fax: (886 2) 2392 6359.

## TURKEY

**Turkish Film and Television Institute**, 80700 Kislaönü-Besiktas, Istanbul. Tel: (90 212) 266 1096. Fax: (90 212) 211 6599. e-mail: sinematv@msu.edu.tr. The Institute is a science and art centre engaged in education, research and archiving on cinema and television. Stock: 6,000 film titles, 3,500 video titles. Library of books, periodicals, newspaper clippings and photos available to researchers.

## UNITED KINGDOM

**Imperial War Museum**, Lambeth Road, London SE1 6HZ. Tel: (44 20) 7416 5291/2. Fax: (44 20) 7416 5299. Stock: over 120 million feet of actuality film relating to conflict in the 20th Century, from Britain and other countries. Viewing facilities for students and researchers, by appointment only; public film screenings.

**National Film and Television Archive**, British Film Institute, 21 Stephen Street, London W1P 1LN. Tel: (44 20) 7255 1444. Fax: (44 20) 7580 7503. Head of Collections, BFI: Caroline Ellis. Curator: Anne Fleming. Stock: 275,000 film and television titles, over 5,000,000 black-and-white stills, 700,000 colour transparencies, 18,000 posters, 2,500 set-designs. Viewing service for students and researchers.

**The Scottish Film and Television Archive**, No. 1 Bowmont Gardens, Glasgow G12 9LR. Tel: (44 141) 337 7400. Fax: (44 141) 337 7413. e-mail: archive@ scottish-screen.com

## UNITED STATES

**Academy of Motion Picture Arts and Sciences**, Centre for Motion Picture Study, Academy Film Archive, 333 South La Cienega Blvd., Beverly Hills, California 90211. Tel: (1 310) 247 3027. Fax: (1 310) 657 5431.

**American Film Institute/National**

**Center for Film and Video Preservation**, 2021 North Western Avenue, Los Angeles, CA 90027. Tel: (1 323) 856 7600.

**Archive Films/Archive Photos**, 530 West 25th Street, New York, NY 10001-5516 USA. Tel: (1 212) 822 7800. Fax: ( 1 212) 645 2137. e-mail: sales@archivefilms.com. Website: www.archivefilms.com. Archive Films is a leading historical footage library with more than 40,000 hours of stock footage, including Hollywood feature films, newsreels, TV news, silent films, documentaries and vintage industrial and educational films, and many special collections. Also 20 million photographs, engravings and drawings spanning 3,000 years of world history.

**George Eastman House/ International Museum of Photography and Film**, 900 East Avenue, Rochester, N.Y. 14607. Tel: (1 716) 271 3361 Fax: (1 716) 271 3970. e-mail: film@geh.org. Website: www.eastman.org.

**Harvard Film Archive**, Carpenter Center for the Visual Arts, Harvard Univ, 24 Quincy Street, Cambridge, MA 02138. Tel: (1 617) 496 6046. Fax: 91 617 495 6197). Films (16mm, 35mm, video); 4,000 titles.

**The Library of Congress**, Motion Picture, Broadcasting and Recorded Sound Division, Washington, DC 20540-4690. Tel: (1 202) 707 8572. Fax: (1 202) 707 2371. Telex: 64198. The nation's largest public research collection and preservation archive for motion pricutres, videos, TV and radio broadcast and sound recordings available to qualified researchers, 8:30 am to 5:00 pm, M-F, through the facilities of the Film and Television Reading Room and the Recorded Sound Reference Center in the James Madison building.

**Museum of Modern Art**, Department of Film and Video,11 West 53rd Street, New York, NY 10019. Tel: (1 212) 708 9600. Fax:

(1 212) 333 1145. Stock: 17,500 film titles, 2,500 books, 250 periodicals, 4,000,000 film stills. The excellent research and screening facilities of the department are available to serious students only, by appointment; 1,000 of its films are available for rental, sale and lease. Stills Archive open by appointment.

**National Museum of Natural History/Human Studies Film Archives**, Rm E307, 123 Smithsonian Institution, Washington DC 20560. Tel: (1 202) 357 3349. Fax: (202) 357 2208.

**Pacific Film Archive**, University Art Museum, 2625 Durant Avenue, Berkeley, California 94720.

**UCLA Film and Television Archive**, 302 East Melnitz Hall, University of California, PO Box 951323, Los Angeles, CA 90095-1323. Tel: (1 310) 206 8013. Fax: (1 310) 206 3129.

**UCLA Film and Television Archive Commercial Services**, 1015 North Cahuenga Blvd, Hollywood, CA 90038. Tel: (1 323) 466 8559. Fax: (1 323) 461 6317.

**The Wisconsin Center for Film and Theater Research**, 816 State Street, Madison, Wisconsin 53706. Tel: (1 608) 264 6466. Fax: (1 608) 264 6472.

**URUGUAY**

**Cinemateca Uruguaya**, Lorenzo Carnelli 1311, Casilla de Correo 1170, Montevideo. Tel: (598 2) 408 2460, 409 5795. Fax: ( 598 2) 409 4572. e-mail: cinemuy@ chasque.apc.org.

# BOOK REVIEWS

The past year has seen some film biographies of considerable stature. Perhaps the most intriguing, and also the most casual, is **Conversations with Wilder**, by Cameron Crowe (Faber, London; Alfred A. Knopf, New York). As the young director interviews the 90-year-old master in a series of sessions at his office and in Hollywood restaurants, a picture emerges of a career that spanned five decades and yielded some of the cinema's wittiest and most acerbic achievements. *Conversations with Wilder* sets some kind of record, with no fewer than 679 illustrations, and deserves to be ranked alongside Truffaut's interview book with Hitchcock.

In a lesser key, but no less engrossing, is Steven Soderbergh's tribute to Richard Lester, in **Getting Away with It** (Faber, London). Flitting between a sequence of encounters with Lester, best-known for *A Hard Day's Night*, and Soderbergh's own anguished attempts to set up a new production, this often hilarious memoir ranges over all kinds of topics germane to the film-maker's craft. The book demonstrates that an independent of one era will always recognise his peer in another.

The most urbane and perceptive of all recent biographies, however, must be Gavin Lambert's **Mainly About Lindsay Anderson** (Faber, London). The screenwriter Lambert and the irascible, iconoclastic Anderson were contemporaries at Oxford, and maintained a lifelong friendship. Lambert enlivens the story with asides about his own career and life (being seduced by Nicholas Ray, for example), but provides a painstaking reconstruction of Anderson's work for stage and screen, and also the first intimate portrayal of his private life and attitudes. This memoir may have been several years in gestation, but its

*Billy Wilder, right, with Walter Matthau*
*photo: Kobal Collection*

*Lindsay Anderson, subject of a fine memoir by his friend Gavin Lambert*

*photo: Kobal Collection*

rich and fastidious appraisal will delight all admirers of Britain's most original director of the past half-century.

Christopher Frayling has written a magnificent account of the career of the father of the spaghetti Western, in **Sergio Leone, Something To Do with Death** (Faber, London). Incomparably researched, judicious in judgement, this substantial tome rates Leone's talent perhaps a shade too highly, in that he was never an originator, only a master of pastiche. The Italian's sheer zest and obsessive temperament, however, give a tragic dimension to his life and work.

Marc Gervais' **Ingmar Bergman, Magician and Prophet** (McGill-Queen's University, Montreal and Kingston) deserves to resuscitate the Swedish master's faded reputation. It's a splendid blend of scholarship and personal experience, for Gervais knew Bergman, Bibi Andersson and others during the 1960's and 1970's. Liv Ullmann's foreword is more than merely decorative.

The troubled odyssey of Elia Kazan through triumph and disgrace has already been well chronicled, both by the director himself and in conversation with critics such as Michel Ciment. Now Jeff Young has collated many hours of interview material, in **Kazan on Kazan** (Faber, London; Newmarket Press, New York), tracing the production of all 19 features directed by the man who launched the careers of Brando and Dean.

More oblique, yet also more effective, is Wim Wenders' approach to **My Time with Antonioni** (Faber, London), the diary he kept over four months in 1994 when Antonioni, left almost speechless by a stroke, was shooting *Beyond the Clouds*. Wenders served as an assistant in the fullest sense of the term, the ultimate *hommage* to one of the cinema's most innovative and uncompromising geniuses.

Thirty-five years ago, Allen Eyles wrote a pioneering study of the Marx Brothers, and in recent times the bookshelf has begun to fill with accounts of life with the individual siblings. Simon Louvish's **Monkey Business, The Lives and Legends of the Marx Brothers** (Faber, London) sparkles with an antic wit, integrating the most diligent of research with some thoroughly entertaining comments on the zany brilliance of the brothers, and placing them in a wider context that includes W.C. Fields and Coney Island.

## Screenplays

**Stanley Kubrick's A Clockwork Orange** (Screenpress Books, Southwold, Suffolk, UK) certainly strives to break new ground in screenplay publishing. Using some 800 images from *A Clockwork Orange*, it brings the film to life on the page as no previous script in book form has done. Originally issued by Ballantine Books of New York in 1972, the paperback version is now available in the UK and should appeal to buffs and libraries, with Kubrick's most controversial movie finally being reissued in cinemas and on DVD.

Even more sumptuous is **The Art of Sleepy Hollow** (Faber, London; Pocket Books, New York), which comprises the screenplay by Andrew Kevin Walker and a tantalisingly brief introduction by the film's creator, Tim Burton. Exquisitely designed in full colour, it is a fitting tribute to one of 1999's most original screen achievements – although it does not reveal how the myriad special effects were accomplished.

Faber has remained loyal to the burgeoning British cinema, and has issued the screenplays of Mike Leigh's **Topsy-**

**Turvy**, Lynne Ramsay's **Ratcatcher** and John Hodge's **The Beach**. The only introduction of note, however, comes from an interview with Ramsay, in which the 29-year-old debutante talks about directing children, and her admiration for Robert Bresson. Part of the joy of re-reading *Topsy-Turvy* stems from the lyrics that are so wittily stitched into the film.

American screenwriting tends to be less academic and more street-smart than its British equivalent, and Charlie Kaufman's coruscating original script, **Being John Malkovich** (Faber, London and New York), is even funnier than Spike Jonze's film. Be sure to catch Kaufman's playful introduction. Almost as amusing, if slightly tending towards the sophomoric, is Wes Anderson and Owen Wilson's **Rushmore** (Faber, London and New York), with its offbeat portrayal of a teenager who breaks all the rules at his 'academy'. Kevin Smith belongs to the same 1990s breed of iconoclastic, questioning and ultimately disarmingly innocent American director. Part parody, part paradigm, **Dogma** (Faber, London and New York) queries the concept of faith in the modern world and creates a gallery of fascinating young characters in the process.

**Girl, Interrupted** won an Oscar for Angelina Jolie, and the screenplay by James Mangold, Lisa Loomer and Anna Hamilton Phelan (Faber, London and New York) has been compared to *One Flew Over the Cuckoo's Nest*. An interview with director Mangold precedes the script and provides a great deal of information about the making of the film.

Finally, a paean for one of the mountain-peaks among Hollywood screenplays – **North by Northwest**, written at the height of his powers by Ernest Lehman and converted in 1959 into a brilliant mystery adventure by Alfred Hitchcock. Released by Faber in its "Classic Screenplays" series, it comes with an afterword by Lehman.

## Reference and History

Einaudi Editore of Torino have continued their massive **Storia del cinema mondiale** project with a 1,015 page tome devoted to the United States. Written by several historians, this scholarly survey is immaculately edited by Gian Piero Brunetta, and will – pending translation into other languages – surely belong on the shelves of any film buff conversant with Italian. The illustrations have been chosen with obvious pleasure and fastidiousness, and the section on the Western typifies the balanced evaluation of the entire project.

Charles Drazin's **In Search of The Third Man** (Methuen, London) serves as an object-lesson in film history, tracing the creation of perhaps the finest of British thrillers through the murk of a post-war era that saw the talents of Reed, Welles, Cotton, Howard and Krasker fusing against all expectations. Geoffrey Macnab, in **Search for Stars** (Cassell, London and New York), produces a thoroughly readable study of the star system, such as it existed in Britain until 1960. Refreshing to find extensive analysis given to the work of James Mason, Ivor Novello, George Formby and Diana Dors (who, it must be remembered, was so admired by the influential magazine, *Sequence*).

**Sin in Soft Focus** sounds like a tabloid serial. In fact it's the title of one of the year's most elegant books, by Mark A. Vieira, and published by Harry N. Abrams, New York. Recapturing the turbulent early 1930s, when Hollywood studios evaded the absurd dictates of the so-called production Code, this volume's beautiful illustrations and well-researched text rekindle the talents of Mae West, Joan Crawford, Claudette Colbert, Fay Wray and other risqué stars of the period.

**Production Design and Art Direction** belies its bald title. Published as part of the "Screencraft" series by Rotovision of Crans-Prés-Céligny, Switzerland, Peter Ettedgui's survey of 16 major designers is incomparably illustrated with sketches, models, frame enlargements and other items that take the reader deep inside the craft of art direction. The interviews are lengthy and informative. Would that all film books were this contemplative and sophisticated.

Books about writing for the movies are headed this year by Peter (*There's Something About Mary*) Farrelly's **The Comedy Writer** (Faber, London; Doubleday, New York). A novel in form, it's a thinly-disguised autobiography tracking the frustrations of trying to become a screenwriter in Hollywood. **Laughing Out Loud**, by Andrew Horton (University of California Press, Berkeley), brings an historical perspective to bear on comedy and writing for laughs, and links both television and movies in creating a primer for the aspiring comic writer, whether Jerry Seinfeld or Woody Allen be his hero.

More theoretical in approach is Sarah Kozloff's **Overhearing Film Dialogue** (University of California Press, Berkeley), which dissects and interprets the very nature of speech in American movies, from the ejaculatory texts of Westerns and gangster films to the pithy exchanges that make up the screwball comedy. Kristin Thompson's **Storytelling in the New Hollywood** discusses narrative traits in the films of the past 70 years, elegantly homing in on ten specific examples of recent Hollywoodiana, from *Amadeus* to *The Silence of the Lambs*.

Students of European cinema may prefer **Heroines without Heroes**, edited by Ulrike Sieglohr (Cassell, London and New York). Dwelling on the post-war period, 1945-1951, this anthology covers France, Germany, Britain, Italy and Spain, with a particular emphasis on the female image and national identities as expressed by such stars as Hildegard Knef and Simone Signoret.

**Projections 10** (Faber, London and New York) consists entirely of interviews conducted by British film-maker Mike Figgis, with 28 Hollywood personalities, from stars to writers, directors and producers. They respond to one of their peers with candour, humour and surprising directness, making the book one of the best bedside reads of the season.

Three unusual areas of film history at last receive their due. **The Art and Politics of Bolivian Cinema**, by José Sánchez-H. (Scarecrow Press, Lanham, Maryland) places this Latin American nation's films in a historical and sociological context, and features interviews with some of the leading directors, above all Sanjines. **Latent Images, Film in Singapore**, by Jan Uhde and Yvonne Ng Uhde (Oxford University Press, Singapore) is a lovingly-produced survey of the individual talents, the trends and the industrial realities governing film in this Southeast Asian community. The Uhdes are especially strong on the exhibition side of the business.

**Magic Moments**, by Robert W. Gutteridge (Gutteridge-Pratley Publications, 104 Ontario Street W, Whitby, Ontario L1N 1P3, Canada), deals with the first 20 years of moving pictures in Toronto (1894-1914). The evident scholarship is leavened with a remarkable selection of illustrations, showing the rise of the Canadian picture house prior to the First World War.

Alison Darren has edited an **A-Z Lesbian Film Guide** (Cassell, London and New York) that is immaculately researched and written, without a shred of inhibition or titillation. Too bad that it does not see the satirical side of Paul Verhoeven's cinema, but, as Joe E. Brown said at the end of *Some Like It Hot*, nobody's perfect.

On a modest scale, the booklets issued by the Brantwood Outline History series (Brantwood Books, St. Paul's Cray, Kent) will be manna for the exhibition fan. Philip Turner charts the history of, respectively, **Cannon Cinemas**, **Warner Cinemas**, **MGM Cinemas**, **Cineplex Odeon**, **Showcase Cinemas** and **Cinecenta Cinemas**.

Finally, a reminder that the Film and TV Documentation Center at the State University of New York, Albany, continues to publish its annual **Film Literature Index**, a prodigious source of reference for anyone involved in film research, indexing as it does nearly every article of consequence in film magazines around the world.

Peter Cowie

# FILM BOOKSHOPS POSTERS & RECORDS

## AUSTRALIA

**Electric Shadows Bookshop**, City Walk, Akuna Street, Canberra, ACT 2601. Tel: (61 262) 488 352. Fax: (61 262) 471 230. e-mail: esb@electricshadowsbookshop. com.au. Website: www.electric shadowsbookshop.com.au. Free quarterly catalogue available. Listing new film books. Australian material highlighted.

**Movie Buffs**, PO Box 36, Kerrimuir, Victoria 3129. Website: www.labyrinth.net.au/~movibuff. Free catalogue available listing movie books, magazines, posters and memorabilia.

## CANADA

**Theatrebooks**, 11 St. Thomas St, Toronto, M5S 2B7. Tel: (1 416) 922 7175. Fax: (1 416) 922 0739. e-mail: action@-theatrebooks.com. Website: www.theatrebooks.com. Founded first as a source of theatre, opera and dance books, Theatrebooks has also been developing a first-class film book collection since 1982. Worldwide mail-order handled.

## FRANCE

**Atmosphère, Libraire du Cinema**, 10 rue Broca, 75005 Paris. Tel: (33 1) 4331 0271. Fax: (33 1 ) 4331 0369. Atmosphère offers a wide range of film publications, with a large stock of stills, postcards, posters of new and old movies of all origins and sizes. Also stocks back issues of magazines. Open every Mon to Sat, 11am to 7pm.

**Cinedoc**, 45-53 Passage Jouffroy, 75009, Paris. Tel: (33 1) 4824 7116. Fax: (33 1) 4483 0634. e-mail: cinedocuments@thema.net. Website: www.cinedoc.com.

Posters, books, stills, press-books, magazines etc.

**Cine-Folie, La Boutique du Cinéma**, 14 rue des Frères Pradignac, 06400 Cannes. Tel: (33 4) 9339 2299. Stills, books, posters, postcards.

**Cinemagence**, 12 rue Saulnier, 75009 Paris. Tel: (33 1) 4246 2121. Fax: (33 1) 4246 2020. Stills, posters, magazines, books. Mail-order service. Free catalogue.

**Contacts Champs-Elysées**, 24 rue du Colisée, 75008 Paris. Tel: (33 1) 4359 1771. Fax: (33 1) 4289 2765. Cinema bookshop established 43 years ago in the Champs-Elysées area, close to the film production companies. Amply stocked with French and foreign-language books on technique, theory, history and director monographs. Also magazines. Reliable mail-order service. Free "new aquisitions" list.

**Gilda**, 36 rue de Boudonnais, 75001, Paris. Tel: (33 1) 42 33 60 00. Videos, books, film magazines, compact disc videos, CDs, CD Roms.

## GERMANY

**Buchhandlung Walther König**, Ehrenstr. 4, 56072 Koln. Tel: (49 221) 205 9625 Fax: (49 221) 205 9640. Website: www.buchhand lung-walther-koenig.de. Offers a comprehensive catalogue of international titles in the film department, also useful anti-quarian department.

**Buchhandlung Langenkamp**, Beckergrube 19, D-2400 Lübeck. Tel: (49 451) 76479. Fax: (49 451) 72645.

**H. Lindemann's Bookshop**, Nadlerstrasse 4+10, D-70173 Stuttgart 1. Tel: (49 711) 2489 9977.

Fax: (49 711) 236 9672. Photography and film literature. Catalogue available.

**Kiepert Taschenbuchladen**, Hardenbergstr. 4-5, D-10623 Berlin. Tel: (49 30) 311 880. Fax: (49 30) 311 88 120. e-mail: keske@kiepert.de. Website: www.kiepert.de. Good selection of film books.

**Sautter + Lackmann**, Film-buchhandlung, Admiralitädstr. 71/72, D-20459 Hamburg; or Postfach 11 04 31, 20404 Hamburg. Tel: (49 40) 373 196. Fax: (49 40) 365 479. Mainly books, but also videos etc.

**Marga Schoeller Bucherstube**, Knesebeckstr. 33, D-10623 Berlin. Tel: (49 30) 881 1122. Fax: (49 30) 881 8479. e-mail: marga. schoeller.buecherstube@glux.de. One of the fabled literary haunts of western Europe, Marga Schoeller's shop is justly proud of its film book selection.

**Verlag für Filmschriften Christian Unucka**, Am Kramerburg 7A, D-85241 Hebertshausen. Tel: (49 8131) 13922. Fax: (49 8131) 10075. Books, posters, pro-grammes, stills, postcards, videos, rare items etc.

## ITALY

**Libreria dello Spettacolo**, via Terraggio 11, 20123 Milan. Tel: (39 02) 864 51730. Fax: (39 02) 864 51730.

**Il Leuto**, via Monte Brianzo 86, 00186 Rome. Tel: (39 06) 868 687. Fax: (39 06) 869 269.

## THE NETHERLANDS

**Ciné-qua-non**, Staalstraat 14, 1011 Amsterdam. Tel: (31 20) 625

5588. Books about film; specialty posters.

## SPAIN

**Alphaville**, Martin de los Heros 14, 28008 Madrid. Tel: (34 91) 559 3836.

**Filmoteca Espanola**, Cine Dore, Santa Isabel 3, Madrid. Tel: (34 91) 369 4673. Well-stocked bookstore dealing with all movie topics.

**El Espectador**, Consell de Cent 475 bis, 08013 Barcelona. Tel: (34 93) 231 6516. Specialising in cinema and video books, magazines etc.

**Ocho y Medio**, Martin de los Heros 23, 28008 Madrid. Tel: (34 91) 559 0628. Fax: (34 91) 540 0672. e-mail: ochoymedio@ arrakis.es. Website: www. ochoymedio.com. Friendly bookstore just up the road from the Alphaville. A wide range of Spanish and foreign-language books.

**Ramon Serina**, Aribay 114, 08026 Barcelona. Tel: (34 93) 454 9633. A specialist collection of books, photos, magazines, press books, posters and programmes on sale to the public in Spain and abroad.

## SWEDEN

**Movie Art of Sweden**, Södra Hamngatan 2, 411 06 Göteborg. Tel: (46 31) 151 412. Fax: (46 31) 115 1445. e-mail: info@movieartof sweden.com. Website: www. movieartofsweden.com. New and vintage film posters, stills, postcards, props, t-shirts. Mail-order available.

## SWITZERLAND

**Filmbuchhandlung Hans Rohr**, Oberdorfstr. 3 CH-8024 Zurich. Tel: (41 1) 251 3636. Fax: (41 1) 251 3344. For many years, Hans Rohr has offered an efficient and reliable service when it comes to dealing with mail-order inquiries for any film, book or magazine in print.

**Librairie du Cinéma**, 9 rue de la Terrassiere, CH-1207, Geneva. Tel: (41 22) 736 8888. Fax: (41 22) 736 6616. e-mail: cinema@ worldcom.ch. Immaculate display of posters, books, stills, postcards, photos, soundtrack CD's and videos. A veritable treasure trove for the movie buff.

## UNITED KINGDOM

**The Cinema Bookshop**, 13-14 Great Russell Street, London WC1B 3NH. Tel: (44 20) 7637 0206. Fax: (44 20) 7436 9979. Fred Zentner's film bookshop close to the British Museum has succeeded by virtue of prompt and friendly service and an eye for rare items.

**The Cinema Store**, Unit 4B/C, Orion House, Upper Saint Martin's Lane, London WC2H 9EJ. Tel: (44 20) 7379 7838. Fax: (44 20) 7240 7689. e-mail: cinemastor@aol.com. Website: www.atlasdigital.com/cinemasto re. Fine selection of magazines, toys and models, laser discs, posters etc. in Paul McEvoy and Neil Palmer's friendly and recently expanded store; now stocking rare/new VHS, soundtracks and trading cards. Mail-order catalogue £1.

**Anne FitzSimons**, 62 Scotby Road, Scotby, Carlisle, Cumbria CA4 8BD. Tel: (44 1228) 513 815. Small stock of ephemera and second-hand and out-of-print books on cinema and other entertainment forms. Catalogue twice a year. Private premises. Postal only.

**Flashbacks**, 6 Silver Place (Beak Street), London W1R 3LJ. Tel/Fax: (44 20) 7437 8562. e-mail: shop@flashbacks.freeserve.co.uk

Website: http://dacre.simplenet. com/. Most impressively stocked establishment which, in London's West End, caters for those interested in movie ephemera – posters, stills, pressbooks – from many countries and every period of cinema history. Also extensive mail-order service. No catalogues issued, but individual requests answered. Mon to Sat, 10.30am to 7pm).

**Greenroom Books**, 11 Bark Lane, Addingham, Ilkley, West Yorkshire LS29 ORA. Tel/Fax: (44 1943) 830 497. Mail-order service for second-hand books on the performing arts.

**Hollywood Superstore**, 16-18 St. Giles High Street, London WC2H 8LN. Tel: (44 20) 7836 3736. Movie photos, posters, books, magazines and vintage memorabilia. Open Mon to Sat, 10am to 6pm.

**Ed Mason**, Tel: (44 20) 7736 8511. Organises the Collector's Film Convention. Held six times a year at Westminster Central Hall, London.

**Movie Boulevard**, 3 Cherry Tree Walk, Leeds LS2 7EB. Tel: (44 113) 242 2888. Fax: (44 113) 243 8840. Welcome north of England addition to the ranks of shops specialising in soundtracks, videos, DVDs and memorabilia. Headed by the enthusiastic Robert Wood.

**Offstage Film & Theatre Bookshop**, Offstage Film & Theatre Bookshop, 37 Chalk Farm Rd, London, NW1. Tel: (44 20) 7485 4996. (44 20) 7916 8046. Bright square space crammed with play and film scripts and books on all aspects of theatrical, broadcast and cinematic media, including criticism, stagecraft, comedy, writing and education.

**Rare Discs**, 18 Bloomsbury Street, London WC1B 32 A. Tel: (44 20) 7580 3516. Specialists in film soundtracks and vinyl and film memorabilia.

**The Reel Poster Gallery**, 72 Westbourne Grove, London W2 5SH. Tel: (44 20) 7727 44 88. Fax: (44 20) 7727 4499. London's first gallery dedicated to original vintage film posters. An extensive yet selective stock includes posters of all genres, from Westerns to science fiction, and Hollywood classics to cult titles, seen through the eyes of artists from various countries.

**Zwemmer Media**, 80 Charing Cross Road, London WC2. Tel: (44 20) 7240 4157. Fax: (44 20) 7240 4186. e-mail: enquires@ zwemmer.co.uk. Website: www. zwemmer.co.uk. Large selection of new and out-of-print film books, from early film-making to digital video. Mail-order inquires.

## UNITED STATES

**Applause**, 211 West 71st Street, New York, NY 10021. Tel: (1 212) 496 7511. Fax: (1 212) 721 2856. Now one of the few – and certainly the only uptown – film and showbiz bookstores in Manhattan.

**Cinema Books**, 4753 Roosevelt Way NE, Seattle, WA 98105. Tel: (1 206) 547 7667. Fine selection of film books and magazines, with space also devoted to TV and theatre. Mail-order welcome.

**Cinema Paradiso**, 162 Bleecker Street, New York, NY 10012. Tel: (1 212) 677-8215. Fax (1 212) 505 0582. Specialising in international movie posters, stills, vintage, originals. Open seven days a week.

**Cinemonde**, 138 Second Ave North, Suite 104, Nashville, TN 37201. Tel: (1 615) 742 3048. Fax: (1 615) 742 1268. Installed in a capacious gallery in Old Nashville, Cinemonde is a poster store for movie buffs. Items are

meticulously stored and displayed, and the colorful catalogue is a collector's item. In addition, Cinemonde has a search service based in San Francisco [1932 Polk St., San Francisco, CA 94109. Tel: (1 415) 776 9988. Fax: (1 415) 776 1424] which can be used to trace hard-to-find vintage posters, headed by the movie poster consultant for Sotheby's, New York .

**Cinematique**, 894 Fourth Street, San Rafael, CA 94901-3224. Tel: (1 415) 456 4577. Fax: (1 415) 456 1951. e-mail: cinematq@pacball. net. Website: www.cinematique online.com. An extensive selection of new and used film and acting books, videos, posters, screenplays, production guides and software, collectibles and film related gifts. Located two blocks from the Northern California Film Institute's Rafael Film Center.

**Collectors Book Store**, 6225 Hollywood Blvd., Hollywood, CA. 90028. Tel: (1 323) 467 3296. Fax: (1 323) 467 4536. Offers a superlative range of posters, stills, lobby cards, TV and film scripts.

**Déjà Vu**, 10956 Weyburn Avenue, Los Angeles, CA 90024. Tel: (1 310) 443 5280. Fax: (1 310) 443 5282. e-mail: dejavucg@earthlink. net. Website: www.dejavue collectibles.com. Collectors gallery. Thousands of auto-graphed photos and original movie posters.

**Dwight Cleveland**, PO Box 10922, Chicago, IL 60610-0922. Tel: (1 773) 525 9152. Fax: (1 773) 525 2969. Buys and sells movie posters.

**Samuel French's Theatre & Film Bookshop**, (2 Locations) 7623 Sunset Boulevard, Hollywood, CA 90046. Tel: (1 213) 876 0570. Fax: (1 213) 876 6822. Extended evening hours at 11963 Ventura Boulevard, Studio City, CA 91604. Tel: (1 818) 762 0535. e-mail: samuelfrench@earthlink.net. Website: www.samuelfrench. com. The world's oldest and largest play publisher (est.1830)

operates a separate film and preforming arts bookshop. Complete range of new movie and performing arts books available: directories, reference, writing, acting biography, screenplays etc. Worldwide mail-order service. Staff prepare meticulous catalogues that include more data than similar publications, and they strive to have any book in the English language from publishers throughout the world.

**Gotham Book Mart**, 41 West 47th Street, New York, NY 10036. Tel: (1 212) 719 4448. This famous literary bookshop (Est. 1920) in mid-Manhattan, is the only New York City bookstore offering new, used and out-of-print film and theatre books. Also, an extensive stock of "quality" film magazines dating from the 1950s to the present.

**Larry Edmund's Bookshop**, 6644 Hollywood Blvd., Hollywood, CA 90028. Tel: (1 323) 463 3273. Fax: (1 323) 463 4245. e-mail: edmunds@artnet.net. Website: www.larryedmunds.com. The stills collection alone is a gold-mine for any film buff. Back numbers of movie annuals, posters, lobby cards and one of the largest collections of new and used books in the world.

**Limelight Film and Theatre Bookstore**, 1803 Market Street, San Francisco, CA 94103. Tel: (1 415) 864 2265. Fax: (1 414) 864 7753. Derek G. Mutch runs this lively store for film and theatre books. Collection includes plays, screenplays, biographies, history and criticism of films and film and television technique.

**Movie Madness**, 1083 Thomas Jefferson St, Washington, DC 20007. Current, classic and campy movie posters available at this unique store in Georgetown.

**Jerry Ohlinger's Movie Material Store Inc.**, 242 West 14th St, New York, NY 10011. Tel: (1 212) 989 0869. Fax: (1 212) 989 1660. Jerry Ohlinger's emporium stocks a wealth of stills from the 1930s through the 1990s, specialising in colour material. Posters are also plentiful, and there are some magazines as well.

Movie Star News, 134 West 18th St, New York, N.Y. 10011. Tel: (1 212) 620 8160. Website: www.moviestarnews.com.

Features the largest stock of movie photos and posters in the world.

# MAGAZINES

The following list amounts to only a selection of the world's hundreds of film publications. Editors wishing to receive a free listing must send sample copies (preferably opening a sample subscription for us), to: IFG, Variety, 6 Bell Yard, London WC2A 2JR, UK.

## ARGENTINA

### ENTERTAINMENT HERALD

Corrieres 2817 3-A 1015, Buenos Aires.

## AUSTRALIA

### CINEMA PAPERS

116 Argyle St, Fitzroy, Victoria. Excellent large-format Australian bi-monthly, packed with information and pictures, useful for anyone monitoring the industry in Oz. Tel: (61 3) 9416 2644. Fax: (61 3) 9416 4088. e-mail: cp-edit@eis.net.au.

### FILM HISTORY

John Libbey and Co. Pty Ltd., Level 10, 15-17 Young Stret, Sydney NSW 2000. Tel: (61 2) 9251 4099. Fax: (61 2) 9251 4428. Articles on the historical development of the motion picture, in a social, technological and economic context. Quarterly.

### THE MACGUFFIN

18 Twyford St, Box Hill North, 3129. e-mail: muffin@labyrinth.net.au. Website: www. labyrinth.au/~muffin. Scholarly newsletter with minimal jargon, focusing on the films of Alfred Hitchcock.

## BELGIUM

### CINE-FICHESDEGRANDANGLE

Rue d'Arschot 29, B-5660 Mariembourg. Monthly review of new films and videos. Tel: (32 60) 312 168. Fax: (32 60) 312 937. e-mail: grand.angle@mail.micro-center.be.

### CINE & MEDIA

Rue du Saphir 15, 1030 Brussels. Tel (32 2) 734 4294. Fax: (32 2) 734 3207. e-mail: sg@ocic.org. Website: www.OCIC.org. Multilingual (French, English and Spanish) bi-monthly published by the International Catholic Organisation for Cinema and the Audiovisual, with reports from all continents.

### CINEMAGIE

Cellebroerstraat 16/2, B-1000 Brussels. Tel: (32 2) 516 0811. Fax: (32 2) 516 0819. e-mail: kfi.brussel@kerknet.be. Extensive treatises on important films, cinematic themes, aspects and trends, TV, music videos; profiles.

### FILM & TELEVISIE + VIDEO

Cellebroerstraat 16/2, B-1000 Brussels. Tel: (32 2) 516 0811. Fax: (32 2) 516 0819. e-mail: kfi.brussel@kerknet.be. Extensive reviews of major new film, video and DVD releases; profiles and interviews; festival news.

### MEDIAFILM

Cellebroerstraat 16, B-1010 Brussels. Serious Belgian quarterly, with extensive reviews, analysis and focus on directors. Quarterly.

### SOUNDTRACK!

Astridlaan 171, 2800 Mechelen. Tel: (32 15) 41 41 07. Fax: (32 15) 43 36 10. e-mail: scq@pophoSteunet.be. Website: www. soundtrack.com. Excellent quarterly for film music collectors.

### STARS

Rue d'Arschot 29, B-5660 Mariembourg. Tel: (32 60) 31 21 68. Fax: (32 60) 31 29 37. e-mail: grand_angle@mail.micro-center.be. Quarterly publication giving actors' biographies and filmographies.

## BOLIVIA

### IMAGEN

Casilla 1733, La Paz. Magazine of the Bolivian New Cinema Movement.

## CANADA

### CINÉ-BULLES

4545 avenue Pierre-de-Coubertin, CP 1000, Succursale M., Montréal H1V 3R2. Remarkable and informative Québécois quarterly; possibly the best in Canada.

### KINEMA

Fine Arts (Film Studies), University of Waterloo, Waterloo, Ont. N2L 3G1. Tel: (1 519) 885 1211 ext. 3709. Fax: (1 519) 746 4982. e-mail: kinema@watarts.uwaterloo.ca. Website: http://arts.uwaterloo.ca/FINE/juhde/kinemahp.htm. A journal of history,

theory and aesthetics of world film and audio-visual media. Twice yearly.

### THE NIGHTINGALE REPORT

45 Barclay Road, Toronto, Ontario M3H 3EZ. Fortnightly newsletter aimed at Canadian film and television industry. News and comprehensive listings.

### 24 IMAGES

3962, rue Laval, Montréal, QC H2W 2J2. Exceptionally attractive French-Canadian quarterly, witty and well-informed.

### SÉQUENCES

2100 rue Saint-Marc, #1702, Montréal, Québec H3H 2G6. Tel: (1 514) 933 9473. Fax: (1 514) 933 0162. e-mail: cast49@hotmail.com

## CHILE

### ENFOQUE

Publicaciones y Audiovisuales, Linterna Mágica Ltda., Casilla 15, Correo 34, Santiago. Occasional quarterly taking an in-depth look at the Chilean/Latin American markets and new-releases.

## CHINA, REPUBLIC OF

### CITY ENTERTAINMENT

Flat B2, 17/F, Fortune Factory Building, 40 Lee Chung Road, Cahiwan, Hong Kong. Tel: (852) 2892 0155. Fax: (852) 2838 49320. e-mail: cityent@wlink.net. Website: www. webhk.com/cityent. Indispensable Hong Kong bi-weekly for anyone interested in Chinese cinema. In Chinese.

### FILM APPRECIATION

The National Film Archive of the R.O.C., 4th Floor, 7 Ching-tao East Road, Taipei, Taiwan R.O.C. Taiwan's leading serious film journal, published as a bi-monthly. Focus on the cinematic output of Taiwan, Hong Kong and mainland China, as well as from Chinese communities overseas.

### POPULAR CINEMA (Dazhong dianying)

22 Beisanhuan donglu 22, Beijing. Leading mainland Chinese monthly, also carrying pieces on Hong Kong, Taiwan and foreign cinema.

## WORLD SCREEN

China Film Press, 22 Beisanhuandonglu, Beijing 100013. Monthly, primarily devoted to new/classic features from around the world, with artist profiles and events.

# COLOMBIA

## KINETOSCOPIO

Carrera 45, no. 53-24, Apartado 8734, Medellin. Tel: (574) 513 4444, ext. 151. Fax: (574) 513 2666. e-mail: aramos@colomboworld.com. Quarterly covering international and Latin American cinema, Colombian directors and festival news.

# CUBA

## CINE CUBANO

Calle 23, no. 1115 Apdo. 55, Havana. Vital information on all Latin American cinema, unfortunately only in Spanish.

# CZECH REPUBLIC

## CINEMA

Václavské nám. 15, 11000 Prague. A glossy Czech monthly.

# DENMARK

## FILM

Gothersgade 55, 1123 Copenhagen K. Tel: (45) 3374 3400. e-mail: susannan@dfi.dk and agnetes@dfi.dk. Published by the Danish Film Institute. Eight issues per year.

## KOSMORAMA

The Danish Film Museum, Vognmagergade 10, 1120-Copenhagen K. Chunky, academic title; twice yearly (in Danish).

# FINLAND

## FILMJOURNALEN

Finlandssvenskt filmcentrum, Nylands-gatan 1, 20500 Åbo. Tel: (358 2) 250 0410. Fax: (358 2) 250 0431. e-mail: filmcent@netti.fi. Passionate Swedish-language quarterly focusing on Nordic and Finnish cinema.

## FILMIHULLU

Malminkatu 36, FI-00100 Helsinki. Finnish film and TV magazine with perverse if passionate critical approach, appearing eight times a year.

# FRANCE

## CAHIERS DU CINEMA

Editions de l'Etoile, 9 passage de la Boule Blanche, 75012 Paris. Celebrated French journal, now enjoying a second lease of life after a long spell in the wilderness.

## POSITIF

Editions Jean-Michel Place, 3 rue Lhomond, 75005 Paris. In-depth interviews, articles, all immaculately researched and highly intelligent. By a clear margin, this is Europe's best film magazine.

## PREMIERE

151 rue Anatole France, 92300 Levallois-

Perret. Tel: (33 1) 4134 9111. Fax: (33 1) 4134 9119. France's familiar movie monthly, packed with information, reviews and filmographies.

## STUDIO MAGAZINE

41/43 rue de Colonel Pierre-Avia, 75015, Paris. Tel: (33 1) 5688 8888. Fax: (33 1) 4566 4852. Glossy, beautifully designed monthly, with reviews, articles and interviews.

# GERMANY

## EPD MEDIEN

Postfach 50 05 50, 60 394 Frankfurt am Main. Tel: (49 69) 580 98141. Fax: (49 69) 580 98 261. e-mail: medien@epd.de. Highbrow publication covering radio, TV and the press. Twice weekly.

## KINO: GERMAN FILM + INTL. REPORTS

c/o Holloway, Helgoländer Ufer 6, 10557, Berlin. Tel: (49 30) 391 6167. Excellent magazine published twice a year, also includes special issues devoted to both German cinema and international festival reports. Features, reviews, interviews and credits.

## THE LIMITED EDITION ONLINE

K.S.Z.-Verlag, Linzer Str. 5, 53604 Bad Honnef. Tel/Fax: (49 22) 241 0468. Website: www.leonline.de. Available only via internet, featuring extensive reviews devoted to movies, DVDs and soundtracks; updated weekly.

## WELTWUNDER DER KINEMATOGRAPHIE

Postfach 100 274, D-10562 Berlin. Tel: (49 30) 6908 8185. Fax: (49 30) 6908 8185. e-mail: DGFK@SNAFU.DE. Fascinating, well-researched new title, with detailed articles on the past, present and future of cinematography and the technical art of film-making. Yearly.

# HUNGARY

## FILMKULTURA

Solymár u. 8, 1032 Budapest. Essays and reviews on Hungarian and international cinema. Six times a year.

## FILMVILAG

Hollan Ernö utca 38/a, H-1137 Budapest. Monthly with reviews and interviews.

# INDIA

## CINEMAYA

B 90 Defence Colony, New Delhi 110 024. Tel: (91 11) 461 7127/464 7482. Fax: (91 11) 462 7211. e-mail: cinemaya@nde.vsni.net.in. Informative, elegant magazine, published quarterly in English since 1988, on all aspects of the Asian film industry. The official journal of NETPAC (Network for Promotion of Asian Cinema).

## FILM INDIA WORLDWIDE

Uma de Cunha, 'Film India Worldwide', PO Box 11158, Mumbai 400020. Fax: (91 22) 287 3513. e-mail: ugmedius@vsnl.com. In addition to news, views and reviews, FIWW offers interactive databank service that covers: film based material referenced for teaching purposes, actors of Indian origin criss-crossing the globe, etc.

## SPECIAL EFFECT

B/4, Balgachia Villa, Calcutta 700 037. Formerly *Magic Lantern*, this Indian film quarterly mixes interviews and reviews with insightful comment; surveys trends in Indian cinema.

# IRAN

## CINEMA

No. 123 Jami, Hafez Avenue, Tehran. Reports and reviews on local and international cinema.

## CINEMA AND THEATRE

No. 1/1 Omrani Alley, North Bahar St, Tehran. Articles on theoretical aspects of cinema and theatre.

## CINEMA AND VIDEO

No. 1073, Rudaki St, Jomhuri Square. Reports and features on cinema and video.

## CULTURE AND CINEMA

PO Box 15175-338 Tehran. Monthly magazine featuring Iranian cinema.

## FILM AND CINEMA

No. 18 Safa Alley, Kushk St, Saadi Avenue, Tehran. Features focusing on theoretical aspects of cinema.

## FILM AND VIDEO

No. 5 Laal Alley, Etesami St, Fatemi Avenue, Tehran. Reports and features on cinema and video.

## FILM INTERNATIONAL

12 Sam Alley, Hafez Ave, Tehran. English-language quarterly journal that offers a cross-cultural review of international cinema, focusing on the film art in Asia.

## FILM REPORT

3rd Floor, 123 Jami St, Hafez Ave, Tehran. Reviews and features on the latest releases.

## THE IMAGE

No. 15 Golriz St, Motahhari Ave, Tehran. Reports and features on cinema and photography.

## PEOPLE AND CINEMA (Mardom va Cinema)

14 Shakid Kamran Saleh Alley, Site Tir St, Tehran. Published by Farabi Cinema Foundation.

# ISRAEL

## CINEMATHEQUE

PO Box 20370, Tel Aviv 61203. Fine monthly Israeli magazine (with summary in English) dwelling on seasons at the Tel-Aviv Cinémathèque, but also reporting on world festivals etc.

# ITALY

## BIANCO E NERO

1524 via Tuscolana, 00173 Rome. Tel/Fax: (39 06) 722 9369. e-mail: biancoen@tin.it. Italian bi-monthly that boasts a reputation for scholarship second to none in its country.

## CINECRITICA

Via Yser, n.8-00198 Rome. Dense Italian quarterly focusing on world cinema.

## CINEMA & CINEMA

1 via Battibecco, 40123 Bologna. Respected quarterly.

## CINEMA & VIDEO INTERNATIONAL

Via Tevere 46B, 00198 Rome. Monthly for audio-visual professionals, in English and Italian.

## CINEMAZERO

Piazza Maestri del Lavoro 3, 33170 Pordenone. Serious bi-monthly covering international cinema, with festival news and book reviews.

## GRIFFITHIANA

Cineteca del Friuli, Via Bini, Palazzo Gurisatti, 33013 Gemona (Udine). Tel/Fax: (39 04) 3297 0542. e-mail: cdf@ cinetecadelfriuli.org. Website: www. cinetecadelfriuli.org/gcm/. Distribution agent in North America: Bilingual Review/ Press, Hispanic Research Center, Arizona State University, PO BOX 872702, Tempe, AZ 85287-2702, USA. e-mail: gary.keller@ asu.edu. Quarterly devoted exclusively to silent cinema and animation. Each issue is a miracle of scholparship and devotion. In English and Italian.

## IMMAGINI & SUONI

FIAIS, Casella postale 6306, 00195 Rome. Tel: (39 06) 370 0266. Fax: (39 06) 3973 3297. Published by the International Federation of Film Archives. In French and Italian.

## LA MAGNIFICA OSSESSIONE

Piazza Palermo, 10B, 16129 Genova. Published by the cinema department of Genova University, this academic quarterly has numerous articles on film history.

## CINEMA & VIDEO INTERNATIONAL

Via delle Cinque Giornate 15, 50129, Florence. Chunky bi-monthly report on Italian film industry, in English with Italian summary. Includes industry news, such as box-office, markets and foreign sales.

## QUADERNI DI CINEMA

Via Benedetto Varchi 57, 50132 Florence. Wide-ranging Italian bi-monthly, striving to match cultural politics with an enthusiastic appreciation of film.

## RIVISTA DEL CINEMATOGRAFO

Via Giuseppe Palombini, 6-165 Rome. Important Italian monthly. Tel: (39 06) 663 7514. Fax: (39 06) 663 7321. e-mail: infoeds@tin.it. Website: www. cinematografo.it.

## SEGNOCINEMA

Via G Prati 34, Vicenza. Glossy bi-monthly packed with profiles, reviews and photographs. September issue lists complete guide to all titles released the previous season.

# NETHERLANDS

## HOLLAND ANIMATION NEWSBRIEF

Hoogt 4, 3512 GW Utrecht. Quarterly newsletter from the Holland Animation Foundation.

## SKRIEN

Vondelpark 3, 1071 AA Amsterdam. Tel: (31 20) 589 1447. Fax: (31 20) 689 0438. e-mail: skrien@xsiall.nl. An excellent, enthusiastic monthly.

# NEW ZEALAND

## ONFILM

PO Box 6374, Wellington. Film, television and video magazine for New Zealand, with location reports and a production survey.

# NORWAY

## Z FILMTIDSSKRIFT

Dronningensgate 16, 0152 Oslo. Enthusiastic quarterly with a focus on film theory and history, both Norwegian and international. Now with useful summaries in English.

# PERU

## EL REFUGIO

José Granda 460, Lima 27. Monthly with reviews and features on world cinema.

## LA GRAN ILUSIÓN

Universidad de Lima, Oficina de Distribución y Venta de Publicaciones, Av. Javier Prado Este s/n Monterrico, Apartado 852, Lima. Weighty journal with essays on international contemporary and classic cinema.

# POLAND

## FILM

Pulawska 61, 02595 Warsaw. Popular monthly with international slant.

## KINO

Chelmska 19/21, 00-724 Warsaw. Tel: (48 22) 841 6843. Fax: (48 22) 841 9057. e-mail: kino@free.ngo.pl. Culturally inclined monthly designed to promote European cinema, with interviews, reviews and essays.

# PORTUGAL

## ESTREIA

Rua de Anibal Cunha 84, Sala 1.6, 4050-846 Porto Tel: (351 22) 207 6050. Fax: (351 22) 207 6059. e-mail: fantas@caleida.pt. Website: www.caleida.pt/fantasporto. Bi-monthly magazine dealing with international and Portuguese topics.

# ROMANIA

## PRO CINEMA

Str. Luterana nr. 11, et. 2, sector 1, Bucharest. Tel: (40 1) 303 3967. Fax: (40 1) 303 3855. Monthly with reviews, profiles and interviews.

# RUSSIA

## ISKUSSTVO KINO

9 ul. Usievicha, 125319 Moscow. Tel (7 95) 151 5651. Fax: (7 95) 151 0272. Website:

www.kinoart.ru. Chunky, theoretical; the most authoritative Russian monthly.

# SOUTH KOREA

## KOREA CINEMA (Yeonghwa)

Korean Film Commission, 206-46 Chongnyangni-dong, Tongdaemun-gu, Seoul. Tel: (82-2) 958 7584. Fax: (82-2) 958 7550. e-mail: dustinyu@hanmail.net Published once a year, a promotional guide for Korean cinema. The commission also publishes Korean Film News twice a year.

# SPAIN

## CINEMANIA

Gran Via 32, 2°, 28013 Madrid. Tel: (34 91) 538 6104. Fax: (34 91) 522 2291. eE-mail: cinemania@progresa.es. Founded in 1995. Upmarket monthly with news, interviews, reports, features and TV and video coverage.

## DIRIGIDO POR

Conseil de Cent 304, 2°, 1°, Barcelona 08007. Tel: (34 93) 487 6202. Fax: (34 93) 488 0896. e-mail: dirigidopor@idgrup.ibernet. com. Handsomely-produced monthly; throws the spotlight each issue on a particular genre, studio or director of international renown.

## FOTOGRAMAS

Gran Via de les Corts Catalanes 133, 3°, 08014 Barcelona. Tel: (34 93) 223 0353. Fax: (34 93) 432 2907. e-mail: fotogramas@ hachette.es. An institution, now 54 years old. A glossy monthly with authoritative film reviews, news, location reports and features.

## IMAGENES DE ACTUALIDAD

Consell de Cent, 304, 2.º, 1.ª, 08007 Barcelona. Tel: (34 93) 487 6202. Fax: (34 93) 488 0896. e-mail: dirigidopor@idgrup. ibernet.com. Glossy, well-presented international magazine with strong Hollywood bias. Monthly.

## NICKELODEON

Bárbara de Braganza 12/5, 28004 Madrid. Tel: (34 91) 308 5238. Fax: (34 91) 308 5885. Website: www.nickel-odeon.com. Quarterly; very well illustrated and researched. The late 1999 issue devoted to Welles should be sought out by every fan of the Master – it's a magnificent publishing achievement.

# SRI LANKA

## CINESITH

Asian Film Centre, 118 Dehiwala Road, Boralesgamuwa. Tel: (94 77) 318 610. Fax: (94 1) 509 553/519 923. e-mail: afc@ sri.lanka.net. Sri Lanka's only serious film magazine focuses on national and international cinema with special reference to Asia. Recognised as a reference journal in the Sri Lankan Universities and libraries.

# SWEDEN

## FILM HÄFTET

Lilla Fiskaregatan 10, SE-222 22 Lund. Tel/fax: (46 46) 137 914. e-mail: Michael. Tapper@swipnet.se.

## FILMRUTAN

Box 82, 851 02 Sundsvall. Organ of the Swedish Federation of Film Societies, this unpretentious quarterly has, with the demise of *Chaplin*, become Sweden's most important film magazine. Features film, book and record reviews.

## SWITZERLAND

### AVANT PREMIERE

Case Postale 5615, 1211 Geneva 11. Colourful monthly with lengthy reviews of new releases, as well as a pull-out brochure on Swiss production and distribution.

### CINE-BULLETIN

Swiss Film Centre, PO Box, Neugasse 6, CH-8031 Zürich. Serious Swiss monthly in French and German with box-office news and films in production.

### FILM

Bederstrasse 76, Postfach, 8027 Zürich. Swiss monthly highlighting new releases, with interviews and good festival coverage. German edition (20,000 copies) and French edition (8,000 copies).

### FILM BULLETIN

Postfach 137, CH-8408 Winterthur. Tel: (41 52) 226 0555. Fax: (41 52) 222 0051. e-mail: info@filmbulletin.ch. Website: www.filmbulletin.ch. Informative, straight-forward look at international cinema, with useful Swiss material also. Bi-monthly. Strong in film history, many essays on the work of famous directors, plus varied interviews.

### RECTANGLE

CAC Voltaire, Rue Général-Dufour 16, 1204 Geneva. Tel: (41 22) 320 7878. Fax: (41 22) 320 8893. e-mail: cacvolt@iprolink.ch. Only film magazine in the Suisse romande, and admirably poised between the theoretical and researchist approach to cinema, with a fresh and lively layout.

## UNITED KINGDOM

### BLACK FILMMAKER

Church Road, Hendon, London, NW4 4EB. e-mail: bfm@ivc.leevalley.co.uk.

### EMPIRE

1st Floor, Mappin House, 4 Winsley St, London W1N 7AR. Supercharged monthly with profiles, reviews and behind-the-scenes reports. Often far ahead of its rivals in breaking news and interviews.

### MUSIC FROM THE MOVIES

1 Folly Square, Bridport, Dorset DT6 3PU. Tel/Fax: (44 1308) 427 057. e-mail: ftmy@halto.co.uk. Informative quarterly devoted to all aspects of film music and its composers, with articles, interviews and soundtrack reviews.

### PICTURE HOUSE

5 Coopers Close, Burgess Hill, W. Sussex RH15 8AN. Admirable quarterly devoted to the cinema buildings of the past.

### SIGHT AND SOUND

British Film Institute, 21 Stephen St, London W1P 1PL. Tel: (44 20) 7255 1444. Fax: (44 20) 7436 2327. e-mail:

s&s@bfi.org.uk. Website: www.bfi.org.uk/ sightandsound. Established in 1932, the UK's leading film journal. Publishes compete cast and crew listings for all films released in the UK.

### TALKING PICTURES

3b Glengarry Road, East Dulwich, London SE22. Quarterly booklet with interviews, reviews and articles on film culture in the UK, now expanding in size and coverage.

### TOTAL FILM

Future Publishing, 99 Baker St, London W1M 1FB. Tel: (44 20) 7317 2600. Fax: (44 20) 7317 2644. e-mail: totalfilm@futurenet. co.uk. The UK's fastest-growing monthly mainstream movie magazine, covering everything from Hollywood blockbusters to European arthouse cinema. Editor: Matt Mueller. Current ABC: 72,225.

## UNITED STATES

### AMERICAN PREMIERE

8421 Wilshire Blvd., Penthouse; Beverly Hills, CA 90211. Bi-monthly industry magazine, free to members of the Academy of Motion Picture Arts and Sciences.

### ANIMATION JOURNAL

Published under auspices of the Chapman University School of Film and Television, 333 N. Glassell, Orange, CA 92866. Tel: (1 714) 744 7018. Fax: ( 1 714) 997 6700. Website: www.chapman.edu/animation. Quarterly.

### ANIMATION MAGAZINE

Bill Buck, 30101 Agoura Court, Suite 110, Agoura, California 91301. Tel: (1 818) 991 2884. Fax: (1 818) 991 3773. Website: www.animag. com. The only international publication focusing on the global animation industry. Monthly.

### AUDIENCE

PO Box 215, Simi Valley, CA 93062-0215. Tel: (1 805) 584 6651. Website: www. audiencemag.com. Billed as an "informal commentary on film", this witty, well-informed online version of the magazine founded in 1968 features articles and reviews.

### CINEASTE

PO Box 2242, New York, NY 10009. Tel/Fax: (1 212) 982 1241. e-mail: cineaste@ cineaste.com. Perhaps the finest anti-establishment movie magazine, never afraid to tackle controversial issues and never prone to Hollywood worship. Its interviews are especially good.

### CINEFANTASTIQUE

PO Box 270, Oak Park, Ill. 60303. Tel: (1 708) 366 5566. Fax: (1 708) 366 1441. e-mail: cmail@cfg.com. An enthusiastic, well-written, beautifully produced bi-monthly with a special emphasis on horror, fantasy and sci-fi; now into its 31st year.

### CINEMA JOURNAL

University of Texas Press, Journals Division, Box 7819, Austin, Texas 78713-7819. Essays concerned with the study of the moving image from diverse method-ological perspectives, with information on upcoming events and research opportunities.

### CLASSIC IMAGES

PO Box 809, Muscataine, IA52761. Formerly *Classic Film Collector*, a good source for film buffs eager to enlarge their library of movies. Monthly.

### FEMME FATALES

5023 Frankford Ave., Baltimore, MD 21206. Tel (1 410) 488 8147. Published every three weeks.

### FILMMAKER MAGAZINE

110 West 57th St, New York, Ny 10019-3319, USA. Tel: 212-581-8080. Fax: 212-581-1857. Website: filmmakermagazine.com. Aimed at independent film-makers, this quarterly offers interviews, news and sound advice.

### FILMS IN REVIEW

PO Box 589, New York, NY 10021. Compact bi-monthly journal, reviewing notable new releases with interviews, retrospective articles and television/video reports.

### FILM COMMENT

Film Society of Lincoln Center, 70 Lincoln Center Plaza, New York, NY 10023. Tel: (1 212) 875 5614. Fax: (1 212) 875 5636. e-mail: rtvfc@aol.com. Informative, feisty and usually uncompromising articles as well as interviews on wide-ranging international topics. Still the best US cinema bi-monthly.

### FILM CRITICISM

Allegheny College, Box D, Meadville, PA 16335. Tel: (1 814) 332 4333/ 4343. Fax: (1 814) 332 2981. e-mail: lmichael@alleg. edu. Scholarly essays on film history, theory and culture. Tri-quarterly.

### FILM JOURNAL INTERNATIONAL

Sunshine Group Worldwide, 244 West 49th St, Suite 200, New York, NY 10019. Tel: (1 212) 246 6460. Fax: (1 212) 265 6428. e-mail: sunshine@maestro.com. Monthly magazine covering international exhibition.

### FILM LITERATURE INDEX

Film and Television Documentation Centre, State University of New York, 1400 Washington Avenue, Albany, NY 12222. Fax: (1 518) 442 5367. e-mail: fatcod@ cnsvax@albany.edu. The most compre-hensive international index to the journal literature of film and television.

### FILM QUARTERLY

University of California Press, 2000 Center St, Suite 303, Berkeley, CA 94704-1223. Tel: (1 510) 642-9740. Fax: (1 510) 642 9917. e-mail: ann.martin@ucpress.ucop.edu. Publishes readable discussions of issues in contemporary, classical and silent film, as well as TV and video. Plus substantial film reviews and interviews, and analyses of independent, documentary, avant-garde and foreign films. Comprehensive book reviews.

### HONG KONG FILM MAGAZINE

601 Van Ness Avenue, Suite E3728, San Francisco, California 94102. Quarterly focusing on the Hong Kong cinema scene, featuring news, reviews and interviews. In English.

### INTERNATIONAL DOCUMENTARY ASSOCIATION (IDA)

1201 West 5th St, Suite M320, Los Angeles, CA 90017. Tel: (1 213) 534 3600. Fax: (1 213) 534 3610. e-mail: info@documentary.org.

Website: www. documentary.org. The only US publication to focus exclusively on non-fiction film and video. Presents new work and ideas in the documentary field, with informative articles, reviews and interviews. Published ten times a year.

### JUMP CUT

PO Box 865, Berkeley, California 94701. Tel: (1 510) 658 2221. Fax: ( 1510) 658 2269. e-mail: jhess@igc.org. Published once or twice a year, this magazine contains an extraordinary amount of closely-woven text.

### LITERATURE/FILM QUARTERLY

Salisbury State University, Salisbury, Maryland 21801. Tel: 1-410 334 3495/ 543 6446. Fax: 1-410 543 6068. e-mail: "jxwelsh@ssu.edu. Almost 30 year-old scholarly quarterly, with film and book reviews, interviews and articles. Manuscripts invited for submission. Circulates coast to coast in the US and Canada and abroad.

### MOVIELINE

1141 South Beverly Drive, Los Angeles, CA 90035. Intelligent, irreverent and refreshingly candid Hollywood monthly. Great interviews.

### MOVIEMAKER

2265 Westwood Blvd., PMB 479, Los Angeles, CA 90064. Tel (1 310) 234 9234. Fax: (1 310) 234 9293. e-mail: staff@moviemaker.com. Published six times a year.

### TM TEEN MOVIELINE

PO Box 469036, Escondido, CA 92046. Tel (1 310) 234 9501. Fax: ( 1 310) 234 0332.

### WIDE ANGLE

The Johns Hopkins University Press, Baltimore, Maryland 212180. Scholarly, thematically arranged journal. Wide range.

## URUGUAY

### CINEMATECA REVISTA

Lorenzo Carnelli 1311, Casilla de Correo 1170, Montevideo. Bright magazine with international slant, published by Cinemateca Uruguaya ten times a year.

# Trade and Technical

## BELGIUM

### MONITEUR DU FILM

36 rue des Frambosiers, 1180 Brussels. Monthly.

## FRANCE

### LE FILM FRANÇAIS

90 rue de Flandre, 75947 Paris Cedex 19. Lightweight weekly, with news, reviews, box-office and production schedules.

## GERMANY

### BLICKPUNKT-FILM

Stahlgruberring 11a, 81829 Munich. Strong on box-office returns and marketing, this

German weekly also covers the video and TV markets. Tel: (49 89) 451 124. Fax: (49 89) 451 14451. e-mail: t.blieninger@e-media.de. Website: www.cinebiz.de.

### ENTERTAINMENT MARKT

Stahlgruberring 11a, 81829 Munich. Bi-weekly business magazine that covers the German video, CD-ROM and computer games, from multimedia to business news. The trade magazine for innovative dealers, distributors and decision-makers. Tel: (49 89) 451 140. Fax: (49 89) 451 14444. e-mail: emv@e-media.de.

### FILM-ECHO/FILMWOCHE

Marktplatz 13, 65183 Wiesbaden. Tel: (49 611) 36 09 80. Fax: (49 611) 37 28 78. E-mail: filmeco@aol.com. Doyen of the German trade. Weekly.

### VIDEO WOCHE

Tel: (49 89) 451 140. Fax: (49 89) 451 14444. E-mail: emv@e-media.de. Trade magazine for software dealers. As the market leader, it provides the latest facts and trends on a weekly basis.

## ITALY

### ECOMONOPRESS ACTING NEWS

Via Belluno 1, 00161 Rome. Comprehensive weekly reports on Italian film starts. Its four market issues have English translations.

### CINEMA D'OGGI

Viale Regina Margherita 286, 00198 Rome. Fornightly interviews with producers.

### GIORNALE DELLO SPETTACOLO

Via di Villa Patrizi 10, 00161 Rome. Box-office data, legal requirements, technical information etc.

## JAPAN

### MOVIE/TV MARKETING

Box 30, Central Post Office, Tokyo, 100-8691 Japan. Tel: (81 3) 3587 2855. Fax: (81 3) 3587 2820. e-mail: info@movietvmarketing.com. Monthly; in English.

## NORWAY

### FILM OG KINO

Dronningensgate 16, PO Box 446 Sentrum, 0104 Oslo. Tel: (47 22) 474 628. Fax: (47 22) 474 698. e-mail: kalle@kino.no. Website: www.filmweb.no/filmogkino/fidsskniftet. Wide-ranging with expressive layout; covers new releases as well as national and international trade news and festival reports. The best film magazine in Scandinavia.

## SPAIN

### CINE & TV INFORME

Gran Via 64, 28013, Madrid. Tel: (34 91) 541 2129. Fax: (34 91) 559 4282. e-mail: exportfilm@cineytele.com. An institution, now 40 years old, a monthly which covers Spanish and international film, video and TV developments.

### CINEVIDEO 20

Clara del Rey 71, bajo B, 28002 Madrid. Tel: (34 91) 519 6586. Fax: (34 91) 519 5119. e-mail: cinevideo@cinevideo20.es. Website: www.cinevideo20.es. Features technologies for film, video, computers, studio facilities, satellite and cable.

### EURO-MOVIES INTERNATIONAL

Jesús y María 32, 2B, 28012, Madrid. Tel: (34 91) 527 6189. Fax: (34 91) 468 7820. Spanish and Latin American panorama, with reviews, festival news and television sections.

### LA GRAN ILUSION

Cuesta de San Vicente 4, 28008 Madrid. Tel: (34 91) 542 2702/03. Fax: (34 91) 542 8777. Enterprising monthly published by distributor/exhibitor Alta Films, with news and views on Alta releases and Spanish cinema in general.

## UNITED KINGDOM

### IMAGE TECHNOLOGY — JOURNAL OF THE BKSTS

5 Walpole Court, Ealing Studios, Ealing Green, London W5 5ED. Tel: (44 20) 7858 45220. Fax: (44 20) 7858 45230. e-mail: movimage@bksts.demon.co.uk. Website: www.bksts. demon. co. uk. Covers technologies of motion picture film, television and sound at professional level. Ten times yearly.

### MOVING PICTURES INTERNATIONAL

38-42 Whitfield St, London W1P 5RF. Tel: (44 20) 7813 9000. Fax: (44 20) 7681 0501. Europe-oriented monthly trade paper, with daily editions at numerous festivals.

### SCREEN INTERNATIONAL

33-39 Bowling Green Lane, London, EC1R 0DA. Tel: (44 20) 7505 8080. Fax: (44 20) 7505 8116. e-mail: Screeninternational@compuserve. com. Website: www. screendaily. com. International film trade magazine.

## UNITED STATES

### AMERICAN CINEMATOGRAPHER

ASC Holding Corp., 1782 N. Orange Dr., Hollywood, CA 90028. Glossy monthly on film and electronic production techniques.

### BOX OFFICE

155 S. El Molino Ave, Suite 100, Pasadena, California, 91101. Tel: (1 626) 396 0250. Fax: (1 626) 396 0248. e-mail: editorial@boxoffice.com; advertising@boxoffice. com. Website: www.boxoffice.com. Business monthly for Hollywood and the movie theatre industry.

### THE HOLLYWOOD REPORTER

5055 Wilshire Boulevard, Los Angeles, CA 90036-4396. Website: www.hollywoodreporter.com. Daily.

### VARIETY

5700 Wilshire Boulevard, Suite 120, Los Angeles, CA 90036. Website: www. variety.com. The world's foremost entertainment industry newspaper (daily and weekly).

# National Organs

## AUSTRALIA

### AFC NEWS

GPO Box 3984, Sydney NSW 2001. Tel: (61 2) 9321 6444. Fax: (61 2) 9357 3631. e-mail: info@afc.gov.au. Website: www. afc.gov.au. Quarterly, with regular production and multimedia reports, industry statistics, funding approvals and news of Australian films at international markets and festivals.

## BELGIUM

### CINEMA, CINEMA

Ministère de la Culture Française, avenue de Cortenbur 158, 1040 Brussels.

## BURKINA FASO

### FESPACO NEWS

01 BP. 2524 Ouagadougou 01. Monthly newsletter of the Pan-African Federation of film-makers.

## CANADA

### FILM CANADA YEARBOOK

Moving Pictures Media (publisher), Box 720, Port Perry, Ontario L9L 1A6. Tel (1 905) 986 0050. Fax: (1 905) 986 1113. e-mail: deborah@filmcanadayearbook.com. Completely updated annually; a comprehensive, national overview of the Canadian film and television industry.

## GERMANY

### KINO

Export-Union des Deutschen Films, Türkenstr. 93, D-80799 München. Tel: (49 89) 390 095. Fax: (49 89) 395 223. e-mail: export-union@german-cinema.de. Information on new German features (in production and on release), and selected German film personalities. Published four times a year in English; yearbook also available.

## ISRAEL

### ISRAEL FILM CENTRE INFORMATION BULLETIN

Ministry of Industry and Trade, 30 Agron St, Jerusalem. Yearly review of Israeli film industry and catalogue of Israeli films.

## NEW ZEALAND

### NZ FILM

PO Box 11546, Wellington. Tel: (64 4) 382 7680. Fax: (64 4) 384 9719. e-mail: marketing@nzfilm.co.nz. Website: www. nzfilm.co.nz. News from the New Zealand Film Commission; a twice-yearly round-up of the country's film industry.

## SPAIN

### ACADEMIA & BOLETÍN

Sagasta 20, 3° dcha., 28004 Madrid. Tel: (34 91) 593 4648/448 2321. Fax: (34 91) 593 1492. e-mail: acaine@render.es. Website: www.sie.es/acacine. Excellent twice-yearly, with articles, news and opinion from members of Spain's Academy of the Arts and Cinematographic Sciences.

# Index to Advertisers

La Rochelle Film Festival 383
Leeds Film Festival 364
Locarno Film Festival 1
London Int'l Film School 394
Malaga Film Festival 365
Manfred Durniok Produktion 2
Mannheim-Heidelberg Film Festival 365
Mill Valley Film Festival 367
Montreal World Film Festival 366
New Zealand Film Commission 229
New Zealand Film Festival 381
Norwegian Film Festival 369
Norwegian Film Institute 234
Odense Film Festival 368
Oulu Children's Film Festival 370
Portland Film Festival 371
Pro Helvetia 292
Productions La Fête Spine
Raindance Film Festival 371
Rotterdam Film Festival 16
San Sebastian Film Festival 372
Sandrew-Metronome 12
Seattle Film Festival 374
Showtime 9
Sitges Film Festival 375
Solothurn Film Festival 375
Stockholm Film Festival 375
Svensk Filmindustri 8
Swiss Film Center 291
Tampere Film Festival 376
Telluride Film Festival Spine
Thessaloniki Film Festival 377
Tromsø Film Festival 379
Umeå Film Festival 379
Valencia Film Festival 380
Valladolid Film Festival 381
Variety 337
Victoria Independent Film & TV Festival 380
Wine Country Film Festival 382
Worldfest Houston 382

Amiens Film Festival 349
ANICA 201
Bergen Film Festival 350
Bermuda Film Festival 5
Brisbane Film Festival 350
CAM Spine
Centro Espressioni Cinematografiche 351
Cinema Tout Ecran 373
Clermont-Ferrand Film Festival 352
Danish Film Institute 124
DB Cine 408
Denver Film Festival 353
Deseo, El 280
Dolby Laboratories Back Cover, 6
Espoo Cine 354
Fantasporto 354
Farabi Film Foundation 182
Filmfest Hamburg 355
Filmfestivals.com 4, 358, 360
Filmstiftung NRW 151
Finnish Film Foundation 136
Flanders Film Festival 355
Fort Lauderdale Film Festival 356
Freedom Film Festival 357
Fribourg Film Festival 382
Gijón Film Festival 356
Giornate del Cinema Muto, Le 364
Greek Film Centre 158
Helsinki Film Festival 370
Hof Film Days 361
Holland Film 223
Hong Kong Film Festival 358
Huelva Film Festival 359
ICAM 57
Icelandic Film Fund 168
Iranian Independents 185
Israel Film Centre 195
Istanbul Film Festival 362
Jerusalem Film Festival 373
Karlovy Vary Film Festival 363